WEST'S LAW SCHOOL
ADVISORY BOARD

UNIFORM COMMERCIAL CODE
IN A NUTSHELL

EIGHTH EDITION

By

BRADFORD STONE

Charles A. Dana Professor of Law Emeritus
Stetson University College of Law
Visiting Professor of Law
Michigan State University
College of Law

and

KRISTEN DAVID ADAMS

Professor of Law
Stetson University College of Law

A Thomson Reuters business

Mat #41179512

Nutshell Series, In a Nutshell and the Nutshell Logo are
trademarks registered in the U.S. Patent and Trademark Office.

COPYRIGHT © 1984, 1989, 1995 WEST PUBLISHING CO.
© West, a Thomson business, 2002, 2005, 2008
© 2012 Thomson Reuters

    610 Opperman Drive
    St. Paul, MN 55123
    1–800–313–9378

Printed in the United States of America

ISBN: 978–0–314–27744–2

For Sarah Stella Chapman

That Love is all there is,
Is all we know of Love.
—Emily Dickinson

PREFACE

"If a statute is to make sense, it must be read in the light of some assumed purpose. A statute merely declaring a rule, with no purpose or objective, is nonsense." Karl N. Llewellyn, The Common Law Tradition 374 (1960).

"The Uniform Commercial Code should be construed in accordance with its underlying purposes and policies. The text of each section should be read in the light of the purpose and policy of the rule or principle in question, as also of the Uniform Commercial Code as a whole, and the application of the language should be construed narrowly or broadly, as the case may be, in conformity with the purposes and policies involved." Comment 1 to Uniform Commercial Code § 1–103.

"Moreover, this case would have been much easier for me to decide if the parties had begun their presentations with an appropriate explanation of the relevant provisions of the statute instead of an unstated assumption that is not entirely obvious." Justice John Paul Stevens, 454 U.S. at 45.

The official text (with comments) of the Uniform Commercial Code embodies more than nine-hundred pages. Its sweeping scope and complexities may appear to discourage summarizing into a Nutshell format. Yet the need to view the Code with some perspective is manifest. This Nutshell endeavors to meet this need.

At the outset, however, the following quote from Section 246 of McCormick's Handbook of the Law of Evidence, Second Edition, should be considered:

"Too much should not be expected of a [summary of the sweeping body of law.] ... The most it can accomplish is to furnish a helpful starting point for discussion of the problems, and a memory aid in recalling some of the solutions. But if [a summary] is to remain brief and understandable, it will necessarily distort some parts of the picture. Simplification has a measure of falsification."

In order to minimize the distortion that comes with simplification, the following techniques have been employed:

First, wherever practicable the actual language of the Code and its comments have been "tracked," even though it may not always have been expedient to indicate this affirmatively.

Second, every Code rule and comment stated is backed up by the relevant UCC citation. Accordingly, the reader—whether law student or practitioner—is given entrée to the Code itself so that an independent judgment may be made as to the rule and application under consideration. Further, the cite will afford ready entrée to a study in depth. For instance, once a relevant UCC cite is obtained, all reported case law construing the language can be located through such publications as the Uniform Laws Annotated—Uniform Commercial Code and the Uniform Commercial Code Reporting Service. The UCC cite also will give ready entrée to the massive legal literature that discusses the Code. On occasion this Nutshell will refer to J. White, R. Summers, Handbook of the Law Under the Uniform Commercial Code (6th ed., Student Edition, 2010) (cited as UCC Hornbook), Gregory M. Travalio, Robert J. Nordstrom & Albert L. Clovis, Nordstrom on Sales & Leases of Goods (2d ed., Aspen 2000) (cited as Sales Hornbook), and R. Henson, Handbook on Secured Transactions Under the Uniform Commercial Code (2d ed., 1979) (cited as Secured Transactions Hornbook) where it is believed such references are particularly helpful.

Third, the purpose or policy of a rule under consideration is frequently stated and an example of the application of the rule is given. Remember: "[A rule] ... with no purpose ... is nonsense." The Code Comments are the principal source for the purpose of the various UCC provisions. These Comments are intended not only to promote uniformity and safeguard against misconstruction but to "aid in viewing the Act as an integrated whole." See the General Comment to the UCC.

Subsequent to the publication of the first edition, the 1978 UCC was promulgated. Other developments included the promulgation of the Restatement (Second) of Contracts, the enactment of the Bankruptcy Reform Act, and the Magnuson–Moss Warranty Act. Further, a revised Uniform Consumer Credit Code was promulgated. The second edition reflected those developments.

The third edition was based upon the 1987 UCC, which added Article 2A, Leases. The edition also cited the Federal Expedited Funds Availability Act, the Federal Food Security Act, FTC Credit Practices Rules, and the Uniform Fraudulent Transfer Act.

The fourth edition was based on the 1990 Code. This Code (1) revised Article 3 (renaming it Negotiable Instruments), and (2) amended Article 4, Bank Deposits and Collections. Additionally, this edition contained the 1990 amendments to Article 2A, Leases. The 1989 official text was also included. This text (1) added Article 4A, Funds Transfers, and (2) contained a revised Article 6, renaming it Bulk Sales.

The fourth edition also cited, throughout Article 2, Sales, the United Nations Convention on Contracts for the International Sale of Goods (CISG). The United States and seventy-eight other countries are parties to the Convention, i.e., are "contracting states."

The fifth edition was based on the 2001 Official Text. Included was (i) revised (1994) Article 8 (Investment Securities), (ii) revised (1995) Article 5 (Letters of Credit), and (iii) revised (2000) Article 9 (Secured Transactions) with conforming amendments to other Articles and errata and amendments to revised Article 9.

The sixth edition was based on the 2004 Official Text. Included was (i) revised (2001) Article 1 (General Provisions), (ii) amended (2003) Article 2 (Sales), (iii) amended (2003) Article 2A (Leases), (iv) amended (2003) Article 3 (Negotiable Instruments), (v) amended (2002) Article 4 (Bank Deposits and Collections), (vi) revised (2003) Article 7 (Documents of Title), (vii) revised (2001) Article 9 (Secured Transactions) with conforming amendments to Articles 1, 2, 2A, 4, 5, 6, 7, and 8. (It is to be noted that Article 7 was the *last* of the articles of the Uniform Commercial Code to be revised.)

The seventh edition incorporated the UCP 600, updated the book's treatment of voidable preferences to mark recent changes in the Bankruptcy Code, and re-oriented the text's treatment of leases to allow for easier comparisons with sales transactions. This edition, which was based on the 2008 Official Text, also marked the inclusion of a second author.

This eighth edition incorporates the 2010 Amendments to Article 9. They are expected to be considered by state legislatures with a view to all states enacting the amendments by a uniform effective date of July 1, 2013. For reasons for the amendments and the process, see E. Smith, A Summary of the 2010 Amendments, 42 UCC L.J. 345–50 (2010).

[Note: See Uniform Electronic Transactions Act (UETA) § 3(b)(2) (does not apply to UCC other than Articles 2 and 2A and §§ 1–107, 1–206 [Rev. 1–306]) and § 16; Electronic Signatures in Global and National Commerce Act (E–Sign), 15 U.S.C.A. § 7001 to § 7031 (especially, §§ 7001(a) and (d)(4), 7002(a)(1) and (c), 7003(a)(3), 7021(a)(1) and (d)–(g). See also UCC §§ 1–108 and Comments, 2–108(4) and Comment 5, 2A–104(4) and Comment 6.]

———————

Bradford Stone expresses appreciation to Charles W. Joiner, Frank R. Kennedy, Marcus L. Plant, and Roy L. Steinheimer, Jr., for their encouragement; to the law student and the practitioner he was privileged to serve for the past thirty-seven years. Kristen Adams adds her appreciation to Bradford Stone for his mentoring and encouragement; to Carol Booth in the Dean's office, and Dianne Oeste in the Office of Faculty Support Services at Stetson University College of Law for excellent assistance, and to Stetson student research assistant Amanda Chazal for her enthusiasm and careful eye for detail.

BRADFORD STONE
and
KRISTEN DAVID ADAMS

St. Petersburg, Florida
and
East Lansing, Michigan
April 2012

INTRODUCTION

History

The present law concerning commercial transactions—the subject of the Uniform Commercial Code—had its modern origins in the law merchant, that is, the system of rules, customs and usages generally recognized and adopted by merchants and traders which constituted the law for the regulation of their transactions and the solution of their controversies. By the end of the seventeenth century, the law merchant had become assimilated by the common law. It should be noted that, in the eighteenth century, many landmark commercial law cases were decided by Lord Mansfield, England's foremost commercial judge.

In 1882, the English Bills of Exchange Act was enacted by Parliament, followed in 1893 by the English Sale of Goods Act. These two acts were the inspiration for the Uniform Negotiable Instruments Law promulgated in 1896 by the National Conference of Commissioners on Uniform State Laws and the Uniform Sales Act promulgated by the Commissioners in 1906.

Other uniform laws relating to the commercial transaction were prepared and promulgated by the Commissioners for adoption by the legislatures of the several states as follows:

Act	Promulgated
Uniform Warehouse Receipts Act	1906
Uniform Bills of Lading Act	1909
Uniform Stock Transfer Act	1909
Uniform Conditional Sales Act	1918
Uniform Trust Receipts Act	1933

While these Uniform Acts had wide acceptance, they were not collectively adopted by every American State.

In the early 1940s, it was recognized that the above uniform acts needed substantial revision to keep them in step with modern commercial practices. Further, since each of the above uniform acts had become a segment of the statutory law relating to commercial transactions, there was a need to integrate each of such acts with the others.

Accordingly, the preparation of the Uniform Commercial Code (UCC) was begun as a joint project of The American Law Institute and the National Conference of Commissioners on Uniform State Laws in 1942. The Chief Reporter of the Code was Professor Karl N. Llewellyn; the Associate Chief Reporter was Professor Soia Mentschikoff. This project resulted in the 1952 Official Text of the UCC. The New York State Law Revision Commission studied the 1952 Code and concluded that it needed extensive revision. The Code was revised and the 1957 Official Text resulted. Subsequently, a 1958 and a 1962 Official Text were promulgated with relatively minor revisions of the 1957 text. The Permanent Editorial Board for the UCC—a body formed to promote uniformity of enactment and construction of the UCC to evaluate and prepare proposals for amendment of the 1962 UCC—promulgated the 1966 Official Recommendations for the Amendment of the Code. Mostly as a consequence of substantial revisions of Article 9 of the UCC, Secured Transactions, a 1972 Official Text was promulgated which incorporated all prior officially approved amendments. A 1978 Official Text was promulgated to permit issuance of corporate stock in uncertificated form. Thus, Article 8, Investment Securities, and related sections of other articles were revised to regulate rights, duties, and obligations of issuers of, and persons dealing with, both certificated and uncertificated investment securities.

INTRODUCTION

In 1987, 1989, and 1990, further official texts were promulgated. The 1987 Official Text added Article 2A, Leases. The 1989 Official Text added Article 4A, Funds Transfers, and contained a revised Article 6, Bulk Sales. The 1990 Official Text contained a revised Article 3 (renamed Negotiable Instruments), an amended Article 4, Bank Deposits and Collections, and included amendments to Article 2A, Leases.

In 1994, 1995, and 2000, revised texts were promulgated covering investment securities, letters of credit, and secured transactions. Most importantly, 2000 revised Article 9 substantially revised Secured Transactions along with conforming amendments to other articles and errata and amendments to revised Article 9. These matters were reflected in the 2001 Official Text.

In 2001, Articles 1 and 9 were revised; in 2002, Article 4 was amended; in 2003, Articles 2, 2A, and 3 were amended; in 2003, Article 7 was revised. These matters are reflected in the 2004 Official Text.

In 2010, amendments to Article 9 were approved with a view to all states enacting the amendments by a uniform effective date of July 1, 2013. In May 2011, the American Law Institute withdrew the 2003 amendments to UCC Article 2 and 2A from the UCC Official Text.

This nutshell will be based on the Official Text, amended through 2010. Remember, though, that while the Code has been enacted in 50 states (Louisiana adopted Articles 1, 3, 4, 5, 7, 8, and 9), the District of Columbia, Guam, and the Virgin Islands, it is important to localize your information as to the Code language of your jurisdiction. Not only might your jurisdiction have enacted a prior Official Text of the UCC, your jurisdiction might have enacted a non-uniform amendment. Also, the UCC itself in some instances includes alternative provisions, e.g., §§ 2–318, 4–106(b), 7–403(a)(2) and Comment 3 (2003).

Rationale for the UCC

The concept of the Uniform Commercial Code is that "commercial transactions" is a single subject of the law, notwithstanding its many facets:

1. A single transaction may well involve a contract for sale of goods followed by a sale. This is the subject of Article 2, Sales, which superseded the Uniform Sales Act.

2. The transaction may well involve the giving of a check or draft for all or part of the purchase price. The check or draft may be negotiated and will ultimately pass through one or more banks for collection. This is the subject of Article 3, Commercial Paper (renamed Negotiable Instruments), and Article 4, Bank Deposits and Collections. These articles superseded the Uniform Negotiable Instruments Law and acts regulating bank collections, such as the American Bankers Association Bank Collection Code.

3. If the goods are shipped or stored, the subject matter of the sale may be covered by a bill of lading or warehouse receipt or both. This is the subject of Article 7, Documents of Title. This superseded certain sections of the Uniform Sales Act, the Uniform Bills of Lading Act, and the Uniform Warehouse Receipts Act.

4. Further, when a transaction involves the giving of a check or draft for a part of the purchase price, it may also involve the acceptance of some form of security for the balance. This is the subject of Article 9, Secured Transactions. This superseded the Uniform Conditional Sales Act, Uniform Trust Receipts Act, and acts regulating chattel mortgages, conditional sales, factor's liens, assignments of accounts receivable, and similar transactions.

5. Or it may be that the entire transaction was made pursuant to a letter of credit, either domestic or foreign. This is the subject of Article 5, Letters of Credit. Except for a few

provisions of the Uniform Negotiable Instruments Law, letters of credit were not previously the subject of statutory enactment.

Obviously, every phase of commerce outlined above is but part of one transaction, namely, the sale of and payment for goods. Accordingly, the Uniform Commercial Code purports to deal with all the phases that may ordinarily arise in the handling of a commercial transaction, from start to finish. See the General Comment to the UCC, § 10–102. Note that the above five phases of a commercial transaction form the organizational basis for this nutshell. Note also that Part Two deals with *leases* of goods under Article 2A. This Article borrows from both Article 2, Sales, and Article 9, Secured Transactions.

Purposes and Construction of the UCC

The Code must be liberally construed and applied to promote its underlying purposes and policies:

> a. to simplify, clarify, and modernize the law governing commercial transactions;
>
> b. to permit the continued expansion of commercial practices through custom, usage, and agreement of the parties; and
>
> c. to make uniform the law among the various jurisdictions.

In addition, the text of each section of the UCC should be read in the light of the purpose and policy of the rule or principle in question (as also of the Code as a whole), and the application of the language should be construed narrowly or broadly, as the case may be, in conformity with the purposes and policies involved. § 1–103(a) and Comment 1.

The Official Comments of the National Conference of Commissioners on Uniform State Laws and The American Law Institute will be of considerable assistance in determining purposes and policies of the Code. This should encourage uniform construction of the UCC among the several jurisdictions. Further, the Permanent Editorial Board for the UCC (PEB) issues supplemental commentary on the UCC from time to time.

In order to permit the continued expansion of commercial practices, the Code drafters adopted a philosophy of open-ended drafting, with room for courts to move in and readjust over the decades. K. Llewellyn, The Common Law Tradition 183, note 186 (1960). Thus, in the main, the Code was not drafted in the manner a conveyancer would. Llewellyn called these persons "The metes and bounds boys." Instead, as Comment 1 to § 1–103 states, "The Uniform Commercial Code is drawn to provide flexibility so that, since it is intended to be a semi-permanent and infrequently-amended piece of legislation, it will provide its own machinery for expansion of commercial practices. It is intended to make it possible for the law embodied in the Uniform Commercial Code to be applied by the courts in the light of unforeseen and new circumstances and practices. The proper construction of the Uniform Commercial Code requires, of course, that its interpretation and application be limited to its reason."

Illustrative of open-ended drafting are Code references to

1. "Usage of trade." § 1–303(c).

2. "Good faith," which means honesty in fact and the observance of reasonable commercial standards of fair dealing. §§ 1–201(b)(20), 1–304; see, e.g., §§ 2–403(1), 2A–304(1), 2A–305(1), 3–302(a)(2), 7–501(a)(5).

3. "Commercially reasonable." See, e.g., §§ 2–706, 2A–527, 7–210, 7–308, 9–610, 9–627.

The Code, accordingly, encourages construction in Llewellyn's "Grand Style" of the common law, which "rests on the court's overt recourse to situation-sense to shape the deciding rule and on constant retest of the rule in the light of reason as it evolves from the situation." S. Mentschikoff, Commercial Transactions 4 note 3 (1970). A Code rule, consequently, should be construed and applied in a manner similar to the method employed by a court in construing and applying a case law (common law) rule. Accordingly, Comment 1 to § 1–103 authorizes reasoning by analogy thus: "The courts have often recognized that the policies embodied in an act are applicable in reason to subject-matter that was not expressly included in the language of the act, ... and did the same where reason and policy so required, even where the subject-matter had been intentionally excluded from the act in general." See also §§ 2–105 Comment 1 (investment securities), 2–313 Comment 2 [Comment 4 (2003) (warranties)].

But what if a fact situation appears to fit the factual preconditions of a Code rule but is not within the reason of the rule? Instead of misconstruing the language of the rule to exclude the fact situation, the Code gives authority to a court, not to mishandle the textual Code rule, but to say this factual situation is different in terms of its reason and therefore the court need not apply the rule. See S. Mentschikoff, Commercial Transactions 11 (1970). Thus, Comment 1 to § 1–103 says, "[Courts have] disregarded a statutory limitation of remedy where the reason of the limitation did not apply.... Nothing in the Uniform Commercial Code stands in the way of the continuance of such action by the courts." See also §§ 1–104 (implied repeal), 1–105 (severability), 1–305 (remedies), 10–103 (general repealer).

Freedom of Contract

Freedom of contract is a principle of the Code, and the effect of its provisions may be varied by agreement. Thus, many Code sections contain gap-filling rules which apply unless the parties otherwise agree. See, e.g., §§ 2–307 (delivery), 2–308 (place of delivery), 2–310 (time of payment), 2–509(4) (risk of loss absent breach). Note that the presence in certain Code provisions of the words "unless otherwise agreed" does not imply that the effect of other provisions may not be varied by agreement. § 1–302(a), (c) and Comments 1 and 3.

This principle is subject to exceptions. First is the general exception that the obligations of good faith, diligence, reasonableness, and care prescribed by the Code may not be disclaimed by agreement. § 1–302(b) and Comment 1, see § 1–304; cf. § 4–103(a). Second, certain sections explicitly preclude variance. See, e.g., §§ 2–318 (third party warranty beneficiaries), 9–602. Third, it is implicit that some sections may not be varied. See, e.g., §§ 1–302 Comment 1, 2–201 (statute of frauds), 9–317 (priority over unperfected interests). Cf. § 9–201(a) and Comment 2.

Further, certain contracts and clauses thereof may not be enforceable due to unconscionability. §§ 2–302, 2–309(3) (notice of termination), 2–719(3) (consequential damages), see §§ 2–718 (damages limited or liquidated) and Comment 1 [Comment 3 (2003)], 2A–108.

Supplementary General Principles

Unless displaced by the particular provisions of the UCC, the principles of law and equity supplement its provisions. § 1–103(b).

Comment 2 to § 1–103 explains: "[W]hile principles of common law and equity may *supplement* provisions of the Uniform Commercial Code, they may not be used to *supplant* its provisions, or the purposes and policies those provisions reflect, unless a specific provision of the [UCC] provides otherwise. In the absence of such a provision, the [UCC] preempts principles of common law and equity that are inconsistent with either [i] its provisions or [ii] its purposes and policies."

OUTLINE

PART TWO.   THE PROCESS OF LEASING GOODS

PART FIVE. FINANCING THE SALE OF GOODS: THE SECURED TRANSACTION

PART SIX. THE ENTIRE TRANSACTION MADE PURSUANT TO A LETTER OF CREDIT [p. 592]

TABLE OF CITATIONS TO THE UNIFORM COMMERCIAL CODE

TABLE OF CITATIONS TO THE UNIFORM COMMERCIAL CODE

TABLE OF CITATIONS TO THE UNIFORM COMMERCIAL CODE

TABLE OF CITATIONS TO THE UNIFORM COMMERCIAL CODE

TABLE OF CITATIONS TO THE UNIFORM COMMERCIAL CODE

C

TABLE OF CITATIONS TO THE UNIFORM COMMERCIAL CODE

TABLE OF CITATIONS TO THE UNIFORM COMMERCIAL CODE

TABLE OF CITATIONS TO THE UNIFORM COMMERCIAL CODE

TABLE OF CITATIONS TO THE UNIFORM COMMERCIAL CODE

TABLE OF CITATIONS TO THE UNIFORM COMMERCIAL CODE

UNIFORM
COMMERCIAL CODE
IN A NUTSHELL

EIGHTH EDITION

PART ONE

THE PROCESS OF SELLING GOODS

[Prefatory Note: In May 2011, the American Law Institute withdrew the 2003 Amendments to Article 2 from the Official Text of the Uniform Commercial Code. Consequently, this Part One will continue to present pre-2003 Article 2. In brackets, however, the proposed changes under Amended (2003) Article 2 are set forth for informational purposes. This Part One does reflect Revised (2001) Article 1 General Provisions and Revised (2003) Article 7 Documents of Title. As to the relation of Articles 1 and 2 to Electronic Signatures in Global and National Commerce Act (E–SIGN), see §§ 1–108 and Comments, 2–108(4) and Comment 5; as to Uniform Electronic Transactions Act (UETA), see § UETA 3(b)(2) and Comments 4 and 7.]

A. SCOPE OF ARTICLE 2 SALES

Since the focal point of the UCC is the sale of and payment for goods, it would seem logical that Article 2, Sales, would apply to *sales* of *goods*. Yet § 2–102 states that Article 2 applies to *transactions* in goods. This indicates a scope broader than sales, e.g., leases, rentals, and gifts of goods, as well as sales. However, most sections of Article 2, e.g., warranties, do relate literally only to sales. For leases, see Part Two infra. CISG 1–6 (scope and applicability), 10 ("place of business" defined), 95 (reservations re: applicability).

A *sale* consists of the passing of title from the seller to the buyer for a *price*. § 2–106(1). The *price* can be payable in money or otherwise, e.g., other goods, services, or realty [real property]. § 2–304. Cf. § 2A–103(1)(j) (2A–103(1)(p) (2003)) ("lease" and "lessor" defined).

Goods means all things that are movable at the time of identification to the contract for sale, that is, tangible personal property, not realty. §§ 2–105(1)–(4) (defining "goods"), 2–501 (identification of goods). Accordingly, *things [choses] in action* (intangibles) are excluded. *Money* as a medium of payment is excluded, but money as a commodity (coin collection for sale) is included. *Investment securities* are excluded since they are covered by UCC Article 8. CISG 2(d). However, an Article 2 section may be applied to investment securities by analogy when the reason of the Article 2 section makes such application sensible and Article 8 does not deal specifically with the problem. §§ 2–105 Comment 1, 1–103 Comment 1, see former § 8–107 Comment 2.

[*2003 Amend.* The term *goods*, now defined at § 2–103(1)(k), also excludes (i) information and (ii) the subject matter of foreign exchange transactions. § 2–103(1)(i) and Comment 7; cf. § 9–102(a)(44) and Comment 4.] The appropriate treatment of "information," specifically "computer information," is also a major focus of the American Law Institute's Principles of the Law of Software Contracts. The Reporters' memorandum provides a useful overview of the project, which was finalized in May 2009, including its relationship to earlier initiatives such as the Uniform Computer Information Transactions Act and the UCC Article 2B project.

Goods v. services

Whether a transaction involves a sale of goods or the rendering of a service has caused considerable difficulty. Courts have disagreed as to whether, for instance, blood furnished in a blood transfusion involves goods or services. The same kind of problem arises with hair dye applied by a beautician in a beauty parlor. The Code does explicitly include specially manufactured goods as goods (not services). § 2–105(1) (2–103(1)(k) (2003)). Also, the Code states that serving food or drink to be consumed either on or off the premises of a restaurateur is a sale of goods, at least for the purpose of the implied warranty of merchantability. § 2–314(1). CISG 3.

[*2003 Amend.* New § 2–108 (Transactions subject to other law) states, e.g., that a transaction subject to Article 2 is also subject to any applicable statute dealing with the transfer of human blood, blood products, tissues, or parts. § 2–108(1)(c)(ii).]

Goods to be severed from realty

Are contracts for the sale of goods to be severed from realty within the scope of Article 2, or are such transactions to be considered contracts affecting land and Article 2 thus inapplicable? The Code answers as follows:

1. A contract for sale of minerals or the like or a structure or its materials to be removed from realty is a contract for sale of goods if they are to be severed from the realty by *seller;* if buyer is to sever, it is considered a land contract.

2. A contract for sale of growing crops or other things attached to realty and capable of severance without material harm (except minerals and structures described in rule 1) or of timber to be cut is a contract for sale of goods, whether the subject matter is to be severed by the buyer or the seller. § 2–107(2) and Comment 2. The 1962 Code included timber within rule 1.

Lastly, Article 2 does not apply to Article 9 security transactions. § 2–107 Comment 3. Article 2 also does not repeal regulatory statutes relating to consumers, farmers, etc., § 2–102. See new § 2–108 (2003). As to multistate transactions, see § 1–105 (§ 1–301 (2001)).

B. THE CONTRACT FOR SALE

It should be noted at the outset that the law of sales of goods is but a part of the law of contracts generally. Thus, general contract law is applicable to sales law unless displaced by the particular provisions of the Code. § 1–103(b). Consequently, unless displaced by Code provisions, the general law of offer and acceptance, consideration, capacity to contract, etc., is applicable. Restatement (Second) of Contracts §§ 9–81. CISG 14–24 (contract formation). The following summarizes the Code's effect on this general law.

1. FORMATION OF THE SALES CONTRACT— MUTUAL ASSENT

A. WHEN AND HOW AGREEMENT IS MADE

It is the Code's basic policy to recognize that a contract may be made in any manner sufficient to show agreement. Such agreement may be oral, written, or manifested by conduct by both parties recognizing the existence of a contract. Of course, provisions such as the statute of frauds may qualify the legal effect of the agreement. §§ 2–204(1), 2–207(3), 2–201, 1–201(b)(3) and (12) (defining "agreement" and "contract").

An agreement frequently arises when an *offer* is followed by an unqualified *acceptance.* Sometimes, however, interchanged correspondence does not disclose the exact point at which the deal was closed, but the actions of the parties (e.g., performance of the agreement) indicate a binding obligation has been undertaken. Thus, the Code states that a contract may be found even if the moment of its making is undetermined. § 2–204(2), see § 2–207(3) (battle of the forms).

[*2003 Amend.* Section 2–204(1) adds that a contract may be made by the interaction of electronic agents and the interaction of an electronic agent and an individual. See new § 2–204 (4) and Comments 1, 4, and 5; §§ 2–211 through 2–213 and Comments.]

B. THE INDEFINITE OFFER

An offer should be sufficiently definite so that, when it is accepted, the terms of the resulting agreement will reasonably inform the parties what they are obligated to do and will enable a court—in the event of litigation—to ascertain the legal obligations the parties assumed. In this vein, the UCC states that, even if one or more terms are left open, a contract for sale does not fail for indefiniteness if (1) the parties have intended to make a contract and (2) there is a reasonably certain basis for giving an appropriate remedy. § 2–204(3). "The test is not certainty as to what the parties were to do nor as to the exact amount of damages due the plaintiff. Nor is the fact that one or more terms are left to be agreed upon enough of itself to defeat an otherwise adequate agreement. Rather, commercial standards on the point of 'indefiniteness' are intended to be applied.... The more terms the parties leave open, the less likely it is that they have intended to conclude a binding agreement, but their actions may be frequently conclusive on the matter despite the omissions [e.g., where they have performed their agreement]." § 2–204 Comment (Comment 3 (2003)(with minor changes)). CISG 14(1).

Counseling point: If open terms remain, state explicitly whether a binding agreement is intended.

To fill in the gaps when the parties have left terms open though they intended a contract, the Code incorporates numerous provisions into the contract absent an *agreement* otherwise. "Agreement" means the bargain of the parties in fact, as found in their language or inferred from other circumstances, including course of performance, course of dealing, or usage of trade. §§ 1–201(b)(3), 1–303.

The most common of these open term provisions relate to price, delivery, payment, duration, options respecting performance, and quantity. These are discussed below.

Open price term

If the parties intend to conclude a contract even though the price is not settled, the price shall be determined thus:

1.   If (a) nothing is said as to price, (b) the price is left to be agreed upon by the parties and they *fail* to agree, or (c) the price is to be fixed in terms of some agreed market or other standard as set or recorded by a third person and it is *not* so set or recorded: Then the price is a reasonable price at the time for delivery. § 2–305(1).

2.   If the price is to be fixed by the seller or by the buyer, then the price is what the designated party fixes in good faith. §§ 2–305(2) and Comment 3, 1–304 (obligation of good faith), 1–201(19) (1–201(b)(20) (2001)) (defining "good faith"), 2–103(1)(b) (2–103(1)(j) (2003)) (defining a merchant's "good faith"), 1–302(b) (good faith cannot be disclaimed).

3.   If a price left to be fixed otherwise than by agreement of the parties fails to be fixed through the fault of one party, then the other party may at his option (a) treat the contract as cancelled, or (b) himself fix a reasonable price. Example: A and B contract for sale of goods, A to fix the price. The agreement becomes economically burdensome to A and A refuses to fix the price. B may either treat the contract as cancelled or himself fix a reasonable price. § 2–305(3). CISG 14(1), 55.

[*2003 Amend.* To achieve gender neutrality, *him, himself, his* are deleted.]

Open delivery term

When no delivery terms are specified,

1. The place for delivery is normally the seller's place of business. § 2–308(a). CISG 31(c).

2. The time for delivery is a reasonable time. § 2–309(1). CISG 33(c).

3. The manner of delivery is by a single lot (not several lots); the seller must put and hold conforming goods at the buyer's disposition and give the buyer any notification reasonably necessary to enable the buyer to take delivery. §§ 2–307, 2–503(1). As to auctions, see 2–328(1).

Open payment term

When parties are silent as to payment terms,

1. Payment is due at the time and place at which the buyer is to receive the goods, i.e., by cash not credit. § 2–310(a). See also §§ 2–307 (single lot or multiple lots), 2–310(d) (credit period), 2–513(1) (inspection), 2–103(1)(c) (2–103(1)(*l*) (2003)) (receipt). CISG 57(1), 58(1).

2. Payment is sufficient when made by any means or in any manner current in the ordinary course of business unless the seller demands payment in legal tender. § 2–511(2). See CISG 54, 59.

Open term as to duration of the contract

Assume A appoints B to be a dealer for A; thus, B is to market goods A will manufacture and sell to B. The agreement does not specify how long A and B are required to deal with each other, thereby raising a potential lack of mutuality of obligation. For what time is the contract valid? Answer: "Where the contract provides for successive performances but is indefinite in duration it is valid for a reasonable time but unless otherwise agreed may be terminated at any time by either party." §§ 2–309(2) (source of quote, with minor changes in 2003) and

Comment 7, 2–106(3). But "[t]ermination of a contract by one party except on the happening of an agreed event requires that reasonable notification be received by the other party and an agreement dispensing with notification is invalid if its operation would be unconscionable." § 2–309(3) and Comment 8, see § 2–302 (unconscionability). Policy involved: good faith and sound commercial practice normally call for notification of the termination of a going contract relationship to give the other party reasonable time to seek a substitute arrangement.

[*2003 Amend.* Section 2–309(3) adds, "A term specifying standards for the nature and timing of notice is enforceable if the standards are not manifestly unreasonable." See Comment 11 and § 1–302(b); § 2–108(1)(c)(iv) and (vi).]

Particulars of performance to be specified by a party

Specifications relating to assortment of the goods are at the buyer's option. Example: Contract for sale of 600 pens; B opts to take 100 blue pens and 500 green pens. Specifications or arrangements relating to shipment will be at the seller's option. § 2–311(1), (2) and Comments 1 and 2. CISG 65.

Quantity: contract for output or requirements

A contract for the seller's "output" or buyer's "requirements" means the actual good faith output or requirements of the particular party. The party who will determine the quantity is required to operate or conduct his business in good faith so that his output or requirements will approximate a reasonably foreseeable figure. §§ 2–306(1) and Comments 1–4, 1–201(19) (1–201(b)(20) (2001)) (defining "good faith"), 2–103(1)(b) (2–103(1)(j) (2003)) (defining "good faith" for merchants), 1–304 (obligation of good faith). An open quantity term—aside from output or requirements contracts—is probably too indefinite to constitute a valid agreement; no commercial standard can readily be applied to determine quantity in order to give a reasonably certain basis for an appropriate remedy. § 2–204(3) and Comment (Comment 3 (2003)) CISG 14(1).

Other omitted terms

The Code also supplies other commonly omitted terms. See, e.g., §§ 2–312 (warranty of title), 2–314 (merchantability), 2–315 (fitness), 2–513 (inspection).

C.   FIRM OFFER TO BUY OR SELL

Assume A offers either to buy goods from B or sell goods to B. A's offer states, ''This offer is firm for a period of 30 days from the date hereof.'' A seeks to withdraw his offer ten days later. At common law, without an ''option'' agreement, A could withdraw his offer since his promise to keep his offer open was not supported by consideration. Under the Code, an offer by a merchant to buy or sell goods in a signed writing that gives assurance that it will be held open is not revocable for lack of consideration. Such an offer is irrevocable for the period of time stated or, if no time is stated, for a reasonable time. But in no event may irrevocability exceed three months. Purpose of rule: to give effect to a merchant's deliberate intention to make a firm offer binding. § 2–205 and Comments 2 and 3.

Thus, in the above example, if A is a merchant and the offer is in a signed writing, effect is given to the merchant's ''firm offer.'' However, if A's firm offer was contained in a form prepared by the offeree, B, such firm offer must be separately signed by the offeror, A. Purpose of rule: to protect A against the inadvertent signing of a firm offer contained in the ''boiler plate'' language on B's form. §§ 2–205, 2–104(1), 1–201(b)(37) and (43). CISG 16(2).

[*2003 Amend. Writing* is changed to *record*. §§ 1–201(b)(31), 2–103(1)(m).]

D. ACCEPTANCE OF OFFER

(1) Manner and Medium of Acceptance

A writes a letter to B offering either to buy or sell goods. A's letter says, "This offer may be accepted only by mail addressed to A at [A's *address*] and shall not be effective unless received at that address prior to [*date*]." Because A stipulated the manner, medium, time, and place of acceptance, any variation from A's stipulation in B's "acceptance" would probably result in a counteroffer under general contract law. Restatement (Second) of Contracts § 59.

Suppose A's offer, however, is silent as to manner, medium, time, and place of acceptance. Some pre-UCC rules required that offers by mail be accepted by mail; telegraphic offers be accepted by telegraphic acceptance, etc. Otherwise, a counteroffer resulted. The Code rejects such rules by stating, "Unless otherwise unambiguously indicated by the language or circumstances [as in the above example which stipulated the manner and medium of acceptance]... an offer to make a contract shall be construed as inviting acceptance in any manner and by any medium reasonable in the circumstances...." § 2–206(1)(a) and Comment 1. Thus, a telegraphic acceptance to a mailed offer—if reasonable—would operate as an acceptance, not a counteroffer. Although the Code does not specifically state that such a telegraphic acceptance would be effective when *dispatched* by the offeree rather than *received* by the offeror, this is the prevailing rule under the general law of contracts. Restatement (Second) of Contracts §§ 63, 67. CISG 18, 20–24.

(2) Acceptance of Ambiguous Offer by Performance or Promise to Perform

B sends A a purchase order stating in part, "Ship at once the following...." Is B's offer to be construed as given in exchange for a *shipment* (resulting in a unilateral contract) or for a *promise* to ship (resulting in a bilateral contract)? Answer: In accordance with ordinary commercial understanding, UCC § 2–206(1)(b) interprets such an order as allowing acceptance *either* by actual *shipment* or by a prompt *promise* to ship, and rejects the artificial theory that only a single mode of acceptance is normally envisaged by an offeror. § 2–206 Comment 2. Thus, A either may ship or promise to ship. If A elects to ship, a unilateral contract results, and nothing in § 2–206 affects the general common-law rule that performance begun (though not yet completed) may temporarily bar revocation of the offer. This is a modification of the general rule that an offer may be revoked any time prior to acceptance. Restatement (Second) of Contracts §§ 42, 50. However, B must be notified of A's acceptance by performance within a reasonable time, or B may treat the offer as having lapsed before acceptance. § 2–206(2) and Comment 3.

Suppose, in the above example, A accepts B's offer by shipping the goods described in the purchase order, resulting in a unilateral contract. If it turns out that the goods did not conform to B's description (see §§ 2–313, 2–314) and B brings suit for breach of warranty, pre-Code, one could argue that A's "acceptance" by shipping nonconforming goods was in fact a counteroffer which B accepted by taking the nonconforming goods. Thus, A did not breach the contract. This has been called "the unilateral contract trick." The UCC position is that a nonconforming shipment is normally to be understood as intended to close the bargain, even though it proves to have been at the same time a breach. Consequently, under the Code, A's shipment of nonconforming goods would constitute both an act of acceptance and a breach of the contract. § 2–206(1)(b) and Comment 4. But what if A does not have the goods described in B's purchase order but believes the goods he has may be an acceptable substitute? May A ship such substitute goods without breaching the contract? Answer: Shipment of nonconforming goods does not constitute an acceptance if A seasonably notifies B that the shipment is offered only as an accommodation to B. § 2–206(1)(b). CISG 18(3).

(3) Acceptance with Additional or Different Terms

Under Amended § 2–206(3) (2003), "[a] definite and seasonable expression of acceptance . . . operates as an acceptance even if it contains terms additional to or different from the offer." See § 2–206 Comments 2 and 3. Cf. former § 2–207(1). See discussion of "Qualified" Acceptance immediately below.

E. "QUALIFIED" ACCEPTANCE CONTAINING ADDITIONAL TERMS

Assume A makes an offer to B, and B in terms accepts, but adds, "Prompt acknowledgment must be made of receipt of this letter," or "Rush." At common law, there would be no contract. Instead, because B's purported acceptance was qualified, in legal effect it constituted a rejection of A's offer and a counteroffer by B. Restatement of Contracts § 60; cf. Restatement (Second) of Contracts §§ 50, 58, 59. Under this view, the acceptance must be a "mirror image" of the offer; stated differently, the offer and acceptance must "ribbon match." The UCC changes this "mirror image" rule by stating that a definite and seasonable expression of acceptance sent within a reasonable time operates as an acceptance *even though* it states terms additional to or different from those offered. § 2–207(1). Rationale: A proposed deal that in *commercial understanding* has been closed should be recognized as a contract. §§ 2–207 Comments 1 and 2, 2–204. Note: Certain comments to § 2–207 were amended or added in 1966.

A common situation with which § 2–207 deals is the exchange of printed purchase order and acceptance (sometimes called "acknowledgment") forms. Because the forms are oriented to the thinking of the respective drafting parties, the terms contained in them often do not correspond. Instead, the seller's form may contain terms different from or additional to those set forth in the buyer's form. This conflict is sometimes known as the "battle of the forms." For example, suppose that in response to A's sales catalogue (an invitation to make an offer), B mails to A a pre-printed form-pad purchase order (an offer) ordering 100 widgets, price $50.00 each, delivery F.O.B. Seller City. These matters are typed in appropriate blanks on the form. On the reverse side are numerous printed "boiler plate" provisions, including this one:

By accepting this order, Seller [A] hereby warrants that the items furnished hereunder will be in full conformity with Buyer's [B's] specifications, and that all items furnished hereunder will be fit for the use intended by Buyer. This warranty is in addition to any warranties, express or implied, given to Buyer by Seller.

A receives the order and sends to B an acknowledgment form reciting the information on B's purchase order form, to wit: the described goods and their quantity, price, and delivery terms. However, on the back of the acknowledgment form is the following printed provision:

Except for the warranty that the goods are made in a workmanlike manner and in accordance with the specifications therefor supplied or agreed to by buyer and are made or packaged pursuant to seller's customary manufacturing procedures, SELLER MAKES NO WARRANTY, EXPRESS OR IMPLIED, AND ANY IMPLIED WARRANTY OF MERCHANTABILITY OR FITNESS FOR A PARTICULAR PURPOSE EXCEEDING THE FOREGOING WARRANTY IS HEREBY DISCLAIMED BY SELLER AND EXCLUDED FROM ANY AGREEMENT MADE BY ACCEPTANCE OF ANY ORDER PURSUANT TO THIS QUOTATION. Seller will not be liable for any consequential damages, loss, or expense arising in connection with the use of or the inability to use its goods for any purpose whatever. Seller's maximum liability shall not in any case exceed the contract price for the goods claimed to be defective or unsuitable.

A further provision states, "Any controversy or claim arising out of or relating to this contract, or the breach thereof, shall be settled by arbitration in accordance with the Rules of the American Arbitration Association, and judgment upon the award rendered by the Arbitrator(s) may be entered in any Court having jurisdiction thereof."

Does the exchange of the above forms result in a contract? If so, what are the terms?

Common-law analysis

If A sent the above acknowledgment to B but did *not* ship the goods, B would be unable to recover damages from A because A's acknowledgment varied from B's purchase order. The acknowledgment constituted a counteroffer which, if not accepted by B, would not ripen into a contract. If A *did* ship the goods to B, B's act of taking the goods—subsequent to the receipt of the acknowledgment—would be an acceptance of A's counteroffer; thus A's terms would prevail. This has been called the "last shot" principle because the terms of the last form sent and received prior to delivery of the goods would govern.

UCC analysis

The Code drafters found these common-law results undesirable. Consequently, under the UCC, A's acknowledgment would probably constitute a definite and seasonable expression of acceptance and would operate as an acceptance even though it stated terms additional to or different from those offered by B. § 2–207(1). Policy: A proposed deal that in *commercial understanding* has in fact been closed should be recognized as a contract. §§ 2–

207 Comment 2, 2–204. Thus, even though A did *not* ship the goods, B would have a remedy against A for breach of contract, contrary to the common-law result.

But what if A *did* ship the goods and B took them after receiving A's acknowledgment? The above analysis shows that we have a contract, even though A's acknowledgment varies from B's purchase order. Now, a difficult question arises: What are the terms of this contract? Recall that A's acknowledgment terms would prevail at common law. The Code intimates that A accepts all of B's purchase order terms, but proposes that the *additional* terms in A's acknowledgment become part of the contract. § 2–207(2). The text does not address how *different* terms should be treated. The Code Comment, however, indicates that the offeree may propose that additional *or different* terms be part of the contract. § 2–207 Comment 3; see also Restatement (Second) of Contracts § 59, Comment a, which states, "The additional or different terms are then to be construed as proposals for modification of the contract.... Such proposals may sometimes be accepted by the silence of the original offeror."

In our example, the *additional* terms in A's acknowledgment are the (1) arbitration term, (2) the preclusion of consequential damages term, and (3) the maximum liability term. The *different* terms are A's exclusion of the implied warranties of merchantability and fitness for a particular purpose, which B's purchase order appears to include. §§ 2–314, 2–315, 2–316.

If we read § 2–207(2) as the Comments do, the additional terms and different terms in A's acknowledgment are to be construed as proposals for modification of the contract. When will such terms become part of the contract? If (1) A and B are merchants, (2) B's offer has not expressly limited acceptance to the terms of his offer, and (3) B has not given appropriate notice of objection to the additional and different terms, then A's proposed terms become part of the contract unless they materially alter it. § 2–207(2).

How do we test materiality? According to the Code Comments, a term would materially alter the contract if it would result in unreasonable surprise or hardship if incorporated without express awareness by the other party. An example of a term that would not "materially alter" the contract is a clause limiting the right of rejection for defects that fall within the customary trade tolerances for acceptance "with adjustment." § 2–207 Comment 5, see §§ 2–601, 2–718, 2–719. Thus, the following rule of thumb may be of some help in determining materiality: If the new clause added is not too different from the ordinary pattern of contracts used in the trade, it may not be a material alteration. See § 1–303.

Although the facts in our example are too sparse to afford a basis for determining the ordinary pattern of contracts in A's and B's trade, we will assume that A's additional and different terms do materially alter the contract. Thus, we would have a contract on B's terms, and none of A's proposals would become part of the contract. This is contrary to the common law where—if delivery occurs and B accepts the goods—a contract would result on A's terms per the "last shot" principle. The Code Comments are not clear as to why the drafters did not apply the "last shot" principle in this context. The policy probably follows this thought process: Offeree A made a definite and seasonable expression of acceptance, but added additional or different terms; then, A shipped the goods. B received A's acknowledgment form containing the equivocal language, and shortly thereafter received the goods. At this late date, B is in great need of the goods and cannot as a practical matter refuse to take them pending negotiation of terms of the contract with A. B's taking the goods under such circumstances is a weak form of acceptance, particularly as it relates to A's additional or different terms. Since A's conduct caused this problem, A should take the risk that B will not expressly assent to the additional or different terms.

But what if the writings of A and B do not establish a contract for sale, yet the goods are accepted and paid for before any dispute arises? There is no question as to whether a contract has been made; the only question is what terms the contract includes. § 2–207 Comment 7. For instance, in the above example suppose B's offer expressly limited A's acceptance to the terms of B's offer (§ 2–207(2)(a)), or A made the acceptance expressly conditional on assent to the additional or different terms (§ 2–207(1)), or most clearly of all, suppose A rejected B's offer and made a counteroffer including the additional or different terms. If B takes the goods in these circumstances, is this an acceptance of A's counteroffer? In other words, should the "last shot" principle govern so that A's additional or different terms prevail? The Code seemingly rejects this result: "Conduct by both parties which recognizes the existence of a contract is sufficient to establish a contract for sale although the writings of the parties do not otherwise establish a contract. In such case the terms of the particular contract consist of those terms on which the writings of the parties agree, together with any supplementary terms incorporated under any other provisions of [the UCC]. "..." § 2–207(3) and Comment 7.

In our example, A and B do not agree on warranties and remedies. A seeks to limit warranties, limit his maximum liability, and exclude liability for consequential damages. Further, A seeks to have disputes settled by arbitration. Thus, under § 2–207(3), these terms not agreed upon drop out, and the Code provisions as to warranties and remedies will be incorporated by default. The resultant contract therefore (1) will include warranties of merchantability and fitness for particular purpose (§§ 2–314, 2–315), (2) will not limit maximum liability to the contract price (e.g., § 2–714), and (3) will include liability for consequential damages (§ 2–715(2)). Further, the Code does not provide for disputes to be settled by arbitration, so the parties' contract will not do so, either. Again as under § 2–207(1) and (2), the resultant contract favors B, whereas the common law would favor A under these facts.

Counseling point to A: You cannot count on the counteroffer and "last shot" principle under the Code. The safe approach is to get B's express assent to your additional or different terms before you ship the goods; alternatively, negotiate in advance an overriding agreement with B that will prevail over the terms of your exchanged order and acknowledgment forms. Example: "This agreement shall replace any provisions other than [*state provisions*], set forth on the face or reverse side of your purchase order, and provisions so replaced shall not be applicable to your purchases from us. Similarly, this agreement shall replace any provisions other than [*state provisions*], set forth either on the face or on the reverse side of our acknowledgment form, and provisions so replaced shall not be applicable to your purchases from us. [*State terms of the overriding agreement.*]" 12 West's Legal Forms § 2.7—Form 19.

Section 2–207 also deals with a written confirmation of an agreement that has already been made either orally or by informal correspondence between the parties. Such a confirmation is normally a formal memorandum embodying the terms agreed upon and adding terms not yet discussed. § 2–207 Comment 1. CISG 19.

[*2003 Amend.* Section 2–207 applies to all contracts for sale of goods, not only to the "battle of the forms," but applies only when a contract has been created under another section (§§ 2–204, 2–206 esp.(3)). The purpose of revised 2–207 is solely to determine the *terms* of the contract. When forms are exchanged before or during performance, revised 2–207 *differs* from prior 2–207 and the common law in that revised 2–207 gives *no preference* to either the *first* or *last* form; the same test is applied to the terms in each. In such a case, the terms of the contract are (a) terms that appear in the records of both parties; (b) terms (whether in a record or not) to which both parties agree; and (c) terms supplied or incorporated under any provision of the UCC, e.g., 2–715(2)(a). Thus, if B and S disagree as to recovery of consequential damages, their competing terms will drop out, and the court will plug in 2–715(2)(a), which *allows* recovery of foreseeable consequential damages. See § 2–207 and Comments.]

F.   OFFER AND ACCEPTANCE IN SALE BY AUCTION

When sale by auction completed

Consistent with general contract law, the Code assumes that an auctioneer invites bids and the bidders are the offerors. Restatement (Second) of Contracts § 28. The auctioneer accepts the winning bid—that is, the sale is complete—when the auctioneer so announces by the fall of the hammer. § 2–328(2), see § 2–328(1). If B makes a bid while the hammer is falling in acceptance of a prior bid by A, the auctioneer may, in the auctioneer's discretion, (1) reopen the bidding, or (2) declare the goods sold under A's bid. § 2–328(2).

Retraction of bid

A bidder may retract the bid until the auctioneer announces the completion of the sale. Restatement (Second) of Contracts § 28. (Offeror may withdraw offer anytime before acceptance.) The retraction does not revive any previous bid. § 2–328(3).

Right to withdraw goods from auction

In an auction *with reserve*, the auctioneer *may* withdraw the goods at any time before announcing completion of the sale. In an auction *without* reserve, *after* the auctioneer calls for bids on an article or lot, that article or lot *cannot* be withdrawn unless no bid is made within a reasonable time. A sale is with reserve unless explicitly labeled as being without reserve. § 2–328(3).

Effect of bid on behalf of seller

Secret bidding by or on behalf of the seller is wrongful. Such a bidder is not seeking to buy, but rather to bid up the price. Here, the buyer (winning bidder) may (a) avoid the sale, or (b) take the goods at the price of the last good faith bid prior to the completion of the sale. § 2–328(4). CISG 2(b).

[*2003 Amend.* Because of different usage, the phrases "with reserve" and "without reserve" are no longer used in § 2–328. See § 2–328 Comment 2. Further, Comment 3 states that, under § 2–328(3), a sale "with reserve" can be converted to a sale "without reserve" during the course of the auction. Original 2–328(3) did not recognize this possibility.]

G. BUYER'S RIGHT TO CANCEL HOME SOLICITATION SALE

Contract principles are modified in a home solicitation sale (door-to-door sale) by allowing a buyer to cancel the sale by midnight of the third business day after the date of the transaction. 16 CFR Part 429, Uniform Consumer Credit Code (UCCC) § 2.501 et seq. (1968), UCCC § 3.501 et seq. (1974). CISG 2(a).

2. THE REQUIREMENT OF CONSIDERATION

A. IN GENERAL

The Code does not alter the general contract rule that an agreement, to be binding, must be supported by consideration. §§ 1–103(b) (Code's relationship to other law), 2–301 (parties' general obligations), 2–106(1) (defining "contract"); Restatement (Second) of Contracts §§ 17, 71. CISG 1(1) (applicability), 30 (seller's obligations), 53 (buyer's obligations). In certain instances, however, the Code does deal with consideration.

B. FIRM OFFER

A firm offer by a merchant is not revocable for lack of consideration. § 2–205. CISG 16(2).

C. CHANGING THE CONTRACT—MODIFICATION, RESCISSION, WAIVER

A agrees to manufacture and sell certain goods to B for $1,500. Subsequently, a shift in the market makes it impossible for A to sell to B at this price without suffering a loss. Thus, B agrees to pay an additional $500 for the goods. Later, B reconsiders and refuses to pay more than the original $1,500 price. At common law, B's promise to pay an additional $500 was not enforceable because it was not supported by consideration. Why? A was under a "pre-existing duty" to deliver the goods. Restatement (Second) of Contracts § 86. UCC § 2–209(1) changes this result: under the Code, an agreement modifying a contract is binding without consideration. See § 2–616 Comment (Comment 1 (2003)). Policy: To protect and make effective all necessary and desirable modifications of sales contracts without regard to technicalities (e.g., pre-existing duty rule) that hampered such adjustments under common law. § 2–209 Comment 1.

However, such modifications must meet the test of good faith. §§ 1–304, 1–201(b)(20) ("good faith" defined), 2–103(1)(j) (2003) (same), see § 2–302 (unconscionability). A market shift as in the above example may provide a good faith reason. But what if there is no market shift but A knows that B needs the goods seasonably delivered and refuses delivery unless B agrees to pay the additional $500? Extortion of a modification without legitimate commercial reason would violate the duty of good faith. Even a technical consideration (A agrees to deliver a cigar to B in addition to delivery of the goods) will not support a modification made in bad faith. § 2–209 Comment 2.

Because of the danger of false allegations of oral modifications, the contract as modified must satisfy the statute of frauds (e.g., contracts for sale of goods for $500 or more must be memorialized in writing). §§ 2–209(3), 2–201. Further, the parties may in effect make their own statute of frauds: a signed agreement that excludes modification or rescission except by a signed writing cannot be otherwise modified or rescinded. However, if a non-merchant is to be held to such a clause in a form supplied by a merchant, it must be separately signed. § 2–209(2) and Comment 3. Cf. "separately signed" requirement of § 2–205 (firm offers).

Despite the provisions in § 2–209(2) and (3), which are designed to prevent contractual modification except by a signed writing, an oral modification or rescission may operate as a *waiver.* Example: A agrees in writing to sell goods to B for $1,500, with delivery to be in ten days. A is able and willing to deliver the goods, but the parties agree orally to extend the delivery date by twenty days. This would constitute an ineffective oral modification of the contract. However, if A relies on the oral modification and delays delivery for the twenty days, B has *waived* the original delivery date. Although B may retract the waiver by reasonable notification that strict performance will be required of any term waived (ten days, not twenty additional days), B may not do so if the retraction would be unjust in view of a material change of position by A (such as deferring delivery) in reliance on B's waiver. § 2–209(4), (5). Policy: To prevent contractual provisions that exclude modification except by a signed writing from limiting in other respects the legal effect of the parties' actual later conduct. § 2–209 Comment 4; see §§ 1–306, 1–308, 2–720. CISG 7(1), 29.

[*2003 Amend. A signed agreement* is now *an agreement in a signed record; writing* is now *record.* § 2–209(2). The Statute of Frauds jurisdictional amount has been amended from $500 to $5,000; *writing* is now *record* for this purpose, also. §§ 2–201, 2–209(3).]

D. THE ILLUSORY PROMISE

Assume A and B agree that A will sell to B certain goods that B may "choose to order," or which B "wishes," "wants," or "desires," for a certain period of time. B's promise is illusory. B has suffered no legal detriment; the agreement is lacking mutuality of obligation. Thus, there is no consideration for A's promise to sell and, accordingly, no legal obligation results. Restatement (Second) of Contracts § 77.

Output contracts

If A agrees to sell to B "all of A's output of [*describe goods*] produced from (*date*) to (*date*)," such promise would not be illusory. B must buy the output; A, if A has an output, must sell to B. § 2–306(1) and Comment 2.

Requirements contracts

If A agrees to sell to B "all of B's requirements of [*describe goods*] during the period from (*date*) to (*date*)," such promise would not be illusory. A must furnish B's requirements; B, if B has requirements, must buy from A. § 2–306(1) and Comment 2.

Problems of indefiniteness relating to output and requirements agreements are further discussed at Part One, B, 1, B supra. Re: "exclusive dealings," see § 2–306(2).

3. FORM OF THE CONTRACT

A. STATUTE OF FRAUDS

A claims B has orally agreed to buy from A certain goods for $1,500. Even before either party has commenced to perform (A by delivery, B by payment), A might wish to claim the "agreement" is enforceable. Because claims like A's could be perjured, the English Statute of Frauds was enacted "for the prevention of many fraudulent practices, which are commonly endeavored to be upheld by perjury and subornation of perjury." Section 17 of that statute referred to sales of goods of at least ten pounds sterling; the statute did not concern itself with smaller sales.

In order to fulfill the policy of the statute of frauds, Section 17 required an appropriate manifestation by B, the party to be charged (i.e., the party against whom enforcement is sought), which corroborated A's assertion of the parties' alleged agreement. Such corroboration could be (1) a note or memorandum of the bargain made and signed by B, the party to be charged, or (2) a part performance by B, i.e., acceptance or receipt by B of part of the goods, something given in earnest to bind the bargain, or part payment.

To put it simply, if the goods to be sold were of at least a certain price, the transaction would be *within* the applicability of the statute of frauds. The statute would then have to be *satisfied* either by a writing signed by the party against whom enforcement is sought or by that party's part performance of the oral agreement. If the statute were not satisfied, the agreement would not be enforceable. The Uniform Sales Act (and now the UCC) builds upon these policy considerations.

Transactions within the UCC statute of frauds

A contract for the sale of goods for the price of $500 or more is not enforceable by way of action or defense unless the requirements of the statute are satisfied in some manner as discussed below. §§ 2–201(1) (statute of frauds), 2–106(1) ("contract" defined), 2–105(1)(2–103(1)(k) (2003)) ("goods" defined), 2–304 ("price" defined). Oral contracts less than $500 need not satisfy the requirements of the statute. Rationale: It is with regard to higher priced goods that persons are tempted to fabricate sales agreements. §§ 2–201(1) (statute of frauds), 2–209(3) (relationship to modification), 2–326(3) (relationship to "sale or return").

Satisfaction of the UCC statute of frauds

Sufficient corroboration of an agreement to satisfy the requirements of the statute of frauds can be accomplished in any one of five ways:

1. Writing signed by defendant

There must be some writing, signed by the party against whom enforcement is sought, that is sufficient to indicate that the parties have made a contract for sale. A writing is not insufficient because it omits or incorrectly states a term agreed upon, but the contract will not be enforceable beyond the quantity of goods shown in such writing. §§ 2–201(1) (statute of frauds), 1–201(b)(37) ("signed" defined) and (43) ("writing" defined). Policy: All that is required is that the writing afford a basis for believing that the offered oral evidence rests on a real transaction.

Thus, the memorandum must (a) evidence a contract for the sale of goods, (b) be signed, and (c) specify a quantity. The contract is not enforceable beyond the quantity of goods shown in such writing. However, price, time and place of payment or delivery, general quality of the goods, or particular warranties may all be omitted. § 2–201 Comment 1.

2. Writing by claimant—reply doctrine

On April 26, A sends to B a written confirmation of an alleged telephone conversation on April 25 wherein B supposedly placed an order for 100 widgets from A. B's office receives this confirmation on April 28 but fails to reply to it. Does A have an enforceable contract? The answer to this question is resolved by the following rule: Between merchants, if, within a reasonable time, a writing in confirmation of the contract and sufficient against the sender is received, and the party receiving it has reason to know its contents, it satisfies the requirements of § 2–201(1) against such party unless written notice of objection to its contents is given within ten days after it is received. § 2–201(2). Thus, in the example, the statute is satisfied and the statute of frauds will be no defense to enforcement, assuming the following:

a. A and B are both merchants.

b. The confirmation meets the minimum writing requirements, e.g., names the quantity of 100 widgets and is signed by A.

c. B receives the confirmation within a reasonable time (presumably from the time of the telephone conversation). April 25–28 seems reasonable.

d. B has reason to know the contents of the writing. See § 1–202 (defining "notice" and "knowledge").

Since B did not give written objection to the contents of the confirmation within 10 days after it was received, it will be treated as the equivalent of a writing signed by B, the party against whom enforcement is sought. § 2–201(2) and Comment 3.

Reason of rule: A professional should object to a confirmation of a fabricated agreement. Failure to do so will remove the statute of frauds defense. Counseling point: Merchant, answer your mail.

Remember, however, that removing the statute of frauds defense does not necessarily mean that A wins. A still has the burden of persuading the trier of fact that a contract was in fact made orally prior to the written confirmation. § 2–201 Comment 3.

3. Partial performance

A contract that does not satisfy the formal requirements of the statute of frauds but is valid in other respects is enforceable with respect to goods (1) for which payment has been made and accepted or (2) which have been received and accepted. §§ 2–201(3)(c), 2–606 (defining "acceptance").

Example 1: A orally agrees to sell to B ten machines for $500 each. Four machines are delivered to B and accepted. B uses the statute of frauds as a defense against A. Is the defense good? Answer: Partial performance—that is, B accepting certain of the goods—is a substitute for a memorandum signed by B, the party against whom enforcement is sought. B's performance, like a writing signed by B, affords a basis for believing that A's offered oral evidence rests on a real transaction. However, the contract is valid only for the goods that have been accepted, i.e., four of the machines. Policy: Acceptance of four units is not sufficiently corroborative of a contract for ten units. The only evidence of ten units is A's uncorroborated, possibly perjured, testimony. § 2–201(3)(c) and Comment 2 (Comment 3 (2003)).

Example 2: In Example 1, suppose A did not deliver any machines; instead, B sent A a check for $2,000, which A cashed. A raises the statute of frauds as a defense against B. Is the defense good? Answer: Per the same reasoning as above, the contract is valid for four machines ($500 per machine times 4 machines equals $2,000), the number for which payment has been made and accepted.

4. Admissions in court

A contract that does not satisfy the formal requirements of the statute of frauds but is valid in other respects is enforceable if the party against whom enforcement is sought admits in his pleading, testimony, or otherwise in court that a contract for sale was made, but the contract is not enforceable beyond the quantity of goods admitted.

Example: Suppose there are no writings of any kind, and there has been no performance under the alleged oral contract between A and B. The contract is enforceable against B if B admits in his pleadings, testimony, or otherwise in court that a contract was made. This corroborates A's assertion. The contract is not enforceable beyond the quantity admitted. Policy: Admission of a sale of four machines does not corroborate a sale of ten. § 2–201(3)(b) and Comment 7.

5. Specially manufactured goods

A contract that does not satisfy the formal requirements of the statute of frauds but is valid in other respects is enforceable if the goods are to be specially manufactured under the circumstances enumerated below.

Example: A orally agrees to specially manufacture for $600 a large set of china for B affixing B's family crest on each piece of china. A begins manufacture and affixation of the crest, and then B repudiates. B raises the statute of frauds. Valid defense?

Observe that there is no corroboration by B of the alleged oral agreement (no writing, no failure to answer a confirmation by A, no partial performance, no admission in court). All that corroborates A's testimony is A's conduct in commencing performance of the alleged oral contract. Yet it is not too likely that A will fabricate a contract wherein the goods are not readily resalable and act unilaterally by making a substantial beginning on their manufacture. Thus, the Code would enforce this contract if each of the following factors are met: (a) the goods are to be specially manufactured for B; (b) they are not suitable for sale to others in the ordinary course of A's business; (c) before notice of repudiation by B is received, A has made either a substantial beginning on their manufacture (or commitments for their procurement), and (d) the circumstances reasonably indicate that the goods are for B. § 2–201(3)(a).

Summary

The five requisites discussed above are intended to fulfill these policies: (1) Corroboration—assurance that there is a basis for believing that the evidence offered by the plaintiff seller rests on a real transaction with this particular buyer, and (2) Economic hardship—protection of the reasonable business expectancy of a plaintiff that has materially changed its position by commencing performance of the contract.

[*2003 Amend. Written* and *writing* are now *record;* the price of *$500* is now *$5,000.* § 2–201(1),(2). The exception for admissions in court has been broadened to include out-of-court admissions *under oath.* § 2–201(3)(b). Section 2–201 now implicitly recognizes the application of nonstatutory exceptions such as promissory estoppel. § 2–201 Comment 2. New § 2–201(4) clarifies that, "A contract . . . is not unenforceable merely because it is not capable of being performed within one year . . . after its making."]

Other Code statutes of frauds are § 1–206 (personal property not otherwise covered) (deleted in 2003) § 8–113 (investment securities), § 9–203 (security agreements). CISG 11–13, 96; see 29.

B. SEALS

Affixing a seal to a writing ["record" (2003)] evidencing a contract for sale or an offer to buy or sell goods does not make the writing ["record" (2003)] a sealed instrument, and the law with respect to sealed instruments (e.g., an extension of the limitations period for contracts under seal) does not apply to such a contract or offer. § 2–203 (seals inoperative), see § 2–725 (statute of limitations), but see Comments to § 2–203.

4. TERMS AND INTERPRETATION OF THE SALES CONTRACT

The terms (§ 1–201(b)(40)) of a sales agreement can be innumerable. The more common terms relate to description, quantity, quality, price, payment (cash or credit), delivery, inspection, warranties, remedies for breach, risk of loss, circumstances excusing performance, etc. Difficulties sometimes arise in determining the meaning of the agreement and its terms. Thus, the question arises: How should a commercial agreement be read?

The UCC rejects both the "lay-dictionary" and the "conveyancer's" reading of a commercial agreement. Instead, the Code determines the meaning of the agreement by the language the parties used and by their actions, read and interpreted in the light of commercial practices and other surrounding circumstances. The commercial context sets the measure and background for interpretation and may explain and supplement even the language of a formal or final writing. § 1–303 Comment 1.

Thus, the Code definitely rejects the premise that language used in the sales agreement should be understood by reference to rules of construction existing in the law rather than the meaning that arises out of the commercial context in which it was used. Consistent with this approach, § 1–201(b)(3) defines *agreement* as "the bargain of the parties in fact, as found in their language or inferred from other circumstances, including [i] course of performance, [ii] course of dealing, or [iii] usage of trade." In addition, § 1–303 states, "A *course of performance* or *course of dealing* between the parties or *usage of trade* in the vocation or trade in which they are engaged or of which they are or should be aware [i] is relevant in ascertaining the meaning of the parties' agreement, [ii] may give particular meaning to specific terms of the agreement, and [iii] may supplement or qualify the terms of the agreement." (Emphasis added.) § 1–303(d). CISG 8, 9.

Usage of trade defined

"A 'usage of trade' is any practice or method of dealing having such regularity of observance in a place, vocation, or trade as to justify an expectation that it will be observed with respect to the transaction in question." § 1–303(c).

Course of dealing defined

"A 'course of dealing' is a sequence of conduct concerning previous transactions between the parties to a particular transaction that is fairly to be regarded as establishing a common basis of understanding for interpreting their expressions and other conduct." § 1–303(b). Note that course of dealing is restricted, literally, to a sequence of conduct between the parties prior to the agreement. Discussed below is *course of performance,* which involves a sequence of conduct *after* or *under* the particular agreement in dispute. § 1–303 Comment 2.

Example 1: Lumberyard A contracts with B to sell B a specified number of "two-by-fours." The lumber actually measures $1\frac{5}{8}$ by $3\frac{1}{2}$ inches, not 2 by 4 inches. Trade usage and course of prior dealing (i.e., in previous transactions, B took $1\frac{5}{8}$ by $3\frac{1}{2}$ lumber without objection) are relevant in determining that the parties meant $1\frac{5}{8}$ by $3\frac{1}{2}$ inches when they specified "two-by-fours."

Example 2: A contracts to sell B a blooded bull. There is no express term in the agreement obligating A to provide pedigree papers showing the animal's conformity to the contract. Such obligation may, however, arise from course of dealing or usage of trade, which may *supplement* the terms of any agreement, to determine the parties' bargain. See § 2–314(3) and Comment 12 (Comment 14 (2003)).

Course of performance defined

A "course of performance" is a sequence of conduct between the parties to a particular transaction that exists if (1) the agreement of the parties with respect to the transaction involves repeated occasions for performance by one party; and (2) the other party, with knowledge of the performance and an opportunity to object, accepts the performance or acquiesces in it without objection. § 1–303(a). Course of performance thus relates to a sequence of conduct *after* or *under* the agreement in dispute. Former § 2–208 Comment 1 observed, "The parties themselves know best what they have meant by their words of agreement and their action under that agreement is the best indication of what that meaning was." CISG 8(3).

Example 3: In Example 1, suppose that A agreed to deliver the lumber in five separate deliveries. The fact that B accepted the lumber without objection in four previous deliveries under this agreement (i.e., in the course of performance) is relevant in determining that the parties had agreed that 2 by 4 means $1\frac{5}{8}$ by $3\frac{1}{2}$.

Construction

Express terms, course of performance, course of dealing, and usage of trade must be construed when reasonable as consistent with each other. If such construction is unreasonable, the following order of priority shall control: (1) express terms, (2) course of performance, (3) course of dealing, (4) usage of trade. § 1–303(e).

It is to be emphasized that *only* when the parties have not agreed—that is, after examining the bargain in fact as found in their language or inferred from other circumstances including course of performance, course of dealing, or usage of trade—does the Code fill in points the parties have not considered and in fact agreed upon. §§ 1–201(b)(3) (defining "agreement"), 1–302(a) (variation of Code terms by agreement). The Code's gap-filling rules include the open term provisions discussed above at Part One, B, 1, B: price term, delivery term, payment term, duration of contract term, particulars of performance terms, output or requirement terms, etc. In addition, the Code provisions on title (§ 2–401), risk of loss (§ 2–509), and inspection (§ 2–513) yield to the contrary agreement of the parties.

In summary, the terms of a contract for sale may be supplied by (1) express language; (2) course of performance, course of dealing, and usage of trade; and (3) gap-filling rules found in the Code (and general law). UCC Hornbook § 4–1 et seq. CISG 6.

Meaning of certain terms

Further, the Code has rules to determine the meaning of certain terms, such as output or requirements terms (§ 2–306(1)); exclusive dealing terms (§ 2–306(2)); terms relating to assignment of the contract (§ 2–210(4) (2–210(3) (2003)); mercantile terms such as "F.O.B." (§§ 2–319 et seq.); auction terms ("with reserve" or "without reserve") (§ 2–328(3)); sale on approval and sale or return terms (§§ 2–326, 2–327); and acceleration "at will" terms (§ 1–309). For additional mercantile terms, see INCOTERMS published by the International Chamber of Commerce.

Legal consequences of terms

Not all terms upon which parties have agreed will necessarily have legal consequences. § 1–201(b)(3), (12) (defining "agreement" and "contract"). For example, the Code's obligation of *good faith* in the performance or enforcement of every contract may prevent enforcement of certain terms or agreements. §§ 1–304 (obligation of good faith), 1–201(b)(20), 2–103(1)(j) (2003) (defining "good faith"); see e.g., § 2–209(1) and Comment 2 (modification without consideration). Further, the duties of good faith, diligence, reasonableness, and care prescribed by the Code may not be disclaimed by agreement. § 1–302(b) and Comment 1. CISG 7(1).

Also, if a court as a matter of law finds a contract or any term of the contract to have been *unconscionable* at the time it was made, the court (1) may refuse to enforce the contract, (2) may enforce the remainder of the contract without the unconscionable term, or (3) may so limit the application of any unconscionable term as to avoid any unconscionable result. § 2–302(1); see §§ 2–309(3) (termination without notification), 2–719(3) (limiting or excluding consequential damages). In determining whether a contract or clause is unconscionable, the *basic test* is whether, in the light of the general commercial background and the commercial needs of the particular trade or case, the clauses involved are so one-sided as to be unconscionable under the circumstances existing at the time of the making of the contract. The goal is prevention of *oppression* (quasi-duress) and *unfair surprise* (quasi-fraud) and not disturbance of the allocation of risks because of superior bargaining power. § 2–302 Comment 1. Unconscionability has been found in warranty disclaimers (particularly when physical injury results), remedy limitations (§ 2–719(3)), situations of gross disparity between the price paid and the market value, etc. CISG 4(a).

Further examples of Code provisions that cannot be varied by agreement are §§ 1–105(2) (1–301(e) and (f) (2001)) (territorial applicability), 2–210(2) (2–210(1)(a) (2003)) (breach or assignment of whole contract), 2–318 (third party beneficiaries of warranties), 2–718(1) (penalties). CISG 12.

5. PAROL EVIDENCE RULE

Terms set forth in a writing intended by the parties as a complete and exclusive statement of their agreement may not be contradicted by evidence of any prior agreement or of a contemporaneous oral agreement. § 2–202. Policy: To prevent the uncertainty in contract enforcement that may occur if evidence is allowed that contradicts the "final writing;" to discourage possibly perjured testimony of oral side agreements.

Of course, the terms set forth in the writing ["record" (2003)] may be explained or supplemented by evidence of course of performance, course of dealing, or usage of trade. § 2–202(a). The goal is that the parties' understanding as to the agreement may be determined. The assumption is that the course of prior dealings and the usages of trade were taken for granted when the writing was phrased. The course of actual performance by the parties, however, is considered the best indication of what the parties intended the writing to mean. § 2–202 Comment 2.

If the writing ["record" (2003)] is not intended as a complete and exclusive statement of the terms of the agreement, evidence of consistent additional terms may be admitted. § 2–202(b), see § 2–326(3) (2001) and Comment 3 (re: sale or return contracts).

[*2003 Amend.* The caption "Final Written Expression" is now "Final Expression in a Record." *Writing* is now *record.* New § 2–202(2) reads, "Terms in a record may be explained by evidence of course of performance, course of dealing, or usage of trade without a preliminary determination by the court that the language used is ambiguous."]

6. ASSIGNMENT OF RIGHTS AND DELEGATION OF PERFORMANCE UNDER THE CONTRACT

A contracts to sell certain goods to B for $1,500, to be delivered in one month. § 2–301 (general obligations of buyers and sellers). May A assign the right to the $1,500 to C? May B assign B's right to the goods to D? May A delegate to C A's duty to deliver the goods to B? May B delegate to D B's duty to pay $1,500 to A?

Generally, the UCC recognizes both delegation of performance and assignability of rights as normal and permissible incidents of a contract for sale of goods. § 2–210 Comment 1 [2003 Comment 2]. Thus, the above questions should all be answered *yes*. Sometimes, however, the answer will be *no*.

Delegation of performance

A and B may always delegate their performance (see § 2–210(5)), *unless* they agree otherwise (see § 2–210(4)) or *unless* the other party has a substantial interest in having the original promisor perform or control the acts required by the contract. § 2–210(1), see § 2–210(6) (post-delegation demand for assurances). Example: A contracts with B to manufacture goods especially for B. For this contract, quality control is extremely important, and A's personal control of this quality is of the essence of the contract. A cannot delegate A's duty to C because B has a substantial interest in having A control the quality of the goods.

Whenever A does delegate his duty of performance to C, A is not relieved from any duty to perform or from any liability for breach. § 2–210(1). C's acceptance of the delegation of duty implies that C has promised to perform the duties so delegated. Either A or B may enforce this promise. § 2–210(5).

Policy: Delegation of performance is recognized as a normal and permissible incident of a contract for the sale of goods so long as there is no substantial reason why the delegated performance will not be as satisfactory as personal performance. § 2–210 Comments 1 and 2.

Assignment of rights

All rights of A or B can be assigned except as follows:

1.   If the assignment would materially affect the duty of the other party. Example: A contracts to sell to B "all B's requirements of widgets during the period from [*date*] to [*date*]." B assigns this right to D. Assuming D's requirements differ from B's, such right could not be assigned because doing so would materially affect A's duties. § 2–210(2).

2.   If the assignment would materially increase the burden or risk imposed on the other party. Example: A contracts to sell to B goods per B's quality specifications. B assigns B's rights in the goods to D. D's specifications vary materially from B's. B cannot assign since doing so would increase materially the burden on A. § 2–210(2).

3.   If the assignment would materially impair the other party's chance of obtaining return performance. Example: "A seller [A] who has a continuing obligation in regard to goods already delivered under a contract by which the buyer [B] is to pay at least a part of the price at future dates may present an example of a case in which the seller [A] may not assign his contractual right to payment. Such an assignment may diminish the seller's [A's] interest in continuing his performance...." R. Nordstrom, Handbook of the Law of Sales § 45, p. 134 (1970). § 2–210(2). As to the creation, attachment, perfection, or enforcement of a security interest in the seller's interest, see § 2–210(3).

4. If the parties have agreed that rights *cannot* be assigned, this agreement will be enforced. § 2–210(2), (4). However, the following two rights *can* be assigned even if the parties have agreed otherwise:

  a. A right to damages for breach of a whole contract.

  b. A right arising out of the assignor's due performance of its entire obligation.

Examples: A delivers goods to B per the contract, or A tenders delivery but B wrongfully rejects and is thus in breach. In either event, since A's obligation is no longer executory because A has fulfilled the obligation to tender or deliver, A may assign the right to payment even if the agreement prohibits assignment. § 2–210(2) and Comment 3.

Note: § 2–210(2) [now 2–210(1)(a) (2003)] is subject to § 9–406 (2001), which "makes rights to payment for goods sold ('accounts'), whether or not earned, freely alienable notwithstanding a contrary agreement or rule of law." § 2–210 Comment 3 (2003). See Part Five, C, 7, B infra.

2–210 is not a complete statement of the law of delegation and assignment; instead, its scope is limited to clarifying a few points that are unclear under the case law. § 2–210 Comment 7. As for "financing assignments" see § 2–210(4) and Comment 5. CISG 1(1), 4 (first sentence).

[*2003 Amend*. If a seller or buyer assigns rights under a contract, see § 2–210 and Comments 3 and 4. If a seller or buyer delegates performance of its duties under a contract, see § 2–210(2) and Comment 5. As to assignment of "the contract" or prohibition of assignment of "the contract," see § 2–210(3),(4) and Comment 6.]

7.   CHECKLIST OF ITEMS TO BE INCLUDED IN CONTRACTS FOR THE SALE OF GOODS

Each contract must be tailored to suit the particular transaction, but the following checklist sets forth items that may be necessary or useful.

a.   Description of the parties (§§ 2–103, 2–104).

b.   Description of the goods.

   (1) Quantity (§ 2–201).

   (2) Quality (§§ 2–313, 2–314, 2–315).

   (3) Manner of selection (§§ 2–311(2), 2–501).

c.   Warranties.

   (1) Title (§ 2–312).

   (2) Quality (§§ 2–313, 2–314, 2–315).

   (3) Disclaimer of warranties (§ 2–316).

   (4) Limitation of liability for breach of warranty (§ 2–719).

d.   Title to the goods (§ 2–401).

e.   Risk of loss and insurance (§§ 2–303, 2–501, 2–509, 2–510).

f.   Seller's obligation to tender delivery of the goods.

   (1) Time of delivery (§§ 2–309, 2–503).

   (2) Place of delivery (§§ 2–308, 2–319 through 2–324, 2–503, 2–504).

   (3) Manner of delivery (§§ 2–311(2), 2–503).

     (a) Delivery in single or several lots (§ 2–307).

     (b) Shipment under reservation (§§ 2–310(b), 2–505).

     (c) Delivery on condition (§ 2–507(2)).

   (4) Seller's right to cure improper tender (§ 2–508).

g.   Buyer's obligation to accept goods (§ 2–507).

(1) Buyer's right to inspect the goods before acceptance (§§ 2–513, 2–606).

(2) Buyer's right to reject goods (§ 2–601).

(a) Manner of rejection (§ 2–602).

(b) Obligation to state reasons for rejection (§ 2–605).

(c) Obligation to care for rejected goods (§§ 2–603, 2–604).

(3) Buyer's obligation to notify seller of breach discovered after acceptance (§ 2–607).

(4) Buyer's right to revoke its acceptance (§ 2–608).

h.   Buyer's obligation to pay for goods (§§ 2–507, 2–606).

(1) Price (§ 2–305).

(2) Medium of payment (§§ 2–304, 2–511).

(3) Time of payment (§ 2–310).

(4) Obligation to pay before inspection of the goods (§ 2–512).

i.   Remedies of seller (§ 2–703).

j.   Remedies of buyer (§§ 2–711, 2–714).

k. Signature of parties (§ 2–201).

l.   Miscellaneous provisions.

(1) Duration and termination of contract term (§§ 2–106(3), 2–309(2)).

(2) Provision forbidding parol modification (§§ 2–202, 2–209).

(3) Provision relating to waiver of rights by course of performance (§§ 2–208 (1–303), 2–209).

(4) Delegation of performance (§ 2–210).

(5) Assignment of rights (§§ 2–210, 9–406(d) (2001)).

(6) Output and requirements clauses (§ 2–306).

(7) Sale on approval terms (§§ 2–326, 2–327).

(8) Sale or return (§§ 2–326, 2–327).

(9) Consignment sale terms (§§ 1–201(b)(35), 2–326 Comment 4 (2001)).

(10) Seller's rights on buyer's insolvency (§ 2–702).

(11) Buyer's rights on seller's insolvency (§ 2–502).

(12) Preservation of goods in dispute (§ 2–515).

(13) Right to adequate assurance of performance (§ 2–609).

(14) Installment contract provisions (§ 2–612).

(15) Force majeure (§§ 2–613 through 2–616).

(16) Liquidated damages (§ 2–718).

(17) Proof of market price (§§ 2–723, 2–724).

(18) Clause shortening the statute of limitations period (§ 2–725).

(19) Acceleration clauses (§ 1–309).

(20) Choice of law clause (§§ 1–105(1–301 (2001))).

For examples of sales agreements, see 12A West's Legal Forms § 17.2. CISG 6.

C. PROPERTY INCIDENTS OF THE SALES CONTRACT

The UCC recognizes four property interests in goods: title, special property, insurable interest, and security interest. §§ 2–401(1), 2–501(1). Historically, the question of risk of loss was also closely related to property interests in goods. § 2–509.

1. TITLE

A sale involves the passing of title from the seller to the buyer for a price. This was true under the Uniform Sales Act (§ 1), and it is true under the UCC. § 2–106(1).

The Uniform Sales Act (USA) placed considerable significance on the location of title, that is, *when* title passed from seller to buyer. For example, suppose a seller and buyer enter into a contract for the sale of certain specific goods. Subsequently, the goods are damaged without either party's negligence. Who bears the *risk* of *loss?* Answer: The goods remain at the seller's risk until title passes to the buyer. USA § 22. Instead of the goods being damaged, suppose the seller repudiates the contract. Is the buyer entitled to the goods or merely money damages? Answer: If title in the goods has passed to the buyer, the buyer may maintain any action allowed to an *owner* of goods, i.e., replevin. USA § 66 (conversion or detention of goods).

Other issues often resolved by title location concerned (1) a seller's right to recover the price of the goods, not merely damages, (2) rights of a buyer's or seller's creditors to levy on the goods of their respective debtors, (3) rights of a seller or buyer to sue third parties for injuries to the goods, (4) rights of a seller or buyer to collect insurance on the goods, (5) the power of a seller or buyer to defeat the other party's interest in the goods by selling them to an innocent third person, (6) the time and place for measuring damages for breach of a contract for sale of the goods, (7) the applicable law in an interstate transaction relating to the goods, (8) infraction of criminal statutes (e.g., "It shall be unlawful to steal *property* of the United

States"), (9) the incidence of taxation (e.g., "There shall be levied a tax . . . on the *sale* of goods"), etc.

When did title pass from seller to buyer under the USA? Simply stated, it passed when they intended it to pass. Absent an expression of contrary intention, title passed as follows:

1.   For goods specifically identified at the time of contracting (i.e., a piano), title passed at the time of contracting unless something remained to be done to the specific goods to put them into a deliverable state (i.e., paint the piano), in which case title passed when such thing was done. USA § 19 Rules 1 and 2 (rules for ascertaining intention).

2.   For goods unascertained at the time of contracting, when the goods were ascertained and delivered to a carrier for shipment to the buyer, title presumptively passed from seller to buyer. If, however, the seller was required to pay the cost of transportation, title passed at the destination. USA § 19 Rules 4 (shipment contract) and 5 (destination contract).

3.   If the goods were sold to a buyer "on approval," title passed when the buyer "approved" the goods; if the goods were delivered to the buyer "on sale or return," title passed to the buyer on delivery but the buyer could revest title in the seller by returning the goods to the seller. USA § 19 Rule 3 (rules for ascertaining intention).

Under UCC Article 2, legal consequences flow directly from the contract and action taken under it *without* considering when property or title passed or was to pass as being the determining factor. The purpose of this change is to avoid making practical issues (e.g., who bears the risk of loss) between practical people turn upon the location of an intangible something, the passing of which no person can prove by evidence, and to substitute for such abstractions proof of words and actions of a tangible character. §§ 2–101 Comment, 2–401 Comment 1.

Accordingly, each provision of UCC Article 2 with regard to the rights, obligations, and remedies of the seller, the buyer, purchasers, or other third parties applies *irrespective* of title to the goods unless the provision specifically refers to such title (e.g., §§ 2–312 (warranty of title), 2–327(1)(a) (re: sale on approval), 2–403(1) (purchaser's title), 2–501(2) (seller's insurable interest), 2–722) (suits against third parties). § 2–401 preamble. Some of the provisions formerly resolved by locating title are the following:

1. Risk of loss. § 2–509.

2. Buyer's right to the goods or damages. §§ 2–716, 2–712, 2–713.

3. Seller's right to the price or damages. §§ 2–709, 2–706, 2–708.

4. The time and place for measuring damages. §§ 2–708(1), 2–713, 2–723.

5. Buyer's right to goods on seller's insolvency. § 2–502.

6. Seller's right to goods on buyer's insolvency. § 2–702.

7. Who may order diversion of goods in transit. § 7–303.

8. Seller's right to goods in a "cash sale." §§ 2–403(1), 2–507(2).

9. Rights of seller's creditors against sold goods. § 2–402.

10. Rights of seller's creditors and purchasers to goods in possession of a bailee that are to be delivered without being moved. § 2–503(4).

11. Rights of buyer's creditors to goods sold "on approval," by "sale or return," or "on consignment." § 2–326 and Comment 4.

12. Insurable interest in goods. § 2–501.

13. Who can sue third parties for injury to goods. § 2–722.

14. Power to transfer goods to others. § 2–403.

15. The applicable law in an interstate transaction. § 1–105 (1–301 (2001)).

16. When title to goods passes under a "sale on approval." § 2–327(1).

The UCC only rarely requires analysis of the location of title to resolve the problem or issue raised by the provisions listed above. Thus, the Code utilizes the "narrow issue" approach to problem-solving. The "lump concept" approach of the USA, which solved the various issues by locating "title," has been virtually abandoned.

The principal disadvantage of the lump concept approach is that it is based upon the wooden notion that title must either pass or not pass from seller to buyer—it cannot be deemed to pass for some purposes but not for others. Thus, for example, consider a hypothetical contract for sale of goods under the Uniform Sales Act: Seller ascertains (identifies) the goods and sets them aside in his warehouse. Per USA § 19 Rule 4 (shipment contract), title will pass upon the goods' delivery to a carrier. Although this might be a satisfactory point at which to pass the risk of loss from seller to buyer, it probably does not follow from this point that the buyer should also have an action to replevy the goods as *owner*. Instead, whether such a cause of action should exist probably requires that we ask a more specific question: Is the buyer, after reasonable effort, able to purchase substitute goods (effect cover)? If the answer is yes, let the buyer simply sue the seller for damages. If the answer is no, allow the buyer a right of replevin for the goods. One can see that in a buyer's-right-to-the-goods issue, delivery to a carrier has no particular policy significance. Yet, under the USA, delivery to a carrier must be the moment that (1) risk passes and (2) the buyer becomes entitled to the goods upon the seller's breach. Cf. §§ 2–509(1)(a) (passage of risk of loss upon delivery to carrier), 2–716(3) (right of replevin).

The UCC "narrow issue" approach frees the problem-solver from the albatross of lump concept thinking and affords a resolution consonant with the relevant policy considerations present in each narrow issue. To under-stand the Code's "step by step performance" rationale and perceive the methodology employed, suppose S and B enter into a contract for sale of certain described goods. The parties then commence to perform such contract. What are the typical *steps* and what *consequences* might result from each such step being performed?

Step One

S identifies the goods. § 2–501(1). *Consequences:* B, under certain circumstances, may have a right to the goods. § 2–716(3). S, under certain circumstances, may have a right to the price. § 2–709(1)(b). B, under certain circumstances, may defeat S's creditors. § 2–502(1). B can sue third parties for injury to the goods. § 2–722.

Step Two

S delivers the goods to a carrier for shipment. *Consequence:* Risk of loss, under certain circumstances, may pass to B. §§ 2–509(1)(a), 2–319(1)(a).

Step Three

The goods reach their destination, and the carrier tenders them to B. *Consequence:* Risk of loss, under certain circumstances, may pass to B. §§ 2–509(1)(b), 2–319(1)(b).

Step Four

B takes receipt (physical possession) of the goods. § 2–103(1)(c)(2–103(1)(*l*) (2003)). *Consequence:* Risk of loss, under certain circumstances, may pass to B. § 2–509(3).

Step Five

B, generally after inspection, accepts the goods. §§ 2–513, 2–606. *Consequences:* S, under certain circumstances, may have a right to the price. § 2–709(1)(a). B's creditors, under certain circumstances, may levy on the goods. § 2–326(2). Risk of loss, under certain circumstances, may pass to B. § 2–327(1).

Of course, the above steps are not exhaustive. Other steps could be involved, e.g., B *rejects* nonconforming goods, § 2–601; S *cures* the nonconformity, § 2–508; or B *revokes acceptance* of the nonconforming goods, § 2–608. When goods are to be delivered by S to B without being moved (i.e., the goods are stored in a warehouse), the third-party-bailee-warehouseman will *receive* notification of B's rights, then *acknowledge* B's rights. § 2–503(4)(b), etc.

These issues will be investigated in due course. What is important here is to understand the methodology employed.

But what if a situation is not covered by any other provision of Article 2, and title becomes material? In such a case, the following rules found in 2–401 apply.

1.   Title to goods cannot pass prior to their identification to the contract. §§ 2–401(1), 2–501, cf. USA § 17 (no property passes until goods are ascertained). This is a matter of logic; how can title pass to goods not yet identified as the goods to which the contract refers?

2.   Title to goods passes from the seller to the buyer in any manner and on any conditions explicitly agreed on by

the parties. § 2–401(1), cf. USA § 18 (property in specific goods passes when parties so intend).

3. Absent contrary agreement, title passes at the time and place at which the seller completes physical delivery of the goods. In particular,

a. In the case of a shipment contract (that is, a contract that requires or authorizes the seller to send the goods to the buyer but does not require the seller to deliver them at a stated destination), title passes to the buyer at the time and place of shipment. §§ 2–401(2)(a), 2–503(2) and Comment 5, 2–504; cf. USA § 19 Rule 4.

b. In the case of a destination contract (that is, a contract that requires the seller to deliver the goods to the buyer at a particular destination), title passes to the buyer upon tender of the goods at their destination. §§ 2–401(2)(b), 2–503(3) and Comment 5, cf. USA § 19 Rule 5.

4. Absent contrary agreement, if (1) delivery is to be made without moving the goods, (2) the goods are already identified at the time of contracting, and (3) no documents [of title] are to be delivered, then title passes at the time and place of contracting. § 2–401(3)(b), cf. USA § 19 Rule 1 (rules for ascertaining intention). If documents of title are involved, see Part Four, B infra.

5. Title to the goods revests in the seller by operation of law if the buyer rejects the goods or revokes acceptance. § 2–401(4).

To what situations will these title-passing rules apply? Not many. It is rare to find a situation in which title was previously relevant, yet uncovered by a provision of Article 2.

Then why do we need title-passing rules under the Code? (1) To cover any unforeseeable situations in which ownership might become relevant, and (2) to deal with other statutes under which ownership or title is relevant. For example, consider 18 U.S.C. § 641: "Whoever ... steals ... any ... thing of value of the United States ... [s]hall be fined under this title or imprisoned not more than ten years, or both." Suppose the United States contracts for the sale of scrap metal to a buyer. Before delivery, X steals the scrap. At the time of the theft, was the scrap "any thing of value of the United States," i.e., did the U.S. still own or have title to the scrap? If the above federal statute does not define *ownership* for its own purposes, a court may determine that Congress intended to incorporate the "private" (UCC) law's rules regarding passage of title. Thus, the UCC must have title-passing rules to accommodate these statutes aside from the Code that have rules dependent upon title or ownership, but leave these terms undefined. § 2–401 Comment 1.

Another example: Consider a statute of State Y that states, "There is hereby levied and there shall be collected and paid ... a tax at the rate of four per cent upon the gross receipts received from the *sale* of tangible personal property at retail *within this state*." Suppose S of State X receives an order for certain goods from B of State Y. S selects the goods and delivers them to a carrier for shipment. B receives the goods in State Y and proceeds to use or consume them. State Y seeks to collect from S a sales tax since the transaction constituted a "sale within this state." S would maintain that, since the "sale within this state" language of the statute was undefined, the legislature intended to incorporate the UCC's definition of sale and its title-passing rules. Thus, S would state that UCC § 2–401(2)(a) would apply and title would pass when the goods were delivered to a carrier in State X. Therefore there would be no sale in State Y, and no sales tax could be levied by State Y. This argument may be persuasive to a court. Suppose, however, State Y points out certain language in the sales contract stating, "If the goods are not satisfactory, B may return them.'' State Y would argue that this language would constitute a "sale on approval." Because B will approve of the goods in State Y where B lives, the sale would take place in State Y, and State Y's sales tax would be proper. §§ 2–327(1)(a), 2–326(1)(a).

To conclude: Under the USA, title location was probably the *first* thing a lawyer looked to in resolving a sales problem; under the UCC, it is the *last* thing he or she looks to. CISG 4(b), 30.

2. SPECIAL PROPERTY

A buyer obtains a *special property* in goods when those goods are identified as being the specific goods to which the contract refers. §§ 2–401(1), 2–501(1). This special property frequently arises before title to the goods passes to buyer, as for example in a shipment contract under which title passes to previously identified goods at the time and place of shipment. § 2–401(2)(a). Simply, goods are deemed identified when it can be said, "*These* are the goods to which the contract refers.''

Of course, as noted, passage of title has minimal significance under the UCC; special property, likewise, has only limited significance. For instance, a buyer will—by having a special property—have certain rights to goods in the event of the seller's insolvency. § 2–502. The seller's unsecured creditors are subject to such a buyer's rights. §§ 2–402(1), 2–502. The buyer will also be entitled to sue third parties for injury to the goods. § 2–722(a). Upon identification—the event which gives rise to the buyer's special property—the buyer, under certain circumstances, will have a right of replevin as against the seller's unsecured creditors. §§ 2–402(1), 2–716. These special property rights are further discussed at Part One, F, 3, A, (5), (c) infra; Part One, F, 4, C infra. See also § 2–401 Comment 3.

3.   INSURABLE INTEREST

"An insurable interest, in its broadest sense, is a relation between the insured and the event insured against, such that the occurrence of the event will cause substantial loss or injury of some kind to the insured." Patterson, Essentials of Insurance Law § 22 (2d ed. 1957). Example: A "insures" certain goods against loss or destruction with the X Insurance Co. The goods are damaged by fire. If A would suffer no injury (i.e., pecuniary loss) as a consequence of the loss, A cannot validly obtain insurance. Instead, any such "insurance" would be void as a wager. If, however, A owned the goods or otherwise would suffer a financial loss if they were damaged, A may validly insure them to protect its interest in them, i.e., A has an "insurable interest" in the goods. Simply stated, the existence of an "insurable interest" distinguishes a wagering agreement from a valid insurance agreement.

Buyer's insurable interest

A buyer obtains an insurable interest (as well as a special property) in goods when they are identified to the contract. § 2–501(1). Example: S and B enter into a contract for the sale of a car. S selects the particular car to be delivered to B. B now has an insurable interest in the car even though B may not yet "own" it. § 2–401. Why? Because B may suffer a financial loss (the loss of B's bargain) if the car is damaged or destroyed.

Seller's insurable interest

A seller retains an insurable interest in goods so long as he or she has title to, or any security interest in, the goods. § 2–501(2). Security interests are discussed below. Insurable interests recognized under other rules of law are not impaired by the UCC. § 2–501(3).

Of course, the principal significance of the insurable-interest concept relates to the law of insurance and not directly to the law of commercial transactions as set forth in the UCC. The Code does recognize, however, that a party with an insurable interest in goods can sue third parties for injury to the goods. § 2–722.

4.   SECURITY INTEREST

A security interest is an interest in personal property or fixtures that secures payment or performance of an obligation. Example: S sells goods to B. B makes a down payment and has 24 monthly installments to pay the balance. S reserves a security interest (this was called a "conditional sale," pre-UCC) to secure the unpaid balance. Upon B's default, S has certain rights against the sold goods (pre-UCC chattel-mortgage language called it "foreclosure") in priority to others claiming an interest in the same goods. This is the subject of UCC Article 9, Secured Transactions, and is discussed in Part Five infra. Of course, security interests can also arise under Article 2, Sales, or Article 2A, Leases. § 9–109(a)(5). These will be discussed later. A buyer's special property in goods, discussed above, is not a security interest. § 1–201(b)(35).

5.   RISK OF LOSS

S and B enter into a contract for the sale of goods; the parties perform their respective obligations—S delivers the goods, and B accepts and pays for the goods—and the contract is fulfilled. § 2–301. Prior to contracting, it seems clear that S bears the risk of the loss of the goods. Subsequent to fulfillment of the contract, it would seem logical that B bears the risk of loss. Query: When does the risk of loss pass from S to B? The resolution of this query does *not,* as noted before, depend upon who had title to the goods at the time of the loss. §§ 2–401 preamble, 2–509. Instead, risk of loss follows its own rules, described below.

Agreement of the parties

Risk of loss passes from S to B when they *agree* it passes. §§ 2–509(4), 2–303 (allocation or division of risks, generally); cf. § 2–401(2) (passage of title), USA § 18 (property in specific goods passes when parties so intend). CISG 6.

Sale on approval

Under a "sale on approval," unless otherwise agreed, risk of loss does not pass to B until B's acceptance. §§ 2–509(4). See also 2–327(1)(a) (special incidents of sale on approval), 2–326(1) ("sale on approval" defined), 2–606 ("acceptance" defined); cf. USA § 19 Rule 3 (rules for ascertaining intention).

Risk of loss in the absence of breach

Subject to the above two rules and the rules to be discussed below concerning the effect of breach on risk of loss (§ 2–510), the following are the rules as to when risk passes from S to B in the absence of breach:

1. When the contract requires or authorizes S to ship the goods by carrier:

a. *Shipment contract.* If the contract does not require S to deliver the goods at a particular destination, the risk of loss passes to B when the goods are duly delivered to the carrier. §§ 2–509(1)(a). See also 2–503(2) and Comment 5 (manner of tender for shipment contract), 2–504 ("shipment contract" defined); cf. § 2–401(2)(a) (passage of title under shipment contract), USA § 19 Rule 4 (rules for ascertaining intention). See § 2–709(1)(a) (re: action for the price). If mercantile terms are employed (e.g., F.O.B. Seller City, F.O.B. Vessel, C.I.F., C & F), see §§ 2–319(1)(a) and (c) (re: "F.O.B." terms), 2–320(2)(a) and (b) (re: "C.I.F." terms), 2–321(2) (re: "C.I.F." terms).

b. *Destination contract.* If the contract requires S to deliver the goods at a particular destination and the goods are duly tendered there while in the possession of the carrier, the risk of loss passes to B when the goods are duly tendered there as to enable B to take delivery. §§ 2–509(1)(b), 2–503(3) and Comment 5 (manner of tender for destination contract), cf. § 2–401(2)(b) (passage of title under destination contract), USA § 19 Rule 5 (rules for ascertaining intention). If mercantile terms are employed (e.g., F.O.B. Buyer City, F.O.B. Vessel, F.A.S., "ex-ship"), see §§ 2–319(1)(b) ("F.O.B." terms), 2–319(1)(c) ("F.O.B." terms), 2–319(2)(a) ("F.A.S." terms), 2–322(2)(b) (delivery "ex-ship"), 2–324 ("No arrival, no sale" terms), CISG 66, 67. For usage of F.O.B. and F.A.S. terms, see INCOTERMS published by the International Chamber of Commerce.

2. If the goods are held by a bailee to be delivered without being moved, risk of loss passes from S to B when bailee W warehouse—after receiving notification of B's rights, i.e., that B has purchased the goods and is entitled to possession—*acknowledges* B's right to possession of the goods. This is sometimes called "attornment." It is the moment when W ceases to be the bailee for S and commences to be the bailee for B. § 2–509(2)(b). For risk-passing rules when documents of title are employed, see Part Four, B infra. See CISG 66, 68.

Example: S and B contract for the sale of certain goods stored in W warehouse. W is a bailee who has agreed to deliver the goods at the termination of the bailment either to S or to another party if S so directs. Although B could obtain delivery by removing the goods from the warehouse, B wishes to have the goods remain in the warehouse because B, a dealer in the goods, does not need them until seasonal demand for the goods commences. Since B could take physical possession of the goods—yet for B's own reasons does not—it would be unfair for risk of loss to remain on S until B takes physical possession.

3. Residuary rules for any case not within 1 or 2 above:

a. If S is a merchant, the risk of loss passes to B upon B's taking physical possession of the goods. §§ 2–509(3), 2–103(1)(c) ("receipt" of goods defined), 2–104(1) ("merchant" defined).

b. If S is not a merchant, risk of loss passes to B on tender of delivery. §§ 2–509(3), 2–503(1).

Underlying *general* policy: Risk of loss falls upon the one who has control of the goods or the right to control the goods. That person is most likely to insure the goods. See § 2–509 Comment 3. (See also § 2–501 Comment 4: "[T]he risk of loss remains on the seller ... until completion of his duties as to the goods...."). CISG 66, 69.

[*2003 Amend.* Section 2–509(2)(b) adds, "on acknowledgment of the bailee *to the buyer.*" Section 2–509(3) has been amended so that the risk of loss for both a *merchant* and a *non-merchant* passes upon the buyer's *receipt* of goods. § 2–103(1)(*l*). Sections 2–319 through 2–324 (mercantile terms) have been deleted as inconsistent with modern commercial practices. § 2–319 Comment (2003).]

Effect of seller's breach on risk of loss

1. If a tender or delivery of goods so fails to conform to the contract as to give the buyer a right of rejection, the risk of their loss remains on the seller until the seller cures the nonconformity or the buyer accepts the goods notwithstanding their nonconformity. §§ 2–510(1). See also 2–601 (buyer's right on improper delivery), 2–508 (cure), 2–606 ("acceptance" defined). Example: S and B contract for sale of goods under a shipment contract in which risk is to pass to B when the goods are delivered to the carrier. S ships the goods. The goods are not of

merchantable quality per § 2–314, and thus are nonconforming. Despite the contract term, risk will not pass upon delivery to the carrier, because of the nonconformity. Risk does not pass to B until either B *accepts* the nonconforming goods or S *cures* the nonconformity.

2. If the buyer rightfully revokes acceptance, the buyer may, to the extent of any deficiency in the buyer's effective insurance coverage, treat the risk of loss as having rested on the seller from the beginning. §§ 2–510(2). See also 2–608 (revocation, generally). Example: To carry forward the example above, suppose B accepted the non-merchantable goods thinking they conformed. B did not discover the nonconformity due to the difficulty of doing so before acceptance. If the nonconformity substantially impairs the value of the goods to B and certain other requisites are fulfilled per § 2–608, B may revoke acceptance of the goods. Doing so gives B the same rights as if B had rejected them initially. § 2–608(3). See also § 2–601 (buyer's rights on improper delivery). See Part One, E, 6, D infra. If B's effective insurance coverage protects only two-thirds of the loss—assuming the goods were damaged subsequent to B's acceptance of them—one-third of the loss rests on the seller. CISG 70. See also 25 and 36(1).

Effect of buyer's breach on risk of loss

The seller may, to the extent of any deficiency in its effective insurance coverage, treat the risk of loss as resting on the buyer for a commercially reasonable time if (a) conforming goods have been identified to the contract and (b) the buyer repudiates or is otherwise in breach before the risk of loss has passed to the buyer. § 2–510(3), cf. USA § 22(b) (risk of loss). Example: S and B contract for sale of goods under a shipment contract in which risk of loss is to pass to B when the goods are delivered to the carrier. S identifies the goods and sets them apart in its warehouse ready for shipment to B. B notifies S not to ship the goods because B is repudiating the agreement (wrongfully). Fire damages the identified goods. S's effective insurance coverage covers only two-thirds of the loss. Because of B's breach, one-third of the loss rests on B despite the contract term (but only if the loss occurred within a commercially reasonable time; S cannot keep this risk on B indefinitely). CISG 69(1).

Underlying general policy: Risk of loss falls—with certain qualifications—upon the one who breached the contract; risk of loss also falls upon the one with effective insurance coverage. CISG 66–70.

D. SELLER'S WARRANTY OBLIGATIONS

1. WARRANTY OF TITLE

Assume B steals goods from A and sells them to innocent C. A reclaims the goods from C pursuant to the general common-law rule that a person (A) may not be deprived of his ownership without his consent even though the goods are in the hands of an innocent purchaser (C). Or, phrased another way: "He who hath not, cannot give." (B, a thief, has no title to stolen goods and cannot, consequently, give good title to C.) Does C have recourse against B? Yes, because B warranted that the title conveyed would be good and its transfer rightful. This warranty was breached. § 2–312(1)(a); cf. §§ 3–416(a)(1) (transfer warranty for negotiable instrument), 7–507(3) (similar warranty for document of title), 8–108(a) (similar warranty for certificated security).

B gives a chattel mortgage in goods to A, who records the mortgage. (This is now called a "security agreement" with A filing a "financing statement" and is governed by UCC Article 9, Secured Transactions.) B sells the goods to innocent C, who does not know of A's interest. A recovers the goods from C due to B's default in payments to A. C is deemed to have constructive notice of A's security interest. §§ 9–201(a), 9–317(b). Does C have recourse against B? Yes, B had warranted to C that the goods shall be delivered free from any security interests, etc., of which the buyer (C) at the time of contracting has no knowledge. This warranty was breached. § 2–312(1)(b). The fact that C had *notice* of A's security interest (thus A recovers the goods from C) is not to be equated with the *actual knowledge* that would preclude C's recovery from B. § 2–312 Comment 1 (Comment 2 (2003)).

Warranties against infringement also are included in § 2–312(3), (2–312(2) (2003)). CISG 41–44.

[*2003 Amend*. Section 2–312(1)(a) adds to the warranty that the title conveyed shall be good and its transfer rightful, the following: "and shall not unreasonably expose the buyer to litigation because of any colorable claim to or interest in the goods." See § 2–312 Comment 1.]

2. WARRANTIES OF QUALITY

A. EXPRESS WARRANTIES

Seller's express warranties rest on "dickered" aspects of an individual bargain. § 2–313(1) and Comment 1. These warranties are as follows:

(1) The goods shall conform to any *affirmation of fact* the seller makes to the buyer relating to the goods. Example: "The goods are 100 per cent wool."

(2) The goods shall conform to any *promise* the seller makes to the buyer relating to the goods. Example: "The color of the cloth supplied by the seller under this contract will not fade."

(3) The goods shall conform to the seller's *description* of the goods. Example: "Seller agrees to supply to

Buyer goods of the following description [*describe* the *goods*]."

(4) The whole of the goods shall conform to any *sample* (or model) of the goods. Example: "Seller agrees to supply the buyer with goods according to the sample [or model] supplied by the buyer."

Basis of the bargain

For an express warranty to be created, such affirmation, promise, description, or sample must become "part of the basis of the bargain." § 2–313(1). A clue as to the significance of this expression may be found in prior law, Uniform Sales Act § 12, which states that "Any affirmation . . . or any promise by the seller relating to the goods is an express warranty if the natural tendency of such affirmation or promise is to induce the buyer to purchase the goods, and if the buyer purchases the goods relying thereon." The Code recognizes that, in actual practice, affirmations, etc. made by the seller are regarded as *part* of the basis of the bargain, hence no particular reliance on the affirmation is needed to weave them into the fabric of the agreement. Rather, any attempt to take such affirmations, etc. out of the agreement requires clear, affirmative proof. § 2–313 Comment 3 [Comment 5 (2003)]. Example: S says, "The goods are 100 per cent wool." B knows that in fact the goods are 50 per cent cotton. Nevertheless, B buys solely on the basis of factors other than S's affirmation. S's affirmation is not "part of the basis of the bargain."

Fact vs. opinion

Formal words such as "warrant" or "guarantee" are not necessary to the creation of an express warranty, nor does the seller need a specific intention to make a warranty. However, the following do not create express warranties: statements of opinion, affirmations of the value of the goods, or statements of commendation (salesperson's puffing). § 2–313(2) and Comment 8 [2–313(3) and Comment 10 (2003)].

Statements made after the sale

The precise time when express warranties are made or samples are shown is not material. The sole question is whether the language or samples are fairly to be regarded as part of the contract. If language is used after the closing of the deal (as when the buyer, when taking delivery, asks and receives an additional assurance), the warranty becomes a modification which—if it is otherwise reasonable and in order—need not be supported by consideration, since an "agreement modifying a contract within [UCC Article 2] needs no consideration to be binding." §§ 2–209(1), 2–313 Comment 7 [Comment 9 (2003)]. (e.g., sales clerk handing over the counter just-purchased eye-shadow says, "This eye-shadow is absolutely harmless to the eyes.").

Express warranties and the parol evidence rule

Assume that, prior to or at the time of closing a deal in writing, S says to B, "These goods are guaranteed for one year." This statement might be kept from the trier of fact by operation of the parol evidence rule: "[A] writing intended by the parties as a final expression of their agreement . . . may not be contradicted by evidence of any prior agreement or of a contemporaneous oral agreement. . . ." § 2–202 ("record" is substituted for "writing" in 2003).

Express warranties and fraud or misrepresentation

Fraud requires (1) a material misrepresentation of fact, (2) made with knowledge of its falsity or recklessly made without knowledge of its truth, (3) with the intention that it be acted upon by another, (4) reliance thereon by another, (5) to its damage. Take away element (2), knowledge of falsity (scienter), and fraud closely resembles breach of an express warranty. This cause of action is also closely related to *innocent misrepresentation.* See Restatement (Second) of Torts §§ 525, 526, 552C. Also note the closely related Restatement (Second) of Torts § 402B, Misrepresentation by Seller of Chattels to Consumer, which states in part,

> "One engaged in the business of selling chattels who, by advertising, labels, or otherwise, makes to the public a misrepresentation of a material fact concerning the character or quality of a chattel sold by him is subject to liability for physical harm to a consumer of the chattel caused by justifiable reliance upon the misrepresentation, even though ... it is not made fraudulently or negligently...."

See Restatement (Third) of Torts: Products Liability § 9.

Magnuson–Moss Federal Warranty Act

Under the Magnuson–Moss Act, certain written consumer product warranties must fully and conspicuously disclose terms and conditions of the warranty, including whether such warranty is "full" or "limited." Under a full warranty, a warrantor must remedy a defect in a consumer product within a reasonable time and without charge. In addition, a warrantor may not limit the duration of implied warranties; exclusion or limitation of consequential damages must appear conspicuously on the face of the warranty; and, after a reasonable number of attempts to remedy defects, the consumer may elect either a refund or replacement. 15 U.S.C. §§ 2303, 2304, 2308, 2311. See also state "lemon laws," 16 CFR Pt. 455 for used car sales and *window form* requirements for consumer sales; and 12 West's Legal Forms § 8.2—Form 33. CISG 35(1), (2)(c), 3 and 36–40; see 44.

[*2003 Amend*. Section 2–313(1) and (2) makes clear that express warranties are made to the *immediate* buyer. New § 2–313(4) asserts that any "remedial promise" S makes to B "creates an obligation that the promise will be performed upon the happening of the specified event." A remedial promise is "a promise by the seller to repair or replace goods or to refund all or part of the price of goods upon the happening of a specified event." § 2–103(1)(n). The category "remedial promise" was created to deal with a statute of limitations problem. See § 2–313 Comments 2, 10, and 11; see § 2–725(2)(c).

New §§ 2–313A and 2–313B create express warranties that run directly from a seller to a *remote* purchaser. The sections are captioned, obligation to remote purchaser created by (i) record packaged with or accompanying goods or (ii) communication to the public. See §§ 2–313A Comment 1, 2–313B Comment 1.]

B. IMPLIED WARRANTIES

Although express warranties rest on "dickered" aspects of an individual bargain, no particular language or action is necessary to evidence implied warranties, and they will arise automatically in certain common factual situations or sets of conditions unless unmistakably negated. Two examples are the implied warranties of merchantability and fitness for a particular purpose. § 2–313 Comment 1 (Comment 3 (2003)).

(1) Implied Warranty of Merchantability

A warranty that the goods shall be merchantable is implied in a contract for their sale *if* the seller is a *merchant* with respect to goods of that kind. §§ 2–314(1). See also 2–104(1) and Comment 2 (defining "merchant"). The warranty requires that the goods be at least fit for the _ordinary_ purposes for which goods of that description are used. § 2–314(2)(c) and Comment 5 (Comment 10

(2003)). See also § 2–314(2)(a)–(f) (defining "merchantability"). Section 2–314 Comment 2 (Comment 3 (2003)) states that "when the warranty is imposed turns basically on the meaning of the terms of the agreement as recognized in the trade. Goods delivered under an agreement made by a merchant in a given line of trade must be of a quality comparable to that generally acceptable in that line of trade under the description or other designation of the goods used in the agreement." Examples of non-merchantable goods are shotgun shells that prematurely explode, shoes with heels that break off under normal use, cattle feed containing sufficient nutrients to keep cattle alive but also causing sterility in bulls, a cocktail robe that bursts into flames upon casual contact with a stove burner, and a soft drink containing small particles of glass. Particular problem areas include design defects and allergies. UCC Hornbook § 10–11 through § 10–13. See § 2–314 Comment 7 (Comment 9 (2003)).

Reliance

Although 2–314 includes no explicit requirement that the buyer rely on the warranty of merchantability, § 2–316(3)(b) (2003) states, "[I]f the buyer before entering into the contract has examined the goods or the sample or model as fully as desired or has refused to examine the goods *after a demand by the seller*, there is no implied warranty with regard to defects that an examination in the circumstances should have revealed to the buyer." (Emphasis added.) (The italicized words were added in 2003.)

Causation   ᴡʜɪʀʟᴘᴏᴏʟ

Of course, it is necessary to show not only the existence of the warranty, but also the fact that the warranty was broken and the breach proximately caused the loss sustained. (i.e., Was B's skin rash caused by S's soap?) § 2–314 Comment 13 (Comment 15 (2003)). See Part One, D, 4, A infra. CISG 35(2)(a) and (d), (3); 36–40, see 44.

(2) Implied Warranties Arising From Course of Dealing or Trade Usage

Implied warranties may arise from course of dealing or trade usage. §§ 2–314(3), 1–303. See Part One, B, 4 supra. Example: For a pedigreed dog or blooded bull to be considered merchantable, trade usage may require that pedigree papers be produced. § 2–314 Comment 12 (Comment 14 (2003)). CISG 8, 9.

(3) Implied Warranty of Fitness for Particular Purpose

When, at the time of contracting, the seller has reason to know (1) any *particular* purpose for which the goods are required and (2) that the buyer is relying on the seller's skill or judgment to select or furnish suitable goods, there is an implied warranty that the goods shall be fit for such purpose. The buyer, of course, must actually rely on the seller. § 2–315 and Comment 1.

A "particular" purpose differs from the "ordinary" purpose for which the goods are used, in that it envisages a specific use by the buyer that is peculiar to the nature of his business, whereas the ordinary purposes for which goods are used are those envisaged in the concept of merchantability (§ 2–314(2)(c)). Example: Shoes are generally used for the purpose of walking upon ordinary ground, but a seller may know that a particular pair was selected for climbing mountains. Assuming that the seller has reason to know that the buyer is relying on the seller's skill or judgment to select or furnish shoes fit for climbing mountains and that the buyer does rely on the seller's judgment, there is an implied warranty that the shoes shall be fit for climbing mountains. § 2–315 Comment 2.

A contract may, of course, include both a warranty of merchantability and one of fitness for a particular purpose. In fact, the two warranties may overlap. Shoes with soles that wear through in one week of ordinary use will not be fit for either a particular or an ordinary purpose. CISG 35(2)(b), (3); 36–40, see 44.

3. CUMULATION AND CONFLICT OF WARRANTIES

Consider the following express warranty under § 2–313(1)(a): "This vehicle is warranted to be free of defects for 12,000 miles or twelve months, whichever occurs first." Does this express warranty displace the implied warranty of merchantability? Warranties, whether express or implied, shall be construed as consistent with each other and as cumulative. If such construction is unreasonable, the intention of the parties shall determine which warranty is dominant. The UCC has rules designed to aid in determining the intention of the parties. For example, express warranties displace inconsistent implied warranties other than an implied warranty of fitness for a particular purpose. § 2–317. CISG 8, 9.

4. DEFENSES TO WARRANTY ACTIONS

A. CAUSATION

In an action based on breach of warranty, it is necessary to show not only the existence of a warranty, but also the fact that the warranty was broken. It is also necessary to show that the breach proximately caused the loss. A seller may defeat recovery by showing that the loss resulted from some action or event following his own delivery of the goods. The buyer's action following an examination of the goods that ought to have revealed the defect complained of can help a court determine whether the breach itself was the cause of the injury. § 2–314 Comment 13 (Comment 15 (2003)), §§ 2–714 (re: damages), 2–715 (incidental and consequential damages). Example: B consumed one-half of a bottle of soft drink. She gagged on some foreign substance. She spit out the substance, then proceeded to finish the drink. As she finished the last draught, she again gagged and discovered that this time she had suffered injuries from the foreign substance, which was particles of ground glass. Held: Action by B (finishing the contents of the bottle) following an examination of the goods that ought to have revealed the defect complained of (gagging upon consuming one-half of the bottle) can affect a court's determination as to whether the breach of warranty (particles of glass in the soft drink), as opposed to B's own conduct, caused the injury. This behavior by B has been called "assumption of risk" or "contributory negligence."

Thus, B's behavior may break the causal chain between the breach of warranty and B's injury. Restatement (Second) of Torts § 402A, Comment n offers similar guidance: "Contributory negligence of the plaintiff [buyer] is not a defense when such negligence consists merely in a failure to discover the defect in the product, or to guard against the possibility of its existence. On the other hand the form of contributory negligence which consists in voluntarily and unreasonably proceeding to encounter a known danger . . . is a defense. . . . If the user or consumer discovers the defect and is aware of the danger, and nevertheless proceeds unreasonably to make use of the product and is injured by it, he is barred from recovery." See §§ 2–314 Comment 13 (last sen.), 2–316 Comment 8 (4th sen.), 2–715 Comment 5 (last sen.). [See §§ 2–314 Comment 15, 2–316 Comment 6, 2–715 Comment 5 (2003).] CISG 2(a), 5, 74. See also Restatement (Third) of Torts: Products Liability § 17 and comment a (describing the rise of comparative fault).

B. STATUTE OF LIMITATIONS

A seller may raise the UCC statute of limitations as a defense to a buyer's breach of contract claim. Under

Article 2, an action for breach of a sales contract must be commenced within four years after the cause of action has accrued. § 2–725. (This statute will be further discussed at Part One, F, 4, D infra.)

C. NOTICE OF BREACH

When a tender has been accepted, the buyer must notify the seller of any breach within a reasonable time after the buyer discovers or should have discovered the breach. § 2–607(3)(a). The *notification* need only inform the seller that the transaction is claimed to involve a breach, and thus open the way for normal settlement through negotiation. The *time* of notification applicable to a merchant buyer is to be determined by applying commercial standards; a retail consumer is to be judged by different standards so that in his case the notification period will be extended. § 2–607 Comment 4. The analysis will be very fact-specific: Five days has been held untimely, and two and one-half years has been held timely, under particular factual settings. See, e.g., UCC Hornbook § 12–10. CISG 39, 40; see 27, 38, 44.

Policy: The notice requirement is designed to defeat commercial bad faith, not to deprive a good faith consumer of a remedy. § 2–607 Comment 4. Consider this pre-UCC explanation: Buyers should be prevented from interposing belated claims for damages (too often a mere afterthought) as an offset to a suit begun by a seller for the purchase price. See 12 West's Legal Forms §§ 8.8, 9.14. The commercial reality is that good faith buyers are timely in reporting defective goods, and sellers should have protection against false, trumped-up claims. Further policy considerations are "to enable the seller to make adjustments or replacements or to suggest opportunities for cure to the end of minimizing the buyer's loss and reducing the seller's own liability to the buyer . . . . to afford sellers an opportunity to arm themselves for negotiation and litigation . . . ." UCC Hornbook § 12–10, p. 564.

[*2003 Amend.* Section 2–607(3)(a) has been amended to provide that failure to give timely notice of breach in the case of accepted goods bars a remedy *only* to the extent the seller is *prejudiced* by the untimely notice.]

For lack of privity as a defense, see Part One, D, 7 infra.

5. EXCLUSION OR MODIFICATION OF WARRANTIES

A. WARRANTY OF TITLE

A warranty of title (§ 2–312(1)) can be excluded or modified only as follows:

(1) by specific *language,* e.g., "Seller does not warrant that the title to the goods conveyed to Buyer is good; nor that the transfer of the goods to Buyer is rightful; nor that the goods are delivered to Buyer free from any security interest or other lien or encumbrance."

(2) by *circumstances* "which give the buyer reason to know that the person selling does not claim title in himself or that he is purporting to sell only such right or title as he or a third person may have," e.g., sales by sheriffs, executors, certain foreclosing lienors, and persons similarly situated. § 2–312(2) and Comment 5. [Foreclosures under Article 9 are another matter. A disposition of collateral under § 9–610 includes warranties of title. § 2–312 Comment 5 (last sentence) (2001).] CISG 6.

[*2003 Amend.* See § 2–312(3) and Comment 6.]

B. WARRANTIES OF QUALITY

(1) Express Warranties

Suppose a sales agreement contains the following language: "The color of the cloth supplied by the seller under this contract will not fade." This is an express warranty per § 2–313(1)(a), (2–313(2)(a) (2003)). Elsewhere, the agreement reads, "Seller hereby excludes all warranties, express or implied." Insofar as it is relates to the express warranty, this exclusion is inoperative by application of the following rules: Express warranties shall be construed, if possible, as consistent with disclaimers of warranty. (In other words, when possible, the court shall find (1) no warranty, (2) no disclaimer, or (3) a limited express warranty.) If such construction is not reasonable, the disclaimer is inoperative. § 2–316(1) and Comment 1. Counseling point: The way to exclude affirmations of fact or promises that relate to the goods is not to make them. CISG 6, 8, 35(2)(c).

(2) Implied Warranties

(a) Examination

"[W]hen the buyer before entering into the contract has examined the goods or the sample or model as fully as (he) desired or has refused to examine the goods [after a demand by the seller] there is no implied warranty with regard to defects which an examination ought in the circumstances to have revealed to him." § 2–316(3)(b) (with minor changes in 2003) and Comment 8 (Comment 6 (2003)). CISG 35(3).

(b) Course of Dealing, Course of Performance, or Trade Usage

An implied warranty can be excluded or modified by evidence of the parties' course of dealing or course of performance, as well as any usage of trade. § 2–316(3)(c). Example: A cattle buyer inspects cattle and cuts out those that do not suit him. Held: According to trade usage, his acceptance of others " 'is irrevocable and without recourse,' and thus excludes all implied warranties." UCC Hornbook § 13–6(c), p. 591. CISG 9.

(c) Language

Unless the circumstances indicate otherwise, all implied warranties (merchantability, fitness for particular purpose) are excluded by language that, in common understanding, calls the buyer's attention to the exclusion of warranties and makes plain that there is no implied warranty. § 2–316(3)(a). Example: "The goods sold under this agreement are sold 'as is' and 'with all faults.' " See UCC Hornbook § 13–6(a).

[*2003 Amend.* Section 2–316(3)(a) adds, "and, in a consumer contract evidenced by a record, is set forth conspicuously in the record." § 2–103(1)(c),(d),(m).]

Other language may also be used to exclude or modify implied warranties:

1.   To exclude or modify the implied warranty of merchantability or any part of it, the language must mention merchantability and, in the case of a writing [record], must be conspicuous. § 2–316(2). A term or clause is conspicuous when it is so written, displayed, or presented that a reasonable person against whom it is to operate ought to have noticed it. § 1–201(b)(10), (2–103(1)(b) (2003)) (e.g. "SELLER MAKES NO WARRANTY OF MERCHANTABILITY WITH RESPECT TO GOODS SOLD UNDER THIS AGREEMENT.").

2.   To exclude or modify any implied warranty of fitness, the exclusion must be by a writing [in a record] and be conspicuous. §§ 2–316(2), 1–201(b)(10)(2–103(1)(b) (2003)) (e.g. "THERE ARE NO WARRANTIES THAT EXTEND BEYOND THE DESCRIPTION ON THE FACE HEREOF.").

[*2003 Amend.* Section 2–316(2) adds, with respect to exclusion or modification of warranty of merchantability, the following: "in a consumer contract the language must be in a record, be conspicuous and state 'THE SELLER UNDERTAKES NO RESPONSIBILITY FOR THE QUALITY

OF THE GOODS EXCEPT AS OTHERWISE PROVIDED IN THIS CONTRACT.' " (Emphasis added). With respect to warranties of fitness, the following language is added: "in a consumer contract [the language] must [be in a record and be conspicuous and] state 'THE SELLER ASSUMES NO RESPONSIBILITY THAT THE GOODS WILL BE FIT FOR ANY PARTICULAR PURPOSE FOR WHICH YOU MAY BE BUYING THESE GOODS, EXCEPT AS OTHERWISE PROVIDED IN THE CONTRACT.' " (Emphasis added). Subsection (2) concludes, "Language that satisfies the requirements of this subsection for the exclusion or modification in a consumer contract also satisfies the requirements for any other contract."]

For limitations on the duration of implied warranties, see "consumer product" warranties under the Magnuson–Moss Warranty Act, 15 U.S.C. §§ 2304(a)(2), 2308(b). CISG 6, 8, 35(2).

Purpose of warranty and disclaimer law

In assessing the law of warranties and disclaimers, be advised of the following observations by the Code drafters:

"In view of the principle that the whole purpose of the law of warranty is to determine what it is that the seller has in essence agreed to sell, the policy is adopted of those cases which refuse except in unusual circumstances to recognize a material deletion of the seller's obligation. Thus, a contract is normally a contract for a sale of something describable and described. A clause generally disclaiming 'all warranties, express or implied' cannot reduce the seller's obligation with respect to such description and therefore cannot be given literal effect under Section 2–316.

This is not intended to mean that the parties, if they consciously desire, cannot make their own bargain as they wish. But in determining what they have agreed upon good faith [§ 1–304] is a factor and consideration should be given to the fact that the probability is small that a real price is intended to be exchanged for a pseudo-obligation." § 2–313 Comment 4 (Comment 6 (2003) (with minor changes)). See also Comment 7 (Comment 9 (2003) (with minor changes)) to § 2–314: "[T]he price at which a merchant closes a contract is an excellent index of the nature and scope of his obligation."

Unconscionability

While freedom of contract is a core principle of the Code (§ 1–302 Comment 1), UCC § 2–302 is intended to make it possible for courts to police contracts or clauses they find unconscionable. Courts may refuse to enforce these contracts, may enforce the remainder of the contract without the unconscionable clause, or may so limit the application of any unconscionable clause as to avoid any unconscionable result. The goal is to prevent oppression and unfair surprise. § 2–302 and Comment 1. See Part One, B, 4 supra.

At least one authority has argued that § 2–302 should have no application to § 2–316 disclaimers because the UCC spells out specifically how to disclaim implied warranties of quality. See discussion in UCC Hornbook § 13–11(b). This may not be the UCC drafters' intention, and we will assume that courts will police all warranty disclaimers which are believed to be oppressive. § 2–302 Comment 1 (citing Bekkevold v. Potts as an example of a court's adverse construction of disclaimer language to avoid an oppressive result).

Karl Llewellyn's statement to the New York Revision Commission [Llewellyn, 1 N.Y.Law Rev.Comm.Rep. 177–178 (1954)] is instructive on this point. He describes the problem of policing against unconscionable contracts and clauses by adverse construction thus:

We have all of us seen this kind of series of cases, haven't we? Case No. 1 comes up. The clause is perfectly clear and the court said, "Had it been desired to provide such an unbelievable thing, surely language could have been made clearer." Then counsel redrafts, and they not only say it twice as well, but they wind up saying, "And we mean it," and the court looks at it a second time and says, "Had this been the kind of thing really intended to go into an agreement, surely language could have been found," and so on down the line.

This kind of thing does not make for good business, it does not make for good counseling, and it does not make for certainty. It means that you never know where you are, and it does a very bad thing to the law indeed. The bad thing that it does to the law is to lead to precedent after precedent in which language is held not to mean what it says and indeed what its plain purpose was, and that upsets everything for everybody in all future litigation.

We believe that if you take this and bring it out into the open, if you say, "When it gets too stiff to make sense, then the court may knock it out," you are going to get a body of principles of construction instead of principles of misconstruction, and the precedents are going to build up so that the language will be relied upon and will be construed to mean what it says.

An appealing case for policing warranties for unconscionability—even those meeting the requirements of § 2–316—is the merchant-seller who has a warranty disclaimer on its pre-printed form-pad contract and does business with a non-merchant consumer buyer who suffers personal injuries as a result of a defect in the goods. Such boiler-plate language "is assented to en bloc, 'unsight, unseen' on the implicit assumption and to the full extent that (1) it does not alter or impair the fair meaning of the dickered terms when read alone, and (2) that its terms are neither in the particular nor in the net manifestly unreasonable and unfair." K. Llewellyn, The Common Law Tradition 371 (1960). Restatement (Second) of Contracts § 211. CISG 4(a), 7(1), 8 (describing a principle often called "blanket assent").

6. LIMITATION OF REMEDIES FOR BREACH OF WARRANTY

Even though a seller may not have excluded or modified its warranties, it may seek in the sales agreement to limit or modify the *remedies* available to the buyer for its breach of warranty. Will this be effective? Generally, a sales agreement may provide for remedies in addition to, or in substitution for, those provided in UCC Article 2, and may limit or alter the measure of damages. §§ 2–316(4), 2–719(1)(a). Examples: "It is expressly understood and agreed that the buyer's sole and exclusive remedy shall be repair or replacement of defective parts, and that the seller shall not be liable for damages for injuries to persons or property." Or, "In no event shall Seller be liable for more than, and the buyer's exclusive remedy shall be limited to, the price of goods alleged to be defective and under no circumstances shall Seller be liable for incidental or consequential damages." Thus, parties are free to shape their remedies to their particular requirements, and reasonable agreements limiting or modifying remedies are to be given effect. § 2–719 Comment 1.

However, it is of the very essence of a sales contract that at least minimum adequate remedies be available. If the parties intend to conclude a contract for the sale of goods, they must accept the legal consequence that there be at least a fair quantum of remedy for breach of the obligations or duties outlined in the contract. Thus, any clause purporting to modify or limit the remedies provisions of Article 2 in an unconscionable manner is subject to deletion. Accordingly, although consequential damages may be limited or excluded, such provisions may not operate in an unconscionable manner. In the case of consumer goods, limitation of consequential damages for injury to the person is prima facie unconscionable. §§ 2–719(3) and Comments 1 and 3, 2–302. Example: B bought a car from S. The contract limited B's remedy to repair or replacement of defective parts; consequential damages were excluded. At 468 miles on the odometer, a defective steering mechanism caused the car to veer sharply to the right and crash into a highway sign and brick wall, injuring B. The clause excluding consequential damages for B's personal injuries is prima facie unconscionable. See Henningsen v. Bloomfield Motors, Inc., 32 N.J. 358 at 375, 161 A.2d 69 at 78 (1960). Note: the Magnuson–Moss Federal Warranty Act does not supersede state law regarding consequential damages for injury to person or property. 15 U.S.C. § 2311(b)(2); see also § 2304(a)(3). CISG 2(a), 5.

Similarly, a term fixing unreasonably large liquidated damages is void as a penalty, while a clause providing for an unreasonably small amount might be stricken for unconscionability. § 2–718 Comment 1. See Part One, F, 4, A, (1) infra. [Under § 2–718(1) (2003), the "unreasonably large liquidated damages" language has been eliminated as unnecessary and misleading. See § 2–718 Comment 3 (2003)].

Finally, if, under the circumstances, an apparently fair and reasonable clause fails in its purpose or operates to deprive either party of the substantial value of the bargain, it must give way to the Code's general remedy provisions. § 2–719(2) and Comment 1. See Part One, F, 4, A, (2) infra. CISG 4(a), 6, 8, 9; see 74–78.

7. BENEFICIARIES OF WARRANTIES

To whom do a seller's warranties in §§ 2–313, 2–314, and 2–315 extend? Clearly they extend to the immediate buyer. Do they extend also to third parties such as remote purchasers, the buyer's family, guests at the buyer's home, a sub-buyer, guests in a sub-buyer's auto, and innocent bystanders hit by an auto driven by a sub-buyer? Insofar as loss is concerned, will the seller's liability to third persons extend only to personal injury, or will such liability extend also to property damage and economic loss such as a buyer's loss of its bargain or loss of profit? See §§ 2–714(2), (3), 2–715(2)(a). CISG 1(1), 4 (first sentence). [See §§ 2–313A, 2–313B, 2–318 (2003).]

History

Historically, a supplier of defective chattels generally was not liable to third persons in the absence of *negligence* or *privity* of contract (a direct contractual relationship between the seller and injured buyer). Privity was not, however, required for a cause of action based on the tort of negligence. MacPherson v. Buick Motor Co., 217 N.Y. 382, 111 N.E. 1050 (1916). There was an exception to this general requirement of privity or negligence for the seller of food and drink for human consumption. Such a seller was held liable for providing unwholesome (defective) food or drink to the consumer even though the seller was not negligent and even though the consumer was not in privity with the seller. To accomplish this result, case law decisions "displayed considerable ingenuity in evolving more or less fictitious theories of liability to fit the case. The various devices included [1] an agency of the intermediate dealer or another to purchase for the consumer, or to sell for the seller; [2] a theoretical assignment of the seller's warranty to the intermediate dealer; [3] a third party beneficiary contract; and [4] an implied representation that the food was fit for consumption because it was placed on the market, as well as numerous others. In later years the courts have become more or less agreed upon the theory of a 'warranty' from the seller to the consumer, either 'running with the goods' by analogy to a covenant running with the land, or made directly to the consumer. Other decisions have indicated that the basis is merely one of strict liability in tort, which is not dependent upon either contract or negligence." Restatement (Second) of Torts § 402A Comment b. See also Restatement (Third) of Torts: Products Liability § 1 comment a.

Since 1950, decisions have extended this rule beyond food for human consumption to cover other products intended for intimate bodily use, e.g., cosmetics. Beginning in 1958 with a Michigan case involving cinder building blocks, a number of decisions have extended the rule of strict liability even further, to cover the sale of any product which, if it should prove to be defective, may be expected to cause physical harm to the consumer or the consumer's property. Spence v. Three Rivers Builders & Masonry Supply, Inc., 353 Mich. 120, 90 N.W.2d 873 (1958). See Restatement (Second) of Torts § 402A Comment b. See also Restatement (Third) of Torts: Products Liability § 1.

Implied warranty of merchantability vs. strict liability in tort

The above discussion has focused primarily on how warranty law has been extended beyond traditional concepts of negligence and privity. An alternative source of liability in situations involving third parties is strict liability in tort, which is reflected in Restatement (Second) of Torts § 402A as follows:

> § 402A. Special Liability of Seller of Product for Physical Harm to User or Consumer

(1) One who sells any product in a defective condition unreasonably dangerous to the user or consumer or to his property is subject to liability for physical harm

thereby caused to the ultimate user or consumer, or to his property if

(a) the seller is engaged in the business of selling such a product, and

(b) it is expected to and does reach the user or consumer without substantial change in the condition in which it is sold.

(2) The rule stated in Subsection (1) applies although

(a) the seller has exercised all possible care in the preparation and sale of his product, and

(b) the user or consumer has not brought the product from or entered into any contractual relation with the seller.

See Reporter's Notes

Caveat:

The Institute expresses no opinion as to whether the rules stated in this Section may not apply:

(1) to harm to persons other than users or consumers;

(2) to the seller of a product expected to be processed or otherwise substantially changed before it reaches the user or consumer; or

(3) to the seller of a component part of a product to be assembled.

See also Restatement (Third) of Torts: Products Liability § 1 (providing a more expansive theory of liability).

Many articles have compared the warranty of merchantability with strict liability in tort. The following chart should afford a basis for analysis:

		Warranty of Merchantability § 2–314	Strict Liability in Restatement, (Second) of Torts § 402A
1.	Condition of goods giving rise to liability	Not merchantable, e.g., not fit for ordinary purpose. § 2–314(1), (2)(c).	Defective condition that is unreasonably dangerous. § 402A(1).
2.	Character of defendant	Must be a seller who is a merchant with respect to goods of that kind. §§ 2–314(1), 2–104(1).	Must be a seller who is engaged in the business of selling such a product. § 402A(1)(a).
3.	Reliance	No explicit requirement. Such warranty "taken for granted." § 2–314 and Comment 11; see, however, § 2–316(3)(b). [See § 2–314 Comment 13 (2003).]	No requirement of "any reliance on the part of the consumer upon the reputation, skill or judgment of the seller." § 402A Comment m.
4.	Disclaimer	Limitation of consequential damages for injury to the person in the case of consumer goods is prima facie unconscionable. §§ 2–316(4), 2–719(3), 2–302; but see § 2–316(1)–(3).	Cause of action not affected by any disclaimer or any other agreement. § 402A Comment m.
5.	Notice	Buyer must, within a reasonable time after he discovers or should have discovered any breach, notify seller of breach or be barred from any remedy. § 2–607(3)(a) and Comments 4 and 5. [See § 2–607(3)(a) (2003).]	Consumer not required to give notice to seller of his injury within a reasonable time after it occurs. § 402A Comment m.
6.	Causation	Buyer may recover consequential damages resulting from seller's breach, including injury to person or property proximately resulting from any breach of warranty. §§ 2–714, 2–	Seller subject to liability for physical harm caused. § 402A(1); see Comment n Contributory negligence; Comment p Further processing or substantial change; Comment q Component

	Warranty of Merchantability § 2–314	Strict Liability in Restatement, (Second) of Torts § 402A
	715(2)(b) and Comment 5, § 2–314 Comment 13, see § 2–316(3)(b) and Comment 8. [See §§ 2–314 Comment 15, 2–316 Comment 6 (2003).]	parts; see also Comments g, h, i, j.
7. Protected persons	Any person who may reasonably be expected to use, consume, or be affected by the goods. § 2–318 Alternative C. [See §§ 2–318 Comments 1–4, 2–313A, 2–313B (2003).]	Ultimate user or consumer. § 402A(1), (2)(b) and Comment *l*.
8. Protected injuries	Injuries to person listed in 7 above or his property. § 2–318 Alternative C and Comment 3; cf. Alternative B. [See § 2–318 Comments 1–4 (2003).]	Physical harm to ultimate user or consumer, or to his property. § 402a(1).
9. Statute of limitations	Four years from tender of delivery. § 2–725(1), (2). [See § 2–725(1)–(3) (2003).]	State law varies (e.g., three years from injury.).

The above chart shows an essential similarity between the implied warranty of merchantability and strict liability in tort. For example, whether a good or condition qualifies as "fit for its ordinary purpose" and "a defective condition unreasonably dangerous" may be similar tests. Of course, under strict liability in tort, the cause of action is not affected by any disclaimer, nor is the plaintiff required to give notice of the injury. However, under the Code, limitation of consequential damages for injury to the person is prima facie *unconscionable*. In addition, the notice requirement is intended to defeat commercial bad faith, not to deprive a good faith consumer of a remedy. Thus, in many if not most instances, an injured consumer could recover under either the Code or under strict liability in tort, even without demonstrating privity or negligence in the preparation and sale of defective goods. Differences between the statutes of limitations, of course, could cause some difficulty. See Part One, F, 4, D infra.

As this discussion suggests, the lawyer's penchant for pigeon-holing a case as arising "in tort" or "in contract" exclusively has not been particularly helpful in analyzing the evolving body of law frequently characterized as "product liability law." Instead, under either theory, the basic inquiries are the same: (1) were the goods defective; and (2) did they cause the plaintiff's injuries?

Policy for strict liability

"On whatever theory [contract or tort], the justification for the strict liability has been said to be that the seller, by marketing his product for use and consumption, has undertaken and assumed a special responsibility toward any member of the consuming public who may be injured by it; that the public has the right to and does expect, in the case of products which it needs and for which it is forced to rely upon the seller, that reputable sellers will stand behind their goods; that public policy demands that the burden of accidental injuries caused by products intended for consumption be placed upon those who market them, and be treated as a cost of production against which liability insurance can be obtained; and that the consumer of such products is entitled to the maximum of protection at the hands of someone, and the proper persons to afford it are those who market the products." Restatement (Second) of Torts § 402A Comment c. Thus, a seller who sends defective goods into the marketplace can calculate the risks, purchase liability insurance, and add it to the price of the product.

Injuries to non-users and nonconsumers

Will persons other than users and consumers be brought within the protection of strict liability principles, e.g., an innocent bystander hit by a defective automobile? Restatement (Second) of Torts § 402A takes no position; (see Caveat and Comments *l* and *o*). See also Restatement (Third) of Torts: Products Liability § 1 (providing a broader theory of liability). Meanwhile, § 2–318 Alternative C extends protection to "any person who may reasonably be … affected by the goods…." (With minor changes in 2003). This may include the innocent bystander mentioned above. In addition, some cases have extended protection to bystanders; e.g., Piercefield v. Remington Arms Company, Inc., 375 Mich. 85, 133 N.W.2d 129 (1965) (innocent bystander injured by defective shotgun shell; privity and proof of negligence deemed unnecessary).

Economic loss

Suppose manufacturer A sold defective golf carts to dealer B who in turn sold them to C, who used them in C's business as a golf course proprietor. The defective golf carts did not injure anyone or harm any property, but did need constant repair. C did not get the benefit of the bargain (see § 2–714(2)); C suffered consequential damages, such as loss of profit, because the defective golf carts caused loss of patronage. (§ 2–715(2)(a)). Whether A should be liable to C in the absence of privity, where no harm to person or property is involved, is controversial. A Michigan court did allow C—on facts similar to those above—to maintain an action against A to recover the loss of C's bargain and the cost of making repairs. Cova v. Harley Davidson Motor Co., 26 Mich.App. 602, 182 N.W.2d 800 (1970). UCC Hornbook §§ 12–5 (direct economic loss), 12–6 (consequential economic loss).

Express warranties vs. seller's misrepresentation

A seller's express warranty, like the implied warranty discussed above, "extends to any person who may reasonably be expected to use, consume or be affected by the goods and who is injured by breach of the warranty." § 2–318 Alternative C. Compare closely related Restatement (Second) of Torts § 402B Misrepresentation by Seller of Chattels to Consumer:

> One engaged in the business of selling chattels who, by advertising, labels, or otherwise, makes to the public a misrepresentation of a material fact concerning the character or quality of a chattel sold by him is subject to liability for physical harm to a consumer of the chattel caused by justifiable reliance upon the misrepresentation, even though
>
> (a) it is not made fraudulently or negligently, and
>
> (b) the consumer has not bought the chattel from or entered into any contractual relation with the seller.

See Reporter's Notes

> Caveat:
>
> The Institute expresses no opinion as to whether the rule stated in this Section may apply
>
> (1) where the representation is not made to the public, but to an individual, or
>
> (2) where physical harm is caused to one who is not a consumer of the chattel.

See Restatement (Third) of Torts: Products Liability § 9.

Vouching-in procedures

Suppose manufacturer A sells goods to dealer B, who sells them to user C. Although C may not want to sue A, the practice of voucher may bring A into C's litigation. Rule: When B is sued for breach of a warranty by C for which A is *answerable over* (A made warranties to B similar to those B made to C), B may give A written notice of the litigation. If the notice states (1) that A may come in and defend, and (2) that if A does not do so, he will be bound in any action against A by B by any determination of fact common to the two litigations, then unless A, after seasonable receipt of the notice, does come in and defend, A is so bound. § 2–607(5).

Products liability

See Restatement (Third) of Torts: Products Liability §§ 1–21 (1998). The Restatement is organized as follows:

- Chapter 1, Liability of Commercial Sellers Based on Product Defects at Time of Sale (§§ 1–8).
- Chapter 2, Liability of Commercial Product Sellers Not Based on Product Defect at Time of Sale (§§ 9–11). See especially § 9 (liability for fraudulent, negligent, or innocent misrepresentation).
- Chapter 3, Liability of Successors and Apparent Manufacturers (§§ 12–14).
- Chapter 4, Provisions of General Applicability (§§ 15–21). The topics covered are causation, affirmative defenses, and definitions (e.g. "product," "one who sells or otherwise distributes," and "harm to persons or property").

Resolving the tension between warranty and tort law

Section 2–314 Comment 7 (2003) states,

When recovery is sought for injury to person or property, whether goods are merchantable is to be determined by applicable state products liability law. When, however, a claim for injury to person or property is based on an implied warranty of fitness under Section 2–315 or an express warranty under Section 2–313 or an obligation arising under § 2–313A or 2–313B, this Article determines whether an implied warranty of fitness or an express warranty was made and breached, as well as what damages are recoverable under Section 2–715.

E. PERFORMANCE OF THE SALES CONTRACT

Generally, the performance obligation of the seller is to transfer (title?) and deliver the goods and the buyer must accept and pay for the goods in accordance with the contract. § 2–301. CISG 30, 53. *Rights* relating to performance include the buyer's right of inspection, § 2–513; buyer's right of rejection if the goods or the tender of delivery fail to conform to the contract, § 2–601; and seller's right to cure improper delivery, § 2–508.

1. GENERAL RIGHTS AND OBLIGATIONS OF SELLERS AND BUYERS

A. PERFORMANCE IN GOOD FAITH

The basic principle

Every contract within the UCC imposes an obligation of good faith in its performance. This obligation may not be disclaimed. §§ 1–201(b)(20) (defining "good faith"), 1–304 (obligation of good faith) and Comments, 1–302(b) (inability to disclaim). CISG 7(1), 60(a).

Cooperation (and options) respecting performance

A contract that leaves particulars of performance to be specified by one of the parties is not thereby made invalid. Specifications must be made in good faith and within limits set by commercial reasonableness. § 2–311(1). Unless otherwise agreed, specifications relating to the assortment of the goods are to be made at the buyer's option (i.e., in a contract for the sale of 600 pens, B may opt to take 100 blue pens and 500 green pens). Specifications or arrangements relating to shipment are to be made at the seller's option (i.e., S may elect to ship goods by X trucking company). § 2–311(2).

When the exercise of an option or cooperation by one party is necessary to, or materially affects, the other party's performance, but it is not seasonably forthcoming, the other party—in addition to all other remedies—is excused from any resulting delay in that party's own performance. And that party may also either (a) proceed to perform in any reasonable manner or (b) after the time for a material part of that party's own performance has passed, treat the failure to specify or to cooperate as a failure to deliver the goods (if breacher is a seller) or a failure to accept the goods (if breacher is a buyer). § 2–311(3) and Comment 3. Illustrative of "other remedies" is the right to adequate assurance of performance, to be discussed presently. See Part One, E, 1, B (2) infra. One example of an option not seasonably forthcoming would be, in a contract for the sale of 600 pens, if B has the option of choosing the styles and colors desired, and B refuses to choose. See also § 2–305(3) and Comment 5. CISG 60(a), 65.

B. RIGHT TO UNIMPAIRED EXPECTATION THAT THE OTHER PARTY WILL DULY PERFORM ITS OBLIGATIONS

Parties bargain, not just for the other party's promise, but the other party's *performance* of that promise. Consequently, the right to unimpaired expectation of proper performance raises (1) the problem of anticipatory repudiation and (2) the right of adequate assurance of performance.

(1) Anticipatory Repudiation

Anticipatory repudiation involves an overt communication of intention or an action that renders performance impossible or demonstrates a clear determination not to continue with performance. § 2–610 Comment 1. Example: B says to S, "Don't deliver the goods next month per our agreement, because I am not going to take them." If the repudiation *substantially impairs* the value of the contract, the aggrieved party may resort to its remedies for breach (see Part One, F infra), or suspend its own performance while negotiating with, or awaiting performance by, the other party. § 2–610. The most useful test of the expression *substantially impairs* is whether material inconvenience or injustice will result if the aggrieved party is forced to wait and ultimately receives tender minus the part or aspect repudiated. § 2–610 Comment 3. Until the repudiating party's next performance is due, the repudiating party may retract the repudiation unless the aggrieved party has, since the repudiation, indicated that the aggrieved party considers the repudiation final, as for example, when the aggrieved party has materially changed its position. § 2–611(1). See also §§ 2–612 (re: installment contracts) and Comment 6, 2–305(3) (failure to fix price term) and Comment 5.

[*2003 Amend*. New § 2–610(2) and Comment 5 provide guidance on when a party can be considered to have repudiated a performance obligation.]

(2) Adequate Assurance of Performance

The right to adequate assurance of performance under § 2–609 rests on recognition of the fact that the essential purpose of a contract between commercial people is actual performance—they do not bargain merely for a promise, or for a promise plus the right to win a lawsuit. Thus, a continuing sense of reliance and security that the promised performance will be forthcoming when due, is an important feature of the bargain. If either the willingness or the ability of Party A to perform declines materially between the time of contracting and the time for performance, Party B is threatened with the loss of a substantial part of what it has bargained for. Yet suppose A has not demonstrated a clear determination not to continue with performance, so as to give B rights under § 2–610 on anticipatory repudiation. In this instance, B has the right to require A to give adequate assurance of A's performance. § 2–609 Comment 1.

For example, a seller may need protection not merely against having to deliver on credit to a shaky buyer, but also against having to procure and manufacture the goods, perhaps turning down other customers. Once the seller has been given reason to doubt the buyer's performance, though it may not rise to the level of an anticipatory repudiation, it is an undue hardship to force the seller to continue his or her own performance. Similarly, a buyer who believes that the seller's deliveries have become uncertain cannot safely wait for the delivery due date to be assured materials for his or her current manufacturing or to replenish his or her stock of merchandise. § 2–609 Comment 1.

Consequently, three measures have been adopted to meet the needs of buyers and sellers in such situations. When reasonable grounds for insecurity arise with respect to the performance of either party, the other (1) may in writing [2003: in a record] demand adequate assurance of due performance and, (2) until that party receives such assurance, may if commercially reasonable suspend any performance for which that party has not already received the agreed return. And (3) after receipt of a justified demand, failure to provide within a reasonable time (not exceeding 30 days) such assurance of due performance as is adequate under the circumstances of the particular case is a *repudiation* of the contract. § 2–609 and Comment 2 et seq. See also §§ 2–210(5) (re: assignment) [2–210(2)(c) (2003)], 2–612(2) and (3) (re: installment contracts) and Comments 5 and 6 [Comments 6 and 8 (2003)], 2–311(3) (failure of specification or cooperation) and Comment 3 and Point 3 of the section's cross references, 2–511 Comment 1 (payment against delivery). CISG 71, 72; see 25–27, 81–84.

2. SELLER'S OBLIGATION TO DELIVER GOODS

A seller's basic obligation is to deliver conforming goods to the buyer. Of course, it is difficult to deliver to an unwilling buyer who wrongfully refuses to accept the goods. Consequently, the seller's obligation is to *tender* delivery of conforming goods to the buyer. §§ 2–301, 2–507(1) (effect of tender), 2–503(1) (manner of tender); see §§ 2–601(a) (right to reject nonconforming tender), 2–106(2) (defining "conforming"), 2–511(1) (tender of payment as a condition to seller's duties). "Tender" contemplates an offer coupled with a present ability to fulfill all the conditions resting on the tendering party and must be followed by actual performance if the other party shows itself ready to proceed. Thus, "tender" connotes such performance by the tendering party as puts the other party in default if such party fails to proceed in some manner. § 2–503 Comment 1. Accordingly, if S duly tenders conforming goods and B does not accept (§ 2–606) them, B is in breach; by contrast, if S does not duly tender delivery of conforming goods, S is in breach. § 2–507(1); see §§ 2–703 (seller's remedies), 2–601(a) (right to reject nonconforming tender), 2–612(3) (re: installment contract), 2–711 (buyer's remedies). As to excuse of the delivery obligation, see Part One, E, 8 infra. CISG 30. [Note minor change in § 2–503 Comment 1 (2003).]

With the significance and importance of tender now established, other matters remain to be determined: What is the time and place for tender? Must goods be delivered in a single lot or several lots? What is the manner of seller's tender of delivery? How long is a contract which provides for successive performance (e.g., deliveries by seller) valid? The parties may determine these matters by their agreement. If they have not otherwise agreed, the following rules apply:

a.   The *time* for tender and delivery shall be a reasonable time. § 2–309(1). CISG 33.

b.   The *place* for tender and delivery is the seller's place of business or, if the seller has none, the seller's residence. Even so, in a contract for sale of identified goods which, to the knowledge of S and B at the time of contracting, are in some other place, that place is the place for their delivery. § 2–308, see § 2–513(4) (re: inspection). Thus, B is to come and pick them up; S need not transport them to B. Where mercantile terms are employed (e.g., F.O.B.), see § 2–319 et seq. CISG 31. [Note: §§ 2–319–2–324 have been eliminated because they are inconsistent with modern commercial practices. § 2–319 Comment (2003).]

c.   *Delivery in single or several lots.* All goods called for by a contract for sale must be tendered in a single delivery. Even so, the circumstances may give either party the right to make or demand delivery in lots, if it is not commercially feasible to deliver or to receive the goods in a single lot. One example is where a contract calls for the shipment of ten carloads of coal and only three cars are available at a given time. § 2–307 and Comment 3.

d.   *Manner of tender of delivery where the contract does not specify same.* (1) The seller (S) must put and hold conforming goods at the buyer's (B's) disposition; (2) S must give B any notification reasonably necessary to enable B to take delivery; (3) tender of delivery must be made at a reasonable hour; (4) the goods tendered must be kept available for the period reasonably necessary to enable B to take possession (that is, B must furnish facilities reasonably suited to the receipt of the goods); and (5) S generally must allow B to inspect the goods. §§ 2–503(1) and Comment 2, 2–513 (re: inspection); but see, e.g., § 2–509(1)(a) (re: risk of loss).

e. *Manner of tender of delivery under a shipment contract.* A shipment contract is one that requires or authorizes S to send the goods to B, but does not require S to deliver them at a particular destination. §§ 2–503(2) and Comment 5, 2–504; cf. §§ 2–401(2)(a) (passage of title under shipment contract), 2–509(1)(a) (risk of loss under shipment contract). Here, S must (1) put the goods in the possession of such a carrier, and make such a contract for their transportation, as may be reasonable under the circumstances (e.g., perishable goods should be refrigerated); (2) obtain and promptly deliver or tender appropriate documents (e.g., bill of lading) to enable B to obtain possession of the goods (this is the subject of Part Four infra); and (3) promptly notify B of the shipment (e.g., send B an invoice). §§ 2–503(2), 2–504; see §§ 2–311(2) (general rule on specifications re: shipping), 2–614 (substituted performance). CISG 31(a), 32, 34. [§ 2–504(a) (2003) reads, "put conforming goods in possession of a carrier and make a proper contract for their transportation having regard to the nature of the goods."]

Specific requirements for tender of delivery under shipment contracts employing mercantile terms are found as follows: F.O.B. place of shipment, § 2–319(1)(a), (3); F.O.B. car or other vehicle at place of shipment, § 2–319(1)(a) and (c), (3); F.O.B. vessel at named place of shipment, §§ 2–319(1)(a) and (c), 2–319(3) and (4), 2–323, 2–308(c); F.A.S. vessel at a named port at the place of shipment, § 2–319(2), (3) and (4); C.I.F. destination or its equivalent, §§ 2–320(1), (2), (4) and Comment 1, 2–321, 2–323, 2–308(c); C & F destination or its equivalent, § 2–320(1), (3) and (4), 2–321, 2–323, 2–308(c). For usage of F.O.B., F.A.S., and C.I.F. terms, see INCOTERMS published by the International Chamber of Commerce. [Note: §§ 2–319–2–324 have been repealed. See 2–319 Comment (2003).]

f. *Manner of tender of delivery under a destination contract.* A destination contract is one that requires S to deliver the goods at a particular destination. § 2–503(3) and Comment 5; cf. §§ 2–401(2)(b) (passage of title under destination contract), 2–509(1)(b) (risk of loss under destination contract). S's duty under such a contract is to tender delivery of conforming goods to B at the agreed destination, and how the goods get there is S's concern. Thus, (1) S must put and hold conforming goods at B's disposition; (2) S must give B any notification reasonably necessary to enable B to take delivery; (3) tender of delivery must be at a reasonable hour, and the goods tendered must be kept available for the period reasonably necessary to enable B to take possession; and (4) in an appropriate case, S must tender documents (e.g., bill of lading) discussed in Part Four, B infra. § 2–503(3).

Specific requirements for tender of delivery under destination contracts employing mercantile terms are found as follows: F.O.B. at named place of destination, § 2–319(1)(b); F.O.B. car or other vehicle at named place of destination, § 2–319(1)(b) and (c), (3); F.O.B. vessel at named place of destination, §§ 2–319(1)(b) and (c), (3) and (4), 2–323, 2–503(5)(b); "ex-ship" at named destination, § 2–322; "no arrival, no sale" or the like, § 2–324. For usage of F.O.B. and other common commercial terms, see INCOTERMS promulgated by the International Chamber of Commerce. [Note: §§ 2–319–2–324 have been repealed. See § 2–319 Comment (2003).]

g. *Manner of tender of delivery when the goods are in a bailee's possession and are to be delivered without being moved.* S bails goods in W warehouse, which holds the goods for S as bailee. S sells the goods to B, who does not intend to remove the goods immediately from the warehouse. S's tender of delivery requires that S procure W's acknowledgment (attornment) of B's right to possession of the goods. § 2–503(4)(a). If documents of title (e.g., warehouse receipts) are involved, see Part Four, B infra. [Note: § 2–503(4)(a) (2003) clarifies that acknowledgment must be made *to the buyer*.]

h. *Contract for successive performances of indefinite duration.* See Part One, B, 1, B supra and § 2–309(2), (3). CISG 30–34.

3.   BUYER'S OBLIGATION TO ACCEPT GOODS

Conforming goods duly tendered

If S duly tenders conforming goods, B must accept them. §§ 2–301, 2–503 Comment 1, 2–507(1), 2–602 Comment 3; see § 2–312 et seq. regarding S's warranties. "Acceptance" means that B takes the goods as B's own. B may accept by words ("The goods conform, I will take them"), action (after reasonable inspection, B pays for and uses the goods), or silence when it is time to speak (B does not reject within a reasonable time). § 2–606 and Comment 1; see §§ 2–512 (payment prior to inspection), 2–503(1)(b) (duty to furnish facilities). Note that B may return goods even if they conform to the contract, under a sale on approval or a sale or return. § 2–326(1). As to B's right of inspection before acceptance, see Part One, E, 5 infra. CISG 53, 60.

Obligation to accept goods that are nonconforming or not duly tendered.

If the goods do not conform or are not duly tendered, B may reject them. Even so, B may opt to take them in spite of the nonconformity. §§ 2–601, 2–606(1)(a). See discussion at Part One, E, 6 infra. Also, S has the right, in appropriate circumstances, to *cure* a nonconformity. See Part One, E, 7 infra. CISG 49(1)(a), 50, 25. In certain situations, however, B will be *obligated* to accept goods even if they are not duly tendered or are nonconforming. These situations are as follows:

1. In a shipment contract, S has certain delivery obligations, including putting the goods in the possession of a carrier and making a proper contract for their transportation, as well as promptly notifying B of the shipment. See Part One, E, 2 supra. Even so, failure to make a proper contract for transportation or to notify B justifies rejection only if material delay or loss ensues. § 2–504.

2. Re: substituted performance: If, without fault of either party, the agreed manner of delivery becomes commercially impracticable but a commercially reasonable substitute is available, the substitute performance must be tendered and accepted. § 2–614(1).

3. Re: installment contract: B may not reject any nonconforming installment if the nonconformity does not substantially impair the value of that installment. Even if the nonconformity does substantially impair the value of the installment, the installment delivery must be accepted if (1) the nonconformity is curable and (2) the seller gives adequate assurance of cure. §§ 2–601 (B's rights), 2–612(1) (defining "installment contract") (2) and Comment 5. As for nonconformity of an installment impairing the value of the whole contract, see § 2–612(3). CISG 73. [See § 2–612(2) and Comments 4, 5, and 8 (2003).]

4. The parties may have agreed that B will accept the goods despite a nonconformity. For example, B may agree to have the defective parts repaired or replaced instead of retaining the right to reject. §§ 2–601, 2–719. These limitations of remedies are discussed at Part One, F, 4, A and B infra. CISG 6.

5. Course of dealing, usage of trade, course of performance, the obligation of good faith, and general contract law may require acceptance if the nonconformity is de minimis. §§ 1–303 (course of performance, course of dealing, and trade usage), 1–304 (obligation of good faith), 1–103(b) (supplemental principles of law). See

§§ 2–314(2)(a), (b) and (d) (role of such evidence in defining merchantability). CISG 8, 9.

Remember: Even when B is required to accept goods that are not duly tendered or are nonconforming, this will not impair B's damage remedies. §§ 2–607(2) and Comment 3, 2–714. See Part One, F, 3 infra.

4.   BUYER'S OBLIGATION TO PAY FOR GOODS

Time and place of payment

Unless otherwise agreed, payment is due at the time and place at which B is to receive the goods. §§ 2–310(a), 2–103(1)(c) [§ 2–103(1)(*l*) (2003)] (defining "receipt"). See §§ 2–307 (delivery in 1 lot or several), 2–507 (tender as a condition to payment). This means the transaction is presumptively for cash not credit. In a cash transaction, when B receives the goods, B pays. In a credit transaction, B has a period thereafter in which to pay, e.g., 30 days. If there is an agreed credit period and S is required to ship the goods, such period normally runs from the time of shipment. § 2–310(d). If documents of title are employed, see § 2–310(b), (c).

Effect of tender of payment

Unless otherwise agreed, a buyer's tender of payment is a condition to the Seller's duty to *tender* and complete any delivery. Recall that Seller's tender of delivery is a condition to Buyer's duty to accept and, unless otherwise agreed, to pay for goods. §§ 2–511(1), 2–507(1), 2–503(1), see § 2–607(1). This normally involves concurrent performance of both at a single place or time. § 2–511 Comment 2.

Example: S and B contract for sale of a single delivery of certain goods for $5000. The contract is otherwise silent. Because the parties did not otherwise specify, the goods are to be delivered at S's place of business at a reasonable time. At such place and time, S must tender delivery by putting and holding the goods at B's disposition and giving B any notification necessary to enable B to take delivery. §§ 2–307, 2–308(a), 2–309(1), 2–503(1). B must now accept and pay for the goods or be in breach of contract. § 2–507(1). Likewise, B's tender of payment is a condition to S's duty to tender and complete delivery. § 2–511(1). If neither party tenders, the other is under no obligation to perform.

Of course, this example does not apply to the great body of commercial contracts with credit terms. § 2–511 Comment 1. In such cases, B need not tender payment as a condition to S's duty to tender and complete delivery.

B's payment obligations under particular contract terms are as follows: payment against documents §§ 2–513(3)(b), 2–310(b) and (c), 2–323(2), 2–605(2), 2–319(4), 2–320(4), 2–321(1) and (3); C.O.D. terms § 2–513(3)(a); and letter of credit terms § 2–325(2). [Note: §§ 2–319, 2–320, and 2–321 have been eliminated. § 2–319 Comment (2003). See §§ 2–513(3)(a), 2–325 (2003).]

Sufficiency of tender of payment

Tender of payment is sufficient when made by any means or in any manner consistent with the ordinary course of business unless the seller (1) demands payment in legal tender and (2) gives any extension of time reasonably necessary to procure it. § 2–511(2). Example: S contracts with B for the sale of certain goods for $5000. S is to deliver to B at B's place of business on February 28. S finds he could now sell the goods to X for $6000 and wishes to get out of the deal with B, but without breaching the contract with B. Thus, when S delivers the goods to B late in the afternoon on February 28 and B tenders a check for $5000, S refuses the check and demands payment in legal tender. B cannot comply because the banks have now closed. The next day, after the banks open and

B obtains the legal tender, S claims B has breached the contract by tendering payment after February 28. This has been called a "forced breach." Under the UCC, B would not be in breach; instead, B would have a reasonable extension of time to procure the legal tender. This could be viewed as a right to *cure* a defective tender of payment similar to S's right to *cure* a defective tender of goods under § 2–508. See Comment 3 to § 2–508 [cf. Comment 3 (2003)]. For S's right to *cure,* see Part One, E, 7 infra.

As to B's right to inspect the goods before payment, see Part One, E, 5 infra. As to S's right to *reclaim* goods if B's check is dishonored, see Part One, F, 2, C infra.

B's payment obligation may be modified if S refuses to cooperate or if an agreed means or manner of payment fails because of certain circumstances. 2–311(3)(b); § 2–614(2). As to the possibility of using what is sometimes called a "full payment" check, see Part Three, C, 8 infra. CISG 53–59.

5. BUYER'S RIGHT TO INSPECT GOODS

Inspection as prerequisite to payment or acceptance

When goods are tendered or delivered or identified to the contract for sale, Buyer has a right *before* payment or acceptance to inspect them at any reasonable place and time and in any reasonable manner. §§ 2–513(1) and (4), 2–310(b), 2–321(3), 2–512(2); see § 2–606(1)(a) and (b) (defining "acceptance"). Any expenses of inspection are normally borne by B. § 2–513(2), see §§ 2–715(1) (expenses as a component of incidental damages), 2–711(3) (B's remedies, including recovery of expenses). See also § 2–613 re: casualty to identified goods. Purpose of inspection: To give B some assurance that the subject goods conform to the contract before B accepts them. [Note: § 2–321 has been eliminated, § 2–319 Comment (2003). See § 2–513 Comment 6 (2003).]

When buyer has no right to inspect before payment

Buyer has no right to inspect the goods before payment:

a. When the parties agreed otherwise. § 2–513(1), see § 2–512(1).

b. When the contract is for delivery C.O.D. § 2–513(3)(a), see § 2–512(1). [See § 2–513(3)(a) (2003).]

c. In most cases when the contract provides for payment against documents of title. § 2–513(3)(b); see §§ 2–310(b), 2–505 (shipment under reservation), 2–512(1). Documents are discussed at Part Four, B infra.

Even when the contract requires payment before inspection, B is excused from making payment if the nonconformity appears without inspection. § 2–512(1)(a) and Comment 3. Example: B agrees to purchase a china vase C.O.D. When the goods are delivered, B takes the package and it rattles, indicating that the vase inside is shattered. B is excused from making payment. Sales Hornbook § 5.06[B], 663–664 (exceptions to the right of inspection).

May buyer agree not to inspect prior to acceptance?

UCC § 2–513(1) states, "Unless otherwise agreed ... buyer has a right before ... acceptance to inspect...." Further, § 2–512(2) states, "Payment ... does not constitute an acceptance ... or impair the buyer's right to inspect...." Some writers believe it is an "extremely odd case in which the parties had agreed that the buyer must accept the goods without having the right to inspect them first.... Therefore, a fairly safe conclusion is that a buyer may always inspect before *acceptance.*" Sales Hornbook § 5.06[B], n. 387. Nevertheless, Buyer may waive the right to reject nonconforming goods. In such case, the right of inspection loses much of its significance. See discussion at Part One, E, 3 supra. CISG 58(3), see 38; see also 35(3) and § 2–316(3)(b).

6. BUYER'S RIGHTS ON IMPROPER DELIVERY

A. IN GENERAL

Perfect tender rule

If the *goods* or *tender* of delivery fail *in any respect* to conform to the contract, the buyer may (a) reject the goods or (b) opt to accept the goods in spite of the nonconformity. Of course, a buyer who accepts a nonconforming tender does not lose any remedy otherwise available, e.g., damages for breach. §§ 2–601 and Comments, 2–606(1)(a), 2–106(2) (defining "conforming"); see § 2–714 and Part One, F, 3, B infra. Further, the buyer may accept some commercial units and reject the rest. Example: S tenders to B two living room suites of furniture. One couch is torn. B may accept one suite (the undamaged one) and reject the other (the one with the damaged couch). B may not, however, reject the damaged couch but accept the rest of that suite. §§ 2–601(c), 2–606(2) (defining "acceptance" of a commercial unit), 2–105(6) (defining "commercial unit") [§ 2–105(5) (2003)]. Simply put, *acceptance* means B takes the goods as B's own; *rejection* means that S must take them back.

The above rule, found in Section 2–601, is often called "the perfect tender rule." General contract law (that is, non-UCC contract law) requires a contracting party to perform (e.g., pay) if the other contracting party *substantially* performs (e.g., substantially builds the house). The Code, by contrast, requires the seller to tender perfectly, that is, the buyer may reject if the goods or the tender fail in *any* respect to conform to the contract. The policy is two fold: "(1) [T]he buyer should not be required to guess at his peril whether a breach is material, and (2) proof of materiality would sometimes require disclosure of the buyer's private affairs such as secret formulas or processes." Braucher & Riegert, Intro. to Comm. Trans. 306 (1977). CISG 53, 60; see 51, 52.

Limitations on the perfect tender rule

The perfect tender rule is, however, subject to certain limitations or exceptions. Part One, E, 3 supra enumerated five situations in which a buyer must accept goods that are *not* duly tendered or are nonconforming:

1.   In a shipment contract, a seller's failure to make proper arrangements for transportation or to notify the buyer justifies rejection only if material delay or loss ensues. § 2–504.

2.   Re: substituted performance: When an agreed manner of delivery becomes commercially impracticable, a commercially reasonable substitute must be tendered and accepted. § 2–614(1).

3.   In an installment contract, a buyer may not reject any nonconforming installment unless the nonconformity substantially impairs the value of that installment. § 2–612(2). CISG 73.

4.   The parties may agree that the buyer will accept goods despite their nonconformity. § 2–601. CISG 6.

5.   Course of dealing, usage of trade, course of performance, and the obligation of good faith may require acceptance of goods that otherwise seem nonconforming. §§ 1–303, 1–304, 2–508 Comment 4 [omitted in 2003], 2–106 Comment 2. CISG 8, 9.

Further, the perfect tender rule is undercut by the following rules:

6.   A seller sometimes has the right to cure an improper tender or delivery. § 2–508. This will be discussed at Part One, E, 7 infra. [See § 2–601 Comment 3 (2003).] CISG 37, 48.

7.   As discussed below, buyers frequently accept by not timely rejecting. § 2–602(1), 2–606(1)(b). CISG 49(2).

8.   After accepting, the buyer may revoke acceptance (which gives the buyer the same rights as if he or she had

rejected them), but only if the nonconformity *substantially* impairs the value of the goods to the buyer. § 2–608. Other requirements for revocation of acceptance are discussed below.

The reluctance of courts to allow a buyer to reject for insubstantial nonconformity, plus the above limitations, may mean that the perfect tender rule is essentially an illusion and the rule applied in fact by courts is more accurately described as a substantial performance rule. See UCC Hornbook §§ 9–3 (buyer's right of rejection), 9–4 (buyer's right to revoke acceptance). CISG 45 esp. (1)(a), 46–52; see 25–27, 81–84.

B. BUYER'S REJECTION

(1) Situations in Which Buyer Has a Right to Reject

As discussed previously, a buyer has the right to reject goods or accept any commercial unit(s) and reject the rest, if the goods or the tender of delivery fail in any respect to conform to the contract. § 2–601. This perfect tender rule, as stated earlier, is limited, as for example, by the seller's right to cure. § 2–508. [See § 2–601 Comment 3 (2003).] CISG 48, 49.

(2) Manner and Effect of Rightful Rejection

The word "reject," although not defined in the UCC, means in effect that a buyer refuses to take particular goods as the buyer's own. Contrast this concept with "acceptance" as found in § 2–606 and Comment 1. Following rejection, Buyer does not keep the goods; instead, Seller takes them back. In addition to rejection and recovery of any payments made, Buyer is entitled to certain damages. § 2–711(1), (3) [§ 2–711 (2003)].

Rejection must occur within a reasonable time of delivery or tender and is ineffective unless Buyer seasonably notifies Seller. § 2–602(1); see §§ 2–503, 1–205, 1–

202(d). The following are some factors relevant in determining a "reasonable time:"

1.   Relative difficulty of discovery of the defect. Contrast, e.g., undersize potatoes with hidden defect in automobile.

2.   The contract terms (if not manifestly unreasonable). Example: "Buyer shall have _____ hours [*or* days] after receipt of the goods to either accept or reject them. If the goods are rejected, notice of rejection must be sent to seller at [*address*] within _____ hours [*or* days] after receipt of goods by buyer."

3.   Perishability of the goods. For example, a buyer's delay of five days in notifying the seller of its rejection of nonconforming shrimp was held unreasonable. Mazur Bros. v. Jaffe Fish Co., Inc., 3 UCC Rep. 419 (1965).

The policy behind the requirement of timely notice of rejection is at least three fold: (1) To give the seller an opportunity to cure; (2) to permit the seller to assist in minimizing the buyer's losses; and (3) to return the goods before they have substantially depreciated. UCC Hornbook § 9–3(c). CISG 49(2), 26, 27.

(3) Requirement That Buyer Specify Reasons for Rejection

Pre-UCC, if a buyer rejected goods based upon an alleged nonconformity (later proved groundless), the buyer frequently was precluded from asserting a different valid nonconformity later. Consequently, buyers were reluctant to identify grounds for rejection, for fear of waiving undiscovered defects.

The Code, by contrast, rests upon a policy of permitting the buyer to give a quick and informal notice of defects without penalizing him or her for omissions. This quick notice allows the seller an opportunity to cure the defect and thus fulfills the general policy of Article 2, which aims to preserve the deal whenever possible. § 2–605 Comments 1 and 2 [Comment 1 (2003)].

But what of the unstated defect, which Seller cannot cure if Buyer does not assert it? In order to protect a seller who may be reasonably misled by Buyer's failure to state curable defects, the Code provides as follows: The buyer's failure to state in connection with rejection a particular defect that is ascertainable by reasonable inspection precludes Buyer from relying on the unstated defect to justify rejection (or to establish breach) where Seller could have cured it if stated seasonably. §§ 2–605(1)(a) and Comments 1 and 2 [Comment 1 (2003)], 2–508. Simply stated, the buyer is required to identify its reason for rejection if (1) the defect is ascertainable by a reasonable inspection, and (2) the seller could have cured it if identified seasonably.

Also note: A buyer who merely rejects goods without stating any particular objections is probably acting in commercial bad faith and seeking to get out of a deal that has become unprofitable. § 2–605 Comment 2 [Comment 1 (2003)].

After a merchant buyer has rejected goods and the time for cure has passed, a merchant seller is entitled to a final statement of the buyer's objections. Such a statement will be important in the event of later litigation. Thus, if a merchant seller makes a request in writing for a full and final written statement of all defects on which the merchant buyer proposes to rely, the buyer's failure to identify a particular defect that is ascertainable by reasonable inspection precludes the buyer from relying on the unstated defect to justify rejection (or to establish breach). §§ 2–605(1)(b) and Comment 3, [Comment 2 (2003) (allowing a "statement in a record" in place of a "writing")] 2–104(3) (defining "between merchants"). Re: documents, see § 2–605(2). CISG 49(2), 26, 27; see 39(1).

[*2003 Amend.* Section 2–605(1) makes three substantive changes:

(i) The failure to particularize affects B's right to reject or revoke acceptance, but not B's right to establish breach.

(ii) It now requires S to have had a right to cure (§ 2–508) in addition to the ability to cure.

(iii) It has been extended to include a notice requirement not only as to rejection, but also as to revocation of acceptance. § 2–605 Comment 1.]

(4) Buyer's Rights and Obligations After Rightful Rejection

(a) When Buyer Has a Security Interest

Upon rightful rejection, Buyer has a security interest in goods it possesses or controls, for any payments made, as well as certain reasonably incurred expenses. Buyer may hold the goods and resell them in good faith and in a commercially reasonable manner, and must then account to Seller for any excess over the amount of Buyer's security interest. §§ 2–602(2)(b), 2–603(1), 2–711(3), 2–706(1) and (6). See CISG 81(2), 84.

(b) When Buyer Has No Security Interest

Buyers generally

If, before rejection, a buyer has taken physical possession of goods in which Buyer does not have a security interest as outlined above (i.e., Buyer has not paid any part of the price), Buyer has a *duty* to hold the rejected goods with reasonable care at Seller's disposition long enough to permit Seller to remove them. Buyer has no further *obligations* if the goods were rightfully rejected. § 2–602(2)(b) and (c). [See § 2–602(2) and Comment 2 and 3 (it is possible for a buyer to effectively reject goods even though the rejection is wrongful and constitutes a breach) (2003)].

If Seller fails to give instructions within a reasonable time after notification of rejection, Buyer has the option to (1) store the goods for Seller's account, (2) reship them to Seller, or (3) resell them for Seller's account. Such action will not be deemed acceptance or conversion. §§ 2–604, 2–606(1)(c), 2–602(2)(a). The basic purpose of § 2–604 is to reduce the stakes in dispute and to avoid pinning a technical "acceptance" on a buyer who has taken steps toward realization on or preservation of the goods in good faith. § 2–604 Comment [Comment 1 (2003)]. [This section no longer refers to "rightful" rejections. § 2–604 Comment 2 (2003).]

Merchant buyers

If the seller has no agent or place of business at the market of rejection, a *merchant* buyer must, after rejecting goods in its possession or control, (1) follow any reasonable instructions the seller gives with respect to the goods and (2) in the absence of such instructions, make reasonable efforts to sell them for the seller's account if they are perishable or threaten to decline in value speedily. This duty arises from commercial necessity and thus is present only in these limited circumstances to prevent serious loss. §§ 2–603(1) and Comments 1 and 2, 2–104(1) (defining "merchant") [Except as otherwise stated in § 2–603, its provisions apply to all rejections, including wrongful rejections. 2–603 Comment 6 (2003).] CISG 86–88, see 85.

(c) Buyer's Remedies in General

See § 2–711 and Part One, F, 3, A infra.

(5) Effect of Wrongful Rejection

If the seller has made a tender that in all respects conforms to the contract, the buyer has a positive duty to accept, and failure to do so constitutes a wrongful rejection. (Contrast the buyer's rightful rejection of an improper tender). § 2–602 Comment 3. In addition, as previously discussed, there are instances in which a buyer must accept the goods even though they are not duly tendered or are nonconforming. See Part One, E, 3 and 6, A supra. Further, the buyer may have waived unstated defects. See Part One, E, 6, B, (3) supra. [§ 2–602 Comment 3 (2003): Elimination of the word "rightful" in the title makes it clear that a buyer can effectively reject goods even though the rejection is wrongful and constitutes a breach. "Rightful" has also been deleted from the titles of §§ 2–603 and 2–604.]

A seller's rights with respect to wrongfully rejected goods are indexed in § 2–703 and are discussed in Part One, F, 2, A infra. See § 2–602(3). CISG 61.

(6) Effect of Failure to Reject

A buyer must take affirmative steps to reject a tender or delivery of goods made pursuant to a contract of sale, or the buyer will be deemed to have accepted them, even if they are wholly nonconforming. Accordingly, once the buyer has had a reasonable opportunity to inspect the goods, unless the buyer makes an effective rejection—that is, the rejection must be within a reasonable time after delivery or tender, and the buyer must seasonably notify seller—*acceptance* of the goods occurs. In this situation buyer's untimely rejection is said to be *ineffective.* §§ 2–602(1) and Comment 1, 2–606(1)(b). For example, a buyer's delay of five days in notifying the seller of its rejection of nonconforming shrimp was held unreasonable. See Part One, E, 6, B, (2) supra. CISG 49(2), 26, 27, 83.

C. BUYER'S ACCEPTANCE

What constitutes acceptance

Acceptance occurs when a buyer, pursuant to a contract for sale, takes particular goods as the buyer's own, by words, action, or silence when it is time to speak. § 2–606 Comment 1. CISG 53, 60.

Example 1: After a reasonable opportunity to inspect, B says to S, "The goods are nonconforming in the following respects: [*specify defects*]. Despite such nonconformity, we have elected to accept the shipment." § 2–606(1)(a) and Comment 3.

Example 2: After having a reasonable opportunity to inspect the goods, B fails to make an effective rejection. § 2–606(1)(b). See Part One, E, 6, B, (2) and (6) supra.

Example 3: B discovers goods are defective and attempts to reject. Notwithstanding this, B uses the goods. B's action is inconsistent with the claim that B has rejected the goods and constitutes an acceptance. § 2–606(1) and Comment 4. But note that, if B's use of the goods is wrongful as against S, it is an acceptance only if ratified by S. §§ 2–606(1)(c), 2–602(2)(a). As to action by a buyer that is not an acceptance, see §§ 2–603, 2–604 [and 2–608(4) (2003)] and see Part One, E, 6, B, (4) supra as to the buyer's rights and obligations after rightful rejection. (For example, the buyer may be able to sell the rejected goods without this act constituting an acceptance.) See also § 2–515 and UCC Hornbook § 9–2.

[*2003 Amend.* Section 2–606(1)(c) deletes, "but if such act is wrongful as against the seller it is an acceptance only if ratified by him."]

Effect of acceptance

The effect of acceptance may be stated as follows:

1.   The buyer must pay the contract rate for the accepted goods, even though the buyer may have remedies for the goods' nonconformity. §§ 2–607(1) and (2), 2–714 (damages for accepted goods), 2–717 (deducting damages from the price). CISG 83, 53, 50; see 45(2).

2.   Acceptance of goods precludes rejection, although sometimes, as is discussed below, the buyer may revoke acceptance. § 2–607(2). CISG 49, 53, 60.

3.   After accepting goods, the buyer must, within a reasonable time after Buyer discovered or should have discovered any breach, notify the seller or be barred from *any* remedy. § 2–607(3)(a). See discussion at Part One, D, 4, C supra. [As of 2003, § 2–607(3)(a) has been amended to provide that failure to give timely notice of breach in the case of accepted goods bars a remedy *only* insofar as the seller is *prejudiced* by the untimely notice.] CISG 39, 40, 44, 27.

4.   The burden is on the buyer to establish any breach with respect to the goods accepted. § 2–607(4).

See also §§ 2–201(3)(c), 2–609(3).

D.   BUYER'S REVOCATION OF ACCEPTANCE

Meaning of revocation of acceptance

A buyer who revokes acceptance has the same rights and duties with regard to the goods as if the buyer had rejected them. §§ 2–608(3), 2–711(1), [§ 2–711(2)(a) (2003).] See Part One, E, 6, B supra. (Pre-UCC law spoke of "rescission," a term capable of ambiguous application. § 2–608 Comment 1.).

Requirements for justifiable revocation of acceptance

A buyer may revoke acceptance when the following four conditions are met:

1.   The nonconformity must *substantially* impair the value of the goods to the buyer. § 2–608(1). (Recall that the buyer could reject if the goods or the tender of delivery failed in *any* respect. § 2–601.)

2.   The buyer must have accepted the goods:

(a) on the reasonable assumption that the nonconformity would be seasonably cured and it has not been; or

(b) without discovery of the nonconformity, so long as the buyer's acceptance was reasonably induced either (i) by the difficulty of discovering the nonconformity before acceptance or (ii) by the seller's assurances. §§ 2–608(1), 2–607(2), 2–508 (re: cure).

3. Revocation of acceptance must occur within a reasonable time after the buyer discovers or should have discovered the ground for it. In addition, the revocation is not effective until the buyer notifies the seller of it. § 2–608(2). Since revocation of acceptance will be generally resorted to only *after* attempts at adjustment have failed, the reasonable time period for notice of revocation should extend in most cases *beyond* the time in which notification of breach must be given (§ 2–607(3)) and *beyond* the time for rejection after tender (§ 2–602(1)). §§ 2–608(2), 1–205(a) (defining "reasonable time"). Some factors relevant in determining a "reasonable time" for revocation are the difficulty of discovering the defect and the perishability of the goods. See Part One, E, 6, B, (2) supra. (As to content of the notice, see § 2–608 Comment 5.).

4. Revocation of acceptance must occur before any substantial change in the condition of the goods not caused by their own defects. § 2–608(2). The policy is to seek substantial justice in regard to the condition of goods restored to the seller. § 2–608 Comment 6. Example: A defective steering mechanism causes a driver to lose control after having driven only 468 miles, and the car is demolished. The substantial change in the car's condition was caused by the defect.

As the previous discussion indicates, it is more difficult for a buyer to revoke acceptance of goods than initially to have rejected them. Why? "[First], . . . the longer the buyer has the goods, the higher the probability that the alleged defect was caused by the buyer or aggravated by its failure properly to maintain the goods. Secondly, the longer the buyer holds the goods, the greater the benefit the buyer may have derived from their use.... These factors support a rule that makes it more difficult for the buyer who has once accepted to cast the goods and attendant loss from depreciation and market factors back on the seller." UCC Hornbook § 9–4, p. 427. CISG 45(1)(a), 49, 81–84, 25–27.

[*2003 Amend.* New § 2–608(4) and Comment 8 deal with the problem of post-rejection or revocation *use* of the goods.]

For discussion of the buyer's potential recovery of money damages, see § 2–711(1) [§ 2–711(2) (2003)] and Part One, F, 3, A, (4) infra.

7. BUYER'S RIGHTS AND OBLIGATIONS WHEN ONE OR MORE NONCONFORMING INSTALL-MENTS ARE DELIVERED UNDER INSTALL-MENT CONTRACT

An installment contract requires or authorizes delivery of goods in separate lots to be separately accepted. §§ 2–612(1), 2–105(5) (defining "lot") [§ 2–105(4) (2003)], 2–606 (defining "acceptance"), 2–607 (effect of acceptance).

The buyer may reject any nonconforming installment if the nonconformity *substantially* impairs the value of *that* installment and cannot be cured. §§ 2–612(2), 2–508 (defining "cure"), see § 2–601. Whenever nonconformity or default with respect to one or more installments substantially impairs the value of the *whole* contract, there is a breach of the whole. § 2–612(3). As to reinstatement of the contract after breach, see § 2–612(3) and Comment 6. [See § 2–608(2) and Comments 4, 5, and 8 (2003).] CISG 73; see 49, 81–84, 25–27.

8. SELLER'S RIGHT TO CURE

As previously discussed, the seller's right to cure significantly limits the "perfect tender rule." Thus, in many circumstances it is not the case that a buyer has the right to reject if the goods or the tender of delivery fail in any respect to conform to the contract for sale. See Part One, E, 6 supra. Instead, in appropriate circumstances, a seller may *cure* an improper tender or delivery by making or substituting a conforming tender or delivery. §§ 2–508, 2–106(2) (defining "conformity"). *Cure* is not defined in the Code, but it undoubtedly refers to repair, adjustment, or replacement of nonconforming goods and arguably also refers to a money allowance (e.g., conforming goods tendered untimely but with a price allowance for late delivery). §§ 2–508 Comment 4 [omitted in 2003], 2–612 Comment 5 [Comment 8 (2003)].

When seller's time for performance has not expired

When goods are rejected as nonconforming and the time for performance has not yet expired, Seller (1) may seasonably notify Buyer of its intention to cure and (2) may then, within the time provided by contract, make a conforming delivery. §§ 2–508(1), 1–202(d) (defining "notice"), 1–205(b) (defining "seasonableness"). Example: S contracts with B to deliver a white stove on or before June 1. S delivers a tan stove, which B rejects, on May 25. S may cure by notifying B of the intention to cure and by delivering a white stove by June 1. CISG 37, see 34.

When Seller reasonably believed the nonconforming tender would be acceptable to Buyer

This rule relates to the situation in which the seller's time for performance has expired. It states as follows: When a buyer rejects a nonconforming tender that the seller had *reasonable grounds to believe* would be acceptable (with or without money allowance), the seller may, after seasonably notifying the buyer, have a further reasonable time in which to substitute a conforming tender. Policy: To avoid the injustice of a surprise rejection. § 2–508(2) and Comment 2; cf. §§ 2–511(2) (tender of payment; legal tender demanded); 2–508 Comment 3; see § 2–106 Comment 2. As to the effect of a "no replacement clause," see § 2–508 Comment 2.

Example: S delivers what S believes to be a newer and better model of hearing aid than was called for in the contract with B. B rejects. S may cure. But what if S is ignorant that the goods are not as agreed? Does S have the right to cure? One approach is as follows: "[Section 2–508(2)] should be limited to sellers who knew their tender was nonconforming but who reasonably believed that their buyers would accept the nonconforming tender—only to meet a surprise rejection." R. Nordstrom, Handbook of the Law of Sales § 105 (1970). Compare this second perspective: "We believe that cure is a remedy which should be carefully cultivated and developed by the courts. To that end we would argue that a seller should be found to have had a reasonable belief that its tender would have been acceptable any time it can convince the court that (1) the seller would have had such reasonable belief had it not been ignorant of the defect, or (2) the seller had some reason, such as prior course of dealing or trade usage, which in fact reasonably led seller to believe that the goods would be acceptable." UCC Hornbook § 9–5. (See also § 2–605 Comment 2 [Comment 1 (2003)], stating that Articles 2's *general policy* is to preserve the deal whenever possible.). CISG 48; see 46(2) and (3), 25.

[*2003 Amend.* Section 2–508(1) and (2) has been amended to provide that, in a nonconsumer contract, the seller has the right to cure if the buyer justifiably revokes acceptance under § 2–608(1)(b). See § 2–508 Comments

1 and 2. The section now predicates the right to cure on good-faith performance by the seller and (under § 2–508(2)), when the time for performance has expired, on the cure being appropriate and timely under the circumstances. See § 2–508 Comments 3 and 4. Another amendment imposes liability on the seller for the buyer's reasonable expenses caused by the breach and subsequent cure. § 2–508(1) (last sentence) and (2) (last sentence) and Comment 5.]

Consider the following case illustrating inspection, rejection, acceptance, revocation of acceptance, and cure: Zabriskie Chevrolet, Inc. v. Smith, 99 N.J.Super. 441, 240 A.2d 195, 5 UCC Rep. 30 (1968). On February 2, B signed a purchase order form for a "brand-new car that would operate perfectly." B made a $124 deposit, followed by a check representing the balance of the purchase price. In the evening of February 10, B's wife took delivery of the car. En route home, about 2 1/2 miles away from home and about 7/10 of a mile from the showroom, the car stalled at a traffic light, stalled again within another 15 feet, and continued to stall at each stop. About half-way home, the car could no longer be driven in "drive" gear at all, and B's wife was obliged to proceed in "low-low" gear at a rate of about five to ten miles per hour, as the vehicle could go no faster. In great distress, B's wife called B, who drove the car in "low-low" gear the remaining seven blocks home. B immediately called his bank (which was open in the evening), stopped payment on the check, and called S to notify them that (1) they had sold him a "lemon," (2) he had stopped payment on the check, and (3) the sale was cancelled. The next day, S sent a wrecker to B's home, brought the vehicle to its repair shop and, after inspection, determined that the transmission was defective. S replaced the transmission with one removed from a vehicle on S's showroom floor, notifying B of what had been done. B refused to take delivery of the repaired vehicle and reasserted his cancellation of the sale. S sued for the balance of the purchase price, and B counter-claimed for return of his deposit.

In rendering judgment for B, the court explained its decision as follows: "[W]e hold that the vehicle ... was substantially defective and constituted a breach of the contract and the implied warranty of merchantability [§ 2–314].... It is clear that a buyer does not accept goods until he has had a 'reasonable opportunity to inspect' [§ 2–606(1)]. Defendant [B] sought to purchase a new car. He assumed ... that his new car, with the exception of very minor adjustments, would be mechanically new and factory-furnished, operate perfectly, and be free of substantial defects.... How long the buyer may drive the new car under the guise of inspection of new goods is not an issue in the present case. It is clear that defendant [B] discovered the nonconformity within 7/10 of a mile and minutes after leaving plaintiff's [S's] show-room. Certainly this was well within the ambit of 'reasonable opportunity to inspect'.... [D]efendant never accepted the vehicle.

Even if defendant [B] had accepted the automobile tendered, he had a right to revoke [acceptance] under ... [§ 2–608]: '(1) The buyer may revoke his acceptance of [goods] ... whose nonconformity *substantially impairs its value* to him....'"

Next, the court found that B had properly rejected the car under §§ 2–601 and 2–602.

Finally, the court assessed S's right to cure under § 2–508(2) and held, "The 'cure' intended under ... the Code does not, in the court's opinion, contemplate the tender of a new vehicle with a substituted transmission, not from the factory and of unknown lineage from another vehicle in plaintiff's possession. It was not the intention of the Legislature that the right to 'cure' is a limitless one to be controlled only by the will of the seller. A 'cure' which endeavors by substitution to tender a chattel not within the agreement or contemplation of the parties is invalid."

For a majority of people, the purchase of a new car is a major investment, rationalized by the peace of mind that flows from its dependability and safety. Once their faith is shaken, the vehicle loses not only its real value in their eyes, but becomes an instrument whose integrity is substantially impaired and whose operation is fraught with apprehension. The attempted cure in the present case was ineffective.

Note: Under the Magnuson–Moss Federal Warranty Act, after a reasonable number of attempts to remedy defects, a consumer may elect either a refund or replacement. 15 U.S.C. § 2304(a)(4). See state "lemon laws," e.g., West's Ann.Cal.Civ.Code § 1793.2.

Summary of seller's right to cure

"Section 2–508 is an important addition to our law. It substantially restricts the right of the buyer to reject, and it substantially complicates the job of the lawyer who represents the buyer who wishes to reject. Although it raises almost as many problems as it answers, in wise judicial hands it offers the possibility of conforming the law to reasonable expectations and of thwarting the chiseler who seeks to escape from a bad bargain." UCC Hornbook § 9–5, p. 444.

9.   DISPUTE AS TO QUALITY OF GOODS: PRESERVING EVIDENCE

Either Seller or Buyer, on reasonable notification to the other and for the purpose of ascertaining the facts and preserving evidence, has the right to inspect, test, and sample the goods (including those that may be in the possession or control of the other). §§ 2–515(a). Seller and Buyer (1) may agree to a third party inspection or survey to determine the conformity or condition of the goods and (2) may agree that the third party's findings shall be binding upon them in any subsequent litigation or adjustment. § 2–515(b) and Comment 1, 1–201(b)(26) (defining "party," as distinguished from "third party").

10.   EXCUSE OF PERFORMANCE

"The Code contains three sections that state the general principles that relieve the seller from full performance of its contractual obligations. These principles are embodied in the common law of contracts in the doctrines of impossibility, impracticability, and implied conditions. The most accurate way of describing these principles is to say that they are all intended to deal with the allocation of risks that the parties have not expressly allocated in their agreement." Sales Hornbook § 5.04, p. 614.

A.   FAILURE OF PRESUPPOSED CONDITIONS

Section 2–615 excuses a seller from timely delivery of the goods contracted for, if the seller's performance has been made commercially impracticable because of supervening circumstances not within the contemplation of the parties at the time of contracting. § 2–615 Comment 1.

The Code itself states that, unless a seller has assumed a greater obligation, the seller's delay in delivery or nondelivery is not a breach of contract for sale if the seller's performance has been made impracticable by the occurrence of a contingency, the *nonoccurrence* of which was a basic assumption on which the contract was made. Of course, the seller must notify the buyer seasonably that there will be a delay or non-delivery. § 2–615(a), (c).

In applying the above rule, note the following observations: Increased cost alone does not excuse the seller's performance unless the rise in cost is due to some unforeseen contingency that alters the essential nature of the performance. Neither is a rise or a collapse in the market a justification, for that is *exactly* the type of *business risk* that contracts are intended to cover. But a severe shortage of raw materials or of supplies due to a contingency such as war, embargo, local crop failure, unforeseen shutdown of major sources of supply, or the like, which either causes a marked increase in cost or altogether prevents the seller from securing supplies *is within* the contemplation of § 2–615. § 2–615 Comment 4.

If delay in delivery or non-delivery affects only part of the seller's capacity to perform, see § 2–615(b), (c). For a discussion of when a supervening and excusing contingency "excuses" the delay, "discharges" the contract, or may result in a waiver of the delay by the buyer, see § 2–616 and Comment. If delay in delivery or non-delivery has been made impracticable by compliance with an applicable governmental regulation, see § 2–615(a), (c). If a "requirements" contract is involved, see §§ 2–615 Comment 9, 2–306.

Along similar lines, sales agreements may contain a *force majeure* clause, similar to this; that modifies §§ 2–615 and 2–616:

> Neither party shall be held responsible for loss resulting from delay in performance or failure of performance of the terms of this contract caused by revolutions or other disorders, wars, acts of enemies, strikes, fires, floods, acts of God or any other cause not within the control of the party whose performance is affected.

> If either party is partially excused from performance for reasons stated above, this contract shall be automatically terminated. No allocation of performance shall be required or permitted.

B. CASUALTY TO IDENTIFIED GOODS

If the contract calls for goods that have already been identified when the contract is made, and the goods suffer a total loss due to no fault of either party, *before* the risk of loss passes to the buyer, the contract is terminated. § 2–613(a). Example: Farmer contracts to sell crops growing on a certain piece of land. Bad climatic conditions cause the crop to fail. If, under the contract, the risk of loss does not pass to the buyer until the crop is duly delivered to a carrier for shipment, Farmer's performance is excused. See §§ 2–615 Comment 9, 2–107(2) (re: contract for sale of growing crops), 2–509(1)(a) (risk of loss in the absence of breach). If the risk of loss has passed to the buyer before the casualty, § 2–613 has no application; instead, under the rules of § 2–509, the buyer bears such risk. § 2–613 Comment 2. See Part One, C, 5 supra, for risk-of-loss discussion.

If the loss is partial or the goods have deteriorated, see § 2–613(b). If the contract contains a "no arrival, no sale" term, see § 2–613 and Comment 3 [omitted in 2003].

C. SUBSTITUTE PERFORMANCE

When, without fault of either party, the agreed manner of delivery becomes commercially impracticable (e.g., the agreed berthing, loading, or unloading facilities fail or an agreed type of carrier becomes unavailable) but a commercially reasonable substitute is available, such substitute performance must be tendered and accepted. § 2–614(1). Example: Sales contract called for delivery of wheat "f.o.b. Kosmos Steamer at Seattle." War led to cancellation of that line's sailing schedule after the space had been duly engaged. Buyer is entitled to demand substituted delivery at the line's loading dock warehouse. Also, Seller would be entitled to make a substituted tender in that manner. § 2–614 Comment 1.

The distinction between this section, § 2–614, and sections 2–613 and 2–615, discussed above, lies in whether the failure or impossibility of performance arises in connection with an *incidental* matter or goes to the *very heart* of the agreement. § 2–614 Comment 1.

If the agreed means or manner of payment fails, see § 2–614(2). CISG 79, 80; see 27.

F. REMEDIES

1. REMEDIES GENERALLY

The UCC's remedies are to be liberally administered to ensure that the aggrieved party is put in as good a position as if the other party had fully performed. § 1–305(a).

First, § 1–305(a) is intended to negate the unduly narrow technical interpretation of some remedial provisions in prior legislation. Consequently, Article 2 rejects the doctrine of election of remedy as a fundamental policy. Thus, the remedies are essentially cumulative in nature, and whether the pursuit of one remedy bars another depends entirely on the facts of the individual case. §§ 1–305 Comment 1, 2–703 Comment 1. Example: B seeks to return defective goods and obtain a refund of the purchase price. In addition, B seeks to recover the expenses of handling and forwarding the goods as well as the profits B would have made on the intended resale of the goods. Pre-UCC courts would often say that B made an election of remedies by seeking rescission of the contract and, accordingly, could not claim the additional expenses and lost profits. The Code rejects this result.

Second, § 1–305(a) is intended to clarify that compensatory damages do not include penal damages. Under §§ 2–720, 2–714, and 2–715, consequential or special damages are included, however. § 1–305 Comment 1.

Third, § 1–305(a) makes it clear that damages need not be calculable with mathematical accuracy. § 1–305 Comment 1.

Insofar as waiver of remedies is concerned, § 2–720 is designed to safeguard a person holding a right of action from any unintentional loss of rights by the ill-advised use of such terms as "cancellation," "rescission" or the like. Such expressions shall not be construed as a renunciation or discharge of any claim in damages for an antecedent breach. §§ 2–720 and Comment, 1–306 (waiver or renunciation); see § 1–308 (reservation of rights). CISG 45, 61, 74.

2. SELLER'S REMEDIES

A. SELLER'S REMEDIES FOR BUYER'S BREACH

A buyer breaches the sales contract by (1) wrongfully rejecting goods, (2) wrongfully revoking acceptance of goods, (3) failing to make a payment that is due on or *before* delivery, or (4) repudiating. The seller's remedies are indexed in § 2–703 and discussed below. If the buyer accepts and retains the goods, but fails to make a payment that is due *after* delivery, see § 2–709(1)(a). See §§ 2–601, 2–606 (defining "acceptance"), 2–607 (effect of acceptance), 2–608 (revocation) and Part One, E, 3 and 6 supra. For a discussion of "installment contracts," see Part One, E, 7 supra. CISG 61.

[*2003 Amend.* Section 2–703 is a list of remedies available under Article 2 to remedy *any* breach by the buyer. It also lists the seller's statutory remedies in the event of the buyer's insolvency. § 2–703 Comment 1. See 2–703(2)(m).]

(1) Seller May Cancel

When the buyer breaches, the seller can cancel the contract. "Cancellation" occurs when S puts an end to the contract due to B's breach. Its effect is the same as "termination" (that is, all obligations that are still executory on both sides are discharged, but any right based on a prior breach or performance survives), *except* that the cancelling party (S) also retains any remedy for breach of the whole contract or any unperformed obligation. §§ 2–703(f), 2–106(3) ("termination" defined), (4) ("cancellation" defined); cf. § 2–711(1). [§§ 2–703(2)(f), 2–711(2) (2003)]. CISG 64, 25–27, 81, 84(1); cf. 49.

(2) Seller May Take Action as to the Goods

(a) Seller May Withhold Delivery of the Goods

S may be unwilling to deliver goods to a breaching B, as for example, if B has failed to make a payment due on or before delivery. S may, accordingly, withhold delivery so as not to be in the unenviable position of an unsecured creditor with goods in the possession of a financially troubled B. Pre-UCC, this was called an "unpaid seller's lien." § 2–703(a) [§ 2–703(2)(a) (2003)]. See CISG 64, 71, 72.

(b) Seller May Stop a Bailee's Delivery of the Goods

Suppose now that S is not in possession of the goods S wishes to withhold from B; instead, S's bailee is. (1) S may stop a carrier or other bailee such as a warehouseman from making any delivery when S discovers B to be insolvent, and (2) in the case of a carload, truckload, planeload, or other larger shipment of express or freight, S may stop delivery when B repudiates or fails to make a payment due before delivery or if, for any other reason, S has a right to withhold or reclaim the goods. Because stoppage is a burden to carriers, the right to stop for reasons other than insolvency is limited to larger shipments. §§ 2–703(b), 2–705(1) and Comment 1.

[*2003 Amend*. For stoppage in cases other than insolvency, § 2–705(1) has been broadened by eliminating the requirement that the goods be by the "carload, truckload, planeload or larger shipments of express or freight."]

When the seller's right of stoppage terminates

S can stop delivery until (1) B's receipt (physical posses-sion) of the goods, (2) acknowledgment (attornment) by a bailee other than a carrier (e.g., a warehouse) that the bailee holds the goods for B, (3) a carrier's acknowledg-ment to B that the carrier holds the goods for B by the act of reshipment or in the capacity of a warehouseman, or (4) negotiation to B of a negotiable document of title (to be discussed in Part Four, B infra). §§ 2–703(b) [§ 2–703(2)(b) (2003)], 2–705(2) and (3), 2–707(b) (a "person in the position of a seller" also has the right of stoppage). Rationale: to protect the bailee for reasons such as the following: (1) When B takes possession, the goods are no longer in possession of the bailee; (2) When a bailee acknowledges (attorns) or has issued a negotiable docu-ment that has been negotiated, the bailee is under an obligation to deliver the goods to B (or some other person than S). Cf. risk of loss § 2–509(2)(b), S's delivery obligation § 2–503(4)(a). As to procedures for stopping delivery, see § 2–705(3). CISG 58(2).

(c) Under § 2–704, Seller May Identify Goods to the Contract Notwithstanding Breach or Salvage Unfinished Goods

Assume S has identified goods to the contract (see § 2–501) and is about to deliver the goods to B when B repudiates. As we will see presently, S will probably resell the goods and seek to recover from B the difference between the resale price and the contract price. § 2–706. But what if the goods to be sold are not yet identified to the contract or are unfinished? May S identify the goods or complete the unfinished goods, then resell them and recover from B the difference between the resale price and the contract price? In answer to these questions, Uniform Sales Act § 64(4) stated that "the buyer shall be liable to the seller for no greater damages than the seller would have suffered if he did nothing towards carrying out the contract or the sale after receiving notice of the buyer's repudiation or countermand." This rule was based on the seller's duty to mitigate damages. Consequently, S was strongly encouraged not to perform further after receiving notice of B's breach. This could prove to be unfair and lead to economically wasteful results. Thus, the UCC gives the aggrieved S the right to identify to the contract any conforming finished goods in S's possession or control regardless of their resalability. §§ 2–703(c) [§ 2–703(2)(c) (2003)], 2–704 and Comment 1. Insofar as unfinished goods are concerned, the Code states as follows: ". . . an aggrieved seller may in the exercise of reasonable commercial judgment for the purposes of avoiding loss and of effective realization either [1] complete the manufacture and wholly identify the goods to the contract or [2] cease manufacture and resell for scrap or salvage value or [3] proceed in any other reasonable manner." § 2–704(2). Further, Comment 2 to § 2–704 states that ". . . the seller is given express power to complete manufacture or procurement of goods for the contract unless the exercise of reasonable commercial judgment as to the facts as they appear at the time he learns of the breach makes it clear that such action will result in a material increase in damages."

When the seller takes appropriate action as to the goods (i.e., seller identifies goods to the contract or salvages unfinished goods), the stage is set for the seller to recover money damages from the buyer. This discussion follows. See CISG 77, 62, 75, 76.

(3) Seller May Recover Monies From Buyer Per §§ 2–706, 2–708, or 2–709

(a) Seller May Resell and Recover Damages

Following Buyer's repudiation, Seller may resell the goods and recover from Buyer the difference between the *contract price* and the *resale price*. Example: S and B contract for the sale of certain goods for $1,000. B repudiates. S resells the goods for $800. S may recover $200, plus incidental damages (e.g., reasonable charges associated with the care and custody of the goods after B's breach), less any expenses saved due to B's breach. §§ 2–703(d) [§ 2–703(2)(g) (2003)], 2–706(1), 2–710. This is S's primary monetary remedy. § 2–704 Comment 1. Note that S's right to the difference between the contract price and resale price is comparable to B's right (when S breaches) to recover the difference between the contract price and the cost of cover. Cf. §§ 2–706(1), 2–712(2). [S may also recover consequential damages under § 2–710 (2003).]

The resale must be made in good faith and in a commercially reasonable manner in every respect, including the method, manner, time, place, and terms of the resale. The resale may be either public (such as a sale by auction) or private. § 2–706(1), (2) and Comment 4 [Comment 5 (2003)]. If the resale is private, S must give B reasonable notification of S's intention to resell; if the resale is public, S must give B reasonable notice of the time and place of the resale. § 2–706(3), (4). For this remedy to be available to S, the goods need not have been identified to the contract before the breach. § 2–706(2). (See also the previous section's discussion of S's right to identify the goods to the contract under § 2–704.) S is not accountable to B for any profit made on any resale. § 2–706(6). The basic policy of § 2–706 is to free the remedy of resale from legalistic restrictions and to enable S to resell in accordance with reasonable commercial practices, so as to realize as high a price as possible under the circumstances. § 2–706 Comment 4 [Comment 5 (2003)].

A purchaser who buys in good faith at a resale takes the goods free of any rights of the original buyer even if the seller fails to comply with one or more of the requirements of § 2–706. § 2–706(5). However, the seller's failure to act properly under § 2–706 deprives him or her of the generous measure of damages provided in § 2–706 and relegates the seller to the more limited recovery provided in § 2–708 (that is, the difference between the contract price and market price). § 2–706 Comment 2. [New § 2–706(7) (2003) adds, S's failure to resell under § 2–706 does not bar S from any other remedy. § 2–706 Comment 11 (2003)]. CISG 61(1)(b), 75, 77.

(b) Seller May Recover Damages for Non-Acceptance or Repudiation

Market-contract price differential

The measure of damages for B's non-acceptance or repudiation is the difference between the *market price* (at the time and place of tender) and the unpaid *contract price*. Example: S and B contract for the sale of certain goods for $1,000. B repudiates. The market price at the time and place of tender is $800. S may recover $200, plus incidental damages (e.g., reasonable charges associated with the care and custody of the goods after B's breach), less any expenses saved due to B's breach. §§ 2–703(e) [§ 2–703(2)(h) and (i) (2003)], 2–708(1), 2–710, 2–723 (proof of market price: time and place), 2–724 (admissibility of market quotations). See § 2–503 (manner of tender) and Part One, E, 2 supra. Note that S's right to recover the difference between the contract price and market price is comparable to B's right (when S breaches) to recover the difference between the contract price and the market price. Cf. §§ 2–708(1), 2–713(1).

Loss of profit

If the measure of damages discussed above is inadequate to put S in as good a position as B's performance would have done, then the measure of damages is the *profit* S would have made from B's full performance. The normal measure of lost profit would be the list price minus the dealer's cost, or the list price minus the cost to the manufacturer. Example: S, a dealer, agrees to sell goods at their list price to B for $1,000. B repudiates. S may recover the list price of $1,000 minus S's cost, plus incidental damages with due allowance for costs reasonably incurred and due credit for any payments or proceeds of resale. §§ 2–708(2) and Comment 2, 2–710. CISG 61(1)(b), 76, 77.

[*2003 Amend.* Section 2–708 Comment 1 contains the following changes from original 2–708:

a.   § 2–708 now provides for consequential as well as incidental damages.

b.   The word "unpaid" in original § 2–708(1) has been deleted as superfluous and misleading.

c.   Section 2–708(1)(a) reverses the terms "market price" and "contract price."

d.   Section 2–708(2) adds, "provided in subsection (1) or in *Section 2–706* is inadequate."

e.   In 2–708(2), the following phrases that appeared in original § 2–708(2) have been deleted: "due allowance for costs reasonably incurred" and "due credit for payments or proceeds of resale."

Under § 2–708(1)(b) and Comment 4, the market price of goods in the case of an *anticipatory repudiation* is measured at the "expiration of a commercially reasonable time after the seller learned of the repudiation."]

(c) Seller May Recover the Price

If B fails to pay the price as it becomes due, S may recover the price (1) of any goods accepted, (2) of any conforming goods lost or damaged within a commercially reasonable time after risk of their loss has passed to B, or (3) of any goods identified to the contract if S is unable after reasonable effort to resell them at a reasonable price (or the circumstances reasonably indicate that such effort will be unavailing). §§ 2–703(e) [§ 2–703(2)(j) (2003)], 2–709(1), 2–501 (B's insurable interest in identified goods), 2–606 (defining "acceptance"), 2–509 (risk of loss). Example: S and B contract for the sale of goods for $1,000. S is to ship the goods to B by carrier pursuant to a "shipment contract" (see 2–504). The goods are lost or damaged in shipment. B bears the risk of loss; S is entitled to the price of $1,000. §§ 2–509(1)(a), 2–709(1)(a). Suppose now that the goods are not damaged, but arrive and are accepted by B. Once again, S is entitled to the price of $1,000. §§ 2–709(1)(a), 2–606 (defining "acceptance"), 2–607(1) (effect of acceptance). Now suppose that S had not yet delivered the goods to the carrier but had identified the goods; that is, S had selected from S's inventory the goods to be sold to B. For example, S might have affixed B's family crest upon the goods per their agreement and set the goods aside for delivery to the carrier. B then repudiated. Since the identified goods could not reasonably be resold with B's family crest affixed, S is entitled to the price of $1,000 from B. This rule is necessary to give S the value of its contract. §§ 2–709(1)(b), 2–704 Comment 1. In fact, S may recover the price together with incidental or *consequential* damages. §§ 2–709(1). [See § 2–710 (2003)]. Even under circumstances in which an action for the price fails, S may nonetheless be entitled to damages for non-acceptance. §§ 2–709(3) and Comment 7, 2–708.

Notice that this monetary remedy is not, like the remedies discussed above in (a) and (b), measured by the difference between the contract price and either the resale price or the market price. §§ 2–706, 2–708. Instead, the price remedy in effect gives S the right to "specifically enforce" the contract. B, being required to pay the contract price, has no rational decision but to accept the goods. For this reason, § 2–709(2) requires that, when S sues for the price, S must hold the identified goods for B. S's right to the price when S is unable reasonably to resell the goods is comparable to B's right to replevy the identified goods (when S breaches the contract) when B is unable to purchase substitute goods. Cf. §§ 2–709(1)(b), 2–716(3). CISG 61(1)(a), 62, 63; see 28, 78; cf. 46, 47.

[*2003 Amend.* Seller may obtain *specific performance* under § 2–716. § 2–703(2)(k). This remedy may be decreed if the goods are unique or in other proper circumstances. In addition, in a nonconsumer contract, it may also be decreed if the parties have *agreed* to that remedy. However, even if the parties agree to specific performance, it may not be decreed if the breaching party's sole remaining contractual obligation is *payment of money.* §§ 2–716(1) and Comments 1 and 3, 2–709, 2–103(1)(c) and (d).]

B. SELLER'S REMEDIES UPON BUYER'S INSOLVENCY

If S discovers B is insolvent, S may *refuse* delivery unless B pays cash, and may *stop* delivery under § 2–705. See Part One, F, 2, A, (2) supra. § 2–702(1). [See § 2–703(3)(a), (b) (2003).] A person is deemed insolvent if he or she has ceased to pay debts in the ordinary course of business, is unable to pay debts as they become due, or is insolvent within the meaning of the federal bankruptcy law. § 1–201(b)(23), B.C., 11 U.S.C. § 101(32) (applying a "balance sheet" test). Policy: It is unfair to require S to deliver on credit to an insolvent B, only to get a small percentage on the dollar in any insolvency proceedings.

But where does S stand if S *delivered* goods to B on credit without taking or retaining some sort of security interest in the goods as an Article 9 Secured Transaction? Such a Seller is an unsecured creditor with no interest in the sold goods. Thus, upon liquidation of B's estate in insolvency proceedings, S would receive only a small percentage of his claim. B.C., 11 U.S.C. § 726. However, suppose S discovers B has received goods on credit while

insolvent. This amounts to a tacit business misrepresentation of solvency and therefore is fraudulent against the
particular S. Likewise, if B furnishes S with a financial
statement falsely indicating solvency, this would probably
be an explicit business misrepresentation of solvency.
Should this "defrauded seller" not be in a somewhat
more favorable position than a nondefrauded unsecured-
seller-creditor?

In response, the Code states that, when S discovers that
B has received goods on credit while insolvent, S may
reclaim the goods following a demand within ten days
after the receipt of the goods. An exception to this ten day
limitation is made when a written misrepresentation of
solvency has been made to the particular S within three
months prior to the delivery. § 2–702(2) and Comment 2;
cf. § 2–502. The seller's right to reclaim is subject to the
rights of certain third parties who may have taken the
goods from B. § 2–702(3). This will be discussed at Part
One, G, 1 and 2 infra. See CISG 81(2), 84(2), 4(b).

[*2003 Amend.* Section 2–702(2) omits the 10-day limitation and the 3-month exception to the 10-day limitation.
§ 2–702 Comment 2. The subsection thus now reads, "the
seller may reclaim the goods upon demand made within a
reasonable time after the buyer's receipt of the goods. See
§ 2–703(2)(d), (3)(c).]

C. SELLER'S REMEDIES IN A "CASH SALE"

S and B contract for the sale of goods whereby S's
delivery and B's payment are to be "concurrent conditions." S hands over the goods to B, who at the same time
hands his currently dated check to S. Commercial people
think of this as a "cash sale," not a "credit sale" as when
B, for example, has thirty days in which to make payment.
A currently dated check is a demand instrument and thus
a cash substitute, not a credit instrument. § 3–104(f). If
the check is dishonored by the bank upon which it is

drawn, we have a "defrauded seller" similar to the seller in 2–702 discussed immediately above. This time, there has been a tacit business misrepresentation either of solvency or of intent to pay, that is, that the check would be honored by the bank. (See the last sentence of § 2–702(2).)

As to this kind of cash sale, wherein S takes B's currently dated check in payment for goods, the UCC says, "Where payment is due and demanded on the delivery to the buyer of goods ... his right as against the seller to retain or dispose of them is conditional upon his making the payment due." § 2–507(2) and Comment 3. "[P]ayment by check is conditional and is defeated as between the parties by dishonor of the check on due presentment." § 2–511(3) and Comments 4–6. Courts have applied these sections to allow the "defrauded seller" to reclaim the goods upon dishonor of the check, provided S acted promptly. If S does not act promptly, S has acquiesced in B's possession and, accordingly, the transaction now becomes a credit transaction, not a cash transaction. This matters because, in an unsecured credit transaction, S generally has no right to reclaim sold goods. The seller's right to reclaim goods in a "cash sale" transaction is similar to the seller's rights under § 2–702 as discussed above. If the check is post-dated by even one day, the transaction amounts to an extension of credit, and S's right to reclaim is determined by § 2–702. § 2–511 Comment 6.

[*2003 Amend.* Section 2–507(2) now states that S may reclaim the goods upon a demand made within a *reasonable time* after S discovers or should have discovered that payment was not made. See § 2–703(2)(d).]

This "cash sale" doctrine had pre-UCC antecedents. The rule was that, in a cash sale transaction, title to the goods would not pass to B until the check was honored. If the check was dishonored and S acted promptly, S could replevy the goods because S still had title.

The Seller's right to reclaim goods as discussed above, may be cut off by certain third parties who take the goods from B. [§ 2–507(3) (2003).] See Part One, G, 1 and 2 infra. See CISG 81(2), 84(2), 4(b).

3. BUYER'S REMEDIES

Buyer's remedies for Seller's breach of a sales contract, when Buyer either has not accepted the goods or has justifiably revoked acceptance, are indexed in § 2–711. When Buyer has "finally accepted," Buyer's remedies appear in § 2–714. § 2–711 Comment 1. See §§ 2–601, 2–606 (defining "acceptance"), 2–607 (effect of acceptance), 2–608 (revocation), and Part One, E, 6 supra. CISG 45. These remedies are discussed below. As to "installment contracts," see Part One, E, 7 supra.

[*2003 Amend.* Section 2–711 now contains a *comprehensive* indexing of Buyer's remedies. See § 2–711(2)(j).]

A. BUYER'S REMEDIES FOR BREACH WHEN BUYER HAS NOT ACCEPTED THE GOODS OR HAS JUSTIFIABLY REVOKED ACCEPTANCE

Buyer has not accepted goods when (1) S fails to make delivery, (2) S repudiates, or (3) B rightfully rejects. Further, acceptance is not final if B justifiably revokes the acceptance. Revocation of acceptance gives B the same rights as if B had rejected them. § 2–608(3). Despite S's breach, however, proper retender of delivery under § 2–508 can effectively preclude B's remedies under § 2–711, except to compensate B for any delay involved. §§ 2–711 and Comment 1, 2–601, 2–606 (defining "acceptance"), 2–607 (effect of acceptance), 2–608 (revocation), and Part One, E, 6 supra. [See § 2–711(1) and (2), but see § 2–711(2)(f) (2003).] CISG 45.

The following are B's remedies for breach when B has not finally accepted the goods and S has not cured any improper tender or delivery.

(1) Buyer May Cancel

One of B's remedies is to cancel. "Cancellation" occurs when B puts an end to the contract due to S's breach. Its effect is the same as that of "termination" (i.e., all obligations still executory on both sides are discharged, but any right based on prior breach or performance survives), *except* that B also retains any remedy for breach of the whole contract or any unperformed balance. §§ 2–711(1), 2–106(3), (4); cf. § 2–703(f) [§§ 2–711(2)(c), 2–703(2)(f) (2003)]. CISG 49, 25–27, 81–84.

(2) Buyer May Recover Price Paid

Upon breach by S (whether or not B cancels), B may recover as much of the price as has been paid. This remedy is important when (1) B has made payment to S prior to delivery of the goods, and the goods are not delivered; (2) B has paid before inspection and then rightfully rejects the goods; or (3) B has paid prior to justifiably revoking acceptance of the goods. § 2–711(1). [See § 2–711(2)(a) (2003).] CISG 81, 84.

(3) Buyer Has a Security Interest in Goods Within Buyer's Possession or Control

Upon rightful rejection or justifiable revocation of acceptance, B has a *security interest* in the goods in B's possession or control for (a) any payments made on their price (see "Buyer May Recover Price Paid" immediately above) and (b) any expenses reasonably incurred in their inspection, receipt, transportation, care, and custody. § 2–711(1), (3) [§ 2–711(2)(a), (3) (2003)]. If, however, S fails to deliver or repudiates, B will not have possession or control of the goods to secure B's right to recover any sums paid.

Buyer may enforce the security interest in the goods by holding and reselling them as an aggrieved seller would under § 2–706, which deals with a seller's right to resell. That is, the resale must be made in good faith, in a commercially reasonable manner, etc. See Part One, F, 2, A, (3) supra. However, while S is not accountable to B under 2–706(6) for any profit made on any resale, B must account for any excess over the amount of B's security interest, under §§ 2–711(3) and 2–706(6). CISG 81(2), 84.

(4) Buyer's Recovery of Money Damages

B's right to cancel and recover as much of the price as has been paid does *not* preclude B from recovering money damages. Instead, the Code provides that, regardless of whether B cancels, he may recover money damages in addition to recovering as much of the price as has been paid. § 2–711(1). This rejects the pre-UCC policy of election of remedies. Under prior law, if B rescinded the contract and either refused the goods or delivered them back to S, B could recover as much of the price as B paid, but no more. If, instead, B sought damages, B would have to affirm the agreement and keep the goods. §§ 2–703 Comment 1, 2–711 Comment 3. [See § 2–711(2)(a) and Comment 3 (2003).] CISG 45(1)(b) and (2).

(a) Buyer May "Cover" and Recover Damages

Buyer may recover from Seller the difference between the *cost of cover* and the *contract price.* Buyer "covers" by making, in good faith and without unreasonable delay, any reasonable purchase of (or contract to purchase) goods to substitute for those due from the seller. Example: S and B contract for the sale of goods for $1,000. S repudiates. B covers by buying substitute goods for $1,200. B may recover $200, plus incidental damages (such as commercially reasonable charges associated with effecting cover) and any consequential damages (of which S had reason to know in advance—see Part One, F, 3, B infra), minus any expenses saved due to S's breach. §§ 2–711(1)(a), 2–712 (defining "cover"), 2–715 and Comment 2. B's right to the difference between the contract price and the cost of cover is comparable to S's right (when B breaches) to the difference between the contract price and resale price. Cf. §§ 2–712(2), 2–706(1) [see § 2–712 Comment 1 (2003)]. B's failure to cover does not bar B from any other remedy, such as B's right to recover damages for non-delivery or repudiation, which will be discussed next. § 2–712(3). CISG 45(1)(b), 75, 77.

[*2003 Amend.* Section 2–712(1) clarifies the circumstances in which B is entitled to cover: (1) if S wrongfully fails to deliver or repudiates, or (2) B rightly rejects or justifiably revokes acceptance. §§ 2–711(2)(d), 2–712 Comment 2.]

(b) Buyer May Recover Damages for Non-Delivery or Repudiation

The measure of damages for S's non-delivery or repudiation is the difference between the *market price* and the *contract price.* The market price is calculated as of the time B learned of the breach and as of the place of tender (or, in the case of revocation or rejection after arrival, as of the place of arrival). Example: S and B contract for the sale of goods for $1,000. S repudiates. The market price at the appropriate time and place is $1,200. B may recover $200, plus incidental damages such as reasonable expenses incident to the breach and any consequential damages of which S had reason to know in advance (see Part One, F, 3, B infra), but minus any expenses saved due to S's breach. §§ 2–711(1)(b), 2–713, 2–715 and Comment 2, 2–723 (proof of market price), 2–724 (admissibility of market quotations), see § 2–503 (manner of tender). Note that B's right to recover the difference between the contract price and the market price is comparable to S's right (when B breaches) to recover the difference between the contract price and the market price. Cf. §§ 2–713, 2–708(1). CISG 45(1)(b), 76, 77.

[*2003 Amend.* Under § 2–713(1)(a), the *market price* in cases other than anticipatory repudiation (i.e., wrongful failure to deliver, rightful rejection, or justifiable revocation) is now measured at the *time for tender*. Under § 2–713(1)(b), the market price in the case of anticipatory repudiation is measured at the "expiration of a commercially reasonable time after the buyer learned of the repudiation." § 2–711(2)(e), 2–713 Comments 1–4; § 2–708(1)(b).]

(5) Buyer's Remedies Reaching the Goods Themselves

(a) In a Proper Case, Buyer May Obtain Specific Performance

When Seller fails to deliver or repudiates, specific performance may be decreed if the goods are unique or in other proper circumstances. §§ 2–711(2)(b), 2–716(1) and (2). This rule is a manifestation of the equitable principle that, when money damages are inadequate, the court of equity will decree that an agreement be specifically performed. Thus, when goods are unique—such as heirlooms or priceless works of art—money damages are inadequate to make a buyer whole. Consequently, Buyer is entitled to specific performance, that is, Seller must deliver to Buyer the heirloom or priceless work of art.

In addition, the UCC demonstrates a more liberal attitude than some courts have shown in connection with specific performance of sales contracts. Thus, in view of UCC Article 2's emphasis on the commercial feasibility of replacement, a new perspective as to what are "unique" goods has been introduced. First, specific performance is no longer limited to goods already ascertained at the time of contracting; second, the determination of uniqueness must consider the total contract situation. Output and requirements contracts involving a particular or peculiarly available source or market are typical commercial specific performance situations today. § 2–716 Comments 1 and 2; see § 2–306. Example of output contract: "The seller hereby agrees to sell and deliver, and the buyer hereby agrees to purchase, accept, and pay for, all of the seller's output of [*description of goods*] produced from (*date*) to (*date*)." Example of requirements contract: "The seller hereby agrees to sell and deliver, and the buyer hereby agrees to purchase, accept, and pay for, all of the buyer's requirements of [*description of goods*] for the buyer's own use and for the purpose of resale by the buyer during the period from (*date*) to (*date*)." In each example, suppose the described goods are available only in a particular or peculiarly available market. If Seller repudiates, Buyer will not be able to obtain the goods elsewhere. Thus, money damages would be inadequate, for example, if the goods were components (not obtainable elsewhere) to be installed in the machinery Buyer manufactures for sale. In the commercial setting, such goods are "unique," and Buyer should be able to obtain specific performance. CISG 45(1)(a), 46 (esp. (1)), 47; see 28; cf. 62, 63.

[*2003 Amend.* Section 2–716(1) (second sentence) adds that, in a nonconsumer contract, specific performance may be ordered if the parties have *agreed* to that remedy. §§ 2–711(2)(h), 2–716(1), (2) and Comments 1–3.

(b) *In a Proper Case, Buyer May Replevy the Goods*

When a seller fails to deliver or repudiates, the buyer has a right of replevin for any goods identified to the contract if, after reasonable effort, he is unable to effect cover for such goods (or the circumstances reasonably indicate that such effort would be unavailing). §§ 2–711(2)(b), 2–716(3), 2–501 (identification of goods to contract). Example: S and B contract for the sale of goods for $1,000. S selected from his inventory the goods to be sold to B, set the goods aside, and tagged them for delivery to B. S then repudiated. B made a reasonable effort to purchase goods in substitution for those due from S, but was unable to do so. B has the right to replevy the goods. § 2–716(3). Compare this right of replevin with the closely associated right of specific performance discussed immediately above. Note that B's right to replevy the identified goods when he is unable to cover is comparable to S's right (when B breaches the contract) to the price if S is unable reasonably to resell. Cf. §§ 2–716(3), 2–709(1)(b).

For B's rights of replevin when the goods have been shipped under reservation, see §§ 2–716(3) and Comment 5 [Comment 4 (2003)], 2–505 and Comments. CISG 45(1)(a), 46 (esp. (1)), 47; see 28; cf. 62, 63.

[Note: Under the 2001 revisions, § 2–716(3) adds the following, "In the case of goods bought for personal, family, or household purposes, the buyer's right of replevin vests upon acquisition of a special property [which occurs upon identification of the goods to the contract], even if the seller had not then repudiated or failed to deliver." See §§ 2–501, 2–716 Comment 3.]

[*2003 Amend.* The last sentence of § 2–716(3) (2001) has been deleted, and new § 2–716(4) states, "The buyer's right under subsection (3) vests upon acquisition of a special property, even if the seller had not then repudiated or failed to deliver." §§ 2–711(2)(h), 2–716 Comments 1(d) and 5.]

(c) Buyer May Recover Identified Goods Upon Seller's Insolvency, Repudiation, or Failure to Deliver

When a seller fails to deliver or repudiates, a buyer who has paid a part or all of the price of goods that have been identified to the contract may, on tendering any unpaid portion of their price, recover them from the seller if the seller becomes insolvent within ten days after receipt of the first installment on their price. §§ 2–711(2)(a), 2–502(1)(b), 2–501 (identification of goods to the contract), 1–201(b)(23) (defining "insolvent"); B.C., 11 U.S.C. § 101(32). Example: B selects a specific dining-room suite on S's showroom floor and enters into a contract to buy said suite for $1,000 with a $300 down payment, the remaining $700 to be paid upon delivery. B pays the $300. Eight days later, S, in great financial difficulty, ceases to pay its debts as they become due (a type of insolvency) and closes its doors for business. B, by tendering the $700 (and keeping the tender good), may recover the dining room suite from S. § 2–502(2) and Comment 3.

Buyer's right to recover goods upon Seller's insolvency is comparable to Seller's right to reclaim goods upon discovery of Buyer's insolvency under § 2–702(2). See Part One, F, 2, B supra. Recall the policy of § 2–702 that, when a buyer receives goods on credit while insolvent, this amounts to a tacit business misrepresentation of solvency and therefore is fraudulent against the particular seller. Consequently, the "defrauded seller" should be in a somewhat more favorable position than an ordinary unsecured seller-creditor. For this reason, the "defrauded seller" can reclaim the sold goods; other unsecured sellers have merely a money claim against the insolvent buyer.

Likewise, under § 2–502, we have a "defrauded buyer" whose seller became insolvent within ten days after receipt of the first installment on their price. Should this "defrauded buyer" not be in a somewhat more favorable position than an ordinary unsecured buyer-creditor? (Note that B's down payment before delivery of goods is an extension of credit to S.) Accordingly, the "defrauded buyer" can recover the goods; other unsecured buyers have merely a money claim against the insolvent seller.

If Buyer seeks greater protection than § 2–502 affords, Buyer must take a security interest against Seller pursuant to UCC Article 9, Secured Transactions, to be discussed in Part Five infra. § 2–502 Comment 2.

Buyer's right to recover may be defeated by certain third parties who claim through Seller. This will be discussed in Part One, G, 3 and 4 infra. CISG 45(1)(a), 46 (esp. (1)), 47; see 28; cf. 62, 63.

[Note: Under the 2001 Revisions to Article 2, § 2–502(1)(a) and (2) allows a buyer to recover goods bought for personal, family, or household purposes if the seller repudiates the contract or fails to deliver the goods. This right vests upon identification of the goods to the contract. § 2–502 Comments 1 and 3; see §§ 2–501, 2–712.]

[*2003 Amend.* Section 2–502(1)(a) substitutes "by a consumer" for the language "for personal, family, or household purposes." §§ 2–103(1)(c), 2–502(1)(a) and (2) and Comments 1 and 3, 2–711(2)(g).]

B. BUYER'S REMEDIES WHEN BUYER HAS FINALLY ACCEPTED THE GOODS

Section 2–714 deals with the remedies available to the buyer after the goods have been accepted and the time for revocation of acceptance has passed. §§ 2–714 Comment 1, 2–606 (defining "acceptance"), 2–607 (effect of acceptance), 2–608 (revocation). In this situation, the damages are measured thus: If Buyer has accepted nonconforming goods, Buyer may recover the loss resulting in the ordinary course of events from Seller's breach as determined in any reasonable manner. § 2–714(1). Of course, Buyer must notify Seller of the breach within a reasonable time after Buyer discovers or should have discovered any breach, or be barred from any remedy. §§ 2–714(1), 2–607(3)(a). CISG 45(1)(b), 74 (first sentence).

[*2003 Amend.* Sections 2–714(1) and 2–607(3)(a) provide that failure to give timely notice of breach in the case of accepted goods bars a remedy only to the extent the seller is prejudiced by the untimely notice. Section 2–711(2)(f) states that the buyer may recover damages with regard to accepted goods *or* breach involving a *remedial promise* under § 2–714. See §§ 2–103(1)(n), 2–313(4) and Comments 2 and 11.]

The usual, standard, and reasonable method of ascertaining damages in the case of breach of warranty, although not intended as an exclusive measure, is the difference (at the time and place of acceptance) between the value of the goods as accepted and the value they would have had if they had been as warranted. § 2–714(2). Example: S and B entered into a contract for the sale of carpeting for $14 per square yard. Lines appeared in the carpeting constituting a breach of warranty as set forth in §§ 2–313, 2–314, and 2–315. The salvage value of the carpeting as scrap was $4 per square yard. B's damages were $10 per square yard, the difference between the value of the goods accepted ($4 per square yard) and the value they would have had if they had been as warranted (the purchase price of $14 per square yard is probably good evidence of the expected value of the goods). On notifying S of B's intention to do so, B may deduct all or any part of the damages from any part of the price still due under the contract. § 2–717. CISG 45(1)(a), 50.

Further, in a proper case, (1) *incidental* and (2) *consequential* damages may also be recovered. §§ 2–714(3), 2–715. Consequential damages resulting from a seller's breach involve both (1) economic loss (e.g., loss of profit) and (2) injury to person or property. § 2–715(2)(a) and (b).

Re: Economic loss

Consequential damages resulting from Seller's breach include any loss resulting from general or particular requirements and needs of which Seller had reason to know at the time of contracting. § 2–715(2)(a). Buyer's particular needs must generally be made known to Seller, while Seller is automatically charged with knowledge of Buyer's general needs. § 2–715 Comment 3. Example: S sells goods to B, who is in the business of reselling. Thus, resale is one of B's particular requirements of which S has reason to know. § 2–715 Comment 6. Thus, loss of profit on resale may be an appropriate element of consequential damages B may recover from S in the event of S's breach.

This approach follows the common-law rule as set forth in the leading case of Hadley v. Baxendale, 9 Exch. 341, 156 Eng.Rep. 145 (1854). The UCC thus rejects the more restrictive "tacit agreement" test. § 2–715 Comment 2. Such a test would require not only that Seller have reason to know or foresee the loss at the time the contract was made, but also that the circumstances of the contract show that the seller expressly or impliedly agreed to be liable for consequential loss of the sort in question. McCormick, Damages § 141 (1935). Example: S contracts with B, a farmer, to deliver a reaping and threshing machine to B by July 14. S knows when contracting that B's wheat will be ready on that date, that it must be harvested promptly, and that B can get no other machine in time. S delays delivery until August 14. B's wheat has to be stacked, is damaged by moisture, and B has to sell at a lower price. S had reason to know or foresee the injuries so caused, so they are included in estimating B's damages. There is no requirement that the circumstances show that S expressly or impliedly agreed to be liable for consequential loss of the sort. See Restatement of Contracts § 330, Illustration 10 (1932). Of course, if B could get another machine in time, B would have a duty to minimize damages and could not recover for any loss that could be reasonably prevented. § 2–715(2)(a) and Comment 2. [Note: Consequential damages arise in situations in which goods are *not* delivered and accepted by B, as well as when goods *are* finally accepted. §§ 2–711(1)[§ 2–711(2) (2003)], 2–712(2), 2–713(1), 2–714(3).]

The UCC's "reason to know" rule takes no formal account of several factors that exert a deep influence on the allowability of consequential damages. Two factors were particularly important, pre-UCC, and remain important under the Code: (1) the relationship between the burden to be imposed on S and the amount of gain that accrued to S under the contract (e.g., $120 sale price, consequential damages of $850,000); and (2) the degree of fault attaching to S. McCormick, Damages § 140 (1935). See Restatement (Second) of Contracts § 351(3). CISG 45(1)(b), 74 (second sentence).

Re: Injury to person or property

Consequential damages resulting from Seller's breach include any injury to persons or property proximately resulting from any breach of warranty. § 2–715(2)(b). If the injury follows use of the goods without discovery of the defect causing the damage, the question of "proximate" cause turns on whether it was reasonable for Buyer to use the goods without having made such inspection as would have revealed the defect. If it was not reasonable for Buyer to do so, or if Buyer did in fact discover the defect prior to Buyer's use, the injury would not proximately result from the breach of warranty. § 2–715 Comment 5. Example: S sells B a bottle of soft drink. The bottle contains ground glass as well as the soft drink. B drinks part of the bottle, notices an unusual sensation in B's throat, spits out the drink, but continues to finish drinking the contents of the bottle, thereby sustaining severe injuries. B's injuries would not proximately result from S's breach of warranty. See § 2–314 Comment 13 [Comment 15 (2003)]. CISG 5.

4. REMEDY PRINCIPLES APPLICABLE
TO SELLERS AND BUYERS

A. TERMS OR CLAUSES IN THE SALES CONTRACT THAT PROVIDE FOR REMEDIES

(1) Liquidated Damages

Damages for breach by either party may be liquidated in the agreement, but only at an amount that is reasonable in light of (1) the anticipated or actual harm caused by the breach, (2) the difficulties of proof of loss, and (3) the inconvenience or nonfeasibility of otherwise obtaining an adequate remedy. § 2–718(1). The following liquidated damages clause is intended to be reasonable in light of these three factors:

"Inasmuch as the failure of the seller to deliver the quantity of commodities specified herein, in accordance with the terms of this agreement will, because of the urgent need for the commodities by the buyer arising from the present emergency conditions, cause serious and substantial damages to the buyer, and it will be difficult or even impossible to prove the amount of such damages, the seller agrees to pay to the buyer, [amount] as liquidated damages for failure to deliver, which sum is computed as follows:

[number]   cents per pound for [identify or designate article];

[number]   cents per pound for [identify or designate article];

[etc.]

The sum is agreed upon as liquidated damages and not as a penalty. The parties hereto have computed, estimated, and agreed upon the sum as an attempt to make a reasonable forecast of probable actual loss because of the difficulty of estimating with exactness the damage which will result."

The requirement that liquidated damages be reasonable is a recognition that damages are intended to compensate the aggrieved party, not penalize the contract breaker. Thus, a term fixing unreasonably large liquidated damages is void as a penalty. §§ 2–718(1), 1–305(a) (remedies to administered liberally). An unreasonably small amount, however, might be stricken under § 2–302 as unconscionable. § 2–718 Comment 1.

[2003 Amend. Section 2–718(1) (first sentence) provides that, in a nonconsumer contract, the test for enforceability of a liquidated damages clause is limited to the reasonableness of the clause in light of the actual or anticipated harm. § 2–718 Comment 2. Former § 2–718(1) stated that an unreasonably large liquidated damages term was void as a penalty. This has been eliminated as unnecessary and misleading. § 2–718 Comment 3. Section 2–718(1) (second sentence) states that enforceability of a term that limits but does not liquidate damages, is determined by § 2–719. § 2–718 Comment 1. See §§ 2–703(2)(l), 2–711(2)(i).]

Retention of buyer's down payment as liquidated damages

Consider the following clause in a sales agreement: "In the event that the buyer fails to perform any of its obligations under this contract, the seller may at its option declare the down payment of [amount] forfeited and may retain such payment as the sole damages to which it will be entitled for breach of the contract by the buyer." Suppose Buyer breaches the agreement and Seller justifiably withholds delivery of goods. Will the Code recognize this forfeiture of Buyer's down payment? Answer: The Code recognizes the forfeiture if the amount forfeited represents a reasonable liquidation of damages as determined under § 2–718(1), discussed above. If Buyer's down payment exceeds the amount to which Seller is entitled under the liquidated damages clause, Buyer is entitled to restitution of this amount. § 2–718(2). Example: Down payment is $100; liquidated damages clause is for $80. Buyer is entitled to restitution of $20.

[*2003 Amend.* Section 2–718(2) expands Buyer's right to restitution of the price paid to *all* circumstances in which Seller stops performance because of Buyer's breach or *insolvency.*]

In the absence of liquidated damages terms, Buyer is entitled to restitution of any amount by which Buyer's payments exceed twenty per cent of the value of the total performance for which the buyer is obligated under the contract, or $500, whichever is smaller. § 2–718(2). Example: Purchase price is $500 (thus, $500 is the value of the total performance for which Buyer is obligated); down payment is $150. Buyer is entitled to restitution of $50 according to the following computation: Twenty per cent of $500 is $100; Buyer's down payment was for $150; Buyer is entitled to $50, the amount by which Buyer's down payment exceeded $100.

[*2003 Amend.* This statutory liquidated-damages deduction from a breaching buyer's restitution remedy under former § 2–718(2)(b) has been eliminated.]

The buyer's right to restitution per the above is subject to offset by the seller per § 2–718(3), see §§ 2–706, 2–708.

If the down payment consists of goods, see § 2–718(4). CISG 6, 4(a).

(2) Contractual Modification or Limitation of Remedy

Parties are free to shape their remedies to fit their particular requirements. Accordingly, a sales agreement may provide for remedies in addition to, or in substitution for, those provided for in Article 2 and may limit or alter the measure of damages recoverable under UCC Article 2, as by limiting the buyer's remedies (1) to return of the goods and repayment of the price or (2) to repair and replacement of nonconforming goods or parts. §§ 2–719(1)(a) and Comment 1, 1–302 (variation by agreement); see, e.g., §§ 2–703, 2–711, 2–714, 2–715. Resort to a remedy provided in the agreement is optional unless the remedy is expressly agreed to be exclusive, in which case it is the sole remedy. Thus, the presumption is that clauses prescribing remedies are cumulative rather than exclusive. § 2–719(1)(b) and Comment 2.

The following is a sample clause modifying or limiting remedies:

> It is expressly understood and agreed that the buyer's sole and exclusive remedy shall be repair or replacement of defective parts, and that the seller shall not be liable for damages for injury to persons or property. Should the goods prove so defective, however, as to preclude the remedying of warranted defects by repair or replacement, the buyer's sole and exclusive remedy shall then be refund of the purchase price.

Note: Under the Magnuson–Moss Federal Warranty Act, exclusion or limitation of consequential damages for a consumer product must appear conspicuously on the face of the warranty. 15 U.S.C. § 2304(a)(3).

When clauses purporting to modify or limit remedies are subject to deletion

Parties are left free to shape their remedies to their particular requirements, and reasonable agreements limiting or modifying remedies are to be given effect. However, it is of the very essence of a sales contract that at least minimum adequate remedies be available. If the parties intend to conclude a contract for sale, they must accept at least a fair quantum of remedy for breach of the obligations outlined in the contract. Consequently, certain clauses limiting remedies are subject to deletion. § 2–719 Comment 1, see § 2–718.

Clause modifying or limiting remedies in an unconscionable manner

Any clause purporting to modify or limit the remedial provisions of UCC Article 2 in an unconscionable manner is subject to deletion. In that event, the remedies under Article 2 apply as if the stricken clause had never existed. § 2–719 Comment 1, see §§ 2–703, 2–711, 2–714, 2–715, 2–302 (unconscionable contract or clause). Thus, consequential damages may be limited or excluded unless the limitation or exclusion is unconscionable. Limitation of consequential damages for injury to the person in the case of consumer goods is *prima facie* unconscionable. § 2–719(3) and Comment 3.

Example: Defective steering mechanism of auto purchased for personal use breaks; auto veers off the road and hits a wall, injuring the buyer-driver and damaging the auto. A warranty clause limiting the buyer's damages to the repair and replacement of the defective steering mechanism and excluding consequential damages is prima facie unconscionable. Thus, the buyer is in all likelihood entitled to consequential damages resulting from the seller's breach, which include "injury to person or property proximately resulting from any breach of warranty." § 2–715(2)(b), see §§ 2–313, 2–314, 2–315. Note the distinction between exclusion or modification of warranties and modification or limitation of remedies. §§ 2–316, 2–719.

Note: The Magnuson–Moss Federal Warranty Act does not supersede state law regarding consequential damages for injury to persons or property. 15 U.S.C. § 2311.

Facially reasonable clause modifying or limiting remedies that fails of its essential purpose

When an apparently fair and reasonable clause, because of the particular circumstances of application, fails in its purpose or operates to deprive either party of the substantial value of the bargain, it must give way to the general remedy provisions of UCC Article 2. § 2–719(2) and Comment 1, see §§ 2–703 (seller's remedies, generally), 2–711 (buyer's remedies, generally), 2–714 (buyer's damages for accepted goods), 2–715 (buyer's incidental and consequential damages).

Example: S sold a car to B. In the sales agreement, S limited S's obligation to repair or replacement of defective parts and excluded responsibility for consequential loss. The car was seriously defective and could not be satisfactorily repaired. Held: The clause failed of its essential purpose, so B's remedies were not limited to repair or replacement of defective parts. UCC Hornbook § 13–10.

Unreasonably large or small liquidated damage clause

See discussion in the section immediately above and §§ 2–719(1), 2–718. CISG 6, 8(2), 4(a).

B. REMEDIES FOR FRAUD

If Seller knowingly misrepresents the quality of goods sold to Buyer, what are Buyer's rights under tort law? Under the Code? Answer: Typically, under tort law, Buyer had an election of remedies: to rescind, or to affirm and sue for fraud. Under the Code, by contrast, remedies for material misrepresentation or fraud include all remedies under Article 2, Sales, for non-fraudulent breach. Accordingly, neither rescission of the contract for fraud nor rejection of the goods bars other remedies under the Code. Purpose: to prevent remedies for fraud from being unduly circumscribed when compared with the more modern and mercantile remedies for breach of warranty. § 2–721 and Comment, see §§ 2–703 and Comment 1, 2–711, 2–714, 2–313 (express warranties). Thus, under the Code, Buyer may both rescind *and* recover damages. CISG 4(a).

C. WHO CAN SUE THIRD PARTIES FOR INJURY TO GOODS

Assume Seller contracts with Buyer for the sale of certain designated goods and reserves a security interest in the goods until Buyer pays the entire purchase price. A third party, X, negligently destroys the goods. Who has the right of action against X, Seller or Buyer or both? Answer: When a third party so deals with goods that have been identified (§ 2–501) to a sales contract as to cause actionable injury to a party to that contract, a right of action exists in *either* party to the contract for sale who:

(1) has title to the goods (§§ 2–401, 2–327),

(2) has a security interest in the goods (§§ 1–201(b)(35), 9–109),

(3) has a special property in the goods (§§ 2–401, 2–501),

(4) has an insurable interest in the goods (§ 2–501),

or (5) bore the risk of loss as to the goods (§§ 2–509, 2–510, 2–327).

See the rules in Part One, C supra. Consequently, it is possible for both Seller and Buyer to have a right of action. § 2–722 and Comment. CISG 1(1), 4 (first sentence).

D. STATUTE OF LIMITATIONS

An action for breach of any sales contract must be commenced within four years after the cause of action accrues. § 2–725(1); see § 2–725(3), (4).

When cause of action accrues

A cause of action accrues when the breach occurs, regardless of whether the aggrieved party knows of the breach. A breach of warranty occurs when tender of delivery is made. § 2–725(2); see §§ 2–503 (manner of tender), 2–313 (express warranties), 2–314 (implied warranty of merchantability), 2–315 (implied warranty of fitness for a particular purpose).

When a warranty explicitly extends to the goods' future performance, discovery of the breach must await the time of such performance. Thus, the cause of action accrues when the breach is or should have been discovered. § 2–725(2); see § 2–313(1)(a) (express warranties). Example: "This vehicle will be free from defects in material and workmanship under normal use and service for 24 months after the date of delivery of the vehicle to the original retail customer or until the vehicle has been driven 24,000 miles, whichever comes first."

Warranty and strict liability in tort compared

Section 2–725 provides a limitations period (except for warranties explicitly extending to future performance) commencing when Seller tenders delivery (regardless of whether the aggrieved party knows of the breach). Under strict liability in tort, by contrast, an illustrative statute of limitations might read, "No action founded upon a tort shall be brought but within three years from the date of the act or omission complained of." The following example shows how both might be applied: S delivers a defective cylinder of gas to B on March 1, 2004. The cylinder explodes December 1, 2005, injuring B. B commences suit against S on July 21, 2008. Has the statute of limitations run? Under the Code, the answer is yes, because more than four years had passed from March 1, 2004 (date of tender of delivery), before B commenced the action. Under tort law, the answer is no, because B commenced his action within three years of "the act or omission complained of" (December 1, 2005). Neither rule is inherently more favorable to B; change the above facts, and the Code statute of limitations may be more favorable to B than the tort statute.

Modification of the limitations period by agreement

In their original agreement, the parties may reduce the limitations period to not less than one year but may not extend it. § 2–725(1). See Convention on the Limitation Period in the International Sale of Goods, especially Article 8 (generally four years).

[*2003 Amend.* The limitations period of § 2–725(1) has been amended from a flat four years to "one year after the breach was or should have been discovered, but no longer than five years after the right of action accrued." The limitations period in a consumer contract may not be reduced. § 2–725(1). In addition to retaining the accrual rules, § 2–275 now provides specific accrual rules for (i) breach by repudiation, (ii) breach of remedial promise, (iii) a claim over (indemnity), (iv) breach of warranty of title, (v) breach of a warranty against infringement, and (vi) breach of a statutory obligation arising under § 2–313A or § 2–313B. § 2–275(2), (3) and Comment 1.]

G. RIGHTS OF THIRD PARTIES—PURCHASERS FROM, AND CREDITORS OF, SELLER AND BUYER

1. PURCHASERS FROM BUYER

Introduction

If B steals goods from A and sells them to innocent C, will A be able to recover the goods from C? Answer: Yes, because one cannot get good title from a thief; stated differently, a thief cannot pass on even to innocent persons better title than he has (which is none); or, he who hath not, cannot give (nemo dat qui non habet); or, as a stream cannot rise higher than its source, a person cannot pass on to another better title than that person has, etc. The Uniform Sales Act stated the rule as follows: "Where goods are sold by a person who is not the owner thereof, and who does not sell them under the authority or with the consent of the owner, the buyer acquires no better title to the goods than the seller had...." USA § 23. Thus, the law will protect ownership; persons may not be deprived of ownership without their consent. For C's rights as against B under § 2–312 title warranties, see Part One, D, 1 supra.

Yet innocent C's plight evokes sympathy. C purchased the goods in good faith and for value. Should not the law protect a BFP? That is, should not the law protect the marketplace by giving C the rights C expected, even though A would be deprived of his ownership without his consent? Thus the question becomes, when should the law protect *ownership* and when should the law protect the *marketplace*?

An old English rule, the doctrine of market overt, protected the marketplace. Thus, if a person purchased goods in good faith at an open and public sale, generally with the further requirement that it be on a certain prescribed day or days and in a prescribed place devoted to sales of goods of the kind in question, the person thereby became owner of the goods, and the former owner lost all property therein, even though the former owner had never consented to the sale. This doctrine has not been recognized in the United States.

Estoppel

However, there are instances in the United States in which the marketplace is protected. Recall under the Uniform Sales Act that a buyer acquired no better title to goods than the seller had. There was an exception to this rule as follows: "... unless the owner of the goods is by his conduct precluded from denying the seller's authority to sell." That is, unless the owner has so clothed the seller with the indicia of ownership that the owner is *estopped* to assert the contrary to a person who has relied (and is entitled to rely) to his detriment. USA § 23. The UCC states the same rule thus: "A purchaser of goods acquires all title which his transferor had or had power to transfer...." § 2–403(1).

When will B have power to transfer to C rights free from a claim by A? Stated differently, when will A be precluded (estopped) from denying B's authority to sell to C? A classic case will illustrate: O'Connor (A) owned a wagon. Tracy (B), a piano mover, with the knowledge and consent of A, had B's name and occupation printed upon the side of the wagon as follows to create the public impression that B was the owner: "George Tracy—Piano Mover" and proceeded to use the same. Thereafter, B, without the knowledge and consent of A, sold the wagon to Clark (C). A sought to recover possession of the wagon from C. In holding for C, the court stated,

> While the soundness of the general rule of law that a vendee of personal property takes only such title or interest as his vendor has and is authorized to transfer cannot for a moment be doubted, it is not without its recognized exceptions. One of these is where the owner has so acted with reference to his property as to invest another with such evidence of ownership, or apparent authority to deal with and dispose of it, as is calculated to mislead, and does mislead, a good faith purchaser for value. In such cases the principle of estoppel applies, and declares that the apparent title or authority, for the existence of which the actual owner was responsible, shall be regarded as the real title or authority, at least so far as persons acting on the apparent title or authority, and parting with value, are concerned. Strictly speaking, this is merely a special application of the broad equitable rule that, where one of two innocent persons must suffer loss by reason of the fraud or deceit of another, the loss should fall upon him by whose act or omission

the wrongdoer has been enabled to commit the fraud. Assuming, in this case, that a jury, under the evidence, should find—as we think they would be warranted in doing—that such marks of ownership were placed on the property by direction of O'Connor, the real owner, as were not only calculated to deceive, but actually intended to deceive, the public, and that by reason thereof, and without any fraud or negligence on his part, the defendant was misled into the belief that Tracy was the real owner, and he accordingly bought and paid him for the property, can there be any doubt, as between the real owner and the innocent purchaser, that the loss should fall upon the former, by whose act Tracy was enabled to thus fraudulently sell and receive the price of the property? We think not. In Bannard v. Campbell, . . . a well-considered case, involving substantially the same principle,—it was held that to create an estoppel by which an owner is prevented from asserting title to and is deprived of his property by the act of a third person, without his assent, two things must concur: "(1) The owner must have clothed the person assuming to dispose of the property with the apparent title to or authority to dispose of it. (2) The person alleging the estoppel must have acted and parted with value upon the faith of such apparent ownership or authority, so that he will be the loser if the appearances to which he trusted are not real." O'Connor's Adm'x v. Clark, 170 Pa. 318, 32 A. 1029 (1895).

Apropos to the above, Comment 1 to § 2–403 (2003) states, "The basic policy that allows the transfer of such title as the transferor has is recognized under subsection (1). . . . Moreover the policy of this Act expressly providing for the application of supplementary general principles of law to sales transactions wherever appropriate (Section 1–103) joins with the present section [§ 2–403] to continue unimpaired all rights acquired under the law of agency or of apparent agency or ownership or other estoppel, whether based on statutory provisions or on case law.''

In § 2–403, the Code deals explicitly with two areas in which certain transferors have "power to transfer:" (1) when goods have been entrusted to a merchant, and (2) when a person has "voidable title."

Entrustment by delivery of goods to a merchant

Suppose A loans goods to B and B, instead of returning the goods to A, wrongfully sells them to innocent C. Case law typically holds that A may recover the goods from C. Merely giving possession to B by way of bailment is not enough to create an estoppel operating against A in favor of C. Instead, possession *plus* some other indicia of ownership or right to sell is required.

Example: A delivers a watch to B for repair. B is a merchant who deals in repairing and selling new and used watches. Without A's consent, B sells the watch to C, who buys in good faith and without knowledge of A's ownership rights. Will A recover the watch from C? No, because "[a]ny entrusting of possession of goods [by A] to a merchant who deals in goods of that kind [B] gives him power to transfer all rights of the entruster [A] to a buyer in ordinary course of business [C]." §§ 2–403(2) and (3) (2003), 2–104(1) (defining "merchant"). The term " 'Buyer in ordinary course of business' means a person [C] that buys goods in good faith, without knowledge that the sale violates the rights of another person [A] in the goods, and in the ordinary, course from a person [B] ... in the business of selling goods of that kind.... Only a buyer that takes possession of the goods or has a right to recover the goods from the seller under Article 2 [see e.g., §§ 2–502, 2–716] may be a buyer in ordinary course of business." § 1–201(b)(9) and Comment 9. Thus, a buyer in ordinary course of business is a buyer who is engaged in *proper* dealings in the *normal* market. § 2–403 Comment 3. Note that, in this example, A has not merely bailed goods; instead, A has bailed goods with a merchant in the business of selling such goods.

Thus, two questions arise: (1) Was B, to whom A entrusted the goods, a merchant dealing in goods of the kind? (2) Is C a buyer in ordinary course of business? Two affirmative answers, and C defeats A, the person who "introduced the goods into the stream of commerce." [But see § 2–108(1)(a), (2), (3) (2003) (referencing other bodies of law that may compel a different result).]

The entrustment principle also manifests itself elsewhere in the UCC: for example, entrusting goods to a warehouse, § 7–205; and a secured party entrusting inventory to a merchant, § 9–320(a). See § 2–403 Comment 2. See Part Four, D, 2, C, (4) and Part Five, C, 5, D, (1), (b) infra. See also §§ 2–507(3) (2003) (BFP may defeat seller's right to reclaim), § 2–702(3) (same rule in pre-2003 code).

A person with voidable title

Assume A sells and delivers goods to B, who in turn sells and delivers them to C. Clearly, since B had title to the goods, C acquires the same good title B had. § 2–403(1). But suppose B obtained the goods from A by some type of fraud and that A, as a result, could avoid the transaction and recover the goods from B. May A likewise recover the goods from C? It depends on whether B's title is deemed void or merely voidable. A person with voidable title has the power to transfer good title to a good faith purchaser for value [C]. § 2–403(1). If no title passed from A to B, A recovers the goods from C; if voidable title passed from A to B, C cuts off A's right to recover the goods and A does not recover the goods from C, if C is a BFP.

Pre-UCC courts sometimes disagreed as to when, if ever, A defeated C. The Code resolves such disputes in § 2–

403(1) (2003): "If goods have been delivered [from A to B] under a transaction of purchase, the purchaser [B] has such power [to transfer good title to a good-faith purchaser for value, C] even if:

(a) the transferor [A] was deceived as to the identity of the purchaser [B];

(b) the delivery [to B] was in exchange for a check that is later dishonored;

(c) it was agreed that the transaction [between A and B] was to be a cash sale; or

(d) the delivery was procured through criminal fraud.

Example 1: A delivers goods on credit to B—a poor individual with bad credit—who represented himself to be X—a rich individual with good credit. If A had known the true facts, A would not have delivered the goods to B on credit. B then sells the goods to C, who purchases in good faith and for value. C gets good title and defeats A. § 2–403(1)(a); cf. § 3–404(a) (checks written by and to impostors).

Example 2: A sells and delivers goods to B, who pays by issuing to A a currently dated check that is later dishonored. We have previously seen that, in this "cash sale" transaction, because B made a tacit representation that the check would be honored, A, the "defrauded seller," would be allowed to reclaim the goods from B. §§ 2–507(2), 2–511(3) (check as conditional payment for goods). See Part One, F, 2, C supra. However, if B sells the goods to C, who purchases in good faith for value, C gets good title and defeats A. §§ 2–403(1)(b) and (c), 2–507(3) (2003).

Example 3: A sells and delivers goods to B on credit. B received the goods on credit while insolvent. This amounts to a tacit business misrepresentation of solvency and therefore is fraudulent against A. Accordingly, upon appropriate demand, A may reclaim the goods from B.

This much we already have investigated. § 2–702(2), see Part One, F, 2, B supra. However, if B sells the goods to C, who purchases in good faith for value, C gets good title and defeats A. § 2–702(3) states, "The seller's [A's] right to reclaim under subsection (2) is subject to the rights of a buyer in ordinary course or other good faith purchaser [for value i.e., C] under this Article (Section 2–403)."

Good faith purchaser for value defined

For C to prevail in the examples above, C must be a BFP, that is, a good faith purchaser for value (§ 2–403(1)).

Good faith means honesty in fact and the observance of reasonable commercial standards of fair dealing. § 1–201(b)(20) and Comment 20 (See former § 1–201(19).)

Purchaser means a person who takes by any voluntary transaction creating an interest in property, such as a sale or security interest. § 1–201(b)(29), (30).

A person gives *value* for rights if the person acquires them in return for any consideration sufficient to support a simple contract. This includes the taking of property in satisfaction of, or as security for, a pre-existing claim. § 1–204. Thus, a donee is not a BFP. CISG 1(1), 4(b).

2. CREDITORS OF BUYER

Review the scenarios presented in Part One, G, 1 immediately above:

a. A entrusted goods to B, a merchant.

b. A sold and delivered goods to B, who represented himself to be X.

c. A sold and delivered goods to B, who paid by issuing to A a currently dated check that was later dishonored.

d. A sold and delivered goods to B on credit while B was insolvent.

In all cases, when B sold the goods to C, a *buyer in ordinary course of business* or a *good faith purchaser* for *value,* the sale cut off A's rights. § 2–403. Now suppose that C—instead of being a buyer from B—was a general or unsecured creditor of B, who in endeavoring to recover an indebtedness, attached or levied upon the goods in B's possession. C is now a "lien creditor," which means "a creditor that has acquired a lien on the property involved by attachment, levy, or the like...." § 9–102(a)(52). Will C, as a lien creditor, defeat A's right to reclaim the goods?

In example *a,* because C does not qualify as a buyer in ordinary course of business, A will reclaim the goods from C. §§ 2–403(2), 1–201(b)(9) (defining "buyer in ordinary course of business").

In examples *b* (B impersonating X) and *c* (the dishonored check), the question is whether C is a good faith *purchaser* for value per § 2–403(1). "Purchaser" means a person who takes by any *voluntary* transaction creating an interest in property, such as a sale or security interest. § 1–201(b)(29), (30). C's lien is obtained involuntarily, since B did not assent. Hence, since C is not a *purchaser,* he cannot be a good faith purchaser for value and, consequently, A can reclaim the goods from C under § 2–403(1). This result reflects the common-law attitude that a creditor is not a "reliance party," that is, the creditor has parted with nothing in reliance on B's ostensible ownership of goods in his possession. Instead, C usually extended unsecured credit to B before B acquired the goods in question. Thus, "[t]he general common law rule is ... that a creditor [C] ... is not protected against latent equities against the judgment debtor [A's right to reclaim goods from a defrauding B] and that he [C] stands in all respects in the shoes of the judgment debtor [B]." S. Riesenfeld, Creditors' Remedies and Debtors' Protection 130 (4th ed. 1987).

Seller's right to reclaim under § 2–702

In example *d* (delivery to insolvent B), it appears that the answer and analysis should be the same as in examples *b* and *c*. Some difficulty arose because § 2–702(3) of the 1962 Code, which allowed A to reclaim from B, stated, "The seller's right to reclaim . . . is subject to the rights of a buyer in ordinary course or other good faith purchaser *or lien creditor* under this Article (Section 2–403)." This italicized language was read in at least two ways: (1) A's right to reclaim was subject to C's interest as a lien creditor, and (2) C's rights were to be determined by § 2–403, which, except for a cross reference in subsection (4), did not discuss lien creditor rights. Accordingly, a court could look to pre-Code law by application of § 1–103 to determine A's rights as against C. In most, but not all, states, prior to the Code, A, the defrauded seller, prevailed over C, a lien creditor of B. In 1966, § 2–702(3) was amended to delete "or lien creditor," with the intention of having A prevail over C. If C is B's trustee in bankruptcy, B.C., 11 U.S.C. § 546(c)(1) allows A to reclaim any goods B has received while insolvent, so long as A demands the goods *in writing* not later than 45 days after receipt of such goods by B. If such 45–day period expires after the commencement of the bankruptcy case, then the deadline for making demand is 20 days after commencement of the case. Reclamation may be denied only if the bankruptcy court grants A priority as an administrative expense or secures A's claim by a lien.

Rights of creditors in a sale on approval, sale or return, or consignment sale

A, who delivers goods to B, also comes into conflict with C, an attaching or levying creditor of B, when A delivers goods to B, if the contract provides that B may return the goods to A even if they conform to the contract. Such a transaction may be characterized either as a sale on approval or a sale or return. Note that, in a usual sales transaction, B may return goods only if they do not conform to the contract. §§ 2–601, 2–608. Now suppose—in a sale on approval or a sale or return—that B's creditor, C, attaches or levies on the goods. Will C's "lien creditor" interest prevail over A's interest in the goods?

Sale on approval

In this situation, A is typically a dealer who seeks to sell goods to B for B's own use (rather than for resale). To overcome B's reluctance to buy, A might deliver the goods to B "on approval" or "on trial" or "on satisfaction." A knows, based on prior use of this technique with other buyers, that B will probably decide to approve and keep the goods. Goods held by B "on approval" are *not* subject to the claims of B's creditors until *acceptance*. §§ 2–326(1)(a), (2) and Comment 1, 2–606 (defining "acceptance"). "The goods are delivered to the proposed purchaser but they remain the property of the seller until the buyer accepts them." § 2–326 Comment 1; cf. USA § 19 Rule 3.

Sale or return

In this situation, A is typically a manufacturer who seeks to sell goods to merchant-dealer B, who would resell the goods. To overcome B's unwillingness to buy, A might agree to take back any unsold commercial unit of goods in lieu of payment. Goods held by B on "sale or return" *are* subject to the claims of B's creditors while in B's possession. § 2–326(1)(b), (2) and Comment 1.

Consignment sale

See e.g., §§ 9–109(a)(4) (consignments fall within Article 9) and Comment 6, 9–102(a)(20) (defining "consignment") and Comment 14, 9–103(d) (consignor's purchase-money security interest in inventory) and Comment

6, 9–319 (consignee's rights with respect to creditors and purchasers) and Comments 2 and 3. See Part Five, C, 2, A infra for discussion of the consignment sale as an Article 9 security transaction. CISG 1(1), 4(b).

3. PURCHASERS FROM SELLER

Entrustment by acquiescence in a merchant's retention of possession—the "seller in possession"

An owner can entrust goods to a merchant, not only by delivery of goods to the merchant—see discussion at Part One, G, 1 supra—but also by buying goods from the merchant but allowing the merchant to retain possession. Example: Merchant A contracts for the sale of certain goods to B. B acquiesces in A's retaining possession for a few days. C sees the goods in A's showroom and offers A a higher price for the same goods, not knowing of the prior sale to B. A sells to C, and C takes delivery of the goods. Assuming B has a right to the goods as against A (see §§ 2–716 (right to replevin), 2–502) (rights to goods upon seller's insolvency), will B recover the goods from C? Answer: No, because B entrusted possession (by acquiescing in A's retention of possession) of the goods to a merchant who deals in goods of that kind, and this gave A power to transfer B's rights to a buyer in ordinary course of business (C). §§ 2–403(2) and (3), 2–104(1), 1–201(b)(9).

Seller's bailee in possession

Buyer can avoid the seller-in-possession risk by taking immediate delivery of the goods. If Seller's goods are in the possession of a bailee who has engaged to deliver the goods back to Seller, Buyer may *notify* the bailee of Buyer's right to take possession and "fix" Buyer's rights against third persons. § 2–503(4)(b), see §§ 7–504(b)(2) and (c) (2003), 9–312(d). CISG 1(1), 4(b).

4. CREDITORS OF SELLER

"Seller in possession"

Assume Merchant A contracts for the sale of certain goods to B, who acquiesces in A's retaining possession for a few days. Now suppose that—instead of C being a buyer in ordinary course of business—C is an unsecured creditor of A, and in seeking to enforce his claim against A, attaches or levies upon the goods in A's possession. Will B's or C's interest in the goods prevail? Answer: B's. Rights of Seller's unsecured creditors (like C) with respect to goods identified (§ 2–501) to a sales contract are *subject to* the buyer's (B's) rights under Sections 2–502, 2–716. § 2–402(1). Recall that Buyer had remedies against Seller reaching the goods themselves: specific performance, replevin if Buyer was unable to cover, or recovery of the goods on Seller's insolvency. §§ 2–716, 2–502. If B, therefore, is able to "reach the identified goods themselves" as against A, then C is subject to B's right to recover the goods. This rule reflects the aforementioned common-law rule that a creditor "stands in all respects in the shoes of the . . . debtor." The buyer's right to reach the goods and to defeat the seller's unsecured creditors is called a *special property.* See Part One, C, 2 supra. If C is A's trustee in bankruptcy, see 11 U.S.C. § 545 (trustee may avoid "statutory lien" that first becomes effective when debtor becomes insolvent), § 507(a)(6) (priority for certain consumer creditors).

Retention of possession as fraudulent

In the example above, even though C is subject to B's right to recover the goods as against A, may C attack the transaction between A and B as fraudulent? Analysis: As early as the landmark Twyne's Case, 76 Eng. Rep. 809 (1601), if A sold goods to B but remained in possession of the goods, such retention, was considered a "badge of fraud." In the language of *Twyne,* "The donor continued in possession, and used them as his own; and by reason thereof he traded and trafficked with others, and defrauded and deceived them." Today, the Code leaves the matter to the state's fraudulent conveyancing law, with one exception: "A creditor of the seller may treat a sale or an identification of goods to a contract for sale as void if as against him [the creditor] a retention of possession by the seller is fraudulent under any rule of law of the state where the goods are situated, except that retention of possession in good faith and current course of trade by a merchant-seller for a commercially reasonable time after a sale or identification is not fraudulent." § 2–402(2).

Example: It is commercially reasonable for A to retain possession of an auto for a few days to service and prepare it for delivery to B.

With this one exception, fraudulent conveyancing law and preference law is applicable. § 2–402(3)(b); see e.g., Uniform Fraudulent Conveyance Act or Uniform Fraudulent Transfer Act, see B.C., 11 U.S.C. §§ 544(b) and 548 (fraudulent transfers), 547 (preferences).

As to C's rights as a *secured* creditor, see § 2–402(3)(a) and Part Five infra. As to a seller's bailee in possession, see Part One, G, 3 above.

5. RIGHTS OF THIRD PARTIES FOUND ELSEWHERE IN THE UCC

Third party rights are addressed in a number of provisions of the UCC. In addition to Article 9, which discusses a myriad of third parties, the following are some specific examples: § 3–306 (holder in due course of a negotiable instrument), § 7–502 (holder of a "duly negotiated" document of title), § 8–303 ("protected purchaser" of an investment security). In each situation, the same ultimate question is presented: When is it more important to preserve prior rights, and when is it more important to protect the marketplace even at the expense of prior rights?

H. BULK SALES

Former Article 6, Bulk Transfers, dealt with the following situation: S, a merchant, owing debts to creditors, sold out S's inventory, pocketed the proceeds, and disappeared leaving S's creditors unpaid. To prevent this kind of commercial fraud, former Article 6 required advance notice to S's creditors of the impending sale. This advance notice would allow S's creditors to take steps to impound the proceeds if they thought it necessary. Former § 6–101 Comments.

Basically, former § 6–104 stated that a bulk transfer falling within Article 6 was *ineffective* against any creditor of the transferor unless advance notice of the impending transfer was given to the transferor's creditors. See former §§ 6–102, 6–103. Thus, creditors who did not receive such notice could disregard the transfer and levy on the goods as if they still belonged to the transferor. "Advance notice" involved the following steps: (1) Transferor furnished a list of Transferor's creditors, (2) Transferor and Transferee prepared a schedule of property to be transferred, (3) Transferee gave notice to Transferor's creditors providing certain information concerning the transfer, and (4) the notice had to be given at least ten days before Transferee took possession of the goods or paid for them (which happened first). Former §§ 6–104 through 6–107.

Under the 1989 Code, Article 6 was renamed "Bulk Sales, and states were invited to select one of two alternatives:" Alternative A repealed Article 6; Alternative B revised Article 6. For those states selecting Alternative B, the Comment to revised § 6–101 recites the major changes from former Article 6:

☐ this Article does not apply to sales in which the value of the property is less than $10,000 or is greater than $25,000,000 (Section 6–103(3)(*l*)).

☐ the choice-of-law provision (Sections 6–103(1)(b) and 6–103(2)) limits the applicable law to that of one jurisdiction.

☐ if the seller is indebted to a large number of persons, the buyer need neither obtain a list of those persons nor send individual notices to each person, but instead may give notice to the group by filing (Sections 6–105(2) and 6–104(2)).

☐ the notice period is increased from 10 days to 45 days (Section 6–105(5)), and the limitations period is extended from six months to one year (Section 6–110).

☐ a buyer's noncompliance does not render the sale ineffective or otherwise affect the buyer's title to the goods; rather, a noncomplying buyer is liable for damages due to noncompliance (Sections 6–107(1) and 6–107(8)).

I. SALE OF INVESTMENT SECURITIES

UCC Article 8, Investment Securities, (e.g., stocks and bonds, as "security" is defined in § 8–102(a)(15)) does not fit within what is normally considered the Code's main purpose: to deal with the normal phases in the handling of a commercial transaction relating to the sale of *goods*. The General Comment to the UCC nevertheless provides this rationale for including investment securities in the Code: "If, instead of goods in the ordinary sense, the transaction involved stocks or bonds, some of the phases of the transaction would obviously be different. Others would be the same. In addition, there are certain additional formalities incident to the transfer of stocks and bonds from one owner to another."

Only a few sections of the former Article 8 dealt with sales aspects of investment securities. For example, § 8–319 (Statute of Frauds) was consistent with the policy of § 2–201, a similar provision relating to the sale of goods. Along the same lines, § 8–107(2), which allowed the seller to recover the price under certain circumstances when the buyer failed to pay, conformed to the policy of § 2–709(1), a similar provision relating to the sale of goods. Further, § 8–314 dealt with aspects of performance of a securities transaction, much like §§ 2–301, 2–507(1), and 2–503 in the sales context.

Revised § 8–113 deletes the statute of frauds provision in former § 8–319. See § 8–113 Comment. With respect to former §§ 8–107 and 8–314, Revision Note 8 to Prefatory Note to Revised Article 8 states,

Article 8 has never been, and should not be, a comprehensive codification of the law of contracts for the purchase and sale of securities. The prior version of Article 8 did contain, however, a number of provisions dealing with miscellaneous aspects of the law of contracts as applied to contracts for the sale of securities. Section 8–107 dealt with one remedy for breach, and Section 8–314 dealt with certain aspects of performance. Revised Article 8 deletes these on the theory that inclusion of a few sections on issues of contract law is likely to cause more harm than good since inferences might be drawn from the failure to cover related issues. The deletion of these sections is not, however, intended as rejection of the rules of contract law interpretation that they expressed.

Under current Article 8, the rules of contract law interpretation may be found by applying non-Code law. See § 1–103(b) and former § 8–107 Comment 2. It is sometimes also appropriate to look to Article 2 by analogy. To make this latter point clear, Comment 1 to § 2–105 states, " 'Investment securities' are expressly excluded from the coverage of [Article 2, Sales of Goods].... It is not intended by this exclusion, however, to prevent the application of a particular section of [Article 2] ... by analogy to securities ... when the reason of that section makes such application sensible and the situation involved is not covered by [Article 8, Investment Securities]...." More broadly, Comment 1 to § 1–103 states, "[C]ourts have often recognized that the policies embodied in an act are applicable in reason to subject-matter that was not expressly included in the language of the act.... and did the same where reason and policy so required, even where the subject-matter had been intentionally excluded from the act in general.... Nothing in the Uniform Commercial Code stands in the way of the continuance of such action by the courts." Accordingly, the Code drafters approve of reasoning by analogy, not only between Article 2, Sales, and Article 8, Investment Securities, but also outside the Code itself, including the law of services, bailments, and perhaps even real estate transactions. See also § 2–313 Comment 2 [Comment 4 (2003)]. CISG 2(d).

PART TWO

THE PROCESS OF LEASING GOODS

[Prefatory Note: Article 2A, Leases, borrows from both Article 2, Sales, and Article 9, Secured Transactions. See Parts One and Five of this Nutshell; see also Comment to § 2A–101. Because of this commonality, each portion of the discussion that follows in Part Two will cite any analogous Article 2 and Article 9 provisions, together with specific page references indicating where the relevant subject matter is discussed.

In May 2011, the American Law Institute withdrew the 2003 Amendments to Article 2A of the Uniform Commercial Code. Consequently, this Part will continue to present pre-2003 Article 2A. In brackets, however, the changes under Amended (2003) Article 2A are set forth for informational purposes. This Part does reflect Revised (2001) Article 1, General Provisions.

As to the relation of Articles 1 and 2A to Electronic Signatures in Global and National Commerce Act (E-Sign), see §§ 1–108 and Comments, [2A–104(4) and Comment 6 (2003)]; as to Uniform Electronic Transaction Act (UETA), see UETA § 3(b)(2) and Comments 4 and 7.]

A. SCOPE OF ARTICLE 2A

Article 2A applies to *leases*, which are transfers of the right to possession and use of *goods* for a period in return for consideration. A *sale* or the retention or creation of a *security interest* is not a lease. §§ 2A–102 (scope), 2A–103(1)(j) [2A–103(1)(p) (2003)] ("lease" defined); Cf.

§§ 2–106(1) ("sale" defined), 1–201(b)(35) ("security interest" defined), 1–203 (leases and security interests distinguished), 9–109(a)(1) and Comment 2 (Article 9 scope), 9–203 Comment 3 (last sentence). *Goods* are all things that are movable at the time of identification to the lease contract or are fixtures, but not, e.g., money, instruments, chattel paper, or minerals before extraction. §§ 2A–103(1)(h) [2A–103(1)(n) (2003)], 2A–217 (identification). Cf. §§ 2–102 (scope of Article 2), 2–106(1) ("sale" defined), 2–105(1) [2–103(1)(k) (2003)] ("goods" defined) at pp. 2–3.

[*2003 Amend.* A license of information is not a lease, § 2A–103(1)(p). "Goods" does not include information, money in which the price is to be paid, investment securities, or choses in action. § 2A–103(1)(n).]

A *consumer lease* is a lease that a lessor who is regularly engaged in the business of leasing or selling makes to an individual lessee (not an organization) who takes the goods primarily for a personal, family, or household purpose. [Further, total payments under the lease contract (excluding payments for options to renew or buy) cannot exceed a designated amount, e.g., $25,000.] § 2A–103(1)(e); Cf. § 9–102(a)(23) ("consumer goods" defined), UCCC § 1.301(14) (1974), Consumer Leasing Act (15 U.S.C. § 1667).

[*2003 Amend.* A consumer lease is one that is made to a *consumer* ("an individual who leases ... primarily for personal, family, or household purposes)." § 2A–103(1)(e), (f).]

A *finance lease* is a three party transaction involving a: lessor, lessee, and supplier. § 2A–103(1)(g), (p), (n), (x) [2A–103(1)(*l*), (v), (t), (ff) (2003)] (defining "finance lease," "lessor," "lessee," and "supplier"). Example 1: Supplier manufactures or supplies goods pursuant to Lessee's specification (perhaps even pursuant to a purchase order, sales agreement, or lease agreement between Supplier and Lessee). After the prospective finance lease is negotiated, Lessor enters a purchase order (or sales agreement, or lease agreement) as buyer or prime lessee, or Lessee assigns an existing order (or agreement or lease) to Lessor, and Lessor and Lessee then enter into a lease or sublease of the goods. Comment: Because Lessor generally performs a limited function, Lessee looks almost entirely to Supplier (or sometimes the manufacturer) for, e.g., warranties. § 2A–103(1)(g) [2A–103(1)(*l*) (2003)] and Comment (g) ("finance lease" defined) and §§ 2A–209 (Lessee as beneficiary of supply contract), 2A–212 (warranty of merchantability), 2A–213 (warranty of fitness for a particular purpose), 2A–407 (irrevocable promises; finance leases).

Example 2 (sale and lease back): Lessee (B) buys goods from Supplier (C) pursuant to a sales contract. After B receives and accepts the goods, B negotiates to sell the goods to Lessor (A) and simultaneously to lease them back from A. In documenting the sale and lease back, B assigns the original sales contract between B (as buyer) and C (as seller), to A. The lease from A to B qualifies as a finance lease, as all three conditions of § 2A–103(1)(g)(i)–(iii) [2A–103(1)(*l*)(i)–(iii) (2003)] are satisfied:

Subparagraph (i) is met: Lessor (A) had nothing to do with the selection, manufacture, or supply of the goods.

Subparagraph (ii) is met: Lessor (A) bought the goods at the same time that A leased the equipment to B, which was in connection with the lease.

Subparagraph (iii)(A) is met: Lessor (A) entered the sales contract with Lessee (B) at the same time that A leased the equipment back to B. B will have received a copy of the contract. See also (iii)(B)–(D).

For a listing of rules that apply only to consumer leases and finance leases, see § 2A–103 Comments (e) and (g). [Amended (g) omits the listing.]

Leases subject to other law

Article 2 leases are also subject to certificate of title statutes, consumer protection statutes, or court decisions. § 2A–104. Cf. §§ 9–201(b)–(d), 9–311 at pp. 445, 449–450, 454, 466, 473, 512–513.

As to territorial application of Article 2A to goods covered by a certificate of title, see § 2A–105; as to limitation of the power of parties to a consumer lease to choose applicable law and a judicial forum, see § 2A–106. See also § 1–105 [§ 1–301 (2001)].

B. THE LEASE CONTRACT

1. FORMATION OF A LEASE CONTRACT

A. MANNER AND MOMENT OF AGREEMENT

A lease contract may be made in any manner sufficient to show agreement; an agreement may be found even if the moment of its making is undetermined. § 2A–204(1), (2). Cf. § 2–204(1), (2) at p. 4.

[*2003 Amend.* "A lease contract may be made in any manner sufficient to show agreement, including offer and acceptance, ... the interaction of electronic agents, and the interaction of an electronic agent and an individual." § 2A–204(1); see §§ 2A–204(4), 2A–222 (legal recognition of electronic contracts, records, and signatures), 2A–223 (attribution), 2A–224 (electronic communication).]

B. THE INDEFINITE OFFER

Even if one or more terms are left open, a lease contract does not fail for indefiniteness if (1) the parties intended to make a lease contract, and (2) there is a reasonably certain basis for giving an appropriate remedy. § 2A–204(3). Cf. § 2–204(3) at pp. 5–9.

C.   FIRM OFFER TO LEASE

A firm offer by a merchant is not revocable for lack of consideration during the time stated or, if no time is stated, for a reasonable time (but in no event may the period of time exceed three months). If the firm offer is in a form supplied by the offeree, it must be separately signed by the offeror. § 2A–205. Cf. § 2–205 at p. 9.

D.   MANNER AND MEDIUM OF ACCEPTANCE

Unless otherwise unambiguously indicated, an offer to make a lease contract must be construed as inviting acceptance in any manner and by any medium that is reasonable under the circumstances. § 2A–206(1). If beginning the requested performance is a reasonable mode of acceptance, see § 2A–206(2). Cf. § 2–206(1)(a), (2) (subsection (1)(b) analogue not made) at pp. 10–12.

2.   THE REQUIREMENT OF CONSIDERATION

A.   IN GENERAL

A lease is a transfer of the right to possession and use of goods for a period in return for consideration. § 2A–103(1)(j) [2A–103(1)(p) (2003)]. Cf. § 2–106(1) ("sale" defined) at p. 1.

B.   FIRM OFFER

As noted before, a firm offer by a merchant is not revocable for lack of consideration. § 2A–205. Cf. § 2–205 at p. 9. [*2003 Amend. Writing* is now *record.*]

C.   MODIFICATION, RESCISSION, WAIVER

An agreement modifying a lease contract needs no consideration to be binding. § 2A–208(1). As to a lease agreement that excludes modification and as to waivers see §§ 2A–208(2)–(4), 2A–107. Cf. §§ 2–209, 1–306 at pp. 21–23; note § 2–209(3) was eliminated in § 2A–208.

3. FORM OF THE LEASE CONTRACT

A. STATUTE OF FRAUDS

Transactions within the statute of frauds

A transaction involving total lease payments (excluding payments for options to renew or buy) of $1,000 or more implicates the statute of frauds. § 2A–201(1)(a), see former § 1–206. Cf. § 2–201(1).

Satisfaction of the statute of frauds

1. *Writing signed by defendant.* The writing must be sufficient to show a lease contract has been made and must describe (i) the goods and (ii) the lease term. § 2A–201(1)(b), (2), (3). Cf. §§ 2–201(1), 9–203(b) (re: enforceability of security interest), 9–108 (collateral description).

2. *Writing by claimant—reply doctrine.* This special rule between merchants of § 2–201(2) was not included. § 2A–201 Comment.

3. *Partial performance.* "A lease contract ... is enforceable with respect to goods that have been received and accepted by the lessee." § 2A–201(4)(c) and (5). (Note that the same rule does not apply where *payment* has been made and accepted.) Cf. § 2–201(3)(c).

4. *Admissions in court.* A lease contract is enforceable if the defendant admits (i.e., in pleadings) that a lease contract was made (but not beyond the quantity of goods admitted). § 2A–201(4)(b) and (5). Cf. § 2–201(3)(b).

5. *Specially manufactured goods.* A lease contract is enforceable (under enumerated circumstances) if the goods are to be specially manufactured. § 2A–201(4)(a). Cf. 2–201(3)(a).

[*2003 Amend.* To accommodate electronic commerce, *record* is substituted for *writing*. § 2A–201(1), (3), (5); §§ 2A–103(1)(cc) ("record" defined), 1–201(b)(31) (same). The exception for admissions in court has been broadened to include out-of-court admissions "under oath." § 2A–201(4)(b). New subsection (6) states, "A lease contract that is enforceable under [§ 2A–201] ... is not unenforceable merely because it is not capable of being performed within one year ... after its making." This provision does not change prior law, but addresses a common misconception.] Cf. § 2–201 at 24–29.

B. SEALS

The affixing of a seal to a lease contract (or an offer to enter into a lease) does not render the writing [record] a "sealed instrument" with particular legal significance. § 2A–203. Cf. § 2–203 at pp. 29–30.

4. TERMS, CONSTRUCTION, AND INTERPRETATION

Course of dealing and usage of trade

See §§ 1–303(b)–(d) (defining "course of perform-ance," "course of dealing," and "trade usage"), 1–201(b)(3), (12), (40) (defining "agreement," "contract," and "term") at pp. 31–32.

Course of performance

If a lease contract involves repeated occasions for per-formance by either party with knowledge of the nature of the performance and opportunity for objection to it by the other, any course of performance accepted or acquiesced in without objection is relevant to determine the meaning of the lease agreement. §§ 2A–207(1), 2A–103(1)(k) and (*l*) ("lease agreement" and "lease contract" defined). See § 1–303(a) (2001) ("course of performance" defined). Cf. §§ 2–208(1), 1–201(b)(3) and (12) at p. 32.

As to construction of lease contract, see 2A–207(2); as to modification and waiver, see § 2A–207(3). See § 1–

303(e), (f) (2001). See also § 1–302 (variation by agreement). Cf. § 2–208(2), (3) at pp. 32–33.

5. PAROL EVIDENCE RULE

Terms set forth in a writing [record] intended by the parties as a complete and exclusive statement of their agreement may not be contradicted by evidence of any prior agreement or of a contemporaneous oral agreement. §§ 2A–202, 1–201(b)(3) ("agreement" defined). (Of course, the terms set forth in the writing [record] may be supplemented by evidence of course of dealing, usage of trade, or course of performance. §§ 2A–202(a), 1–303, 2A–207 [2A–202(1)(a) (2003)].)

If the writing [record] is not intended as a complete and exclusive statement of the terms of the agreement, evidence of consistent additional terms may be admitted. § 2A–202(b) [2A–202(1)(b), see new 2A–202(2) (2003)]. Cf. § 2–202 at p. 35.

C. PROPERTY INCIDENTS OF THE LEASE CONTRACT

1. TITLE TO AND POSSESSION OF GOODS

With some exceptions, each provision of Article 2A applies regardless of whether the lessor or a third party has title to the goods, and whether the lessor, the lessee, or a third party has possession of the goods. § 2A–302. Cf. §§ 2–401, 9–202 at pp. 41–50, 424 (para. [4]).

2. SPECIAL PROPERTY

Section 2A–217, which discusses identification of goods to a contract, omits any discussion of whether the lessee has a "special property" in the leased goods, deeming the concept irrelevant to the leasing context. § 2A–217 Comment. Cf. §§ 2–401(1), 2–501 at p. 50.

3.   INSURABLE INTEREST

A lessee *obtains* an insurable interest when existing goods are identified to the lease contract. § 2A–218(1), see § 2A–217 (re: identification). The lessor *retains* an insurable interest until (1) the lessee exercises an option to buy and (2) risk of loss passes to the lessee. § 2A–218(3), see § 2A–219. A lessee with an insurable interest in the goods has standing to sue third parties for injury to the goods. § 2A–531(1). Cf. §§ 2–501, 2–722 at pp. 51–52. (See § 2A–218(5) (2003) re: the common practice of shifting the responsibility and cost of insuring the goods by contract.)

4.   SECURITY INTEREST

Retention or creation of a security interest does not create a lease under Article 2A. § 2A–103(1)(j) [2A–103(1)(p) (2003)]. Instead, Article 9 (Secured Transactions) applies to a transaction that creates a security interest regardless of its form or the name the parties have given it, e.g., a self-styled "lease." §§ 9–109(a)(1) and Comment 2, 9–203 Comment 3. Whether a transaction creates a lease or a security interest is determined by the facts of each case. § 1–203. See hypotheticals at § 2A–103 Comment (j). [For discussion of "true" leases vs. security interest "leases," see pp. 52, 437–442.] [*2010 Amendment*. [The parties' subjective intent regarding how the transaction is to be characterized does not affect whether Article 9 applies. § 9–109 Comment 2.]

5.   RISK OF LOSS

Lease other than finance lease

For non-finance leases, risk of loss is retained by the lessor and does not pass to the lessee. § 2A–219(1).

Finance lease

For finance leases, risk of loss passes to the lessee. § 2A–219(1). Finance leases are discussed at Part Two, A supra at pp. 170–171. For hypos, see §§ 2A–103(1)(g) [2A–103(1)(*l*) (2003)] and Comment (g), 2A–407 Comments.

Risk of loss in the absence of default

In the absence of default, if risk of loss is to pass to the lessee at an unspecified time, the following rules apply:

1.   If the lease contract requires or authorizes the goods to be shipped by carrier:

a.   *Shipment contract.* If the contract does not require delivery at a particular destination, risk of loss passes to the lessee when the goods are duly delivered to the carrier. § 2A–219(2)(a)(i). See § 2A–529(1)(a) (lessor's action for rent), cf. § 2–709(1)(a) (action for the price). Cf. § 2–509(1)(a) at p. 53.

b.   *Destination contract.* If the contract requires delivery at a particular destination and the carrier duly tenders the goods there, the risk of loss passes to the lessee when the goods are tendered for the lessee to take delivery. § 2A–219(2)(a)(ii). Cf. § 2–509(1)(b) at p. 54.

2.   If the goods are held by a bailee to be delivered without being moved:

Risk of loss passes to the lessee upon the bailee's acknowledgment of the lessee's right to possession of the goods. § 2A–219(2)(b). Cf. § 2–509(2)(b) at pp. 54–55.

3.   Residuary rules. (In any case not within 1 or 2 above):

a.   If Lessor (or Supplier in a finance lease) is a merchant, the risk of loss passes to the lessee upon the lessee's receipt of the goods. § 2A–219(2)(c), see § 2A–103(1)(g) ("finance lease" defined) [2A–103(1)(*l*) (2003)]. Cf. § 2–509(3) at p. 55.

b.   If Lessor is not a merchant, risk passes to the lessee on tender of delivery. § 2A–219(2)(c). Cf. § 2–509(3). [*2003 Amend.* Section 2A–219(2)(b) adds "on acknowledgment by the bailee *to the lessee,*" thus clearing up some confusion in the case law as to which party must be given the acknowledgment. See, e.g., Jason's Foods, Inc. v. Peter Eckrich & Sons, Inc., 774 F.2d 214 (7th Cir.1985) (Posner decision).

Section 2A–219(2)(c) has been amended so that risk of loss for both *Merchant* and *Non-merchant* passes upon Lessee's *receipt* of goods.]

Effect of default by lessor on risk of loss

When the risk of loss is to pass to the lessee at an unrelated time,

a.   If a tender or delivery of goods fails to conform to the lease contract, so as to create a right of rejection, the risk of their loss remains with the lessor (or supplier in a finance lease) until the lessor's cure or the lessee's acceptance. §§ 2A–220(1)(a), 2A–509 (rightful rejection), 2A–513 (cure), 2A–515 (acceptance). Cf. § 2–510(1) at pp. 55–56.

b.   If the lessee rightfully revokes acceptance, the lessee, to the extent of any deficiency in its own effective insurance coverage, may treat the risk of loss as having remained with the lessor from the beginning. §§ 2A–220(1)(b), 2A–517. Cf. 2–510(2) at p. 56.

Effect of default by lessee on risk of loss

The lessor (or supplier in a finance lease) may, to the extent of any deficiency in its effective insurance coverage, treat the risk of loss as resting on the lessee for a commercially reasonable time if: (a) conforming goods are already identified to a lease contract, and (b) the lessee repudiates or is otherwise in default under the lease contract. (This rule applies regardless of whether the parties agreed by contract that risk of loss is to pass to the lessee.) §§ 2A–220(2), 2A–217 (re: identification), see § 2A–103(1)(g) ("finance lease" defined) [2A–103(1)(*l*) (2003)]. Cf. § 2–510(3) at pp. 56–57.

Casualty to identified goods

If a lease contract requires goods that are identified when the lease contract is made, and (1) *before* delivery, the goods suffer casualty without fault of the lessee, the lessor, or the supplier, or (2) *before* risk of loss passes to the lessee pursuant to the lease agreement or § 2A–219, the goods suffer casualty, if the loss is total, the lease contract is terminated. §§ 2A–221(a), 2A–217 (identification). Cf. § 2–613(a). Where the loss is partial or the goods have deteriorated, see § 2A–221(b). Cf. § 2–613 at pp. 117–118.

D. LESSOR'S WARRANTY OBLIGATIONS

1. EXPRESS WARRANTIES

The following constitute express warranties:

(1) The goods will conform to any *affirmation of fact* the lessor makes to the lessee relating to the goods.

(2) The goods will conform to any *promise* the lessor makes to the lessee relating to the goods.

(3) The goods will conform to any *description* of them.

(4) The whole of the goods will conform to any *sample* (or model) of the goods.

Basis of the bargain

For an express warranty to be created, the affirmation, promise, description, or sample must become "part of the basis of the bargain." § 2A–210(1).

Fact vs. opinion

Formal words such as "warrant" or "guaranty" are not necessary to the creation of an express warranty, but an affirmation merely of the value of the goods or a statement of commendation does not create a warranty. § 2A–210(2). Cf. § 2–313 at pp. 58–61.

Note: All of Article 2's express and implied warranties are included in Article 2A, revised to reflect the differences between a sale of goods and a lease of goods. Leases and sales of goods are sufficiently similar to justify this decision. § 2A–210 Comment.

[*2003 Amend.* Article 2A does not contain provisions analogous to §§ 2–313A and 2–313B (re: obligations to remote purchasers). § 2A–101 Comment (2003 Amendments).]

2. WARRANTIES AGAINST INTERFERENCE AND INFRINGEMENT

A lease contract includes a warranty that, for the lease term, no person holds a claim to or interest in the goods arising from any act or omission of the lessor (other than a claim by way of infringement), which will interfere with the lessee's enjoyment of its leasehold interest. § 2A–211(1). Note: This section is modeled on § 2–312 [Warranty of Title], with modifications to reflect the limited interest transferred by a lease. Although the warranty of quiet possession was abolished with respect to sales of goods, § 2A–211(1) reinstates it with respect to leases. § 2A–211 Comment. Cf. § 2–312 at pp. 57–58. As to warranties against infringement, see § 2A–211(2), (3). Cf. § 2–312(3).

[*2003 Amend.* A lessor (other than a finance lessor) warrants (1) that no person holds an interest that will interfere with the lessee's enjoyment of its leasehold (a warranty of quiet enjoyment) and (2) the transfer does not unreasonably expose the lessee to litigation, i.e., when a third person has or asserts a "colorable" claim to, or interest in, the goods. § 2A–211(1) and Comments 1 and 2. As to the warranty against infringement, see § 2A–211(3) and Comment 3.]

3. IMPLIED WARRANTY OF MERCHANTABILITY

Except in a finance lease, a warranty that the goods will be merchantable is implied in a lease contract *if* the lessor is a *merchant* with respect to goods of that kind. §§ 2A–212(1), 2–104(1) ("merchant" defined). The warranty requires that the goods be at least fit for the *ordinary* purposes for which goods of that type are used. § 2A–212(2)(c). Cf. § 2–314(1), (2)(c) at pp. 62–64.

Note: The lessor's function in a finance lease is extremely limited. § 2A–103(1)(g) ("finance lease" defined) [2A–103(1)(*l*) (2003)] and Comment (g). Thus, the lessee looks to the *supplier* of the goods for warranties. That expectation is reflected in § 2A–209(1): "The benefit of a supplier's promises to the lessor under the supply contract and of all warranties, whether express or implied, including . . . [in some cases warranties of a manufacturer provided under] the supply contract, extends to the lessee to the extent of the lessee's leasehold interest under a finance lease related to the supply contract. . . ." See also § 2A–209 Comment 1.

Other implied warranties may arise from course of dealing or usage of trade. §§ 2A–212(3), 1–303 ("course of dealing" and "trade usage" defined), cf. § 2–314(3).

[For guidance in resolving the tension between merchantability in warranty and defect in tort, see § 2A–212 Comment 2 (2003).]

4. IMPLIED WARRANTY OF FITNESS FOR PARTICULAR PURPOSE

Except in a finance lease, if the lessor at the time the lease contract is made has reason to know (1) of any *particular* purpose for which the goods are required and (2) that the lessee is relying on the lessor's skill or judgment to select or furnish suitable goods, the lease contract will include an implied warranty that the goods will be fit for that purpose. § 2A–213, cf. § 2A–212(2)(c) (implied warranty of merchantability). Cf. §§ 2–315, 2–314(2)(c) at pp. 64–65.

With respect to a finance lease, see Note to Implied Warranty of Merchantability immediately above and § 2A–209(1) and Comments.

5. CUMULATION AND CONFLICT OF WARRANTIES

Warranties (express or implied) must be construed as (1) consistent with each other and (2) cumulative, but if that construction is unreasonable, the parties' intention determines which warranty is dominant. § 2A–215 contains rules for ascertaining that intention. Cf. § 2–317 at p. 65.

6. DEFENSES TO WARRANTY ACTIONS

A. CAUSATION

Causation language in the following damages sections provides a defense, where relevant, to a warranty action.

1. "Loss resulting in the ordinary course of events" § 2A–519(3).

2.   "Unless special circumstances show proximate damages of a different amount" § 2A–519(4).

3.   "Incidental damages resulting from a lessor's default" § 2A–520(1).

4.   "Consequential damages resulting from a lessor's default include:

a.   any loss resulting from ... requirements ... of which the lessor ... had reason to know ...; and

b.   injury to person or property proximately resulting from any breach of warranty." § 2A–520(2). Cf. §§ 2–714, 2–715 at pp. 65–66.

B. STATUTE OF LIMITATIONS

An action for default under a lease must be commenced within 4 years after the cause of action accrued. § 2A–506. See Part Two, G, 2, C infra. Cf. § 2–725 at pp. 66–67.

[*2003 Amend*. Section 2A–506 (1) (second sentence) now reads, "Except in a consumer lease or an action for indemnity, the original lease agreement may reduce the period of limitations to not less than one year."]

C. NOTICE OF BREACH

Within a reasonable time after the lessee discovers or should have discovered any default, the lessee must notify the lessor, and the supplier under a finance lease, or be barred from any remedy against the party not notified. § 2A–516(3)(a). See § 2A–103(1)(g), (x) and Comment (g) ("finance lease" and "supplier" defined) [2A–103(1)(*l*), (ff) (2003)]. Cf. § 2–607(3)(a) at pp. 67–68.

[*2003 Amend*. Section 2A–516(3)(a) now concludes, "failure to give timely notice bars the lessee from a remedy only to the extent that the lessor or supplier is prejudiced by the failure."]

7. EXCLUSION OR MODIFICATION
OF WARRANTIES

Express warranties

Express warranties and disclaimers are to be construed as consistent. If the construction is not reasonable, the negation is inoperative. § 2A–214(1). Cf. § 2–316(1).

Implied warranties

Implied warranties can be excluded or modified as follows:

1. *Examination.* If, before entering into the lease contract, the lessee has examined the goods, etc., or has refused to examine the goods, [after a demand by the lessor] there is no implied warranty with regard to defects that an examination ought to have revealed. § 2A–214(3)(b). Cf. § 2–316(3)(b).

2. *Course of dealing, course of performance, or usage of trade.* An implied warranty may also be excluded or modified by course of dealing, course of performance, or usage of trade. § 2A–214(3)(c). Cf. § 2–316(3)(c).

3. *Language.* Unless the circumstances indicate otherwise, all implied warranties are excluded by expressions like "AS IS," or "WITH ALL FAULTS," or other language that in common understanding calls the lessee's attention to the exclusion of warranties and makes plain that there is no implied warranty, so long as the language is in writing [a record] and conspicuous. §§ 2A–214(3)(a), 1–201(b)(10) ("conspicuous" defined), 2A–103(1)(d) (2003) (same). Cf. § 2–316(3)(a).

Other language may be used to exclude or modify implied warranties:

a. To exclude or modify the implied warranty of merchantability or any part of it, the language must mention "merchantability," be in a writing [record], and be conspicuous. §§ 2A–214(2), 1–201(b)(10) ("conspicuous" defined), 2A–103(1)(d) (2003) (same). Cf. § 2–316(2).

b.   Any exclusion or modification of an implied warranty of fitness must be written and conspicuous, e.g., "THERE IS NO WARRANTY THAT THE GOODS WILL BE FIT FOR A PARTICULAR PURPOSE." §§ 2A–214(2), 1–201(b)(10) ("conspicuous" defined). Cf. § 2–316(2).

[*2003 Amend.* Excluding or modifying the implied warranty of *merchantability* in a *consumer lease* requires the following language: "THE LESSOR UNDERTAKES NO RESPONSIBILITY FOR THE QUALITY OF THE GOODS EXCEPT AS OTHERWISE PROVIDED IN THIS CONTRACT." (The language must be in a record and conspicuous; in any other contract the language must mention merchantability.) §§ 2A–214(2), 1–201(b)(10), (31) ("conspicuous" and "record" defined); § 2A–103(1)(d), (f), (cc) ("conspicuous," "consumer lease," and "record" defined). Excluding all implied warranties of *fitness* in a *consumer lease* requires the following language: "THE LESSOR ASSUMES NO RESPONSIBILITY THAT THE GOODS WILL BE FIT FOR ANY PARTICULAR PURPOSE FOR WHICH YOU MAY BE LEASING THESE GOODS, EXCEPT AS OTHERWISE PROVIDED IN THE CONTRACT." (The exclusion or modification must be in a record and be conspicuous; in any other contract, the language is sufficient if it states, e.g., "THERE ARE NO WARRANTIES THAT EXTEND BEYOND THE DESCRIPTION ON THE FACE HEREOF.") §§ 2A–214(2), 1–201(b)(10), (31) ("conspicuous" and "record" defined), § 2A–103(1)(d), (f), (cc) ("conspicuous," "consumer lease," and "record" defined). Section 2A–214(2) (last sentence) reads, "Language that satisfies the requirements of this subsection for a consumer lease also satisfies its requirements for any other lease contract."]

Warranties against interference or infringement

Excluding or modifying these warranties requires a conspicuous writing unless the circumstances give the lessee reason to know that the goods are being leased subject to a claim or interest of any person. §§ 2A–214(4), 1–201(b)(10) ("conspicuous" defined). Cf. § 2–312(2).

[*2003 Amend.* Section 2A–211(4) (moved from 2A–214(4)), deals with the disclaimer or modification of the warranty of title or against infringement, and it states the general standard: to be effective as against an immediate lessee, the language must be conspicuous and in a record. § 2A–211 Comment 4, § 1–201(b)(10), (31) ("conspicuous" and "record" defined); § 2A–103(1)(d), (cc) (same).]

Unconscionability

If a court finds a lease contract or any clause of a lease contract to have been unconscionable at the time it was made, see § 2A–108(1) and (3). Cf. § 2–302. As to consumer leases, see §§ 2A–108(2) and (4), 2A–103(1)(e) ("consumer lease" defined). [2A–103(1)(f) (2003)].

Cf. §§ 2–312(2), 2–316 at pp. 68–74.

8. LIMITATION OF REMEDIES FOR BREACH OF WARRANTY

See §§ 2A–214(4), 2A–503, 2A–504 (liquidated damages), 2A–108 (2003) (unconscionability) at Part Two, G, 2, A infra. Cf. §§ 2–316(4), 2–718, 2–719 at pp. 74–75.

9. THIRD–PARTY BENEFICIARIES OF WARRANTIES (PRIVITY)

A warranty to or for the benefit of a lessee under Article 2A extends to any person who may reasonably be expected to use, consume, or be affected by the goods and who is injured by breach of the warranty. § 2A–216 (Alternative C). As to vouching-in procedures, see § 2A–516(4). Cf. §§ 2–318, 2–607(5) at pp. 75–77.

10.   WARRANTIES, ETC., UNDER FINANCE LEASE

The function performed by the *lessor* in a finance lease is extremely limited. § 2A–103(1)(g) ("finance lease" defined) [2A–103(1)(*l*) (2003)] and Comment (g). See Part Two, A supra. The lessee looks to the *supplier* of the goods for warranties. Thus, the benefit of the supplier's promises to the lessor under the supply contract and of all warranties (express or implied) under the supply contract, including in some cases a manufacturer's warranty, extend to the lessee to the extent of the lessee's leasehold interest. § 2A–209(1), see § 2A–407. As to modification of the supply contract and imposition of duties on the lessee, see § 2A–209(2) and (3). Cf. § 9–405 at p. 566.

E.   REPUDIATION, SUBSTITUTED PERFORMANCE, AND EXCUSED PERFORMANCE OF A LEASE CONTRACT

1.   REPUDIATION

A.   INSECURITY AND ADEQUATE ASSURANCES

If reasonable grounds for insecurity arise with respect to the performance of either party, the insecure party (1) may demand in writing [a record] adequate assurance of due performance and, until he receives that assurance, (2) may suspend any performance for which he has not already received the agreed return. (3) *Repudiation* of the lease contract occurs if adequate assurance of due performance is not provided to the insecure party within a reasonable time (not to exceed 30 days) after the other party receives the demand. § 2A–401; see §§ 2A–303

Comment 5, 2A–510(1) (installment contracts). Cf. §§ 2–609, 2–210(6) [2–210(2)(c) (2003)], 2–612(2) at pp. 87–89.

B.   ANTICIPATORY REPUDIATION

If either party repudiates with respect to a performance, not yet due, the loss of which will *substantially impair* the value of the lease contract to the other, the aggrieved party may (1) await retraction of repudiation, (2) demand adequate assurance of future performance, or (3) resort to any right or remedy upon default. § 2A–402. As to retraction of anticipatory repudiation, see § 2A–403. Cf. §§ 2–610, 2–611 at pp. 86–87.

[*2003 Amend.* New § 2A–402(2) explains when a party has repudiated a performance obligation.]

2.   SUBSTITUTED PERFORMANCE

If, without fault of the lessee, lessor, or supplier, the agreed manner of performance becomes commercially impracticable but a commercially reasonable substitute is available, the substitute must be tendered and accepted. § 2A–404(1). If the agreed means or manner of payment fails, see § 2A–404(2). Cf. § 2–614 at pp. 118–119.

3.   EXCUSED PERFORMANCE

Delay in delivery or non-delivery by a lessor or supplier is not a default under the lease contract if the agreed performance has been made impracticable by the occurrence of a contingency the *nonoccurrence* of which was a basic assumption on which the lease contract was made. Of course, the lessor must notify the lessee (in case of a finance lease, the supplier must notify the lessor and, if known, the lessee), of the delay or non-delivery. §§ 2A–405(a) and (c), 2A–103(1)(g) ("finance lease" defined)

[2A–103(1)(*l*) (2003)]; see § 2A–404 (substituted performance).

If delay in delivery or non-delivery affects only part of the lessor's or supplier's capacity to perform, see § 2A–405(b), (c). Where delay in delivery or non-delivery has been made impracticable by compliance with any applicable governmental regulation, see § 2A–405(a), (c). As to the appropriate procedure on excused performance, see § 2A–406. As to casualty to identified goods, see § 2A–221. Cf. §§ 2–615, 2–616, 2–613 at pp. 116–117.

4. IRREVOCABLE PROMISES: FINANCE LEASES

In the case of a *finance lease* that is not a *consumer lease*, the lessee's promises under the lease contract become irrevocable and independent upon the lessee's acceptance of the goods. § 2A–407(1); § 2A–103(1)(e), (g), (j) ("consumer lease," "finance lease," and "lease" defined) [2A–103(1)(f), (*l*), (p) (2003)]. Cf. § 9–404. See Part Two, A supra re: leases, finance leases, and consumer leases. Re: acceptance of goods, see § 2A–515. (Note that § 2A–407 extends the benefits of the classic "hell or high water" clause to a finance lease that is not a consumer lease. This section is self executing; *no special provision* need be added to the contract. § 2A–407 Comment 1.)

Example: A (potential lessor) has been contacted by B (potential lessee) to discuss the lease of a line of equipment B has recently ordered from C (supplier/manufacturer of the goods). The negotiation is completed, and A and B sign a lease with a 60 month term. B (as buyer) assigns the purchase order to A. This transaction should qualify as a finance lease. § 2A–103(1)(g), (j) [2A–103(1)(*l*), (p) (2003)].

Assume C delivers the line of equipment to B's place of business. After C installs the goods and B tests them, B accepts the goods by signing a certificate of delivery and acceptance, a copy of which B sends to A and C. One year later, the line of equipment malfunctions, and B falls behind in its manufacturing schedule.

Because the transaction is a finance lease, A makes no warranty of fitness or merchantability to B. §§ 2A–212(1), 2A–213. See Part Two, D, 3 and 4 supra. B's obligation to pay rent to A continues because the obligation became *irrevocable* and *independent* when B accepted the equipment. § 2A–407(1). B has no right of set-off with respect to any payment still due under the lease. § 2A–508(6) [2A–508(5) (2003)].

However, B may have another remedy. Despite the lack of privity between B and C, now that B has assigned the purchase order with C to A, B may have a claim against C. § 2A–209(1). See Part Two, D, 10 supra. See hypothetical at § 2A–407 Comments 3–5.

Section 2A–407 does not address whether a "hell or high water" clause is enforceable when included in (1) a finance lease that *is* a consumer lease, or (2) a lease that is *not* a finance lease. § 2A–407(3). See §§ 2A–104(1)(c) (effect of consumer protection law), 2A–103(4) (referencing Article 1), 9–403 (agreement not to assert defenses against assignee), 9–404 (rights of and claims & defenses against assignee). See discussion of consumer protection legislation at Part Three, B, 2, C infra at pp. 273–276; see also p. 565. The following "hell or high water" provision was enforced in In re O.P.M. Leasing Servs., 21 B.R. 993, 1006 (Bankr. S.D.N.Y. 1982) (cited in § 2A–407 Comment 6):

> (West Virginia's [Lessee's]) obligation to pay directly to such assignee [of Lessor] the amounts due from Lessee under any Equipment Schedule (whether as rent or otherwise) shall be *absolutely unconditional* and shall be payable whether or not *any* Equipment Schedule is terminated by operation of law, any act of the parties or otherwise . . . [Emphasis added].

Also read § 2A–407(2) and Comment 7.

F.   EFFECT OF LEASE CONTRACT

1.   VALIDITY AND ENFORCEABILITY

A.   GENERAL RULE

Generally, a lease contract is effective and enforceable between the parties and against third parties. Exceptions to this rule arise when Article 2A provides a specific rule to the contrary. Enforceability depends on the contract's meeting the requirements of the statute of frauds (§ 2A–201). Enforceability is also a function of the contract's conformity to Article 1's principles of construction and interpretation (§ 2A–103(4)). The effectiveness or enforceability of a lease contract does not depend on whether the lease contract or financing statement has been filed (re: priority of fixtures, see § 2A–309(9)). § 2A–301 and Comment 2. Further, § 2A–302 provides that separation of ownership and possession *per se* does not affect the enforceability of the lease contract. § 2A–302 Comment. Cf. §§ 9–201, 9–202 at pp. 449–450.

B.   TRANSFER OF RIGHTS AND DUTIES

On February 1, A (prime lessor) leased six combines to B (prime lessee/sublessor), a corporation engaged in the business of farming, for a 12-month term. On March 1, may B sublease two combines to C for an 11 month term?

Answer: Yes. Generally, any interest of a party under a lease contract, including subleases, may be transferred. However, the rule has two significant qualifications:

1.   If the prime lease contract between A and B prohibits B from subleasing the combines, or makes such a sublease an event of default, § 2A–303(2) applies; thus, while B's interest under the prime lease contract may be transferred under the sublease to C, A may have a remedy

pursuant to § 2A–303(4). See § 2A–303(7) (in a consumer lease, the prohibition or default provision must be specific, by a writing [record], and conspicuous).

2.   Absent a prohibition or default provision in the prime lease contract, A might be able to argue that the sublease to C materially increases A's risk; thus, while B's interest under the prime lease may be transferred under the sublease to C, A may have a remedy pursuant to § 2A–303(4). §§ 2A–303(2), 2A–303(4)(b)(ii). Cf. Bankruptcy Code § 365(b)(1) (executory contracts and unexpired leases); cf. §§ 2–210(6) [2–210(2)(c) (2003)] (assignment that delegates performance), 2–609 (right to adequate assurance of performance). See also § 9–403 through 9–406 (assignment under Article 9); § 9–407 (restrictions on assignment) and Comments 2 and 3.

As to transfers of Lessor's residual interest in the goods, see §§ 2A–303(2), 2A–103(1)(q) [2A–103(1)(w) (2003)]; as to an assignment of "the lease" or of "all my rights under the lease," see § 2A–303(5). Cf. § 2–210(5) [2–210(3) (2003)]; as to delegation of performance, see § 2A–303(6). Cf. § 2–210(1) and (6) [2–210(1) and (2)(a) (2003)]; as to transfer of a right to damages for default, etc., see § 2A–303(3). Cf. § 2–210(2) (second sentence) [2–210(1)(a) (second sentence) (2003)].

See § 2A–301 Comment 3 (Hypothetical (a)–(d)). Cf. §§ 2–210, 9–403 through 9–406 at pp. 36–38, 274–275, 562–567.

2.   PRIORITY OF VARIOUS CLAIMS TO GOODS

A.   LESSOR'S SUBSEQUENT LEASE OF GOODS

"Sections 2A–304 [discussed here] and 2A–305 [discussed immediately below] are twins that deal with good faith transferees of goods subject to the lease contract. Section 2A–304 creates a set of rules with respect to transfers by the lessor of goods subject to a lease contract; the transferee considered is a subsequent lessee of the goods. The priority dispute covered here is between the *subsequent* lessee and the *original* lessee of the goods...." § 2A–301 Comment 4(c) [Emphasis added].

Example: A leases goods to B. Later, A leases the goods to C. Will C take subject to the lease contract between A and B? Answer: Generally, C—a subsequent lessee from a lessor of goods under an existing lease contract—obtains (to the extent of the leasehold interest transferred) the leasehold interest in the goods that A *had* or *had power* to transfer, and takes subject to the existing lease contract. But a subsequent lessee (C) in ordinary course of business from a lessor (A) who is a merchant dealing in goods of that kind, to whom the existing lessee (B) entrusted the goods before the interest of the subsequent lessee (C) became enforceable against the lessor (A), obtains (to the extent of the leasehold interest transferred) the lessor's (A's) and existing lessee's (B's) rights to the goods and takes free of the existing lease contract. §§ 2A–304(1) and (2), 2–403(3) (entrustment). Cf. § 2–403(2).

As to a lessor with voidable title, see § 2A–304(1)(a)–(d), cf. § 2–403(1); as to lessor's rights to dispose of goods after a lessee's default, see §§ 2A–527(4), 2A–304(1); as to certificates of title, see § 2A–304(3). Note that § 2A–304(1) is subject to § 2A–303 discussed at Part Two, F, 1, B supra. Cf. § 2–403 at pp. 151–158.

[*2003 Amend.* See §§ 2A–104(2), 2A–105(3).]

B.   LESSEE'S SALE OR SUBLEASE OF GOODS

Like § 2A–304, § 2A–305 deals with good faith transferees of goods subject to the lease contract. "Section 2A–305 creates a set of rules with respect to transfers by the lessee of goods subject to a lease contract; the transferees considered are buyers of the goods or sublessees of the goods. The priority dispute covered here is between the *transferee* and the *lessor* of the goods...." § 2A–301 Comment 4(c). See § 2A–301 Comment 3(e) [Emphasis added].

Example: A leases goods to B. Later, B either sells or leases the goods to C. Will C take subject to the lease contract between A and B? Answer: Generally, C—a buyer or sublessee from the lessee (B) of goods under an existing lease contract—obtains (to the extent of the interest transferred) the leasehold interest in the goods that B *had* or *had power* to transfer, and takes subject to the existing lease contract. But C, as either a buyer in ordinary course of business (BOCB) or a sublessee in ordinary course of business (LOCB), from a lessee (B) who is a merchant dealing in goods of that kind, to whom the lessor (A) entrusted the goods, obtains (to the extent of the interest transferred) the lessor's (A's) and lessee's (B's) rights to the goods and takes free of the existing lease contract. §§ 2A–305(1) and (2), 2–403(3) (entrustment). Cf. § 2–403(2).

As to a lessee with a voidable leasehold interest, see § 2A–305(1)(a)–(c). Cf. § 2–403(1); as to a merchant lessee's duties to dispose of rightfully rejected goods for the lessor's account, see §§ 2A–511(4), 2A–305(1); as to certificates of title, see § 2A–305(3). Note that § 2A–305(1) is subject to § 2A–303, discussed at Part Two, F, 1, B supra. Cf. § 2–403 at pp. 151–158.

[*2003 Amend.* See §§ 2A–104(2), 2A–105(3).]

C. PRIORITY OF LIENS ARISING BY OPERATION OF LAW

Section 2A–306 creates a rule governing priority disputes between holders of liens for services or materials that are furnished with respect to goods subject to a lease contract, and the lessor or lessee under that contract. § 2A–301 Comment 4(d).

Example: Lessor leases goods to Lessee. Later, Lessee—in satisfaction of its maintenance covenant—takes the goods to Repairman for maintenance and repairs. Repairman asserts a possessory lien to secure payment of the charges. Do Lessor and Lessee's interests have priority over this lien that arises by operation of law? Answer:

> If a person in the ordinary course of [his or her] business furnishes services or materials with respect to goods subject to a lease contract, a lien upon those goods in the possession of that person given by statute or rule of law for those materials or services takes priority over any interest of the lessor or lessee under the lease contract or [Article 2A] [1] unless the lien is created by statute and the statute provides otherwise or [2] unless the lien is created by rule of law and the rule of law provides otherwise.

§ 2A–306; see particularly, § 2A–301 Comment 3(f) (enforceability of lease contract). Cf. § 9–333 at pp. 512–513.

D. PRIORITY OF (1) LIENS ARISING BY ATTACHMENT OR LEVY, (2) SECURITY INTERESTS, AND (3) OTHER CLAIMS TO GOODS

Section 2A–307 governs priority disputes between (1) a lessee and creditors of the lessor and (2) a lessor and creditors of the lessee. § 2A–301 Comment 4(d).

Example 1: Lessor leases goods to Lessee. Later, *Lessee* is in financial straits, and one of Lessee's creditors obtains a judgment against Lessee. If Creditor levies on Lessee's leasehold interest in the goods, who will prevail? Answer: Unless the levying creditor also holds a repairman's lien covered by § 2A–306, discussed immediately above, the judgment creditor will take its interest *subject to* Lessor's contractual rights. § 2A–307(1), see § 2A–301 Comment 3(g).

Example 2: Lessor leases goods to Lessee. Later, *Lessor* is in financial straits and Lessor's creditor holds the judgment. The judgment creditor takes *subject to* the lease contract *unless* the *lien* attached to the goods *before* the lease contract became enforceable. §§ 2A–307(2), 2A–103(1)(r) [2A–103(1)(x) (2003)], see § 2A–301 Comment 3(g).

Exceptions to Section 2A–307(2) are provided in (i) § 2A–306, priority of liens arising by operation of law, discussed immediately above; (ii) § 2A–308, special rights of creditors, discussed below at Part Two, F, 2, E infra; and (iii) § 2A–307(3) regarding the priority of a lessee against the security interest of a lessee's creditor, which is presented presently:

Lessee vs. secured party creditor of lessor. A lessee takes a leasehold interest subject to a security interest held by the lessor's creditor, with these exceptions:

(1) § 9–317 (interests that take priority over, or take free of, a security interest).

(2) § 9–321 (lessee of goods in ordinary course of business).

(3) § 9–323(f) and (g) and Comments 2 and 6 (future advances).

E. SPECIAL RIGHTS OF LESSOR'S OR SELLER'S CREDITORS

Section 2A–308 governs transfers and preferences claimed to be fraudulent. § 2A–301 Comment 4(e). Subsection (1) states that a creditor of a lessor who is in possession of goods subject to a lease may treat the lease as void if, as against the creditor, Lessor's retention of possession is fraudulent under any statute or rule of law, e.g., Uniform Fraudulent Conveyance Act, or Uniform Fraudulent Transfer Act. Note, however, that retention of possession of goods for a commercially reasonable time after the lease becomes enforceable is not fraudulent. § 2A–308. Cf. § 2–402(2). As to fraudulent transfer or voidable preference, see § 2A–308(2). Cf. § 2–402(3)(b).

Subsection (3) states a new rule with respect to sale-leaseback transactions, i.e., transactions in which Seller sells goods to Buyer but retains possession of the goods pursuant to a lease contract between Buyer as lessor and Seller as lessee. Notwithstanding any statute or rule of law that would treat such retention as fraud, whether *per se* or *prima facie,* the retention is not fraudulent if Buyer bought for value and in good faith. (This provision overrides § 2–402(2) to the extent it would otherwise apply to such a transaction.) § 2A–308(3) and Comment, see § 2A–302 discussed at Part Two, F, 1, A supra. Cf. § 2–402(2) and (3)(b) (retention of possession as fraudulent) at pp. 163–164.

F. LESSOR'S AND LESSEE'S RIGHTS IN FIXTURES

Section 2A–309 governs priority disputes between various third parties and a lessor of fixtures with respect thereto. §§ 2A–301 Comment 4(f), 2A–309(1)(a).

Lessor vs. subsequent land mortgagee

Basically, Lessor has priority if its interest is "perfected" by a "fixture filing" before the mortgagee's interest is recorded. Simply: first to file or record prevails. § 2A–309(1)(a) and (b) and (e), (4)(b), (9). §§ 9–501 (filing office), 9–502 (contents of filing), 9–505 (other law); cf. 9–334 (priority in fixtures, etc.). Note: Even though the lease agreement does not create a security interest, the interest of a lessor of fixtures, including the lessor's residual interest in leased goods that are or are to become fixtures per Article 9, is perfected by a fixture filing. § 2A–309(9).

Lessor vs. prior land mortgagee

Basically, a lessor's "purchase money lease" in the fixture has priority as against a mortgagee's *prior* recorded real estate interest, provided that Lessor's "fixture filing" is filed in the real estate records before the goods become fixtures or within 10 days thereafter. § 2A–309(1)(b) and (c), (4)(a), (9). See §§ 9–501 (filing office), 9–502 (contents of filing), 9–505 (other law). Cf. § 9–334 (priority in fixtures, etc.) (note 20-day grace period at § 9–334(d)(3)).

As to the priority of a lessor of certain readily removable fixtures, regardless of whether the interest is perfected, see § 2A–309(5); as to a construction mortgage, see § 2A–309(1)(d), (6).

As to removal of fixtures, see § 2A–309(8), cf. § 2A–310(5). Cf. § 9–334 at pp. 520–523.

G. LESSOR'S AND LESSEE'S RIGHTS IN ACCESSIONS

Section 2A–310 governs priority disputes between various third parties and a lessor of accessions with respect thereto. §§ 2A–301 Comment 4(f), 2A–310(1).

With two exceptions, the interest of a lessor or lessee under a lease contract entered into *before* the goods become accessions is *superior* to all interests in the whole. § 2A–310(1) and (2).

Two exceptions

The interest of a lessor or lessee under a lease contract is *subordinate* to the interest of (a) a buyer or lessee in ordinary course of business of any interest in the whole acquired *after* the goods become accessions; or (b) a creditor with a security interest in the whole perfected before the lease contract was made, to the *extent* that the creditor makes *subsequent* advances without knowledge of the lease contract. § 2A–310(4).

As to removal of accessions, see § 2A–310(5), cf. § 2A–309(8). Cf. § 9–335 at pp. 523–524.

[*2003 Amend.* Section 2A–310 Comment adds this paragraph: "Unlike the rules governing a security interest under Article 9, there is never a requirement in this Article that a lessor make a public filing to fully protect its interest in the leased goods against third party claims. Similarly, a lessor need not make a public filing to protect any interest in accessions to those leased goods. Accordingly, priority rules involving leased accessions should not be resolved by reference to Article 9's filing rules."]

H. PRIORITY SUBJECT TO SUBORDINATION

Sections 2A–304 through 2A–310 deal with priority. As § 2A–311 states, a person entitled to priority may agree to subordinate the claim. § 2A–301 Comment 4(g). Cf. § 9–339.

G. DEFAULT

1. DEFAULT PROCEDURE

A. WHAT CONSTITUTES DEFAULT

Whether a lessor or lessee is in default is determined by the lease agreement and Article 2A. § 2A–501(1); see §§ 2A–508(1) (lessee's remedies), 2A–523(1) (lessor's remedies). See §§ 2A–109, 3–108 re: acceleration clauses. Cf. §§ 9–601(a), 1–309 at p. 568.

B. ENFORCEMENT WHEN LESSOR OR LESSEE DEFAULTS

In the event of default, the party seeking enforcement has rights and remedies as provided in Article 2A and the lease agreement. The party may reduce its claim to judgment or otherwise enforce the lease contract by self-help or any available judicial or nonjudicial procedure. Rights and remedies are generally cumulative. § 2A–501(2)–(4). If the lease agreement covers both real property and goods, see § 2A–501(5). Cf. § 9–604 at p. 569.

C. NOTICE AFTER DEFAULT

Generally, the party in default is not entitled to notice of default or notice of enforcement from the party seeking enforcement. § 2A–502 and Comment.

2. DEFAULT PROVISIONS APPLICABLE TO LESSORS AND LESSEES

A. TERMS OR CLAUSES IN THE LEASE AGREEMENT PROVIDING FOR REMEDIES OR DAMAGES

(1) Modification or Impairment of Rights and Remedies

A lease agreement (1) may include rights and remedies for default in addition to or instead of those provided in Article 2A, and (2) may limit or alter the measure of damages recoverable under Article 2A. [§§ 2A–508(1)(j), 2A–523(1)(h) (2003).] Resort to a remedy under Article 2A or in the lease agreement is optional unless the parties agreed the remedy would be exclusive. § 2A–503(1), (2) (first sentence).

If the remedy fails of its essential purpose, see § 2A–503(2) (second sentence); if a provision for an exclusive remedy is unconscionable, see § 2A–503(2) (second sentence); as to limitation, etc., of consequential damages, see § 2A–503(3); as to rights and remedies re: collateral contracts, see § 2A–503(4) and Comment 4. Cf. §§ 2–719, 2–701, 2–302, 2–316 at pp. 145–148.

(2) Liquidation of Damages

Damages for default may be liquidated, but only at an amount or by a formula that is reasonable in light of the then-anticipated harm caused by the default. [§§ 2A–508(*l*)(i) (lessee's remedies), 2A–523(*l*)(g) (2003) (lessor's remedies).] § 2A–504(1) and (2), see §§ 2A–108 (unconscionability), 1–305 (liberal administration of remedies). As to a lessee's right to restitution of payments, see § 2A–504(3), (4). Cf. §§ 2–718(1)–(3), 2–719(2), 2–302 at pp. 143–145.

B. REMEDIES FOR FRAUD

Rights and remedies for material misrepresentation or fraud include all of Article 2A's rights and remedies for default. § 2A–505(4) and (5); see §§ 2A–508 (lessee's remedies), 2A–523 (lessor's remedies). Cf. § 2–721 at p. 148.

C. STATUTE OF LIMITATIONS

An action for default under a lease contract must be commenced within 4 years after the cause of action accrued. § 2A–506(1); see § 2A–506(3) and (4). As to when a cause of action for *default* accrues, see § 2A–506(2) (first sentence); as to when a cause of action for *indemnity* accrues, see § 2A–506(2) (second sentence); as to breach of warranty, see §§ 2A–210 (express warranties), 2A–212 (merchantability), 2A–213 (fitness).

In the original lease contract, the parties may reduce the limitations period to not less than one year. § 2A–506(1). Cf. § 2–725 at pp. 149–151.

[*2003 Amend.* Section 2A–506(1) adds, "*Except in a consumer lease or an action for indemnity,* the original lease agreement may reduce the period of limitations to not less than one year."] [Emphasis added].

D. SUITS AGAINST THIRD PARTIES FOR INJURY TO GOODS

If a third party deals with goods that have been identified (§ 2A–217) to a lease contract, in a way that causes actionable injury to a party to the lease contract,

(a) the *lessor* has a right of action against the third party, and

(b) the *lessee* also has a right of action against the third party if the lessee:

(i) has a security interest in the goods (§§ 1–201(b)(35) ("security interest" defined), 9–109 (scope of Article 9));

(ii) has an insurable interest in the goods (§ 2A–218, see § 2A–217 (identification to the contract)); or

(iii) bears the risk of loss as to converted or destroyed goods (§§ 2A–219, 2A–220 (effect of default)).

See Part Two, C supra; § 2A–531. Cf. §§ 2–722, 2–501, 2–509, 2–510 at p. 149.

3. LESSOR'S DEFAULT

A. WHAT CONSTITUTES LESSOR'S DEFAULT

Lessor defaults by

(1) failing to deliver goods that conform to the lease contract. § 2A–509; cf. §§ 2–601 (buyer's rights on improper delivery), 2–602(1) (rightful rejection); or

(2) repudiating the lease. § 2A–402, cf. § 2–610.

Further, Lessor defaults when Lessee:

(1) rightfully rejects the goods. § 2A–509; cf. §§ 2–601, 2–602(1); or

(2) justifiably revokes acceptance of the goods. § 2A–517; cf. § 2–608.

§ 2A–508(1) (index of lessee's remedies). Cf. § 2–711 at pp. 131–141.

When Lessor is otherwise in default, see § 2A–508(3) [2A–508(2) (2003)]; see §§ 2A–503 (modification or impairment of rights and remedies), 2A–504 (liquidated damages). Cf. §§ 2–718(1)–(3), 2–719 at pp. 145–148. If Lessor has breached a warranty, see §§ 2A–508(4) [2A–508(3) (2003)], 2A–519(4).

[*2003 Amend.* Section 2A–508 is an index to §§ 2A–503 through 2A–505 (modification of remedies, liquidated damages) and §§ 2A–509 through 2A–522, which set out Lessee's rights and remedies after Lessor's default. § 2A–508 Comments 1, 2, 5.]

B. LESSEE'S RIGHTS ON IMPROPER DELIVERY TO (1) REJECT, OR (2) ACCEPT

(1) In General—Perfect Tender Rule

If the goods or the tender of delivery fail *in any respect* to conform to the lease contract, the lessee may (a) reject the goods or (b) opt to accept the goods in spite of the nonconformity. Further, Lessee may accept any commercial unit and reject the rest. § 2A–509(1).

For limitations on the perfect tender rule, see §§ 2A–404(1) (substituted performance), 2A–510 (installment contracts), 2A–513 (cure and replacement), 2A–509(2) (reasonable time, notice) (see 2A–515(1)(b)), 2A–517. Cf. §§ 2–601, 2–602, 2–612, 2–614, 2–606, 2–508, 2–608 at pp. 100–101.

[*2003 Amend.* The perfect tender rule is also subject to §§ 2A–503, 2A–504 (modification of remedies, liquidated damages).]

(2) Lessee's Rejection of Goods

(a) Situations When Lessee Has Right to Reject

See Part Two, G, 3, B, (1) immediately above (perfect tender rule).

(b) Manner and Effect of Rightful Rejection

Rejection of goods is ineffective unless (1) it is within a reasonable time after tender or delivery of the goods, and

(2) the lessee seasonably notifies the lessor [or supplier]. §§ 2A–509(2), 1–202 (notice), 1–205 (reasonable time); see § 2A–515(1)(b) (failure to reject is acceptance). Cf. § 2–602(1) at pp. 101–102.

(c) Requirement That Lessee Particularize Reasons for Rejection

A lessee's failure to identify and state a particular defect that is ascertainable by reasonable inspection precludes the lessee from relying on the defect to justify rejection (or to establish default) if, had it been stated seasonably, the lessor or the supplier could have cured it. §§ 2A–514(1)(a), 2A–513. Re: merchant lessor or supplier's request for a statement of defects, see § 2A–514(1)(b); re: payment against documents, see § 2A–514(2). Cf. § 2–605 at pp. 102–104.

[*2003 Amend*. Section 2A–514(1) makes three substantive changes: (i) failure to particularize affects only Lessee's right to reject or revoke acceptance (not Lessee's right to establish a breach of the agreement); (ii) it now requires that Lessor have a right to cure (§ 2A–513) in addition to the ability to cure; and (iii) it now includes a notice requirement not only as to rejection, but also as to revocation of acceptance. § 2A–514 Comment.]

(d) Rights and Obligations of Lessee After Rightful Rejection

(i) When Lessee Has a Security Interest

On rightful rejection or justifiable revocation of acceptance, a lessee has a security interest in goods in its possession or control, for any rent and security that has been paid and certain reasonably incurred expenses. [§ 2A–508(1)(f) (2003).] §§ 2A–508(5) [2A–508(4) (2003)], 2A–512(1) (lessee's duties as to rightfully rejected goods), 2A–511(1) (same, for merchant lessee). As to disposition of the goods, see §§ 2A–508(5), [2A–508(4) (2003)], 2A–527(5). Cf. §§ 2–602(2)(b) and (c), 2–604, 2–603, 2–706 esp. (6) at p. 104.

(ii) When Lessee Has No Security Interest

Lessees generally

After rejecting goods and seasonally notifying the lessor or supplier, the lessee shall hold the goods with reasonable care at Lessor's or Supplier's disposition for a reasonable time. If Lessor or Supplier gives no instructions within a reasonable time after notification, Lessee may (1) store the rejected goods for Lessor's or Supplier's account, (2) ship them to Lessor or Supplier, or (3) dispose of them for Lessor's or Supplier's account (with reimbursement for expenses). Lessee has no further *obligations* with regard to rightfully rejected goods. § 2A–512(1), see § 2A–512(2). Cf. §§ 2–602(2)(b) and (c), 2–604 at pp. 104–105.

[*2003 Amend.* Former § 2A–512(1)(a) and (c) has been moved to 2A–509(3); former § 2A–512(1)(b) is now § 2A–512(1).]

Merchant lessees

If Lessor or Supplier has no agent or place of business at the market of rejection, a *merchant* lessee who rejects goods in his possession or control shall follow Lessor or Supplier's reasonable instructions with respect to the goods. In the absence of instructions, a merchant lessee shall make reasonable efforts to dispose of the goods for Lessor's account if they threaten to decline in value speedily. § 2A–511(1), (3). As to Lessee's right of reimbursement for expenses, see §§ 2A–511(2), 2A–512(1)(b) [2A–512(1) (2003)]; as to the rights of a purchaser at disposition, see § 2A–511(4), see § 2–706(5). Cf. §§ 2–603 at p. 105.

(e) Effect of Wrongful Rejection

A lessee who wrongfully rejects is in default, and Lessor has the remedies indexed in § 2A–523. § 2A–509(3)(d). See Part Two, G, 4, A and C infra. Cf. §§ 2–602(3), 2–703 at pp. 105–106.

(f) Effect of Failure to Reject

Rejection of goods is *ineffective* unless timely and accompanied by seasonable notification. *Acceptance* of goods occurs when Lessee fails to make an effective rejection. §§ 2A–509(2), 2A–515(1)(b). Cf. §§ 2–602(1), 2–606(1)(b) at p. 106.

[*2003 Amend.* Rejection is ineffective unless the lessee seasonably notifies the lessor or supplier. 2A–509(2).]

(3) Lessee's Acceptance of Goods

What constitutes acceptance

Acceptance occurs after

(1) Lessee has had a reasonable opportunity to inspect the goods, and

(2) Lessee—

(a) signifies or acts with respect to the goods in a manner that signifies to Lessor or Supplier (i) that the goods are conforming or (ii) that Lessee will take or retain them in spite of their nonconformity; or

(b) fails to make an effective rejection. §§ 2A–515(1), 2A–509(2); see § 2A–515(2). Cf. § 2–606 at pp. 106–107 (note that § 2–606(1)(c) was not incorporated into § 2A–515).

[*2003 Amend.* Section 2A–515(1)(c) adds that acceptance occurs when the lessee (subject to 2A–517(6)), uses the goods in any manner that is inconsistent with the lessor's or supplier's rights. Section 2A–517(6) deals with post-rejection or revocation *use of the goods.*]

Effect of acceptance

1.   Lessee must pay rent according to the lease contract for any goods accepted, even though Lessee may have remedies for the goods' nonconformity. §§ 2A–516(1) and (2), 2A–519(3) and (4), 2A–508(6). Cf. § 2–607(1).

2.   Acceptance of goods precludes rejection, although sometimes a lessee may revoke acceptance. This will be discussed presently. § 2A–516(2). Cf. § 2–607(2).

3.   If a tender has been accepted, Lessee must give notice of default, within a reasonable time after Lessee discovered or should have discovered any default, or be barred from any remedy. In a finance lease, notice must be given either to the supplier, the lessor, or both, but no remedy exists against the party not notified. §§ 2A–516(3)(a) and Comment 2, 2A–103(1)(g) and (x) ("finance lease" and "supplier" defined) [2A–103(1)(*l*) and (ff) (2003)]. Cf. § 2–607(3)(a). [Section 2A–516(3)(a) (2003) adds that "failure to give timely notice bars the lessee from a remedy only to the extent that the lessor or supplier is prejudiced by the failure."]

4.   The burden is on the lessee to establish any default. § 2A–516(3)(c). Cf. § 2–607(4).

See also §§ 2A–201(4)(c) (statute of frauds), 2A–401(5) (adequate assurances); cf. §§ 2–201(3)(c), 2–609(3), 2A–407 (irrevocable promises; finance leases). Cf. § 2–607 at pp. 107–108.

(4) Lessee's Revocation of Acceptance

Meaning of revocation of acceptance

A lessee who revokes acceptance has the same rights and duties with regard to goods as if Lessee had rejected them. § 2A–517(5), see § 2A–508(1) and (5) [(4) (2003)]. Cf. §§ 2–608(3), 2–711(1) at p. 108.

Requirements for justifiable revocation of acceptance

Lessee may revoke acceptance when the following conditions are met:

1. The nonconformity must *substantially* impair the value of the goods to Lessee. § 2A–517(1).

2. Lessee must have accepted the goods

(a) on the reasonable assumption that the nonconformity would be cured and it has not been seasonally cured (except in the case of a finance lease); or

(b) without discovery of the nonconformity, if Lessee's acceptance was reasonably induced either by (i) Lessor's assurances, or (ii) the difficulty of discovery before acceptance (except in the case of a finance lease). §§ 2A–517(1), 2A–516(2), 2A–513 (cure; replacement), 2A–103(1)(g) ("finance lease" defined), [2A–103(1)(*l*) (2003); see § 2A–516 Comments re: finance lease.

3. Revocation must occur within a reasonable time after Lessee discovers or should have discovered the ground for it, and is not effective until Lessee notifies Lessor. § 2A–517(4).

4. Revocation must occur before any substantial change in the goods' condition that is not caused by the nonconformity. § 2A–517(4). Cf. §§ 2–608(1) and (2), 2–601, 2–602(1), 2–607(2), 2–703, 2–508 at pp. 108–110.

As to revocation of acceptance of a lot or commercial unit, see § 2A–517(2) and (3).

[*2003 Amend.* New § 2A–517(6) and Comment 3 deals with post-rejection or revocation *use* of the goods.]

C. LESSOR'S RIGHT TO CURE IMPROPER TENDER OR DELIVERY

If lessor's or supplier's time for performance has not expired

In this situation, see § 2A–513(1).

If lessor or supplier had reasonable grounds to believe the nonconforming tender would be acceptable

If Lessee rejects a nonconforming tender that Lessor or Supplier had *reasonable grounds to believe* would be acceptable (with or without money allowance), Lessor or Supplier may have a further reasonable time (beyond the time for performance) to substitute a conforming tender if he seasonably notifies Lessee. § 2A–513(2). Cf. § 2–508 at pp. 111–115.

[*2003 Amend.* Section 2A–513(1) and (2) now provides (in a nonconsumer contract) the lessor the right to cure if the lessee justifiably revokes acceptance under § 2A–517(1)(b). See §§ 2A–513 Comment, 2–508 Comments 1 and 2. The section now predicates the right to cure on good-faith performance by the lessor and (under § 2A–513(2)), when the time for performance has expired, on the cure being appropriate and timely under the circumstances. See § 2–508 Comments 3 and 4. Another amendment imposes liability on the lessor for the lessee's reasonable expenses caused by the breach and subsequent cure. § 2A–513(1) (last sentence) and (2) (last sentence).]

D. NONCONFORMITY OF INSTALLMENT(S) IN INSTALLMENT LEASE CONTRACT

See § 2A–510; see also §§ 2A–103(1)(i) and (s) ("installment lease contract" and "lot" defined) [2A–103(1)(*o*) and (y) (2003)], 2A–513 (cure; replacement), 2A–509 (lessee's rights on improper delivery), 2A–515. Cf. §§ 2–612, 2–105(5), 2–508 [2–105(4) (2003)], 2–601, 2–602(1), 2–606 at p. 110.

E. LESSEE'S REMEDIES WHERE (1) GOODS ARE NOT ACCEPTED, OR (2) ACCEPTANCE IS REVOKED

Lessee's non-acceptance may be found when (1) Lessor fails to deliver goods in conformity to the lease contract,

(2) Lessor repudiates, or (3) Lessee rightfully rejects goods. Further, acceptance is not final when Lessee justifiably revokes acceptance of the goods. Revocation of acceptance gives Lessee the same rights as if he had rejected the goods. § 2A–517(5). § 2A–508 (index section); see §§ 2A–509, 2A–402 (anticipatory repudiation), 2A–515 (acceptance), 2A–516 (effect of acceptance), 2A–517 (revocation), 2A–510 (installment lease). See Part Two, G, 1 through 3, D supra. Cf. §§ 2–711, 2–601, 2–602(1), 2–610, 2–606, 2–607, 2–608, 2–612 at pp. 131–139.

[*2003 Amend.* Section 2A–508 indexes §§ 2A–503 through 2A–505 and 2A–509 through 2A–522, which set out the lessee's rights and remedies after the lessor's default. § 2A–508 Comment 1; see Comments 2–9.]

The following remedies are available to a lessee who has not finally accepted the goods.

(1) Lessee May Cancel the Lease Contract

Lessee may cancel per § 2A–508(1)(a) and (3). See § 2A–505(1)–(3), cf. § 2A–523(1)(a) and (3) (lessor's remedies). Cf. §§ 2–711(1), 2–106(3) and (4), 2–720, 2–703(f) at p. 132. [*2003 Amend.* See § 2A–508(1)(a) and (2), cf. § 2A–523(1)(f) and (4); § 2–711(2)(c), 2–703(2)(f).]

(2) Lessee May Recover Rent and Security Paid

Lessee may recover as much of the rent and security as has been paid and is just under the circumstances. §§ 2A–508(1)(b) and Comment 2. Cf. § 2–711(1) [2–711(2)(a) (2003)] at p. 132.

(3) Lessee's Security Interest in Goods in Lessee's Possession or Control

On rightful rejection or justifiable revocation of acceptance, Lessee has a *security interest* in goods it possesses or controls for (a) any rent and security that has been paid and (b) any expenses reasonably incurred in their inspection, receipt, transportation, and care and custody. § 2A–508(1), (5) [2A–508(1)(b), (4) (2003)]. As to enforcement of the security interest, see §§ 2A–508(5) [2A–508(4) (2003)], 2A–527(5). Cf. § 2–711(1), (3) at pp. 132–133.

(4) Lessee's Recovery of Money Damages

(a) Lessee May "Cover" and Recover Damages

After Lessor's default, Lessee may cover by purchasing or leasing goods to substitute for those due from Lessor. If (i) Lessee covers by leasing goods, (ii) the lease agreement is substantially similar to the original lease agreement, and (iii) the cover is made in good faith and in a commercially reasonable manner, Lessee may recover from Lessor the present value (as of the date of the commencement of the term of the *new* lease agreement) of the rent under the *new* lease agreement that is comparable to the then-remaining term of the *original* lease agreement, less the present value of the rent reserved for the remaining term under the *original* lease agreement (together with incidental or consequential damages, less expenses saved). §§ 2A–508(1)(c), 2A–518(1) and (2) and Comment 2. § 2A–520. Cf. § 2A–527.

If the substitute *lease* agreement does *not* qualify for treatment under § 2A–518(2) (see criteria (i)–(iii) in the prior paragraph), or Lessee's cover is by *purchase*, Lessee may recover from Lessor *as if* Lessee elected not to cover and § 2A–519 governs (which is discussed immediately below). § 2A–518(3). Cf. §§ 2–711(1)(a) [2–711(2)(d) (2003)], 2–712, 2–706 at pp. 133–134.

(b) Lessee May Recover Damages for (i) Lessor's Non-Delivery or Repudiation, or (ii) Lessee's Rejection or Revocation

If Lessee elects *not* to cover, or the cover (a) is by lease agreement that does *not* qualify for treatment under § 2A–518(2) (discussed immediately above), or (b) is by *purchase,* the measure of damages is the present value (as of the date of default) of the *then market rent* (§ 2A–519(2)) minus the present value as of the same date of the *original rent*, computed for the remaining term of the original lease agreement (together with incidental and consequential damages, less expenses saved). §§ 2A–508(1)(c) [2A–508(1)(d) (2003)], 2A–519(1) and (2), 2A–507 (proof of market rent), 2A–520 (incidental and consequential damages); cf. § 2A–528 (lessor's damages). Cf. §§ 2–711(1)(b) [2–711(2)(e) (2003)], 2–713, 2–723, 2–724, 2–715, 2–708 at pp. 134–135.

(5) Lessee May Exercise Contractual Remedies

Lessee may exercise any other remedies provided in the lease contract. § 2A–508(1)(d); see § 2A–503; cf. § 2A–523(1)(f). Cf. § 2–719(1) at pp. 133–135.

[*2003 Amend.* See § 2A–508(1)(k),(2) and Comment 4; see also § 2A–508(1)(i) and (j).]

(6) Lessee's Remedies Reaching the Goods Themselves

(a) On Lessor's Insolvency, Lessee May Recover Identified Goods

If Lessor fails to deliver or repudiates, a lessee who has paid a part or all of the rent and security for goods identified to a lease contract, on making and keeping good a tender of any unpaid portion of the rent and security due under the lease contract, may recover the goods from Lessor if Lessor becomes insolvent within 10 days after receipt of the first installment of rent and security. §§ 2A–508(2)(a) [2A–508(1)(g) (2003)], 2A–522; cf. § 2A–525(2) (lessor's right to possession of goods). Cf. §§ 2–711(2)(a) [2–711(2)(g) (2003)], 2–502, 2–501, 2–702(2), 9–609 at pp. 137–139.

[*2003 Amend.* New § 2A–522(1)(a) allows a lessee to recover the identified goods if, "in the case of goods leased by a consumer, the lessor repudiates or fails to deliver as required by the lease contract..." § 2A–103(1)(e), see § 2A–522 Comments.]

(b) In a Proper Case, Lessee May Obtain Specific Performance

If Lessor fails to deliver or repudiates, specific performance may be decreed if the goods are unique or in other proper circumstances. §§ 2A–508(2)(b), 2A–521(1) and (2). Cf. §§ 2–711(2)(b) [2–711(2)(h) (2003)], 2–716(1) and (2) at pp. 135–136.

[*2003 Amend.* Section 2A–521 has been moved to § 2A–507A because it has been amended so that the remedy is available to both lessors and lessees. Section 2A–507A(1) (second sentence) adds that, in a contract other than a consumer lease, specific performance may be decreed if the parties have *agreed* to that remedy. §§ 2A–508(1)(h), 2A–507A(1), 2A–103(1)(f).]

(c) In a Proper Case, Lessee May Replevy the Goods

If Lessor fails to deliver or repudiates, Lessee has a right of replevin, etc., for goods identified to the lease contract if, after reasonable effort, Lessee is unable to effect cover for those goods, or the circumstances reasonably indicate that the effort will be unavailing. §§ 2A–508(2)(b), 2A–521(3), 2A–217 (identification); cf. § 2A–529(1)(b) (lessor's action for the rent). Cf. §§ 2–711(2)(b) [2–711(2)(h) (2003)], 2–716(3), 2–501, 2–709(1)(b) at pp. 136–137.

[*2003 Amend.* Lessee's right of replevin has been moved to § 2A–507A(3). § 2A–508(1)(h).]

F. LESSEE'S REMEDIES WHEN GOODS ARE FINALLY ACCEPTED

Section 2A–519(3) and (4) deals with the measure of damages when goods have been accepted and acceptance is not revoked. §§ 2A–508(1)(e) (2003), 2A–519 Comments 4 and 5, 2A–515 (acceptance), 2A–516 (effect of acceptance), 2A–517 (revocation). Such damages consist of the loss flowing from the default in the ordinary course of events. §§ 2A–508(3) [2A–508(2) (2003)], 2A–519(3). Of course, Lessee must notify Lessor and, where relevant, Supplier, within a reasonable time after Lessee discovers or should have discovered any default, or lose any remedy against the party not notified. § 2A–516(3)(a). [Under 2A–516(3)(a) (2003), failure to give timely notice bars Lessee from a remedy *only* to the extent that Lessor or Supplier is *prejudiced* by the failure.]

The general measure of damages for breach of warranty is the present value of the difference between the value of the goods as accepted and their value if they had been as warranted. §§ 2A–508(4) [2A–508(3) (2003)], 2A–519(4). Subject to § 2A–407 (irrevocable promises in finance leases), Lessee, on notifying Lessor of Lessee's intention to do so, may deduct all or any part of the damages resulting from any default under the lease contract from any part of the rent still due under the contract. § 2A–508(6) [2A–508(5) and Comment 8 (2003)].

Further, *incidental* and *consequential* damages (less expenses saved) may be recovered. §§ 2A–519(3) and (4), 2A–520. Cf. §§ 2–714, 2–715, 2–717, 2–606, 2–607, 2–608 at pp. 139–142.

G. LESSEE'S REMEDIES FOR LESSOR'S DEFAULT UNDER AN INSTALLMENT LEASE CONTRACT

See §§ 2A–508(1) (lessee's remedies), 2A–510 (installment contracts), 2A–103(1)(i) and (s) ("installment lease contract" and "lot" defined) [2A–103(1)(*o*) and (y) (2003)], 2A–513 (cure; replacement), 2A–509 (rightful rejection), 2A–515 (acceptance). Cf. §§ 2–612, 2–105(5) [2–105(4) (2003)], 2–508, 2–601, 2–602(1), 2–606 at p. 110.

4. LESSEE'S DEFAULT

A. WHAT CONSTITUTES LESSEE'S DEFAULT

Lessee is in default if Lessee:

(1) wrongfully rejects goods. See § 2A–509, cf. §§ 2–601, 2–602(1).

(2) wrongfully revokes or attempts to revoke acceptance of goods. See § 2A–517, cf. § 2–608.

(3) fails to make payment when due. Cf. § 2–310(a).

(4) repudiates. See § 2A–402, cf. § 2–610.

§ 2A–523(1) (index section). Cf. § 2–703 at pp. 120–131.

B. WHEN LESSEE IS OTHERWISE IN DEFAULT UNDER LEASE CONTRACT

See § 2A–523(3) [2A–523(4) (2003)] and Comment 20[19]; see also §§ 2A–503 (modification or impairment of rights and remedies), 2A–504 (liquidated damages). Cf. §§ 2–718, 2–719 at pp. 143–148.

C. LESSOR'S REMEDIES WHEN LESSEE DEFAULTS

These remedies are indexed at § 2A–523(1). Cf. § 2–703. To better understand subparagraphs (a) through (f) of § 2A–523(1), set forth below, study the hypothetical at Comments 5–18 to § 2A–523.

[*2003 Amend.* § 2A–523(1), is an index to §§ 2A–503 through 2A–505, § 2A–507 and §§ 2A–524 through 2A–531. See § 2A–523 Comments 1–3, study hypotheticals at Comments 4–17.]

(1) Lessor May Cancel the Lease Contract

Lessor may cancel per § 2A–523(1)(a) and (3) [2A–523(1)(f) and (4) (2003)]. See § 2A–505(1)–(3), cf. § 2A–508(1)(a) and (3)[2]. Cf. § 2–703(f) [2–703(2)(f) (2003)],

2–106(3) and (4), 2–720, 2–711(1) [2–711(2) (2003)] at pp. 120–121.

(2) Lessor May Take Action As to the Goods

(a) Lessor May Identify Goods to the Lease Contract Notwithstanding Default or Salvage Unfinished Goods

This section gives an aggrieved lessor the right to identify to the lease contract conforming goods not already identified (if, at the time the lessor learned of the default, they were in the lessor's or supplier's possession or control). Lessor may also dispose of goods that have been intended for the particular lease contract, even if these goods are unfinished. §§ 2A–523(1) [2A–523(1)(c) (2003)], 2A–524(1), 2A–527(1), 2A–103(1)(p) and (x) ("lessor" and "supplier" defined) [2A–103(1)(v) and (ff) (2003)].

"If the goods are unfinished ... an aggrieved lessor or the supplier may either [1] complete manufacture and wholly identify the goods to the lease contract or [2] cease manufacture and lease, sell, or otherwise dispose of the goods for scrap or salvage value or [3] proceed in any other reasonable manner." § 2A–524(2). This rule is intended to minimize loss and promote effective realization in the exercise of reasonable commercial judgment. Cf. §§ 2–703(c) [2–703(2)(c) (2003)], 2–704 at pp. 122–123.

(b) Lessor May Withhold Delivery of Goods and Take Possession of Goods Previously Delivered

If Lessor discovers Lessee is insolvent, Lessor may refuse to deliver the goods. In addition, upon Lessee's default, Lessor has the right to take possession of or reclaim the goods. Lessor may (1) take possession without judicial process, if that can be done without breach of the peace, or (2) proceed by action. §§ 2A–523(1)(c) [2A–523(1)(a) (2003)], 2A–525 and Comment 2, §§ 1–201(b)(23) ("insolvent" defined), 1–305(b) (liberal administration of remedies).

As to Lessee's duty to assemble the goods, see § 2A–525(2) (second sentence); as to rendering the goods unusable, see § 2A–525(2) (third sentence). Cf. §§ 2–703(a) [2–703(2)(a) (2003)], 2–702(1) and (2), 9–609 at pp. 121, 572–573.

(c) Lessor May Stop Delivery of the Goods by Any Bailee

Lessor (1) may stop delivery of goods in possession of a carrier or other bailee (e.g., warehouseman) if Lessor discovers Lessee is insolvent, and (2) may stop larger shipments (carload, truckload, planeload) of express or freight if Lessee repudiates or fails to make a payment due before delivery, etc. §§ 2A–523(1)(d) [2A–523(1)(b) (2003)], 2A–526(1), 1–201(b)(23) ("insolvent" defined).

Lessor may stop delivery until (1) Lessee comes into physical possession of the goods, (2) any bailee other than a carrier acknowledges to Lessee that it holds the goods for the lessee, or (3) such acknowledgment is made to Lessee by a carrier via reshipment or as a warehouse. § 2A–526(2). As to procedures for stopping delivery, see § 2A–526(3). Cf. §§ 2–703(b) [2–703(2)(b) (2003)], 2–705 at pp. 121–122.

[*2003 Amend.* For stoppage in cases other than insolvency, § 2A–526(1) has been broadened by eliminating the requirement that the goods be by the "carload, truckload, planeload, or larger shipments of express or freight." If Lessee is insolvent but *not* in default, see § 2A–523(2).]

(3) Lessor May Recover Monies From Lessee

(a) Lessor May Dispose of the Goods and Recover Damages

After Lessee's default (or after Lessor refuses to deliver or takes possession of goods per §§ 2A–525 or 2A–526 as discussed at Part Two, G, 4, C, (2), (b) and (c) supra),

Lessor may dispose of the goods or the undelivered balance thereof by *lease* or *sale*. If (i) Lessor disposed of the goods by lease, (ii) the new lease agreement is substantially similar to the original lease agreement, and (iii) such disposition was in good faith and in a commercially reasonable manner, the lessor may recover the following damages from the lessee: (a) accrued and unpaid rent (as of commencement of the *new* lease), (b) the present value (as of the same date), of the rent under the *original* lease for the then-remaining term, minus the present value (as of the same date), of the rent under the *new* lease agreement for a comparable period, and (c) incidental or consequential damages per § 2A–530 (less expenses saved). §§ 2A–523(1)(e) [2A–523(1)(e) (2003)], 2A–527(1) and (2). Cf. § 2A–518.

If Lessor's disposition is by a lease agreement that does *not* qualify for treatment under § 2A–527)(2) (see criteria (i)–(iii) in the prior paragraph), or is by *sale*, Lessor may recover from Lessee *as if* Lessor had elected not to dispose of the goods, and § 2A–528 (which is discussed immediately below) governs § 2A–527(3).

As to the rights of a subsequent buyer or lessee, see § 2A–527(4); as to accountability for any profit made on disposition, see § 2A–527(5). Cf. §§ 2–703(d), [2–703(2)(g) (2003)], 2–706, 2–712 at pp. 123–125.

(b) Lessor May Retain the Goods and Recover Damages

If Lessor elects to retain the goods, or Lessor elects to dispose of the goods, but the disposition (a) is by *lease* agreement that does *not* qualify for treatment under § 2A–527(2) (discussed immediately above), or (b) is by *sale*: Lessor may, under appropriate circumstances, recover from Lessee (i) accrued and unpaid rent as of the date of default, if Lessee has never taken possession of the goods, or if Lessee has taken possession, as of the date Lessor repossesses the goods or an earlier date on which

Lessee tenders the goods to Lessor, (ii) the present value (as of the date determined under (i) above) of the total rent for the then-remaining term of the *original* lease agreement, minus the present value as of the same date of the market rent at the place where the goods are located, computed for the same lease term, and (iii) incidental or consequential damages per § 2A–530 (less expenses saved). §§ 2A–523(1)(e) [2A–523(1)(e) (2003)], 2A–528(1), 2A–507. Cf. § 2A–519(1), (2).

Loss of profit

If the above measure of damages is inadequate to put Lessor in as good a position as if Lessee had fully performed, the measure of damages is the present value of the *profit* Lessor would have made from Lessee's full performance. §§ 2A–528(2), 2A–530 (incidental damages), see § 1–305(a) (liberal administration of remedies). Cf. §§ 2–703(e) [2–703(2)(h) and (i) (2003)], 2–708, 2–723, 2–724, 2–713 at pp. 125–126.

(c) *Lessor May Recover the Rent*

After Lessee's default (see Part Two, G, 4, A and B supra), Lessor may have an action for the rent:

1. for goods *accepted* by Lessee (and not repossessed, etc.). § 2A–515.

2. for conforming goods lost or damaged within a commercially reasonable time after *risk of loss* passes to Lessee. § 2A–219.

3. for goods *identified* to the lease contract, if Lessor is unable after reasonable effort to dispose of them at a reasonable price, or the circumstances reasonably indicate that effort will be unavailing. § 2A–217.

In these situations, Lessor may recover from Lessee as damages

(i) accrued and unpaid rent as of the date of entry of judgment in favor of Lessor,

(ii) the present value as of the same date of the rent for the then-remaining lease term of the lease agreement, and

(iii) any incidental or consequential damages allowed under § 2A–530 (less expenses saved). §§ 2A–523(1)(e) [2A–523(1)(d) (2003)], 2A–529(1) and (4) (action for the rent). Cf. § 2A–521(3) [2A–507A(3) (2003)].

With one exception, a lessor who is able and elects to sue for the rent must hold any goods not lost or damaged for the lessee. § 2A–529(2), (3) and Comment 3. (If Lessor is not entitled to rent, see § 2A–529(5).) Cf. §§ 2–703(e) [2–703(2)(j) (2003)], 2–709, 2–501, 2–509, 2–606, 2–716 at pp. 126–128.

[*2003 Amend.* Lessor may obtain specific performance under § 2A–507A, but not if the breaching party's sole remaining contractual obligation is the payment of money. § 2A–523(1)(d), 2A–507A(1) and Comment 2.]

(4) Lessor May Exercise Contractual Remedies

Lessor may exercise any other rights or pursue any other remedies provided in the lease contract. §§ 2A–523(1)(f) [2A–523(1)(i) (2003)]; 2A–503 (modification or impairment of rights and remedies); cf. § 2A–508(1)(d) [2A–508(1)(k) (2003)]. Cf. § 2–719(1) at pp. 143–148.

(5) Lessor May Recover Loss Resulting in Ordinary Course of Events

A lessor who does not fully exercise a right or obtain a remedy to which he or she is entitled under § 2A–523(1) may recover the loss resulting in the ordinary course of events from the lessee's default as determined in any reasonable manner, together with incidental or consequential damages, less expenses saved in consequence of

Lessee's default. § 2A–523(2) [2A–523(3), 2A–530 (2003)]. See Part Two, G, 4, C, (1)–(4).

(6) Lessor May Recover for Loss to Residual Interest

In addition to any other recovery under Article 2A or other law, the lessor may recover from the lessee an amount that will fully compensate the lessor for any loss of, or damage to, the lessor's residual interest in the goods caused by the lessee's default. § 2A–532 and Comment.

D. LESSOR'S REMEDIES WHEN LESSEE DEFAULTS UNDER AN INSTALLMENT LEASE CONTRACT

See §§ 2A–523(1) and (2) [2A–523(1) and (3) (2003)], 2A–510 (installment contracts), 2A–103(1)(i) and (s) ("installment lease contract" and "lot" defined) [2A–103(1)(o) and (y) (2003)]; see §§ 2A–513 (cure; replacement), 2A–509 (rightful rejection), 2A–515 (acceptance). Cf. §§ 2–703, 2–612 at pp. 99–101.

PART THREE

THE PROCESS OF PAYING FOR GOODS WITH NEGOTIABLE INSTRUMENTS

A. INTRODUCTION TO NEGOTIABLE INSTRUMENTS

Recall from the introduction to this nutshell that a "commercial transaction" may involve not only the sale of goods, but also the giving of a check or draft for all or part of the purchase price. Further, the check or draft may be "negotiated" and ultimately pass through one or more banks for collection. This Part deals with negotiable instruments and the bank operations related to them.

Of course, negotiable instruments are used for purposes other than payment for goods. Negotiable instruments also may be used as a means to repay loans or to pay for land, services, or other purchases.

Subject matter

UCC Article 3, entitled Negotiable Instruments, applies to notes (including certificates of deposit) and drafts (including checks). It does not apply to money, payment orders (which fall within Article 4A), or securities (e.g., stocks and bonds) (which are covered by Article 8). If there is a conflict as to which Article governs a particular transaction, Article 4 (Bank Deposits and Collections) and Article 9 (Secured Transactions) prevail over Article 3. §§ 3–101 (short title), 3–102 (subject matter), 3–104(e)–(j) (defining "note," "check," "cashier's check," "teller's check," "traveler's check," and "certificate of deposit").

A draft is an instrument Drawer issues to Drawee unconditionally ordering Drawee to pay to the order of Payee or Bearer, a fixed amount of money, payable on demand or at a definite time. The draft is a check if (1) Drawee is a bank and (2) the instrument is payable on demand. § 3–104(a), (c), (e), (f)–(i) (defining "negotiable instrument," "note," "draft," "check," etc.).

A note is an instrument Maker issues, unconditionally promising to pay to the order of Payee or Bearer, a fixed amount of money, payable on demand or at a definite time. A certificate of deposit is a note acknowledging receipt of a sum of money and promising to repay it. § 3–104(a), (e), (j).

Drafts and checks are "three party paper:" (1) Drawer, (2) Drawee, and (3) Payee. Notes and certificates of deposit are "two party paper:" (1) Maker (or Issuer) and (2) Payee.

For examples of various negotiable instruments, see 13 West's Legal Forms, Ch. 11.

UCC Article 4, entitled Bank Deposits and Collections, applies to *items*, while UCC Article 3, entitled Negotiable Instruments, applies to *instruments*. "Item" means a promise or order to pay money, handled by a bank for collection or payment. It does not include a "payment order" (§ 4A–103) or a credit or debit card slip. "Instrument" denotes Article 3 negotiable instruments but not Article 8 investment securities. §§ 4–101 (short title), 4–104(a)(9) (defining "item") and Comment 8; see §§ 3–103(a)(8) and (12) (defining "order" and "party"), 3–104 (defining "negotiable instrument"), 8–102(a)(15) (defining "security"). If there is a conflict, Article 4 trumps Article 3; Article 8 trumps Article 4. § 4–102(a). Article 4 also applies to the collection of documentary drafts. §§ 4–501 et seq., 4–104(a)(6) (defining the term).

Overview of contracts and warranties between parties to negotiable instruments

The *Maker* of a promissory note undertakes to pay the note according to its terms. Because there is no need for Payee (or a subsequent taker) to seek payment first from another party before pursuing Maker, Maker's obligation is sometimes called a contract of primary liability. §§ 3–412, 3–105(c) (defining "maker").

The *Drawer* of a draft such as a check is obliged to pay the check according to its terms *if* the check is dishonored by Drawee. A check is dishonored when Payee (or a subsequent taker) duly presents it for payment to Drawee and it is not paid. Former § 3–413(2) commonly required Payee (or a subsequent taker) to give notice of dishonor to Drawer as a precondition of Drawer's obligation to pay the item. Under the 1990 Revised Code, Drawer is entitled to have the check presented to Drawee and dishonored before Drawer must pay, but notice of dishonor is no longer a condition of Drawer's liability. §§ 3–103(a)(5) (defining "drawer"), 3–104(f) (defining "check"), 3–414(b) (drawer's liability), and Comment 2, 3–501(a) (defining "presentment"), 3–502(b)(1) and (2), 3–503 Comment 1 (notice of dishonor). Drawer's obligation is sometimes called a contract of secondary liability because payment is sought first from Drawee.

Although Payee may present a draft directly to Drawer (or a note directly to Maker) for payment, Payee may also indorse and transfer the item to a subsequent taker/indorsee, typically in return for some consideration. In such cases, if the item is a check, *Payee–Indorser* must (like Drawer) pay the check according to its terms *if* the check is dishonored by Drawee. A check is dishonored when Indorsee duly presents it for payment to Drawee and it is not paid. Before payment can be sought from Indorser, Indorser is generally entitled to notice of dishonor. §§ 3–104(f) ("check" defined), 3–415(a) (indorser's liability),

3–501(a) ("presentment" defined), 3–502(b)(1) and (b)(2) (dishonor), 3–503(a) (notice of dishonor). Indorser's obligation, like Drawer's, is sometimes called a contract of secondary liability.

Along the same lines, if the item is a note, *Payee–Indorser* is obliged to pay a note according to its terms *if* Maker dishonors the note. For example, assume Maker issues a note on May 1 promising to pay $1,000 on November 1 to the order of Payee. Payee–Indorser indorses the note to Indorsee. This note is dishonored if not paid on November 1. (There need not be a presentment for payment as under former §§ 3–414(1), 3–501(1)(b).) Indorser's obligation normally may not be enforced unless Indorser is given due notice of dishonor. §§ 3–104(e) (defining "note"), 3–415(a) (indorser's liability), 3–502(a)(3) (dishonor), 3–503(a) (notice of dishonor). Again, this is sometimes called a contract of secondary liability.

Indorser, by transferring the check or note, makes a *transfer warranty* that (1) Indorser is a "person entitled to enforce" the instrument (e.g., there are no unauthorized or missing indorsements), (2) all signatures are authentic and authorized, (3) the instrument has not been altered, (4) the instrument is not subject to a defense or claim in recoupment (partial defense), and (5) Indorser has no knowledge of any insolvency proceeding. §§ 3–416(a) and (b) and Comment 2, 3–301 ("person entitled to enforce"); cf. § 2–312 (warranty of title). See § 3–416(a)(6) and Comment 8 (remotely-created consumer items).

Acceptor (such as Drawee who certifies a check) is obliged to pay the draft according to its terms. Because there is no need for Payee (or a subsequent taker) to seek payment first from another party, this is sometimes called a contract of primary liability. §§ 3–103(a)(1) ("acceptor" defined), 3–413(a) (acceptor's liability), 3–409(a) and (d) (defining "acceptance" and "certified check").

Common uses of negotiable instruments

(1) A negotiable instrument may be used as a cash substitute, as when a check is used to transmit funds safely from Buyer to Seller through the mail. (2) As detailed later, a draft may be used as a collection device. Example: Seller–Drawer (creditor) draws a draft on Buyer–Drawee (debtor) payable to order of Seller. Seller negotiates the draft to a bank for collection. (3) A note is often used as a deferred payment device. Example: If Buyer wishes to pay for goods in twenty-four monthly installments, Buyer may sign a promissory note promising to pay a sum of money each month for twenty-four months.

History

Negotiable instruments law had its modern origins in the Law Merchant, which eventually was absorbed into the common law. In 1882, the English enacted the Bills of Exchange Act. In the United States, this Act inspired the Uniform Negotiable Instruments Law (NIL), which was superseded by UCC Article 3, first entitled Commercial Paper and renamed Negotiable Instruments in 1990.

B. THE NEGOTIABILITY CONCEPT— RIGHTS OF TAKERS OF NEGO- TIABLE INSTRUMENTS

1. INTRODUCTION TO NEGOTIABILITY

Property law and negotiable instruments

Assume Wrongdoer (W) steals goods and money from Owner (O) and sells the goods and transfers the money to innocent Transferee (T) for value. Will O be able to recover the goods and money from T? Answer: Under property law, O may recover the goods, since a thief generally cannot pass any greater title than the thief has. (Recall the discussion in Part One, G supra and § 2–403.) But what of the money? O cannot recover the money from T, even if O could identify the stolen money by serial number. Why? To protect the free circulation of money, so that persons may accept money without fear of any claims of prior putative owners. Here, the law protects the marketplace rather than the owner.

Similarly, suppose W steals O's paycheck, issued by X Corp., which O had indorsed by signing his or her name on the back. W sells the check to innocent T for value. O cannot recover the check from T. Why? To protect the free circulation of negotiable instruments, which are instruments representing money. Again, the law protects the marketplace rather than the owner. Cf. §§ 2–403 (power to transfer), 3–306 (claims to an instrument), 3–203(b) (to third comma) (implications of transfer). As later discussion will show, the result would be different if O had not indorsed or had indorsed differently.

Contract law and negotiable instruments

Suppose Buyer (B) buys goods that end up being defective, on credit from Seller (S). B has a valid defense against any claim by S for the unpaid monies. See, e.g., §§ 2–711 (buyer's remedies in general), 2–714 (remedies if goods are accepted) and Part One, D and F, 3 supra. If S assigns his or her contract rights to Transferee (T), will B's defense likewise be valid as against T? Answer: Yes. Generally, under contract law, assignees stand in the shoes of their assignors. Restatement (Second) of Contracts § 336. Thus, under contract law, as under property law, a person generally cannot pass to others greater rights than the person has. Now suppose, however, that buyer B paid seller S for the goods by issuing a negotiable promissory note, which S negotiates to innocent T for value. Will B's failure of consideration defense, valid as against S, likewise be valid against T? Answer: No. T cuts off B's defense and thus gets greater rights against B than S has. Why? To protect the free circulation of negotiable instruments. The law protects the marketplace even though doing so cuts off most of B's otherwise valid defenses on the instrument. § 3–305(a) and (b).

Greater rights for good faith purchasers

Thus, contrary to the general law of property and contracts, by negotiating a negotiable instrument to T, S may pass on to T greater rights as against B than S has. If the instrument is not negotiable, however, T is subject to all claims and defenses available under ordinary property and contract law. §§ 3–305(a), 3–306 (first sentence).

Merger or symbolism

In addition to the fact that negotiability gives greater rights to the good faith purchaser, there is another attribute of great importance. Suppose B contracts to purchase goods from S, and S assigns his or her right to payment to T. Before T notifies B of this assignment, B pays S. May T recover payment from B? No. Debtor B may safely pay his or her creditor S until B receives notification of the assignment, and payment to S discharges B's obligation as against both S and T. Restatement (Second) of Contracts § 338. Suppose, however, that B issued a negotiable note to S, which S negotiated to T. B should refuse to pay S unless S presents and surrenders the note because, if B pays S when innocent T has possession of the note, T can recover on the note from B. Thus, in this situation, B will pay twice. §§ 3–601(b), 3–602(a), 3–301. This attribute of negotiability is sometimes called *merger*; that is, the debt is so merged into the instrument evidencing the claim to the debt that the instrument must be treated in many situations as if it were the claim itself. This concept is also called *symbolism*; that is, the instrument symbolizes the claim itself. This means an obligor on a negotiable instrument cannot safely pay off the obligation without presentation and surrender of the properly indorsed instrument. When S surrenders the instrument upon payment, B is assured that such instrument is not in the hands of an innocent T, and thus the risk of double payment is avoided. See §§ 3–601(b) (discharge), 3–602(a) (payment), 3–301 (person entitled to enforce instrument), 1–201(b)(21)(A) (defining "holder") 3–501(b)(2) (presentment and surrender); cf. § 7–403(c) (in case of bailment). But see § 3–602(b) (notification of transfer) and Comments 2 and 3.

Procedural aspects of negotiability

In addition to the substantive consequences of negotiability discussed above, there are procedural consequences. Example: Maker (M) issues a note to Payee (P), who indorses it to Transferee (T). In an action on the note, T merely attaches the note to his or her complaint and alleges the note was executed by M, properly transferred to T, and has not been paid. See, e.g., § 3–308(b). It is not necessary to allege and prove the underlying sale or other transaction giving rise to the note or the consideration for it, as would be the case for assignments of choses in action generally.

These attributes and consequences of negotiability are further discussed below.

2. EFFECTIVENESS OF DEFENSES AND
CLAIMS IN RECOUPMENT
AGAINST SUBSEQUENT TAKERS
OF INSTRUMENTS

A. REQUISITES TO GREATER RIGHTS FOR GOOD FAITH PURCHASERS

Three factual settings to consider

One: Assume Seller enters into a sales contract with Buyer. Buyer (drawer) gives a check to Seller (payee) in payment. Seller indorses the check to Bank A. The goods are either not delivered to Buyer, or are delivered but defective, and Buyer rejects them. Due to this failure of consideration, Buyer orders Drawee Bank to stop payment on the check. Consequently, when Bank A duly presents the check for payment, Drawee Bank dishonors it. Bank A then gives Buyer notice of dishonor pursuant to § 3–503(a) and Comment 1, to invoke Buyer's obligation to pay the check under § 3–414(b) and Comment 2. Buyer asserts against Bank A the failure of consideration defense Buyer holds against Seller. See § 2–711.

Two: Assume Seller enters into a sales contract with Buyer. Buyer (maker) issues an installment note to Seller (payee) in payment. Seller indorses the note to Bank A. The goods are either not delivered to Buyer, or are delivered but defective, and Buyer rejects them. Bank A seeks payment on the note from Buyer pursuant to § 3–412. Buyer asserts against Bank A the failure of consideration defense Buyer holds against Seller.

Three: Assume Seller enters into a sales contract with Buyer. As a vehicle for payment, Seller (drawer) draws a draft upon Buyer (drawee) payable to the order of Seller, and Buyer accepts the draft, just as a bank would when certifying a check. Seller indorses the draft to Bank A. The goods either are not delivered to Buyer, or are delivered but defective, and Buyer rejects them. Bank A seeks payment on the draft from Buyer under § 3–413. Buyer asserts against Bank A the failure of consideration defense Buyer holds against Seller.

Requisites to greater rights for good faith purchasers

In the above three situations, under ordinary contract principles, Bank A would merely stand in the shoes of Seller. Any defense of Buyer that is valid against Seller would thus also be valid as against Seller's assignee, Bank A. Under Article 3, however, Bank A can sometimes obtain greater rights than Seller; that is, Bank A may be able to cut off Buyer's defense. For Bank A to cut off the defense of Buyer that is valid as against Seller:

    (1) the instrument must be negotiable;

    (2) the taker must be a holder;

    (3) the holder must be a holder in due course; and

    (4) the defense the obligor is asserting must *not* be a "real defense"; that is, a defense to which even a holder in due course is subject.

This holds regardless of whether Buyer is a drawer (as in factual setting 1 above), a maker (as in factual setting 2), or a drawee/acceptor (as in factual setting 3). Detailed discussion of these four requisites follows. These requisites are found in § 3–305(a) and (b), which states, "The right of a *holder in due course* to enforce the obligation of a party to pay the instrument is subject to [real] defenses of the obligor [§ 3–305(a)(1) and (b)], but is not subject to [personal] defenses of the obligor [§ 3–305(a)(2) and (b)] or claims in recoupment [§ 3–305(a)(3) and (b)] against a person other than the holder." § 3–305(b).

" 'Holder in due course' means the *holder* of an *instrument* if [it] ... is not ... irregular or incomplete ... and the holder took [it] (i) for value, (ii) in good faith, [iii–vi] without notice" of certain claims or defenses to payment that will be discussed later in this Part. § 3–302(a).

" 'Instrument' means a negotiable instrument." § 3–104(b). " 'Holder' means the person in possession of a negotiable instrument that is payable either to bearer or to an identified person who is the person in possession." § 1–201(b)(21)(A).

(1) The Instrument Must Be Negotiable

For a draft (including a check, § 3–104(e)–(i)) or a note (including a certificate of deposit, § 3–104(e) and (j)) to be negotiable, it must meet the following formal requisites per § 3–104(a)–(d).

(a) There Must Be a Written Promise or Order to Pay, Signed by Maker or Drawer

Signed writing

The term "negotiable instrument" is limited to a *signed writing* that orders or promises payment of money. §§ 3–103(a)(8) and (12), 3–104 Comment 1. A complete signature is not necessary. Instead, a signature can be any symbol executed or adopted with the present intention to adopt or accept a writing. §§ 1–201(b)(37), 3–401. The symbol may be printed, stamped, or written; it may consist of initials or a thumbprint. It may be on any part of the document. No catalog of possible signatures can be complete, so a court must use common sense and commercial experience. § 1–201 Comment 37. "Writing" is also a broad term, including printing, typewriting, or any other intentional reduction to tangible form. § 1–201(b)(43). It appears that the writing could be other than on paper, e.g., auto fenders, brick walls, gravestones, cows, people, etc. However, because negotiable instruments are expected to circulate in commerce more or less freely, the writing will virtually always be on paper. Indeed, Article 3 was formerly entitled, "Commercial Paper."

Note how the Uniform Electronic Transactions Act (UETA) fits in here. The purpose of the Act is to remove barriers to electronic commerce by validating and effectuating electronic records and signatures. Notably, UETA does not apply to a transaction to the extent it is governed by certain other law, including UCC Article 3 §§ 3(a) and (b)(2), 7. Similarly, see Electronic Signatures in Global and National Commerce Act (E–SIGN), 15 U.S.C. §§ 7001(a), 7003(a)(3). As to "transferable record," see UETA §§ 3 (Comment 6) and 16 esp. (a), (d), and (e); E–SIGN § 7021 esp. (a)(1), (d), and (e).

Promise or order

To be negotiable, a note must contain a Maker's *promise* to pay; a draft must contain a Drawer's *order* to pay. §§ 3–104(a) and (e), 3–103(a)(5) and (7) (defining "drawer" and "maker"). A "promise" is a written undertaking to pay money, signed by the person undertaking to pay. An acknowledgment of an obligation, standing alone, is not a promise. Thus, an I.O.U. is not a note unless it also includes an undertaking to pay. § 3–103(a)(12) and Comment 3.

An "order" is a written instruction to pay money, signed by the person giving the instruction. It may be addressed to any person (including the same person who gives the instruction, e.g., cashier's check (§ 3–104(g)), or to one or more persons jointly or in the alternative but not in succession. An authorization to pay, standing alone, is not an order. § 3–103(a)(8) and Comment 2. Example: Drawer instructs Drawee to "*Pay* to the order of...." The word *pay* is the instruction. (Former § 3–102(1)(b) defined an order as a *direction* to pay.) [For a draft that is *payable through* or *payable at* a bank, see § 4–106.]

A promise or order is not a negotiable instrument if it states conspicuously that it is not negotiable. §§ 3–104(d) and (f) and Comments 2 (paragraphs 3–5) and 3, 1–201(b)(10) (''conspicuous'' defined) In the case of a check, such statements are ineffective.

(b) The Promise or Order Must Be Unconditional

Express condition

A promise or order is unconditional and thus potentially negotiable unless it states an *express* condition to payment. Example: The statement, ''I promise to pay . . . John Doe if he conveys title to Blackacre to me'' includes an express condition that defeats negotiability. §§ 3–104(a), 3–106(a)(i) and Comment 1. But suppose a promise states, ''In consideration of John Doe's promise to convey title to Blackacre, I promise to pay . . . John Doe.'' Although the recital of Doe's executory promise to convey Blackacre might be read as an *implied* condition that the promise be performed for payment to be made, the condition is not express and therefore does not defeat negotiability. § 3–106(a)(i) and Comment 1. As to traveler's checks, see § 3–106(c) and Comment 2; as to FTC legend, see § 3–106(d) and Comment 3 and Part Three, B, 2, C, infra.

Incorporating or referencing another record

A mere reference to another writing does not make a promise or order conditional. Instead, a promise or order is unconditional unless it states (1) that the promise or order is *subject to* or *governed by* another record, or (2) that rights or obligations with respect to the promise or order are *stated in* another record. The following are three examples of conditional promises: (1) ''This note is subject to a contract of sale dated. . . .''; (2) ''This note is governed by a loan and security agreement dated. . . .''; (3) ''Rights and obligations of the parties with respect to this note are stated in an agreement dated [*date*] between the payee and maker of this note." §§ 3–104(a), 3–106(a)(ii) and Comment 1; see 3–117. It is not relevant whether any condition to payment is actually stated in the writing to which reference is made. Rationale: The holder of a negotiable instrument should not be required to examine another document to see what the holder's rights are with respect to payment. §§ 3–104(a), 3–106(a)(iii) and Comment 1. Even so, § 3–106(b)(i) states that a promise or order is not made conditional by a reference to another record for a statement of rights with respect to *collateral, prepayment,* or *acceleration.* Example: "This note is secured by a security interest in collateral described in a security agreement dated [*date*] between the payee and maker of this note. Rights and obligations with respect to the collateral are [stated in] [governed by] the security agreement." § 3–106 Comment 1. [*Record* is defined at §§ 1–201(b)(31), 3–103(a)(14); see § 9–102 Comment 9.]

Engagement of general credit

Former § 3–105(2)(b) stated that a promise or order was conditional if an instrument stated that it was to be paid only out of a particular fund or source. *See* Former § 3–105(1)(f)–(h), (2)(b) (also listing some exceptions). Example: "I promise to pay ... only out of my cotton profits." Revised § 3–106(b)(ii) changes the result such that a promise or order is not conditional just because payment is promised from a particular fund or source. Rationale: "There is no cogent reason why the general credit of a legal entity must be pledged to have a negotiable instrument. Market forces determine the marketability of instruments of this kind. If potential buyers don't want promises or orders that are payable only from a particular source or fund, they won't take them, but Article 3 should apply." § 3–106 Comment 1 (last paragraph).

(c) The Unconditional Promise or Order Must Be for a Fixed Amount of Money

Former §§ 3–104 and 3–106 required that the instrument contain an unconditional promise or order to pay a *sum certain* in money. Revised § 3–104(a) uses somewhat different language, requiring "a *fixed amount of money,* with or without interest or other charges described in the promise or order." The new language is more flexible, allowing for variable interest rates.

Fixed amount

The following examples satisfy the *fixed amount* requirement: "[P]ay ... $1,000 on [*date*];" "[P]ay ... 36 monthly installments of $256.86...." The "fixed amount" requirement applies only to principal. Interest may be stated in the instrument as a fixed or variable amount of money, or it may be expressed as a fixed or variable rate. For examples of notes with variable interest rates, see 13 West's Legal Forms § 11.5—Form 19 et seq. (If the instrument includes interest at an unspecified rate, the judgment rate applies.) § 3–112 and Comments.

The above discussion leaves the "with... other charges" language unexplained. "Other charges" would include costs of collection or attorney's fees upon default, if the instrument allows for such costs. § 3–104(a), see former § 3–106(1)(e).

Money

" 'Money' means a medium of exchange authorized or adopted by a domestic or foreign government..." as part of the official currency of that government. § 1–201(b)(24) and Comment 24. Unless the instrument states otherwise, an instrument that states an amount in foreign money may be paid in foreign money or in an equivalent amount in U.S. dollars. § 3–107. For calculation of the conversion rate, see §§ 3–107 and Comment, 3–111.

(d) The Writing Must Be Payable to Bearer or to Order

"To bearer" and "to order" are the so-called "magic" words of negotiability. This language indicates affirmatively that the instrument is intended to be negotiable.

Bearer

A promise or order is payable to *bearer* if it states, "Pay to bearer," "Pay to the order of bearer," "Pay to cash," or "Pay to the order of cash." If the promise or order states, "Pay [to the order of] a bucket of bolts," it is payable to bearer since the language chosen makes it clear that it is not payable to an identified person." Suppose the promise or order states, "Pay to the order of _____" and the instrument is delivered without the _____ having been filled in. Such an instrument is payable to bearer. Of course, the deliveree will probably fill in the blank. §§ 3–104(a)(1), 3–109(a), 1–201(b)(5) (defining "bearer"); cf. former § 3–111(c) and Comment 2.

Order

A promise or order is payable to *order* if it states, "Pay to the order of [*an identified person*]," or "Pay to [*an identified person*] or order." § 3–109(b), see § 3–110 (identifying to whom instrument is payable). If the instrument states, "Pay to the order of John Doe or bearer," the instrument is payable to bearer. § 3–109 Comment 2, cf. former §§ 3–110(3) and Comment 6, 3–111(b).

But what if an instrument read, "Pay John Doe"? This is neither bearer nor order paper. Under former § 3–805, Article 3 applied to this instrument (assuming it was otherwise negotiable), but there could be no holder in due course of the instrument. Under present § 3–104(a) and (c), the instrument is excluded from Article 3. If, however, the instrument is a check, the check *is* governed by Article 3 and there *can* be a holder in due course of it. § 3–104(c) and (f) and Comment 2.

If the instrument states that it is NOT NEGOTIABLE, see discussion in subsection (a), above. For guidance in applying Article 3 to a non-negotiable instrument by analogy, see § 3–104 Comment 2 (third through fifth paragraphs).

Significance of order vs. bearer distinction

If an instrument is payable to bearer, it can be negotiated by transfer of possession alone. Negotiation of an instrument that is payable to order—and thus to an identified person—requires both transfer of possession and the indorsement of the identified person. §§ 3–109 Comment 1, 3–201(b). Ultimately this is why the earlier hypothetical involving the stolen paycheck assumed the owner had indorsed the check before the theft.

(e) The Writing Must Be Payable on Demand or at a Definite Time

On demand

A promise or order is payable on demand if it (1) states that it is payable at the will of the holder, e.g., if it states it is payable "on demand," or "at sight," or (2) does not state any time of payment, as in the case of a check. §§ 3–104(a)(2) and (f), 3–108(a). Post-dated checks are a special case covered by later discussion. The date on a check is otherwise typically its date of issuance, which is different and, for this purpose, superfluous.

Definite time

A promise or order is payable at a definite time if it is

- payable on lapse of a definite period after sight or acceptance ("Ten days after sight pay . . ."), or

- payable at a fixed date or dates ("Pay . . . on June 1, 2008"), or

- payable at a time or times readily ascertainable when issued (a note payable "one year after the war," or "on death," does not qualify),

subject to rights of

(i) prepayment ("Maker reserves the right at any time to pay all installments remaining due on this note with interest to the time of payment,"), or

(ii) acceleration ("Holder may declare the entire unpaid balance of this note immediately due and payable whenever holder deems [himself] [herself] insecure." See § 1–309), or

(iii) extension at the holder's option ("The due date of this instrument may be extended at the holder's option from time to time and for any term or terms."), or

(iv) extension to a further definite time at the option of the maker or acceptor or automatically upon or after a specified act or event ("The maturity of this instrument shall be automatically extended for a period of _____ days [*or* weeks *or* months] if [*specify the event that 'triggers' extension.*"]). §§ 3–104(a)(2), 3–108(b). See § 3–113.

If an instrument is payable at a fixed date and is also payable upon demand, see § 3–108(c).

(f) The Writing Must Not State Any Other Undertaking or Instruction to Do Any Act in Addition to Payment of Money

To pass as negotiable, an instrument should have the characteristics of *simplicity* and *singleness of purpose.* Or, to use the oft-quoted statement, a negotiable instrument must be "a courier without luggage." Consequently, the promise or order may not state "any other undertaking or instruction by the person promising or ordering payment to do any act in addition to the payment of money," with

three exceptions as discussed below. § 3–104(a)(3) and
Comment 1, see § 3–117.

Exceptions

The promise or order may, however, contain

(i) an undertaking or power to give, maintain, or
protect collateral to secure payment. § 3–104(a)(3)(i).
Example: "Maker agrees to maintain the collateral that
is security for the payment of this note in good repair
and free from damage, injury, and deterioration and to
keep said collateral free of all conflicting claims, liens,
and encumbrances."

[*or*]

(ii) an authorization or power to the holder to confess judgment or realize on or dispose of collateral.
§ 3–104(a)(3)(ii); but see UCCC § 3.306 (1974) and
FTC Credit Practices Rules, 16 CFR § 444.2(a)(1). Example: "Maker hereby authorizes the holder of this note,
after default, to enter an appearance on Maker's behalf
and as Maker's attorney to confess judgment in any
court of record for any amount due on this note."

[*or*]

(iii) a waiver of the benefit of any law intended to
protect or benefit an obligor. § 3–104(a)(3)(iii); but see
FTC Credit Practices Rules, 16 CFR § 444.2(a)(2). Example: "In the event that judgment is obtained on this
note, Maker waives all rights of any law exempting his
property from execution or attachment."

(2) The Taker of the Instrument Must Be a "Holder"

Because a "holder in due course" must be a "holder,"
we must first discuss issuance and negotiation. See § 3–
301(i). The following subsections will illustrate these concepts. " '*Holder*' means the person in possession of a
negotiable instrument that is payable either to bearer or to

an identified person that is the person in possession."
§ 1–201(b)(21)(A). " '*Bearer*' means a person in possession of a negotiable instrument ... payable to bearer or
indorsed in blank." § 1–201(b)(5); see § 3–109(a) re:
bearer, § 3–109(b) re: identified person. " '*Issue*' means
the first delivery of an instrument by the maker or drawer,
whether to a holder or nonholder...." §§ 3–105(a), 1–
201(b)(15). " '*Negotiation*' means a transfer of possession
... of an instrument by a person other than the issuer to
a person who thereby becomes its holder." § 3–201(a).

In applying the above definitions, it may be determined
that "[a] person can become holder of an instrument
when the instrument is issued to that person, or the status
of holder can arise as the result of an event that occurs
after issuance. 'Negotiation' is the term used in Article 3 to
describe this post-issuance event." § 3–201 Comment 1.

(a) How Issuance and Negotiation to a Holder is Effected

First transaction—issuance

Assume Buyer buys goods from Seller and *issues* a draft,
check, or note "to the order of Seller". §§ 3–105(a)
("issue" defined), 1–201(b)(15) ("delivery" defined).
When Buyer completes the instrument, signs it, and voluntarily transfers it to Seller (i.e., delivery per § 1–
201(b)(15)), Seller is "the identified person [who is] in
possession" of the instrument, and is thus a "holder."
§ 1–201(b)(21)(A). Alternatively, Buyer could have written
the instrument "to bearer." In such a case, Seller is "the
person [who is] in possession [of] the instrument ...
payable to bearer, and again is a 'holder'." § 1–201(b)(5)
and (21)(A).

Second transaction—negotiation

Assume Seller now wishes to *negotiate* the instrument
to Adams. If the instrument is payable "to the order of
Seller," it is negotiated by transfer of possession to Adams,

along with Seller's indorsement. §§ 3–201(a) and (b) (first sentence), 3–204(a) and (b) (defining "indorsement" and "indorser"), 1–201(b)(21)(A) (defining "holder"), see § 3–110 (identifying to whom instrument is payable). If the instrument is payable "to bearer," it is negotiated merely by Seller's transfer of possession to Adams (i.e., no indorsement is required). §§ 3–201(a) and (b) (second sentence), 1–201(b)(21)(A) (defining "holder"); see § 3–109(c) (first sentence).

Third transaction—negotiation

Assume Adams now wishes to *negotiate* the instrument to Baker:

If the instrument is payable "to bearer" and was negotiated to Adams by mere transfer of possession, Adams likewise may negotiate to Baker by mere transfer of possession to Baker (no indorsement is required). §§ 3–201(b) (second sentence), 1–201(b)(5) and (21)(A) (defining "bearer" and "holder").

If the instrument was issued payable "to the order of Seller" and was indorsed in blank by Seller (a blank indorsement is usually the signature of the indorser without other words (§ 3–205(b) (first sentence) and Comment 2 (second paragraph))), the instrument thereby became payable to bearer and may be negotiated by transfer of possession alone (until specially indorsed). §§ 3–205(b) (second sentence), 1–201(b)(5) and (21)(A) (defining "bearer" and "holder"); see §§ 3–205(c) (converting blank indorsement to special indorsement), 3–109(c) (second sentence). Thus, Adams could negotiate the instrument to Baker by merely transferring possession of it to Baker (no indorsement is required).

If the instrument was issued payable "to the order of Seller" and was specially indorsed by Seller "Pay to Adams, (signed) Seller" (a special indorsement identifies a person to whom the indorsement is payable (§ 3–205(a) (first sentence)), the instrument became payable to the identified person and may be negotiated *only* by the indorsement of that person. §§ 3–205(a), (c), 1–201(b)(21)(A) (defining "holder"). Thus, Adams could negotiate the instrument to Baker by indorsing it and transferring possession of it to Baker. Note: Even if the instrument was issued payable to bearer, if it was specially indorsed by Seller, an indorsement by special indorsee Adams would be required. §§ 3–109(c), 3–205(a).

To recap, for an order instrument to be negotiated to a holder requires indorsement and transfer of possession. An order instrument is any instrument issued to order, or any instrument that is specially indorsed. For a bearer instrument to be negotiated to a holder requires only transfer of possession. A bearer instrument is any instrument issued to bearer or an order instrument that is indorsed in blank.

(b) *The Indorsement Requirement*

We have just observed that, to be negotiated to a holder, order paper must be indorsed. Now let us investigate certain matters regarding this indorsement.

(i) *Indorsement defined.* Indorsement means a signature (other than that of a maker, drawer, or acceptor) made on an instrument—usually on the back—for the purpose of (i) negotiating it (by special or blank indorsement), (ii) restricting payment of it (by restrictive indorsement, e.g., "for deposit only"), or (iii) incurring the indorser's liability on it. § 3–204(a) and (b); see §§ 3–205 (special, blank, and anomalous indorsements), 3–206 (restrictive indorsements), 3–415(a) and (b) (indorser liability).

(ii) *Who must indorse.* "[I]f an instrument is payable to an identified person, negotiation requires ... its indorsement by the holder." §§ 3–201(b), 1–201(b)(21)(A) (defining "holder"). "When specially indorsed, an instrument becomes payable to the identified person and may be negotiated only by that person." § 3–205(a) (second sentence), see § 3–109 Comment 1 (esp. last sentence).

(iii) *Where the indorsement must be written.* An indorsement is to be made *on an instrument.* For the purpose of determining whether a signature is made on an instrument, a paper affixed to the instrument (an allonge) is a part of the instrument. § 3–204(a) (esp. last sentence) and Comment 1 (last paragraph).

(iv) *Validity of indorsement(s) in name of payee.* "Section 3–110 states rules for determining the identity of the person to whom an instrument is initially payable if the instrument is payable to an identified person. [See § 3–109(b).] This issue usually arises in a dispute over the validity of an indorsement in the name of the payee." § 3–110 Comment 1. See §§ 3–404 esp. (b) (impostors; fictitious payees), 3–405 esp. (a)(2)(ii) (employer's liability), 3–406 (negligence).

(AA) *Intent of person signing as or for issuer.* The identity of the payee is determined by the intent of the person signing as (or in the name of) the issuer. Example: Drawer issues a check payable to John Smith. Many persons are named John Smith. Drawer's intention determines which John Smith is the payee. § 3–110(a) (first and second sentences). If more than one person signs, see § 3–110(a) (third sentence). See also § 3–110 Comment 1 (first and second paragraphs).

(BB) *Signature made by automated means.* In this case (e.g., check-writing machine), the payee's identity is determined by the intent of the person supplying the name. § 3–110(b) and Comment 1 (third paragraph).

(CC) *Instruments payable to bank accounts.* If the instrument is payable to an account number, the instrument is payable to the person to whom the account is payable. § 3–110(c)(1) and Comment 2.

(DD) *Instruments payable to trusts and estates, agents, informal organizations, public offices.*

Section 3–110(c)(2)(i) covers trusts and estates. Example: An instrument payable to "Estate of Anna Hoffman" is payable to the estate's representative.

Section 3–110(c)(2)(ii) covers instruments payable to an agent of a named person. Example: Instrument payable to "Jane Doe, President of X Corporation." Either Doe or X Corporation can be the holder of the instrument.

Section 3–110(c)(2)(iii) covers instruments payable to funds or organizations that are not legal entities. Example: Instrument payable to "Stetson Law Student Association." Any representative of the members of the organization can act as holder.

Section 3–110(c)(2)(iv) covers instruments payable to an office or a person described as holding an office. Example: Instrument payable to "Pinellas County Tax Collector" is payable to the incumbent of the office.

Section 3–110(c)(2) merely determines who is the holder of the instruments discussed therein. (§ 1–201(b)(21)(A)). It does not determine ownership of the instrument. § 3–110 Comment 3.

(EE) *Instruments payable to two or more persons.* If an instrument is payable to two or more persons alternatively ("to X or Y"), it is payable to *any* of them and may be negotiated by *any* of them. If an instrument is payable to two or more persons not alternatively ("to X and Y"), it is payable to *all* of them and may be negotiated only by *all* of them. If the instrument is ambiguous ("to X and/or Y"), it is payable to the persons alternatively. §§ 3–110(d) and Comment 4, 3–201 (defining "negotiation"), 1–201(b)(21)(A) (defining "holder").

(v) *Unindorsed order instruments—right to indorsement.* If an instrument is payable to order or specially indorsed to the transferor, the transferee has a specifically enforceable right to the transferor's unqualified indorsement. Even so, negotiation does not occur until indorsement is made. § 3–203(c) and Comment 3.

(vi) *Unindorsed items delivered to depositary bank for collection.* Suppose Payee receives a check payable "to the order of Payee." Payee deposits the check with Depositary Bank, but does not indorse it. Former § 4–205 not only permitted the bank to supply Payee's indorsement, but also required that it do so as a requisite to negotiation. Under present § 4–205(1), Depositary Bank becomes a *holder* regardless of whether Payee indorses the check, because Payee was a holder. Therefore, Depositary Bank can—but need not—supply Payee's indorsement. If the bank satisfies the other requisites of § 3–302, it is a holder in due course. §§ 4–105(1) and (2) ("depositary bank" defined), 1–201(b)(4) ("bank" defined); see § 4–206 (transfer between banks).

(vii) *Indorsement purporting to transfer less than entire amount of instrument.* In this case, negotiation does not occur. Instead, the transferee has only the rights of a partial assignee. Examples: Under the language, "Pay A two-thirds and B one-third," neither A nor B becomes a holder. "Pay A and B" transfers the entire cause of action to A and B as tenants in common. § 3–203(d) and Comment 5.

(viii) *Indorsement transferring security interest.* Under § 3–204(c), even if Payee's indorsement to Creditor mentions creation of a security interest, it is an unqualified indorsement that gives Creditor the right to enforce an instrument as its holder. § 3–204 Comment 2.

(ix) *Indorsement payable to holder under name that is not the name of holder (e.g., misspelling).* Example: Frank Smythe, a payee on a note or draft, is incorrectly designated "Frank Smith." Frank is the holder despite the error and may indorse in both names, first, "Frank Smith," then "Frank Smythe." § 3–204(d) and Comment 3.

(x) *Negotiation subject to rescission.* Even if, under other law, the negotiation may be rescinded, the remedy may not be asserted against a holder in due course or a payor bank. Thus, negotiation is effective even if obtained (i) from an infant, a corporation exceeding its powers, or a person without capacity, or (ii) by fraud, duress or mistake, etc. Example: Payee, an infant, indorses and transfers possession of a note to Indorsee, who negotiates it to a holder in due course. Payee may not raise infancy as a defense against the holder in due course. § 3–202 and Comments. See especially Comment 2 for extreme application of negotiability principle. See § 3–306.

(xi) *Restrictive indorsement—effect on further transfer or negotiation.* Previous discussion has explored two aspects of indorsements. Indorsements can be (1) special or blank and (2) unqualified or qualified. Indorsements also have a third aspect; they are either nonrestrictive or restrictive. Restrictive indorsements are made for the purpose of restricting payment of the instrument, e.g., "for deposit only". § 3–204(a) and (b), see §§ 3–205 (special, blank, and anomalous indorsements), 3–206 (restrictive indorsements), 3–415(a) and (b) (indorser's obligations). Example 1: Payee indorses, "Without recourse, (signed) P. Payee." This indorsement is in blank, qualified, and nonrestrictive. Example 2: Payee indorses, "Pay to XYZ Bank for deposit only, (signed) P. Payee.'' This indorsement is special, unqualified, and restrictive. See § 3–205 Comment 2 (second paragraph).

The great majority of restrictive indorsements fall within § 3–206(c), i.e., ''pay any bank,'' ''for deposit,'' or ''for collection.'' These words show the intention to have an instrument collected by a bank. §§ 3–206 Comment 3, 3–201(b) (''negotiation'' defined).

Effect of restrictive indorsements

Example: Assume Payee X indorses a check, ''For deposit only, (signed) X.'' The check is stolen by T, a thief, who cashes it at Grocery Store. Grocery Store indorses the check and deposits it in Depositary Bank (§ 4–105(2)). Grocery Store's account is credited, and the check is forwarded to Intermediary Bank (§ 4–105(4)) which forwards it to drawee Payor Bank (§ 4–105(3)) which pays the check. Who is liable to X in conversion? Answers:

    1.   A person other than a bank (i.e., Grocery Store), who purchases an instrument indorsed ''for deposit only, (signed) X'' converts the instrument unless the amount paid for the instrument is (i) received by indorser X or (ii) applied consistently with the indorsement (i.e., put in X's account). Because the amount paid for the check was not received by indorser X or applied consistently with the indorsement, Grocery Store is a converter and liable to X. § 3–206(c)(1) and Comment 3.

    2.   A depositary bank that takes a check for collection when indorsed ''for deposit only, (signed) X'' converts the check unless the amount paid by the bank with respect to the check is (i) received by indorser X or (ii) applied consistently with the indorsement. Because the amount paid for the check was not received by indorser X or applied consistently with the indorsement, Deposi-

tary Bank is a converter and liable to X. § 3–206(c)(2) and Comment 3.

3. Payor Bank and Intermediary Bank may disregard the indorsement and will not be liable if the proceeds of the check are not received by indorser X or applied consistently with the indorsement. § 3–206(c)(4) and Comment 3. For the policy behind this rule, see former § 4–205 Comment 2 ("For the purpose of permitting items to move rapidly through banking channels, intermediary banks and payor banks which are not also depositary banks are permitted to ignore restrictive indorsements.").

For other varieties of indorsements, see § 3–206(a) ("Pay A only"—subsequent holders may ignore the restriction), § 3–206(b) ("Pay A if A ships goods complying with our contract"—Code makes the conditional indorsement ineffective with respect to parties other than the indorser and indorsee), § 3–206(d) ("Pay T in trust for B"—subsequent transferees are not affected by the restriction unless they have knowledge that T dealt with the instrument in breach of trust). § 3–206 Comments 2 and 4.

Note: "The presence on an instrument of an indorsement to which [§ 3–206] applies does not prevent a purchaser of the instrument from becoming a holder in due course...."§ 3–206(e).

(xii) *Reacquisition.* Reacquisition of an instrument occurs if it is transferred to a former holder, by negotiation or otherwise. A former holder who reacquires the instrument may cancel indorsements made after the reacquirer first became a holder of the instrument. § 3–207 and Comment (esp. Case #1 and #2); see §§ 3–201 (defining "negotiation"), 3–203(a) and (b) (re: transfer).

For check indorsement standards under the federal Expedited Funds Availability Act, see 12 U.S.C. §§ 4001–

4010 and Regulation CC, 12 CFR Part 229. See 13 West's
Legal Forms § 8.1—Form 36.

(3) The Holder Must Be a "Holder in Due Course"

Simply, a holder in due course is a holder of a negotiable instrument who takes the instrument for value in good
faith without notice of certain claims and defenses described below. § 3–302(a). This is Negotiable Instrument
law's version of Sales law's bona fide purchaser. See § 2–403.

(a) Requisites to Holder in Due Course Status

(i) The Taker Must Be a Holder of a Negotiable Instrument

We have already seen that a holder in due course must
be (1) a holder of (2) a negotiable instrument. §§ 3–302(a) (defining "holder in due course"), 3–104(a)–(d)
(defining "negotiable instrument"), 1–201(b)(21)(A) (defining "holder").

(ii) The Instrument Must Not Be So Irregular or Incomplete
as to Call Its Authenticity Into Question

The instrument, when issued or negotiated to the holder, must not bear such apparent evidence of forgery or
alteration or otherwise be so irregular or incomplete as to
call its authenticity into question. § 3–302(a)(1) and Comment 1. Example: An apparent alteration in amount that
causes the word "void" to appear on the check. No holder
of this item could be a holder in due course.

(iii) The Holder Must Take the Instrument for Value

To qualify as a holder in due course, the holder must
take the instrument for value. §§ 3–302(a)(2)(i), 3–303, cf.
§ 1–204. For purposes of UCC Articles 3 and 4, it is

important to distinguish between *value* and *consideration*. Pursuant to § 3–303(a)(1), "An instrument is issued or transferred for value if the instrument is issued or transferred for a promise of performance, to the extent the promise has been performed." Under § 3–303(b), " 'Consideration' means any consideration sufficient to support a simple contract." Example: On April 1, Issuer I issues a check to Payee, P. P indorses the check to Seller S as a down payment for goods to be delivered by S to P on May 1. The check is dishonored April 2. S has not taken the check for value because it had not yet delivered the goods to P. Under § 3–303(a)(1), S would be a taker for value only "to the extent the promise [to deliver the goods] has been performed." Policy: Until S delivers the goods, it has not suffered an out-of-pocket loss. And, under § 2–703, S is excused from performing the promise to deliver the goods because P failed to make payment when due. § 3–303 Comment 2.

A holder also takes an instrument for value if (1) it acquires a security interest in the instrument (Payee borrows money from Holder and pledges the instrument to Holder as security, § 3–303(a)(2), see § 3–302(c)(i)); (2) it takes the instrument as payment for an antecedent claim (Payee indorses an instrument to Holder for services previously performed for Payee by Holder, § 3–303(a)(3)); or (3) it takes the instrument in exchange for a negotiable instrument (Payee indorses an instrument to Holder in exchange for Holder's promissory note issued to Payee, § 3–303(a)(4) and Comment 5). As to Holder taking the instrument and issuing a letter of credit, see § 3–303(a)(5) and Comment 5; see Part Six infra for discussion of letters of credit.

If the promise of performance that is the consideration for an instrument has been *partially* performed, see §§ 3–303(a)(1), 3–302(d) and Comment 6 (Case #5).

When a bank gives value

Assume Payee P indorses and deposits a check to its account in Bank A (depositary bank). § 4–105(2). The deposit creates a credit that can be revoked by Bank A if a claim or defense to payment appears. See former § 3–303 Comment 3. Clearly, Bank A has not paid value merely by crediting P's account. § 4–214(a) and Comment 1. If, however, Bank A allows P to withdraw the funds relating to the check, then Bank A has paid value. Query: How may we ascertain when P has withdrawn the funds? Answer: By adopting the "first in, first out" rule (FIFO). Example: On May 1, P has $500 in its account with Bank A. On May 2, a $250 check is deposited. On May 3, P deposits $800 in its account. On May 4, P withdraws $500. On May 5, P withdraws $250. On May 5, after the withdrawal, Bank A has paid value for the $250 check. The May 4 withdrawal depleted the $500 balance that existed on May 1; the May 5 withdrawal depleted the May 2 $250 deposit. (First monies in, first monies out.) The UCC confirms this rule by stating that a bank gives value for holder-in-due-course purposes to the extent that it has a security interest in the item; it has a security interest if credit given for the deposited item has been withdrawn according to the FIFO rule. §§ 4–211, 4–210(a)(1) and (b) (last sentence) and Comment 2.

Moreover, sometimes Bank A gives value and acquires a security interest in the item even before withdrawal. This occurs when Bank A has given credit that is available for withdrawal *as of right,* to the extent of the credit given, regardless of whether the credit is drawn upon. § 4–210(a)(2).

Finally, as in contract law generally, the courts are not concerned with the economic adequacy of the consideration given for the instrument. Restatement (Second) of Contracts § 79. Even so, as will be discussed presently, taking a $100 note, due in 30 days, for $25 may raise the issue of "good faith."

(iv) The Holder Must Take the Instrument Without Notice That It Is Overdue or Has Been Dishonored

To qualify as a holder in due course, a holder must take the instrument before maturity, without notice that it is overdue, has been dishonored, or that there is an uncured default with respect to payment of another instrument issued as part of the same series. §§ 3–302(a)(2)(iii), 1–202 (defining "notice"), 3–302(f) (when notice is effective). Policy: An instrument that remains in circulation after it is due generates suspicion. Why is it in circulation; that is, why is it not already paid?

Instruments Payable on demand

An instrument payable on demand (§ 3–108(a)) becomes overdue at the earliest of the following times:

(1) the day after demand for payment is duly made.

[or]

(2) if the instrument is a check, 90 days after its date. Former § 3–304(3)(c) stated that a domestic check was overdue when more than a reasonable length of time had elapsed after its issue, which was presumed to be 30 days.

[or]

(3) if the instrument is not a check, when the instrument has been outstanding for an unreasonably long period of time. §§ 3–304(a), 1–303 (esp. c).

Instruments Payable at a definite time

An instrument payable at a definite time (§ 3–108(b)) becomes overdue as follows:

(1) *Single payment instruments.* Instruments for a single payment of *principal* are overdue the day after

the due date. Example: A note due June 1 is overdue if unpaid on June 2. § 3–304(b)(2).

(2) *Installment instruments.* If the *principal* is payable in installments and an installment is late (e.g., installment number five is due June 1, and is unpaid as of June 2), the instrument is overdue until the default is cured. § 3–304(b)(1) and Comment 2.

(3) *Accelerated payments.* If a due date with respect to *principal* has been accelerated, the instrument becomes overdue the day after the accelerated due date. §§ 3–304(b)(3), 3–108(b)(ii).

(4) *Overdue interest.* An instrument does not become overdue if there is a default in payment of interest but no default in payment of principal, unless the due date of principal has been accelerated. § 3–304(c). Policy: Former § 3–304 Comment 6 states, "notice that interest is overdue [is] insufficient [to give notice that the instrument is overdue], on the basis of banking and commercial practice, . . . and the frequency with which interest payments are in fact delayed."

Dishonor

See generally § 3–502 and Part Three, C, 3, B, (1) infra.

(v) The Holder Must Take the Instrument in Good
     Faith, Without Notice of Claims or Defenses

Good faith

To qualify as a holder in due course, the holder must take the instrument in good faith. § 3–302(a)(2)(ii). " 'Good faith' means honesty in fact and the observance of reasonable commercial standards of fair dealing." §§ 3–103(a)(6), 1–201(b)(20). The former § 3–302 (see former § 1–201(19)) defined good faith as "honesty in fact in the conduct or transaction concerned." See former §§ 2–

103(1)(b), 2A–103(3). Revised Article 3 essentially returns to the 1952 Official Text, which defined good faith as "including observance of the reasonable commercial standards of any business in which the holder may be engaged."

Without notice

To qualify as a holder in due course, the holder must take the instrument without notice of claims or defenses. § 3–302(a)(2)(iv)–(vi). Under § 1–202(a), a person has *notice* of a fact if (1) the person has actual knowledge of it; (2) the person has received a notice or notification of it (see §§ 1–202(e), 3–302(f)); or (3) from all the facts and circumstances *known* to the person at the time in question (not facts that should have been known to a reasonable person), the person has *reason to know* it exists.

Without notice of unauthorized signature or alteration

The holder must take the instrument without notice that it contains an unauthorized signature or has been altered. §§ 3–302(a)(2)(iv), 1–201(b)(41) (defining "unauthorized signature"), 3–407(a) (defining "alteration"). The statute addresses notice of forgery or alteration separately from "claims or defenses" because these are not technically defenses. § 3–302 Comment 2 (last sentence).

Without notice of any claim to the instrument

The holder must take the instrument without notice of any *claim to the instrument.* §§ 3–302(a)(2)(v), 3–306, 3–307 (notice of breach of fiduciary duty); see § 3–302(b) (second sentence). Example: Drawer issues a paycheck to Payee, who indorses it in blank and leaves it on her dressing table. Thief steals it and sells it to Holder. Payee has a "claim to the instrument."

Without notice that any party has a defense or claim in recoupment

The holder must take the instrument without notice that any party has a *defense* or *claim in recoupment.* §§ 3–302(a)(2)(vi), 3–305(a) and Comment 3; see § 3–302(b); see also § 7–501 Comment 1 (second paragraph, last two sentences) (2003) (foundation of good-faith-purchase doctrine). Example: B issues a $10,000 note to the order of S in exchange for S's promise to deliver certain equipment. If S fails to deliver the equipment or delivers defective equipment that is rightfully rejected, B has a *defense* to the note. §§ 2–711, 2–601 et seq. If B accepts the defective equipment and has a breach of warranty claim against S for $1,000, B has a *claim in recoupment* against S for $1,000, which will reduce the amount owing on the note to $9,000. See §§ 3–305 Comment 3, 2–606 (defining "acceptance"), 2–607 (effect of acceptance), 2–714 (buyer's remedies upon accepting nonconforming goods). For further discussion, see Part Three, B, 2, B, (4), (b) and (c) infra.

Good faith and *notice* are dealt with by both case law and the UCC.

1.   *Case law.* The following three illustrations show how *courts* have dealt with the good faith and lack of notice requirements:

   a.   *Disparity between face value of instrument and sum paid by purchaser.* Example: Drawer D issues check to Payee P for $675. P negotiates the check to Transferee T, who pays $50 for it. A court or jury would probably find T was not acting in good faith and without notice. Why? Purchasing the check for such a low sum suggests T had knowledge of something wrong. Of course, an instrument is frequently discounted, e.g., Maker M issues a note to Payee P for $500 due in 60 days, and P discounts (sells) it with Bank A for $475. This discount probably does not preclude Bank A's taking in good faith and without notice. A note due in 60 days is not of the same value in the marketplace as a note due now. Why? Because Bank A will hold the note for 60 days before it is due, it is entitled to be compensated by earning interest for the use of the money. Further, evaluating the risk that the obligors on the instrument may not honor the instrument is an important factor in determining the sum Bank A will pay.

b. *Effect of the subsequent taker's closeness to the original transaction.* Example: M bought goods from P and issued to P an installment note and security agreement, which P discounted to Bank A. P used Bank A's regular form contract for the note and security agreement. Bank A had a thorough knowledge of P's business and exercised extensive control over its operation. Courts have held that this kind of closeness may preclude Bank A from having holder-in-due-course status. However, P's mere use of Bank A's forms, standing alone, would not preclude Bank A from being a holder in due course. Indeed, doing so would seem desirable so that the transactions may be conducted as routinely as possible with resulting cost savings. To understand the distinction, note that the holdings denying holder-in-due-course status generally reflect a concern for consumer protection. See Part Three, B, 2, C infra.

c. *Duty of inquiry.* Example: M issues a note to P, who indorses it to A. Does A have a duty to ask whether M has any defenses against P? Generally, no. Such a duty would put too great a burden upon the free flow of negotiable instruments. Of course, knowledge of suspicious facts will give notice to A and might dictate that A should inquire. § 1–202(a)(3).

2. *UCC provisions.* Sections 3–302(b) and 3–307 set forth specific provisions that deal with notice:

a. *Notice of discharge.* Except for discharge in bankruptcy, notice of discharge does not disqualify a person from being a holder in due course. Even so, discharge is effective against a person who became a holder in due course *with notice* of the discharge. § 3–302(b) (first sentence) and Comment 3 (see example), see § 3–305(a)(1)(iv).

b. *Filing or recording as constituting notice.* Public filing or recording of a document does not of itself constitute notice of a defense, claim in recoupment, or claim to the instrument. § 3–302(b) (second sentence). This is consistent with the negotiability concept: Rights concerning instruments intended to circulate freely in the marketplace should be determined as far as possible by the four corners of the instrument. Thus, by possessing the instrument, the holder has assurance that he or she controls the debt represented by the instrument without reference to outside considerations such as constructive notice by the filing-and-recording acts. Example: Maker issues a note to Payee secured by a mortgage on land (or by a security interest in personalty under UCC Article 9). Payee assigns the note and mortgage to A without indicating on them, by indorsement or otherwise, the fact of the assignment. A records the assignment and then gives the note and mortgage to Payee for servicing. Payee fraudulently negotiates the note (with the mortgage) to B, who takes in good faith and without knowledge of the assignment to A. Recording the assignment does not of itself constitute notice to B of A's interest. See § 9–331(c), and Nelson & Whitman, Real Estate Finance Law § 5.34 (4th Practitioner's Ed. 2002).

c. *Notice of breach of fiduciary duty.* Section 3–307 deals with the situation in which (1) an instrument is taken from a "fiduciary" (e.g., agent or corporate officer), (2) the taker has knowledge of the fiduciary status of the fiduciary, and (3) the "represented person" (e.g., principal or corporation) makes a claim to the instrument on the basis that the transaction is a breach of fiduciary duty. Example: Check payable to Corporation is indorsed in the name of Corporation by Doe as its President. Doe gives the check to Bank as partial repayment of a personal loan that Bank made to Doe. Under these facts, Bank has notice of Corporation's claim that Doe breached the fiduciary relationship, according to the following rule: In the case of an instrument payable to the represented person (or the fiduciary as such), the taker has notice of the breach of fiduciary duty if the instrument is taken in payment for a debt the taker knows to be the fiduciary's personal debt. § 3–307(a) and (b)(1) and (2)(i) and Comment 3, see 3–306 (re: claims to an instrument). If the instrument is issued by the represented person, see § 3–307(3) and (4); if an instrument is indorsed "Pay to T in trust for B" (restrictive indorsement), see § 3–206(d) and Comment 4.

Forgotten notice

Assuming Holder has notice of a defense or claim, is there a time when, and are there circumstances under which, the notice may cease to be effective? The UCC does not address this matter. Former § 1–201(25) and Comment 25. Thus, the pre-UCC "forgotten notice" or "temporary amnesia" doctrine has not been overruled. Consider bearer bonds stolen from A, and assume A sent printed notices of the theft, along with adequate descriptions of the bonds, to dealers throughout the country. B received such a notice. Later, B, forgetting the notice, took the bonds in good faith. Held: B wins. "Though one has received actual notice, if by forgetfulness or negligence he does not have it in mind when he acquires the bonds, he may still be a good faith purchaser. . . . [B]ut he may not willfully close his eyes to the notice, or resort to trick or artifice to avoid knowledge of its contents, or purposefully forget it." See Graham v. White–Phillips Co. case cited in former § 1–201 Comment 25. See § 8–102(a)(4) and (15) re: securities, e.g., bonds. Under revised § 1–202 and Comment, the reference to the "forgotten notice" doctrine has been deleted.

Notice of any defense or claim vs. notice of a particular defense or claim

Suppose Drawer issues a check to Payee Corporation in payment for goods that turn out to be defective. Payee Corporation's President indorses the check to A in payment for an automobile A knows President will use personally, not for corporate purposes. A does not, however, have notice of Drawer's defense (or claim in recoupment) arising from the defective goods. Does the fact that A has notice of one claim to the instrument (Payee Corporation's claim that its fiduciary breached his trust per § 3–307(b)) preclude A from being a holder in due course as to Drawer's failure-of-consideration defense (or claim in recoupment) of which A did not have notice? Answer: Yes. To be a holder in due course, the holder must take without notice of *any* claim to the instrument *and* without notice that *any* party has a defense or claim in recoupment. § 3–302(a)(2)(v) and (vi); see §§ 3–305(a), 3–306. Rationale: The object is to require a thoroughly honest and fair transaction, for a holder to qualify as a holder in due course.

(b) Payee as a Holder in Due Course

Assume Buyer–Maker issues a note to Seller–Payee, who negotiates to Bank A, who takes it for value in good faith and without notice of any defense or claim. Under these facts, Bank A is a holder in due course. But Seller–Payee, an immediate party to the underlying sales transaction who breached some or all of the quality warranties under §§ 2–313 through 2–315, is not a holder in due course. Suppose, however, the following: Buyer–Maker issues the note making Bank A the payee at Seller's request, because Seller planned to deliver the note to Bank A. Seller indorses its name on the back of the note and delivers it to Bank A. Here, Bank A, while seeming to be an immediate party because of how the note is written, is actually a remote party insofar as the underlying sales transaction is concerned. Consequently, Bank A may be a holder in due course, though normally the payee—as an immediate party to the underlying transaction—would not be. See § 3–302 Comment 4 and examples.

(c) Unusual Circumstances in Which a Holder Does Not Become a Holder in Due Course

When an instrument is taken (i) by legal process or by purchase at an execution, bankruptcy, creditor's sale, etc., (ii) by purchase as part of a bulk transaction not in the ordinary course of the transferor's business, or (iii) as successor in interest to an estate, etc., the taker will not be a holder in due course. § 3–302(c) and Comment 5 (see § 3–203(b) (shelter doctrine)), cf. § 7–501(a)(5) (re: documents of title). However, under governing federal law, when the Federal Deposit Insurance Corporation takes over an insolvent bank in a purchase-and-assumption transaction, it is given holder-in-due-course status. See 12 U.S.C. § 1823(e); Campbell Leasing, Inc. v. F.D.I.C., 901 F.2d 1244 (5th Cir. 1990), Desmond v. F.D.I.C., 798 F.Supp. 829 (D. Mass. 1992).

(d) Holder of Security Interest as Holder in Due Course

Assume Payee negotiates Maker's $1,000 note to Holder as security for Payee's $600 debt to Holder, and Maker has a defense against Payee (§ 3–305(a)(2)) of which Holder has no notice. Under these facts, Holder may qualify as a holder in due course only to the extent of $600. Section 3–302(e) states the rule: If Holder has only a security interest in the instrument and Maker has a defense, Holder may assert rights as a holder in due course only up to the amount of the unpaid obligation secured. §§ 3–302(e) and Comment 6 (Case #6); 3–301; see §§ 3–204(c) (re:

indorsement that transfers a security interest), 9–109 (scope of Article 9), 1–203 (lease vs. security interest), cf. § 2–403(1) (first sentence) (re: transfer of interest in goods).

(e) Successors to Holders in Due Course—Shelter Principle

Transfer of an instrument (regardless of whether the transfer is a negotiation) vests in the transferee any right of the transferor to enforce the instrument (including any right as a holder in due course). Example 1: Assume that, by fraud, Payee induced Maker to issue a note to Payee. Such fraud is a personal defense to Maker's obligation to pay the note under § 3–305(a)(2) and (b). Payee negotiated the note to X, a holder in due course. After the instrument became overdue, X negotiated the note to Y, who had notice of Payee's fraud. See § 3–302(a)(2)(iii) and (vi). Under what is called "the shelter principle," Y succeeds to X's rights as a holder in due course and takes free of Maker's defense of fraud. Policy: To assure the holder in due course (X) a free market for the instrument. § 3–203(b) and Comments 2 and 4 (Case #1). Cf. 2–403(1) (first sentence) (re: transfer of interest in goods).

There is an exception to the shelter principle: "[T]he transferee cannot acquire rights of a holder in due course by a transfer, directly or indirectly, from a holder in due course if the transferee engaged in fraud or illegality affecting the instrument." § 3–203(b). Example 2: In Example 1, assume Payee negotiated the note to X, a holder in due course. Payee then repurchased the note from X. Payee, the fraudster, does not succeed to X's rights as a holder in due course and is subject to Maker's defense of fraud. Policy: A party to fraud or illegality affecting an instrument is not permitted to wash the instrument clean by passing it to a holder in due course and then repurchasing it. § 3–203(b) and Comments 2 and 4 (Case #2).

(f) Burden of Establishing Signatures and Status as Holder in Due Course

Assume the following: Buyer issues a note or draft to Seller in payment for goods. Seller indorses the instrument to Adams. Adams now sues Buyer on the instrument.

Signatures

In an action on an instrument, the authenticity of Buyer's signature on the instrument is admitted unless specifically denied in the pleadings. § 3–308(a) (first sentence). If the validity of a signature is denied in the pleadings, see § 3–308(a) (second sentence); as to undisclosed principals, see § 3–308(a) (third sentence).

Defenses or claims in recoupment

If the validity of Buyer's signature is admitted (or proved per § 3–308(a)), plaintiff Adams will be entitled to payment, just by producing the instrument, if Adams proves he or she is a "holder" (§§ 3–301, 1–201(b)(21)(A)), *unless* defendant Buyer proves a defense or claim in recoupment, i.e., the goods were not delivered or, if delivered, they did not conform to the sales contract. §§ 3–308(b) (first sentence), 3–103(a)(13) (defining "prove"), 1–201(b)(8) ("burden of establishing"). See, e.g., §§ 2–711 (buyer's remedies for rejected goods), 2–714 (buyer's remedies for accepted goods), 2–717 (deducting damages from price), 3–305(a)(2), (3) and (b).

Due Course

If Buyer proves a defense or claim in recoupment, Adams' right to payment is subject to the defense or claim, *except* to the extent Adams proves rights of a holder in due course that are not subject to the defense or claim. §§ 3–308(b) (second sentence), 3–103(a)(13) (defining "prove"), (1–201(b)(8)) ("burden of establishing"), 3–302 (holder in due course), 3–203(b) (shelter doctrine). Note that, until proof of a defense or claim in recoupment is made, whether Adams qualifies as a holder in due course does not matter. In the absence of a defense or claim in recoupment, *any* person entitled to enforce the instrument is entitled to recover. § 3–308 Comment 2.

(4) Holder in Due Course Is Subject to "Real Defenses" But Not "Personal Defenses" or "Claims in Recoupment"

Although a *holder* of an instrument is a "person entitled to enforce" it, the holder may be subject to defenses and claims in recoupment of prior parties. If the holder is a holder in due course, however, the holder will *not* be subject to "personal defenses" or "claims in recoupment" of prior parties (but will be subject to "real defenses"). §§ 3–301 ("holder" defined), 3–305(a) and (b) ("real" and "personal" defenses defined).

(a) Real Defenses

A holder in due course's right to enforce an instrument is *subject to* the "real defenses" of the obligor (e.g., maker or drawer) as stated in § 3–305(a)(1). § 3–305(b); see §§ 3–407(c)(i) (re: fraudulent alterations), 3–403(a) (effect of unauthorized signature), 3–406 (role of contributory negligence), 3–302 Comment 2 (last sentence) (forgery and alteration technically not defenses). The "real defenses" are as follows:

1. Infancy of the obligor, to the extent it is a defense to a simple contract under other law. § 3–305(a)(1)(i), (b) and Comment 1. The *policy* is one of protecting the infant even at the expense of occasional loss to innocent purchasers. The UCC makes no attempt to state when infancy is a defense. In some jurisdictions, an infant cannot rescind the transaction or set up the defense without first restoring the holder to the position held before the instrument was taken. In other jurisdictions,

an infant who misrepresents his or her age may not assert infancy. See Restatement (Second) of Contracts § 14.

2.   Duress that (under other law) nullifies the obligation.   § 3–305(a)(1)(ii), (b) and Comment 1. Examples: An instrument signed at gunpoint is null and void even in the hands of a holder in due course; one signed under threat to prosecute the maker's son for theft, by contrast, may be voidable so that the defense is cut off by a holder in due course.

3.   Lack of legal capacity that (under other law) nullifies the obligation. § 3–305(a)(1)(ii), (b) and Comment 1. Examples: mental incompetence, guardianship, ultra vires acts or lack of corporate capacity, or any other incapacity apart from infancy. Such incapacity is typically statutory. The key is whether the effect of the state law is to render the obligation entirely null and void (creating a real defense) or merely to render the obligation voidable at the election of the obligor (creating a personal defense).

4.   Illegality of the transaction that (under other law) nullifies the obligation. § 3–305(a)(1)(ii), (b) and Comment 1. Examples: gambling or usury.

5.   Fraud in the execution (also known as real or essential fraud, fraud in the essence, fraud in the inception, fraud in the factum, or fraud in esse contractus). This is fraud that induced the obligor to sign the instrument with neither (i) knowledge nor (ii) reasonable opportunity to learn of its character or essential terms.   § 3–305(a)(1)(iii), (b) and Comment 1 (fifth paragraph). Common illustration: Maker is tricked into signing a note, believing it is merely a receipt or some other document. Theory of defense: Maker's signature on the instrument is ineffective because Maker did not intend to sign such an instrument at all. This defense also extends to an instrument signed with knowledge

that it is a negotiable instrument, but without knowledge of its essential terms. Example: Maker is about to sign a $100 note. Payee knocked over a lamp to distract Maker. When Maker reached to catch the lamp, Payee substituted a note for $1,000, which Maker signed without noticing the switch. Contrast the personal defense of fraud in the inducement, wherein Maker *did* intend to sign the negotiable instrument as issued, and voluntarily "set it afloat upon a sea of strangers." "The *test* of the defense is that of excusable ignorance of the contents of the writing signed. The party must not only have been in ignorance, but must also have had no reasonable opportunity to obtain knowledge. All relevant factors are to be taken into account, including the intelligence, education, business experience, and ability to read or understand English of the signer. Also relevant is the nature of the representations that were made, whether the signer had good reason to rely on the representations or to have confidence in the person making them, the presence or absence of any third person who might read or explain the instrument to the signer, or any other possibility of obtaining independent information, and the apparent necessary, or lack of it, for acting without delay. Unless the misrepresentation meets this test, the defense is cut off by a holder in due course." § 3–305 Comment 1 (fifth paragraph).

6. Discharge of the obligor in insolvency proceedings. Example: Maker's debts are discharged under the federal Bankruptcy Code. See 11 U.S.C. §§ 727, 523, 524. §§ 3–305(a)(1)(iv), 1–201(b)(22) ("insolvency proceedings" defined); see §§ 3–601(b) (re: effect of discharge on one who lacks notice), 3–302 Comment 3, 3–305 Comment 1 (last paragraph).

7. Alteration, to the extent altered, unless a party who would have asserted the defense is estopped by negligence from doing so. Example: Maker issues a note

to Payee for $100. Payee skillfully alters it to $1,000 and negotiates it to Adams, a holder in due course. Adams recovers only $100 from Maker. Rules: A fraudulent alteration discharges a party whose obligation is affected by the alteration. However, a holder in due course such as Adams may enforce the note according to its *original* terms (not the altered terms). Note: In the case of an incomplete instrument altered by unauthorized completion, Adams may recover according to the note's terms as completed, i.e., $1,000. §§ 3–407 esp. (c)(i) and (ii), 3–302 Comment 2 (last sentence). Also note: If Maker's negligence in completing the note substantially contributes to an alteration, Maker is precluded from asserting the alteration against a person who, in good faith, takes the note for value such as Adams. §§ 3–406(a), 3–103(a)(9) ("ordinary care" defined), see § 3–406(b) (which adopts a comparative negligence test). As to the burden of proof, see § 3–406(c).

8. Unauthorized signature (including forgery) unless the party who would have raised the defense is estopped by ratification or negligence from doing so. Example: Forger forges Drawer's name on a check and delivers it to Payee, who negotiates it to Adams, a holder in due course. Adams cannot recover from Drawer but may recover from Forger. Rules: An unauthorized signature is wholly inoperative as that of the person whose name is forged, functioning only as the forger's signature, insofar as a holder in due course is concerned. (Of course, Drawer may ratify the unauthorized signature.) §§ 3–403(a), 1–201(b)(41) ("unauthorized signature" defined); see § 3–401(a) (liability on signature), § 3–302 Comment 2 (last sentence) (forgery and alteration technically not defenses). Note: If Drawer's negligence substantially contributes to the forgery, Drawer is precluded from asserting the forgery against a person who, in good faith, takes the check for value such as Adams. §§ 3–406(a), 3–103(a)(9) ("ordinary

care" defined), see § 3–406(b) (which adopts a comparative negligence test). For cases illustrating conduct that can be the basis of preclusion under § 3–406(a), see Comment 3 (e.g., drawer is negligent in failing to secure an automatic signing device).

(b) Personal Defenses and Claims in Recoupment

The right of a holder in due course to enforce the instrument is *not* subject to "personal defenses" stated in § 3–305(a)(2) or claims in recoupment stated in § 3–305(a)(3) against a person other than the holder. § 3–305(b).

(i) Personal Defenses of the Obligor
Found Elsewhere in Article 3

These personal defenses (§ 3–305(a)(2) and (b)) are listed in Comment 2 to § 3–305 as follows:

1. Nonissuance (non-delivery), conditional issuance, and issuance for a special purpose. § 3–105 esp. (b) and Comment 2. Example: B steals from A's office two signed but otherwise incomplete checks. B completes the checks and indorses them to C, a holder in due course. C cuts off A's defense.

2. Failure to countersign a traveler's check. § 3–106(c) and Comment 2.

3. Modification of the obligation by a separate agreement. § 3–117 and Comment 1.

4. Payment that violates a restrictive indorsement. § 3–206(f) and Comment 5.

5. Instruments issued without consideration, or for which the promised consideration has not been given. § 3–303(b). Example: Buyer issues a note to the order of Seller in exchange for Seller's promise to deliver specified equipment. If Seller fails to deliver the equipment or delivers equipment that is rightfully rejected,

Buyer has a defense to the note because the consideration for the note was not given. § 3–303(b). [For Buyer's Article 2 rights, see §§ 2–301, 2–601 through 2–605, 2–711.] Although that defense can be asserted against Seller, Buyer could not assert the defense against a holder in due course. § 3–305 Comment 3. (If Buyer accepts the defective equipment from Seller, see "claims in recoupment" discussed below.)

6. Breach of warranty when a draft is accepted. § 3–417(b) (fourth sentence).

7. Unauthorized completion. §§ 3–115 (incomplete instruments), 3–407 esp. (c) and Comments (fraudulent alteration), 3–302 Comment 2 (last sentence) (forgery and alteration technically not defenses). Example: A signs and hands B a check naming B as payee. The amount is left blank. A tells B to fill in the amount but not to exceed $300. B fills in $500 and indorses to C, a holder in due course. C cuts off A's defense. Contrast the real defense of alteration discussed at (a), 7 above.

(ii) Personal Defenses Available at Common Law in an Action to Enforce a Right to Payment Under a Simple Contract

The most prevalent common-law defenses are fraud in the inducement, misrepresentation, or mistake in the issuance of the instrument. These are cut off by a holder in due course. § 3–305(a)(2) and (b) and Comment 2, 1–103(b) (common-law defenses supplement UCC), see § 3–303(b) ("consideration" defined). Example: S, in selling goods to B, makes fraudulent representations regarding them. Relying on S's representations, B buys the goods and gives S a note. S indorses the note to H, a holder in due course. H cuts off B's defense of fraud in the inducement. Rationale: B knowingly issued a negotiable instrument and "set it afloat upon a sea of strangers." Contrast the real defense of fraud in the execution discussed at (a), 5 above and § 3–305(a)(1)(iii).

(iii) Claims in Recoupment

The right to enforce an instrument is subject to the obligor's claim against the original payee if the claim arose from the transaction that gave rise to the instrument. (But the obligor's claim may be asserted against a transferee of the instrument only to reduce the amount owing on the instrument at the time the action is brought.) However, a holder in due course's right to enforce the instrument is not subject to claims in recoupment against a person other than the holder. § 3–305(a)(3), (b).

Example from § 3–305(b) and Comment 3: "Buyer issues a note to the order of Seller in exchange for a promise of Seller to deliver specified equipment. ... Seller delivered the promised equipment and it was accepted by Buyer. [§ 2–606.] The equipment, however, was defective. Buyer retained the equipment and incurred expenses with respect to its repair. In this case, Buyer does not have a defense under Section 3–303(b). Seller delivered the equipment and the equipment was accepted. Under Article 2, Buyer is obliged to pay the price of the equipment which is represented by the note. [§ 2–607(1).] But Buyer may have a claim against Seller for breach of warranty. [§§ 2–313 through 2–317, 2–714.] If Buyer has a warranty claim, the claim may be asserted against Seller as a counterclaim or as a claim in recoupment to reduce the amount owing on the note."

"Suppose Seller negotiates the note to Holder. If Holder had notice of Buyer's warranty claim at the time the note was negotiated to Holder, Holder is not a holder in due course (Section 3–302(a)(2)(iv)) and buyer may assert the claim against Holder (Section 3–305(a)(3)) but only as a claim in recoupment, i.e., to reduce the amount owed on the note. If the warranty claim is $1,000 and the unpaid note is $10,000, Buyer owes $9,000 to Holder. If the warranty claim is more than the unpaid amount of the note, Buyer owes nothing to Holder, but Buyer cannot recover the unpaid amount of the warranty claim from Holder. If Buyer had already partially paid the note, Buyer is not entitled to recover the amounts paid. The claim can be used only as an offset to amounts owing on the note. If Holder had no notice of Buyer's claim and otherwise qualifies as a holder in due course, Buyer may not assert the claim [in recoupment] against Holder."

Note: Under former § 3–408, the claim in recoupment was called the personal defense of "partial failure of consideration."

(c) Effectiveness of Discharge

Example: Maker issues a note to Payee. Maker pays Payee, endeavoring to discharge Maker's obligation on the note. Maker, however, did not take up the note from Payee. (It either had been negotiated to Adams or it subsequently was negotiated to Adams.) Held: Discharge of Maker's obligation to pay the note is not effective against Adams if Adams is a holder in due course *without notice of the discharge*. §§ 3–601, 3–602(a) (payment and discharge), 3–301(i) (holder's right to enforce), 1–201(b)(21)(A) ("holder" defined); see 3–302(b) (first sentence) and Comment 3. For discharge of obligations, see Part Three, C, 8 infra.

The above example illustrates *merger*. That is, the debt is so merged into the paper evidencing the debt that the paper must be treated in many situations as if it were the debt claim itself. Simply stated, an obligor cannot safely discharge its obligation without requiring the party receiving payment to present and surrender the paper. This will assure the obligor that the paper is not in the possession of a holder in due course who lacks notice of the discharge. See § 3–501(b)(2).

[Note: Section 3–602(a), discussed above, covers payments made in a traditional manner to the "person entitled to enforce" the instrument (e.g., the "holder"). Amended § 3–602(b) (2002) provides an alternative method of payment. This deals with the situation in which a holder transfers the instrument without giving notice to the parties obligated on the instrument. See § 3–602(b) and Comments 2 and 3.]

(d) Discharge, Defenses, and Claims in Recoupment of Accommodation Parties

See §§ 3–302(b) (first sentence), 3–601(b). See also §§ 3–305(d) and Comment 5, 3–419(c) (determining accommodation party status), 3–605(e) (discharge of secondary obligors) and Part Three, C, 6 infra.

B. EFFECT OF CONSUMER PROTECTION LEGISLATION ON THE RIGHTS OF A HOLDER IN DUE COURSE

Negotiable instruments under UCC Article 3

Assume Buyer–Maker issues a negotiable installment note to Seller–Payee in payment for goods, which are defective. If Seller negotiates the note to Bank, a holder in due course, then Bank takes free of Buyer's personal defense against Seller. Rationale: Bank is financing Buyer's purchase. Thus, while Bank should bear the *credit* risk, it should not be involved in disputes concerning the underlying sales transaction. Accordingly, Bank takes the note free of most defenses Buyer could assert against Seller. Note that this would also be the result if Buyer borrowed directly from Bank, then bought the goods from Seller with the borrowed money. Either way, Buyer would be required to pay Bank even if the purchased goods were defective.

In the context of consumer goods, however, some courts and legislatures believed it inappropriate to have a buyer's defenses cut off by a holder in due course, and thus limited or precluded holder-in-due-course status. Statutes having this effect are often entitled, Retail Installment Sales Act, Home Improvement Finance Act, etc. An illustrative statute is Uniform Consumer Credit Code § 3.307 [Certain Negotiable Instruments Prohibited] (1974) which states,

> With respect to a consumer credit sale or consumer lease, [except a sale or lease primarily for an agricultural purpose,] the creditor may not take a negotiable instrument other than a check dated not later than ten days after its issuance as evidence of the obligation of the consumer.

Under this section, Bank takes the note or draft subject to Buyer's defenses against Seller. See FTC rule, 16 CFR § 433.2; §§ 3–106(d) and Comment 3 (such language does not render an instrument conditional and thus non negotiable), 3–302(g) and Comment 7 (UCC definition of "holder in due course" is limited by such laws).

Secured transactions under UCC Article 9

In the factual setting above, suppose Buyer did not sign a negotiable installment note, but instead executed a security agreement under UCC Article 9. (Article 9 is discussed at Part Five infra.) Suppose the following waiver-of-defense clause appears in the security agreement: "Buyer/debtor waives the right to assert against any assignee of the seller/secured party, or any subsequent assignee, any defense, counterclaim, or setoff he could assert against the seller/secured party in an action brought by him upon the debt of the buyer/debtor or upon the security agreement." Such a waiver—if enforceable—would give Bank rights similar to a holder in due course. As to this clause, UCC § 9–403(b) states,

[A]n agreement between an account debtor [e.g., Buyer] and an assignor [e.g., Seller] not to assert against an assignee any claim or defense that the account debtor may have against the assignor is enforceable by an assignee that takes an assignment [for value, in good faith, and without notice]. [See § 9–403(c).]

"[Section 9–403(b)] is subject to law ... which establishes a different rule for an account debtor who is an individual and who incurred the obligation primarily for personal, family, or household purposes." § 9–403(e). One such law is Uniform Consumer Credit Code § 3.404 (Assignee Subject to Claims and Defenses], subsection (1) of which states,

With respect to a consumer credit sale or consumer lease [, except one primarily for an agricultural purpose], an assignee of the rights of the seller or lessor is subject to all claims and defenses of the consumer against the seller or lessor arising from the sale or lease of property or services, notwithstanding that the assignee is a holder in due course of a negotiable instrument issued in violation of the provisions prohibiting certain negotiable instruments (Section 3.307).

See FTC rule, 16 CFR § 433.2.

Finance leases under UCC Article 2A

For discussion of irrevocable promises under finance leases and the classic "hell or high water" clause, see §§ 2A–103(1)(g), 2A–209 and 2A–407 and Part Two, D, 10 and E, 4 supra.

Consumer credit contract notice

In connection with any sale or lease of goods or services to consumers in or affecting commerce, it is an unfair or deceptive act or practice within the meaning of Section 5 of the Federal Trade Commission Act for a seller to take or receive a "consumer credit contract" that fails to contain a notice that any holder of such contract is subject to all claims and defenses a debtor could assert against the seller. 16 CFR § 433.1 et seq. The text of such notice should be as follows:

NOTICE

ANY HOLDER OF THIS CONSUMER CREDIT CONTRACT IS SUBJECT TO ALL CLAIMS AND DEFENSES WHICH THE DEBTOR COULD ASSERT AGAINST THE SELLER OF GOODS OR SERVICES OBTAINED PURSUANT HERETO OR WITH THE PROCEEDS HEREOF. RECOVERY HEREUNDER BY THE DEBTOR SHALL NOT EXCEED AMOUNTS PAID BY THE DEBTOR HEREUNDER.

[Note: Amended § 3–305(e)(2002) has been added to clarify the treatment of an instrument that omits the above notice. It adopts the view that the instrument should be treated as if the language required by the FTC Rule were present. § 3–305(e) and Comment 6, cf. § 9–404(d).]

Credit cards

Assume Buyer purchases goods from Seller in a "consumer credit" transaction using a credit card, and the goods turn out to be defective. May the cardholder (Buyer) assert against the card issuer (Buyer's bank—arguably analogous to a holder in due course) claims and defenses arising out of the transaction with Seller (the person who had honored the credit card)? Answer: Sometimes. Subject to certain limitations, Buyer may have the right not to pay the remaining amount due on the purchase. 15 U.S.C. § 1666i, 12 CFR § 226.12(c). Cf. §§ 5–102(a)(10) ("letter of credit" defined), 5–108(a) and (f) (doctrine of strict compliance and independence principle), 5–103(d) (independence principle).

3. EFFECTIVENESS OF CLAIMS TO A NEGOTIABLE INSTRUMENT AS AGAINST A SUBSEQUENT TAKER

Stolen bearer paper and claims to the instrument

Assume A issues a note or draft to B, who, in turn, negotiates it to C, a holder in due course. We know from prior discussion that C takes the instrument free of A's personal defenses against B. Now suppose A issues the note or draft designating payment "to bearer." Alternatively, assume A issues the item payable "to the order of B," and B indorses in blank. §§ 1–201(b)(5) ("bearer" defined), 3–109(a) (instrument payable to bearer), 3–201(b) (negotiation), 3–205(b) (blank indorsement). In either case, further suppose C steals the bearer paper and sells it to D, a holder in due course. May B, the "true owner" of the paper, recover it from D? Answer: D takes the paper free of B's claim. § 3–306 (second sentence). Our analysis of how D can take free of B's *claim* is similar to our analysis of how D can take free of A's defenses or claims in recoupment: (1) the instrument must be negotiable; (2) the taker must be a holder; (3) the holder must be a holder in due course; and (4) A's defense must be a personal defense rather than a real defense. See Part Three, B, 2, B supra.

Stolen order paper and claims of ownership

Now suppose, in the above example, A issues the note or draft "to the order of B." B does *not* indorse; rather, C steals the item and forges B's indorsement. C sells the instrument to D, who takes for value in good faith without notice of B's claim to the instrument. "An indorsement that is payable to an identified person [B] cannot be negotiated without the indorsement of the identified person [B]. § 3–201(b). Thus, an instrument payable to order *requires* the indorsement of the person to whose order the instrument is payable [B]." § 3–109 Comment 1.

[Emphasis added.] Since B did not indorse the order paper, D cannot become a *holder* (§ 3–201(a)); therefore, D cannot be a holder in due course, and will be *subject to* B's claim to the instrument. § 3–306 (first sentence).

Other claims

The claims referred to in § 3–306 "include not only claims to ownership but also any other claim of a property or possessory right. This includes the claim to a lien or the claim of a person who was wrongfully deprived of possession of an instrument. Also included is a claim based on Section 3–202(b) for rescission of a negotiation of the instrument by the claimant." § 3–306 Comment. Example: A issues a negotiable note "to order of B." B, an infant, indorses and delivers the note to C, who indorses and delivers it to D, a holder in due course. B now wishes to rescind the transaction and recover the note under state law allowing infants to disaffirm their contracts. Held: B's indorsement and transfer to C was effective as a negotiation, and B's remedy of rescission may not be asserted against D. §§ 3–202 (negotiation subject to rescission), 3–306 and Comment (claims to an instrument). Remember, though: D, even as a holder in due course, is subject to B's real defense of infancy on B's indorsement contract. § 3–305(a)(1)(i) and (b).

4. JUS TERTII—CLAIMS AND DEFENSES OF THIRD PERSONS

"[Generally,] in an action to enforce the obligation of a party to pay [an] instrument, the obligor may not assert against [a] person entitled to enforce the instrument a defense, claim in recoupment, or claim to the instrument (Section 3–306) of another person. . . ." §§ 3–305(c), 3–301 ("person entitled to enforce" defined). Example: B buys goods from S and negotiates to S a cashier's check, issued by Bank, in payment of the price. Shortly after delivering the check to S, B learns that S defrauded B in the sales transaction. S may enforce the check against Bank even though S is not a holder in due course. Bank has no defense to its obligation to pay the check, and it may not (with one exception described below) assert B's defenses, claims in recoupment, or claims to the instrument (with an exception). B may have a claim to the instrument under Section 3–306 based on a right to rescind the negotiation to S because of S's fraud. §§ 3–202(b), 3–201 Comment 2. Bank cannot assert that claim unless B is joined in the action in which S is trying to enforce payment of the check. In that case, an exception applies, and Bank may pay the amount of the check into court. The court will decide whether that amount belongs to B or S. § 3–305 Comment 4.

5. ELECTRONIC NOTES

A person having control of a "transferable record" is deemed the holder (§ 1–201(b)(21)) of it and has the same rights and defenses as a holder of a writing under the UCC, including the rights and defenses of a holder in due course. 15 U.S.C. § 7021(d) (E–SIGN). A "transferable record" is an electronic record that (a) would be a note under UCC Article 3 if it were in writing; (b) the issuer has expressly agreed is a transferable record; and (c) relates to a loan secured by real property. § 7021(a)(1); see § 7021(e)–(g). See UETA § 16.

C. LIABILITIES OF PARTIES: CONTRACT, WARRANTY, TORT

1. LIABILITY ON AN INSTRUMENT

A. SIGNATURE IN GENERAL

A person is not liable on an instrument unless he or she (or his or her agent) signed it. (See below for discussion of when an agent's signature binds the principal.) A signature is a word, mark, or symbol executed by a person "with present intention to authenticate a writing." It may be made manually or by a device or machine and by use of any name, including a trade or assumed name. §§ 3–401, 1–201(b)(37) ("signed" defined); see § 3–204(a) ("indorsement" defined).

B. SIGNATURE BY REPRESENTATIVE

When principal is bound

If a person acting as a representative [agent (A)] signs an instrument with either the name of the represented person [principal (P)] or the name of the signer (A), P is bound by the signature to the same extent P would be bound by A's signature on a simple contract. If P is bound, A's signature functions as P's authorized signature, and P is liable on the instrument, regardless of *whether* P is identified in the instrument. Example: Assume P authorized A to borrow money on P's behalf, and A signed A's name to a note without disclosing that the signature was on behalf of P. A is liable on the instrument. But if the person entitled to enforce the note [third party (T)] can prove that P authorized A to sign on P's behalf, P also is liable on the instrument. §§ 3–402(a) and Comment 1, 3–401(a), 1–201(b)(33) ("representative" defined). This rule gives T the choice of holding P liable when discovered. Restatement (Third) of Agency § 6.03 and Comment b.

When agent is bound

If A signs A's name to an instrument and A's signature is an authorized signature of P, the following rules apply:

1. If the form of the signature shows *unambiguously* that the signature is made on behalf of P, who is identified in the instrument, A is not liable on the instrument. § 3–402(b)(1). Example: Peter Principal Corporation, by Alice Agent, Treasurer.

2. If (i) the form of the signature does *not* show unambiguously that the signature is made in a representative capacity (Case #3 in § 3–402 Comment 2) or (ii) P is not identified in the instrument (Cases #1 & 2 in § 3–402 Comment 2), A is liable on the instrument to a holder in due course who took the instrument without notice that A was not intended to be liable on the instrument. With respect to any other person, A is liable on the instrument *unless* A *proves* the original parties (e.g., issuer and payee) did not intend A to be liable on the instrument. §§ 3–402(b)(2) and Comment 2, 1–201(b)(33) ("representative" defined), 3–103(a)(13) (§ 1–201(b)(8)) (defining "prove" and "burden of establishing," respectively).

Consider three illustrative cases: In each, suppose Alice Agent, the authorized agent of Peter Principal, signs a note on behalf of Peter Principal. Further assume that the original parties to the note intended that Principal (but not Agent) be liable on the note.

Case #1: Alice signs, "Alice Agent."

Case #2: Alice signs, "Alice Agent, Treasurer."

Case #3: The name "Peter Principal" is written on the note and, immediately below that name, Alice signs, "Alice Agent."

In each case, Alice is liable to a holder in due course who does not know that Alice was not intended to be liable.

§ 3–402 Comment 2. Policy: In none of the cases does Alice's signature unambiguously show that she was signing as an agent for Principal. A holder in due course should be able to resolve any ambiguity against Alice. However, the situation is different if no holder in due course is involved (e.g., if the payee is seeking to enforce the note). In such a situation, in Cases #1–3, only Principal is liable on the note. § 3–402(a). Policy: If the original parties to the note did not intend that Alice also be liable, imposing liability on Alice is a windfall to the person enforcing the note.

When principal or agent is bound—check cases

The rules are different when a check is involved. If (1) A, an authorized agent for P, signs A's name as drawer of a check without indicating A's representative status, and (2) the check is payable from an account of P who is identified on the check, then signer A is not liable on the check. Example: "Peter Principal Corporation, Alice Agent." Rationale: If the check identifies P, A does not have to indicate his or her agency status, because nobody is deceived into thinking that the person signing the check is meant to be personally liable. § 3–402(c) and Comment 3.

C. UNAUTHORIZED SIGNATURE

Suppose Alice Agent signs an instrument as follows:

Peter Principal Corporation

by Alice Agent, Treasurer

This signature clearly binds Principal, assuming Alice is an authorized representative. See § 3–402(b)(1), discussed immediately above. Now assume Alice Agent's signature lacks actual, implied, or apparent authority. Is Principal bound? Is Agent? Answer: An unauthorized signature is ineffective as Principal's signature, but is effective as the unauthorized signer's signature in favor of a person who in good faith pays the instrument or takes it for value.

§§ 3–403(a) and Comment 2, 1–201(b)(41) ("unauthorized signature" defined). Thus, Agent would be liable to such a taker but Principal is not. For discussion of signatures of more than one person, ratification of unauthorized signatures, and preclusion from asserting forgeries, see §§ 3–403(a) (last sentence) and (b) (see § 1–201(b)(25) and (27) (defining "organization" and "person")), 3–406 (role of contributory negligence).

2. OBLIGATION OF MAKER OF NOTE OR ISSUER OF CASHIER'S CHECK

The maker of a note or the issuer of a cashier's check is obliged to pay the item according to its terms at the time it was issued. If the maker or issuer signed an incomplete instrument, he or she must pay according to its terms when completed. This obligation is owed to a "person entitled to enforce" the instrument, e.g., holder (or to an indorser who paid the instrument). §§ 3–412, 3–301 ("person entitled to enforce"), 1–201(b)(21)(A) ("holder" defined), 3–104(e) and (g) (defining "note" and "cashier's check"); see §§ 3–116(a) (co-makers are jointly and severally liable) and 3–419(b) (surety may sign a note as maker). Examples: "On June 1, I promise to pay to the order of Paula Payee, One Thousand Dollars." "On demand, I promise to pay Bearer $_____." Jones fills in $1,000 in the blank space. The maker's or issuer's obligation is sometimes called a contract of primary liability since the instrument need not first be dishonored by someone else.

By long-established custom and usage, a signature in the lower right hand corner of an instrument indicates intent to sign as a maker of a note or issuer of a cashier's check. Sometimes, however, a lower-right-hand-corner signer may be an indorser. Example: Instrument reads, "John Johnson promises to pay. . . ." In the lower right hand corner are the signatures of John Johnson and Mike

Gunter. Mike might be held to be an indorser per the rule, "[R]egardless of the intent of the signer [Mike], a signature ... is an indorsement unless ... circumstances *unambiguously* indicate that the signature was made for a purpose other than indorsement." [Emphasis added.] § 3–204(a) and Comment 1.

If bank refuses to pay a cashier's check, see §§ 3–411 and Comment 1 (including consequential damages), 3–302 Comment 4 (Case #1), 3–305(c) and Comment 4 (Example).

3. OBLIGATION OF DRAWER OF DRAFT OR INDORSER OF INSTRUMENT

A. DRAWER OR INDORSER'S GENERAL OBLIGATION

Drawer

If an unaccepted draft (e.g., uncertified check) is *dishonored,* the drawer must pay the draft according to its terms at issuance. If the drawer signed an incomplete instrument, he or she must pay according to its terms when completed. This obligation is owed to a "person entitled to enforce" the draft, e.g., holder (or to an indorser who paid the draft). The drawer may escape liability if the draft is drawn "without recourse." §§ 3–414(b) and (e), 3–301 ("person entitled to enforce"), 1–201(b)(21)(A) ("holder" defined), 3–116(a) (joint and several liability), 3–419(b) (accommodation parties). As to the drawer of an accepted draft, see § 3–414(d); as to the obligation of an issuer of a cashier's check, see §§ 3–414(a), 3–412.

This is sometimes called a contract of secondary liability, because several preliminary steps are required: (1) the obligee presents the draft to the drawee, (2) the drawee dishonors the draft, (3) the obligee gives notice of dishonor to the drawer. By custom and usage, a signature in the lower right hand corner of a draft indicates an intent to sign as a drawer. § 3–204(a) and Comment 1.

Indorser

If an instrument is *dishonored,* an indorser must pay the amount due on the instrument according to its terms at the time it was indorsed. If the indorser indorsed an incomplete instrument, he or she must pay according to its terms when completed. This obligation is owed to a "person entitled to enforce" the instrument, e.g., holder (or to a subsequent indorser who paid the instrument). Generally, indorsers are liable to one another in the order their signatures appear on the instrument. If an indorsement states that it is made "without recourse" (called a qualified indorsement), the indorser escapes liability under this section. §§ 3–415(a) and (b) and Comment 1, 3–116(a) (joint and several liability); see § 3–117 (other agreements affecting instrument).

This is sometimes called a contract of secondary liability, because several preliminary steps are required: (1) the obligee presents the item to the maker (if a note) or the drawee (if a draft), (2) the maker or drawee dishonors the note or draft, (3) the obligee gives notice of dishonor to the indorser. See § 3–415(c). By custom and usage, a signature on the back of an instrument signals an intent to sign as an indorser. § 3–204(a).

B. PRESENTMENT, DISHONOR, NOTICE OF DISHONOR, EVIDENCE OF DISHONOR (PROTEST)

We have just discussed drawers' and indorsers' contracts of secondary liability. These parties must pay if the draft or note is dishonored. Here, we detail (1) when an instrument is deemed dishonored and (2) when notice of dishonor is required.

(1) Dishonor

(a) When Note is Dishonored

Demand note

Assume a note states, "On demand, I promise to pay to the order of Paul Payee...." Such a "demand note" is dishonored if presentment is duly made to the maker and the note is not paid on the day of presentment. § 3–502(a)(1).

Time note

Assume a note states, "On June 1, 2010, I promise to pay to the order of Paula Payee...." Such a note payable at a definite time ("time note") is dishonored if not paid on its due date (June 1, 2010). This rule allows holders to collect notes in ways that make sense commercially *without* having to be concerned about making a formal *presentment* on a given day. § 3–502(a)(3) and Comment 3. If a time note is payable at or through a bank, or presentment is expressly required, see § 3–502(a)(2).

(b) When Unaccepted Draft is Dishonored

Demand draft

Check presented for immediate payment over the counter: Assume Drawer issues an uncertified check to Payee who, at 11:00 a.m. on June 1, presents it personally to Drawee–Payor Bank for immediate payment over the counter. Such a check is dishonored if presentment for payment is duly made and the draft is not paid on the day of presentment (June 1). §§ 3–502(b)(2), 3–501(b)(4).

Check presented through the check-collection system: Instead of Payee seeking immediate payment over the counter, suppose Payee deposits the check with Depositary Bank, who forwards it to Intermediary Bank, who forwards it to Payor Bank (drawee) for payment. Here, the check is dishonored if Payor Bank makes timely return of the check or sends timely notice of dishonor or nonpayment (or, less commonly, becomes accountable for the amount of the check under § 4–302). § 3–502(b)(1) and Comment 4.

Time draft—payable on date stated in draft

Assume Drawer issues a draft on March 1 stating, "On June 1 [*year*], pay to the order of. . . ." Dishonor occurs if presentment for payment is made and payment is not made on (1) the day the draft becomes payable (June 1) or (2) the day of presentment, if after the due date. Note: The holder of an unaccepted draft payable on a stated date can choose to present the draft for *acceptance* before the stated date to establish whether the drawee is willing to assume liability by accepting. Dishonor occurs when a draft is presented and not accepted. § 3–502(b)(3) and Comment 4.

Time draft—payable a period of time after sight or acceptance

See § 3–502(b)(4).

Documentary draft

See §§ 3–502(c), 3–103(c) (4–104(a)(6)) (defining the term).

(c) When Accepted Draft (e.g., Certified Check) Is Dishonored

A certified check is dishonored if presentment for payment is duly made to the drawee–acceptor and the draft is not paid that day. §§ 3–502(d) and Comment 6, 3–501(b)(4) (presentment after cut-off hour); see §§ 3–409 ("acceptance" and "certified check" defined), 3–413 (acceptor's obligation).

(d) Requisites for Presentment (If Required for Dishonor)

Presentment defined

Presentment means a demand by a "person entitled to enforce" an instrument (e.g., holder): (i) to *pay* the instrument, to the drawee or a party obliged to pay the instrument (e.g., maker) or (ii) to *accept* a draft, made to the drawee. §§ 3–501(a), 3–301 ("person entitled to enforce"). (For a note or accepted draft payable at a bank, demand is made to the bank.)

Place and manner of presentment

Presentment (1) either may or must be made at the *place* of payment; (2) may be made by any commercially reasonable means (e.g., oral, written, electronic); and (3) is effective when the demand for payment or acceptance is received. §§ 3–501(b)(1), 3–111 ("place of payment"). See §§ 4–110 (electronic presentment), 4–212 (items not payable by, at, or through a bank).

Time of presentment

See § 3–502(a)(1) and (2), (b)–(d) ("the day it [instrument] becomes payable;" "the day of presentment"). Note: Because a payor must decide whether to pay or accept on the day of presentment, § 3–501(b)(4) allows the payor to set a cut-off hour (not earlier than 2 p.m.) for receipt of instruments presented.

Rights of person to whom presentment made

Upon demand of the person to whom presentment is made, the person making presentment must (i) exhibit the instrument, (ii) give reasonable identification, and (iii) *sign* a *receipt* on the instrument for any payment made, or *surrender* the instrument if full payment is made. § 3–501(b)(2).

Without dishonoring the instrument, the party to whom presentment is made may (i) return the instrument for lack of a necessary indorsement or (ii) refuse payment or acceptance for failure to comply with applicable law or rule (e.g., terms of the instrument). § 3–501(b)(3).

Excused presentment

Presentment for payment or acceptance is excused if

(i) the person entitled to present the instrument cannot with reasonable diligence make presentment,

(ii) the maker or acceptor has repudiated an obligation to pay the instrument or is dead or in insolvency proceedings (§ 1–201(b)(22) ("insolvency proceedings" defined)),

(iii) by the terms of the instrument, presentment is not necessary to enforce the obligation of indorsers or the drawer,

(iv) the drawer or indorser whose obligation is being enforced has waived presentment (see § 3–504(b) (last sentence)) or otherwise has no reason to expect, or right to require, that the instrument be paid or accepted, or

(v) the drawer instructed the drawee not to pay or accept the draft, or the drawee was not obligated to the drawer to pay the draft. §§ 3–504(a), 3–502(e).

Note: "In the great majority of cases presentment and notice of dishonor are waived with respect to notes." § 3–502 Comment 2.

Failure timely to present or initiate collection

Indorser: If a check is not presented for payment, or given to a depositary bank for collection, within 30 days after indorsement, the indorser's secondary liability is discharged. § 3–415(e). Policy: Although an indorser who pays will have recourse against prior indorsers and the drawer, §§ 3–414(b) (last sentence), 3–415(a) (last sentence), the indorsee's failure timely to present or initiate bank collection may prejudice the indorser's chances for recovery. Note: "[Section 3–415(e)] modifies former §§ 3–503(2)(b), 3–502(1)(a) by stating a 30-day period rather than a seven-day period, and stating it as an absolute rather than a presumptive period." § 3–415 Comment 4.

Drawer: If

(i) a check is not presented for payment or given to a depositary bank for collection within 30 days after its date,

(ii) the drawee suspends payments after expiration of the 30-day period without paying the check, and

(iii) because of the suspension of payments, the drawer is deprived of funds maintained with the drawee to cover payment of the check,

then the drawer, to the extent it is deprived of funds, may discharge its obligation to pay the check by assigning its rights against the drawee with respect to the funds to the "person entitled to enforce" the check. §§ 3–414(f), 3–301 ("person entitled to enforce"). The existence of federal bank deposit insurance minimizes this risk. See example at § 3–414 Comment 6. Simply put, after the passage of the 30-day period, the risk of the drawee's insolvency passes from the drawer to the payee (or other holder).

(2) Notice of Dishonor

(a) When Notice of Dishonor is Required

Indorser

An indorser's obligation may not be enforced unless the indorser is given notice of dishonor. §§ 3–503(a)(i), 3–415(a); see § 3–415(c).

Drawer

Notice of dishonor is no longer relevant to a drawer's liability. Drawers are entitled to have the draft presented to the drawee and dishonored before they are liable to pay, but no notice of dishonor need be made to them *as a condition of liability.* § 3–503(a)(i) and Comment 1, see former § 3–501(2)(a). Exception: The obligation of a drawer stated in § 3–414(d) may not be enforced unless the drawer is given notice of dishonor. Section 3–414(d) covers drafts accepted other than by a bank. Example: S sells goods to B. As a collection device, S draws a draft on B payable to the order of Bank. B accepts the draft. S's obligation to pay the draft if B dishonors it is the same as the obligation of an indorser, i.e., S's obligation may not be enforced unless S is given notice of dishonor. § 3–414 Comment 4.

(b) How Notice of Dishonor is Given

Notice of dishonor

(1) may be given by any person;

(2) may be given by any commercially reasonable means (e.g., orally, in writing, or electronically); and

(3) is sufficient if it (i) reasonably identifies the instrument and (ii) indicates it has been dishonored.

Note: Return of an instrument given to a bank for collection is sufficient notice of dishonor. § 3–503(b). Example: Bank returns to its customer a check with a ticket attached stating, "The attached check was presented to the drawee on [*date*] for payment. Payment was refused. [*signed*] Depositary Bank."

(c) Time for Giving Notice of Dishonor

Instrument taken for collection by collecting bank

A collecting bank must give notice of dishonor before midnight of the next banking day following the banking day on which the bank receives notice of dishonor of the instrument. Any other person must give notice of dishonor within 30 days of the day on which the person receives notice of dishonor. §§ 3–503(c) (first sentence), 3–103(c) (§ 4–104(a)(3)). The 30-day rule replaces the three-day period in former § 3–508(2). § 3–503 Comment 2.

Any other instrument

For any other item, notice of dishonor must be given within 30 days following dishonor. § 3–503(c) (second sentence).

(d) When Notice of Dishonor is Excused

Notice of dishonor is *excused* if

(i) by the terms of the instrument, notice of dishonor is not necessary to enforce the instrument, or

(ii) the party whose obligation is being enforced waived notice of dishonor. (A waiver of presentment is also a waiver of notice of dishonor.) §§ 3–504(b), 3–503(a)(ii).

Delay in giving notice of dishonor is *excused* (1) if the delay was caused by circumstances beyond the control of the person giving notice *and* (2) the person giving the notice exercised reasonable diligence after the cause of the delay ceased to operate. §§ 3–504(c), 3–503(c).

(e) Effect of Failure to Give Timely Notice of Dishonor

Indorser

If notice of dishonor of an instrument is required—see above discussion—and is not given to an indorser, the indorser's liability is discharged. § 3–415(c) and Comments 1 and 2.

Drawer

Recall that notice is no longer required to invoke the liability of a drawer. Also recall the exception that, if a draft is drawn on an acceptor who is not a bank (i.e., a seller draws a draft on the buyer, who accepts the draft), the drawer's obligation is the same as an indorser's. § 3–414(d) and Comments 2 and 4. In such a case, failure to give timely notice of dishonor discharges the drawer.

(3) Evidence of Dishonor and Notice of Dishonor

Evidence of dishonor and notice of dishonor may be accomplished, among other ways, by a protest, which is a certificate of dishonor. Protest is no longer mandatory. § 3–505 and Comment; see § 3–102 Comment 5.

4. LIABILITY OF TRANSFERORS— TRANSFER WARRANTIES

Example 1: A issues to B a draft or note payable "to the order of B," which B indorses and delivers to C. Example 2: A issues to B a draft or note payable "to bearer," which B delivers to C without indorsement.

From previous discussion, we know that in both examples, C takes as a "holder" and, accordingly, may also qualify for holder-in-due-course status. §§ 1–201(b)(21)(A) ("holder" defined), 3–302 (holder in due course). Further, we know that, in Example 1, B, as an indorser, must pay the amount due on the instrument if it is dishonored (unless B indorsed "without recourse"). §§ 3–415, 3–501 et seq. This is sometimes called an indorser's contract of secondary liability. In Example 2, B has not indorsed the "bearer" paper and thus has undertaken no secondary liability. See § 3–401(a).

In both examples, however, B has transferred the "property" in the instrument to C. The purpose of B's transfer is to give the person receiving delivery, C, the right to enforce the instrument. § 3–203(a) and (b). Accordingly, B's transfer warranties (whether or not B has indorsed the instrument) are as follows. § 3–416 Comment 1 (second sentence).

A person who transfers an instrument for consideration warrants to the transferee that

(1) the warrantor is a "person entitled to enforce" the instrument, e.g., a "holder." §§ 3–416(a)(1), 3–301 ("person entitled to enforce"), 1–201(b)(21)(A) ("holder" defined). This is in effect a warranty that there are no unauthorized or missing indorsements preventing the transferee from being a person "entitled to enforce" the instrument. § 3–416 Comment 2. Cf. former § 3–417(2)(a) (transferor warrants "he has good title to the instrument").

(2) all signatures on the instrument are authentic and authorized. § 3–416(a)(2), cf. § 1–201(b)(41) ("unauthorized signature" defined).

(3) the instrument has not been altered, e.g., the amount has not been raised. §§ 3–416(a)(3), 3–407(a) ("alteration" defined).

(4) the instrument is not subject to a defense or claim in recoupment that can be asserted against the warrantor. § 3–416(a)(4). Rationale: "[T]he transferee does not undertake to buy an instrument that is not enforceable in whole or in part. . . . Even if the transferee takes as a holder in due course who takes free of the defense or claim in recoupment, the warranty gives the transferee the option of proceeding against the transferor rather than litigating with the obligor on the instrument the issue of the holder-in-due-course status of the transferee." § 3–416 Comment 3, see § 3–305(a) and (b). Example: In Examples 1 and 2 above, suppose B sells defective goods to A, who rejects the goods. A's *defense* on the draft or note would be cut off by C if C is a holder in due course. § 3–305(a)(2) and (b) and Comment 2. If A accepts the defective goods, A is

obliged to pay the price, but A has a claim against B for breach of warranty; the claim may be asserted against B as a *claim in recoupment* to reduce the amount owing on the draft or note. If C qualifies as a holder in due course, A may not assert the claim against C. § 3–305(a)(3) and (b) and Comment 3. However, § 3–416(a)(4) gives C the option of proceeding against B rather than litigating the issue of holder-in-due-course status with A.

(5) the warrantor has *no knowledge* of any insolvency proceeding commenced with respect to the maker or acceptor or the drawer (of an unaccepted draft). Policy: Concealment of known insolvency proceedings is a fraud upon the transferee. §§ 3–416(a)(5) and Comment 4, 1–201(b)(22) ("insolvency proceedings" defined).

(6) the person on whose account the item is drawn (e.g., drawer of check) *authorized* the issuance of the item in the *amount* for which the item is drawn. §§ 3–416(a)(6), 4–207(a)(6), 3–103(c), 4–104(a)(9) ("item" defined). This warranty applies to a "remotely-created consumer item," that is, an item drawn on a consumer account that is not created by the payor bank and does not bear the drawer's *handwritten* signature. §§ 3–103(a)(2) ("consumer account" defined) and (16), 4–105(3) ("payor bank" defined). The provision deals with responsibility for unauthorized telephone-generated checks (e.g., telemarketer check fraud) and rests on the premise that depositary banks can control this type of fraud more effectively than payor banks. §§ 3–416 Comment 8, 4–207 Comment 2.

Beneficiaries of transfer warranties

A person who transfers an instrument for consideration makes a transfer warranty to the transferee and, if the transfer is by *indorsement,* to any *subsequent* transferee.

Thus, if there is an indorsement, the warranty runs with the instrument and a remote holder may sue any indorser-warrantor directly and thus avoid a multiplicity of suits. § 3–416(a) and Comment 1. (Recall that bearer paper may be transferred/negotiated without an indorsement.)

For the measure of damages for breach of a transfer warranty, see § 3–416(b); for disclaimer of transfer warranties, see § 3–416(c); for similar warranties in the collection process, see § 4–207(a), (c) and (d). But note § 4–207(b) ("If an item is dishonored, a customer or collecting bank transferring the item and receiving settlement . . . is obliged to pay the amount due on the item. . . ."), cf. § 3–415(a); see Regulation CC, 12 CFR §§ 229.34, 229.35(b).

5. LIABILITY OF DRAWEE AND ACCEPTOR

A. CONTRACT LIABILITY ON THE DRAFT

(1) Drawee

Assume Drawer issues a check to Payee, who presents it to Drawee Bank for payment. Although there are sufficient funds, Drawee refuses to pay. Does Payee have rights against Drawee? Answer: Drawee is not liable on the instrument until Drawee accepts (certifies) it. § 3–408, see § 3–401(a). But has not Drawee broken its contract of deposit with Drawer wherein Drawee has engaged to honor Drawer's order if there are sufficient funds, and cannot the check be considered an assignment of Drawer's rights against Drawee? Answer: Perhaps, as will become apparent in the discussion of wrongful dishonor below at Part Three, D, 3, but (1) this is a separate issue from Drawee's contract liability on the instrument, and (2) only Drawer (not Payee) has a claim for wrongful dishonor. Further, a check or other draft does not of itself operate as an assignment of funds in the hands of Drawee available for its payment. § 3–408.

(2) Acceptor

Acceptance defined

Acceptance means the drawee's signed agreement to pay a draft as presented. A certified check is a check that is *accepted* by the bank on which it is drawn. § 3–409(a) (first sentence) and (d) (first sentence).

Obligation of acceptor

The acceptor of a draft is obliged to pay a draft according to its terms at the time it was accepted (even if the acceptance states that the draft is payable "as originally drawn"). Example: Draft is issued for $1,000; X skillfully alters it to read $10,000. If Acceptor accepts it, Acceptor must pay $10,000. § 3–413(a)(i). If the acceptance varies the terms of the draft or the draft is an incomplete instrument, see § 3–413(a)(ii) and (iii). If the certification of a check (or other draft) does not state an amount and the amount is raised, see § 3–413(b) and Comment. The obligation is owed to a "person entitled to enforce" the draft, e.g., holder (or to the drawer or an indorser who paid the draft). §§ 3–413, 3–301 ("person entitled to enforce"), 1–201(b)(21)(A) ("holder" defined), 3–104(e) ("draft" defined), 3–103(a)(1) ("acceptor" defined); see §§ 3–116(a) (joint and several liability), 3–419(b) (accommodation parties). This is sometimes called a contract of primary liability because the draft need not be dishonored by someone else to trigger the acceptor's liability. Simply put, a drawee becomes an acceptor by signing the draft agreeing to pay it. § 3–408. See §§ 3–409(b)–(d) (draft not signed by drawer, draft payable at a fixed period after sight, drawee has no duty to certify check), 3–410 (acceptance varying draft).

Where acceptance must be written

An acceptance must be written on the draft and may consist solely of the drawee's signature. Customarily, the signature is written vertically across the face of the instrument, but, since the drawee has no reason to sign for any other purpose, a signature in any other place, even on the back of the instrument, is sufficient. It need not be accompanied by such words as "Accepted," "Certified" or "Good." It must not, however, bear any words indicating an intent to dishonor the draft. § 3–409(a) (second sentence) and Comment 2. As to an agreement to accept a draft in a separate writing, see §§ 3–409 Comment 4, 5–102(a)(10) (letter of credit).

When acceptance becomes effective

Acceptance may be made at any time and becomes effective when the drawee *notifies* the holder or *gives notice* according to instructions, or the accepted draft is *delivered.* § 3–409(a) (third sentence) and Comment 2.

Examples illustrating acceptance and certification

One: Assume Buyer seeks to pay Seller for goods by check. Because Seller wants more than Buyer–Drawer's contract of secondary liability on the check, further assume Seller has Drawee–Bank certify the check. The result is that Drawee, as Acceptor, has undertaken primary liability on the check.

Two: Assume Manufacturer–Seller contracts to sell goods to Dealer–Buyer. Further assume Seller wants cash terms, but Buyer wants sixty-day credit terms so Buyer may resell the goods and pay Seller out of the proceeds. Thus, Seller draws a draft on Buyer (sometimes called a trade acceptance) payable in sixty days, naming Seller or Bank A as Payee. Next, assume the following 3 transactions: (1) Seller discounts (sells) the draft with Bank A. (2) Buyer accepts the draft—that is, Buyer agrees to pay it in sixty days. (3) Seller gets cash from Bank A in return for the draft. The net effect is that Seller gets cash immediately, while Buyer gets sixty-day credit terms. Buyer is expected to discharge the obligation to pay by paying Bank A at the end of the sixty days. For a discussion of a draft with a bill of lading attached, see Part Four, B infra.

B. CONVERSION (TORT) LIABILITY

(1) When Instrument is Paid on a Forged Indorsement

Assume the following 3 transactions: (1) Drawer issues a check to the order of Payee. (2) Forger steals the check from Payee and forges Payee's name on the check. (3) Forger presents the check to Drawee, who pays Forger. Does Payee, the "true owner" of the check, have rights against Drawee? Answer: Yes. "An instrument is . . . converted if . . . a bank [e.g., Drawee] makes or obtains payment with respect to the instrument for a person *not* entitled to enforce the instrument or receive payment [i.e., Forger]." [Emphasis added.] "This [rule] covers cases in which a depositary or payor bank [Drawee] takes an instrument bearing a forged indorsement." §§ 3–420(a) (second sentence) and Comment 1 (first paragraph, fifth sentence et seq.), 3–301 ("person entitled to enforce"), 1–201(b)(21)(A) ("holder" defined), 3–201(b) (negotiation), 3–109 Comment 1 (last sentence). See §§ 3–406 (role of negligence), 1–201(b)(41) (defining "unauthorized signature"). The measure of liability is presumed to be the amount payable on the instrument. § 3–420(b). Note: If Forger had deposited the check with Depositary Bank, this bank would be liable in conversion, though other collecting banks would normally not be liable in conversion beyond the amount of proceeds not yet paid out. § 3–420(a) (and Comment 1 (sixth sentence)) and (c) (and Comment 3). Further note that issuers (e.g., drawers), acceptors, payees, or indorsees who did not receive delivery do not have an action for conversion. § 3–420(a) (third sentence) and Comment 1 (second paragraph et seq.).

(2) When Instrument is Delivered for Payment or Acceptance and Not Accepted, Paid, or Returned on Demand

Assume Drawer issues a check to Payee, who in turn presents it to Drawee for payment. Further suppose Drawee takes the check, but subsequently refuses either to pay or return it. Does Payee have rights against Drawee? Answer: Yes. Under former § 3–419(1)(a) and (b) and Comment 2, "An instrument is converted when [Drawee] refuses on demand either to pay or return it." Reason: "A negotiable instrument is the property of the holder. It is a mercantile specialty which embodies rights against other parties [e.g., Drawer], and a thing of value.... A refusal to return it on demand is a conversion." Former § 3–419 Comment 2. See § 3–414(b).

Revised § 3–420(a) (first sentence) states that the law of conversion applicable to personal property generally also applies to instruments. Former § 3–419(1)(a) and (b) have been "deleted as inappropriate in cases of noncash items that may be delivered for acceptance or payment in collection letters that contain varying instructions as to what to do in the event of nonpayment on the day of delivery. It is better to allow such cases to be governed by the general law of conversion that would address" whether the *presenter's right to possession* has been *denied.* § 3–420 Comment 1 (first four sentences).

Note: Even *without* a demand for return of an item (e.g., a check), the payor (e.g., drawee) will be responsible for late return. See §§ 4–302, 4–104(a)(3) and (9) and (10) (defining "banking day," "item," and "midnight deadline"). (Pre-UCC: constructive acceptance or conversion); § 3–408 Comment 2. See Part Three, E, 1 and 3 infra. Note also § 3–206(c) (restrictive indorsement—payor bank as converter).

6. OBLIGATION OF ACCOMMODATION PARTY

A. INTRODUCTION

Suppose Buyer wants to buy goods from Seller on credit. To induce Seller to sell, Surety promises to pay Seller if Buyer does not.

This is a suretyship relation. To paraphrase Restatement of Security § 82 and Restatement (Third) of Suretyship and Guaranty § 1, Suretyship exists when (1) there is one creditor [Seller] and two debtors [Buyer and Surety]; (2) the creditor can recover only once; and (3) as between the two debtors, one [Buyer] rather than the other [Surety] ought to pay. Thus, a simple suretyship relation involves three contracts: One, the underlying sale contract between Seller and Buyer; two, Surety's promise to the Seller to pay if Buyer does not; three, since as between Buyer and Surety it is Buyer's debt, Buyer as the principal obligor expressly or impliedly promises to *reimburse* Surety if Surety is called upon to pay. Further, if Surety pays Seller, equity dictates that Surety be equitably substituted to Seller's rights against Buyer under the sales contract. This is called the right of *subrogation*. Thus, Surety has the direct right of reimbursement against Buyer and the derivative right of subrogation.

B. ACCOMMODATION PARTY DEFINED

Suppose now that Buyer (the principal obligor) and Surety (the secondary obligor) are parties to a note. Surety is now called an "accommodation party," Buyer is called an "accommodated party," and the instrument is signed by Surety "for accommodation." "An accommodation party is a person who signs an instrument to benefit the accommodated party either by signing at the time value is obtained by the accommodated party or later, and who is not a direct beneficiary of the value obtained." Example: "If X cosigns a note of Corporation that is given for a loan to Corporation, X is an accommodation party if no part of the loan was paid to X or for X's direct benefit. This is true even though X may receive indirect benefit from the loan because X is employed by Corporation or is a stockholder of Corporation, or even if X is the sole stockholder so long as Corporation and X are recognized as separate entities." § 3–419(a) and Comment 1. As to an accommodation party's entitlement to reimbursement and subrogation, see §§ 3–419(f) (first sentence) and 1–201(b)(39); as to exoneration, see § 3–419(f) (second sentence.)

C.　OBLIGATION OF ACCOMMODATION PARTY

An accommodation party (Surety) may sign the instrument as maker, drawer, acceptor, or indorser, and is obliged to pay the instrument in the capacity in which Surety signs. § 3–419(b); see §§ 3–412 through 3–415 (respective obligations of issuers, acceptors, drawers, and indorsers described), 3–501 et seq. (presentment, dishonor, etc.). Even so, Surety will usually be a co-maker or anomalous indorser. Example 1: Buyer and Surety sign as co-makers, naming Seller as payee. In such a case, as a co-maker, Surety is bound to a contract of primary liability. § 3–412. Example 2: Buyer signs a note as maker, naming Seller as payee. Surety indorses the back of the note, and it is delivered to Seller. In such a case, Surety, as an anomalous indorser who has thus taken on secondary liability, is obliged to pay the note *if* it is *dishonored*. §§ 3–415, 3–205(d) and Comment 3. Note: Surety's obligation may be enforced notwithstanding any statute of frauds and regardless of whether Surety receives consideration for the accommodation. § 3–419(b) (last sentence). Also note: Surety's obligation to pay the note is not changed if Seller had notice, when Seller took the note, that Surety had signed for the purpose of accommodation. § 3–419(c) (second sentence). As to Surety's special defenses, see § 3–605.

If Surety's signature is accompanied by words indicating unambiguously that Surety is *guaranteeing collection* rather than *payment* of Buyer's obligation, then Surety must pay the amount due on the note to a "person entitled to enforce" the note (Seller), but only if "execution of judgment against [Buyer] has been returned unsatisfied . . . or it is otherwise apparent that payment cannot be obtained from [Buyer]." § 3–419(d). If Surety does not unambiguously limit its exposure to guaranteeing collection, Surety will be deemed to have guaranteed payment. § 3–204(a)(iii) and Comment 1; see §§ 3–414 Comment 4, 3–416 Comment 3, 3–419 Comment 4; cf. former § 3–416(1), (3) and (5). Further, § 3–419(e)(2002) states that, if the signature of a party is accompanied by the words "payment guaranteed," or the like, it means that the signer is obligated to pay the amount due on the instrument without prior resort to the accommodated party (principal obligor). Cf. Restatement (Third) of Suretyship and Guaranty § 15(a).

D. ACCOMMODATION PARTY'S RIGHT TO CONTRIBUTION FROM COSURETIES

Assume Maker issues a note to Payee, and on the reverse side of the note are the anomalous indorsements of A, then B, then C, then D. Normally, an earlier indorser is liable to a later indorser. Thus, A would be liable to B, C, and D. B would be liable to C and D, etc. §§ 3–415 Comment 1 (second sentence), 3–205(d); see former § 3–414(2). But two or more anomalous indorsers such as our hypothetical presents can have joint and several liability. § 3–116(a). An anomalous indorsement normally indicates that the indorser signed as an accommodation party (surety). If more than one accommodation party indorses a note, the indorsers have joint and several liability (§ 3–116(a)), and § 3–116(b) applies: "[A] party having joint and several liability who pays the instrument is entitled to receive from any party having the same joint and several

liability contribution in accordance with applicable law."
§ 3–116 Comment 2. Example: A, B, C, and D in the
above facts agreed to be cosureties for Maker and to
contribute pro rata to the common loss that would be
caused by Maker's default. This is called a surety's right of
contribution against cosureties. Thus, if A pays Maker's
entire obligation on the note, A is entitled to twenty-five
percent contribution each from B, C, and D. See L.
Simpson, Suretyship § 49 (1950). See also, Restatement
(Third) of Suretyship and Guaranty §§ 55–58.

E. ACCOMMODATION PARTY'S ASSERTION OF AC-COMMODATED PARTY'S DEFENSES OR CLAIMS IN RECOUPMENT AGAINST PERSON ENTITLED TO ENFORCE INSTRUMENT

Assume that, to induce Seller to deliver goods to Buyer
on credit, Surety cosigns with Buyer, as comakers, a note
naming Seller as payee. Seller delivers the goods to Buyer.
Buyer inspects and rejects them as nonconforming. See
§§ 2–313, 2–314, 2–315, 2–513, 2–601, 2–703, 2–711 (re:
causes of action and potential remedies for breach of
warranty and delivery of nonconforming goods). Seller
seeks recovery from Surety. May Surety assert Buyer's
defense(s)? Answer: Yes. "In an action to enforce the
obligation of [Surety] to pay an instrument, [Surety] may
assert against [Seller] any defense or claim in recoupment
. . . that [Buyer] could assert against [Seller]." Surety may
not, however, assert Buyer's defenses of discharge in
bankruptcy, infancy, and lack of legal capacity. § 3–305(d)
and Comment 5. Cf. obligation of issuer of letter of credit.
§§ 5–102(a)(10), 5–103(d), 5–108(f)(1).

F. ACCOMMODATION PARTY'S SPECIAL DEFENS-ES

We have seen that an accommodation party (surety) is
liable in the capacity in which he or she signed, e.g., as a
comaker or anomalous indorser. Here we will see that the

accommodation party may assert defenses that may not apply to other signers. Note that the surety's defenses are not dealt with exhaustively by the Code. See L. Simpson, Suretyship, Part 4 (1950); see Restatement (Third) of Suretyship and Guaranty §§ 37–49.

(1) No Liability of Accommodation Party to Accommodated Party

Example: Surety signs a note as an accommodation maker for Buyer, who is named as payee. Buyer indorses the note to Seller, who then delivers goods to Buyer. If Buyer–Indorser pays the note and takes it up, will Buyer have recourse against Surety–Maker? Also, if Surety pays the note and takes it up, will Surety have recourse against Buyer? Answer: Ordinarily, an indorser who pays a note will have recourse against the maker. § 3–412 (esp. last sentence). However, here Surety was merely facilitating Buyer's transaction with Seller. It was not expected that Surety would be liable to Buyer on the note; rather the anticipation was that, if Surety paid off the note, Surety would have a right of reimbursement against the principal debtor (Buyer) and be subrogated to the rights of the creditor (Seller) against the principal debtor (Buyer). Hence the rules, "An *accommodation* party [Surety] who pays the instrument [i] is entitled to reimbursement from the accommodated party [Buyer] and [ii] is entitled to enforce the instrument against the accommodated party [Buyer] [i.e., the right of subrogation] ... An *accommodated* party [Buyer] that pays the instrument has no right of recourse against, and is not entitled to contribution from, an accommodation party [Surety]." (Emphasis added.) § 3–419(f), see § 3–116(b).

(2) Discharge of Secondary Obligors

Amended § 3–605 (2002) deals with suretyship defenses concerning *impairment* of the right of *recourse* or of *collateral.* At the outset, observe that Restatement (First) of Security referred to the three parties to a surety relationship as creditor (C), principal debtor (P), and surety (S), while Article 3 calls them "person entitled to enforce," "accommodated party," and "accommodation party." Restatement (Third) of Suretyship and Guaranty refers to them as obligee, principal obligor, and secondary obligor. Amended § 3–605 designates them "person entitled to enforce", "principal obligor," and "secondary obligor." See §§ 3–103(a)(11) and (17), 3–301. Here, we will use these letters: C (creditor, person entitled to enforce, obligee), P (principal debtor, principal obligor, accommodated party), and S (surety, secondary obligor, accommodation party).

Hypothetical case: Bank (C) agrees to lend $10,000 to Borrower (P), but only if Backer (S) also agrees to be liable for repayment of the loan. P signs a note undertaking to pay $10,000 to the order of C on a due date stated in the note. S also undertakes the repayment obligation by signing the note as a *co-maker* (§§ 3–419(b), 3–412, 3–116(a)) or *indorser* (§§ 3–419(b), 3–415(a)). Now assume C and P agree to a modification of their rights and obligations after the note is signed. We discuss below whether the modification (e.g., a release or an extension of the due date) discharges S. § 3–605 (Comments 1 and 2). (The following rules also apply to indorsers who are not accommodation parties. Reason: "Unless an indorser signs without recourse, the indorser's liability under Section 3–415(a) is functionally similar to that of a guarantor of payment." § 3–605 Comment 3, see § 3–412 (last sentence).)

(a) Impairment of Recourse

Discharge of S by C's releasing P's obligation to pay

Example 1: In the above hypothetical case, assume that, as the due date of the $10,000 note approaches, it becomes obvious that P cannot pay the full amount of the note and may soon be facing bankruptcy. C, to collect as much as possible from P and lessen the need to seek recovery from S, agrees to release P from its obligation under the note in exchange for $3,000 in cash. (The agreement is silent as to the effect of the release on S.) Rule: Releasing P also discharges S. § 3–605(a)(2) and Comment 4 and Case 1.

Example 2: Same facts as Example 1 except that the terms of the release provide (i) that C retains its right to enforce the instrument against S, and (ii) that S retains its recourse against P. (According to 3–605(g) and Comment 10, a release preserves S's recourse if the terms of the release provide that C retains the right to enforce the instrument against S.) Thus, S is not discharged from its obligations to C, and P is not discharged from its obligation to reimburse S. § 3–605(a)(2) and (a)(1) and Comment 4 and Case 3. Because S's claims against P are preserved, S's recourse is not impaired. But see § 3–605(a)(3), (g) and Comment 4 (paragraph 6) (notwithstanding language in the release that prevents discharge of S under § 3–605(a)(2), 3–605(a)(3) discharges S from its obligation to C to the extent that the release otherwise would cause S a loss).

Section 3–605(a) facilitates negotiated workouts between C and P, so long as they are not at the expense of S, who has not consented to the arrangement (either specifically or by waiving its rights to discharge). See example in § 3–605 Comment 4 (seventh paragraph) (P pays some portion of a guaranteed obligation, C releases P in exchange for that payment, and C pursues S for the remainder of the obligation). Counseling point: Obtain S's consent or waiver. § 3–605(f).

If the instrument is a check and the obligation of S is based on indorsement of the check, see § 3–605(a)(2)(last sentence).

Discharge of S by C's extension of the due date

In the above hypothetical case, suppose P and C agree that P may repay the $10,000 loan at some date after the due date. Will this modification discharge S? Answer:

Normally, such an extension will occur only when P is unable to pay on the due date; thus, S normally would acquiesce in C's willingness to wait for payment from P rather than preferring to pay C right away and rely on an action against P that may have little or no value. The hope is that the additional time may enable P to obtain funds to pay the note. "In some cases, however, the extension may cause loss to [S], particularly if deterioration of the financial condition of [P] reduces the amount that [S] is able to recover on its right of recourse when default occurs. [Thus, Section 3–605(b)(2)] provides that an extension of time results in a discharge of [S], but only to the extent that [S] proves that the extension caused loss." § 3–605(b), (h) and Comment 5.

As to reservation of rights, see § 3–605(b)(1), (2); as to S's *consent* to the extension, or if the note (or a separate agreement) provides for *waiver* of discharge, see § 3–605(f) discussed below.

Discharge of S by modification of P's obligation to C other than release or extension of due date

See § 3–605(c) and Comment 6.

(b) *Impairment of Collateral*

In the above hypothetical case, suppose P's obligation to pay the $10,000 note to C is secured by collateral (see, e.g., § 9–109), and S, another party to the note, is an accommodation party. If C impairs the value of the interest in the collateral, S's obligation is discharged to the extent of the impairment. § 3–605(d) and Comment 7. S has the burden of persuasion. § 3–605(h), see § 1–201(b)(8) (defining "burden of establishing" a fact). Example: C, the payee of a secured note, fails to perfect the security interest (i.e., the financing statement was not filed). The collateral is owned by P, who subsequently files for bankruptcy. As a result of the failure to perfect, the security interest is not enforceable in bankruptcy. § 9–317(a)(2), B.C. § 544(a). S's right to be subrogated to C's security interest in the collateral is impaired, and S's obligation is discharged to the extent of the impairment. Section § 3–605(d) (last sentence) states four common examples of impairment.

(c) Effect of Lack of Knowledge or Notice That Instrument Was Signed for Accommodation

S is not discharged under the suretyship defenses of impairment of recourse or collateral found in § 3–605(a)(3), (b), and (d) unless C (i) knows S is an accommodation party, or (ii) has notice under § 3–419(c) that the instrument was signed for accommodation. § 3–605(e). S is presumed to be an accommodation party, and there is thus notice that the instrument is signed for accommodation, if the signature (i) is an anomalous indorsement or (ii) is accompanied by words indicating the signer is acting as a surety or guarantor with respect to the obligation of another party to the instrument. §§ 3–419(c), 3–205(d). Example: S is an accommodation maker, and nothing on the note shows S has signed for accommodation. C negotiates the note to X, who is ignorant of that fact. In this case, X is entitled to proceed according to what is shown by the face of the note or what X otherwise knows, and S is not discharged if X acts in ignorance of the relation. See former § 3–606 Comment 3.

(d) Consent to Event or Conduct, or Waiver of Discharge

S is not discharged if (i) S *consents* to the event or conduct that is the basis of the discharge or (ii) the instrument (or a separate agreement) provides for *waiver* of discharge. It is standard practice to include a waiver of suretyship defenses in notes prepared by financial institutions, such as the following: "The makers, indorsers, and guarantors of this note, and the sureties hereon, consent that the time of its payment may be extended without notice, all defenses on the ground of any extension of time of payment being hereby expressly waived." Thus, § 3–605 will discharge an accommodation party only if the note does not include a waiver clause and C takes actions that would give rise to a discharge without obtaining S's *consent*. § 3–605(f) and Comment 9.

(e) Effectiveness of Discharge against Holder in Due Course

Discharge of the obligation of an accommodation party (surety) is not effective against a holder in due course who lacks notice of the discharge. § 3–601(b); see § 3–302(b) (first sentence).

G. CONCLUSION

Counseling point: "A man void of understanding striketh hands and becometh surety in the presence of his friend." "He that is surety for a stranger shall smart for it; and he that hateth suretyship is sure." Proverbs 17:18 and 11:15.

[See 16 CFR § 444.3 for the Federal Trade Commission rule regarding notice to sureties in consumer credit transactions apprising them of the nature and extent of their liability. See 13 West's Legal Forms § 6.11—Form 32; see also UCCC § 3.208(1974).]

7.   ACCRUAL OF CAUSE OF ACTION AND STATUTE OF LIMITATIONS

Former § 3–122 stated when a cause of action accrued, but Revised § 3–118 does not. Instead, the only purpose of Revised § 3–118 is to define the time within which an action to enforce an obligation, duty, or right arising under Article 3 must be commenced. In addition, Revised § 3–118 is not exhaustive: the circumstances under which a limitations period may be tolled, for example, is left to other law. §§ 3–118 Comment 1, 1–103(b).

Common statutes of limitations are as follows:

1. *Personal uncertified checks.* "[A]n action to enforce the obligation of a party to an unaccepted draft [e.g., uncertified check] to pay the draft must be commenced within three years after dishonor of the draft or 10 years after the date of the draft, whichever period expires first." § 3–118(c), see § 3–502(b).

2. *Notes payable at a definite time.* Action must be commenced within six years after the due date(s) stated in the note (or, if a due date is accelerated, within six years of the accelerated due date). § 3–118(a).

3. *Certificates of deposit.* Action must be commenced within six years after *demand* for payment is made to the maker. § 3–118(e). (If the instrument states a due date, see § 3–118(e) and Comment 4.)

For notes payable on demand, see § 3–118(b); for teller's checks, cashier's checks, certified checks, and traveler's checks, see § 3–118(d); for accepted drafts other than certified checks, see § 3–118(f); for warranty and conversion cases, etc., see §§ 3–118(g), 3–416(d), 3–417(f), 4–207(e), 4–208(f); see §§ 3–420, 4–111.

8. DISCHARGE OF OBLIGATIONS

We have assessed the obligations of makers, acceptors, drawers, and indorsers. Now, we will survey the *discharge* of parties from their obligations. § 3–601(a); see §§ 3–602(b) (by payment), 3–302(b) (re: holder in due course), 3–305(a)(1)(iv) and (b).

Simple contract discharge

The obligation of a party to pay an instrument is discharged by an act or agreement that would discharge an obligation to pay money under a simple contract. § 3–601(a). Examples: accord and satisfaction, novation, running of statute of limitations, discharge in bankruptcy, etc. See, e.g., §§ 3–118, 3–311.

Discharge by payment

An instrument is paid to the extent payment is made by (or on behalf of) a party obliged to pay the instrument, and to a "person entitled to enforce" the instrument, e.g., "holder." §§ 3–602(a), 3–301 ("person entitled to enforce"), 1–201(b)(21)(A) ("holder" defined). To the extent of the payment, the party is *discharged* (even if payment is made with knowledge of another person's claim to the instrument). § 3–602(c); see Part Three, B, 4 *supra* (jus tertii—claims and defenses of third persons) and §§ 3–305(c) and Comment 4, 3–306.

The party is not discharged in certain situations: (1) if the payor (i) knows of an injunction against payment, or (ii) has accepted indemnity against loss; or (2) if the person making payment *knows* the instrument has been stolen and pays a person it *knows* is in wrongful possession of the instrument. § 3–602(e).

But remember: Discharge by payment is not effective against a holder in due course who lacks notice of the discharge. Thus, if an instrument is paid without being surrendered, a subsequent holder in due course who lacks notice of the discharge cuts off this personal defense. §§ 3–305(a)(2) and (b), 3–601(b); see § 3–501(b)(2) (re: surrender).

[Note: § 3–602(a) covers payments made in a traditional manner to the person entitled to enforce the instrument. Amended § 3–602(b) (2002), "which provides an alternative method of payment, deals with the situation in which a person entitled to enforce the instrument transfers the instrument without giving notice to the parties obligated to pay the instrument. If that happens and one of those parties subsequently makes a payment to the transferor, the payment is effective even though it is not made to the person entitled to enforce the instrument." § 3–602 Comment 2, see §§ 3–602(c) and (d) (2002), 9–406(a) (discharge of account debtor).]

Discharge by tender of payment

If tender of the amount due on an instrument is made to a person entitled to enforce the instrument (and refused), the obligation to pay after-accruing *interest* on the amount tendered is discharged. §§ 3–603(c) (first sentence), 3–301. As to tender of payment if presentment is required, see §§ 3–603(c) (second sentence), 3–502.

"Further, refusal of a tender of payment discharges any indorser or accommodation party having a right of recourse against the party making the tender." § 3–603(b) and Comment. Example: A issues a note to B, who indorses it to C, who indorses it to D. B tenders payment to D, who refuses the tender. C is discharged. See § 3–415(a).

As to tender discharging a mortgage, see Nelson and Whitman, Real Estate Finance Law § 6.7 (5th Practitioner's Ed. 2007); see also § 3–603(a).

Discharge by cancellation or renunciation

A person entitled to enforce an instrument may discharge the obligation of a party (e.g., indorser) to pay the instrument:

   (i) by an intentional voluntary act (e.g., surrender of the instrument, destruction or cancellation of the instrument, or striking out the party's signature),

(ii) by agreeing not to sue (or otherwise renouncing rights against) the party by a signed record. §§ 3–604(a), 1–201(b)(31) ("record" defined). Example: "I hereby renounce all rights and claims against you [*maker, indorser, etc.*] on [*describe the instrument*]."

Discharge by impairment of collateral or right of recourse

See Part Three, C, 6, F, (2) supra and § 3–605.

Discharge of one party with joint and several liability

The discharge of a jointly and severally liable obligor (e.g., one of several comakers, § 3–116(a)) does not affect the right of other obligors to seek contribution from the discharged obligor. § 3–116(b) and (c) and Comment 1.

[Note: § 3–116(c) has been deleted under Amended § 3–116 (2002). See Amended Comment 1.]

Discharge by reacquisition of an instrument

Assume a note is payable to A, and A indorses in blank and delivers it to B who, in turn, indorses in blank and delivers it to C. C indorses in blank and delivers it to A. Are B and C discharged from their obligations to A? Answer: "A former holder [A] who reacquires the [note] may cancel indorsements [of B and C] made after the reacquirer [A] first became a holder of the [note].... An indorser [B and C] whose indorsement is canceled is discharged, and the discharge is effective against any subsequent holder." § 3–207 and Comment (see two examples).

Discharge by accord and satisfaction

Assume S sells and delivers goods to B, who asserts that it is not obliged to pay full price for the goods because they are defective. §§ 2–709 (action for the price), 2–606 (acceptance of goods), 2–607 (acceptance, notice, and burden of proof), 2–714 (buyer's damages for accepted goods), 2–717 (deducting damages from price). Further assume B seeks an accord and satisfaction of this disputed claim by, in good faith, tendering a check to S for some amount less than the full amount, bearing conspicuous language indicating that it is offered as "full payment" or "full satisfaction" of the claim.

Common-law rule: By obtaining payment of the check, S accepts B's offer of compromise, even if S adds a notation that the check is accepted "under protest" or in only "partial satisfaction" of the claim. S can refuse the check or accept it subject to the condition stated by B, but cannot obtain payment of the check yet refuse to be bound by the condition. § 3–311 Comments 1–3.

Section 3–311 rule: 3–311 follows the common-law rule, with minor variations to reflect modern business conditions. Thus, if B proves (i) B tendered the check in good faith as full satisfaction of the claim, (ii) the amount was unliquidated or subject to bona fide dispute, and (iii) S obtained payment of the check, then S's claim will be discharged if B proves the check contained a conspicuous statement that it was tendered in full satisfaction of the claim. §§ 3–311(a) and (b), 3–103(a)(13) ("prove" defined), 1–201(b)(10) ("conspicuous" defined), 1–308(b) (reservation of rights inapplicable). There are two limitations, designed to protect S against inadvertent accord and satisfaction:

  1. Section 3–311(c)(1) allows S (if an organization) to protect itself by advising customers (e.g., B) by a conspicuous statement that communications regarding disputed debts must be sent to a particular person, office, or place. If the full satisfaction check is sent to the designated destination and paid, the claim is discharged. If S proves the check was not received at the designated destination, the claim is not discharged unless S or its agent knew the check was tendered in full

satisfaction of the claim. § 3–311(c)(1) and (d) and Comments 5 and 7.

2.   Section 3–311(c)(2) can be used by an S other than an organization or as an alternative to subsection (c)(1). Thus, if S discovers it has obtained payment of a full satisfaction check, it may prevent accord and satisfaction if, within 90 days of payment, S tenders repayment to B. §§ 3–311(c)(2) and Comment 6, see § 3–311(d) and Comment 7.

"Section 3–311 is based upon a belief that the common law rule produces a fair result and that informal dispute resolution by full satisfaction checks should be encouraged." § 3–311 Comment 3.

Discharge by alteration of instrument

Assume A issues a draft or note to B for $100, and B raises the amount to $1,000. Will B recover $1,000, $100, or nothing on the instrument? Answer: An alteration fraudulently made discharges a party (A) whose obligation is affected by the alteration (unless A assents or is precluded from asserting the alteration). Thus, assuming B's alteration is fraudulent and there is no assent or estoppel by A, B recovers nothing. But what if B's alteration is not fraudulent? Suppose A intended to issue the instrument for $1,000 but mistakenly issued it for $100, and B remedied the matter by altering the paper. Here, the instrument may be enforced according to its original terms ($100). § 3–407(a) and (b). B may be able to recover the additional $900 under ordinary contract law, depending on the circumstances. As to a person taking the instrument for value, in good faith, and without notice of the alteration, see § 3–407(c).

Discharge by acceptance varying a draft

See § 3–410(c).

Discharge by bank's certification or other acceptance of draft

A *drawer* is discharged of liability on a draft accepted by a bank (e.g., certified check) regardless of when or by whom acceptance was obtained. This changes former § 3–411(1), under which the drawer was discharged only if the holder obtained acceptance. §§ 3–414(c) and Comment 3, 3–409(d). If a draft is accepted by a bank after an *indorsement* is made, the liability of the indorser is discharged. § 3–415(d).

Discharge of drawer when holder delays collection

See Part Three, C, 3, B, (1), (d) supra and §§ 3–414(f) and Comment 6, 3–501.

Discharge of indorser of check not presented for payment (or given to depositary bank for collection) within 30 days after indorsement

See Part Three, C, 3, B, (1), (d) supra and § 3–415(e) and Comment 4.

Discharge of indorser if required notice of dishonor is not given

See Part Three, C, 3, B, (2), (e) and §§ 3–415(c) and Comments 1 and 2, 3–414(d), 3–503 esp. (c).

Discharge of warrantors by untimely notice of claim for breach of transfer and presentment warranties

See §§ 3–416(c) (4–207(d)), 3–417(e) (4–208(e)).

9. EFFECT OF INSTRUMENT ON UNDERLYING OBLIGATION

Typical case (uncertified check or note): Assume Buyer (B) pays for goods or services by giving Seller (S) B's personal check, or B signs a note for the purchase price.

In either case, B's obligation to pay the price (§ 2–301) is suspended when S takes the note or check. If the check or note is *dishonored* (§ 3–502(a) and (b)), S may sue on either the dishonored instrument or the contract of sale (if S has possession of the instrument and is the "person entitled to enforce" it). If the check or note is *paid*, payment *discharges* the obligation (§ 2–301) to the extent of the amount of the check or note. §§ 3–310(b) and Comment 3, 3–301(i) ("person entitled to enforce"), see §§ 3–602(a), 3–308(b). These rules reflect this commercial understanding: "It is commonly said that a check or other negotiable instrument is 'conditional payment.' By this it is normally meant that taking the instrument is a surrender of the right to sue on the obligation until the instrument is due, but if the instrument is [dishonored,] the right to sue on the obligation is revived." Former § 3–802 Comment 3. Note: If the right to enforce the instrument is held by somebody other than S, S cannot enforce the right to payment of the price under the sales contract because that right is represented by an instrument that is enforceable by somebody else. Thus, if S sold the note or the check to a holder (H) (and has not reacquired it after dishonor), the only right that survives is H's right to enforce the instrument. § 3–310 Comment 3 (first paragraph).

Where an instrument is indorsed over to the obligee in payment of another person's obligation, see § 3–310(b)(3) (last sentence) and Comment 3 (last paragraph); where an instrument is lost, stolen, or destroyed, see § 3–310(b)(4) (last sentence) and Comment 4; where a certified or cashier's or teller's check is taken for an obligation, see §§ 3–310(a) and Comment 2 and 3–414(c); in rare cases where other instruments are taken for obligations, see § 3–310(c) and Comment 5.

10. LOST, DESTROYED, OR STOLEN
INSTRUMENTS

Assume the following: (1) Drawer issues and delivers a check to Payee "to order of Payee." (2) While in Payee's possession, the check is lost, destroyed, or stolen. (3) Payee seeks to have Drawer issue a replacement check. Drawer would naturally be reluctant to do so since it is possible, if Payee indorsed the check in blank, that the check is in the possession of a holder in due course. Of course, if the signature of Payee is forged, no one thereafter can qualify as a "holder" so as to be a holder in due course. See Part Three, B, 3 and 4 supra and §§ 3–305(c), 3–306.

Accordingly, § 3–309(a) provides that Payee, although not in possession of the check, is entitled to enforce the check if (1) Payee was entitled to enforce the check when loss of possession occurred (or Payee acquired ownership of the check from a person who was entitled to enforce it when loss of possession occurred), (2) the loss of possession was not the result of a transfer by Payee or a lawful seizure, and (3) Payee cannot reasonably obtain possession of the check because the check was *destroyed* or *lost* or *stolen* by an unknown person (or a person who cannot be found or is not amenable to service of process). § 3–309 Comments 2 and 3. In our example, because (1) Payee was entitled to enforce the check when it was stolen, (2) the check was not transferred or seized, and (3) Payee cannot obtain possession of the check because of the theft, Payee is entitled to enforce the check *but*, under § 3–309(b), must prove the terms of the check and Payee's right to enforce it. Note: A court may not enter judgment for Payee unless it finds Drawer is adequately protected against any loss that might occur due to a claim by another person (e.g., a holder in due course) to enforce the check. Adequate protection may be provided by any reasonable means, e.g., security indemnifying

Drawer against loss. § 3–309(b) (third and fourth sentences) and Comment 1. Cf. §§ 7–601, 8–405, 8–406.

In August 1991, the National Conference of Commissioners on Uniform State Laws promulgated new § 3–312, entitled, "Lost, Destroyed, or Stolen Cashier's Check, Teller's Check, or Certified Check." Under this rule, certain claimants can notify the bank of their claim and, if a certain period of time has passed (e.g., 90 days) and the check has not been presented for payment, obtain payment from the bank without providing security. See § 3–312 Comments (especially cases in Comment 4).

D. THE RELATIONSHIP BETWEEN A PAYOR BANK AND ITS CUSTOMER

1. FACTUAL SETTING

Here, we investigate the relationship between the customer who draws a check and the payor bank. See §§ 4–104(a)(5) ("customer" defined), 4–105(3) ("payor bank" defined). Example: Customer opens a checking account with Bank. Customer deposits monies with Bank and signs a signature card evidencing a certain contractual relationship between them. The relationship created is that of a debtor and a creditor. Per the deposit contract, Bank (drawee–debtor) engages to pay checks that Customer (drawer–creditor) may issue from time to time. After Customer issues a check to Payee, Payee presents the check to Bank for payment. Bank then charges the amount of the check against Customer's account.

2. RIGHTFUL VS. WRONGFUL PAYMENT

A. **WHEN A BANK MAY CHARGE ITS CUSTOMER'S ACCOUNT**

A drawee–payor–bank may charge an item (e.g., a check) against the account of a drawer–customer–depositor if the item is "properly payable" from the account. §§ 4–401(a), 4–104(a)(1) and (5) and (9) (defining "account," "customer," and "item"), 4–105(3) (defining "payor bank"). By inference, a bank may *not* charge an item against a customer's account if the item is *not* "properly payable" from the account. An item is "properly payable" if it is authorized by the customer and is in accordance with any agreement between the customer and bank. § 4–401(a) (last sentence). Examples: "An item containing a *forged drawer's* signature or *forged indorsement* is not properly payable." [Emphasis added.] § 4–401 Comment 1. Another example of a payment made without authority is a check that is altered after issuance (e.g., the amount is raised). "[Here,] bank . . . may charge the indicated account of its customer according to the *original* terms of the altered item [not the terms as altered]." [Emphasis added.] § 4–401(d)(1), cf. § 3–407(c)(i).

As Aigler and Steinheimer point out in Cases on Bills and Notes 10–11 (1962),

It cannot be overemphasized that the bank's duty to the depositor is to make payments only in accordance with his *genuine* orders. Expressed in bookkeeping terms, it is warranted in charging to the depositor's account, and thus reducing its indebtedness to him, only when the payments are made strictly as the depositor ordered. This duty on the bank's part is not merely that it use care; it is absolute, subject only to possible breaches of duty on the part of the depositor that will free the bank from this strict obligation.

Example: On May 1, Bank sends to Customer a statement of account accompanied by cancelled checks paid by Bank. On May 2, Customer, in reconciling his account, discovers that one of the checks was not issued by him; his signature on the check was forged. He also discovers that another check was issued by him but—notwithstanding his exercise of reasonable care in drawing the check— was skillfully raised from $100 to $1,000. Customer immediately notifies Bank and demands that Bank recredit his account (1) for the amount of the forged check; and (2) for the amount by which the altered check was raised.

A few weeks later, a payee of another one of the checks Bank returned to Customer on May 1 reported to Customer that Payee had not been paid by Customer. After several exchanges of correspondence, it was determined that someone had wrongfully taken the check from Payee's mailbox, forged Payee's signature, and cashed the check at Bank. On discovery of this, Customer issues another check to Payee (see § 3–309), promptly notifies Bank of the forged indorsement, and demands that Bank recredit his account for the amount of the check.

Bank must recredit Customer's account for the amount of both the forged drawer check and the forged indorsement check. These checks are not "properly payable." Further, Bank must recredit Customer's account for the amount by which the altered check was raised ($900). Bank may charge Customer's account according to the original terms of the check ($100), but the other $900 was not Customer's genuine order. § 4–401(a), (d).

Bank's payment of overdraft

Bank may charge an item against Customer's account even if doing so creates an overdraft. If more than one customer can draw on the account, the nonsigning customer is not liable for an overdraft unless that person benefits from the proceeds of the item. § 4–401(a) and (b) and Comments 1 and 2.

Bank's payment of postdated check

Bank may charge against Customer's account a check that is otherwise properly payable, even if payment was made before the date of the check, unless Customer notified Bank of the postdating in advance, describing the check with reasonable certainty. §§ 4–401(c), 3–113(a) and Comment (re: date of instrument). Reason: The automated check collection system cannot accommodate postdated checks. § 4–401 Comment 3.

Order in which items may be charged or certified

Generally, items may be accepted, paid, certified, or charged to the indicated account of Customer in any order. § 4–303(b) and Comment 7.

B. CUSTOMER'S DUTIES TO BANK—EFFECT ON BANK'S LIABILITY FOR WRONGFUL PAYMENT

We have learned from the preceding discussion that the liability of a bank for paying a forged or altered instrument is absolute. However, as the Aigler and Steinheimer quotation above stated, the bank's absolute duty to follow the drawer-depositor's genuine order is "subject only to possible breaches of duty on the part of the depositor that will free the bank from this strict obligation." The drawer's duties are basically (1) to prepare and issue an instrument non-negligently, and (2) to exercise reasonable care and promptness in examining bank statements and items to discover and report forgeries and alterations. Discussion of these duties follows.

(1) Preparation and Issuance of Instruments

(a) Negligence Contributing to Forged Signature or Alteration

A customer whose failure to exercise ordinary care substantially contributes to an ***alteration*** of an instrument or a *forged* signature on an instrument, is *precluded* from asserting the alteration or forgery against a bank that, in good faith, pays the instrument. If, however, Bank, the entity asserting the preclusion, fails to exercise ordinary care in paying the instrument and that failure substantially contributes to the loss, the loss is *allocated* between Customer and Bank according to the extent to which the failure of each contributed to the loss. §§ 3–406(a) and (b), 3–103(a)(9) ("ordinary care" defined).

Example 1: Customer writes a check for $10. The figure '10' and the word 'ten' are typewritten in the appropriate spaces on the check form, but a large blank space is left after the figure and the word. The payee, using a typewriter with a typeface similar to that used on the check, writes the word 'thousand' after the word 'ten' and a comma and three zeroes after the figure '10'. Bank in good faith pays $10,000 when the check is presented for payment and debits Customer's account in that amount. The trier of fact could find that the drawer failed to exercise ordinary care in writing the check and that the failure substantially contributed to the alteration. In that case, the drawer is precluded from asserting the alteration against the drawee if the check was paid in good faith. However, if the drawee failed to exercise ordinary care and that failure substantially contributed to the loss, the loss will be allocated between the drawer and drawee on a *comparative negligence* basis. § 3–406 Comment 3 (Case #3); see §§ 3–406(b) and Comment 4, 3–406(c) (regarding burden of proof).

Example 2: "Employer [Customer] signs checks drawn on Employer's account by use of a rubber stamp of Employer's signature. Employer keeps the rubber stamp along with Employer's personalized blank check forms in an unlocked desk drawer. An unauthorized person fraudulently uses the check forms to write checks on Employer's account. The checks are signed by use of the rubber stamp. If Employer demands that Employer's account in the drawee [Bank] be recredited because the forged check was not properly payable [§ 4–401(a)], the drawee [Bank] may defend by asserting that Employer is precluded from asserting the forgery. The trier of fact could find that Employer failed to exercise ordinary care to safeguard the rubber stamp and the check forms and that the failure substantially contributed to the forgery of Employer's signature by the unauthorized use of the rubber stamp." § 3–406 Comment 3 (Case #1).

Section 3–406(a) also precludes a negligent customer-drawer from asserting the "real defenses" of forgery and alteration against a person who, in good faith, takes the item for value. See Part Three, B, 2, B, (4) supra.

(b) Completion of Incomplete Instrument

Example: Customer issues a check to Payee, but leaves the amount blank. Payee was authorized to fill in the amount of $100, but improperly fills in an amount of $1,000. May Bank charge $1,000 to Customer's account? Answer: A bank that in good faith makes payment to a holder may charge the indicated account of its customer according to the terms of the *completed* item ($1,000), even though the bank knows the item was completed after issuance (unless the bank has notice that the completion was improper). § 4–401(d)(2) and Comment 4; cf. §§ 3–115 (incomplete instruments), 3–407(c)(ii) and see Part Three, B, 2, B, (4) supra (rights of holder in due course).

(c) Instruments Payable to Impostors or Fictitious Payees

(i) Impostors

Example: In a certain business transaction, Impostor represents himself to Customer as Smith and induces Customer to draw a check to the order of Smith. Impostor indorses the check in the name of Smith and cashes it at drawee Bank. Customer discovers that Impostor was an impostor and now wants Bank to recredit Customer's account because the check was not "properly payable" (§ 4–401(a)) for the reason that it was paid over a forged indorsement. ("An item containing a ... forged indorsement is not properly payable." § 4–401 Comment 1.) Will customer prevail? Answer: If Impostor (by use of the mails or otherwise) induces Customer to issue the check to Impostor, Impostor's indorsement in Smith's name *is effective* as Smith's indorsement in favor of Bank who, in good faith, pays the instrument. Accordingly, Customer's account need not be recredited, so long as Bank acted in good faith in paying the check. § 3–404 Comment 3. However, if Bank fails to exercise ordinary care in paying the check and that failure substantially contributes to the loss resulting from payment of the check, Customer may recover from Bank *to the extent* Bank's failure to exercise ordinary care contributed to the loss. § 3–404(d). In sum, § 3–404 "codifies the proposition that certain behavior [e.g., issuing a check to an impostor] is negligent and thus renders signatures resulting from that behavior effective against the negligent party"; section 3–404 "is a kind of codified negligence liability." UCC Hornbook §§ 17–1, 17–4. Cf. § 2–403(1)(a) (re: power to transfer title to goods in the face of similar deceit). Note: Impostor's indorsement in Smith's name is also effective as Smith's indorsement in favor of a holder in due course. (Recall that a person taking through a forged indorsement is not a "holder" and thus cannot qualify as a "holder in due course." See Part Three, B, 2, B, (2) and Part Three, B, 3 supra.) Simply, the Code's position is that a drawer, rather than a drawee or holder in due course, bears the risk of imposture.

(ii) Fictitious Payees

Assume Treasurer, who is authorized to draw checks on behalf of Corporation, fraudulently draws a check payable to Supplier Co., a non-existent company (i.e., a "fictitious person"). (Treasurer did not intend "Supplier Co." to have any interest in the check.) Treasurer indorses the check in the name of "Supplier Co." and deposits it in Depositary Bank. The check is paid by drawee Payor Bank, which charges Corporation's account. Corporation discovers the fraud after Treasurer has departed for unknown parts with the proceeds of the check, and seeks to have Payor Bank recredit Corporation's account since the check was not "properly payable," on the theory that it bore a forged indorsement of "Supplier Co." § 4–401(a) and Comment 1. Will Corporation win? Answer: No. "If the person identified as payee of an instrument [Supplier Co.] is a fictitious person ... any person in possession of the [check] is its holder. An indorsement by any person [e.g., by Treasurer] in the name of the payee [Supplier Co.] is *effective* as the indorsement of the payee in favor of a person who, in good faith, pays the check." Accordingly, the check is "properly payable." §§ 3–404(b)(2) and (c)(i) and Comment 2 (Case #1), 4–401(a) (defining "properly payable"). If, however, Payor Bank fails to exercise ordinary care, Corporation may recover from Payor Bank *to the extent* the failure to exercise ordinary care *contributed* to the loss. § 3–404(d) and Comment 3.

Note: If Supplier is an actual company that does business with Corporation and Treasurer intended to steal the check when it was drawn, the result is the same as in the example above, i.e., the indorsement is *effective.* Section 3–404(b) applies because Treasurer did not intend Supplier Co. to have any interest in the check. § 3–404(b)(1) and Comment 2 (Case #2). Note also: The indorsement is effective in favor of a person who, in good faith, takes it for value (e.g., holder in due course) or for collection (e.g., Depositary Bank). § 3–404(b) and Comments 2 (Cases #1 through #5) and 3.

(d) Employees' Fraudulent Indorsements of Instruments Issued by Employers

Example: Treasurer signs checks on behalf of Corporation as drawer. Clerk's duties include preparing these checks to be signed and issued. Clerk prepares a check payable to the order of Supplier Co. for Treasurer's signature. Clerk fraudulently informs Treasurer that the check is needed to pay a debt owed to Supplier Co., a company that does business with Corporation. No money is owed to Supplier Co.; Clerk intends to steal the check. Treasurer signs it and returns it to Clerk for mailing. Clerk does not indorse the check, but deposits it to an account in Depositary Bank that Clerk opened in the name "Supplier Co." The check is honored by the drawee, Payor Bank. Must Payor Bank recredit Corporation's account? Answer: "If [Corporation] entrusted [Clerk] with responsibility with respect to the [check] and the [Clerk] ... makes a fraudulent indorsement of the [check], the indorsement is effective as the indorsement of the person to whom the [check] is payable [i.e., Supplier Co.] if it is made in the name of that person." § 3–405(b). Accordingly, § 3–405 treats Clerk's deposit as an effective indorsement because Clerk was entrusted with responsibility with respect to the check. The drawee, Payor Bank, may debit the account of Corporation for the amount of the check. § 3–405, especially (a)(2)(ii), (a)(3)(iii), (b) and Comment 3 (Case #7). If, however, Payor Bank fails to exercise ordinary care in paying the check and that failure substantially contributes to the loss resulting from the fraud, Corporation may recover from Payor Bank *to the extent* the failure to exercise ordinary care contributed to the loss. § 3–405(b) and Comment 4; cf. 3–404(d), 3–406(b), 4–406(e) (re: bank statement rule). Note: The fraudulent indorsement is also effective against a person who in good faith takes it for value or for collection. § 3–405(b).

Policy: "Section 3–405 is based on the belief that the employer is in a far better position to avoid the loss by care in choosing employees, in supervising them, and in adopting other measures to prevent ... fraud in the issuance of instruments in the name of the employer." § 3–405 Comment 1.

(2) When Bank Sends or Makes Available a Statement of Account or Items—Customer's Duty to Discover and Report Unauthorized Signature or Alteration

(a) Requisites to Impose on Customer the Duty to Discover and Report Unauthorized Signature or Alteration

Customer's duty to discover and report to Bank instances of alteration of customer's checks or forgery of its signature becomes operative only if Bank sends or makes available to Customer a statement of account pursuant to § 4–406(a). § 4–406(c). Subsection (a) provides, "[Bank] that sends or makes available to [Customer] a statement of account showing payment of [checks] for the account shall either [i] return or make available to [Customer] the [checks] paid or [ii] provide information in the statement of account sufficient to allow [Customer] reasonably to identify the [checks] paid." See § 4–104(a)(9).

Whether Bank returns to Customer the paid checks is to be determined by the Bank–Customer agreement. If Bank does not return the checks, the standard is that Customer must be given information "sufficient to allow Customer reasonably to identify the [checks] paid." If Bank supplies Customer with an image of the paid check, it complies with this standard. If the check is described by check number, amount, and date of payment, Bank also complies. § 4–406(a) (safe harbor rule, especially second sentence), (b) and Comments 1–3.

(b) Customer's Duty to Discover and Report Customer's Unauthorized Signature or Any Alteration

If Bank sends or makes available a statement of account or checks, as discussed above, Customer must exercise reasonable promptness in examining the statement or checks to determine whether any payment was not authorized (i) because of an alteration of a check or (ii) because a purported signature of Customer was not authorized. If Customer should reasonably have *discovered* the unauthorized payment, Customer must promptly *notify* Bank of the relevant facts. § 4–406(c); see § 4–401(a) and (d)(1) (when bank may charge customer's account).

If Bank *proves* that Customer failed to comply with its duties per the previous paragraph, Customer cannot proceed against Bank for Customer's unauthorized signature or any alteration on the check, if Bank *also proves* that it suffered a loss by reason of the failure. §§ 4–406(d)(1), 4–104(c) (3–103(a)(13) ("prove" defined), 1–201(b)(8)) ("burden of establishing" defined). This rule is akin to requiring Customer to close the barn door after the horse has been stolen. How does Bank prove it suffered a loss? Perhaps by proving that customer's prompt discovery and notification to Bank of a forged Customer's signature or alteration would have resulted in apprehending the person who forged or altered the check while the person had the ill-gotten gains.

As to Customer's duty to discover Customer's unauthorized signature or alteration by the *same* wrongdoer on any *other* check paid in good faith by Bank, see § 4–406(d)(2). One of the most serious consequences of Customer's failure to comply with the requirements of § 4–406(c) is the opportunity for a wrongdoer to repeat the misdeeds. One of the best ways to keep down losses is for Customer to *promptly* examine the statement within a reasonable time not to exceed 30 days and notify Bank of any unauthorized signature or alteration so Bank can stop paying further checks. § 4–406 Comment 2 (last paragraph).

(c) Bank's Failure to Exercise Ordinary Care—Comparative Negligence Test

In the above discussion, we learned the circumstances under which Customer is precluded from asserting Customer's unauthorized signature, or any alteration, against Bank. §§ 4–401, 4–406(a)–(d). However, if Customer *proves* that Bank failed to exercise *ordinary care* in paying the check and that the failure substantially contributed to the loss, the loss is *allocated* between Customer and Bank according *to the extent* to which the conduct of each contributed to the loss. §§ 4–406(e) and Comment 4, 4–104(b) (§ 3–103(a)(9)) ("ordinary care" defined); cf. §§ 3–404(d) (re: impostors and fictitious payees), 3–405(b) (re: employees fraudulent indorsement), 3–406(b). If Bank did not pay the check in good faith, see § 4–406(e) (second sentence).

The above rules are summarized as follows:

1.   Bank may charge against Customer's account a check that is "properly payable," that is, authorized by Customer. Thus, Bank's liability for paying over a forged drawer–customer's signature or paying an altered instrument is absolute, because such a check is not properly payable. § 4–401 and Comment 1.

2.   Customer's failure to comply with its duty to discover and report an alteration or customer's own unauthorized signature *may* preclude Customer from asserting these against Bank. § 4–406(a)–(d).

3.   If Customer proves that Bank failed to exercise ordinary care in paying the check and that the failure substantially contributed to the loss, the loss is allocated between Customer and Bank using a modified comparative negligence test. § 4–406(e) and Comment 4.

(d) No Duty to Discover and Report Unauthorized Indorsement

"Section 4–406 imposes no duties on the drawer [Customer] to look for unauthorized indorsements." § 4–406 Comment 5. Why? Although there is little excuse for Customer not detecting its own forged signature (reconciliation of its own records with the statement or checks should quickly reveal discrepancies), Customer does not know the signatures of indorsers.

(e) Time Limit on Customer's Right to Assert Against Bank (i) Customer's Unauthorized Signature, (ii) Any Alteration, or (iii) An Unauthorized Indorsement

Customer must discover and report Customer's unauthorized signature on, or any alteration on, the check within one year of when the statement or checks are made available to it or will be precluded from asserting either against Bank. § 4–406(a), (f). Further, § 4–111 provides a statute of limitations allowing Customer three years to seek to have its account recredited following payment of a check with an unauthorized indorsement. § 4–406 Comment 5.

C. EVENTS OR CIRCUMSTANCES THAT SUSPEND OR TERMINATE BANK'S AUTHORITY TO PAY

A draft (e.g., check) authorizes (orders) the drawee Bank to make payments on behalf of drawer Customer. If Bank pays in strict accordance with Customer's genuine order, Bank may charge that payment to Customer's account. § 4–401. Customer's relationship with Bank in placing this order may be likened to a principal–agent relationship. Restatement (Third) of Agency § 3.09 (2006) states, "An agent's actual authority terminates ... (2) upon the occurrence of circumstances on the basis of which the agent should reasonably conclude that the principal no longer would assent to the agent's taking action on the principal's behalf."

Accordingly, the following discussion centers on events or circumstances that may affect Bank's authority to pay as customer's agent: (1) Customer's stop-payment order, (2) a stale check, (3) Customer's death or incompetence, and (4) Customer's bankruptcy or assignment for benefit of creditors.

(1) Customer's Right to Stop Payment

Factual setting

By telephone, Customer ordered Bank to stop payment on a previously issued check. Ten days later, Payee presents the check, and Bank pays. Is Bank liable for making payment despite the stop-payment order?

Analysis

1.   Customer may stop payment of any check drawn on Customer's account (or may close the account) by giving Bank an order describing the check (or account) with reasonable certainty. (A payee or indorsee has no such right.) See one exception where Customer has died. § 4–403(a) and Comments 1 and 2. See §§ 4–405(b), 4–401(c).

2.   A stop-payment order is effective for six months, but lapses after 14 calendar days if the original order was oral and was not confirmed in a record (e.g., a writing) within that period. § 4–403(b). As to renewal of stop-payment orders, see § 4–403(b) (second sentence).

3.   A stop-payment order must be received at a time and in a manner that affords Bank a reasonable opportunity to act on it before taking any action on the check, e.g., before Bank certifies the check or pays it in cash. §§ 4–403(a) and Comment 4, 4–303(a), 4–107 Comment 4.

From the above analysis, it would appear that Bank improperly paid over Customer's stop-payment order. (Assume the order was duly confirmed in a record.) But Bank is only prima facie liable. The burden of establishing the fact and amount of loss resulting from payment of the check is on Customer. §§ 4–403(c), 1–201(b)(8) ("burden of establishing" defined), see § 4–407 Comment 1.

Example 1: Buyer buys, receives, and accepts goods from Seller for $1,000. Buyer draws a check on Bank payable to Seller. Even though the goods are not defective, Buyer nevertheless orders Bank to stop payment. Although the order to stop payment was timely, Bank paid the $1,000 to Seller when Seller subsequently presented the check for payment. Buyer seeks to have Bank recredit its account. Must Bank recredit? No, because Buyer cannot establish any loss resulting from payment of the check contrary to the stop-payment order. Buyer obtained non-defective goods for which Buyer had agreed to pay Seller $1,000. Even if payment had been stopped, Buyer would have been liable to Seller for the $1,000 under its contract of secondary liability as a drawer. §§ 4–403(a) and (c), 3–414.

Example 2: Same as Example 1 except that the goods are defective. The value of the defective goods accepted is $600; if they had been as warranted, their value would be the same as the purchase price, $1,000. (Thus, Buyer's damages are $400.) § 2–714(2). Now, Bank must recredit Buyer's account, but only for $400. Reasons:

(1) $400 is the amount of loss resulting from payment of the check over the stop-payment order (§ 4–403(c)).

(2) Bank is subrogated to the rights of payee–Seller against drawer–Buyer either on the check or under the transaction out of which it arose (the sale of the defective goods). Seller is not entitled to the full price ($1,000), but the goods are still worth a portion of the contract price ($600). Since Buyer retained the goods, it must pay part of the agreed price ($600). Accordingly, Bank should be subrogated to Seller's claim for $600

against Buyer. § 4–407(2) and Comment 2. Therefore, Bank can deduct $600 from Buyer's $1,000 claim against Bank for improper payment. As a result, Bank's liability to Buyer is $400. § 4–407(2) and Comment 2. See UCC Hornbook § 19–6.

Buyer thus owed $600 for the goods. But remember that Bank has paid Seller $1,000 (even though the goods were actually worth only $600 due to the defect). What are Bank's rights? Answer: Bank is subrogated to Buyer's rights against Seller with respect to the transaction out of which the check arose. §§ 4–407(3) and Comment 3, 2–714(2) (Buyer's remedies for accepted goods). Consequently, Bank can recover $400 from Seller.

In short: Buyer ends up paying $600, the value of the goods; Seller ends up with $600, the value of the goods; Bank (which paid the $1,000 check) ends up deducting $600 from Buyer's account and recovering $400 from Seller.

Example 3: Same as Example 2 except that payee–Seller indorses the check to Adams, a holder in due course. Adams takes free of Buyer's personal defense of failure of consideration against payee–Seller. § 3–305(a)(2) and (b). Must Bank recredit Buyer's account? No. Reasons:

(1) Buyer cannot establish any loss resulting from payment of the check contrary to the stop-payment order. Although Buyer may have received defective goods, this defense is cut off by Adams, a holder in due course. Even if payment had been stopped, Buyer as drawer would have been liable for the $1,000 check to Adams as a holder in due course (§§ 4–403(c), 3–414).

(2) Bank is subrogated to the rights of holder in due course Adams on the check against drawer–Buyer. And since Adams has a valid claim against drawer–Buyer for the $1,000, Bank is subrogated to such right and can

assert it as a defense against Buyer for paying over the stop-payment order. §§ 4–407(1) and Comment 1, 3–414, 4–403 Comment 7. See UCC Hornbook § 19–6.

As to whether Bank may vary any of the above rules by its contract of deposit with Customer, see §§ 4–403 Comment 7, 4–103 and UCC Hornbook §§ 19–2, 19–5.

(2) Checks Presented More than Six Months Old

Example: Customer dates a check April 1 and issues it to Payee. The check is subsequently presented to Drawee Bank on December 10. Is Bank obligated to pay? Answer: No. Bank owes no obligation to Customer to pay a check (other than a certified check, which constitutes Bank's own engagement to pay) presented more than six months after its date. Banking and commercial practice regards a check that is outstanding for longer than six months as stale, and a bank will normally not pay such a check without consulting the depositor.

But Bank may charge Customer's account for a payment made after the six month period in good faith, for example, if Bank is in a position to know, as in the case of dividend checks, that Customer wants payment made. § 4–404 and Comment; see §§ 3–414(f) (obligation of drawer), 3–415(e) (obligation of indorser), 3–304(a)(3) (overdue instrument).

(3) Death or Incompetence of Customer

Example: Customer either is incompetent when he or she issues a check or becomes incompetent thereafter. When is Drawee Bank's authority to pay rendered ineffective? Answer: Bank's authority to pay is not rendered ineffective by Customer's incompetence at the time the check is issued or its collection undertaken, if Bank does not *know* of an adjudication of incompetence. Customer's incompetence does not revoke Bank's authority to pay until Bank *knows* of an adjudication of incompetence and has reasonable opportunity to act on it. §§ 4–405(a) and Comment 1, 1–202(b) ("knows" defined).

Example: On June 1, Customer dies, having recently issued a check. Drawee Bank learns of the death on June 2. The check is presented to Bank on June 6 for payment. May Bank pay? Answer: Even if it knows Customer has died, Bank may, for ten days after the date of death, pay (or certify) checks drawn on or before that date, unless ordered to stop payment by a person claiming an interest in the account, e.g., Customer's surviving relative or creditor. Purpose: To permit holders of checks drawn and issued shortly before death to cash them without filing a claim in probate. Such checks normally are given for immediate payment of an obligation; there is almost never any reason why they should not be paid, so filing in probate is a useless and burdensome formality to the holder, the executor, the court, and the bank. § 4–405(b) and Comments 2 and 3, see § 4–403(a) and Comment 2.

Compare the above rules with the general rule of agency law that death of the principal "terminates the agent's actual authority." Restatement (Third) of Agency § 3.07(2). See also §§ 3.07(4) and 3.08.

(4) Customer's Bankruptcy

See Bank of Marin v. England, 385 U.S. 99, 87 S.Ct. 274, 17 L.Ed.2d 197 (1966). "We cannot say that the act of filing a voluntary petition in bankruptcy *per se* is reasonably calculated to put the bank on notice. Absent revocation by the drawer or his trustee or absent knowledge or notice of the bankruptcy by the bank, the contract between the bank and the drawer remains unaffected by the bankruptcy and the right and duty of the bank to pay duly presented checks remain as before." See B.C., 11 U.S.C. § 542(c). See also § 4–303 Comment 1 (bankruptcy petition and assignment for creditors' benefit.)

3. WRONGFUL DISHONOR

We have seen that Drawee Bank may charge against Customer's account only checks that are "properly payable," that is, Bank must pay strictly in accordance with Customer's order (at least if there are sufficient funds). § 4–401(a). With certain exceptions—i.e., breach of Customer's duties of care to Bank—Bank will face liability for "wrongful payment." See §§ 3–404, 3–405, 3–406, 4–406. Now we look at Bank's liability to Customer for "wrongful dishonor" of a check that is "properly payable." (But note that Bank may dishonor a check that would create an overdraft unless it agreed to pay the overdraft.) §§ 4–402(a), 4–401(a).

Example: Customer deposited $1,000 in his account with Bank, giving him a balance of $2,500. Because of a clerical error, Bank did not credit the $1,000 to his account. Several days later, Customer drew a check for $2,000. It was dishonored by Bank, which erroneously believed there were insufficient funds in Customer's account to cover the $2,000 check. As a consequence, Customer's credit rating was impaired. Further, a sheriff appeared at Customer's office with a warrant and arrested him. Customer was booked, fingerprinted, brought before a magistrate, and finally released on bond. What is Bank's liability to Customer for wrongful dishonor? Answer: (1) Bank is liable for damages proximately caused by wrongful dishonor of the check. (2) Liability is limited to actual damages proved and may include damages for an arrest or prosecution, or other consequential damages. (3) Whether any consequential damages are proximately caused by the wrongful dishonor is a question of fact to be determined in each case. § 4–402(b) and Comment 3. Thus, in the above example, the trier of fact may well find Customer's arrest was proximately caused by wrongful dishonor of the check.

As to Bank's determination of Customer's account balance on which a decision to dishonor for insufficiency of available funds is based, see § 4–402(c).

E. THE BANK COLLECTION PROCESS

1. THE PROCESS DESCRIBED

In payment for goods sold, Buyer draws a $500 check on Drawee Bank and issues it to Seller as payee. Although Seller could take the check directly to Drawee Bank for payment in cash, it is more likely that Seller will deposit the check in its account with its bank, Depositary Bank, to have the check forwarded to and paid by Drawee Bank (also known as Payor Bank). § 4–105(3). This deposit is effected typically by having Payee–Seller complete a "deposit ticket" such as the following:

CASH	CURRENCY		
	COIN		
C H E C K S		*5* 00	oo
TOTAL FROM OTHER SIDE			
TOTAL		*5* 00	oo
LESS CASH RECEIVED			
NET DEPOSIT		*500*	oo

USE OTHER SIDE FOR ADDITIONAL LISTING

Seller presents the check, properly indorsed, with the "deposit ticket" to Depositary Bank's teller. The teller furnishes a receipt showing a $500 provisional credit to Seller's account. If the check is not collected, the credit will be revoked.

Depositary Bank (§ 4–105(2)) will now seek to collect the "item" (§ 4–104(a)(9)), as the check is called in the collection process

1. *"On us" items.* If Depository Bank (Seller's bank) is also Drawee Bank (Buyer's bank)—referred to in the collection process as Payor Bank (§ 4–105(3))—this depositary-payor bank will determine whether (1) the check is in good form (e.g., not forged) and (2) there are sufficient funds in Buyer's account, and if the answer is "yes" to both, the $500 is "paid" (by deducting $500 from Buyer's account and crediting Seller's account). See § 4–401(a). The provisional credit given to Payee–Seller is now final, and Payee–Seller may withdraw the funds. More on how Payor Bank "pays" is discussed presently.

2. *"City" or "clearing house" items.* If Depository Bank (Seller's bank) and Payor Bank (Buyer's Drawee Bank) are not the same bank, but are located in the same vicinity, they may daily forward checks drawn on each other—including Buyer's $500 check—and provisionally settle by striking a balance. Example: Depository Bank has checks in the amount of $750,000 drawn on Payor Bank; Payor Bank has checks in the amount of $650,000 drawn on Depository Bank. Payor Bank would "owe" $100,000 to Depository Bank. This difference may be paid by debiting and crediting accounts.

When several banks are located in the same vicinity, they may find it convenient to establish a clearing house to handle their items. § 4–104(a)(4). These banks (a) send the clearing house the checks deposited with them but drawn on other banks and (b) receive from the clearing house checks drawn on them but deposited with other banks. Similar to the two-bank situation, a balance will be struck between the amount of the checks forwarded to the clearing house and the checks received from the clearing house, and a *provisional settlement* made.

3. *"Country" or "transit" items.* If the Depository Bank and Payor Bank are not in the same vicinity, more steps may be required to forward the check to Payor

Bank. Assume a California Seller and a Maine Buyer. Seller deposits Buyer's check in Depositary Bank in California. The item moves through two or three California banks to the Federal Reserve Bank of San Francisco, to the Federal Reserve Bank of Boston, then to Payor Bank in Maine. See § 4–215 Comment 2. Each bank will provisionally credit the account of its transferor. Note that the Federal Reserve Bank fulfills a country-wide clearing-house function. The banks in the chain are called Depositary Bank (the first bank to take the item); Collecting Bank (a bank handling an item for collection except the payor bank); Presenting Bank (a bank presenting an item except a payor bank); and Payor Bank (a bank that is the drawee of a draft). § 4–105.

Upon receipt of an item, Payor Bank must decide whether to "finally pay" it. See § 4–215 discussed later. This is so regardless of whether the item was received over the counter ("on us"), by mail, or through a clearing house. In former times, when check collection was done manually at Payor Bank, the process was described as follows: "After the initial receipt the item moves to the sorting and proving departments. When sorted and proved it may be photographed. Still later it moves to the bookkeeping department where it is examined for form and signature and compared against the ledger account of the customer to whom it is to be charged [buyer–drawer]. If it is in good form [e.g., no forgeries or alterations] and there are funds to cover it [and no stop-payment orders, garnishments, etc.], it is posted to the drawer's account, either immediately or at a later time. If paid, it is so marked and filed with other items of the same customer. This process may take either a few hours or substantially all of the day of receipt and of the next banking day." Former § 4–213 Comment 3. In modern-day practice, by contrast, such "process of posting" events do not occur. See former § 4–109. Instead, "checks enter payor banks in large sacks with many other checks, are run through the payor bank's [electronic and mechanical] processing equipment and are charged to various accounts without human intervention." UCC Hornbook § 18–4. Periodically, Payor Bank will send to its customer (Buyer–Drawer) a statement of account. § 4–406(a).

The following diagrams of the bank collection process may be useful:

Reprinted from King, Barnhizer, Knight, Payne, Starnes & Stone, Commercial Transactions Under the Uniform Commercial Code and Other Laws, with permission. Copyright 2011 Matthew Bender & Company, Inc., a member of the LexisNexis® Group. All rights reserved.

COLLECTION OF CHECKS—SCHEMATIC DIAGRAM

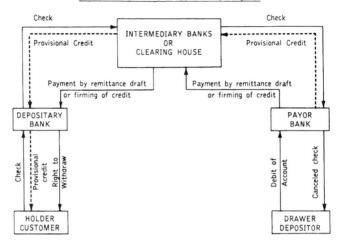

IF CHECK IS HONORED

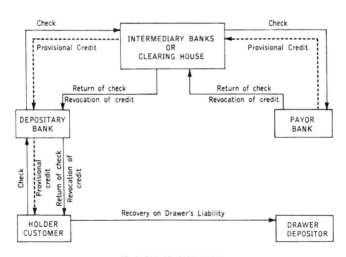

IF CHECK IS DISHONORED

[B87]

To summarize, suppose Mrs. Henderson of Albany, New York, buys a painting from Art Dealer in Sacramento, California. She sends her check, drawn on Albany Bank, to Art Dealer. (1) Dealer deposits the check in his account at Sacramento Bank. (2) Sacramento Bank deposits the check in its account at the Federal Reserve Bank of San Francisco. (3) San Francisco Fed sends the check to New York Fed for collection. (4) New York Fed sends Mrs. Henderson's check to Albany Bank, which deducts the amount from her account. (5) Albany Bank tells New York Fed to deduct the amount of the check from its account. (6) New York Fed pays San Francisco Fed from its share in the interdistrict settlement fund. (7) San Francisco Fed adds the amount to Sacramento Bank's account, and Art Dealer's account is increased. (Federal Reserve Banks use the interdistrict settlement fund in Washington, D.C. as their switching mechanism. The fund settles net amounts due between Reserve Banks daily.) [Adapted from The Story of Checks and Electronic Payments at 13, published by Federal Reserve Bank of New York (1987).]

[Note: The collection of items (e.g., checks) is governed by Article 4, agreement of the parties, clearing-house rules, and Federal Reserve regulations and operating circulars. §§ 4–102 (applicability of Article 4), 4–103(a) and (b) (variation by agreement and clearing-house and federal guidance). "Regulation J, 12 CFR 210, governs the rights of parties in the collection process through the Federal Reserve Banks. Originally Regulation J prescribed rules similar to Article 4; a number of the rules, however, have been changed by Regulation CC." UCC Hornbook § 18–5, p. 850. Note also the Expedited Funds Availability Act, 12 U.S.C. § 4000 et seq., and its implementing Regulation CC, 12 CFR Pt. 229, which provide, *inter alia,* restrictions on the length of time banks may hold a customer's funds after checks are deposited. These supersede "any provision of the law of any state, including the Uniform Commercial Code . . ., which is inconsistent with this chapter or such regulations." § 4–103 Comment 3 (third paragraph). The Comments to the following sections cite Reg. CC: 3–102, 3–104, 3–111, 3–415, 4–102, 4–103, 4–109, 4–110, 4–201, 4–202, 4–204, 4–207, 4–214, 4–215, 4–301, 4–302, 4–303.]

See also, "Check Clearing for the 21st Century Act" ("Check 21"), 12 U.S.C. §§ 5001–5018 (Purpose: To facilitate check truncation by authorizing substitute checks, to foster innovation in the check collection system without mandating receipt of checks in electronic form, etc.).

2. STATUS OF COLLECTING BANK AS AGENT

Agency presumed

Unless a contrary intent clearly appears, during the time when an item is in the collection process, a collecting bank acts as an agent or sub-agent of the item's owner (e.g., a payee who deposited it with a depositary bank for collection) and any settlement given for the item is *provisional.* This presumption of agency applies regardless of the form of indorsement (e.g., in blank, special, or restrictive) or lack of indorsement. Thus, questions once litigated as to whether ordinary indorsements "for deposit," "for collection," or in blank have the effect of creating an agency status or a purchase are no longer an issue. See § 4–201(b). Policy: Because the tremendous volume of items handled (numbering annually in the billions) makes it impossible for banks to examine all indorsements on all items—in fact, this examination is not made, except perhaps by depositary banks—it is unrealistic to base a bank's rights and duties on variations in the form of indorsements. Similarly, the nature of the credit given for an item, or whether it is subject to immediate withdrawal as of right (or is in fact withdrawn) does not rebut the general presumption. (Historically, much time has been spent and effort expended in determining or attempting to determine whether a bank was a purchaser of an item or merely a collection agent.) § 4–201(a) and Comments 1, 2, 6. See also §§ 4–203 (effect of instructions), 3–206(c)(4) and (d) (restrictive indorsement), 3–420(c) (conversion).

But the ownership of an item (e.g., by the payee) and any rights of the owner to proceeds of the item are subject to the rights of a collecting bank, such as those resulting from advances on the item and rights of recoupment or setoff. § 4–201(a) and Comment 5.

Note well: If an item is handled by banks for presentment, payment, collection, or return, the relevant provisions of UCC Article 4 apply even if the parties' action clearly establishes that a particular bank has *purchased* the item and is the owner of it. Thus, the general approach of Article 4, similar to that of other articles, is to provide, within reasonable limits, rules or answers to major problems known to exist in the bank collection process without regard to questions of status and ownership, but to keep general principles such as status and ownership available to cover residual areas not covered by specific rules. § 4–201(a) and Comment 1. (See, e.g., Part One, C, 1 supra explaining that "title" to goods is no longer a principal problem-solving device under Article 2, Sales, but is reserved for residual areas not covered by specific rules. § 2–401.)

The specific rules in Article 4 are generally consistent with the agency status of the collecting banks. Certain of these rules are discussed below.

3. RIGHTS, OBLIGATIONS, AND RESPONSIBILITIES OF COLLECTING BANKS

Basic responsibilities of collecting bank

A collecting bank must exercise *ordinary care* in the following types of basic action:

(1) presenting or sending an item for presentment,

(2) sending notice of dishonor or nonpayment, or returning an item,

(3) settling for an item,

(4) notifying its transferor of any loss or delay in transit.

The *time* for taking proper action is before its "midnight deadline" following receipt of an item, notice, or settlement. §§ 4–202(a) and (b) and Comments 1–3, 4–104(a)(10) (defining "midnight deadline"). See, §§ 4–103 (ordinary care and measure of damages), 4–104(c) (3–103(a)(9)) ("ordinary care" defined), 4–106 ("payable through" or "payable at"), 4–107 (separate office), 4–108 (time of receipt), 4–109 (delays), 4–110 (electronic presentment); 4–203 (effect of instructions), 4–204 (methods of sending), 4–205 (unindorsed item), 4–206 (transfer between banks), 4–212 (items not payable by, through, or at bank), 4–213 (medium and time of settlement). As to presentment, dishonor, and notice of dishonor, see § 3–501 et seq. and Part Three, C, 3, B supra. As to a bank's non-liability for the insolvency, neglect, etc., of others, see § 4–202(c) and Comment 4.

Collecting bank's right of charge-back

See §§ 4–214, 4–201 Comment 3; Reg. CC, 12 CFR 229.36(d).

Risk of loss in the event of insolvency

See §§ 4–216, 4–201 Comment 3.

Collecting bank as holder in due course: value

Holder-in-due-course status is usually associated with an "owner" of an item rather than an "agent." Even so, a depositary bank may enjoy this status. Why? A depositary bank may make advances on paper it holds for collection. When it does, it obtains a "security interest" in the item. This "value" may support holder-in-due-course status. §§ 4–211, 4–210(a) and (b) and Comments 1 and 2. See Part Three, B, 2, B, (3), (a), (iii) supra.

Collecting bank as holder in due course: effect of restrictive indorsement

See §§ 3–206(c) and (e), 3–420(c), 4–201(b); see also Part Three, B, 2, B, (2), (b), (xi) supra.

Transfer, presentment, encoding, and retention warranties of collecting banks

See §§ 4–207, 4–208, 4–209 and Part Three, F infra.

Federal Regulations

See Reg. CC, 12 CFR § 229.30 through 229.42; Reg. J, 12 CFR §§ 210.1 through 210.15.

4. FINAL PAYMENT OF ITEM BY PAYOR BANK

Provisional credits

"Under current bank practice [see above discussion], in a major portion of cases banks make *provisional settlement* for items when they are first received and then await subsequent determination of whether the item will be *finally paid*. . . . Statistically, this practice of settling provisionally first and then awaiting final payment is justified because the vast majority of . . . items are finally paid, with the result that in this great preponderance of cases it becomes unnecessary for the banks making the provisional settlements to make any further entries. In due course the provisional settlements become final simply with the lapse of time. [No news is good news.] However, in those cases in which the item being collected is not finally paid ... provision is made in [§ 4–214(a)] for the reversal of the provisional settlements, charge-back of provisional credits and the right to obtain refund." § 4–214 Comment 1 (emphasis added). As to federal preemption under Reg. CC, see cites at § 4–214 Comment 4.

When item is finally paid by Payor Bank

When is an item "finally paid" by drawee Payor Bank? Answer: When Payor Bank does any of the following:

(1) Pays the item in cash. Example: Payee presents a check to the teller at Payor Bank, who pays cash for it. § 4–215(a)(1).

(2) *Finally* settles for the item, i.e., settles for the item *without* having a right to revoke the settlement under a statute, clearing-house rule, or agreement. §§ 4–215(a)(2), 4–104(a)(11) ("settle" defined). For Payor Bank's *statutory right* to revoke settlement, see §§ 4–215 Comment 4 (first and second paragraphs), 4–301(a); for an *agreement* allowing Payor Bank to revoke a settlement, see § 4–215 Comment 4 (fourth paragraph). Example of Payor Bank's right to revoke a settlement, arising under a *clearing-house rule:* Clearing-house rule provides that items exchanged and settled for in a clearing (e.g., before 10:00 a.m. on Monday) may be returned (and the settlements revoked) up to but not later than 2:00 p.m. on the same day (Monday) or, under deferred posting, at some hour on the next business day (e.g., 2:00 p.m. Tuesday). Under this type of rule, the Monday morning settlement is provisional and thus does not constitute final payment. § 4–215 Comment 4 (third paragraph).

(3) Makes *provisional* settlement for the item and fails to revoke the settlement in the time and manner permitted by statute, clearing-house rule, or agreement §§ 4–215(a)(3), 4–104(a)(11) ("settle" defined). An example is the clearing-house settlement above: "In the illustration there given if the time limit for the return of items received in the Monday morning clearing is 2:00 p.m. on Tuesday and the provisional settlement has not been revoked at that time in a manner permitted by the clearing-house rules, the provisional settlement made on Monday morning becomes final at 2:00 p.m. on Tuesday. [Section 4–215(a)(3)] provides specifically that in this situation the item is finally paid at 2:00 p.m. Tuesday. If on the other hand a payor bank receives an item in the mail on Monday and makes some provisional settlement for the item on Monday, it has until midnight on Tuesday to return the item or give notice and revoke any settlement under Section 4–301. In this situation . . . if the provisional settlement made on Monday is not revoked before midnight on Tuesday as permitted by Section 4–301, the item is finally paid at midnight on Tuesday." § 4–215(a)(3) and Comment 7; see §§ 4–215(b)–(d), 4–301, 4–302 (late return). With respect to checks, see Reg. CC, 12 CFR §§ 229.30 and 229.38.

Note: The "process of posting test" for determining when final payment is made has been abandoned. § 4–215 Comment 5, see former § 4–109.

Reasons why final payment is important

"Final payment of an item is important for a number of reasons. [1] It is one of several factors in determining the relative priorities between items and notices, stop-payment orders, legal process and setoffs (Section 4–303). [2] It is the 'end of the line' in the collection process and the 'turn around' point commencing the return flow of proceeds. [3] It is the point at which many provisional settlements become final. See Section 4–215(c). [See also § 4–214 Comment 1.] [4] Final payment of an item by the payor bank fixes preferential rights under Section 4–216." § 4–215 Comment 1.

When credits become available for withdrawal as of right

See § 4–215(e) and (f) and Comments 11 and 12. With respect to checks, Reg. CC, 12 CFR §§ 229.10—229.13 or similar applicable state law controls. 12 CFR § 229.20.

5. PRIORITIES IN CUSTOMER'S ACCOUNT—WHEN ITEMS ARE SUBJECT TO (1) NOTICE, (2) STOP–PAYMENT ORDER, (3) LEGAL PROCESS, OR (4) SETOFF

"While a payor bank is processing an item presented for payment, it [1] may receive knowledge or a legal notice affecting the item, such as knowledge or a notice that the drawer has filed a petition in bankruptcy or made an assignment for the benefit of creditors; [2] may receive an order of the drawer stopping payment on the item; [3] may have served on it an attachment of the account of the drawer; or the bank itself [4] may exercise a right of setoff against the drawer's account. Each of these events affects the account of the drawer and may eliminate or freeze all or part of whatever balance is available to pay the item. Subsection (a) [of 4–303] states the rule for determining the relative priorities between these various legal events [usually described as the 'four legals'] and the item." § 4–303 Comment 1.

The rule is, if any one of several things has been done to the item or it has reached any one of several stages in its processing *at the time* the knowledge, notice, stop-payment order, or legal process is received or served *and a reasonable time* for the bank to act thereon *expires* or the setoff is *exercised,* the knowledge, notice, stop-payment order, legal process, or setoff comes too late, the item has priority, and a charge to the customer's account may be made and is effective. Thus, at the time the reasonable time *expires* (or the setoff is *exercised*), if the payor bank has *done* any of the following, or if any one of the following *stages* in the processing of the item has been reached, the item has priority:

(a) Payor Bank *accepts* or *certifies* the item, or *pays* the item in *cash.* § 4–303(a)(1) and (2) and Comments 2, 3 and 6.

(b) Payor Bank *settles* for the item without having a right to revoke the settlement. (Example: "If a payor bank settles for an item presented over the counter for immediate payment by a cashier's check ... which the presenting person agrees to accept, [§ 4–303(a)(3)] would control and the event determining priority has occurred." § 4–303(a)(3) and Comment 3 (second sentence).

(c) Payor Bank becomes *accountable* for the amount of the item under Section 4–302 dealing with late return of items. § 4–303(a)(4) and Comment 5. ("If the payor bank is not the depository bank it is accountable if it retains the item beyond midnight of the banking day of receipt without settling for it." §§ 4–302(a)(1) and Comment 1, 4–104(a)(3) and (11) and Comments 2 and 10 ("banking day" and "settle" defined), 4–108 (time of receipt).

With respect to checks, Section 4–303(a)(5) provides that the determining event for priorities is a given hour ("a cutoff hour") on the day after the check is received. The hour may be fixed by the payor bank no *earlier* than one hour after the opening of the next banking day after the bank received the check and no *later* than the close of that banking day. If a check is received after the payor bank's regular cutoff hour (e.g., 2:00 p.m.), it is treated as received the next banking day. §§ 4–303(a)(5) and Comment 4, 4–104(a)(3) ("banking day" defined), 4–108 (time of receipt). (If no cutoff hour is fixed, see § 4–303(a)(5).) Example: Drawer issues a check to Payee, who deposits it in Depositary Bank, who forwards it to Collecting Bank. On Monday morning, Collecting Bank presents it to drawee–Payor Bank for collection. A provisional settlement is made by midnight on Monday, and by 2:00 p.m. on Tuesday the internal process of posting the check is completed. (Payor Bank has decided to pay the check.) At 2:30 p.m. on Tuesday, Payor Bank is served a writ of garnishment to collect a judgment obtained by Creditor in a suit against Drawer. There are insufficient funds in Drawer's account to cover both the check and the garnishment. Who has priority? (Assume Payor Bank has fixed a cutoff hour of 2:00 p.m.) Answer: Payee, the owner of the check, has priority. Rule: "Any ... legal process served upon ... a payor bank comes too late to terminate ... the bank's ... duty to pay an item ... if the ... legal process is ... served and a reasonable time for the bank to act thereon expires ... after ... a cutoff hour no earlier than one hour after the opening of the next banking day after the banking day on which the bank received the check and no later than the close of that next banking day...."§§ 4–303(a)(5), 4–104(a)(3) ("banking day" defined), 4–108 (time of receipt). Here, the cutoff hour is 2:00 p.m. on Tuesday; the expiration of the reasonable time for the garnishment is sometime after 2:30 p.m. on Tuesday, the time the garnishment was served on Payor Bank. The garnishment "comes too late."

For discussion of customer's (1) right to stop payment and (2) bankruptcy, see Part Three, D, 2, C supra.

6. PRIORITIES IN CUSTOMER'S ACCOUNT—ORDER IN WHICH ITEMS MAY BE CHARGED OR CERTIFIED

Items may be accepted, paid, certified, or charged to a customer's account in any order. § 4–303(b) and Comment 7.

F. FINALITY OF PAYMENT OR ACCEPTANCE (1) BY MISTAKE OR (2) IN GOOD FAITH—RELATIONSHIP BETWEEN PAYOR OR ACCEPTOR AND PRESENTER

1. FINALITY OF PAYMENT

A. TYPICAL FACTUAL SETTING

Drawee Bank pays a check drawn upon it. Subsequently, Drawer determines that (1) its signature was forged, (2) Payee's indorsement was forged, or (3) the amount of the check was altered (e.g., raised from $100 to $1,000). We already know—assuming Drawer breached no duties to Drawee—that Drawer may not charge against Drawer's account a check that bears a forged Drawer's signature or a forged indorsement of Payee. The check is not "properly payable." § 4–401(a) and Comment 1. Likewise, Drawee may charge Drawer's account only according to the original terms ($100) of the altered check ($1,000). § 4–401(d). See Part Three, D, 2, A and B supra. Now, Drawee Bank—who bears the loss at this point—seeks to recover the amount of the check from the person who *presented* the check for payment. Thus the issue: May Drawee Bank (payor) recover from Presenter, or is payment final?

In seeking an answer, Comment 1 to § 3–418 states, "Subsections (a) and (c) are consistent with former Section 3–418 and the rule of Price v. Neal;" also, Comment 3 to § 3–417 says that "subsection (a)(3) retains the rule of Price v. Neal, 3 Burr. 1354 (1762)." Let us briefly survey Price v. Neal and former § 3–418.

B.   PAYMENT BY MISTAKE RULES—PRE-UCC

The rule of Price v. Neal is actually an exception to a general rule, so let us begin at the beginning.

General rule

Payor (Drawee) can recover from Presenter monies paid by mistake. This is a quasi-contract (restitutionary) rule intended to prevent unjust enrichment.

Example 1: Drawee Bank pays a check bearing the forged indorsement of Payee. Bank can recover from Presenter because Drawee mistakenly thought the indorsement was genuine.

Example 2: Drawee Bank pays a check that was raised from $100 to $1,000. Drawee can charge $100 to Drawer's account (see § 4–401(d)(1)) and recover $900 from Presenter because Drawee mistakenly thought the check was not altered.

Exception to general rule: The rule of *Price v. Neal*

A drawee who pays an instrument on which the drawer's signature is forged (as contrasted with a forged *indorsement*) *cannot* recover the payment from the presenter, notwithstanding the general rule allowing recovery of monies paid by mistake. Reason: Drawee Bank is in a superior position to detect a forgery because it has the drawer's signature on file (Drawer signed signature card when Drawer opened checking account with Drawee) and is expected to know and compare it. A less fictional rationalization is that it is highly desirable to end the transaction when the instrument is paid rather than re-open and upset a series of commercial transactions at a later date when the forgery is discovered. Former § 3–418 Comment 1. Note that the drawee is not in a superior position to detect a forged indorsement or an alteration, and thus the drawee is entitled to recover from the presenter under the general rule allowing recovery of monies paid by mistake.

Limitation or qualification to the exception to the general rule

There is a limitation or qualification to the rule that a drawee bank cannot recover payment to the presenter because the drawee was in a superior position to detect or determine certain facts. Such a payor *may* recover from a bad faith presenter or a presenter who was a mere donee. Example: Drawee Bank pays Presenter on a draft bearing Drawer's forged signature. Drawee Bank was in a superior position to detect the forgery, so it cannot recover its payment (Price v. Neal rule). However, if Presenter was the forger or received payment with knowledge of the forgery, then Drawee may recover the monies paid. Courts applying this pre-UCC rule disagreed as to whether such a drawee could recover from a good faith but negligent presenter.

C. PAYMENT BY MISTAKE RULES—FORMER ARTICLES 3 AND 4

Former Articles 3 and 4 closely followed the above common-law principles. But instead of employing rules of restitution allowing Drawee to recover from Presenter the monies paid by mistake, former Articles 3 and 4 stated simply that payment was final unless Presenter breached a presentment warranty. Former §§ 3–418, 3–417(1), 4–207(1). Consider the following examples:

Examples per pre-UCC general rule

Assume Drawee pays over a forged indorsement of Payee or pays over an altered check. Pre-UCC rule: Drawee may recover from Presenter monies paid by mistake, because Drawee is *not* in a superior position to detect the forged indorsement or alteration. Former UCC rule: Drawee may recover from Presenter, even though payment is final as a general rule, per former § 3–418. Reason: Presenter breached its *presentment* warranty that it has good title per former §§ 3–417(1)(a), 4–207(1)(a), and that the instrument has not been materially altered per former §§ 3–417(1)(c), 4–207(1)(c).

Examples per pre-UCC exception to general rule

Assume Drawee pays over Drawer's forged signature. Pre-UCC: Under the rule of Price v. Neal, because Drawee *is* in a superior position to detect the forgery of its own drawer, Drawee may *not* recover from Presenter. Former UCC rule: Because payment is final per former § 3–418, Drawee may *not* recover from Presenter unless a presentment warranty is breached. Reason: Presenter does not warrant that Drawer's signature is not forged—only that Presenter has no knowledge that it is. Former §§ 3–417(1)(b), 4–207(1)(b). We assume for purposes of this example that Presenter has no such knowledge.

Examples per pre-UCC limitation or qualification to the exception to the general rule

Assume Drawee makes payment over Drawer's forged signature to the forger himself or to a person who either takes the item with knowledge of the forgery or obtains this knowledge after taking the item but before presenting it. Pre-UCC rule: Even though Drawee was in a superior position to detect the forgery, Drawee may recover from this *bad faith* presenter. Former UCC rule: Drawee may recover from Presenter because payment is not final to a Presenter who is not either a holder in due course per § 3–302 or a person who in good faith changed his position in reliance on the payment. If, however, Presenter took the item as a holder in due course but obtained knowledge of the forgery prior to presentment, Drawee may recover on the basis that Presenter breached the presentment warranty due to Presenter's *knowledge* of Drawer's forged signature. Former §§ 3–418, 3–417(1)(b), 4–207(1)(b).

To summarize these rules simply, if Drawee *was not* in a superior position to detect certain facts (such as a forged indorsement or alteration), Drawee may recover from Presenter. If the drawee *was* in a superior position to detect certain facts (such as Drawer's forged signature), Drawee may not recover from Presenter, unless Presenter lacked good faith. Pre-UCC cases reached these results through rules of restitution; former UCC did so by focusing on the presence or absence of presentment warranties.

D. PAYMENT BY MISTAKE RULES—REVISED ARTICLES 3 AND 4

Under former § 3–418, the remedy for a drawee that paid an item by mistake was based on the law of mistake and restitution, but was not specifically stated. Revised § 3–418, by contrast, specifically sets forth the right of restitution. Further, revised § 3–418 does not limit the remedies provided by § 3–417 (Presentment Warranties). § 3–418(c) (second sentence) and Comment 1.

Restitution

Section 3–418(a) provides that, if Drawee pays an item on the mistaken belief that (i) payment had not been stopped or (ii) Drawer's signature was authorized, Drawee may recover the amount of the draft from Presenter. Subsection (b) of § 3–418 states that, if an instrument has been paid by mistake and the case is not covered by subsection (a), the person paying (e.g., Drawee) may, to the extent permitted by the law governing mistake and restitution, recover payment from Presenter. The following are two common examples of mistake under subsection (b): (1) Drawer has no account with Drawee, and (2) available funds do not cover the amount of the check. § 3–418(a) and (b) and Comments 1–3, Restatement of Restitution §§ 29, 33.

The remedies provided above, however, may *not* be asserted against a person who took the instrument in good faith and for value (or who in good faith changed position in reliance on the payment). "[T]he drawee in most cases will not have a remedy against the person paid because there is usually a person who took the check in good faith and for value or who in good faith changed position in reliance on the payment." §§ 3–418(c) and Comment 1, 1–201(b)(20) ("good faith" defined), 3–103(a)(6) (same), 3–303 ("value" defined). Even so, all is not lost. Below, we consider how presentment warranties may provide a remedy. § 3–418(c) (second sentence).

Presentment warranties to drawees of unaccepted drafts

If an uncertified check is presented to Drawee Bank, which pays the check, the person obtaining payment (Presenter) makes the following warranties to Drawee Bank:

(1) The warrantor is a "person entitled to enforce" the check. In almost all instances, this means a "holder" of the check. §§ 3–417(a)(1), 3–301 ("person entitled to enforce"), 1–201(b)(21) ("holder" defined); cf. § 4–208(a)(1). This in effect is a warranty that there are no unauthorized or missing indorsements. § 3–417 Comment 2. Remember: A person cannot be a "holder" after a forged indorsement. §§ 3–109 Comment 1 (last sentence), 3–201 (re: negotiation), 3–205(a) (re: indorsement). See §§ 3–417(c), 1–201(b)(41) (unauthorized signature); cf. § 4–208(c).

(2) The check has not been altered. §§ 3–417(a)(2), 3–407(a) ("alteration" defined); cf. § 4–208(a)(2).

(3) The warrantor has *no knowledge* that the drawer's signature is unauthorized. §§ 3–417(a)(3), 1–201(b)(41) ("unauthorized signature" defined), 1–202(b) ("knowledge" defined); cf. § 4–208(a)(3). "[S]ubsection (a)(3) retains the rule of Price v. Neal ... that the drawee takes the risk that the drawer's signature is unauthorized unless the person presenting the draft has knowledge that the drawer's signature is unauthorized.... [T]he warranty of no knowledge that the drawer's signature is unauthorized is also given by prior transferors of the [check]." § 3–417 Comment 3.

(4) The drawer *authorized* issuance of the item in the *amount* for which the item is drawn. §§ 3–417(a)(4), 3–103(c), 4–104(a)(9) ("item" defined), 4–208(a)(4). This warranty applies to a "remotely-created consumer item," that is, an item drawn on a consumer account that is not created by the payor bank and does not bear a *handwritten* signature purporting to be the drawer's. §§ 4–104(c), 3–103(a)(2) and (16) ("consumer account" and "remotely-created consumer item" defined), 4–105(3) ("Payor bank" defined). The provision deals with responsibility for unauthorized telephone-generated checks (e.g., telemarketer check fraud). Sections 3–417(a)(4) and 4–208(a)(4) "implement [ ] a limited rejection of *Price v. Neal* ... so that in certain circumstances ... the payor bank can use a warranty claim to absolve itself of responsibility for honoring an unauthorized item." Premise: "Monitoring by depository banks can control this type of fraud more effectively than any practices readily available to payor banks." §§ 3–416 Comment 8, 4–208 Comment 2.

As to the measure of damages for breach of a present-ment warranty, see §§ 3–417(b), 4–208(b) (e.g., an amount equal to what Drawee paid Presenter).

Presentment warranties in all other cases

In all cases not covered by subsection (a) of § 3–417, discussed above, there is only one warranty: Presenter warrants that he or she is a "person entitled to enforce" the instrument (e.g., there are no forged indorsements). §§ 3–417(d)(1), 3–301 ("person entitled to enforce"); cf. § 4–208(d).

Example 1: Maker issues a note to Payee. The note is eventually taken by Presenter, who receives payment from Maker. Presenter warrants only that there are no forged indorsements. There is no warranty with respect to alteration or knowledge that Maker's signature is unauthorized. Maker *should know* what the terms of the note were and whether its own signature was authorized. (Cf. Price v. Neal.) § 3–417 Comment 4, see § 3–412.

Example 2: Drawer issues a check for $100 to Payee. Payee skillfully raises it to $1,000. Drawee Bank accepts (certifies) it for $1,000. See § 3–409(a), (d). Payee negotiates it to Presenter, who presents it to Drawee Bank, which pays. Drawee Bank cannot recover the payment. Instead, Drawee Bank is obliged to pay the check according to its *terms* at the *time* it was *accepted* (i.e., $1,000). § 3–413(a)(i). If the amount of the check is raised *after* the certification, see §§ 3–413(b), 3–417 Comment 4.

2. FINALITY OF ACCEPTANCE

The finality-of-acceptance rules parallel the finality-of-payment rules with regard to the effect of a mistake. Example: Drawee Bank has accepted (certified) a check drawn upon it but has not yet paid it. See § 3–409(a), (d). Subsequently, it is determined that (1) Drawer's signature was forged, (2) Payee's indorsement was forged, or (3) the amount of the check was altered prior to acceptance (e.g., from $100 to $1,000). May Drawee refuse to pay, or is its acceptance final?

Acceptance by mistake

If a drawee accepts an item on the mistaken belief that (i) payment had not been stopped or (ii) the drawer's signature was authorized, the drawee may revoke its acceptance. In other cases of mistake (e.g., Drawer has no account with Drawee or there are insufficient funds in the account), the drawee may revoke its acceptance. § 3–418(a), (b). However, revocation of acceptance may *not* be asserted against a person who took the item in good faith and for value, as is most often the case, or who in good faith changed position in reliance on the payment. § 3–418(c).

Presentment warranties to drawees of unaccepted drafts

If an uncertified check is presented to Drawee Bank for acceptance (certification—§ 3–409(a) and (d)) and the bank accepts (certifies) the check, the person obtaining certification (Presenter), at the time of presentment, warrants to Drawee Bank that (1) Presenter is a "person entitled to enforce" the check (e.g., there are no forged indorsements), (2) the check has not been altered, and (3) Presenter has no knowledge that Drawer's signature is unauthorized. Breach of a presentment warranty is a *defense* to Drawee Bank's obligation to pay. §§ 3–417(a) and (b), 3–301 ("person entitled to enforce"); cf. § 4–208(a) and (b). Note: This parallels the warranties given to Drawee Bank when Presenter presents an item for *payment* (discussed above).

If an item is altered (e.g., the amount is raised) prior to acceptance, see § 3–413(a) (acceptor is obliged to pay draft according to its *terms* at acceptance); if a check is certified and subsequently altered (raised), see § 3–413(b). Cf. former §§ 3–417(1)(c)(iii) and (iv), 4–207(1)(c)(iii) and (iv). See also §§ 3–417(d)(1) and Comment 4, 4–208(d).

3. WARRANTOR/PRESENTER AS BENEFICIARY OF DRAWEE/PAYOR'S RIGHTS AGAINST DRAWER

Example: Drawer issues a check for $100. Payee skillfully raises it to $1,000 and indorses the check to Adams, a holder in due course. Adams presents it to Drawee for payment. Drawee pays $1,000 in good faith. Drawee returns the check to Drawer, along with others and a statement of account. Drawer delays reconciling its own records with the statement of account. Months later, Drawer discovers the alteration and seeks to have Drawee recredit Drawer's account for the $900 amount by which the check was raised. § 4–401(d)(1). Assume Drawee can prove that Drawer breached its duty to examine the checks promptly to discover and report the alteration and that Drawee suffered a loss thereby. § 4–406 (esp. (d)(1)). Even so, assume Drawee, rather than pursuing Drawer, asserts a claim against Adams for breach of the presentment warranty that the check had not been altered. §§ 3–417(a)(2), 4–208(a)(2). Will Drawee recover from Adams? Answer: No. Adams may defend by proving that Drawer is precluded under § 4–406 (Drawer's duty to discover and report alteration) from asserting the alteration against Drawee. §§ 3–417(c), 4–208(c), 3–103(a)(13). Rationale: "[Section 3–417(c)] gives to the warrantor [Adams] the benefit of rights that the drawee has against the drawer under . . . 4–406. If the drawer's conduct contributed to a loss from . . . alteration, the drawee should not be allowed to shift the loss from the drawer to the warrantor [presenter Adams]." § 3–417 Comment 6.

4. ENCODING AND RETENTION WARRANTIES

See § 4–209(a) and (c) and Comments 1 and 2 for encoding warranty; see § 4–209(b) and (c) and Comments 1 and 3 for retention warranty.

G.   REVIEW OF LIABILITY FOR ALTERED AND FORGED INSTRUMENTS

The law of negotiable instruments is frustrating in that it is difficult to see the forest for the trees. To assist in this task, the following problems review the liabilities discussed above.

1.   ALTERED INSTRUMENT

Problem A. Drawer issues a check to Payee for $100. Payee raises it to $1,000 and indorses it to Adams, a holder in due course. Adams presents the check to Drawee for payment, and Drawee pays.

☐☐ *Drawer vs. Drawee.* Drawer discovers the alteration and wants Drawee to recredit Drawer's account for $900. Will Drawer win? Yes. Drawee may charge Drawer's account only according to the check's *original* terms ($100). § 4–401(d)(1). See discussion at Part Three, D, 2 supra.

☐☐ *Drawee vs. Adams.* May Drawee now recover the $900 from Adams? Yes. Adams breached a presentment warranty because the check was altered. §§ 3–418(c), 3–417(a)(2) and (b) (first sentence), 4–208(a)(2) and (b) (first sentence). See discussion at Part Three, F supra.

☐☐ *Adams vs. Payee.* May Adams now recover the $900 from indorser Payee? Yes. Payee breached a transfer warranty because the check was altered. §§ 3–416(a)(3) and (b), 4–207(a)(3) and (b). See discussion at Part Three, C, 4 supra.

Problem B. Now suppose that—instead of Drawee paying—Drawer stops payment on the check.

☐☐ *Adams vs. Drawer.* Assuming Adams duly presents the item for payment to Drawee, and Drawee dishonors it, will Adams recover from Drawer? Yes, but only $100, the original amount of the check. The additional $900 was not Drawer's obligation. Alteration is a "real defense" good against Adams. § 3–407(c)(i), see § 3–406. See discussion at Part Three, B, 2, B, (4) supra.

☐☐ *Adams vs. Drawee.* May Adams now recover the $900 from Drawee? No. Drawee is not liable on the check until Drawee accepts it. § 3–408, see § 3–401. See discussion at Part Three, C, 5 supra.

☐☐ *Adams vs. Payee.* May Adams now recover the $900 from indorser Payee? Yes, based either on Payee's indorsement or breach of a transfer warranty that the check was not altered. §§ 3–415, 3–416(a)(3) and (b), 4–207(a)(3) and (b) and (c). See discussion at Part Three, C, 3 and 4 supra.

2. FORGED DRAWER'S SIGNATURE

Problem A. Forger forges Drawer's name on a $1,000 check and issues it to Payee, who indorses and delivers it to Adams, who takes it for value in good faith without notice of the forgery. Adams presents it to Drawee, who pays.

☐☐ *Drawer vs. Drawee.* Drawer discovers the forgery and wants Drawee to recredit Drawer's account for $1,000. Will Drawer win? Yes. The check was not "properly payable" because Drawer never authorized it. § 4–401(a) and Comment 1. See discussion at Part Three, D, 2 supra.

☐☐ *Drawee vs. Adams.* May Drawee now recover from Adams? No. Drawee's payment to Adams is final because Adams had no knowledge that Drawer's signature was forged and thus breached no presentment warranty. §§ 3–417(a)(3), 3–418(a) and (c), 4–208(a)(3). See discussion at Part Three, F supra.

☐☐ *Drawee vs. Forger.* May Drawee now recover from Forger? Yes. An unauthorized signature is effective as the signature of the unauthorized signer. § 3–403(a). See discussion at Part Three, C, 1, C supra.

Problem B. Now suppose that—instead of Drawee paying—Drawer stops payment on the check.

☐☐ *Adams vs. Drawer.* Assuming Adams duly presents the item to Drawee for payment and Drawee dishonors it, will Adams recover from Drawer? Answer: No. An unauthorized signature is wholly inoperative as that of the person whose name was signed (here, Drawer). Thus, forgery is a "real defense" against Adams. § 3–403(a) and Comment 2, see § 3–406. See discussion at Part Three, B, 2, B, (4) supra.

☐☐ *Adams vs. Drawee.* May Adams recover from Drawee? No. Drawee is not liable on the check until Drawee accepts it. § 3–408, see § 3–401. See discussion at Part Three, C, 5 supra.

☐☐ *Adams vs. Payee.* May Adams recover from indorser Payee? Yes, based either on Payee's indorsement or breach of a transfer warranty that all signatures are authentic and authorized. §§ 3–415, 3–416(a)(2), 4–207(a)(2). See discussion at Part Three, C, 3 and 4 supra.

☐☐ *Payee vs. Forger.* May Payee recover from Forger? Yes. An unauthorized signature is effective as the signature of the unauthorized signer. §§ 3–403(a), 3–414. See discussion at Part Three, C, 1, C supra.

3.   FORGED INDORSEMENT

Problem. Drawer issues a check "to the order of Payee" for $1,000. Forger steals the check from Payee, forges Payee's name on the check, and sells the check to Adams, who deposits it with Depositary Bank. The check goes through the collection process and is paid by Drawee.

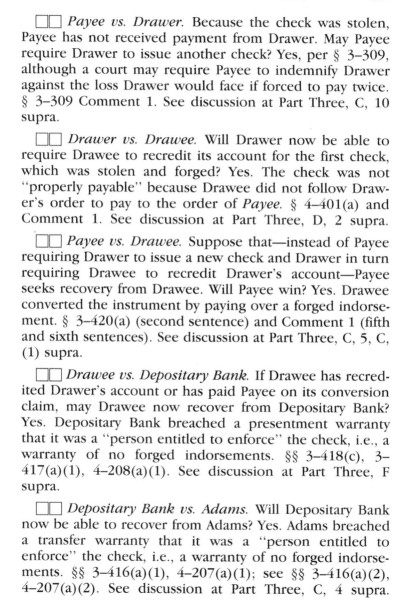

☐☐ *Payee vs. Drawer.* Because the check was stolen, Payee has not received payment from Drawer. May Payee require Drawer to issue another check? Yes, per § 3–309, although a court may require Payee to indemnify Drawer against the loss Drawer would face if forced to pay twice. § 3–309 Comment 1. See discussion at Part Three, C, 10 supra.

☐☐ *Drawer vs. Drawee.* Will Drawer now be able to require Drawee to recredit its account for the first check, which was stolen and forged? Yes. The check was not "properly payable" because Drawee did not follow Drawer's order to pay to the order of *Payee.* § 4–401(a) and Comment 1. See discussion at Part Three, D, 2 supra.

☐☐ *Payee vs. Drawee.* Suppose that—instead of Payee requiring Drawer to issue a new check and Drawer in turn requiring Drawee to recredit Drawer's account—Payee seeks recovery from Drawee. Will Payee win? Yes. Drawee converted the instrument by paying over a forged indorsement. § 3–420(a) (second sentence) and Comment 1 (fifth and sixth sentences). See discussion at Part Three, C, 5, C, (1) supra.

☐☐ *Drawee vs. Depositary Bank.* If Drawee has recredited Drawer's account or has paid Payee on its conversion claim, may Drawee now recover from Depositary Bank? Yes. Depositary Bank breached a presentment warranty that it was a "person entitled to enforce" the check, i.e., a warranty of no forged indorsements. §§ 3–418(c), 3–417(a)(1), 4–208(a)(1). See discussion at Part Three, F supra.

☐☐ *Depositary Bank vs. Adams.* Will Depositary Bank now be able to recover from Adams? Yes. Adams breached a transfer warranty that it was a "person entitled to enforce" the check, i.e., a warranty of no forged indorsements. §§ 3–416(a)(1), 4–207(a)(1); see §§ 3–416(a)(2), 4–207(a)(2). See discussion at Part Three, C, 4 supra.

□□ *Adams vs. Forger.* May Adams now recover from Forger? Yes, based either on breach of a transfer warranty or Forger's indorsement. §§ 3–416(a)(1), 3–418(d), 3–415(a), 3–403(a). See discussion at Part Three, C, 1 and 4 supra.

□□ *Payee vs. Depositary Bank.* Suppose that—instead of Payee requiring Drawer to issue a new check or Payee seeking recovery against Drawee—Payee seeks recovery against Depositary Bank. Will Payee win? Yes, because Payee may recover from Drawee for making payment over a forged indorsement (§ 3–420(a) (second sentence) and Comment 1) and Drawee, in turn, may recover from Depositary Bank for breach of the presentment warranty that there are no forged indorsements (§ 4–208(a)(1) ("person entitled to enforce")), Section 3–420(a) allows Payee to recover directly from Depositary Bank. Comment 1 to § 3–420 states in part, "[A]n instrument is converted if it is … taken for collection … from a person not entitled to enforce the instrument or receive payment…. This covers cases in which a depositary bank … takes an instrument bearing a forged indorsement." Comment 3 explains, "The depositary bank is ultimately liable in the case of the forged indorsement check because of its warranty to the payor bank under Section 4–208(a)(1) and it is usually the most convenient defendant in cases involving multiple checks drawn on different banks. There is no basis for requiring the owner of the check to bring multiple actions against the various payor banks and to require those banks to assert warranty rights against the depositary bank." Note: As to liability of collecting banks other than the depositary bank, see § 3–420(c).

□□ *Drawer vs. Depositary Bank.* Alternatively, suppose Drawer has issued another check to Payee but—instead of Drawer requiring Drawee to recredit Drawer's account because the first check was not "properly payable" in that payment was made over a forged indorsement (§ 4–401(a) and Comment 1), and then Drawee recovering from Depositary Bank for breach of the presentment warranty that it was a "person entitled to enforce" the check, i.e., a warranty that there are no forged indorsements (§ 4–208(a)(1))—Drawer seeks recovery against Depositary Bank. Will Drawer win? No. "An action for conversion of an instrument may not be brought by ... the issuer [e.g., drawer] of the instrument." § 3–420(a) (last sentence). "Under former Article 3, the cases were divided on the issue of whether the drawer of a check with a forged indorsement can assert rights against a depositary bank that took the check. The last sentence of Section 3–420(a) resolves the conflict.... There is no reason why a drawer should have an action in conversion. The check represents an *obligation* of the drawer rather than *property* of the drawer. The drawer has an adequate remedy against the payor bank for recredit of the drawer's account for unauthorized payment of the check [§ 4–401(a).]" § 3–420 Comment 1 (second paragraph) [Emphasis added].

H. INVESTMENT SECURITIES AS NEGOTIABLE INSTRUMENTS

Certificated securities as negotiable instruments

UCC Article 8, Investment Securities, is like a negotiable-instruments law dealing with *securities,* e.g., stocks and bonds. §§ 8–102(a)(15) ("security" defined), former § 8–105(1). Thus, Article 8, which deals with investment paper, may be likened to Article 3, which deals with money paper. That is, negotiable-instruments principles frequently find an analogue in Article 8. For example, (1) certain good-faith purchasers may obtain greater rights to the paper than their transferors had; and (2) the obligee's claim is so merged into the paper evidencing the claim that the paper must be treated in many situations as if it were the claim itself. More information follows below on the doctrine of merger or symbolism.

Greater rights for good-faith purchasers

Assume A issues paper to B, who indorses and delivers it to C, who in turn indorses and delivers it to D. Regardless of whether the paper is Article 3 "money paper" or Article 8 "investment paper," if D is a good-faith purchaser, D takes it free from B's claims and most of A's potential defenses. Under Article 3, a good-faith purchaser is called a holder in due course. The analogous Article 8 term is "protected purchaser."

Example 1: A issues a stock certificate to B. B indorses the certificate on the reverse side. C steals the certificate and sells it to D, a "protected purchaser." Will B recover the certificate from D? No. "A protected purchaser ... acquires its interest in the security free of any adverse claim [including B's claim of ownership]." § 8–303(b); cf. § 3–306 (second sentence).

Example 2: Corporation A issues a stock certificate to B in return for B's promissory note, which was never paid. B sells the stock certificate to C. A state statute provides, "[N]o corporation shall issue any certificates of shares of stock until the corporation has received the par value thereof." Stock issued in violation of this provision is voidable at the election of the corporation. Will A be able to assert this defect against C? No. "A security ... even though issued with a defect going to its validity, is valid in the hands of a purchaser for value and without notice of a particular defect." § 8–202(b)(1); cf. § 3–305(a)(2) and (b) and Comment 2 (instruments issued for which promised performance has not been given.)

Merger or symbolism

A issues a stock certificate to B, who indorses and delivers it to C. To register the transfer, C must present the security to A (§ 8–401). To be a "protected purchaser," C must take delivery of the security (§§ 8–303(a)(3), 8–106(a) and (b) ("control" defined), 8–301(a)(1)) (re: delivery). A creditor of C who wants to attach or levy upon the security must cause it to be seized (§ 8–112(a)). See also, e.g., §§ 8–204 (re: restrictions on transfer), 8–209 (issuer's lien), 8–301 (delivery). These are manifestations of the concept of merger, that is, C's right to the shares is so merged into the paper evidencing the claim (e.g., the stock certificate) that the paper is treated as if it were the claim itself. Further, Article 9, Secured Transactions, allows for *pledges of certificated securities* as collateral, i.e., a possessory security interest. See §§ 9–313(a), 8–301(a)(1).

Note: Revised Article 8, Investment Securities, deals not only with certificated and uncertificated securities, but also with direct and indirect holding systems. For an excellent analysis, see Prefatory Note to Revised Article 8.

I. FUNDS TRANSFERS

Assume Buyer wants to pay Seller for goods. Instead of delivering to Seller a negotiable instrument such as a check or some other writing such as a credit card slip that enables Seller to obtain payment from a bank, Buyer may transmit an instruction to Buyer's bank to credit a sum of money to Seller's bank account. This "instruction" is called a "payment order" and is the subject of Article 4A, Funds Transfers. §§ 4A–102, 4A–108 (excluding consumer transactions). " 'Funds transfer' means a series of transactions, beginning with the *originator's payment order,* made for the purpose of making payment to the *beneficiary* of the order. The term includes any payment order issued by the *originator's bank* or an *intermediary bank* intended to carry out the originator's payment order. A funds transfer is completed by *acceptance* by the *benefi-*

ciary's bank of a payment order for the benefit of the beneficiary of the originator's payment order." § 4A–104(a). Italicized words are defined at §§ 4A–103, 4A–104, 4A–209 (see 4A–301).

Example: "[Buyer] X transmits an instruction to X's bank to credit a sum of money to the bank account of [Seller] Y. In most cases X's bank and Y's bank are different banks. X's bank may carry out X's instruction by instructing Y's bank to credit Y's account in the amount that X requested. The instruction that X issues to its bank is a 'payment order.' X is the 'sender' of the payment order and X's bank is the 'receiving bank' with respect to X's order. Y is the 'beneficiary' of X's order. When X's bank issues an instruction to Y's bank to carry out X's payment order, X's bank 'executes' X's order. The instruction of X's bank to Y's bank is also a payment order. With respect to that order, X's bank is the sender, Y's bank is the receiving bank, and Y is the beneficiary. The entire series of transactions by which X pays Y is [known] as the 'funds transfer.' With respect to the funds transfer, X is the 'originator,' X's bank is the 'originator's bank,' Y is the 'beneficiary' and Y's bank is the 'beneficiary's bank.' In more complex transactions there are one or more additional banks known as 'intermediary banks' between X's bank and Y's bank. In the funds transfer the instruction contained in the payment order of X to its bank is carried out by a series of payment orders by each bank in the transmission chain to the next bank in the chain until Y's bank receives a payment order to make the credit to Y's account. In most cases, the payment order of each bank to the next bank in the chain is transmitted electronically, and often the payment order of X to its bank is also transmitted electronically." From Prefatory Note to Article 4A.

See the following diagram:

Funds Transfer

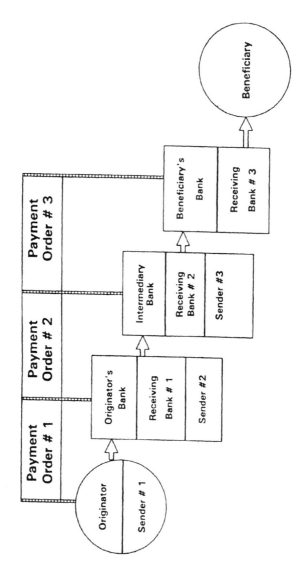

Of course, problems can arise in the consummation of a funds transfer. The following list includes some of them:

1. An unauthorized payment order. See §§ 4A–201 through 4A–204, see § 4A–304.

2. Erroneous payment orders or erroneous execution of payment orders, viz., a beneficiary not intended by the sender, payment in an amount greater than the sender intended, or a duplicate payment order. See §§ 4A–205, 4A–206, 4A–303.

3. Misdescription of the beneficiary, an intermediary bank, or the beneficiary's bank. See §§ 4A–207, 4A–208.

4. Late or improper execution or a failure to execute a payment order. See § 4A–305.

5. Insolvency of a bank obliged to pay. See, e.g., § 4A–403(b) and Comment 4.

See Model Law on International Credit Transfers adopted by the United Nations Commission on International Trade Law [UNCITRAL]. "It covers basically the same type of transaction as does Article 4A, although it requires the funds transferred to have an international component." Prefatory Note to Article 4A (last paragraph).

PART FOUR

SHIPPING AND STORING
GOODS COVERED BY DOCUMENTS OF
TITLE

[Prefatory Note: Article 7 was revised in 2003. The 2003 revision provides a framework for the development of electronic documents of title. See § 1–201(b)(16) (document of title, tangible document of title, electronic document of title). For example, a person takes "possession" of a negotiable tangible document of title; a person takes "control" of a negotiable electronic document of title. See § 7–106. Cf. chattel paper, tangible chattel paper, electronic chattel paper. § 9–102(a)(11), (31), (78); §§ 9–105, 9–313(a). "To the extent possible, the rules for electronic documents of title are the same or as similar as possible to the rules for tangible documents of title." Prefatory Note to Revised Article 7. See § 7–105 (a) and (c). This section allows documents of title issued in one medium to be reissued in another medium, e.g., an issuer of an electronic document may issue a tangible document as a substitute for the electronic document.]

A. INTRODUCTION

Recall from the introduction to this nutshell that a "commercial transaction" dealing with the sale of and payment for goods, may also involve the shipment or storage of goods covered by a bill of lading or warehouse receipt, that is, a document of title. Such documents of title are the subject of Article 7. § 7–101.

Scope

A *document of title* under Article 7 "means a record (i) that in the regular course of business or financing is treated as adequately evidencing that the person in possession or control of the record is entitled to receive, control, hold, and dispose of the record and the goods the record covers and (ii) that purports to be issued by [a bailee, e.g., carrier or warehouse] or addressed to a bailee [i.e., a delivery order] and to cover goods in the bailee's possession which are either identified or are fungible portions of an identified mass. The term includes a bill of lading[,] . . . warehouse receipt, and order for delivery of goods. An *electronic document of title* means a document of title evidenced by a record consisting of information stored in an electronic medium. A *tangible document of title* means a document of title evidenced by a record consisting of information that is inscribed on a tangible medium [i.e., traditional paper documents]." [Emphasis added.] § 1–201(b)(16), (31) ("document of title" and "record" defined), § 7–102(a)(1), (10) ("bailee and "record" defined). See § 7–401 (re: irregularities).

Bill of lading means a document of title evidencing the receipt of goods for shipment, issued by a person engaged in the business (directly or indirectly) of transporting or forwarding goods. § 1–201(b)(6).

Warehouse receipt means a document of title issued by a person engaged in the business of storing goods for hire. § 1–201(b)(42), see § 7–201 ("person that may issue a warehouse receipt"). For the form and terms of a warehouse receipt, see § 7–202.

Delivery order means a record containing an order to deliver goods, directed to a warehouse, carrier, or other person who, in the ordinary course of business, issues warehouse receipts or bills of lading. § 7–102(a)(5).

For a list of laws repealed by Article 7 (e.g. Uniform Bills of Lading Act, Uniform Warehouse Receipts Act, and Uniform Sales Act), see § 10–102(1). For the relation of Article 7 to a treaty or statute (e.g., FBLA, UETA, E–SIGN), see §§ 7–103, 1–108 (re: E–SIGN).

Also note the existence of paramount federal law (see § 7–103(a)), the Federal Bills of Lading Act (49 U.S.C. §§ 80101–80116). Section 80102 describes the Act's scope:

This chapter applies to a bill of lading when the bill is issued by a common carrier for the transportation of goods—

(1) between a place in the District of Columbia and another place in the District of Columbia;

(2) between a place in a territory or possession of the United States and another place in the same territory or possession;

(3) between a place in a State and a place in another State;

(4) between a place in a State and a place in the same State through another State or foreign country; or

(5) from a place in the State to a place in a foreign country.

Overview of the law of documents of title

Simply, a document of title evidences (1) receipt of goods by a bailee–carrier (for bills of lading) or by a bailee–warehouse (for warehouse receipts) and (2) a contract for shipment of identified goods (for bills of lading) or for storage of identified goods (for warehouse receipts). Further, if the document of title is negotiable—as when the goods are to be delivered to *bearer* or to the *order* of a named person (§ 7–104)—certain important attributes of negotiability are manifested: (1) the person in *possession* of the document of title is entitled to receive, hold, and dispose of both the document and the goods it covers (invoking the concept of "merger" or "symbolism" whereby the possessor of the paper controls that which the paper represents, e.g., money, goods); (2) a good-faith purchaser of the document may acquire greater rights to the document and the goods it covers than the purchaser's transferor, thus taking free of the claims and defenses of prior parties.

Thus, it can be seen that Article 7 invokes both the law of bailments and the law of negotiable instruments:

1. *Bailment.* A bailee has lawful possession of goods but not title. See § 7–102(a)(1). The bailee generally has a duty to exercise ordinary care toward the goods. See §§ 7–204, 7–309. The bailee contracts to deliver the goods pursuant to the bailment agreement. See § 7–403. The bailee may be entitled to a possessory lien for storage or transportation charges. See §§ 7–209, 7–307.

2. *Document of title as negotiable instrument.* A negotiable warehouse receipt or bill of lading is analogous to an Article 3 promissory note. Article 3 paper involves an engagement to pay money "to order" or "to bearer." §§ 3–412, 3–104(a). Similarly, Article 7 negotiable paper involves an engagement to deliver identified goods "to order" or "to bearer." §§ 7–104, 7–403. But note one important distinction: Article 7 paper purports to cover *identified* goods; Article 3 paper does *not* cover or represent any particular money. Cf. §§ 1–201(b)(16), 3–106(b)(ii) and Comment 1 (last paragraph).

Further, a delivery order under Article 7 is analogous to an Article 3 draft, which is a drawer's order to a drawee to pay money to a payee. A delivery order is a bailor's order to a bailee to deliver goods to a deliveree (e.g., consignee). Cf. §§ 3–104(a) and (e), 7–102(a)(3) and (5).

For a form bill of lading, warehouse receipt, and delivery order, see 15 West's Legal Forms § 18.3.

B. BAILEE'S DELIVERY OBLIGATION: THE DOCUMENT AS A SYMBOL OR REPRESENTATIVE OF GOODS

A bailee–warehouse or carrier must deliver the bailed goods to a "person entitled under the document" if the person:

(1) has satisfied the bailee's lien (if the bailee so requests or if the bailee is prohibited by law from delivering the goods until the charges are paid), and

(2) (if the outstanding document is negotiable)—has surrendered possession or control of the document for cancellation or indication of partial deliveries (with a certain exception to be discussed later). §§ 7–403(a), (b) and (c), 7–104, 7–102(a)(9).

A "person entitled under the document" is defined as follows:

1. In the case of a *negotiable* document of title, "person" means the *holder*. §§ 7–102(a)(9), 7–104.

a. "Holder" means the person in *possession* of a negotiable *tangible* document of title if the goods are deliverable either (i) to bearer or (ii) to the order of the person in possession. § 1–201(b)(21)(B). "Bearer" means a person in *possession* of a negotiable tangible document of title payable to bearer or indorsed in blank, § 1–201(b)(5). See § 7–501(a)(1) (re: negotiation). Cf. §§ 3–602(a) (discharge by payment of an Article 3 negotiable instrument), 3–301(i) (holder of Article 3 negotiable instrument), 1–201(b)(21)(A).

[or]

b. "Holder" means the person in *control* of a negotiable *electronic* document of title. §§ 1–201(b)(21)(C), 7–106 and Comment 2 (Control of an electronic document substitutes for the indorsement and possession of a tangible document of title). For the general test for control and a safe harbor test, see § 7–106(a) and (b) and Comments. [*2010 Amendment.* The amended definition of "control" of electronic chattel paper conforms the Article 9 definition to the Uniform Electronic Transactions Act and the 1999 revisions to Article 7. The amendment provides a safe harbor test, but permits other forms of control as well. §§ 7–106, 9–105, UETA § 16.]

2. For a nonnegotiable document of title, "person" means the person to whom delivery of the goods is to be made by the terms of the document. §§ 7–104, 7–102(a)(9).

3. For a delivery order, "person" means the person to whom delivery of the goods is to be made pursuant to instructions in the order. §§ 7–104, 7–102(a)(5) ("delivery order" defined).

(For situations in which delivery to a "person entitled under the document" is excused, see Part Four, E infra.)

Example 1 (receipt or bill): A delivers goods to Bailee (a warehouse or carrier), who issues a tangible document of title (a warehouse receipt or bill of lading) wherein Bailee contracts to deliver the goods "to A," "to B," "to the order of A," or "to the order of B." Who is the "person entitled under the document" to whom Bailee must deliver the goods? Answer: If Bailee contracts to deliver "to A" or "to B," Bailee fulfills this obligation by delivering the goods to A or to B, respectively. The nonnegotiable document need not be surrendered to Bailee. However, if the contract is to deliver "to the order of A" or "to the order of B," Bailee fulfills this obligation when A or B, respectively, *surrenders* the negotiable document to Bailee and Bailee delivers the goods.

Example 2 (receipt or bill): Now suppose that, under a tangible document of title, Bailee contracts to deliver goods "to bearer," or "to the order of A," and A indorses in blank (by merely signing A's name). If A delivers the document to B, B becomes the "person entitled under the document" to whom Bailee must deliver the goods upon surrender of the document. However, if under the document Bailee contracts to deliver "to the order of A" and A delivers the document to B but does *not* indorse it, B is *not* "the person entitled under the document" to whom Bailee must deliver the goods. B is in possession of the document, but B is not a *holder*, and Bailee's contract thus does not run to B.

Example 3 (delivery order): S delivers 100 cases of goods to W warehouse. W issues a tangible nonnegotiable warehouse receipt and contracts to deliver the bailed goods "to S." S is the "person entitled under the document," to whom W is to make delivery. There is no need for the nonnegotiable document to be surrendered. §§ 7–102(a)(9), § 7–403(a) and (c); see 7–502(a)(4). S now contracts to sell 25 cases of the goods to B and issues to B a "delivery order," i.e., a written order directed to W to deliver goods as follows: "Please deliver to the order of B 25 cases of [*describe goods*], cases no. 1–25. W/R #4321. Yours truly, (signed) S." § 7–102(a)(1), (5), (8). (The delivery order is analogous to a draft under UCC Article 3.) B is now the "person entitled under the document" to whom W must deliver the goods. §§ 7–102(a)(9), 7–502(a)(4).

Of course, W has no obligation to hold the goods for B or deliver them to B until W accepts the delivery order. After W accepts, the delivery order is for practical purposes indistinguishable from a warehouse receipt issued by W. §§ 7–502(a)(4), 7–102 Comment 3. Indeed, W will not know that S (the person entitled under the warehouse receipt) has ordered delivery "to order of B" until W receives notification of B's rights. Analogy: Under Article 3, Drawee is not liable on a draft until it accepts or certifies it, at which time it is similar to a promissory note issued by Drawee. §§ 3–408, 3–409(a) and (d), 3–413(a). Sample language for an accepted delivery order: "This is to certify that the goods covered by this delivery order are actually at Warehouse, [*address*] and are to the order of B."

As a result of Bailee's obligation under a tangible negotiable document to deliver to a holder who surrenders the document to Bailee, a negotiable document is said to be symbolic or representative of the goods themselves. That is, the claim is so merged into the paper evidencing the claim that the paper is treated as if it were the claim itself. Thus, the document's holder controls the right to possession of the goods the document represents. This obligation to deliver to the holder is stated on a bill of lading, thus: "The surrender of the original order bill of lading, properly indorsed, shall be required before the delivery of property covered by the bill." (An "order bill" means a negotiable bill; a "straight bill" means a nonnegotiable bill.) Also, recall that a tangible document of title is defined as a document that adequately evidences that the person in possession of it is entitled to receive, hold, and dispose of the document and the goods it covers. § 1–201(b)(16).

Note § 7–302 on "through" bills of lading, the purpose of which is to subject the initial carrier to suit for breach of the contract of carriage (e.g., delivery obligation) by any performing carrier (connecting carrier). § 7–302 Comment 1.

When a document of title—especially a negotiable one—is utilized in a commercial transaction, there are several consequences under Articles 2, 7 and 9:

1. *Passing title—Article 2.* Unless otherwise explicitly agreed, (1) title passes to the buyer at the time and place at which the seller completes physical delivery [§ 2–103(1)(e)] of the goods even if a document of title is to be delivered at a different time or place; (2) when delivery is to be made without moving the goods (e.g., goods stored in a warehouse) and the seller is to deliver a tangible document of title, title passes when and where the seller delivers the document. § 2–401(2), (3)(a). For the limited effect of title-passing rules generally, see Part One, C, 1 supra.

2. *Risk of loss—Article 2.* In a shipment contract, risk of loss passes to the buyer when goods are delivered to the carrier, even if the shipment is made under reservation. §§ 2–509(1)(a), 2–505. When the goods are held by a bailee to be delivered without being moved (e.g., goods stored in a warehouse), risk of loss passes to the buyer (1) on receipt of a negotiable tangible document of title covering the goods; or (2) *after* the buyer's receipt of a nonnegotiable document of title (or other direction in a record to deliver, see § 7–102(a)(5)) as provided in § 2–503(4)(b), to wit: risk of loss remains on the seller until the buyer has had a reasonable time to present the document (or direction). Simply: Risk of loss remains on the seller during a period that is reasonable to secure acknowledgment of the transfer from the bailee. §§ 2–509(2)(a) and (c), 2–503(4)(b) and Comment 6. Compare § 3–414(f), wherein risk of a drawee's insolvency shifts from the drawer to payee if "a check is not presented for payment . . . within 30 days after its date. . . ." For a general discussion of risk of loss, see Part One, C, 5 supra.

3. *Seller's delivery obligation—Article 2.* Tender of delivery requires that Seller (1) put and hold conforming goods at Buyer's disposition and (2) give Buyer any notification reasonably necessary to enable Buyer to take deliv-

ery. §§ 2–503(1), 2–301, 2–507(1). In a *shipment* contract, Seller must obtain and promptly deliver or tender in due form any document necessary to enable Buyer to obtain possession of the goods. §§ 2–503(2), 2–504(b). In a *destination* contract, tender requires that Seller tender any appropriate documents. § 2–503(3)–(5) and Comment 5.

When goods are in the possession of a bailee and are to be delivered without being moved (e.g., goods stored in a warehouse), tender requires that the seller tender a negotiable document of title covering such goods. § 2–503(4)(a). If the document is nonnegotiable, tender of it or of a record directing the bailee to deliver (delivery order) is sufficient unless the buyer seasonably objects. But the risk of the bailee's failure to honor the nonnegotiable document (or obey the direction) remains on the seller until the buyer has had a reasonable time to present the document (or direction). Refusal by the bailee to honor the document or to obey the direction defeats the tender. § 2–503(4)(b). For the seller's delivery obligation generally, see Part One, E, 2 supra. Compare Buyer's payment by check, which is defeated by its dishonor. § 2–511(3). As to mercantile terms, see § 2–319 et seq. and INCOTERMS.

4. *Buyer's obligation to accept and pay—Article 2.* Unless otherwise agreed, if Seller is authorized to send the goods, Seller may ship them under reservation and tender the documents of title, but Buyer may inspect the goods before payment will be due (unless inspection is inconsistent with the terms of the contract). §§ 2–310(b), 2–505 (shipment under reservation), 2–513 (inspection), see § 2–310(a) (payment normally due at receipt). If delivery is authorized and made by way of documents of title otherwise than by the previous sentence, then payment is due when and where the buyer is to receive delivery of

the tangible documents. §§ 2–310(c), 2–511(1) and Comment 1 (tender as a precondition to payment); see §§ 2–319(4) (shipment "F.O.B." or "F.A.S."), 2–320(4) (shipment "C.I.F." or "C. & F."), 2–321(1) and (3) (specific terms for "C.I.F." or "C. & F." shipment). See § 2–319 Comment (2003).

For Buyer's obligation to accept and pay for goods generally, see Part One, E, 3 and 4 supra.

5. *Buyer's right to inspection of goods—Article 2.* Recall that Buyer generally has a right to inspect goods before payment. § 2–513(1) and Part One, E, 5 supra. But Buyer may not have this right if the contract provides for payment against documents of title. § 2–513(3)(b). As to Buyer's right to inspect before payment in a cash transaction or shipment-under-reservation transaction, see §§ 2–310(a)–(c) and Comments 1 and 4, 2–505 (shipment under reservation), 2–320 Comments 1 and 12.

6. *Buyer's right of rejection on improper delivery—Article 2.* Generally, if the goods or the *tender of delivery* fail in any respect to conform to the contract, Buyer may reject the whole or accept any commercial unit and reject the rest. § 2–601. *Tender of delivery* may be accomplished by tendering goods or, in some instances, by tendering documents. § 2–503. See Part One, E, 6 supra.

7. *Stoppage of delivery in transit—Article 2.* For Seller's stoppage of delivery in transit, see Part One, F, 2, A, (2), (b) supra. If a negotiable document is involved, Seller may stop delivery until negotiation to the buyer of any negotiable document covering the goods. § 2–705(2)(d), see §§ 2–705(3)(c) and (d), 7–501(a) (re: negotiation), 7–504(d). See § 2A–526.

8. *Seller's remedies in a cash-sale transaction—Article 2.* When payment is due and demanded upon delivery to the buyer of goods or documents of title, Buyer's right as

against Seller to retain or dispose of them is conditioned upon Buyer's making the payment due. §§ 2–507(2), 2–511(3). For discussion of "cash sale" transactions generally, see Part One, F, 2, C supra.

9. *Buyer's right of replevin—Article 2.* Buyer has a right of replevin for goods identified to the contract that have been shipped under reservation, if satisfaction of the security interest in them has been made or tendered. §§ 2–716(3), 2–505 (shipment under reservation). If a negotiable document is outstanding, Buyer's right of replevin relates to the document, not directly to the goods. § 2–716 Comment 5. For discussion of Buyer's right of replevin generally, see Part One, F, 3, A, (5), (b) supra.

10. *Diversion—Article 7.* Carrier *may* deliver goods to a person or destination other than is stated in the bill, on instructions from the holder of a negotiable bill. § 7–303(a)(1) and Comment 1. If the bill is nonnegotiable, Carrier *may* divert the goods upon instructions from (1) the consignor, even if the consignee has given contrary instructions; (2) the consignee in the absence of contrary instructions from the consignor (if the goods have arrived at the billed destination or if the consignee is in possession of the tangible bill or in control of the electronic bill); or (3) the consignee, if entitled as against the consignor to dispose of the goods (see Part Four, E infra re: delivery to person with paramount title). § 7–303(a)(2)–(4).

11. *Lost or missing documents—Article 7.* If a document has been lost, stolen, or destroyed, a court may order delivery of the goods or issuance of a substitute document, and the bailee, without liability to any person, may comply with the order. If the document was negotiable, a court may not order delivery of the goods (or issuance of a substitute document) without the claimant's

posting security unless it finds that any person who may suffer loss as a result of nonsurrender of possession or control of the document is adequately protected against the loss. § 7–601, cf. §§ 3–309, 8–405, 8–406 (similar rules for negotiable instruments and security certificates).

12. *Attachment of goods covered by documents—Article 7.* Generally, a lien does not attach by virtue of any judicial process to goods in the possession of a bailee for which a negotiable document of title is outstanding unless possession or control of the document is first surrendered to the bailee or the document's negotiation enjoined. The bailee may not be compelled to deliver the goods pursuant to process until possession or control of the document is surrendered to the bailee or court. § 7–602, cf. § 8–112 (similar rule for security certificate). Example: S delivers goods to W warehouse and receives a negotiable warehouse receipt "to order of S." S contracts to sell the goods to B and negotiates (indorses and delivers) the receipt to B. C, a creditor of S, causes a writ of garnishment to be served on W. Held: No lien attaches by virtue of the garnishment. If the receipt were nonnegotiable ("to S" not "to order of S"), a lien would have attached by virtue of the garnishment, unless W previously received notification of B's rights. Such notification "fixes" B's rights as against W and all third persons (e.g., C). § 2–503(4)(b), see § 7–504(b)(1).

Note: One who purchases a negotiable document for value without notice of the process or injunction takes free of the lien imposed by judicial process. § 7–602.

13. *Secured transactions—Article 9.* A delivers goods to bailee W warehouse, who issues a tangible negotiable warehouse receipt "to order of A." A indorses and delivers the receipt to B by way of pledge to secure repayment of a loan from B to A. §§ 9–102(a)(30) ("document" defined),

9–312(c) (perfection of interest in goods covered by nego-tiable document), 9–313(a) (perfection by possession of document). If W issues a nonnegotiable document "to A" (not "to order of A"), B perfects its security interest by possession when W receives notification of B's rights. § 9–312(d). See Part Five, C, 4, C infra.

14. *Secure payment of purchase price: exchange of goods or document for price.* Seller may be unwilling to deliver goods to Buyer without receiving payment. Like-wise, Buyer may be unwilling to pay for goods before receiving them. Thus, they can agree to exchange the goods for the purchase price simultaneously. See §§ 2–310(a) (time for payment), 2–507(1) (effect of seller's tender), 2–511(1) (tender of payment). If Seller and Buyer are at a great distance, an intermediary (e.g., letter carrier, truck driver) may deliver the goods in exchange for the price and remit the monies to Seller, i.e., a C.O.D. transac-tion. Alternatively, the sales agreement may provide for "sight draft against order bill of lading," "payment against documents," or "shipment under reservation." See § 2–505(1)(a) re: reservation of a security interest in the goods. This documentary sale is outlined thus:

(1) Seller delivers the goods to Carrier, who issues to Seller a seller's (shipper's) order bill:

Consigned to ORDER OF *Seller*

Notify *Buyer*

(2) Seller draws a sight draft (§§ 3–104(a) and (e) (defining "negotiable instrument" and "draft"), 3–108(a) (payable on sight)) on Buyer:

At Sight

Pay to the order of *Seller*

Five Thousand and no/100 . . . . Dollars

To: Buyer

(signed) Seller

Seller indorses the draft either in blank or "Pay Seller City Bank, for collection"; Seller indorses the bill of lading in blank. See §§ 3–205 (various kinds of indorsements), 1–201(b)(21)(A) ("holder" defined), 7–501(a). The draft and bill are then delivered to Seller City Bank for collection.

(3) Seller City Bank forwards the draft and bill to Buyer City Bank. See § 4–501 et seq. re: collection of documentary drafts.

(4) Buyer City Bank notifies Buyer that the draft and bill have arrived. Buyer pays the draft, and the draft and bill are delivered to Buyer. See § 3–501(b)(2).

(5) Buyer is now the *holder* of the bill of lading, since Buyer is in possession of a document issued to order and indorsed in blank. § 1–201(b)(21)(B). Buyer is the "person entitled under the document" to whom Carrier must deliver the goods. § 7–102(a)(9). Thus, Buyer surrenders the bill to Carrier and receives the goods. § 7–403(c). See §§ 2–310(b) and (c) (re: time for payment), 2–513(3)(b) (re: inspection).

(6) Buyer City Bank transmits the proceeds (e.g., by transfer(s) of bank credits) to Seller City Bank.

(7) Seller City Bank remits the proceeds to Seller (e.g., by crediting Seller's account).

The above may be diagrammed thus: Copyright © 1997, by Matthew Bender & Co., Inc., and reprinted with permission from King, Kuenzel, Stone, Commercial Transactions Under the Uniform Commercial Code: Cases and Materials, 5th Edition.

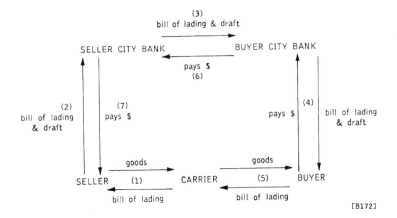

[B172]

Use of "order bills" may be impeded by the fact that the goods may arrive at their destination before the documents. Thus, the Code provides that bills may be issued at the goods' destination. See § 7–305 and Comment re: destination bills.

A nonnegotiable document can reserve possession of goods as security thus: Suppose Carrier issued a nonnegotiable bill "to Seller" (not "to the order of Seller"). Seller is the "person entitled under the document" to whom Carrier must deliver the goods. Although the nonnegotiable bill need not be surrendered, Carrier will not deliver to anyone (e.g., Buyer) until it receives instructions (a delivery order) from Seller. Seller will not do so until Buyer has made satisfactory arrangements to pay for the goods. § 2–505(1)(b) (shipment under reservation); see § 7–403(a), (c) (obligation to deliver); § 7–102(a)(9) ("person entitled under the document").

As to the other UCC sections that allow Seller to control possession of goods or to recover possession of goods, see §§ 2–507(2), 2–702, 2–703, 2–705, 9–609.

C. OBLIGATION OF BAILEE–WAREHOUSE TO KEEP THE GOODS COVERED BY EACH WAREHOUSE RECEIPT SEPARATE

General rule

Unless the warehouse receipt otherwise provides, a warehouse shall keep separate the goods covered by each receipt, to permit identification and delivery. § 7–207(a).

Exception for fungible goods

Different lots of fungible goods *may* be commingled. §§ 7–207(a), 1–201(b)(18) (defining "fungible goods"). Commingled fungible goods are owned in common by the persons entitled thereto (and the warehouse is severally liable to each owner for that owner's share). § 7–207(b).

As to holders of overissued receipts being permitted to share in the mass of fungible goods, see § 7–207(b) and Comment.

D. NEGOTIATION AND TRANSFER OF DOCUMENTS OF TITLE

1. INTRODUCTION

Assume Bailee A (a warehouse or carrier) issues to B a warehouse receipt or bill of lading agreeing to deliver the bailed goods "to B," "to the order of B," or "to bearer." C steals the document (or defrauds B out of possession) and transfers or negotiates it to D. Does D acquire title to the document and goods free of B's claim?

In answering the above query, observe the parallel between a promissory note (UCC Article 3) and document of title (UCC Article 7). In the above example, if A had issued a promissory note to B, and C had negotiated the note to D, a holder in due course, then D would take the note *free of* claims to the instrument (including B's claim). § 3–306 (second sentence). If, however, D did not have the rights of a holder in due course, then D would take the note *subject to* all valid claims on the part of any person (including B's claim). § 3–306 (first sentence). See Part Three, B, 1 and 3 supra.

Similarly, under Article 7, if D takes a negotiable document by "due negotiation," D will take free of B's claim. (B's claim is valid against C; a thief or defrauder has no right to the document or goods as against B.) On the other hand, if D takes by transfer rather than "due negotiation," D will be subject to B's claim. § 7–501 et seq.

Simply: a negotiable document "duly negotiated" gives certain good-faith purchasers greater rights to the document and goods it represents than the person negotiating it had.

2. NEGOTIATION OF WAREHOUSE RECEIPTS AND BILLS OF LADING BY "DUE NEGOTIATION"

A. REQUIREMENTS OF "DUE NEGOTIATION"

For a tangible document of title to be "duly negotiated",

1. The document must be negotiable. A document is negotiable if, by its terms, the goods are to be delivered to *bearer* or the *order* of a named person. §§ 7–104(a), 7–501(a)(5); see §§ 7–104(b) and (c) (nonnegotiable), 7–501(c) (indorsement of nonnegotiable document) and (d) (naming of person to be notified). As to overseas trade, see § 7–104 Comment 1 (first paragraph). Cf. § 3–104 (negotiable instruments).

2. The document must be negotiated to a *holder*. (defined at 1–201(b)(21)(B)).

☐ ☐ *Example 1*: A issues and delivers to B a document mandating delivery "to the order of B." B negotiates the document to C by B's indorsement and delivery. After B's indorsement in blank or to bearer, any person may negotiate it by delivery alone. § 7–501(a)(1) and (5).

☐ ☐ *Example 2*: A issues and delivers to B a document mandating delivery "to bearer." The document has thus been negotiated to B. If the document is written "to the order of B," the effect is the same. § 7–501(a)(2) and (3).

☐ ☐ *Example 3*: A issues and delivers to B a document mandating delivery "to the order of B." B indorses, "To C, (signed) B." C's negotiation of such document requires C's indorsement and delivery. § 7–501(a)(4) and (5).

☐ ☐ *Simply*: To be negotiated, order paper must be indorsed and delivered; bearer paper may be negotiated by delivery alone. See comparable requirements of UCC Article 3. §§ 3–201, 3–204, 3–205 and Part Three, B, 2, B, (2), (a) supra. As to the right to compel indorsement, see § 7–506; cf. §§ 3–203(c) (re: negotiable instruments), 8–307 (re: securities).

3. The holder must purchase the document in *good faith*, without *notice* of any defense against or claim to it on the part of any person. §§ 1–201(b)(20) ("good faith" defined), 1–202 ("notice" defined); § 7–501(a)(5), (d).

4. The holder must purchase the document for *value*. § 7–501(a)(5). A person gives value, for example, if he acquires the document in return for a binding commitment to extend credit, or as *security* for a pre-existing claim. § 1–204, cf. § 3–303 (re: negotiable instruments).

5. The document must be negotiated in the regular course of business or financing and not in settlement or payment of a money obligation. A document is presumed to be "duly negotiated" unless otherwise established.

§§ 7–501(a)(5), 1–201(b)(8) ("burden of establishing" defined). Policy:

> The foundation of the mercantile doctrine of good faith purchase for value has always been . . . the furtherance and protection of the regular course of trade. The reason for allowing a person, in bad faith or in error, to convey away rights which are not its own has from the beginning been to make possible the speedy handling of that great run of commercial transactions which are patently usual and normal.

* * *

> A pre-existing claim constitutes value, and "due negotiation" does not require "new value." . . . But the matter has moved out of the regular course of financing if the debtor is thought to be insolvent, the credit previously extended is in effect cancelled, and the creditor snatches a plank in the shipwreck under the guise of a demand for additional collateral. Where a money debt is "paid" in commodity paper [document of title], any question of "regular" course disappears, as the case is explicitly excepted from "due negotiation." § 7–501 Comment 1.

The holder of a "duly negotiated" document is Article 7's holder in due course. Cf. §§ 7–501(a)(5), 3–302.

For an electronic document of title, see similar rules in § 7–501(b)(3). Note, however, that the "control" concept as applied to negotiable electronic documents of title substitutes for *both possession* and *indorsement*. § 7–501(b)(1) and Comment 1.

B. RIGHTS ACQUIRED BY "DUE NEGOTIATION"

Subject to certain qualifications to be discussed presently, a holder to whom a negotiable document of title has been "duly negotiated" acquires thereby

(a) Title to the document;

(b) Title to the goods;

(c) All rights accruing under the law of agency or estoppel; and

(d) The direct obligation of the issuer (warehouse, carrier) to hold or deliver the goods according to the terms of the document free of any defense or claim by the issuer (except those arising under the terms of the document or under Article 7, e.g., the defense of non-negligent destruction of the goods). § 7–502(a) and Comment 3. "[T]itle and rights acquired by due negotiation ... are not impaired even if ... (2) any person has been deprived of possession of a negotiable tangible document or control of negotiable electronic document by misrepresentation, fraud, accident, mistake, duress, loss, theft or conversion. ..." § 7–502(b).

Example 1: B delivered goods to bailee A (warehouse or carrier), who issued and delivered to B a tangible document (warehouse receipt or bill of lading) under which A agreed to deliver the goods "to bearer" or "to the order of B," after which B indorsed (if order paper) in blank. C steals the instrument (or defrauds B out of possession) and delivers the document to D, who takes by "due negotiation." D acquires title to the document and the goods free from B's valid claim against C.

Example 2: Suppose in Example 1 the document stated, "Deliver to the order of B," and C indorsed B's name and delivered it to D. Here, D does not take by negotiation, much less "due negotiation." Order paper requires the indorsement of B (not C as forger), to be negotiated. § 7–501(a)(1), (5). D thus takes subject to B's claim. See § 7–504(a) to be discussed presently.

Note the parallel with Article 3. See Part Three, B, 3 supra and § 3–306.

C. CERTAIN CASES WHEN HOLDER'S RIGHTS ARE DEFEATED DESPITE "DUE NEGOTIATION"

(1) Unauthorized Bailment

If a person has bailed goods with a warehouse or carrier without the authority of the goods' "true owner," the bailment is unauthorized. "A document of title [even though "duly negotiated,"] confers no right in goods against a person who, *before* issuance of the document, had a legal interest or a perfected security interest [per UCC Article 9] in the goods and did not

1.   deliver or entrust the goods or any document of title covering the goods to the bailor or bailor's nominee with:

   a.   actual or apparent authority to ship, store, or sell;

   b.   power to obtain delivery under § 7–403; or

   c.   power of disposition under §§ 2–403, 2A–304(2), 2A–305(2), 9–320, or 9–321(c) or other statute or rule of law; or

2.   acquiesce in the procurement by the bailor (or bailor's nominee) of any document." § 7–503(a).

Simply: A person who owned goods before issuance of a document will defeat even a person to whom a document representing the goods has been "duly negotiated" unless the owner is estopped from asserting his or her ownership. Or, as Comment 1 to § 7–503 states,

In general it may be said that the title of a purchaser by due negotiation prevails over almost any interest in the goods which existed prior to the procurement of the document of title if the possession of the goods by the person obtaining the document derived from any action by the prior claimant which introduced the goods into the stream of commerce or carried them along that stream. A thief of the goods cannot indeed by shipping or storing them to the thief's own order acquire power to transfer them to a good faith purchaser.

Example 1: B steals goods from A and sells them to C, a good-faith purchaser for value. A will recover the goods from C because B, a thief, cannot pass on to C greater rights than B has. See Part One, G, 1 supra.

But suppose that B—instead of selling the goods directly to C—delivers the goods to X bailee (a warehouse or carrier) who issues a negotiable tangible document (a warehouse receipt or bill of lading) "to order of B." B indorses to C, who takes by "due negotiation." A will recover the goods even from a holder by due negotiation such as C. § 7–503(a). As to A's rights if faced with a warehouse's or carrier's lien, see §§ 7–209(c), 7–307(b).

Example 2: A delivers goods to B, a merchant who deals in goods of that kind. B sells the goods to C, a buyer in ordinary course of business. A cannot recover the goods from C. By entrusting the goods to a merchant who deals in goods of that kind, A gives B the power to transfer A's rights to C, a buyer in ordinary course of business. § 2–403(2), (3).

But suppose that B—instead of selling the goods directly to C—delivers the goods to X bailee (a warehouse or carrier), who issues a negotiable tangible document (a warehouse receipt or bill of lading) "to order of B." B indorses to C, who takes by "due negotiation." A cannot recover the goods from C. A gave B the power of disposition under § 2–403. §§ 7–501(a)(5), 7–502(a), 7–503(a).

(2) Two or More Documents Issued by Different Issuers Representing the Same Goods

Unaccepted delivery order

First Rule: "Title to goods based upon an unaccepted delivery order is subject to the rights of any person to which a negotiable warehouse receipt or bill of lading covering the goods has been duly negotiated." § 7–503(b). Example: W issues a negotiable warehouse receipt "to order of S." S sells the goods covered by the receipt to B–1 per a delivery order ordering W to deliver "to order of B–1." S then "duly negotiates" the warehouse receipt to B–2. B–1 is subject to B–2's rights. (Compare the payee of an uncertified check, who loses to others who get to the drawee first.)

Second Rule: Title to goods based upon an unaccepted delivery order "may be defeated under § 7–504[(b)(2)] to the same extent as the rights of the issuer or a transferee from the issuer." § 7–503(b) (second sentence). For an example, see § 7–503 Comment 2.

The above rules reflect the "seller in possession" concept that buyers who acquiesce in a merchant seller's retention of possession give the seller power to transfer the buyers' rights to certain third parties. § 2–403(2), (3). See Part One, G, 3 and 4 supra; Part Four, D, 3, C, (1) supra.

Freight forwarder's bill

Title to goods based upon a bill of lading issued to a freight forwarder is subject to the rights of any person to whom a freight forwarder's bill is duly negotiated. § 7–503(c), see § 1–201(b)(6) ("bill of lading" defined). Example: S delivers goods to F freight forwarder. (Freight forwarders take goods from different sellers and consolidate them into carloads for lower transport costs.) F issues a negotiable bill to S, which S duly negotiates to A. F in turn delivers a carload of goods (including S's goods) to C railroad. C issues to F a negotiable bill, which F duly negotiates to B. B's title to the goods is subject to A's rights.

(3) Two or More Documents Issued by the Same Issuer Representing the Same Goods

Overissue

Bailor delivers goods to Bailee (a warehouse or carrier), who issues a negotiable document (a warehouse receipt or bill of lading), which Bailor duly negotiates to A. Later, Bailee issues another negotiable document, which Bailor duly negotiates to B. A acquires title to the goods; B acquires only a cause of action against Bailee, who made the deception possible. Section 7–402 states the rule:

> A duplicate or any other document of title purporting to cover goods already represented by an outstanding document of the same issuer does not confer any right in the goods.... The issuer is liable for damages caused by its overissue or failure to identify a duplicate document by a conspicuous notation.

For exceptions to the above rule, see § 7–304 (tangible bills of lading in a set); § 7–205 (overissue of documents for fungible goods); § 7–601 (substitutes for lost, stolen, or destroyed documents); or substitute documents issued per § 7–105.

(4) Fungible Goods

Example: A delivers grain for storage to W warehouse, which both stores and sells grain. W issues a negotiable warehouse receipt, which A duly negotiates to B. W sells and delivers certain of the grain to C, who buys in ordinary course of business. W is now insolvent. Who gets the grain: B, the holder of the "duly negotiated" document or C, the buyer in ordinary course of business? Answer: "A buyer in ordinary course of business [C] of fungible goods sold and delivered by a warehouse [W] that is also in the business of buying and selling such goods takes the goods free of any claim [e.g., B's] under a warehouse receipt even if the receipt is negotiable and has been duly negotiated." §§ 7–205, 1–201(b)(18) ("fungible goods" defined).

This rule is an application of the principle of § 2–403(2) that an entruster to a merchant loses to a buyer in ordinary course of business. § 2–403 Comment 2; see § 9–320(a) re: similar principle.

As to B's right to share in the remaining grain stored with W, see §§ 7–205 Comments, 7–207(b).

3.   TRANSFER IN THE ABSENCE OF "DUE NEGOTIATION"

A.   WHEN DOCUMENT OF TITLE IS TRANSFERRED RATHER THAN "DULY NEGOTIATED"

A nonnegotiable document may be transferred but cannot be "duly negotiated." A negotiable document is transferred rather than "duly negotiated" if the taker does not take (a) by negotiation, (b) in good faith and without notice of defenses, (c) for value, and (d) in regular course of business or financing, etc. §§ 7–104, 7–501(a)(5) and (b)(3), 7–504(a).

B.   RIGHTS ACQUIRED BY A TRANSFEREE OF A DOCUMENT NOT "DULY NEGOTIATED"

A transferee of a document, whether negotiable or nonnegotiable, to whom the document has been delivered but not "duly negotiated" acquires the title and rights that

1.   its transferor had, or

2.   its transferor had *actual* authority to convey. § 7–504(a) and Comment 1.

Contrast a taker by "due negotiation," who acquires all rights under the law of agency (including apparent authority) or estoppel. §§ 7–502(a)(3), 1–103(b).

Example: A issues and delivers to B a negotiable document stating, "Deliver to order of B." C steals the document from B, forges B's name, and delivers it to D, who takes in good faith, without notice of defenses, for value, in regular course of business. D takes subject to B's conversion claim against C because D did not take by negotiation and therefore did not take by "due negotiation." The result would be the same if B had indorsed in blank—rather than C forging B's signature—if D took with notice of B's claim or if the document was not negotiable, i.e., stated, "Deliver to B."

Simply: Transferee D stands in the shoes of Transferor C and gets no greater rights. Cf. § 3–306 (first sentence).

Note the following comparison (from Comment 1 to § 7–504) between the rights acquired by a transferee of a document in the absence of "due negotiation" and the rights acquired by transfer of the goods themselves:

> Under the general principles controlling negotiable documents, it is clear that in the absence of due negotiation a transferor cannot convey greater rights than the transferor has, even when the negotiation is formally perfect. This section recognizes the transferor's power to transfer rights which the transferor has or has "actual authority to convey." Thus, where a negotiable document of title is being transferred the operation of the principle of estoppel is not recognized, as contrasted with situations involving the transfer of the goods themselves. (Compare Section 2–403 on good faith purchase of goods.) This section applies to both tangible and electronic documents of title.

> A necessary part of the price for the protection of regular dealings with negotiable documents of title is an insistence that no dealing which is in any way irregular shall be recognized as a good faith purchase of the document or of any rights pertaining to it. So, where the transfer of a negotiable document fails as a negotiation because a requisite indorsement is forged or otherwise missing, the purchaser in good faith and for value

may be in the anomalous position of having less rights, in part, than if the purchaser had purchased the goods themselves.

Example 1: A sells and delivers goods to B, relying on B's misrepresentation that B is X. B sells the goods to C, a good-faith purchaser for value. C takes *free from* A's claim against B. § 2–403(1)(a). See Part One, G, 1 supra.

Example 2: A sells and delivers goods to B, relying on B's misrepresentation that B is X. B delivers the goods to Warehouse (or Carrier), who issues a negotiable document "to order of B." B delivers the document without indorsement to C, who takes for value in good faith and without notice of defenses, etc. C takes *subject to* A's claim against B since C did not take by "due negotiation." § 7–504(a). The result would be the same if the document were nonnegotiable ("deliver to B") even if it were indorsed. See § 7–501(c).

C. CERTAIN CASES IN WHICH TRANSFEREE OR CONSIGNEE'S RIGHTS IN A NONNEGOTIABLE DOCUMENT MAY BE DEFEATED

(1) Defeat of Transferee's Rights Prior to Notification to Bailee of Transfer—The "Seller in Possession"

"In the case of a transfer of a nonnegotiable document of title, until (but not after) the bailee receives notice of the transfer, the rights of the transferee may be defeated

1. by any creditors of the transferor who could treat the transfer as void under §§ 2–402 or 2A–308 [e.g., when the seller's retention of possession is a "badge of fraud," see Part One, G, 4 supra];

2. by a buyer from the transferor in ordinary course of business [§ 1–201(b)(9)], if the bailee has delivered the goods to the buyer or received notification of the buyer's rights;

3. by a lessee from the transferor in ordinary course of business [§ 2A–103(1)(u)], if the bailee has delivered the goods to the lessee or received notification of the lessee's rights; or

4. as against the bailee, by good-faith dealings of the bailee with the transferor." § 7–504(b).

Example 1: S, a merchant, contracts to sell goods to B–1. S retains possession of the goods, which S later sells to B–2, a buyer in ordinary course of business. B–2 keeps the goods, since B–1's "entrusting of possession of goods to a merchant [S] who deals in goods of that kind gives [S] power to transfer all rights of the entruster to a buyer in ordinary course of business [B–2]." § 2–403(2). " 'Entrusting' includes ... any acquiescence in retention of possession...." § 2–403(3). See Part One, G, 3 supra.

Example 2: S, a merchant, delivers goods to X, a bailee-warehouse (or carrier) who issues a nonnegotiable document engaging to deliver the goods "to S" (*not* to the "order of S"). S then contracts to sell the goods to B–1. Later, S sells the same goods to B–2, a buyer in ordinary course of business; X is then notified of B–2's rights. Who has priority as to the goods, B–1 or B–2? Answer: B–2. Until X receives notification of the transfer to B–1, B–1's rights may be defeated by B–2, a buyer in ordinary course of business, if bailee X received notification of B–2's rights. Here, X received notification of B–2's rights before receiving notification of the transfer to B–1. § 7–504(b)(2), see § 2–503(4)(b).

Note that Example 2 is a variant of Example 1. In Example 1, S as a "seller in possession" had the power to transfer B–1's rights to B–2, a buyer in ordinary course of business. In Example 2, S was the bailor of the bailee in possession and still controlled the goods (X engaged to deliver to S). S had the power to transfer B–1's rights to B–2, a buyer in ordinary course of business. Once X is notified of the transfer to B–1, however, S no longer controls the right to possession of the goods held by X. Per X's delivery obligation—after receiving notification of the transfer to B–1—X will no longer follow S's delivery instructions. See §§ 7–403(a), 7–102(a)(9) ("person entitled under the document"), 7–603 (conflicting claims).

If the document had been negotiable, i.e., X engaged to deliver the goods "to the order of S," and S indorsed and delivered the document to B–1, B–1's rights would not be defeated. Why? Because S no longer controls the right to possession of the goods. Bailee X's obligation is to deliver to the *holder* (B–1) who surrenders the document, not to deliver to S. § 7–403(a), (c); § 7–102(a)(9).

Here and elsewhere, we have observed several Code sections involving goods in possession of a bailee who has issued a nonnegotiable document. The following chart will help to interrelate these sections:

Rights, Obligations, Risks, etc.	Determining Event	Nutshell Discussion
1. Seller's tender of delivery obligation	Tender of nonnegotiable document § 2–503(4)(b)	Part One, E, 2; Part Four, B and H
2. Risk of Loss	Risk of loss remains on seller until buyer has had a reasonable time to present the nonnegotiable document § 2–509(2)(c), § 2–503(4)(b) and Comment 6	Part One, C, 5; Part Four, B and H
3. Buyer's rights as against bailee and all third parties (e.g., creditors of and purchasers from seller)	Receipt by bailee of notification of buyer's rights "fixes" buyer's rights § 2–503(4)(b) and comment 6	Part One, G, 3 and 4; Part Four, B and H
4. Seller's right to stop delivery of goods in possession of bailee	May stop until acknowledgment to buyer by bailee that bailee holds for buyer § 2–705(2)(b), (c)	Part One, F, 2, A, (2), (b)
5. Defeat of transferee's rights	Until bailee receives notification of the transfer § 7–504 (b)	Part Four, D, 3, C, (1); Part Four, H.

Rights, Obligations, Risks, etc.	Determining Event	Nutshell Discussion
6. Perfection of security interest	Perfected by bailee's receipt of notification of secured party's interest § 9–312(d), but see § 9–313(c)	Part Five, C, 4, C, (2).

(2) Diversion or Other Change of Shipping Instructions—Loss of Consignee's Title as Against Buyer in Ordinary Course of Business

A diversion or other change of shipping instructions by the consignor in a nonnegotiable bill of lading that causes the bailee not to deliver the goods to the consignee defeats the consignee's title to the goods if the goods have been delivered to a buyer in ordinary course of business or a lessee in ordinary course of business. § 7–504(c). "Consignor" means a person named in a bill of lading as the person from whom the goods have been received for shipment. "Consignee" means a person named in a bill of lading to whom (or to whose order) the bill promises delivery. § 7–102(a)(3), (4).

Example: Manufacturer, having shipped a lot of standardized goods to A on a nonnegotiable bill of lading (e.g., a bill promising to "deliver to A"), diverts the goods to customer B who pays for them. A may not reclaim the goods from B, a buyer in ordinary course of business. Rationale: No policy supports the involvement of innocent third party B in the manufacturer's default on its contract to A; and the common commercial practice of diverting goods in transit suggests a trade understanding in accordance with the above rule. § 7–504 Comment 3. See § 7–303 and Part Four, B supra and E infra for discussion of diversion.

(3) Stoppage of Delivery in Transit

Delivery to a buyer pursuant to a nonnegotiable document of title may be stopped by a seller pursuant to § 2–

705 or a lessor under § 2A–526. § 7–504(d). See Part One, F, 2, A, (2), (b) supra.

4. OBLIGATIONS OF INDORSERS AND PERSONS WHO NEGOTIATE OR DELIVER DOCUMENTS

A, a warehouse or carrier, issues a warehouse receipt or bill of lading engaging to deliver bailed goods "to B" or "to the order of B." B indorses and delivers the receipt or bill to C. What are B's obligations to C? Answer:

1. *Indorsement.* Indorsement of a tangible document of title (receipt or bill) does not make the indorser (B) liable for any default by the bailee–issuer (A) or by previous indorsers. § 7–505 and Comment. Contrast indorsements of promissory notes, wherein the indorser contracts, upon dishonor and notice of dishonor, to pay the instrument. § 3–415(a), (c). Cf. §§ 8–304(f), 8–305(b) (re: securities).

2. *Warranties on negotiation or delivery.* A person (B) who negotiates or delivers for value a receipt or bill warrants to B's immediate purchaser (C), in addition to any warranty made in selling or leasing the goods (§§ 2–312 through 2–318, 2A–210 through 2A–216), that

a. The document is genuine; and

b. B has no knowledge of any fact that would impair the document's validity or worth; and

c. B's negotiation or delivery is rightful and fully effective with respect to the title to the receipt or bill and the goods it represents. § 7–507; cf. transfer warranties re: negotiable instruments. §§ 3–416, 4–207. Cf. § 8–108(a).

As to an intermediary's warranty of good faith and its authority, see § 7–508. Cf. § 8–108(g).

Obligation of indorser and issuer of delivery order

The holder of a delivery order (one can be a "holder" only of a *negotiable* delivery order) acquires the obligation of the issuer (e.g., a seller of goods) and any indorser to procure the bailee's acceptance. §§ 7–502(a)(4), 1–201(b)(21) ("holder" defined); see §§ 7–505 (indorser is not a guarantor), 7–507 (warranties on negotiation or delivery). Cf. contract of secondary liability of drawers and indorsers of drafts and transfer warranties per §§ 3–414, 3–415, 3–416. As to *acceptance* under Article 3, see §§ 3–409, 3–410, 3–413; cf. § 7–102(a)(5) and Comment 3.

E. SITUATIONS EXCUSING DELIVERY TO A "PERSON ENTITLED UNDER THE DOCUMENT"

In Part Four, B supra we discussed the fact that the bailee–warehouse or carrier must deliver the bailed goods to a "person entitled under the document." However, in certain instances, delivery to such person is *excused*. That is, the bailee must deliver the goods to a "person entitled under the document," *unless* the *bailee* establishes any of the following excuses (§§ 7–403(a)(1)–(7), 1–201(b)(8) ("person entitled under the document")):

1. *Delivery to person with paramount title.* Delivery to a person entitled under the document is excused if delivery is made to a person whose receipt was rightful as against the claimant. § 7–403(a)(1).

Example 1: Recall Example 1 at Part Four, D, 2, C, (1) supra wherein B stole goods from A, then delivered the goods to X bailee (a warehouse or carrier), who issued a negotiable document (a warehouse receipt or bill of lading) "to order of B." B indorsed to C, who took by due negotiation. We learned that A would be entitled to the goods as against C, even though C took by due negotiation. § 7–503(a). Accordingly, if X delivers the goods to "true owner" A, it *excuses* X's delivery to C, the "person entitled under the document," because X delivered to someone with paramount title (A).

Example 2: Suppose in Example 1 that—instead of delivery to "true owner" A—X delivered the goods to C, the "person entitled under the document." Is X liable for making delivery to a person who does not have paramount title? Answer: Generally, no. "A bailee [X] that in good faith has received goods and delivered ... the goods according to the terms of a document of title ... is not liable for the goods even if (1) the person from which the bailee received the goods [B] did not have authority to procure the document or to dispose of the goods; or (2) the person to which the bailee delivered the goods [C] did not have authority to receive the goods." § 7–404 and Comment. Thus, if X acted in good faith, X is not liable for delivery to C. If, however, X knew of A's claim of paramount title, but nevertheless delivered the goods to C, then X may be liable. Section 7–603 "enables a bailee [X] faced with conflicting claims to the goods to compel the claimants to litigate their claims with each other rather than with [bailee X]" § 7–603 Comment 1.

Example 3: Suppose in Example 1 that—instead of B stealing the goods from A—A entrusted goods to merchant B, who dealt in goods of that kind, which gives B the power to transfer A's rights to a buyer in ordinary course of business. Here, A would *not* be entitled to the goods as against C, who took by "due negotiation." §§ 7–502(a)(2) and (b), 7–503(a)(1), 7–403 Comment 2. See discussion at Part Four, D, 2, C, (1) supra. Accordingly, when X delivered the goods to A, X did *not* deliver the goods to a person whose receipt was rightful as against the claimant (C). Thus, X misdelivered because X did not deliver either to the person entitled under the document or to a person whose receipt was rightful as against the claimant. § 7–403(a)(1).

To conclude, X may in good faith deliver the goods to the "person entitled under the document" even if the person does not have paramount title. If X delivers to a person *other than* the "person entitled under the document," however, X delivers at X's peril, that is, X is liable for misdelivery unless the person does have paramount title. This is true even if X delivers in good faith.

2.   *Damage to or delay or loss of goods.* Damage to, or delay, loss, or destruction of, the goods for which the bailee is not liable excuses delivery to a person entitled under the document. § 7–403(a)(2). This rule is, in essence, a cross-reference to the entire body of tort law determining the varying responsibilities and standards of care applicable to commercial bailees. § 7–403 Comment 3. The Code spells out the minimum standards thus: Warehouses and carriers must exercise the degree of care that "a reasonably careful person would exercise under similar circumstances." §§ 7–204(a) and (d), 7–309(a). States and the federal government may apply more rigid standards, e.g., absolute liability of common carriers, with certain enumerated exceptions (act of God, act of public enemy, act of shipper, act of public authority, or inherent nature of the goods). § 7–103. See UCC Hornbook §§ 28–3, 29–3 (Practitioner's Edition).

As to contractual limitation of a carrier's or warehouse's liability, see §§ 7–204(b), 7–309(b). As to the time and manner of presenting claims and commencing actions, see §§ 7–204(c), 7–309(c).

3.   *Enforcement of lien or lawful termination of storage.* Previous sale or other disposition of the goods in lawful enforcement of a lien or upon a warehouse's lawful termination of storage excuses delivery to a person entitled under the document. § 7–403(a)(3).

Warehouse's or carrier's lien

Generally, a warehouse or carrier has a specific lien on the stored or shipped goods for charges associated with storage or transportation, etc. In addition, a warehouse may have a general lien or a security interest in the goods. §§ 7–209(a), (b) and Comments 1 and 2, 7–307(a). As to effectiveness of lien vs. third parties, see §§ 7–209(c) and (d), 7–307(a) and (b). As to loss of lien, see §§ 7–209(e), 7–307(c).

Enforcement of warehouse's or carrier's lien

"Foreclosure" upon a warehouse's or carrier's lien is effected by a public or private sale of the goods. "Commercial reasonableness" (except for noncommercial storage with a warehouse per § 7–210(b)) is the standard for such proceedings. §§ 7–210, 7–308. The warehouse or carrier satisfies its lien from the proceeds of the sale. §§ 7–210(f), 7–308(e). As to rights of purchasers at the sale, see §§ 7–210(e), 7–308(d). Compare the above "foreclosure" with §§ 2–706, 9–601 et seq.

Warehouse's termination of storage

A warehouse may terminate storage at its own option, as for example when the goods are about to deteriorate or decline in value to less than the amount of the warehouse's lien, or are hazardous. § 7–206 and Comments. If the goods are not removed, the warehouse may sell them per § 7–210 (Enforcement of Warehouse's Lien) or otherwise sell or dispose of them as appropriate per § 7–206(b), (c).

4. *Seller's right to stop delivery.* A seller's exercise of its right to stop delivery per Section 2–705 or a lessor's exercise of its right to stop delivery per Section 2A–526 excuses delivery to a person entitled under the document. § 7–403(a)(4). See Part One, F, 2, A, (2), (b) supra; Part One, F, 2, B supra; Part Two, G, 4, C, (2), (c) infra.

5. *Diversion.* A diversion, reconsignment, or other disposition pursuant to § 7–303 excuses delivery to a person entitled under the document. § 7–403(a)(5). Section 7–303 states that a carrier *may* deliver the goods to a person or destination other than that stated in the bill, on instructions from the holder of a negotiable bill. § 7–303(a)(1) and Comment 1. If the bill is nonnegotiable, the carrier may do so on instructions from (1) the consignor, even if the consignee has given contrary instructions; (2) the consignee, in the absence of contrary instructions from the consignor (if the goods have arrived at the billed destination or if the consignee is in possession of the tangible bill or in control of the electronic bill); (3) the consignee, if entitled as against the consignor to dispose of the goods (see Part Four, E supra re: delivery to a person with paramount title). § 7–303(a)(2)–(4).

6. *Release, satisfaction, etc.* Release, satisfaction, or any other personal defense against the claimant (person entitled under the document), excuses delivery to him or her. § 7–403(a)(6).

7. *Other lawful excuse.* Any other lawful excuse excuses delivery to a person entitled under the document. § 7–403(a)(7). For example, if more than one person claims title or possession of the goods, the bailee (warehouse or carrier) is excused from delivery until it has had a reasonable time to ascertain the validity of the adverse claims or to bring an action for interpleader. § 7–603; see §§ 7–601 (lost, stolen, or destroyed documents), 7–602 (judicial process against goods covered by document).

F. NONRECEIPT OR MISDESCRIPTION OF GOODS

Assume A (either a warehouse or carrier) issues a document (a warehouse receipt or bill of lading) to B acknowledging possession of certain goods even though no goods were in fact received. B indorses and delivers the document to C. What are C's rights as against A? The following rules apply:

Warehouse receipt

"A party to or a purchaser for value in good faith [C] of a [warehouse receipt] . . . that relies upon the description of the goods in the [warehouse receipt] may recover from the issuer [A] damages caused by the nonreceipt or misdescription of the goods. . . ." § 7–203.

Bill of lading

"A consignee of a nonnegotiable bill of lading which has given value in good faith, or a holder to which a negotiable bill has been duly negotiated [C], relying upon the description of the goods in the bill or upon the date shown in the bill, may recover from the issuer [A] damages caused by the misdating of the bill or the nonreceipt or misdescription of the goods. . . ." § 7–301(a).

Disclaimer

A may avoid the above responsibility—if A does not know whether the goods were received (e.g., a box is bailed but may be empty)—by employing words on the receipt or bill such as, "said to contain," "contents or condition of contents of packages unknown," or "shipper's weight, load and count," if the indication is true. §§ 7–203, 7–301(a).

Compare the above with a promissory note A issues to B in payment for goods B agreed to sell to A. If B negotiates the note to C, who takes it for value, in good faith, and without notice of defenses to its enforcement, and the goods are never delivered, A's personal defense of failure of consideration is cut off by C, a holder in due course. §§ 3–305(a)(2) and (b), 3–303(b).

If B subsequently delivers the goods to A, see § 7–502(a)(3) and Comment 2.

G. FORGED OR ALTERED DOCUMENTS

Alteration

Assume A (either a warehouse or carrier) issues a document (a warehouse receipt or bill of lading) to B, who fills in a blank in the document to reflect more goods than were in fact received by A. B indorses and delivers the paper to C. What are C's rights as against A? The following rules apply:

☐ ☐ 1. *Warehouse receipt.* "If a blank in a negotiable tangible warehouse receipt has been filled in without authority, a good-faith purchaser for value and without notice of the lack of authority [e.g., C] may treat the insertion as authorized. Any other unauthorized alteration [e.g., changing the number of goods stated on the receipt to have been received by A] leaves any tangible or electronic warehouse receipt enforceable against the issuer [A] according to its original tenor." § 7–208.

☐ ☐ 2. *Bill of lading.* "An unauthorized alteration or filling in of a blank in a bill of lading leaves the bill enforceable according to its original tenor." § 7–306.

Compare the above with §§ 3–407(c) and 3–406: If A issues an altered note, even a person taking the note for value in good faith and without notice of the alteration takes subject to the alteration because it is a "real" defense. Cf. § 8–206.

Forgery

Assume B forges A's name to a document (a warehouse receipt or bill of lading) that purports to be issued to B. B then indorses and delivers the paper to C. What are C's rights against A? Answer: C, even as a holder of a "duly negotiated" document, has no rights. A is neither a *bailee* nor an *issuer* and consequently should not be required to take on the liability of such persons. § 7–102(a)(1), (8) ("bailee" and "issuer" defined); see § 1–201(b)(6), (16), (42) ("bill of lading," "document of title," and "warehouse receipt" defined). Similarly, under Article 3, forgery of a note constitutes a "real" defense that is valid as against a holder in due course. §§ 3–403 (unauthorized signature), 3–406 (role of negligence); see § 3–401(a) (effect of signature). Cf. § 8–205.

What are C's rights against B in the above examples? See § 7–505; § 7–507 re: warranties on negotiation (e.g., warranty that the document is genuine). See Part Four, D, 4 supra. Compare obligations of indorsers and transferors of notes. §§ 3–415, 3–416, 4–207. Cf. §§ 8–304(f), 8–305(b), 8–108(a).

PART FIVE

FINANCING THE SALE OF GOODS: THE SECURED TRANSACTION

[Prefatory Note: This Part Five incorporates the 2010 Amendments to Article 9. They are expected to be considered by state legislatures with a view to all states enacting the amendments by a uniform effective date of July 1, 2013.

This Part will continue to present the pre–2010 Article 9. In brackets, however, the changes under Amended (2010) Article 9 are set forth.]

A. FUNDAMENTALS OF A SECURED TRANSACTION

The introduction to this nutshell explained that a "commercial transaction" may involve not only a contract for sale of goods followed by a sale and the giving of a check or draft for a part of the purchase price, but also the acceptance of some form of *security* for the balance. Such security is the subject of Article 9, Secured Transactions.

To understand the fundamentals of a secured transaction, consider the following:

Assume debtor D owns certain property (e.g., a house, goods, or stocks) and needs cash for an emergency. D may sell the property to creditor C to raise the cash. Alternatively, D may borrow cash from C and give C a security interest in the property (called collateral) to secure repayment of the loan.

Now suppose D does not own certain property (e.g., a house or a refrigerator) but wishes to acquire it. D may pay a down payment to seller C and pay C the remainder of the purchase price in installments. D may further agree that C will have a security interest in the property to secure payment of the balance. Alternatively, D may obtain a loan from lender C, pay seller X cash for the property, and give lender C a security interest in the goods to secure repayment of the loan.

The above security transactions involve (1) a debt, (2) a debtor, (3) a creditor, (4) property making up the security (collateral), and (5) an agreement (which may take the form of a pledge, chattel mortgage, conditional sale, etc.) that gives the creditor an *interest* in the collateral (sometimes called a lien, title, or a security interest) so that, if the debtor defaults, the creditor is secured, i.e., the creditor can proceed against the collateral (through foreclosure) and apply it toward the debt.

Thus, C's fundamental rights are (a) to recover the amount of the debt from D, and (b) to have the collateral applied toward the debt in the event of default, a right generally enforced in preference to the claims of third persons. D's fundamental rights are (a) to redeem the collateral by paying the debt (a power to destroy C's interest in the property) and (b) to have general rights of ownership in the collateral except insofar as they are conferred upon C by the particular transaction.

Several of these fundamentals will now be examined more closely:

Foreclosure

The secured creditor's right to have the collateral applied toward the debt in the event of default is often referred to as foreclosure—the right to cut off the debtor's interest in the collateral and also junior third party interests. Thus, the secured creditor may take or keep the collateral in satisfaction of the debt (strict foreclosure); alternatively, a foreclosure sale is conducted wherein the purchaser from such sale cuts off the interests of the debtor, the secured creditor, and junior third-party interests (foreclosure by sale). The proceeds of such sale are used to pay off the debt to the secured creditor. Any excess is paid to junior interests, and any remaining monies returned to the debtor. If the sale is insufficient to satisfy the debt, the secured creditor may be entitled to a deficiency judgment.

Redemption

Of course, the secured creditor's interest in the collateral is only for the purpose of securing repayment of the debt. Consequently, any time before foreclosure, the debtor may pay the debt and thereby cut off the secured party's interest in the collateral.

Priority

The secured party's right to proceed against the collateral after the debtor's default—with a right of priority over third-party claims—is the essence of a security transaction. It is this right, most clearly illustrated once a bankruptcy proceeding is underway, that distinguishes a secured creditor from an unsecured creditor.

The *unsecured* creditor has no rights against specific property of the debtor. The unsecured creditor may obtain a judgment against the debtor, cause a writ of execution to be issued, and have the property levied upon be sold at an execution sale with the proceeds used to pay the claim. In this process, the unsecured creditor becomes a "lien creditor." This "lien" arises very late in the drama, when earlier secured claims will likely have exhausted the debtor's property. The unsecured creditor is the subject of law school courses entitled, Creditors' Rights, Debtor–Creditor Relations, etc.

For a secured creditor to have rights that prevail over third-party claims, security law often requires some form of public notice so that third parties may be apprised of the secured creditor's interest. This notice may be given by the secured creditor taking possession of the collateral (pledge) or by a certain paper being filed or recorded in an appropriate public office (e.g., register of deeds). Without such notice, the secured creditor may not have priority over certain third parties.

Example illustrating the above fundamentals: On February 1, in return for a credit extension of $1,000, D gives a security interest in certain goods to C–1, who promptly files or records or takes possession of the goods. On March 1, C–2 loans $1,500 to D and takes a security interest in the same goods. C–1 has priority over the later interest in the same goods. C–1 may foreclose upon its interest by having the goods sold to X, who takes the goods free of the interests of D, C–1, and C–2. The amount paid at the foreclosure sale ($800) is paid to C–1 in partial satisfaction of the debt. C–1 may be entitled to a $200 deficiency judgment against D ($1,000 minus $800), the amount by which the value of the collateral was insufficient to satisfy D's debt to C–1. If, however, the price paid at the foreclosure sale exceeded $1,000, the excess may be paid to C–2 to the extent necessary to satisfy its claim, and any remaining surplus returned to D.

B. PRE-CODE PERSONAL PROPERTY SECURITY LAW

We shall very briefly survey the law of personal property security prior to the enactment of UCC Article 9. Pre-Code law was characterized by a variety of independent security devices arising at different times to facilitate different kinds of secured financing: pledge, chattel mortgage, conditional sale, trust receipt, factor's lien, and assignment of accounts receivable were among the most common.

Pledge

Restatement of Security § 1 defines a pledge as "a security interest in a chattel or an intangible represented by an indispensable instrument [e.g., negotiable tangible warehouse receipt], the interest being created by a bailment for the purpose of securing the payment of a debt or the performance of some other duty." Comment a to § 1 states, "The pledge is one of the simplest of the security devices. The fundamental idea of the pledge is possession by the pledgee. If the creditor's security interest depends upon possession obtained and held primarily for security, he has a pledge." Restatement of Security §§ 28 and 35 state that a pledgee's interest in pledged personal property is generally superior to subsequent interests, but not prior interests.

Chattel mortgage

The chattel mortgage was a response to the need for a nonpossessory security device. Example: Assume Seller sold and delivered goods to Buyer. As part of this transaction, Buyer might sign a chattel mortgage agreement stating,

> For valuable consideration, and as security for the unpaid Principal Balance and Service Charges, Buyer (mortgagor) hereby mortgages and conveys the within described merchandise to Seller (mortgagee), to have and to hold the same forever, upon condition that if Buyer promptly pays or causes to be paid the indebtedness corresponding to said merchandise and performs all the conditions hereof ... at the time and in the manner specified ... then this mortgage shall be void, otherwise to remain in full force and effect.

The chattel mortgage took the form of a conveyance (from Buyer to Seller) subject to defeasance; that is, if the debt were paid, the conveyance would be void. Some states called Seller–mortgagee's interest "title." Other states looked through the transaction's form to its substance and called the mortgagee's interest a "mere lien." As to the mortgagee's rights against third parties, a typical chattel-mortgage statute stated,

Every mortgage or conveyance intended to operate as a mortgage of goods or chattels that is not accompanied by an immediate delivery, and followed by an actual and continued change of possession of the things mortgaged, is absolutely void (as against creditors of the mortgagor and purchasers of the goods or chattels from the mortgagor) unless the mortgage or a true copy thereof is filed as directed in this article.

Conditional sale

The conditional sale device was used to finance a buyer's purchase of goods. Example: Seller sells and delivers goods to Buyer, who signs a conditional sales agreement stating,

Title to the described equipment shall remain in Seller until the purchase price therefor ... is paid in full in cash. Upon full performance and observance by the purchaser of all the terms and conditions hereof, at the times specified therefor, title to said equipment shall, without further action on the part of Seller, be transferred to and vested in Purchaser.

The sale was "conditional" in the sense that Buyer would not get title to the goods until and unless Buyer paid in full. Some states did not require a filing or recording to afford public notice to third parties who dealt with Buyer. The Uniform Conditional Sales Act § 5 (enacted in a few states), however, stated,

Every provision in a conditional sale reserving property in the seller shall be void as to any purchaser from or creditor of the buyer, who, without notice of such provision, purchases the goods or acquires by attachment or levy a lien upon them, before the contract or a copy thereof shall be filed as hereinafter provided, unless such contract or copy is so filed within ten days after the making of the conditional sale.

Financing collateral that "turns over"—trust receipts, factor's liens, assignments of accounts receivable

The chattel mortgage and conditional sale were suited to a single transaction in goods. They were not suited to transactions dealing with inventory and accounts wherein the collateral was changing. Example: Manufacturer obtains raw materials that become work in process and end up as finished goods. The finished goods are delivered to Dealer, who holds them for sale. User buys the goods from Dealer for personal or business use. User has thirty days in which to pay for the goods. Manufacturer wishes to borrow against its inventory of raw materials, work in process, and finished goods; Dealer wishes to borrow against its inventory of goods and its accounts receivable, e.g., the money User owes Dealer. These types of collateral are constantly changing as goods are produced, sold, and paid for on a continuing basis. Thus, the Uniform Trust Receipts Act, non-uniform factor's lien acts, and legislation addressing assignment of accounts receivable were promulgated to accommodate such transactions. A device called field warehousing, which will be discussed later, was also utilized.

The Code's assessment of prior law is seen in the following Comment to former § 9–101:

Pre-Code law recognized a wide variety of security devices, which came into use at various times to make possible different types of secured financing. Differences between one device and another persisted, in formal requisites, in the secured party's rights against the debtor and third parties, in the debtor's rights against the secured party, and in filing requirements, although many of those differences no longer served any useful function. Thus an unfiled chattel mortgage was by the law of many states "void" against creditors generally; a conditional sale, often available as a substitute for the chattel mortgage, was in some states valid against all creditors without filing, and in states where filing is required was, if unfiled, void only against lien creditors. The recognition of so many separate security devices had the result that half a dozen filing systems covering chattel security devices might be maintained within a state, some on a county basis, others on a state-wide basis, each of which had to be separately checked to determine a debtor's status.

Nevertheless, despite the great number of security devices, there remained gaps. In many states, for example, a security interest could not be taken in inventory or a stock in trade despite the need for such financing. It was often baffling to try to maintain a technically valid security interest when financing a manufacturing process, wherein the collateral starts out as raw materials, becomes work in process, and ends up as finished goods. Furthermore, it was by no means clear, even to specialists, how a security interest might be taken under pre-Code law in many kinds of intangible property—such as television rights or motion-picture rights—that have come to be important commercial collateral.

Although the chattel mortgage could be adapted for use in almost any situation involving goods as collateral, there were limitations, sometimes highly technical, on the use of other devices, such as the conditional sale and particularly the trust receipt. In many cases, a security transaction described by the parties as a conditional sale or a trust receipt was later determined by a court to be something else, usually a chattel mortgage. The consequence of such a determination was typically to void the security interest against creditors because the security agreement was not filed *as a chattel mortgage* (even though it may have been filed as a conditional sale or a trust receipt). The aforementioned difficulty inherent in using inventory as collateral has been avoided to some extent by the device known as "field warehousing" as well as by the use of the trust receipt. In addition, after 1940, a number of states authorized inventory financing by enacting similar (although not uniform) statutes known as "factor's lien" acts. During the same period, the increasingly common practice of lending against accounts receivable inspired new statutes in that field in more than thirty states.

The growing complexity of financing transactions forced legislatures to keep piling new statutory provisions on top of inadequate and already sufficiently complicated nineteenth-century security law. The results were increasing costs to both parties and increasing uncertainty as to both their rights and the rights of third parties dealing with them.

C. SECURED TRANSACTIONS UNDER UCC ARTICLE 9

1. PURPOSE AND POLICY OF UCC ARTICLE 9

UCC Article 9 is intended to provide a simple and unified structure within which the immense variety of present-day secured-financing transactions can proceed with less cost and greater certainty. The Comment to former § 9–101 states,

[1.] This Article sets out a comprehensive scheme for the regulation of security interests in personal property and fixtures. It supersedes prior legislation dealing with such security devices as chattel mortgages, conditional sales, trust receipts, factor's liens and assignments of accounts receivable. [See also revised § 9–101 Comment 1.]

[2.]　Consumer installment sales and consumer loans present special problems of a nature which makes special regulation of them inappropriate in a general commercial codification. Many states now regulate such loans and sales under small loan acts, retail installment selling acts and the like. [See, e.g., Uniform Consumer Credit Code. Under revised § 9–101 Comment 4.j., see also reference to consumer and consumer goods transactions.] . . .

[3.]　Under this Article the traditional distinctions among security devices, based largely on form, are not retained; the Article applies to all transactions intended to create security interests in personal property and fixtures, and the single term "security interest" substitutes for the variety of descriptive terms which had grown up at common law and under a hundred-year accretion of statutes. This does not mean that the old forms may not be used. . . . [Former § 9–102(2), revised § 9–109(a) and Comment 2.]

[4.]　This Article does not determine whether "title" to collateral is in the secured party or in the debtor and adopts neither a "title theory" nor a "lien theory" of security interests. Rights, obligations and remedies under the Article do not depend on the location of title (Section 9–202). The location of title may become important for other purposes—as, for example, in determining the incidents of taxation—and in such a case the parties are left free to contract as they will. In this connection the use of a form which has traditionally been regarded as determinative of title (e.g., the conditional sale) could reasonably be regarded as evidencing the parties' intention with respect to title to the collateral.

[5.]　Under the Article distinctions based on form (except as between pledge and non-possessory interests) are no longer controlling. For some purposes there are distinctions based on the type of property which constitutes the collateral—industrial and commercial equipment, business inventory, farm products, consumer goods, accounts receivable, documents of title and other intangibles—and, where appropriate, the Article states special rules applicable to financing transactions involving a particular type of property. Despite the statutory simplification a greater degree of flexibility in the financing transaction is allowed than ... [was] possible under ... [pre-UCC] law.

[6.]   The scheme of the Article is to make distinctions, where distinctions are necessary, along functional rather than formal lines.

This has made possible a radical simplification in the formal requisites for creation of a security interest.

[7.]   A more rational filing system replaces the present system of different files for each security device which is subject to filing requirements. Thus not only is the information contained in the files made more accessible but the cost of procuring credit information, and, incidentally, of maintaining the files, is greatly reduced. [See former § 9–401, revised § 9–501.]

[8.]   The Article's flexibility and simplified formalities should make it possible for new forms of secured financing, as they develop, to fit comfortably under its provisions, thus avoiding the necessity, so apparent in recent years, of year by year passing new statutes and tinkering with the old ones to allow legitimate business transactions to go forward.

[9.]   *The rules set out in this Article are principally concerned with the limits of the secured party's protection against purchasers from and creditors of the debtor.* [Emphasis added.]

[10.]   Except for procedure on default, freedom of contract prevails between the immediate parties to the security transaction. [See § 1–302(a) and Comment 2, revised § 9–602.]

As the above Comment shows, the UCC adopts a unitary approach to personal property secured transactions. Gone are mortgagors and mortgagees, conditional sale vendors and vendees, pledgors and pledgees, entrusters and trustees, etc. These persons are now called *debtor* and *secured party*. For example, a pre-Code chattel mortgage lawyer might say, "A mortgagor, pursuant to a mortgage agreement, gives a mortgage lien to a mortgagee covering furniture as collateral to secure a loan. The mortgage is recorded to protect against third party claims to the collateral." The Code lawyer would say, "A *debtor* [§ 9–102(a)(28) (debtor), (59) (obligor)], pursuant to a *security agreement* [§ 9–102(a)(73)], gives a *security interest* [§ 1–201(b)(35)] covering furniture as *collateral* [§ 9–102(a)(12)] (e.g., *consumer goods, inventory* [§ 9–102(a)(23), (33), (48)]) to a *secured party* [§ 9–102(a)(72)] to secure a loan. Upon granting the loan, the security interest *attaches* [§ 9–203(a)] to the collateral. A *financing statement* [§§ 9–102(a)(39), 9–502, 9–521(a)] is *filed* [§ 9–501] to *perfect* [§ 9–308(a)] the security interest against third party claims to the collateral." (The citations above and to follow are to revised Article 9 (2001), revised Article 1 (2001), and conforming amendments to Articles 2, 2A, and 7 (2003). The 2010 Amendments are presented in brackets following the relevant discussion. These amendments have a uniform effective date, where adopted by state law, of July 1, 2013. Section 9–102(a) provides many of the definitions that apply to Article 9 transactions. [*2010 Amendment*: Subsections 9–102(a)(68)–(80) are redesignated 9–102(a)(69)–(81).]

Since pre-Code vocabulary is sometimes still used in business, it is helpful to be able to express the concepts either in pre-Code or Code terms. See the following chart:

PERSONAL PROPERTY SECURITY NOMENCLATURE

	Secured Transaction (UCC)	Chattel Mortgage	Conditional Sale	Pledge	Assignment of Accounts	Trust Receipt	Factor's Act (see also Assignment of Accounts)
1. Name of Parties:							
a. Debtor	Debtor	Mortgagor	Conditional Sales Vendee	Pledgor	Assignor	Trustee	Borrower
b. Secured Creditor	Secured Party	Mortgagee	Conditional Sales Vendor	Pledgee	Assignee	Entruster	Factor
2. Creditor's Interest in Collateral	Security Interest	Lien (or Title)	Title	Lien	Outright Sale, Security Transfer	Security Interest	Lien
3. Name of Agreement	Security Agreement	Chattel Mortgage	Conditional Sales Contract	Pledge Agreement	Assignment	Trust Receipt	Factoring Agreement
4. Method of Perfection	1. File Financing Statement 2. Possession 3. Control 4. Automatic	1. Record Mortgage 2. Possession	1. File Conditional Sales Contract 2. Automatic	1. Possession	1. File 2. Mark Books 3. Notify Account Debtor 4. Automatic ("Validation")	1. File 2. Possession	1. Record or File 2. Put Up Sign 3. Possession

The Comment to former § 9–101 also shows that, while Article 9 does not make distinctions based on form, there are functional distinctions based on the type of property that constitutes the collateral. The type of collateral is determined by either (1) the *nature* of the collateral or (2) its *use*. Thus, although many sections of Article 9 apply to all personal property, some important sections state special rules with reference to particular types of collateral, e.g., sections dealing with filing, priorities, and default. The different types of collateral are as follows:

1. *Goods* means all things that are movable when a security interest attaches (tangible personal property). The term includes fixtures, certain timber, unborn young of animals, crops, manufactured homes, and certain computer programs embedded in goods. The term does not include, e.g., documents, instruments, investment property (stocks and bonds), money, and minerals (before extraction). § 9–102(a)(41) and (44) ("fixtures" and "goods" defined); cf. § 2–105(1) (§ 2–103(1)(k) (2003)) ("goods" defined). See § 9–102(a)(1), (30), (47), (49), (53), (75) ("accession," "document," "instrument," "investment property," "manufactured home," and "software" defined).

a. *Consumer goods* are goods used or bought for use primarily for personal, family, or household purposes. § 9–102(a)(23). Example: Debtor gives Secured Party a security interest in household furniture. See 16 CFR 444.2(a)(4).

b. *Farm products* means goods (other than standing timber) with respect to which Debtor is engaged in a farming operation and which are (A) crops (including those growing on trees, vines, and bushes, and aquatic goods); (B) livestock (including aquatic goods); (C) supplies used or produced in a farming operation; or (D) products of crops or livestock in their unmanufactured states. § 9–102(a)(34) and Comment 4.a. Examples: Corn growing on Farmer's land; two cows and their calves; 50 chickens and a quantity of their eggs; catfish raised on a catfish farm; ginned cotton; wool-clip; maple syrup; and milk, even if pasteurized by Farmer. See § 9–324 Comment 11.

c. *Inventory* means goods (other than farm products) that (i) are leased by a lessor or held by a person for sale or lease; (ii) are to be furnished or are furnished by a person under a contract of service; (iii) consist of raw materials or work in process; or (iv) consist of materials used or consumed in a business (e.g., fuel used in operations). Examples: Dealer gives Secured Party a security interest in Dealer's cars that it holds for sale or lease; Manufacturer gives Secured Party a security interest in raw materials, work in process, and finished furniture. § 9–102(a)(48) and Comment 4.a.

d. *Equipment* means goods other than inventory, farm products, or consumer goods. § 9–102(a)(33). For instance, goods are equipment if they are used or bought for use primarily in business. Example: Security interest in furniture delivery truck.

Comment 4.a to § 9–102 observes,

The classes of goods are mutually exclusive. For example, the same property cannot simultaneously be both equipment and inventory. In borderline cases—a physician's car or a farmer's truck that might be either consumer goods or equipment—the principal use to which the property is put is determinative. Goods can fall into different classes at different times. For example, a radio may be inventory in the hands of a dealer and consumer goods in the hands of a consumer. As under former Article 9, goods are "equipment" if they do not fall into another category.

e. *Fixtures* are goods that have become so related to particular real property that an interest in them arises under real property law. § 9–102(a)(41). Example: Furnace permanently affixed to a building. Cf. *as-extracted collateral*. § 9–102(a)(6).

f. *Accession* means goods that are physically united with other goods in such a manner that the identity of the original goods is not lost. § 9–102(a)(1). Example: Motor installed in automobile.

2. *Indispensable paper.* This concept does not appear in the Code as such, even though the Comment to former § 9–106 refers to an "indispensable writing." This term covers various categories of paper that are either negotiable or to some extent dealt with as if negotiable. This category has also been referred to as *semi-intangibles* or *commercial specialties.* [Simply, this means that the transfer of some interest in property (e.g., money or goods) is accomplished by delivery, with any necessary indorsement, of the "indispensable writing" representing the property, e.g., a promissory note or negotiable tangible warehouse receipt.]

a. *Document* means document of title, e.g., bill of lading or warehouse receipt. §§ 9–102(a)(30) ("document" defined), 7–201(b) (storage under bond), 1–201(b)(6), (16), (42) ("bill of lading," "document of title," and "warehouse receipt" defined).

b. *Instrument* means most commonly a negotiable instrument (draft, check, certificate of deposit, or note), or any other writing that evidences a right to payment of a money obligation and that is transferred by delivery with any necessary indorsement. The term does not include, e.g., *investment property.* § 9–102(a)(47), (49).

c. *Promissory note* means an instrument that evidences a promise to pay a monetary obligation (but is not a check, draft, or certificate of deposit). § 9–102(a)(65) and Comment 5.c.

d. *Investment property* means a certificated (or uncertificated) security, a security entitlement, securities account, commodity contract, or account. § 9–102(a)(49) and Comment 6 ("investment property" defined); § 8–102(a)(4), (15)–(18) and Comments 4, 16–18 ("certificated security," "security," "security certificate," "security entitlement," and "uncertificated security" defined). Example: stock certificate or bond certificate.

e. *Chattel paper* consists of (i) a monetary obligation (that is, a right to payment) together with (ii) a security interest in or a lease of specific goods, if the obligation and security interest or lease are evidenced by a "record" or "records." (The definition has been expanded from former Article 9 to include software and a license of software used in the goods.) Traditional written chattel paper is included in the definition of *tangible chattel paper. Electronic chattel paper* is chattel paper that is stored in an electronic medium instead of in tangible form. § 9–102(a)(11), (31), (78) and Comment 5.b. "Record" is defined at § 9–102(a)(69). Example: "A dealer sells a tractor to a farmer on conditional sales contract. . . . The conditional sales contract is a 'security agreement,' the farmer is the 'debtor,' the dealer is the 'secured party' and the tractor is the type of 'collateral' defined in Section 9–109 [revised § 9–102(a)(33)] as 'equipment.' But now the dealer transfers the contract to his bank, either by outright sale or to secure a loan. Since the conditional sales contract is a security agreement relating to specific equipment, the conditional sales contract is now the type of collateral called 'chattel paper.' In this transaction between the dealer and his bank, the bank is the 'secured party,' the dealer is the 'debtor,' and the farmer is the 'account debtor.' " Former § 9–105 Comment 4.

3. *Intangibles.* This type of collateral is purely intangible; that is, intangibles are not evidenced by an indispens-

able writing, but may be the subject of commercial financing transactions.

a. *Account* under former Article 9 meant any right to payment for goods sold or leased *or* for services rendered that was not evidenced by an indispensable writing (such as an instrument or chattel paper), regardless of whether earned by performance. Former § 9–106 and Comment. Under revised Article 9, the definition has been expanded and reformulated and is no longer limited to payment rights relating to goods or services. Many categories of payment rights that were "general intangibles" under former Article 9 are "accounts" under the revision. For example, the revised definition of "account" includes a right to payment of a monetary obligation for real property sold; for intellectual property licensed; for an insurance policy issued; for a secondary obligation incurred (such as a suretyship obligation); from the use of a credit card; or as winnings in a lottery operated or sponsored by a State. § 9–102(a)(2) and Comment 5.a.

A *health-care-insurance receivable* is an interest in or claim under a policy of insurance; specifically, a right to payment for health-care goods or services provided. This is a subset of "account." § 9–102(a)(2), (46) and Comment 5.a.

The term "account" does *not* include (i) payment rights evidenced by chattel paper or an instrument (as under former § 9–106), (ii) commercial tort claims, (iii) deposit accounts, (iv) investment property, (v) letter-of-credit rights, or (vi) payment rights for money or funds advanced or sold (other than arising out of the use of a credit card). § 9–102(a)(2).

Example: Dealer sells goods (such as equipment or consumer goods) to users on open account (that is, on an unsecured basis) wherein each user has 60 days in which to pay. Dealer assigns the accounts to its bank, either by outright sale or to secure a loan. In this transaction between Dealer and its bank, the bank is the "secured party," Dealer is the "debtor," and the users are the "account debtors." § 9–102(a)(2), (3).

b. *General intangible* is the residual category of personal property collateral (including things in action) that is *not* included in the other defined types of collateral (e.g., accounts, chattel paper, instruments, investment property, or money). Examples: intellectual property, rights to payment of a loan that is not evidenced by chattel paper or an instrument, or rights that arise under a license of intellectual property. § 9–102(a)(42) and Comment 5.d.

The definition has been revised to exclude the following three separate types of collateral:

(i) *commercial tort claim* (includes the claim of an individual arising in tort if the claim arose out of its business, but does not include damages for the personal injury or death of an individual). § 9–102(a)(13), see § 9–109(d)(12).

(ii) *deposit account* (a demand, time, or savings account maintained by a bank, but not investment property or accounts evidenced by an instrument). § 9–102(a)(29), see § 9–109(d)(13).

(iii) *letter-of-credit right* (a right to payment or performance under a letter of credit). § 9–102(a)(51).

The following are subsets of "general intangible":

(i) *Payment intangible* (a general intangible under which the account debtor's principal obligation is monetary). § 9–102(a)(3), (61) ("account debtor" and "payment intangible" defined), see § 9–109(a)(3), (d)(4) and (5) and (7) (re: scope of Article 9). Example: a loan not evidenced by an instrument or chattel paper.

(ii) *Software* (a computer program and supporting information; but not a program embedded in goods, e.g., automobile brakes controlled by an on-board computer). § 9–102(a)(44), (75) and Comments 4.a., 5.d., and 25 ("goods" and "software" defined).

4. *Proceeds* includes whatever is acquired upon the sale, lease, license, exchange, or other disposition of collateral. § 9–102(a)(64)(A). ·See § 9–102(a)(9) (cash proceeds) and (58) (noncash proceeds). Example: Dealer gives a security interest to Bank in its inventory of cars. Dealer sells a car from its inventory to User–Buyer. User–Buyer pays a cash down payment and trades in its used car. User pays the balance by certified check. The cash, trade-in car, and check are proceeds of inventory collateral.

2. APPLICABILITY OF UCC ARTICLE 9

A. GENERAL SCOPE OF ARTICLE 9

Unless excluded (see below), Article 9 applies to the following:

1. *Basic Scope Provision.* Article 9 applies to a transaction, regardless of its form or name assigned by the parties (e.g., pledge, chattel mortgage, conditional sale, or trust receipt), that creates a *security interest* in *personal property* or *fixtures* by *contract.* § 9–109(a)(1) and Comment 2. Thus, all consensual security interests in personal property and fixtures are covered by Article 9 (unless excluded under § 9–109 (c) and (d)).

"Security interest" means an interest in personal property or fixtures that secures payment or performance of an obligation. § 1–201(b)(35). See definitions of types of personal property (e.g., goods, documents, instruments, general intangibles, chattel paper, and accounts) and fixtures at § 9–102 discussed immediately above.

As to a security interest in an obligation secured by a non-Article 9 transaction (such as a land mortgage), see

§ 9–109(b) and Comment 7. See §§ 9–203(g) (attachment and enforceability of lien securing payment right), 9–308(e) (perfection of same).

2. *Agricultural Lien.* Article 9 applies to an agricultural lien. § 9–109(a)(2) and Comment 3. This lien is created by statute and not dependent on possession of the collateral. It is not a "security interest." § 9–102(a)(5). See, e.g., Iowa Code Ann. § 570A.3 (e.g., an agricultural supply dealer furnishing feed to a farmer has a lien for the unpaid amount of the retail cost of the feed, including labor. The lien attaches to all livestock consuming the feed).

3. *Sale of Accounts, Chattel Paper, Payment Intangibles, or Promissory Notes.* Former Article 9 applied to *sales* of "accounts" or "chattel paper." Revised Article 9 adds "payment intangibles" or "promissory notes." § 9–109(a)(3) and Comments 4 and 5. See definitions at § 9–102(a)(2), (11), (61), (65). See also § 9–318 (a), which facilitates securitization deals. Securitization consists of isolating a pool of receivables and packaging them into securities that can be traded in the capital markets.

4. *Consignment.* Former Article 9 applied to a consignment intended as security. Former §§ 9–102(2), 1–201(b)(35) ("security interest"), 2–326 ("sale on approval," "sale or return"). Revised Article 9 applies to every "consignment." § 9–109(a)(4) and Comment 6. Caution: study the definition, which excludes small transactions and consumer goods. § 9–102(a)(20) and Comment 14.

The difference between a "true" consignment and a consignment intended as security is stated in 5 Collier, 16th ed., Bankruptcy para. 541.05[1][b] as follows: "In ordinary commercial practice, a consignment is equivalent to a bailment for care or resale, wherein there is no obligation of purchase in the consignee.... Consignments of personal property are, for the most part, governed by [Revised Article 9 of the U.C.C.], which distinguishes between consignments that satisfy the definition in Revised [9–102(a)(20)] and those that do not. Those in the former category are treated as purchase-money security interests; the consignor is a secured creditor and the consignee is the owner. If the consignee is a debtor, its interest in the consigned property will become part of the bankruptcy estate.... The situation is less clear with respect to consignments that do not fall within the U.C.C. definition...."

As to consignments not intended as security, see former § 1–201(37); § 2–326(1)(b), (2), (3)(c) (consignor should file even if a true consignment).

5. *A Security Interest Arising Under Articles 2 (Sales) or 2A (Leases)*. These interests are subject to Article 9. §§ 9–109 (a)(5), 9–110. See, e.g., § 2–505 (shipment under reservation). "[H]owever, until the seller or lessor [buyer–debtor] obtains possession of the goods, the security interest is enforceable even in the absence of a security agreement, filing is not necessary to perfect the security interest, and the secured party's (buyer's or lessee's) rights on the debtor's (seller's or lessor's) default are governed by Article 2...." § 9–110 Comment 3. Example: S ships goods to B "under reservation." S procures a negotiable tangible bill of lading to its own order and, accordingly, reserves a security interest in the goods to secure payment of the purchase price. See §§ 9–110 Comment 5, 1–201(b)(35) and Comment 35 ("security interest" defined).

6. *A Security Interest Arising Under Articles 4 or 5*. For a collecting bank's security interest in items in the collection process and the analogous security interest of an issuer (or nominated person) of a letter of credit, both of which are within Article 9's scope, see §§ 4–210, 5–118 and Comment 1. § 9–109(a)(6).

The following language would indicate in a forthright manner that a transaction creates a security interest:

To secure the full and timely payment of the sums owing to the Secured Party hereunder, and to secure the performance of the Debtor's obligations set forth herein, the Debtor hereby grants to the Secured Party a security interest in the following described property. * * *

Creation of a security interest is not always as clearly signalled as in the above illustration. The following situations give insight.

Leases

Former Article 9 applied to a lease intended as security. Former § 9–102(2). Revised Article 9 applies to a transaction that creates a security interest, regardless of its form or the name the parties have given to it. §§ 9–109(a)(1) and Comment 2, 9–203. Thus, a self-styled "lease" may serve as a security agreement if it creates a security interest. §§ 9–203 Comment 3 (last two sentences), 9–102, Comment 3.b (last paragraph). Significance: Article 9 leases are subject to the Code's filing requirements; true leases are not. Consequently, in a true lease, the lessor will generally prevail over claims to the leased goods by creditors of (or purchasers from) the lessee, without the necessity of filing to put third parties on notice. But see § 2A–309(4) regarding fixture filing. See also § 9–505 (precautionary filing; compliance with other law). [*2010 Amendment.* The parties' subjective intent regarding how the transaction is to be characterized does not affect whether Article 9 applies. § 9–109 Comment 2.]

Whether a transaction in the form of a lease creates a *lease* or *security interest* is determined by the facts of each case. §§ 1–201(b)(35) (last sentence) ("security interest" defined), 1–203(a) (distinguishing leases from security agreements); see § 2A–103(1)(j) and Comment (j) [§ 2A–103(1)(p) (2003)] ("lease" defined). Section 1–203(b) further provides that a transaction in the form of a lease creates a security interest

a.   if the lessee has an obligation to continue paying consideration for the term of the lease,

b.   if the obligation is not terminable by the lessee, and

c.   if one of four additional tests is met:

(1) the original lease term is equal to or greater than the "remaining economic life of the goods" [at the time the transaction is entered into]. § 1–203(b)(1), (e);

(2) the lessee is bound to renew the lease for the "remaining economic life of the goods" or is bound to become the owner of the goods. § 1–203(b)(2), (e);

(3) the lessee has an option to renew the lease for "the remaining economic life of the goods" for no additional consideration or for "nominal additional consideration" upon compliance with the lease agreement. § 1–203(b)(3), (d), (e); or

(4) the lessee has an option to become the owner of the goods for no additional consideration or for "nominal additional consideration" upon compliance with the lease agreement. [Additional consideration is "nominal" if it is less than lessee's "reasonably predictable" cost of performing under the lease agreement if the option is not exercised. "Reasonably predictable" is determined at the time the transaction is entered into]. § 1–203(b)(4),(d),(e).

All of these tests focus on economics, not party intent. § 1–203 Comment 2.

UCC § 1–203(c)(1)–(6) states that a transaction in the form of a lease does *not* create a security interest *merely* because the transaction has certain characteristics listed therein. For example, a fixed-price purchase option in a lease does not of itself create a security interest. § 1–203 Comment 2 (eighth and ninth paragraphs).

Example 1 (option to purchase for nominal additional consideration—security interest created): Seller/Secured Party sold certain goods to Buyer/Debtor on an installment basis, with Seller reserving title to secure payment of the sums owing. (Pre-Code, this was called a conditional sale.) Buyer agreed to pay $60.67 a month for 36 successive monthly installments. ($60.67 times 36 equals $2,184.12.) This is clearly an Article 9 secured transaction. Now suppose the following: Lessor leased certain goods to Lessee. Lessee agreed to lease for 36 successive monthly lease payments of $60.64. ($60.64 times 36 equals $2,183.04.) At the end of 36 months, Lessee had the option to purchase the goods upon payment of $1.08. Because this is nominal additional consideration, the transaction creates a security interest. In sum, this lease is merely a disguised secured installment-sales contract.

Example 2 (option to purchase for additional consideration that is not nominal—lease created): Lessor leased an accounting machine to Lessee for 3 years for $118.00 a month. Lessee had the option to purchase the machine during the three year term at the list price of $4,690.00 less a deposit of $234.00 and subject to a credit of 75% of the monthly payments if purchased during the first year or 70% if purchased thereafter. Regardless of whether the option were exercised at the end of the first year, the second year, or the third, the optionee [Lessee] would have had to pay an amount at least roughly equivalent to the then fair market value of the machine. Held: This is a true lease. In re Alpha Creamery Co., Inc., Bankruptcy No. 29,264–B, 1967 WL 8996 (Bankr.W.D.Mich. June 8, 1967). The court in Alpha Creamery identified these factors as characteristics of a true lease:

(a) Purchase option price that approximates the goods' market value at the time of the exercise of the option.

(b) Rental charges indicating an intention to compensate Lessor for loss of value over the term of the lease due to aging, wear, and obsolescence.

(c) Rentals that are not excessive and an option purchase price that is not too low.

(d) Facts showing that the lessee is acquiring no equity in the leased article during the term of lease.

In this case, the option price was more than nominal, the lessee acquired no equity during the lease term, and the option purchase price at the termination of the lease term was approximately 32% of the list price, indicating that the parties did not intend to create a security interest in the personal property described in the lease.

In applying the economic-realities test, some courts [e.g., *Alpha*] stated that, if the amount the lessee must pay to exercise his option is roughly equal to the fair market value of the asset at that time, the transaction is not a secured sale. This equivalence would indicate that the lessee was not really paying installments on the price, but instead was paying a true rent (a sum for wear and tear plus reasonable profit). But merely adopting the economic realities test does not necessarily resolve all issues.

J. White & R. Summers, Uniform Commercial Code § 30–3 at 20 (5th Practitioner's Ed., 2002) ask,

When does one measure the "economic reality?" Intending a true lease, parties might at the signing select an option price that they believe will equal the fair market value of the property at the end of the lease. Yet actual value at the end of the lease may be substantially higher or lower than their estimate. If the leased goods retain their value longer than expected, the option price should still be tested against the prediction, not the actuality.

Parties make their agreement at the outset. Only there do they have the common intention to create a lease or security agreement, and it is at that time we should determine their true intention. If subsequent events make the option price small in comparison with the asset's value at the end of the lease, so be it. That fact does not change what was once a true lease into a security agreement. The courts have not always been careful to distinguish between the predicted value established at the outset and the actual value. The drafters of the revised section 1–201(37) [§ 1–203] have adopted the approach that the market value agreed to by the parties is to be judged by the standard of the "reasonably predicted" fair market value when the transaction was entered into.

Example 3 (no option to purchase—security interest created): Lessor leased certain equipment to Lessee. The equipment was estimated to have a useful life of three years, after which it would have little or no remaining value. The "lease" required Lessee to pay, during the three years, an amount equivalent to the purchase price (or purchase price less scrap value) and provided that, at the end of the term, Lessor would retake the goods. This transaction creates a secured transaction, not a true lease. Lessee's obligation was not subject to termination by Lessee, and the term was equal to the economic life of the machine. § 1–203(b)(1). See UCC § 2A–103(1)(j) and Comment (j) (paragraphs 3–6) [§ 2A–103(1)(p) (2003)].

Summary: "[T]he key feature that distinguishes leases from [secured installment] sales [is] the lessor's retention of a meaningful residual. . . . In determining whether a purchase option is 'nominal' . . . [t]he correct analysis should be to determine whether, *at the inception of the lease*, the amount of the purchase option is sufficiently small (or nominal) in relation to the anticipated value at the expiration of the term of the lease that the lessee would (or should) be economically compelled to exercise the option. Under these circumstances, the exercise of the option is (or should be) a foregone conclusion and the lease should be characterized as a secured transaction." Bayer, Personal Property Leasing: Article 2A of the Uniform Commercial Code, 43 Bus. Law. 1491 at 1496 (1988) [Emphasis added]. Notably, having the lessee assume incidences of ownership (such as paying insurance) during the lease does not transform the transaction into a sale. See § 1–203(c).

Re: federal tax deductions, local tax or regulations that apply to owners (not lessees), and unexpired leases under Bankruptcy Code § 365, see J. White & R. Summers § 30–3 at 20–24 (4th Practitioner's Ed., 1995).

Subordination Agreements

A subordination agreement has the effect of making one claim junior to another. Such an agreement does not create a security interest unless so intended. § 1–310 (subordinated obligations); see § 9–339 (priority subject to subordination).

Debtor's Covenant Not to Transfer or Encumber Property

Suppose Debtor enters into the following agreement:

Negative Covenant Regarding Encumbrances

The undersigned hereby covenants that, so long as the indebtedness evidenced hereby is outstanding, he will not mortgage, pledge, encumber, grant a security interest in, or assign or transfer by way of security any of his property, real or personal, tangible or intangible, unless the indebtedness evidenced hereby is rateably secured by such mortgage, pledge, encumbrance, security interest, assignment, or transfer.

This agreement probably does not create an Article 9 security interest. § 9–109(a)(1) (scope of Article 9); but see § 9–401(b) and Comment 5 (negative pledge covenant).

Surety's Right of Subrogation

P, a contractor, agrees to build a building for C. Per the agreement, P applies to S, a surety, for a performance bond and in the application *assigns* to S all payments to become due to P under the contract with C. Due to financial difficulties, P is unable to complete the building and S, per the performance bond, assumes responsibility for completion. Accordingly, S pays large sums of money to subcontractors who furnished labor and materials for the building. S claims the monies C would otherwise owe P. Are S's rights within the scope of Article 9? Answer:

If S claims "the balance due under the contract by virtue of the assignment to it in the contractor's [P's] bond application, it would be fairly arguable that it was claiming a security interest in a contract right [under the 1962 Code or an "account" or "general intangible" under the 1972 Code. But] [t]he surety makes an alternative claim, not resting on the assignment to it by the contractor, that it is subrogated to the rights of the contractor for the contract balance ... [e.g., C], and to the rights of the subcontractors it paid.... Of basic importance is the general rule of [UCC] Section 9–102(2) that Article 9 "applies to security interests *created by contract.*" * * * Rights of subrogation, although growing out of a contractual setting and ofttimes articulated by the contract, do not depend for their existence on a grant in the contract, but are created by law to avoid injustice. Therefore, subrogation rights are not "security interests" within the meaning of Article 9.

[Canter v. Schlager, 358 Mass. 789, 267 N.E.2d 492, at 499 (1971)].

The result should be the same under Revised § 9–109(a)(1).

B.   TRANSACTIONS EXCLUDED FROM ARTICLE 9

1.   **Extent to which Article 9 does not apply.** Article 9 does not apply *to the extent* federal law preempts it. § 9–109(c)(1) and Comment 8. See, e.g., Federal Aviation Act, Ship Mortgage Act, and Federal Copyright Act. Former § 9–104 Comment 1. Re: certain governmental debtors, see § 9–109(c) (2) and (3) and Comment 9; re: rights of certain persons under a letter of credit, see § 9–109(c)(4).

2.   **Inapplicability of Article 9.** Article 9 does not apply to the following:

(a) *Nonconsensual liens.* Landlord's liens and liens for services or materials (other than agricultural liens). § 9–109(d)(1) and (2). (With few exceptions, Article 9 applies to *consensual* security interests. § 9–109 Comment 10.)

(b) *Wage and Similar Claims.* See § 9–109(d)(3) and Comment 11.

(c) *Certain Sales and Assignments of Receivables.* E.g., a sale of accounts, chattel paper, payment intangibles, or promissory notes as part of the sale of a business out of which they arose. § 9–109(d)(4)–(7) and Comment 12. By their nature, these sales and assignments do not concern commercial financing transactions. Id.

(d) *Assignments of Judgments.* Such judgments are excluded (other than judgments on a payment right that itself was Article 9 collateral). § 9–109(d)(9) and Comment 12.

(e) *Insurance.* Interests in insurance policies are excluded, but assignments of "health-care insurance receivables" by or to a health-care provider are covered by Article 9. §§ 9–109(d)(8) and Comment 13, 9–102 (a)(46).

(f) *Set-off.* Section 9–109(d)(10) adds two exceptions to the general exclusion of set-off rights (i.e., "banker's lien") from Article 9.

(g) *Interests in Real Property.* Section 9–109(d)(11) excludes leases and most other interests in, or liens on, real property. This exclusion generally reiterates the limitation made explicit in § 9–109(a)(1) ("personal property and fixtures"). § 9–109 Comment 10.

(h) *Tort Claims.* Section 9–109(d)(12) narrows the broad exclusion of transferred tort claims under former § 9–104(k). Article 9 now applies to assignments of "commercial tort claims" (§ 9–102(a)(13)) as well as security interests in tort claims that constitute proceeds of other collateral. § 9–109 Comment 15.

(i) *Deposit Accounts.* Under former § 9–104(*l*), deposit accounts were excluded as original collateral. Under § 9–109(d)(13), a deposit account (§ 9–102(a)(29)) may be taken as original collateral under Article 9, but an *assignment* of a deposit account in a consumer transaction is excluded.

C. STATUTES NOT AFFECTED BY ARTICLE 9

A transaction subject to Article 9 is subject to applicable consumer laws and other law (e.g., Uniform Consumer Credit Code, local statutes regulating small loans, retail installment sales, and the like). § 9–201(b)–(d).

3. REQUISITES TO AN ENFORCEABLE SECURITY INTEREST

A security interest *attaches* when it becomes enforceable against the debtor with respect to the collateral (unless an agreement expressly postpones the time of attachment). Three basic prerequisites to the existence of a security interest are

a.   the existence of an appropriate agreement;

b.   the fact that value has been given; and

c.   the fact that the debtor has rights in the collateral (or the power to transfer rights in the collateral to a secured party). § 9–203(a), (b) and Comment 2. [But this rule is subject to § 9–203(c) (security interest of a collecting bank or a letter-of-credit issuer; security interest arising under Article 2 or 2A; security interest arising in the purchase of a financial asset).] See also § 9–203(d)–(i) and Comments 6–10.

Discussion of these three prerequisites follows.

A.   REQUISITE OF AN AGREEMENT

(1) Formal Requisites of a Security Agreement

A security interest cannot attach until there is an agreement that it attach. § 9–203(a), (b)(3). For a security agreement to exist, the following formal requisites must be satisfied:

1.   Debtor must "authenticate" it. § 9–203(b)(3)(A) and Comment 3. "Authentication" can involve not only a signature on a writing, but also an electronic transmission. § 9–102(a)(7) ("authenticate"), (69) ("record") and Comment 9. [*2010 Amendment.* The definition of "authenticate" is modified to conform to the definition of "sign" in §§ 1–201(b)(27) and 7–102(a)(11).]

2.   It must create or provide for a security interest. §§ 9–203(b)(3)(A), 9–102(a)(73) ("security agreement" defined), 1–201(b)(35) ("security interest" defined); see § 1–201(b)(3) ("agreement" defined). Example: "Debtor hereby grants to Secured Party a security interest in the following goods. . . ."

3. It must provide a description of the collateral and, if the security interest covers timber to be cut, a description of the land concerned. A description of personal or real property is sufficient, whether or not it is specific, if it reasonably identifies what is described. §§ 9–203(b)(3)(A), 9–108(a) and Comment 2. For examples of reasonable identification, see § 9–108(b) (e.g., specific listing, category, collateral type as defined in the UCC (with exceptions), quantity, allocational formula, etc., if the identity of the collateral is objectively determinable). Note that a super-generic description is not sufficient (e.g., "all the debtor's assets"), § 9–108(c). In addition, certain descriptions by type are inadequate (e.g., "commercial tort claim," in a consumer goods transaction). § 9–108(e).

Note: Under § 9–203(b)(3), enforceability requires compliance with an evidentiary requirement in the nature of a Statute of Frauds. However, a debtor may show by parol evidence that a debt purporting to be absolute was in fact for security. Similarly, a "lease" may serve as a security agreement if it creates a security interest. §§ 9–203 Comment 3, 1–201(b)(35).

(2) Possession, Delivery, or Control of Collateral Pursuant to Security Agreement

Section 9–203(b)(3)(B)–(D) dispenses with the requirement of an authenticated security agreement and provides alternative evidentiary tests:

1. When collateral is in Secured Party's *possession* pursuant to Debtor's security agreement. Here, Secured Party's possession substitutes for Debtor's authentication under § 9–203(b)(3)(A). § 9–203(b)(3)(B).

2. When the collateral is a certificated security in registered form and the security is *delivered* to Secured Party (i.e., Secured Party acquires possession of the certificate per § 8–301(a)(1)) pursuant to Debtor's security agreement. Here, delivery to Secured Party is sufficient to

substitute for an authenticated security agreement. §§ 9–203(b)(3)(C), 8–301, 8–102(a)(4) and (13).

3.   When the collateral is deposit accounts, electronic chattel paper, investment property, letter-of-credit rights, or electronic documents, and Secured Party has *control* pursuant to the debtor's security agreement. Here, "control" satisfies the evidentiary test. § 9–203(b)(3)(D); see § 9–102(a) (29), (30), (31), (49), (51) (defining the enumerated types of collateral). For "control," see §§ 7–106, 9–104 through 9–107. For example, § 8–106 Comment 1 states,

> Obtaining "control" means that the purchaser [e.g., secured party] has taken whatever steps are necessary . . . to place itself in a position where it can have the securities sold, without further action by the owner.

The purpose of Article 9's evidentiary requirement is to ensure that Debtor's conduct corroborates Secured Party's testimony that there is a security transaction, to guard against perjury. Appropriate corroboration can be found in the following conduct by Debtor: (i) authenticating a security agreement, (ii) giving possession of the collateral to the secured party, or (iii) allowing Secured Party to "control" the collateral. Another evidentiary purpose is "to minimize the possibility of future disputes as to the terms of a security agreement (e.g., as to the property that stands as collateral for the obligation secured)." § 9–203 Comment 5.

(3) Terms of Security Agreement

The above formal requisites of a security agreement are the minimum requirements. A security agreement will usually contain many other terms addressing such matters as (a) the amount of the indebtedness and terms of payment, (b) risk of loss or damage to the collateral, (c) insurance on the collateral, (d) maintenance and repair of the collateral, (e) debtor's warranty of ownership of the collateral free from liens or security interests, (f) debtor's rights (if any) as to moving the collateral to another location, and (g) events that constitute default by debtor. Examples of security agreements with such terms may be found in Volumes 14, 14A, and 14B West's Legal Forms. (5th ed. 2009).

Effectiveness of terms

Except as otherwise provided by the UCC, a security agreement is *effective* according to its terms (1) between the parties, (2) against purchasers of the collateral, and (3) against creditors. § 9–201(a). Thus, the Code embraces freedom of contract. § 1–302(a) and Comment 1. But see § 9–602 and Comment 2 regarding the procedure to be followed upon the debtor's default.

Some terms that may be included in a security agreement will be given only *limited effect*. Examples: option to accelerate (§ 1–309); after-acquired-property clause (§ 9–204); retention-of-title term (§§ 9–202, 1–201(b)(35)); waiver-of-defense clause (§ 9–403); in installment-purchase agreements (both a sale and a security transaction), warranty disclaimers and limitation or modification of seller's warranties and buyer's remedies (§§ 2–312, 2–316, 2–718, 2–719, see § 2–302); and parties' power to choose applicable law (§ 1–301).

Some terms are *ineffective* if included in a security agreement. Examples: term relieving a party from the obligations of good faith, diligence, reasonableness, or care (§ 1–302(b), see § 9–207(a)); term prohibiting transfer of debtor's rights in collateral (§ 9–401); unconscionable terms in an installment sale (or security transaction, by analogy?) (§ 2–302); term varying Article 9 priority rules (§§ 1–302 Comment 1 (first paragraph, last sentence), 9–201 Comments); and terms waiving or varying certain rights and duties upon default. (§ 9–602). Other terms may be ineffective pursuant to non-Code law, e.g., usury laws, small loan acts, retail installment sales acts, Uniform Consumer Credit Code, etc. § 9–201(b)–(d). See FTC Credit Practices Rules, 16 CFR Part 444.

Two clauses merit separate discussion—the after-acquired-property clause and the future-advance clause.

After-acquired-property clause

"[A] security agreement may create or provide for a security interest in after-acquired collateral." § 9–204(a). Example:

> The secured party's security interest under this agreement extends to all collateral of the kind that is the subject of this agreement that the debtor may acquire at any time during the continuation of this agreement in connection with the operation of the debtor's business.

However, no security interest attaches under an after-acquired-property clause (i) to consumer goods, other than an accession when given as additional security, unless the debtor acquires rights in them within 10 days after the secured party gives value; or (ii) to a commercial tort claim. §§ 9–204(b), 9–102(a)(1) and (13) ("accession" and "commercial tort claim" defined). See 16 CFR § 444.2(a)(4).

The nineteenth-century prejudice against the "mortgage on after-acquired property" was based on a feeling, often inarticulate in courts' opinions, that a borrower should not be allowed to encumber all of his or her present and future assets, and that for the protection not only of the borrower, but also of other creditors, a cushion of free assets should be preserved. Although the Code rejects this view, it does limit the attachment of a security interest in the case of consumer goods, for similar policy reasons. Former § 9–204 Comments 2 and 4. See Uniform Consumer Credit Code §§ 3.301, 3.302, 3.303 (1974) re: cross-collateral.

Future-advance clause

"A security agreement may provide that collateral secures ... future advances ... whether or not the advances are given pursuant to commitment." §§ 9–204(c), 9–102(a)(68) ("pursuant to commitment" defined).

Example:

> The security interest herein created shall also secure all other indebtedness, obligations, and liabilities of the debtor to the secured party, now existing and hereafter arising, including future advances, howsoever evidenced or created, actual, direct, contingent, or otherwise.

At common law and under chattel mortgage statutes, there seems to have been a vaguely articulated prejudice against future-advance agreements comparable to the prejudice against after-acquired-property interests. Under the Code, by contrast, collateral may secure future advances. Former § 9–204 Comment 5.

Recognition of the validity of the security interest on after-acquired property and the security interest for future advances facilitates the financing of inventory and accounts receivable where the collateral turns over (e.g., shifting stock). A secured party thus may make present and future advances to Debtor, secured by both present and after-acquired inventory or accounts (or both). This results in a "floating lien." Such a lien is useful when Debtor's inventory turns over frequently. Former § 9–204 Comment 2.

(4) Effect of Debtor's Use or Disposition of Collateral Without Accounting to Secured Party

Assume a dealer in goods gives a security interest in accounts (arising from sales of goods) to Secured Party. Dealer collects the accounts and uses the monies to purchase more goods from Manufacturer to replace the goods Dealer has sold. Is Debtor's (Dealer's) use or disposition of the collateral (accounts) without accounting to Secured Party fraudulent? Answer:

"[Section 9–205] provides that a security interest is not invalid or fraudulent by reason of the debtor's liberty to dispose of the collateral without being required to account to the secured party for proceeds or substitute new collateral.... [T]his section repeals the rule of Benedict v. Ratner ... and other cases which held such arrangements void as a matter of law because the debtor was given unfettered dominion or control over collateral." § 9–205 Comment 2.

B. REQUISITE THAT VALUE BE GIVEN

A security interest cannot attach until the secured party gives *value*. § 9–203(b)(1). "Value" is any consideration sufficient to support a simple contract, including the taking of property in satisfaction of, or as security for, a pre-existing claim. § 1–204 and Comment 1.

Example 1: Pursuant to a security agreement wherein Debtor gives Secured Party a security interest in certain collateral, Secured Party (1) loans Debtor money, or (2) commits itself to loan Debtor money. Value is given when Secured Party loans or agrees to loan the funds. § 1–204(1), (4) ("value" defined).

Example 2: Pursuant to a security agreement (or conditional sales contract), Secured Party sells or agrees to sell certain goods to Debtor on an installment basis and reserves a security interest in the goods to secure the balance of the purchase price. Value is given when Secured Party sells or agrees to sell the goods. § 1–204(1), (4).

Example 3: Debtor owes Creditor a sum of money on an unsecured basis. Debtor and Creditor enter into a security agreement wherein Debtor gives Creditor a security interest in certain goods to secure repayment of the pre-existing unsecured claim. Taking property as security for a pre-existing claim constitutes value. § 1–204(2).

C. REQUISITE THAT DEBTOR HAVE RIGHTS IN THE COLLATERAL

A security interest cannot attach until the debtor has rights in the collateral (or the power to transfer rights in the collateral to a secured party). § 9–203(b)(2).

Example 1: D *owns* certain goods and wishes to borrow from C. Even prior to giving C a security interest in the goods, D has rights in the collateral. D *owns* the collateral.

Example 2: Buyer D goes to seller C's store and selects certain goods D wishes to purchase pursuant to a conditional sales contract (security agreement). When the contract is signed binding both D and C, D has rights in the collateral. Why? Identification of particular goods as goods to which the sales contract refers gives D a special property and an insurable interest in the goods. § 2–501(1). If the goods are not identified at the time of entering into the contract, D has no interest in any particular goods until they are subsequently identified to the contract per § 2–501.

Example 3: X sells goods to D and takes a currently dated check as payment. The check is dishonored due to insufficient funds. Meanwhile, D pledges the goods to SP. Will X recover the goods from SP? Answer: D has voidable title to the goods and has the *power* to transfer good title to a good-faith *purchaser* for value. "Purchaser" includes a secured party. §§ 2–403(1)(b), 1–201(b)(29) and (30); see §§ 2–507(2) (buyer's rights to retain goods conditioned on payment), 2–511(3) (conditional payment by check), 9–102(a)(72) ("secured party" defined). [See § 2–507(3) (2003).]

4.   REQUISITES TO PROTECTION OF SECURED
PARTY AGAINST THIRD-PARTY CLAIMS—
PERFECTION OF A SECURITY INTEREST

A.   HOW AND WHEN A SECURITY INTEREST IS PER-FECTED AND EFFECT OF PERFECTION

A security interest or agricultural lien is perfected if it has attached *and* all of the applicable requirements for perfection have been satisfied. §§ 9–308(a), 9–203(a) and (b). A list of possible methods of perfection follows.

1.   Perfection can be accomplished by filing a financing statement pursuant to § 9–501 et seq. § 9–310(a). Policy: to give public notice of the security interest or agricultural lien.

2.   Perfection can be accomplished by filing or registration pursuant to certain statutes, regulations, and treaties. § 9–310(b)(3). Examples:

(a) Federal statutes, regulations, and treaties providing for registration or filing, e.g., aircraft. §§ 9–310(b)(3), 9–311(a)(1) and Comment 2 (Filing under Article 9 is not an alternative).

(b) State certificate-of-title statutes for, e.g., motor vehicles, which provide for a security interest to be indicated on the certificate. §§ 9–311(a)(2) and (3) and Comment 3, 9–102(a)(10) ("certificate of title" defined). As to inventory, see § 9–311(d) and Comment 4. [*2010 Amendment.* The amended definition of "certificate of title" includes language covering electronic records where such records are permitted by the relevant governmental unit as an alternative to a certificate of title. § 9–102(a)(10).]

3.   Placing certain collateral (e.g., goods) in the secured party's possession accomplishes perfection. §§ 9–310 (b)(6), 9–313; see §§ 9–310(b)(4) (goods in possession of bailee), 9–310(b)(7) (certificated security perfected by delivery). Policy: The fact that Debtor is not in possession

puts third parties dealing with him or her on notice that Debtor's interest may be encumbered.

4. A security interest in certain collateral (e.g., deposit accounts) can be perfected by the secured party's "control." §§ 9–310(b)(8), 9–314(a); see § 8–106 Comment 1. Simply: Control is analogous to possession, for intangible property.

5. A security interest in some collateral is perfected when it attaches (automatic perfection), e.g., a purchase-money security interest in consumer goods. §§ 9–310(b)(2), 9–309, 9–203 (a) and (b) ("attachment" and enforceability); see § 9–310(b)(5) (temporary perfection).

As to perfection of agricultural liens, see § 9–308(b); see also, § 9–308(d)-(g). As to continuous perfection, see § 9–308(c).

Filing or possession prior to attachment

"If the steps for perfection have been taken in advance, as when the secured party files a financing statement before giving value or before the debtor acquires rights in the collateral, then the security interest is perfected when it attaches." § 9–308(a) (second sentence) and Comment 2 (source of quote). Example: D wishes to borrow money from C and gives C a security interest in goods D owns. C files a financing statement, then C and D sign a security agreement that commits C to loan to D. The security interest is perfected, not when the financing statement is filed, but when the security agreement is signed. See § 9–502(d).

Effect of perfection

"A perfected security interest may still be or become subordinate to other interests.... However, in general, after perfection the secured party is protected against creditors and transferees of the debtor and, in particular, against any representative of creditors in insolvency proceedings [e.g., trustee in bankruptcy] instituted by or against the debtor." § 9–308 Comment 2. See priorities discussed at Part Five, C, 5 infra.

B. PERFECTION BY FILING

(1) Types of Collateral Perfected by Filing

Most types of collateral either may or must be perfected by filing under Article 9: goods (including fixtures), chattel paper, negotiable documents, instruments, investment property, accounts, and general intangibles. §§ 9–310(a), 9–312(a) and (d). However, security interests in "deposit accounts" and "letter-of-credit rights" may be perfected only by "control"; and a security interest in "money" may be perfected only by the secured party's taking possession. § 9–312(b).

(2) What Is Filed—A Financing Statement

Contents of financing statement

A financing statement is sufficient only if it (i) provides the name of the debtor, (ii) provides the name of the secured party or its representative, and (iii) indicates the collateral covered by the financing statement. § 9–502(a).

Sufficiency of Debtor's name. If Debtor is a "registered organization" (corporation, limited partnership, or limited liability company), then Debtor's name is the name shown on the public record of Debtor's "jurisdiction of organization." §§ 9–503(a)(1), 9–102(a)(50) and (70) ("jurisdiction of organization" and "registered organization" defined). (Section 9–503(a)(2) and (3) contains special rules for decedent's estates and common-law trusts.)

In other cases, if Debtor has a name, the financing statement is sufficient only if it provides Debtor's individual or organizational name. Debtor's name is not rendered ineffective by the absence of a trade name. Conversely, a financing statement that provides *only* Debtor's trade name is not sufficient. § 9–503(a)(4)(A), (b)(1), (c). Example: Edmund Carroll d/b/a Kozy Kitchen. "Trade names are deemed to be too uncertain and too likely not to be known to the secured party or person searching the record, to form the basis for a filing system." Former § 9–402 Comment 7. If Debtor does not have a name, see § 9–503(a)(4)(B).

"The requirement that a financing statement provide the debtor's name is particularly important. Financing statements are indexed under the name of the debtor, and those who wish to find financing statements search for them under the debtor's name." § 9–503 Comment 2.

[*2010 Amendment*. Sufficiency of debtor's name–A financing statement sufficiently provides the name of the debtor as follows:

1. *Individuals*. Article 9 provides alternative approaches toward the requirement for providing the name of an individual debtor.

Alternative A. For individual debtors holding an unexpired driver's license issued by the State where the financing statement is filed (ordinarily the State where the debtor maintains the debtor's principal residence), the financing statement sufficiently provides the name of the debtor, *only if* it provides the name indicated on the license. (The "only if" rule.) § 9–503(a)(4) and Comment 2.d. As to multiple driver's licenses, see § 503(g). (Note: when a debtor does not hold an unexpired driver's license issued by the relevant State, the requirement can be satisfied in either of two ways: If the financing statement provides (i) the "individual name" of the debtor (cf. current § 9–503(a)(4)(A)), or (ii) if it provides the debtor's surname (family name) and first personal name (first name other than the surname). § 9–503(a)(5) and Comment 2.d.

Alternative B. This alternative provides three ways in which a financing statement may sufficiently provide the name of an individual debtor: (i) if it provides the "Individual name" of the debtor (cf. current § 9–503(a)(4)(A)); (ii) if it provides the surname and first personal name of the debtor; (iii) if the individual holds an unexpired driver's license issued by the State where the financing statement is filed (ordinarily the State of the debtor's principal residence), the name indicated on the driver's license. (The "safe harbor" approach.) § 9–503(a)(4)(A)-(C) and Comment 2.d; see § 9–503(e) and (g).

Rationale. "The rationale for choosing the driver's license name as the name of the debtor . . . is that in most cases an individual debtor holds a driver's license that is offered as a form of identification when the debtor seeks to obtain secured financing." E. Smith, A Summary of the 2010 Amendments to Article 9, 42 UCC L.J. 345 at 353 (2010). "[D]etermination of a debtor's name . . . must take into account the needs of both filers and searchers. Filers need a simple and predictable system in which they can have a reasonable degree of confidence that, without undue burden, they can determine a name that will be sufficient so as to permit their financing statements to be effective. Likewise, searchers need a simple and predictable system in which they can have a reasonable degree of confidence that, without undue burden, they will discover all financing statements pertaining to the debtor in question." § 9–503 Comment 2.d. (para.12).

2. *Name of Registered Organizations*. As a general matter, if the debtor is a "registered organization" (corporations, limited partnerships, limited liability companies, and statutory trusts) per § 9–102(a)(71), then the debtor's name is the name shown on the "public organic record" of the debtor's "jurisdiction of organization," that is, the jurisdiction under whose law the organization is organized. §§ 9–503(a)(1), 9–102(a)(50) and Comment 2.a.

See § 9–503(h). In most cases a "public organic record" means a record that is available to the public for inspection and that is a record filed with the State to form or organize the registered organization.§ 9–102(a)(68) and Comment 11 (6th para.); see § 1–201(b)(25) and (27).

3. *Name of Debtor When Collateral is Held in Trust.* When collateral is held in a trust that is not a registered organization, see §§ 9–503(a)(3) and Comment 2.b, 9–503(h).

4. *Name of Debtor When Collateral is Administered by a Personal Representative.* See §§ 9–503(a)(2) and Comment 2.c, 9–503(f).

5. *Name of Debtor in Other Cases.* If the debtor is an organization, then the name is its organization name. §§ 9–503(a)(6)(A), 1–201(b)(25) and (27) ("organization" defined). If the debtor does not have a name, see § 9–503(a)(6)(B).

Note: A financing statement that provides the name of the debtor per § 9–503(a) is not rendered ineffective, e.g., by the absence of a trade name or other name of the debtor. § 9–503(b). See § 9–503(c) (Debtor's trade name insufficient) and (e) (Multiple debtor's) and Comment 4. For a draft of financing statement form, see § 9–521.]

Secured party's name. See § 9–503(d) and (e) and Comments 3 and 4.

Indication of collateral. A financing statement sufficiently indicates the collateral that it covers if it provides (1) a description pursuant to § 9–108 (e.g., specific listing, category, type of collateral as defined under the Code (with exceptions), quantity, allocational formula, etc., if the identity of the collateral is objectively determinable); or (2) an indication that it covers all assets or all personal property. § 9–504. Note: a supergeneric description is sufficient for a financing statement, but not a security agreement. §§ 9–108(c), 9–203(b)(3), 9–504(2) and Comment 2. As to after-acquired property and future advances, see §§ 9–204 Comment 7, 9–502 Comment 2.

Deletion of provisions of former § 9–402(1). Section 9–502(a) does not require the debtor's signature. (Of course, the filing must be authorized.) §§ 9–502 Comment 3, 9–509, 9–510, see § 9–511. Other provisions of former § 9–402(1) are deleted (real-property description for financing statements covering crops, adequacy of copies of financing statements, and copy of security agreement as financing statement). Note that the filing office must reject a financing statement lacking other information formerly required as a condition of perfection (e.g., an address for debtor, secured party). §§ 9–502 Comment 4, 9–516(b)(4) and (5), 9–520 (a) and (c).

Counseling points: (1) Include the mailing address for the secured party and debtor and other information per § 9–516(b)(4) and (5) in the financing statement. (2) Use Uniform Form of Written Financing Statement at § 9–521(a) ("Safe Harbor Form"; filing office normally may not refuse to accept this form). § 9–521 Comment 2.

Real-Property-Related filings

As to fixture filings, financing statements covering timber to be cut, and as-extracted collateral, see § 9–502(b) and Comment 5.

Record of mortgage as a financing statement

See § 9–502(c) and Comment 6.

Filing for consignments, leases, etc.

See § 9–505 and Comments.

Errors or omissions in financing statement

A financing statement substantially satisfying the filing requirements is effective even if it has minor errors or omissions unless they are seriously misleading. § 9–

506(a). Concerning the effectiveness of financing statements in which the debtor's name is incorrect, the *general rule* is that "a financing statement that fails sufficiently to provide the name of the debtor in accordance with Section 9–503(a) is seriously misleading." § 9–506(b) and Comment 2 (source of quote). For example, § 9–503(a)(1) provides that, if Debtor is a "registered organization" (e.g., corporation), then Debtor's name is the name shown on the public record of Debtor's jurisdiction of organization. *Exception*: If the financing statement nevertheless would be discovered in a search under the debtor's correct name using the filing office's standard search logic, the incorrect name does not make the financing statement seriously misleading. §§ 9–503(a), 9–506 and Comment 2. Illustration: "Hanson," "Hansen," "Hanssen."

Post-filing changes

This section deals with situations in which information becomes inaccurate after the financing statement is filed.

Post-filing disposition of collateral. "[A] financing statement remains effective even if the collateral is sold or otherwise disposed of." § 9–507(a) and Comment 3 (source of quote) and Example; see § 9–508(c).

Other post-filing changes. "[A]s a general matter, post-filing changes that render a financing statement inaccurate and seriously misleading have no effect on a financing statement. The financing statement remains effective." § 9–507(b) and Comment 4 (source of quote). Two exceptions:

1. *Changes in debtor's name.* This addresses a "pure" change in Debtor's name, i.e., a change that does not implicate a new debtor (e.g., partnership named Jupiter changes its name to Zeus—see UCC Hornbook § 23–14). § 9–507(c). Here, "[i]f a name change renders a filed financing statement seriously misleading, . . . [it] is effec-

tive only to perfect a security interest in collateral acquired ... within four months after the change...." § 9–507 Comment 4.

2. *When financing statement is effective against a new debtor.* Section 9–508 addresses the effectiveness of a financing statement filed against an "original debtor" when a "new debtor" becomes bound by the "original debtor's" security agreement (e.g., an individual debtor who operates a business as a sole proprietorship and then incorporates it, or an original debtor who is a corporation that is merged into another corporation). § 9–102(a) (56), (60) ("new debtor" and "original debtor" defined); see § 9–508 Comments 2 and 3. Comment 4 states,

[Section 9–508 (a)] provides that a filing against the original debtor generally is effective to perfect a security interest in collateral that a new debtor has at the time it becomes bound by the original debtor's security agreement and collateral that it acquires after the new debtor becomes bound. Under subsection (b), however, if the filing against the original debtor is seriously misleading as to the new debtor's name, the filing is effective as to collateral acquired by the new debtor more than four months after the new debtor becomes bound only if a person files during the four-month period an initial financing statement providing the name of the new debtor. Compare Section 9–507(c) (four-month period of effectiveness with respect to collateral acquired by a debtor after the debtor changes its name)....

Illustration: Raymond B. Brooks d/b/a Carpet Castle incorporates the proprietorship as Carpet Castle, Inc.

(3) When a Financing Statement May Be Filed

"A financing statement may be filed before a security agreement is made or a security interest otherwise attaches." § 9–502(d), see § 9–308(a). This rule is a manifestation of the "notice filing" concept. Comment 2 to § 9–502 states,

> This section adopts the system of "notice filing." What is required to be filed is not, as under pre-UCC chattel mortgage and conditional sales acts, the security agreement itself, but only a simple record providing a limited amount of information (financing statement). The financing statement may be filed before the security interest attaches or thereafter. . . .
>
> The notice itself indicates merely that a person may have a security interest in the collateral indicated. Further inquiry from the parties concerned will be necessary to disclose the complete state of affairs. . . .
>
> Notice filing has proved to be of great use in financing transactions involving inventory, accounts, and chattel paper, because it obviates the necessity of refiling on each of a series of transactions in a continuing arrangement under which the collateral changes from day to day. However, even in the case of filings that do not necessarily involve a series of transactions (e.g., a loan secured by a single item of equipment), a financing statement is effective to encompass transactions under a security agreement not in existence and not contemplated at the time the notice was filed, if the indication of collateral in the financing statement is sufficient to cover the collateral concerned. Similarly, a financing statement is effective to cover after-acquired property of the type indicated and to perfect with respect to future advances under security agreements, regardless of whether after-acquired property or future advances are mentioned in the financing statement and even if not in the contemplation of the parties at the time the financing statement was authorized to be filed.

Remember: Filing before a security interest attaches does not constitute perfection. In such an instance, perfection occurs when the security interest attaches. § 9–308(a).

(4) Place of Filing

Introduction: pre-Code filing or recording

Comment 1 to former § 9–401 states,

Under chattel mortgage acts, the Uniform Conditional Sales Act, and other conditional sales legislation, the geographical unit for filing or recording was local: the county or township in which the mortgagor or vendee resided or in which the goods sold or mortgaged were kept. The Uniform Trust Receipts Act used the state as the geographical filing unit: under that Act statements of trust receipt financing were filed with an official in the state capital and were not filed locally. The statewide filing system of the Trust Receipts Act has been followed in many accounts receivable and factor's lien acts.

Both systems have their advocates and both their own advantages and drawbacks. The principal advantage of statewide filing is ease of access to the credit information which the files exist to provide. Consider for example the national distributor who wishes to have current information about the credit standing of the thousands of persons he sells to on credit. The more completely the files are centralized on a statewide basis, the easier and cheaper it becomes to procure credit information; the more the files are scattered in local filing units, the more burdensome and costly. On the other hand, it can be said that most credit inquiries about local businesses, farmers and consumers come from local sources; convenience is served by having the files locally available and there is no great advantage in centralized filing.

Filing pursuant to Article 9 of the Code

Former § 9–401(1) afforded each State three alternative approaches depending on the extent to which the State desired central filing (usually with the Secretary of State), local filing (usually with a county office), or both. For example, former § 9–401(1) (Second Alternative) required local filing with respect to farm-related collateral and consumer goods; filings for land-related collateral (e.g., fixtures) took place in the office where a mortgage on the real estate would be filed or recorded. All other cases (e.g., inventory, nonfarm equipment, most accounts) called for filing in the Secretary of State's office.

"Any benefit that local filing may have had in the 1950s is now insubstantial. Accordingly, ... [revised Article 9] dictates central filing for most situations, while retaining local filing for real-estate-related collateral and special filing provisions for transmitting utilities." § 9–501 Comment 2. Thus, § 9–501(a) indicates where *in a given State* a financing statement is to be filed:

1.   Local filing in real-property-mortgage office: (i) "as-extracted collateral" (minerals); (ii) timber to be cut; and (iii) fixtures. § 9–501(a) and Comments 3 and 4; § 9–102(a)(6), (40), (41) ("as-extracted collateral," "fixture filing," and "fixtures" defined).

2.   Central filing (normally in the Secretary of State's office) in all other cases. § 9–501(a)(2).

3.   Special filing provisions for transmitting utilities (e.g., railroad or electric company). See §§ 9–501(b), 9–102(a)(80) ("transmitting utility" defined).

Note: Former § 9–401(2) and (3) (filing in improper place(s), effect of change in debtor's place of business or location of collateral) has been omitted. These subsections dealt primarily with local filing situations. Under Revised Article 9, most filings will occur centrally.

Law governing perfection by filing

In what State does a secured party file? Answer: Under Section 9–301(1), the law governing perfection by filing of security interests in both tangible and intangible collateral is the law of the jurisdiction of the *debtor's location*, as determined under § 9–307. § 9–301 Comment 4. This general rule is subject to several exceptions. See § 9–301 Comment 5.a.–d.

Under former § 9–103(1)(b), perfection (e.g., filing) of a security interest in "ordinary goods" was governed by the law of the jurisdiction where the *collateral* was located. There were several exceptions. For example, for most accounts, the jurisdiction in which the *debtor* was located governed. Former § 9–103(3)(b). See Part Five, C, 6 infra.

Filing or registration pursuant to certain statutes, regulations, and treaties

Filing a financing statement is not necessary or effective to perfect a security interest in property subject to

1.   Federal statutes, regulations, and treaties that provide for registration or filing, e.g., civil aircraft. §§ 9–310(b)(3), 9–311(a)(1) and Comment 2 (filing under Article 9 is not a permissible alternative); or

2.   State certificate-of-title statutes covering, e.g., motor vehicles, and providing for a security interest to be indicated on the certificate. §§ 9–311(a)(2) and (3) and Comment 3, 9–102(a)(10) ("certificate of title" defined). As to inventory, see § 9–311(d) and Comment 4 (governed by the normal perfection rules). [*2010 Amendment.* The amended definition of "certificate of title" includes language covering electronic records where such records are permitted by the relevant governmental unit as an alternative to a certificate of title. § 9–102(a)(10).]

Note: Insofar as priority is concerned, compliance with the requirements of a statute, regulation, or treaty described in § 9–311(a) is equivalent to filing a financing statement under Article 9. § 9–311(b).

(5) Filing Fees

See § 9–525.

(6) What Constitutes Filing

Communication of a record to a filing office and tender of the filing fee, or *acceptance* of the record by the filing office *constitutes filing*. §§ 9–516(a), 9–102(a)(18) and (69) ("communicate" and "record" defined). Former § 9–403(1) used the word *presentation* and explained in the Comment, "Prior law was not always clear whether a mortgage filed for record gave constructive notice from the time of presentation to the filing officer or only from the time of indexing. Subsection (1) adopts ... [the time of presentation]."

Rightful rejection. However, *filing* does *not* occur when a filing office refuses to accept a record for any of the reasons enumerated in § 9–516(b). See § 9–516(c). This is an exclusive list of grounds upon which the filing office may reject a record. § 9–516 Comment 3. Examples of grounds: an initial financing statement does not (i) provide Debtor's name, (ii) provide a mailing address for the debtor or secured party of record, or (iii) indicate whether the debtor is an individual or an organization. Other grounds: (i) unauthorized communication of the record, and (ii) applicable filing fee not tendered. [*2010 Amendment*. A filing office will not be permitted to reject a financing statement that fails to provide the type of organization of the debtor, the jurisdiction of organization of the debtor, or organizational identification number of the debtor, or a statement that the debtor has none. § 9–516(b)(4) and (5).]

Wrongful rejection. If the filing office refuses to accept a record for any reason other than one set forth in § 9–516(b) (discussed immediately above), the record is *effective* as if accepted, *except* as against a purchaser of the collateral who gives value in reasonable reliance upon the absence of the record from the files. § 9–516(d) and Comment 3; § 1–201(b)(29), (30) ("purchase" and "purchaser" defined); § 9–102 (a) (69)("record" defined). Example: "State A filing office may not reject . . . an initial financing statement indicating that the debtor is a State A corporation and providing a three-digit organizational identification number, even if all State A organizational identification numbers contain at least five digits and two letters." § 9–516 Comment 3.

Safe harbor rule. "A filing office that accepts written records may not refuse to accept a written initial financing statement [in the form and format set forth at § 9–521] except for a reason set forth in Section 9–516(b)." § 9–521(a).

Effect of indexing errors. The filing office's failure to index a record correctly does not affect the record's effectiveness. Policy: "[T]his section imposes the risk of filing-office error on those who search the files rather than on those who file." § 9–517 Comment 2.

(7) Duration of Effectiveness of Filing

A filed financing statement is normally effective for a period of five years after the date of filing. § 9–515(a). A financing statement that relates to a public-finance transaction or a manufactured-home transaction and so indicates is effective for 30 years. §§ 9–515(b), 9–102(a)(54) and (67) ("manufactured-home transaction" and "public-finance transaction" defined). As to a transmitting-utility financing statement and a record of mortgage as a financing statement, see § 9–515(b), (g) and Comment 2; § 9–102(a)(55), (80) ("mortgage" and "transmitting utility" defined). As to the effect of a debtor's bankruptcy, see § 9–515 Comment 4. [*2010 Amendment*. If a debtor is a transmitting utility (and a filed *initial* financing statement so states), the financing statement is effective until a termination statement is filed; thus, the financing statement remains effective indefinitely (until a termination statement is filed). §§ 9–515(f) and Comment 2, 9–102(a)(81).]

(8) Effect of Lapsed Filing

The effectiveness of a filed financing statement lapses when the period of its effectiveness (generally, five years) expires. Upon lapse, any security interest (or agricultural lien) perfected by the financing statement becomes unperfected and is deemed *never* to have been perfected *as against a purchaser* of the collateral for value. § 9–515(c); § 1–201(b)(29), (30) (*purchase* includes security interest).

Example: SP–1 files against Debtor's collateral, and then SP–2 files. SP–1 has priority under the first-to-file rule. § 9–322(a)(1). Then SP–1's filing lapses. As long as SP–2's security interest remains perfected, SP–2 is entitled to priority over SP–1's security interest, which is deemed never to have been perfected against a purchaser for value (SP–2) (see § 9–322(a)(2)). § 9–515 Comment 3, Example 1. This rule avoids a circular-priority problem. Former § 9–403 Comment 3. As to lapsed SP–1 vs. judicial lien creditor (LC), see Example 2 to § 9–515 Comment 3 and § 9–102(a)(52).

(9) Continuation of Effectiveness of Filing

The effectiveness of a filed financing statement lapses when the period of its effectiveness (generally, five years) expires *unless* a continuation statement is filed before the lapse. A continuation statement may be filed only within six months before the period expires (see § 9–510(c)). Upon timely continuation, the effectiveness of the initial financing statement continues for a period of five years (commencing on the day on which the financing statement would have expired). Upon expiration of the five-year period, the financing statement lapses, unless another

470 THE SECURED TRANSACTION Pt. 5

continuation statement is filed. §§ 9–515(c)–(e) and Comment 5, 9–102(a)(27) ("continuation statement" defined).

(10) Amendment of a Financing Statement

Generally, a person may add or delete collateral covered by, or otherwise amend the information provided in, a financing statement by filing an amendment. §§ 9–512(a), 9–509(a). An amendment does not extend the financing statement's period of effectiveness. §§ 9–512(b), 9–515. If the amendment adds collateral, it is effective as to the added collateral only from the date of filing of the amendment. § 9–512(c); see § 9–512(d) and (e).

"[Section 9–512] revises former Section 9–402(4) to permit secured parties of record to make changes in the public record without the need to obtain the debtor's signature. However the filing of an amendment that adds collateral or adds a debtor must be authorized by the debtor or it will not be effective." §§ 9–509(a), 9–510(a); § 9–512 Comment 3 (source of quote).

Note: Although termination statements, assignments, and continuation statements are types of amendments, these particular types of amendments are contained in §§ 9–513, 9–514 and 9–515. § 9–512 Comment 2. See § 9–521(b) (uniform form of written amendment). See, particularly, box 2 Termination, box 3 Continuation, box 4 Assignment. For "correction statement," see § 9–518. [*2010 Amendment*. "Correction statement" has been changed to "information statement." § 9–518.]

(11) Assignment of Secured Party of Record's Powers

"[A] secured party of record may effectuate an assignment of its power to affect a financing statement. It may also be useful for a secured party who has assigned all or part of its security interest or agricultural lien and wishes to have the fact noted of record, so that inquiries concerning the transaction would be addressed to the assignee.

See Section 9–502, Comment 2. Upon the filing of an assignment, the assignee becomes the 'secured party of record' and may authorize the filing of a continuation statement, termination statement, or other amendment. Note that under Section 9–310(c) no filing of an assignment is required as a condition of continuing the perfected status of the security interest against creditors and transferees of the original debtor." § 9–514(a) and (b) and Comment 2 (source of quote). See § 9–310 Comment 4, Example 1. As to assignment of record of mortgage, see § 9–514(c).

(12) Termination Statement

Consumer goods collateral

A secured party of record must file a termination statement for the financing statement if (1) it covers consumer goods and (2) there is no obligation secured by the collateral covered by the financing statement and no commitment to make an advance, incur an obligation, or otherwise give value. The secured party must comply (i) within one month after there is no such obligation or commitment, or (ii) if earlier, 20 days after receiving an authenticated demand from Debtor. §§ 9–513(a) and (b), 9–102(a)(7) and (79) ("authenticate" and "termination statement" defined).

Collateral other than consumer goods

In cases of other collateral, within 20 days after receiving an authenticated demand from a debtor, the secured party of record shall (i) send the debtor a termination statement for the financing statement or (ii) file a termination statement in the filing office if there is no obligation secured by the collateral covered by the financing statement and no commitment to make an advance, incur an obligation, or otherwise give value. § 9–513(c). If Debtor did not authorize filing of the financing statement, see § 9–513(a)(2) and (c)(4); as to *buyers* of receivables, see § 9–513(c)(2) and Comment 4; as to certain consignments, see § 9–513(c)(3).

Note: "Because most financing statements expire in five years unless a continuation statement is filed (Section 9–515), no compulsion is placed on the secured party to file a termination statement unless demanded by the debtor, except in the case of consumer goods. Because many consumers will not realize the importance to them of clearing the public record, an affirmative duty is put on the secured party in that case." § 9–513 Comment 2.

Effect of filing termination statement

Upon filing a termination statement, the financing statement ceases to be effective. § 9–513(d) and Comment 5.

Damages for noncompliance

In the event of noncompliance, Debtor may recover $500, and in addition, damages in the amount of any loss caused. §§ 9–513 Comment 2 (last two sentences), 9–625(b) and (e)(4).

(13) Functions, Duties, Etc., of Filing Office

The functions of a filing office include filing records and related duties. §§ 9–519 through 9–527. See § 9–521 (Uniform Form of Written Financing Statement and Amendment). [*2010 Amendment*. Uniform forms have been updated to reflect the amendments. § 9–521.]

C. PERFECTION BY POSSESSION

(1) Types of Collateral Perfected by Possession or Delivery

A secured party may perfect a security interest in (i) tangible negotiable documents, (ii) goods, (iii) instruments, (iv) money, or (v) tangible chattel paper, by taking *possession* of the collateral (pledge). It may perfect a security interest in certificated securities by taking *delivery*. §§ 9–313(a) and Comment 6, 8–102(a)(4), 8–301. Example: A stock certificate is registered in the name of Shareholder. Delivery of the stock certificate to the secured party occurs when it acquires possession of the certificate. § 8–301(a)(1). As to goods covered by a certificate of title, see §§ 9–313(b), 9–316(d) and Comment 5; see § 9–311 Comment 7.

Note: [1] Except as otherwise provided with respect to proceeds, a security interest in money may be perfected *only* by the secured party's taking possession. § 9–312(b)(3). [2] A security interest in purely intangible collateral (e.g., accounts) *cannot* be perfected by possession. There is nothing to possess. See discussion of "control," "filing," and "automatic perfection." § 9–313 Comment 2.

(2) Requirement of Secured Party's Possession

Generally

Section 9–313 does not define "possession," but adopts the general concept as it developed under former Article 9. For example, former § 9–205 Comment 6 stated, "The common law rules on the degree and extent of possession which are necessary to perfect a pledge interest ... are not relaxed by ... [Article 9]." In determining whether a particular person has possession, the principles of agency apply. Thus, if the collateral is in the possession of an agent of the secured party who is not also an agent of the debtor, the secured party has possession. § 9–313 Comment 3, see § 9–205(b).

When collateral is in possession of a third party–document of title not issued.

Under former § 9–305, if collateral (other than goods covered by a negotiable document) was held by a third party bailee rather than the debtor, the secured party was deemed to have possession from the time the bailee *received notification*. Rationale: See Restatement of Security § 8 Comment a. Cf. §§ 2–503(4) (re: seller's tender of delivery), 2–509(2) (re: risk of loss), 2–705(2)(b) and (c) (re: stoppage of delivery), 7–504(b) and (c) (re: shipment by seller).

Revised § 9–313(c) provides a method of perfection by possession when the collateral is possessed by a third person who is not the secured party's agent. Notification to a third person does not suffice to perfect. Perfection does not occur unless the third person *authenticates* an *acknowledgment* that it holds the collateral for the secured party's benefit. § 9–313(c), (f)–(i); see § 9–102(a)(7) ("authenticate" defined).

When goods in possession of a bailee—covered by document of title

While goods are in the possession of a bailee that has issued a *tangible negotiable* document covering goods, a security interest in the goods may be perfected by perfecting a security interest in the document, i.e., the security interest is perfected by taking *possession* of the negotiable document. §§ 9–312(c)(1), 9–313(a), 9–102(a)(30) ("document" defined), 7–104 (negotiable and nonnegotiable documents of title). See Part Four, B supra for a discussion of how controlling a document of title controls the goods represented by the document. See also § 7–403 (bailee's obligation to deliver); cf. §§ 2–401(3) (passage of title), 2–503(4) (seller's tender of delivery), 2–509(2) (risk of loss), 2–705(2)(d) (stoppage of delivery), 7–303(a)(1) (diversion; reconsignment; change of instructions).

While goods are in the possession of a bailee that has issued a *nonnegotiable* document covering the goods, a security interest in the goods may be perfected by (i) issuance of a document in the name of the secured party,

(ii) the bailee's *receipt* of *notification* of the secured party's interest, or (iii) filing as to the goods. § 9–312(d).

Example 1: W issues a tangible negotiable warehouse receipt "to the order of D." D gives a security interest in the warehouse receipt to SP. D indorses it and hands it to SP, who takes possession. SP is perfected by possession. See §§ 1–201(b)(16) and (42) ("document of title" and "warehouse receipt" defined), 7–104 (negotiable and non-negotiable documents of title).

Example 2: W issues a nonnegotiable warehouse receipt "to D." D gives SP a security interest in the warehouse receipt. SP notifies D of the security interest. SP is perfected when W obtains notification. §§ 1–201(b)(16) and (42), 7–104.

See §§ 9–312 Comment 7, 9–313 Comment 4.

(3) When Security Interest Becomes Perfected by Possession

"If perfection of a security interest depends upon possession of the collateral by a secured party, perfection occurs no earlier than the time the secured party *takes* possession and continues only while the secured party *retains* possession." § 9–313(d) [Emphasis added]. See § 9–313(e) re: a certificated security. Note the 20-day periods provided in § 9–312(e), (f), and (g) during which a debtor may have possession of collateral in which there is a perfected security interest. § 9–313 Comment 5.

D. PERFECTION BY CONTROL

(1) Types of Collateral Perfected by Control

A security interest in (i) investment property, (ii) deposit accounts, (iii) letter-of-credit rights, (iv) electronic chattel paper, or (v) electronic documents, may be perfected by control. § 9–314(a), § 9–102(a)(29) ("deposit account"), (30) ("document"), (31) ("electronic chattel paper"), (49) ("investment property"), (51) ("letter-of-credit right"); § 1–201(b)(16) ("document of title"). See § 9–312(b)(1), (2).

(2) Requirements for Control

A secured party has control of a *deposit account* (e.g., savings account) if, for example, the debtor, secured party, and bank with which the account is maintained have agreed in an authenticated record that the bank will comply with Secured Party's instructions directing disposition of account funds without Debtor's further consent. § 9–104(a)(2), see § 9–104(a)(1) and (3). As to control of electronic chattel paper, electronic documents, and letter-of-credit rights, see §§ 7–106, 9–105, 9–107.

Section 9–106 deals with control of *investment property*. § 9–102(a)(49) ("investment property" defined). For example, a secured party has control of a certificated security in "bearer form" (bearer bond) when it acquires possession of the security certificate. §§ 9–106(a), 8–106(a) ("control defined"), 8–301(a)(1) ("delivery" defined), 8–102(a)(2) ("bearer form" defined). If a certificated security is in "registered form" (stock registered in the name of Shareholder), the secured party has control if the certificated security is delivered *and* the certificate is indorsed to the secured party or in blank by an effective indorsement. §§ 8–106(b)(1) ("control" defined), 8–304(a) and (c) (re: indorsement), 8–102(a)(13) ("registered form" defined). Obtaining control means that the secured party has taken whatever steps are necessary, given the manner in which the securities are held, to place itself in a position where it can have the securities sold without further action by the owner. § 8–106 Comment 1. [*2010 Amendment.* The Amendments reject the holding of *Highland Capital Management LP v. Schneider*, 8 N.Y.3d 406 (2007) and clarify "the registrability requirement in the definition of 'registered form,' and its parallel in the definition of 'security.' " § 8–102 Comment 13.]

(3) Time of Perfection by Control

A security interest is perfected by control when (and only while) the secured party obtains control. § 9–314(b). As to investment property, see § 9–314(c) and Comment 3.

E. AUTOMATIC PERFECTION

In some instances, no additional steps beyond *attachment* are necessary to perfect a security interest. §§ 9–308(a), 9–203(a) ("attachment" defined). In such cases, automatic perfection, also known as perfection by attachment, occurs without filing, possession, or control. Section 9–309(1)–(14) contains the rules for automatic perfection. The following security interests are *perfected* when they *attach*:

1. *Purchase-money security interest (PMSI) in consumer goods*, except, for example, as to certificate-of-title statutes covering automobiles, etc., which provide for a security interest to be indicated on the certificate as a condition or result of perfection. §§ 9–309(1) and Comment 3, 9–102(a)(23) ("consumer goods" defined), 9–103(a) and Comment 3 ("PMSI" defined); cf. former § 9–107(a) and (b). Note: "The concept of 'purchase-money security interest' requires a close nexus between the acquisition of collateral and the secured obligation." In a PMSI transaction, the debt is incurred to purchase the very collateral it secures. § 9–103 Comment 3. Example 1: S sells consumer goods to B. S takes or retains a PMSI to secure the unpaid balance of the purchase price. Example 2: S agrees to sell consumer goods to B for cash. X, a financing agency (e.g., bank), lends the purchase price to B. B uses the money to buy the goods from S and gives X a security interest in the

purchased goods to secure repayment of the loan. X has a PMSI in the consumer goods. (This is sometimes called an enabling loan.)

Revised Article 9 approves the "dual-status" rule, under which a security interest may be a purchase-money interest to some extent and a non-purchase-money security interest to some extent. The revision rejects the "transformation" rule, under which any cross-collateralization, refinancing, or the like destroys the purchase-money status entirely. § 9–103(b)(2) and (3), (e)–(g) and Comments 4, 7. But as to consumer goods transactions, see § 9–103(h) and Comment 8.

As to software, see § 9–103(a)–(c) and Comment 5; as to consignments, see § 9–103(d) and Comment 6; as to the significance of a PMSI, see § 9–103 Comment 2.

2.   The following *rights* to *payment*: (i) casual or isolated assignments of accounts or payment intangibles, and (ii) *sales* of payment intangibles and promissory notes. § 9–309(2)–(4) and Comment 4; see § 9–109(a)(3).

3.   Health-care-insurance receivables under § 9–309(5). See § 9–309 Comment 5.

4.   Security interests under UCC Articles 2, 2A, 4, and 5. § 9–309(6)–(8).

5.   Certain security interests in *investment property*. § 9–309(9)–(11) and Comment 6.

6.   An *assignment for benefit of creditors*. § 9–309(12) and Comment 8.

7.   A security interest created by an assignment of a beneficial interest in a decedent's estate. § 9–309(13) and Comment 7.

8.   Sale (by an individual) of a right to payment of winnings in a lottery (or other game of chance). § 9–309(14) and Comment 4 (last paragraph).

Temporary perfection

In certain situations, a security interest in negotiable documents, goods in possession of a bailee, instruments, or certificated securities may be temporarily perfected for 20 days (without filing or possession). § 9–312(e)–(h). Former § 9–304(4) and (5) allowed 21 days.

As to proceeds, see § 9–315 Comments 4–8 (automatic perfection: 20-day period; formerly 10-day).

5. PRIORITIES AMONG CONFLICTING INTERESTS IN THE SAME COLLATERAL

A. INTRODUCTION TO PRIORITY RULES

"The rules set out in ... [Article 9] are principally concerned with the limits of the secured party's protection against purchasers from and creditors of the debtor." Former § 9–101 Comment. We already know that the limits of a secured party's protection typically depend on whether the secured party has *perfected* its security interest. See Part Five, C, 4 supra. "A perfected security interest may still be or become subordinate to other interests.... However, in general, after perfection the secured party is protected against creditors and transferees of the debtor and, in particular, against any representative of creditors in insolvency proceedings instituted by or against the debtor." § 9–308 Comment 2. See, e.g., §§ 9–317 (a)(2)(A), 9–102(a)(52)(C) (trustee in bankruptcy as lien creditor). Bankruptcy Code § 544(a). Note: Even an *unperfected* security interest may afford protection as against some third parties (e.g., general creditors). See §§ 9–201(a), 9–317(a)(2). Now is the time to detail these priority rules.

The conflicting interests

The interests that compete with the secured party fall into two categories: purchasers from the debtor and creditors of the debtor. These parties include (i) other secured parties under UCC Articles 2, 2A, 4, 5, or 9; (ii) general (unsecured) creditors; (iii) lien creditors (by attachment, levy, or the like); (iv) buyers, (v) lessees, (vi) licensees, (vii) lienors by operation of law (e.g., repairperson's possessory lien); (viii) liens and priorities of governmental units (e.g., federal tax lien); and (ix) the trustee in bankruptcy. Some of these interests are more difficult to obtain priority over than the others.

The priority rules—former Article 9

Former § 9–312 Comment 1 stated, "In a variety of situations two or more people may claim an interest in the same property. The several sections specified in ... [§ 9–312(1)] contain rules for determining priorities between security interests and such other claims in the situations covered in those sections. For cases not covered in those sections this section [§ 9–312(2)–(7)] states general rules of priority between conflicting security interests."

These priority rules may be analyzed by reducing them into three categories:

1.   Priority rules in situations specified in § 9–312(1) (e.g., secured party vs. lien creditor or certain buyers).

2.   Priority rules in situations specified in § 9–312(2), (3) and (4) (conflicting security interests in (i) production-money security interest in crops, (ii) purchase-money security interests in inventory, and (iii) purchase-money security interests in collateral other than inventory).

3.   General or residual rules of priority in § 9–312(5): In all cases not governed by the other rules above, conflicting security interests rank according to priority in time of filing or perfection (first-to-file-or-perfect rule).

These rules may be likened to a number of specific bequests and a million-dollar residuary clause.

The priority rules—revised Article 9

Revised § 9–322 states *general rules* of priority among conflicting security interests, most importantly the "first-to-file-or-perfect" rule. § 9–322(a)(1); see (a)(2) and (3). (With respect to proceeds and supporting obligations, see § 9–322(b)–(e)). The *general rule* of first-to-file-or-perfect is *subject to:*

1.   The rule in § 9–322(g) governing priority of agricultural liens. § 9–322(f)(1);

2.   The other priority rules found in Part 3 of Article 9. § 9–322(f). (See §§ 9–301 through 9–339.); and

3.   Priority rules governing security interests under Articles 2, 2A, 4, and 5. § 9–322(f)(2)–(4). See §§ 4–210, 5–118, 9–110 (§§ 2–401, 2–505, 2–711(3), 2A–508 (5) (§ 2A–508(4) (2003)).

The priority rules found in Part 3 of Article 9 are set forth in the following sections:

a.   § 9–317, priority of security interest (or agricultural lien) vs. (i) lien creditors, (ii) buyers, (iii) lessees, and (iv) licensees (re: other security interests, see §§ 9–317(a)(1), 9–322.)

b.   § 9–318, priority in sale of account or chattel paper.

c.   § 9–319, priority of consignor vs. creditors and purchasers of consignee.

d.   § 9–320, priority rule regarding goods: (i) buyer in ordinary course of business, and (ii) buyer of consumer goods.

e.   § 9–321, priority regarding (i) licensee of general intangible and (ii) lessee of goods in ordinary course of business.

f.   § 9–323, priority of future advances (secured party vs. other secured party, lien creditor, buyer, or lessee).

g. § 9–324, priority of purchase-money security interests; cf. § 9–317(e) (second in time, first in right). (As to priority of production-money security interests, see Model § 9–324A.)

h. § 9–325, priority of security interest in transferred collateral.

i. § 9–326, priority of security interests created by new debtor.

j. special priority in particular types of collateral: § 9–327 (deposit accounts), § 9–328 (investment property), § 9–329 (letter-of-credit rights), § 9–330 (chattel paper and instruments), § 9–331 (purchase of instruments, documents, and securities, priority of interests in financial assets and security entitlements), § 9–332 (transfer of money or of funds from deposit account), § 9–334 (fixtures and crops), § 9–335 (accessions), § 9–336 (commingled goods), § 9–337 (goods covered by certificate of title), and § 9–312(c) (goods covered by negotiable document).

k. § 9–338, priority when a financing statement contains incorrect information.

l. § 9–333, priority of liens arising by operation of law.

m. § 9–339, priority subject to subordination.

Principal inquiries regarding the priority rules

A study of the priority rules outlined above should reveal that certain inquiries must be made to locate the governing priority rule in a given situation:

1. Who is our secured party's competitor (e.g., another secured party, lien creditor, buyer, etc.)?

2. What type of collateral is involved (e.g., consumer goods, equipment, inventory, instruments, accounts, proceeds, etc.)?

3. Is the security interest a purchase-money security interest?

In certain instances, additional inquiries may be required:

(a) Is the security interest related to other jurisdictions?

(b) Does the security interest secure future advances or after-acquired property?

B. OVERVIEW OF PRIORITY RULES IN COMMON SITUATIONS INVOLVING GOODS

Let us now apply the priority rules outlined above in common goods-collateral situations. This will afford a basic understanding of the operation of § 9–322.

In the following examples, these abbreviations are used:

"SP–1" means Secured Party Number One (*our* party).

"SP–2" means Secured Party Number Two (the *other* party).

"D" means Debtor.

"LC" means Lien Creditor, i.e., a creditor who has acquired a lien on the property by attachment, levy, or the like. (A state's non-UCC law determines when and how the lien is acquired.)

"B" means Buyer of the collateral.

(1) When No Purchase-Money Security Interest Is Involved

(a) Equipment or Consumer Goods Collateral

Example: D owns and possesses a machine, which D uses either in D's business or for personal purposes, i.e., equipment or consumer goods. § 9–102(a)(23), (33) (defining "consumer goods" and "equipment"). D wishes to borrow from SP–1. Thus, on May 1, SP–1 loans $5,000 to D and takes a security interest in D's machine to secure repayment of the loan. SP–1 duly files its financing statement on May 2.

Now assume the following occurs:

1.   On May 5, SP–2 loans D $2,500 and takes a security interest in the same machine. SP–2 files its financing statement on May 6; *or*

2.   On May 5, LC, a creditor of D, acquires a lien on the same machine by attachment, levy, or the like; *or*

3.   On May 5, B buys the same machine from D and receives delivery that very day.

Questions: Does SP–1's security interest have priority over (1) SP–2's security interest; (2) LC's lien; or (3) B's interest?

Answers: (1) *SP–1 v. SP–2.* SP–1 has priority over SP–2 because SP–1 was the first to file. SP–1 filed on May 2; SP–2 filed on May 6. Rule: "Conflicting [non-purchase-money] perfected security interests ... rank according to priority in time of filing or perfection." § 9–322(a)(1). Note: to get to § 9–322(a)(1), one must first determine that none of the priority rules in the special situations referenced in § 9–322(f) govern the conflict.

(2) *SP–1 v. LC.* SP–1 has priority over LC because SP–1 perfected by filing prior to LC's becoming a lien creditor. SP–1's security interest attached on May 1 (§ 9–203(a)) and was perfected by filing on May 2. LC became a lien creditor on May 5. Rule: "A security interest ... is subordinate to the rights of ... a person that becomes a lien creditor before ... the security interest is ... perfected." § 9–317(a)(2). And by implication and per § 9–201, a *perfected* security interest is *not* subordinate to the rights of a person who becomes a lien creditor *after* the security interest is perfected. Section 9–201(a) states, "Except as otherwise provided in [the Uniform Commercial Code], a security agreement is effective according to its terms between the parties, against purchasers of the collateral, and

against creditors." The *Code* does provide otherwise as to *unperfected* security interests.

(3) *SP–1 v. B.* SP–1 has priority over B, a buyer not in ordinary course of business, because SP–1 perfected by filing prior to B's giving value and receiving delivery of the machine without knowledge of the security interest. SP–1's security interest attached on May 1 (§ 9–203(a)) and was perfected by filing on May 2. B bought and received delivery on May 5. Rule: "[a] buyer ... of ... goods ... takes free of a security interest ... if the buyer gives value and receives delivery of the collateral without knowledge of the security interest ... and before it is perfected." § 9–317(b). And by implication and per § 9–201(a) (as pointed out immediately above), a *perfected* security interest is *not* subordinate to such buyer who gives value and receives delivery of the collateral without knowledge of the security interest *after* it is perfected.

Simply stated, "First in time, first in right."

(b) Inventory Collateral

Note in the following example that the facts are essentially the same as in the example above, except that SP–1 loans to D, a *dealer* in goods, *not an ultimate user* of goods. Thus, the goods in question constitute inventory rather than equipment or consumer goods.

Example: D, a dealer, owns and possesses certain machinery as inventory for sale or lease. § 9–102(a)(48) ("inventory" defined). D wishes to borrow from SP–1. Thus, on May 1, SP–1 loans $5,000 to D and takes a security interest in D's inventory to secure repayment of the loan. SP–1 duly files its financing statement May 2. Now assume the following occurs:

1. On May 5, SP–2 loans $2,500 to D and takes a security interest in the same machinery. SP–2 files its financing statement on May 6; *or*

2.   On May 5, LC, a creditor of D, acquires a lien on the same machinery by attachment, levy, or the like; *or*

3.   On May 5, B in good faith buys one of the machines from D and receives delivery the same day.

Questions: Does SP–1's security interest have priority over (1) SP–2's security interest; (2) LC's lien; or (3) B's interest?

Answers: (1) *SP–1 vs. SP–2*. SP–1 has priority over SP–2 because SP–1 was the first to file. SP–1 filed on May 2; SP–2 filed on May 6. The rule is the same as for the equipment or consumer-goods hypothetical discussed above. § 9–322(a)(1).

(2) *SP–1 vs. LC*. SP–1 has priority over LC because SP–1 perfected by filing before LC became a lien creditor. SP–1's security interest attached on May 1 (§ 9–203(a)) and was perfected by filing on May 2. LC became a lien creditor on May 5. The rule is the same as for the equipment or consumer-goods hypothetical discussed above. §§ 9–317(a)(2), 9–201(a).

(3) *SP–1 vs. B*. SP–1 does *not* have priority over B, even though SP–1's security interest attached on May 1 (§ 9–203(a)) and was perfected by filing on May 2 before B bought and received delivery on May 5. Rule: "[A] buyer in ordinary course of business . . . takes free of a security interest created by the buyer's seller [i.e., D], *even if* the security interest is *perfected* and the buyer *knows* of its existence." § 9–320(a) [Emphasis added]. 'Buyer in ordinary course of business' means a person [B] that buys goods in good faith, without knowledge that the sale violates the rights of another person in the goods, and in the ordinary course from a person . . . in the business of selling goods of that kind . . . 'Buyer in ordinary course of business' does not include a person that acquires goods in a transfer in bulk . . . ." § 1–201(b)(9). Note the similar policy considerations in § 2–403(2), under which a party

entrusting goods to a merchant lost to a buyer in ordinary course of business. See Part One, G supra. See also § 9–320 Comments 2 and 3.

In our example, if B buys all of D's inventory (a transfer in bulk) or otherwise fails to qualify as a buyer in ordinary course of business, B takes subject to SP–1's security interest. §§ 9–201(a), 9–317(b), 9–315(a)(1). See the discussion of SP–1 vs. B in the hypothetical addressing equipment or consumer goods above.

Simply stated, "First in time, first in right" except with regard to a buyer in ordinary course of business.

(2) When a Purchase-Money Security Interest Is Involved

(a) Introduction

A secured party who holds a "purchase-money security interest" may have priority over competing interests in the same collateral even if the purchase-money secured party was second to perfect or file, i.e., "second in time, first in right."

Example: A secured party (SP–2) takes a security interest in industrial equipment owned by D and industrial equipment to be after-acquired by D. SP–2 promptly files. Later, Seller (our secured party, i.e., SP–1) sells new industrial equipment to D and retains or takes back a security interest in the industrial equipment to secure payment of the unpaid purchase price. SP–1 promptly files. SP–1's interest is a purchase-money security interest because it was taken or retained by Seller to secure all or part of its price. § 9–103(a) and (b), cf. former § 9–107(a). See esp., § 9–103(a)(2).

Question: Does SP–2 (who filed first) have priority over SP–1 (who filed later), or does an earlier mortgage with an after-acquired-property clause prevail over a subsequent purchase-money mortgage? (The earlier mortgagee (SP–2) claims a security interest in the goods as after-acquired property; the later mortgagee (SP–1) claims the goods by virtue of the security interest in them SP–1 took or retained to secure their purchase price.)

Answer: Revised § 9–324 follows former § 9–312(3) and prior law: SP–1 has priority. Comment 3 to former § 9–312 states,

> Prior law, under one or another theory, usually contrived to protect purchase money interests over after-acquired property interests (to the extent to which the after-acquired property interest was recognized at all). For example, in the field of industrial equipment finance it was possible, by manipulation of title theory, for the purchase money financer of new equipment (under conditional sale or equipment trust) to protect himself against the claims of prior mortgagees or bondholders under an after-acquired clause in the mortgage or trust indenture: the result was arrived at on the theory that since "title" to the equipment was never in the vendee or lessee there was nothing for the lien of the mortgage to attach to. While . . . [Article 9] broadly validates the after-acquired property interest, it also recognizes as sound the preference which prior law gave to the purchase money interest. That policy is carried out in . . . [former § 9–312(3) and (4) and revised § 9–324].

Or, as Nelson & Whitman state in Real Estate Finance Law § 9.1 at 1111–1113 (5th Practitioner's Ed. 2007),

> Several rationales have been advanced for this favoritism for the purchase money . . . [secured party]. The traditional and frequently stated explanation is that of transitory seizin. The idea is that title shot into the grantee [D] and out of him again into the purchase money . . . [secured party SP–1] so fleetingly—*quasi uno flattu,* in one breath, as it were—that no other interest [e.g., SP–2] had time to fasten itself to it. . . . A

better statement of the reason for the rule is that the title comes to the purchaser [D] already charged with the ... [security interest] in favor of the ... [seller–secured party SP–1]; that regardless of the form all that the transaction ever transfers [to D] is the redemption right.

Nelson & Whitman then give a more illuminating answer for the law's favoritism for the purchase-money secured party:

The other answer justifies the doctrine [of giving the purchase-money secured party priority] on the fairness of protecting one [SP–1] who has parted with property on the faith of having a security interest in it until the money for which [he or] she was exchanging it is received as against persons [e.g., SP–2] who, for different reasons, have inferior claims.... As against other ... [secured party] claimants [SP–2] to the property ... [the purchase-money secured party SP–1] has the edge because the property [he or] she is relying on for payment was previously [his or] hers up to the time of ... [the purchase-money secured transaction]; there was never an instant when [he or] she relinquished a hold on it; and [he or] she would never have parted with it at all except upon the belief and faith that if [his or] her buyer [D] defaulted [he or] she could either recapture the property or get paid out of it.... Other ... [secured parties, e.g., SP–2], on the other hand, ... parted only with money in which they retained no interest whatsoever, and placed their reliance for repayment of their debts on getting a security interest in other property not only never previously owned by them but not even owned by the ... [debtor D] at the time the money was loaned.... This difference in attitude toward the hazard of losing property previously owned and that of not getting an interest in property which had never before belonged to the claimant [SP–2] is an old and important one. Here it justifies preferring the ... [purchase-money secured party seller] over ... [the secured party SP–2] under an after-acquired property clause. [Id. at 1114–1115.]

When a *third party* lends purchase-money, much the same reasoning applies, and priority is given to the third-person lender over a prior secured party claiming under an after-acquired-property clause. The rationale for the law's favoritism for the third-party purchase-money lender is set forth by Nelson & Whitman:

It relied upon getting security upon this very property and its money went into the payment of it. Without this advance of money, the ... [debtor] would [n]ever have received the property. It is this last feature that serves to give it priority over other ... [secured parties] whose loans were not limited in their use to the acquisition of the property which was to be security for repayment. [Id. at 1116.]

Example: A secured party (SP–2) takes a security interest in industrial equipment owned and to be after-acquired by D. SP–2 promptly files. Later, Seller agrees to sell new industrial equipment to D for cash. Lender (SP–1), a financing agency, advances funds to enable D to buy the equipment, and D uses the money for that purpose. D gives SP–1 a security interest in the equipment to secure repayment of the loan. SP–1 promptly files. SP–1's interest is a "purchase-money security interest" because SP–1 supplied value (the loan) in return for the security interest to enable D to acquire rights in the collateral, and the loan was in fact so used. § 9–103(a) and (b), cf. former § 9–107(b) (enabling loan). See esp. § 9–103(a)(2).

A third party financing agency can also have a purchase-money security interest: "[S]eller has a purchase money security interest if he retains a security interest in the goods; a financing agency has a purchase money security interest when it advances money to the seller, taking back an assignment of chattel paper...." Former § 9–107 Comment 1.

Further policies support the purchase-money priority:

[A] seller ... should not be obliged to inspect public filings (with respect to his purchaser) in order for the seller to maintain priority in goods which it owns and proposes to sell.... [T]he debtor needs some protection from an earlier secured creditor who may have filed a financing statement with respect to many of debtor's assets (including after-acquired), but who is unwilling to advance additional funds. UCC Hornbook § 25–4.

If such a debtor can't find a lender willing to finance a new line of merchandise, the purchase-money provisions enable him to give that new lender a first claim on the new merchandise notwithstanding a prior filing by another creditor. Thus, the purchase-money provisions give the debtor somewhat greater bargaining power and at least theoretically enlarge his ability to get credit. [UCC Hornbook § 24–5 at 1138 (4th ed.)]

Now to examine purchase-money priority under the Code.

(b) Equipment Collateral

Example: On May 1, SP–1, a dealer, sells and delivers to D a machine to be used in D's business, i.e., equipment. § 9–102(a)(33) ("equipment" defined). SP–1 takes or retains a security interest in the machine to secure payment of the purchase price. SP–1 files its financing statement on May 8.

Now assume the following occurs:

1. On May 5, SP–2 loans D $2,500 and takes a security interest in the same machine. SP–2 files its financing statement on May 6; *or*

2. On May 5, LC, a creditor of D, acquires a lien on the same machine by attachment, levy, or the like; *or*

3. On May 5, B buys the same machine from D and receives delivery the same day.

Questions: Does SP–1's security interest have priority over (1) SP–2's security interest; (2) LC's lien; or (3) B's interest?

Answers: (1) *SP–1 vs. SP–2*. SP–1 has priority over SP–2 even though SP–2 filed on May 6 and SP–1 filed on May 8. Rule: "[A] perfected purchase-money security interest in goods other than inventory or livestock [e.g., equipment] has priority over a conflicting security interest [of SP–2] in the same goods . . . if the purchase-money security interest is perfected when the debtor receives possession of the collateral or within 20 days thereafter." §§ 9–324(a), 9–103(a) and (b). SP–1's security interest was perfected on May 8, which was within 20 days of D's receiving possession of the machine on May 1.

(2) *SP–1 vs. LC*. SP–1 has priority over LC even though LC became a lien creditor on May 5 and SP–1 filed on May 8. Rule "[I]f a person [SP–1] files a financing statement with respect to a purchase-money security interest before or within 20 days after the debtor receives delivery of the collateral, the security interest takes priority over the rights of a . . . lien creditor [LC] which arise between the time the security interest attaches and the time of filing." §§ 9–317(a)(2) and (e) (source of quote), 9–103(a) and (b), 9–203(a) and (b). SP–1's security interest was filed on May 8, which was within 20 days after D received delivery of the collateral on May 1.

(3) *SP–1 v. B*. SP–1 has priority over B even though B bought and took delivery of the machine on May 5 and SP–1 filed on May 8. Rule: "[I]f a person [SP–1] files a financing statement with respect to a purchase-money security interest before or within 20 days after the debtor receives delivery of the collateral, the security interest takes priority over the rights of a buyer [B], . . . which arise between the time the security interest attaches and

the time of filing." §§ 9–317(b) and (e) (source of quote), 9–103(a) and (b), 9–203(a) and (b). [Of course, a buyer in ordinary course of business takes free of a security interest even if the security interest is perfected and the buyer knows of its existence. §§ 9–317(e), 9–320(a).]

Note in the above equipment-collateral example that SP–1's purchase-money security interest had priority over earlier security interests waiting to attach to after-acquired property. Also, SP–1 had a 20 day grace period after D received possession of the equipment. Here, SP–2 was claiming an interest, not in after-acquired property, but in property in D's possession during a period when SP–1 had not filed. Why does SP–1 have priority here? Answer: To afford SP–1 a limited time to get the financing statement filed. SP–2, as a sophisticated lender, should know that a purchase-money secured party can file after it (for a limited 20 day period) and have priority.

"[Revised § 9–317(e)] differs from former Section 9–301(2) in two significant respects. First, subsection (e) protects a purchase-money security interest against all buyers and lessees, not just against transferees in bulk. Second, subsection (e) conditions this protection on filing within 20, as opposed to ten, days after delivery." § 9–317 Comment 8.

(c) Consumer Goods Collateral

Example: On May 1, SP–1, a dealer, sells and delivers to D a machine to be used for D's personal purposes, i.e., consumer goods. § 9–102(a)(23) ("consumer goods" defined). SP–1 takes or retains a security interest in the machine to secure payment of the purchase price. SP–1 does not file a financing statement.

Now assume the following occurs:

1.   On May 5, SP–2 loans D $2,500 and takes a security interest in the same machine. SP–2 files its financing statement on May 6; *or*

2.   On May 5, LC, a creditor of D, acquires a lien on the same machine by attachment, levy, or the like; *or*

3.   On May 5, B buys the same machine from D and receives delivery the same day.

Questions: Does SP–1's security interest have priority over (1) SP–2's security interest; (2) LC's lien; or (3) B's interest?

Answers: (1) *SP–1 vs. SP–2*. SP–1 has priority over SP–2 even though SP–2 filed on May 6 and SP–1 never filed. Rule: "[A] perfected purchase-money security interest [of SP–1] in goods other than inventory or livestock [e.g., consumer goods] has priority over a conflicting security interest [of SP–2] in the same goods … if the purchase-money security interest is perfected when the debtor receives possession of the collateral or within 20 days thereafter." §§ 9–324(a), 9–103 (a) and (b). SP–1's security interest was *automatically* perfected because it was a purchase-money security interest in consumer goods and was *perfected* (by attachment) when D received possession of the collateral. §§ 9–201(a), 9–203(a) and (b), 9–308(a), 9–309(1). See automatic perfection discussed at Part Five, C, 4, E supra.

(2) *SP–1 vs. LC.* SP–1 has priority over LC even though LC became a lien creditor on May 5 and SP–1 never filed. Rule: "A security interest … is subordinate to the rights of … a person that becomes a lien creditor before … the security interest … is perfected." § 9–317(a) (2)(A). And by implication, as previously discussed, a *perfected security interest* is *not* subordinate to the lien creditor. SP–1's security interest was *automatically* perfected because it was a purchase-money security interest in consumer goods and thus was perfected (at attachment) when D received delivery of the collateral. §§ 9–201(a), 9–203(a) and (b), 9–308(a), 9–309(1). See automatic perfection discussion at Part Five, C, 4, E supra.

(3) *SP–1 vs. B.* SP–1 does *not* have priority over B (under appropriate circumstances) even though SP–1 was automatically perfected. Rule: "[A] buyer of goods [B] from a person who used or bought the goods for use primarily for personal, family, or household purposes takes free of a security interest, even if [automatically] perfected, if the buyer buys (1) without knowledge of the security interest; (2) for value; (3) primarily for the buyer's personal, family, or household purposes; and (4) before the filing of a financing statement covering the goods." § 9–320(b). For other buyers of consumer goods, see § 9–317(b) and (e) (e.g., if B is a second-hand machine dealer and buys the goods for resale).

(d) Inventory Collateral

Example 1: On April 1, SP–2 loans $25,000 to D, a dealer in machinery, and takes a security interest in D's present and after-acquired inventory of machines. SP–2 files its financing statement on April 2. SP–1, a manufacturer, is considering selling machines to D and taking or retaining a security interest in them as inventory (§ 9–102(a)(48)), to secure payment of the purchase price. Consequently, SP–1 does the following:

1. On May 1, SP–1 files a financing statement naming D as debtor and appropriately describing the collateral.

2. On May 2, SP–1 sends notification to SP–2 of SP–1's forthcoming purchase-money security interest in the machines SP–1 plans to sell to D, properly describing the machines. SP–2 receives the notification on May 3.

3. On May 5, SP–1 delivers machines to D, who receives possession of the machines the same day.

Question: Does SP–1's security interest have priority over SP–2's?

Answer: *SP–1 vs. SP–2*. SP–1 has priority over SP–2 even though SP–2 filed on April 2 and SP–1 filed on May 1.

Rule: "[A] perfected purchase-money security interest [of SP–1] in inventory has priority over a conflicting security interest [of SP–2] in the same inventory, . . . if:

(1) the purchase-money security interest is perfected when the debtor receives possession of the inventory;

(2) the purchase-money secured party sends an authenticated notification to the holder of the conflicting security interest;

(3) the holder of the conflicting security interest receives the notification within five years before the debtor receives possession of the inventory; and

(4) the notification states that the person sending the notification has or expects to acquire a purchase-money security interest in inventory of the debtor and describes the inventory." §§ 9–324(b), 9–103, 1–202(d) and (e) (re: notice and receipt of notice).

Note: These notification requirements apply only if the holder of the conflicting security interest [SP–2] had filed a financing statement covering the same types of inventory (if the purchase-money security interest [of SP–1] is perfected by filing), before the date of the filing. § 9–324(c) and Comments 4–6. As to conflicting purchase-money security interests, see § 9–324(g) and Comment 13.

Observe that § 9–324(a) (purchase-money priority for, e.g., equipment) has a 20-day grace period for filing but no notification requirement, whereas § 9–324(b) (purchase-money priority for inventory) has a notification requirement but no grace period. See § 9–324 Comment 4.

Example 2: On May 1 SP–1, a manufacturer, sells and delivers to D, a dealer, machines that D will resell to ultimate users. SP–1 takes or retains a security interest in the machines to secure payment of the purchase price. SP–1 files its financing statement on May 8.

Now assume the following occurs:

1.   On May 5, LC, a creditor of D, acquires a lien on the same machinery by attachment, levy, or the like; *or*

2.   On May 5, B–1 in good faith buys a machine from D's inventory and receives delivery the same day; *or*

3.   On May 5, B–2 in good faith buys *all* of the machines in D's inventory.

Questions: Does SP–1's security interest have priority over (1) LC's lien; (2) the interest of B–1 who bought one machine; or (3) the interest of B–2 who bought all of the machines?

Answers: (1) *SP–1 vs. LC.* SP–1 has priority over LC even though LC became a lien creditor on May 5 and SP–1 filed on May 8. Rule: "[I]f a person [SP–1] files a financing statement with respect to a purchase-money security interest before or within 20 days after the debtor receives delivery of the collateral, the security interest takes priority over the rights of a . . . lien creditor which arise between the time the security interest attaches and the time of filing." §§ 9–317(a)(2) and (e) (source of quote), 9–103(a) and (b), 9–203(a) and (b).

(2) *SP–1 vs. B–1.* SP–1 does *not* have priority over B–1. Section 9–317(b) states that a buyer of goods takes free of a security interest if the buyer gives value and receives delivery of the collateral without knowledge of the security interest and before it is perfected. B–1 bought and took delivery on May 5; SP–1 did not perfect until May 8. Thus, under this analysis, B–1 should take free from SP–1's unperfected security interest. But see § 9–317(e) (20-day grace period good as against buyers). However, if B–1 is a buyer in ordinary course of business, it would take free of even a perfected security interest; accordingly, B–1 would take free of an *unperfected* one. §§ 9–320(a) and Comment 2, 1–201(b)(9) ("buyer in ordinary course of business" defined). See also answer 3 below.

(3) *SP–1 vs. B–2.* SP–1 has priority over B–2 even though B–2 bought on May 5 and SP–1 filed on May 8. B–2, who bought D's entire inventory of machines, is a transferee in bulk and thus not a buyer in ordinary course of business. § 1–201(b)(9). Thus the rule: "[I]f a person [SP–1] files a financing statement with respect to a purchase-money security interest before or within 20 days after the debtor receives delivery of the collateral, the security interest takes priority over the rights of a buyer [B–2] ... which arise between the time the security interest attaches and the time of filing." §§ 9–317(b) and (e) (source of quote), 9–103(a) and (b), 9–203(a) and (b). SP–1's security interest was perfected on May 8, which was within 20 days of D's receiving delivery on May 1.

Note: "Subsection (e) differs from former Section 9–301(2) in two significant respects. First, subsection (e) protects a purchase-money security interest against *all buyers and lessees*, not just transferees in bulk. Second, subsection (e) conditions this protection on filing within 20 days, as opposed to ten days, after delivery." § 9–317 Comment 8. [Emphasis added].

C. OPERATION OF ARTICLE 9 PRIORITY RULES

We have just surveyed Article 9 priority rules in common goods-collateral situations. Thus, we should have a basic familiarity with Article 9 rules and methodology. Now we will take a closer look at certain aspects of the Article 9 priority rules, especially the general priority rules of § 9–322(a). This subsection states,

> Except as otherwise provided in this section, priority among conflicting security interests and agricultural liens in the same collateral is determined according to the following rules:
>
> (1) Conflicting perfected security interests and agricultural liens rank according to priority in time of filing or perfection. Priority dates from the earlier of

the time a filing covering the collateral is first made or the security interest or agricultural lien is first perfected, if there is no period thereafter when there is neither filing nor perfection.

(2) A perfected security interest or agricultural lien has priority over a conflicting unperfected security interest or agricultural lien.

(3) The first security interest or agricultural lien to attach or become effective has priority if conflicting security interests and agricultural liens are unperfected.

See § 9–322(f) (limitations on subsection (a)).

Comment 4 to § 9–322 gives three examples illustrating the operation of § 9–322(a)(1) (competing perfected security interests) and comments on them as follows:

EXAMPLE 1: On February 1, A files a financing statement covering a certain item of Debtor's equipment. On March 1, B files a financing statement covering the same equipment. On April 1, B makes a loan to Debtor and obtains a security interest in the equipment. On May 1, A makes a loan to Debtor and obtains a security interest in the same collateral. A has priority even though B's loan was made earlier and was perfected when made. It makes no difference whether A knew of B's security interest when A made its advance.

The problem stated in Example 1 is peculiar to a notice-filing system under which filing may occur before the security interest attaches (see Section 9–502). The justification for determining priority by order of filing lies in the necessity of protecting the filing system—that is, of allowing the first secured party who has filed to make subsequent advances without each time having to check for subsequent filings as a condition of protection. Note, however, that this first-to-file protection is not absolute. For example, Section 9–324 affords priority to certain purchase-money security interests, even if a competing secured party was the first to file or perfect.

[*2010 Amendment*. Section 9–322 Comment 4 has been expanded to address a financing statement that was ineffective when filed, but later becomes effective. Based on notice-filing principles, the time of the ineffective filing becomes the "timing of filing" within the language of § 9–322(a)(1). § 9–322 Comment 4.]

EXAMPLE 2: A and B make non-purchase-money advances secured by the same collateral. The collateral is in Debtor's possession, and neither security interest is perfected when the second advance is made. Whichever secured party first perfects its security interest (by taking possession of the collateral or by filing) takes priority. It makes no difference whether that secured party knows of the other security interest at the time it perfects its own.

The rule of subsection (a)(1), affording priority to the first to file or perfect, applies to security interests that are perfected by any method, including temporarily (Section 9–312) or upon attachment (Section 9–309), even though there may be no notice to creditors or subsequent purchasers and notwithstanding any common-law rule to the contrary. The form of the claim to priority, i.e., filing or perfection, may shift from time to time, and the rank will be based on the first filing or perfection as long as there is no intervening period during which perfection lapses. See Section 9–308(c).

EXAMPLE 3: On October 1, A acquires a temporarily perfected (20-day) security interest, unfiled, in a tangible negotiable document in the debtor's possession under Section 9–312(e). On October 5, B files and thereby perfects a security interest that previously had attached to the same document. On October 10, A files. A has priority, even after the 20-day period expires, regardless of whether A knows of B's security interest when A files. A was the first to perfect and maintained continuous perfection or filing since the start of the 20-day period. However, the perfection of A's security interest extends only "to the extent it arises for new value given." To the extent A's security interest secures advances made by A beyond the 20-day period, its security interest would be subordinate to B's, inasmuch as B was the first to file.

Since Example 3 above relates to a type of collateral not yet discussed (documents), let us add the following:

Example 3(a). On May 1, B (SP–2) loans $1,000 to D and takes a security interest in D's machine. On May 2, D pledges the machine to A (SP–1) to secure a loan of $500. A takes immediate possession. On May 5, B duly files a financing statement. On May 10, A files a financing statement and on May 11 returns the machine to D. A has priority, regardless of whether A knows of B's interest when A files, because A perfected first (by possession on May 2) and has maintained continuous perfection by filing. However, if A redelivers the machine to D and *then* files, B has priority because there is a period in which A is neither filed nor perfected by possession, and B filed first. See also § 9–308(c) (re: continuous perfection).

Section 9–322(a) and the above examples show that this is a pure "*race type*" statute; the one who files or perfects first wins. Knowledge of a competing secured party when an advance is made or when filing or perfection occurs does not alter the priority rules. This is contrasted with some pre-Code "*notice type*" statutes, which allowed an earlier unfiled SP–1 to have priority over a subsequent SP–2 with actual knowledge (or non-record notice) of SP–1's earlier interest even though SP–2 filed first. (Some pre-Code statutes were of a "*notice-race*" type whereby SP–2 must have had neither notice nor knowledge of SP–1's unfiled interest and must have filed before SP–1.) The virtue of a race type statute is certainty; priority is determined by a race to the filing office.

Note, however, that SP–1's unperfected security interest is not subordinate to a *buyer* of the goods *with knowledge* of the security interest before it is perfected. § 9–317(b). As to lessees and licensees, see § 9–317(c) and (d); as to purchasers of chattel paper or instruments, see § 9–330(b) and (d). Further, Comment 3 to § 9–324 states, "A purchase-money security interest qualifies for a priority under subsection (a), even if the purchase-money secured party *knows* that a conflicting security interest has been created and/or that the holder of the conflicting interest has filed a financing statement covering the collateral." [Emphasis added.]

Application of priority rules to after-acquired property

Comment 5 to § 9–322 states, "The application of the priority rules to after-acquired property must be considered separately for each item of collateral. Priority does not depend only on time of perfection but may also be based on priority in filing before perfection." Remember: filing may occur before a security interest attaches. §§ 9–308(a), 9–203(a) and (b) ("attachment" defined). Clearly, Debtor does not have rights in after-acquired collateral until Debtor acquires it; thus, *perfection* cannot occur until that time. § 9–308(a). Comment 5 gives the following example:

> Example 4: On February 1, A makes advances to Debtor under a security agreement covering "all Debtor's machinery, both existing and after-acquired." A promptly files a financing statement. On April 1, B takes a security interest in all Debtor's machinery, existing and after-acquired, to secure an outstanding loan. The following day, B files a financing statement. On May 1, Debtor acquires a new machine. When Debtor acquires rights in the new machine, both A and B acquire security inter-

ests in the machine simultaneously. Both security interests are perfected simultaneously. However, A has priority because A filed before B.

Why are the interests perfected simultaneously? Because A and B's pre-attachment filings do not accomplish perfection; instead, for perfection to occur, there must be an attachment, which will happen here when the debtor acquires rights in the after-acquired collateral. When the property is acquired, *zing*, the security interests of A and B are perfected simultaneously.

The following checklist may assist in understanding the requirements for perfection by filing.

Checklist

☐ Agreement (security agreement)

☐ Value given by Secured Party

☐ Debtor has rights in the collateral

☐ Filing

When all of the boxes are checked (in whatever order), Secured Party has perfected. See § 9–308(a).

Note: When after-acquired collateral is encumbered by more than one security interest, one of the interests often is a purchase-money security interest that is entitled to special priority under Section 9–324. Thus, in Example 4, if B's loan enabled Debtor to acquire the new machine and created a purchase-money security interest, B would have priority under § 9–324(a). § 9–103 (a) and (b).

Application of priority rules to future advances

We already know that a security agreement may include future advances, regardless of whether the advances are given pursuant to commitment. (An advance is made "pursuant to commitment" if the secured party has bound itself to make it, i.e., an obligatory future advance rather than an optional or voluntary future advance.) §§ 9–204(c), 9–102(a)(68). Accordingly, a secured party may make periodic advances against a debtor–dealer's incoming inventory. Alternatively, a secured party may provide financing to a debtor-manufacturer by advancing monies in installments as the goods progress from raw materials and components to work-in-progress to completed goods (e.g., financing the construction of a jumbo-jet aircraft).

But what is the priority of a security interest based on future advances as against conflicting interests in the same collateral? Example: On February 1, D gives SP–1 a security interest in goods worth $25,000 to secure a loan of $10,000. The security agreement includes a provision for future advances. SP–1 promptly files. On March 1, LC levies on the goods, or SP–2 takes a security interest in the same goods and promptly files. LC's or SP–2's claim is for $7,500. On April 1, SP–1 makes a future advance of $10,000 under the February 1 security agreement. LC's intervening lien or SP–2's intervening security interest is clearly junior to SP–1's security interest because SP–1 filed and perfected before LC acquired its lien or SP–2 filed. §§ 9–201(a), 9–317(a)(2), 9–322(a)(1). But the burning question is whether SP–1's security interest has priority only as to the February 1 loan or also as to the April 1 loan.

Pre-Code analysis: Priority of SP–1's future advances vs. intervening LC or SP–2

The majority pre-Code rule as to the priority of a secured party's future advances as against intervening interests may be stated thus:

1. *Obligatory future advances.* If the future advance is legally obligatory, SP–1 has priority over LC or SP–2 as to the future advance (as well as the original advance), regardless of whether SP–1 has knowledge or notice of the intervening interests.

2. *Optional or voluntary future advances.* If the future advance is optional or voluntary, SP–1 has priority over LC or SP–2 if SP–1 makes the future advance without actual knowledge (as distinguished from constructive notice by filing or recording) of the intervening interest(s). If SP–1 has actual knowledge of these interests when it makes the second advance, SP–1 has priority as to the February 1 advance but *not* the April 1 advance.

Rationale: If SP–1 has actual knowledge of a later encumbrancer yet gives an advance SP–1 was not obligated to make, SP–1 should not be able to squeeze out a subsequent and junior encumbrancer by later enlarging the SP–1 security interest by the additional advance. Recall the above example: The goods were worth $25,000; SP–1's security interest was to secure the original advance of $10,000. This left a $15,000 equity for junior interests. Thus, LC's or SP–2's $7,500 claim could be satisfied from D's equity. If SP–1's subsequent advance of $10,000 also had priority over LC or SP–2, D's equity would be only $5,000, which would not wholly satisfy the interest of LC or SP–2. (It should be noted, however, that, although D's equity in the encumbered goods has been depleted, D's assets have been enhanced by the addition of SP–1's $10,000 April 1 advance.) See discussion of future advances in 2 G. Gilmore, Security Interests in Personal Property § 35.1 et seq. (1965).

Code analysis: Priority of SP–1's future advances vs. intervening secured party (SP–2)

"Under ... the first-to-file-or-perfect rule of Section 9–322(a)(1), ... the time when an advance is made plays no role in determining priorities among conflicting security interests.... Thus, a secured party [SP–2] takes subject to *all advances* secured by a competing security interest [SP–1] having priority under Section 9–322(a)(1) [first-to-file or perfect]. This result generally obtains regardless of how the competing security interest is perfected and regardless of whether the advances are made 'pursuant to commitment' [§ 9–102(a)(68)]." § 9–323 Comment 3. (For the scope of § 9–323, see Comment 2.) Further, Comment 4 to § 9–322 states, "In general the rule in . . . [§ 9–322(a)(1) (first-to-file-or-perfect)] does not distinguish among various advances made by a secured party. The priority of *every advance* dates from the earlier of filing or perfection." [Emphasis added.]

Comment 3 to § 9–323 gives the following example that illustrates the analysis above:

> EXAMPLE 1: On February 1, A makes an advance [of $10,000] secured by machinery [worth $25,000] in the debtor's possession and files a financing statement. On March 1, B makes an advance [of $7,500] secured by the same machinery and files a financing statement. On April 1, A makes a further advance [of $10,000], under the original security agreement, against the same machinery. A was the first to file and so, under the first-to-file-or-perfect rule of Section 9–322(a)(1), A's security interest has priority over B's, both as to the February 1 and as to the April 1 advance. It makes no difference whether A knows of B's intervening advance when A makes the second advance. Note that, as long as A was the first to file or perfect, A would have priority with respect to both advances if either A or B had perfected by taking possession of the collateral. Likewise, A would have priority if A's April 1 advance was not made under the original agreement with the debtor, but was under a new agreement.

Note that, in rare instances, the priority of an advance dates from the time the advance is made, e.g., when the security interest is perfected automatically or temporarily and the advance is not made pursuant to a commitment entered into while the security interest was perfected by another method. Thus, an advance has priority from the date it is made without commitment and while the security interest is perfected only temporarily. §§ 9–323 Comment 3 and Example 2, 9–322 Comment 4 and Example 3.

But what is SP–2 to do when the UCC filing officer discloses to it that SP–1 has filed a financing statement previously? Dean Steinheimer, in the Practice Commentary to Michigan Compiled Laws Annotated § 440.9402 (see revised § 9–502), states,

Notice filing. As stated in [§ 9–502(d)], a financing statement may be filed at any time—even before there is a security agreement or before the security interest attaches. The code philosophy is that a simple filed notice to third parties that the secured party and debtor *may* be financing with respect to collateral described in the financing statement should be a "red flag" warning third parties not to proceed with any financing on the same collateral of the debtor until investigation is made to see that the road ahead has been cleared. Because of the priority given to the first person to file a financing statement under the first-to-file rule of [§ 9–322(a)(1)], a second lender must always proceed cautiously before he does any financing of the debtor if there is already a financing statement on file covering the collateral in which he is interested. If there is such a prior filing, the second lender should do one of the following things:

(a) Insist that the record be cleared by the filing of a termination statement as to the financing statement which is on file. If there is, in fact, no outstanding indebtedness between the first lender and debtor, the debtor can demand such a termination statement [§ 9–513]. The second lender should not simply rely on the fact that he is satisfied that there is no actual loan outstanding between the first lender and debtor for so long as the first financing statement remains on file any subsequent advance made by the first lender to debtor would be fatal to second lender's rights under the first-to-file priority rule [§ 9–322(a)(1)].

(b) Enter into a subordination agreement with the first lender which appropriately apportions priorities in the collateral [§ 9–339].

(c) Have the first lender file a partial release of collateral [§ 9–512(a)].

A statement of account and list of collateral claimed by the first lender [§ 9–210], does not satisfactorily clear the way for the second lender because of the priorities given first lender under the first-to-file rule [§ 9–322(a)(1)].

Code analysis: Priority of SP–1's future advances vs. intervening lien creditor (LC)

"[A] security interest [of SP–1] is subordinate to the rights of a person that becomes a lien creditor [LC] to the extent that the security interest secures an advance made more than 45 days after the person becomes a lien creditor unless the advance is made:

(1) without knowledge of the lien; or

(2) pursuant to a commitment entered into without knowledge of the lien."

Sections 9–323(b) and Comment 4, 9–102(a)(52); cf. Federal Tax Lien Act, § 6323 (c)(2). ("It seems unfair to make it possible for a debtor and secured party with knowledge of the judgment lien to squeeze out a judgment creditor who has successfully levied on a valuable equity subject to a security interest, by permitting later enlargement of the security interest by an additional advance, unless that advance was committed in advance without such knowledge." 1972 UCC Official Text, § 9–312, Reasons for 1972 Change (5) (Paragraph 2, Appendix)).

Code analysis: Priority of SP–1's future advances vs. intervening buyer (B)

Section 9–323 (d) and (e) state as follows:

(d) **Buyer of goods.** Except as otherwise provided in subsection (e), a buyer of goods [B] other than a buyer in ordinary course of business takes free of a security interest [of SP–1] to the extent that it secures advances made after the earlier of:

(1) the time the secured party acquires knowledge of the buyer's purchase; or

(2) 45 days after the purchase.

(e) **Advances made pursuant to commitment: priority of buyer of goods.** Subsection (d) does not apply if the advance is made pursuant to a commitment entered into without knowledge of the buyer's purchase and before the expiration of the 45-day period.

"Of course, a buyer in ordinary course of business who takes free of the security interest under Section 9–320 . . . [is] not subject to any future advances." § 9–323 Comment 6.

For analogous rules for lessees, see § 9–323 (f) and (g) and Comment 6; for buyers of receivables or consignments, see § 9–323(c) and Comment 5.

D. PRIORITY RULES FOR VARIOUS TYPES OF COLLATERAL

(1) Goods Collateral

(a) Goods for Use—Equipment and Consumer Goods

Secured party vs. other secured parties, lien creditors, buyers, lessees

These priority questions may be analyzed on the basis of whether a purchase-money security interest is involved.

a. Non-purchase-money security interests. With respect to equipment or consumer goods, we have already seen that the priority of non-purchase-money security interests will be ranked according to time of filing or perfection. Further, we learned that the form of the claim to priority, i.e., filing or perfection, may shift from time to time, and the rank will be based on the first filing or perfection as long as there is no intervening period without filing or perfection. See § 9–322(a) and Comment 4. For detailed discussion see Part Five, C, 5, B, (1), (a) supra; Part Five, C, 5, C supra.

As to lien creditors, buyers, and lessees: A perfected security interest has priority over later lien creditors, buyers, and lessees. §§ 9–201(a), 9–317(a)–(c); see § 9–317(a)(2)(B). For detailed discussion, see Part Five, C, 5, B, (1), (a) supra. For discussion of after-acquired property and future advances, see Part Five, C, 5, C supra.

Simply: First in time, first in right.

b. Purchase-money security interests. We have also already seen that a perfected purchase-money security interest in equipment or consumer goods has priority over a conflicting security interest in the same collateral (SP–1 vs. SP–2) if the purchase-money security interest is perfected (e.g., by filing as to equipment, automatic as to certain consumer goods) when the debtor receives possession of the collateral *or* within 20 days thereafter. § 9–324(a) and Comment 3. As to lien creditors, buyers, and lessees, SP–1 has a 20 day grace period for perfection by filing. Such grace period cuts off intervening buyers, lessees, or lien creditors. (Former § 9–301(2) included lien creditors and transferees in bulk but not buyers generally.) Recall, however, that a buyer takes free of an automatically perfected purchase-money security interest in consumer goods if the buyer buys without knowledge of the interest, for value, and for the buyer's own personal, family, or household purposes. But note that filing is required for a motor vehicle that is subject to a registration requirement, even if it involves a purchase-money security interest in consumer goods. § 9–309(1). See § 9–311(a)(2), (b), (c); § 9–320.

For detailed discussion, see Part Five, C, 5, B, (2), (b) and (c) supra. For discussion of after acquired-property and future advances, see Part Five, C, 5, C supra.

Simply: Second in time, first in right.

Priority of security interests (SP–1 vs. SP–2) in transferred collateral

Section 9–325 addresses the "double debtor" problem, which arises when a debtor acquires property that is subject to a security interest created by another debtor. Comment 3 gives this example:

> EXAMPLE 1: A owns an item of equipment subject to a perfected security interest in favor of SP–A. A sells the equipment to B, not in the ordinary course of business. B acquires its interest subject to SP–A's security interest. See Sections 9–201, 9–315(a)(1). Under this section, if B creates a security interest in the equipment in favor of SP–B, SP–B's security interest is subordinate to SP–A's security interest, even if SP–B filed against B before SP–A filed against A, and even if SP–B took a purchase-money security interest. Normally, SP–B could have investigated the source of the equipment and discovered SP–A's filing before making an advance against the equipment, whereas SP–A had no reason to search the filings against someone other than its debtor, A.

Rule: "[A] security interest created by a debtor [B] is subordinate to a security interest in the same collateral created by another person [A] if:

(1) the debtor [B] acquired the collateral subject to the security interest created by the other person [A];

(2) the security interest created by the other person [A] was perfected when the debtor acquired the collateral; and

(3) there is no period thereafter when the security interest is unperfected." § 9–325(a); for limitation on rule, see subsection (b) and Comments 4–6.

Secured party vs. holder of lien arising by operation of law (SP–1 vs. LBOL)

Suppose SP–1 sold a car to D and retained a security interest in it to secure the unpaid balance of the purchase price. A financing statement is duly filed (or the security interest is noted on the certificate of title). Later, D takes the car to a garage for repair. Garage asserts a possessory lien to secure payment of the repair charges. Does SP–1's security interest have priority over the garage's lien arising by operation of law (LBOL)? Answer:

A *possessory lien* [LBOL] on goods has priority over a security interest in the goods unless the lien is created by a statute that expressly provides otherwise.

§ 9–333(b) (emphasis added). Section 9–333(a) defines "possessory lien":

In this section, "possessory lien" means an interest, other than a security interest or an agricultural lien:

(1) which secures payment or performance of an obligation for services or materials furnished with respect to goods by a person in the ordinary course of the person's business;

(2) which is created by statute or rule of law in favor of the person; and

(3) whose effectiveness depends on the person's possession of the goods.

Cf. § 2A–306.

Thus, Garage (LBOL) will have priority over SP–1 unless the lien [LBOL] is created by a statute that expressly provides otherwise. Example, from Iowa Code Ann. § 577.1:

Any person who renders any service or furnishes any material in the making, repairing, improving, or enhancing the value of any inanimate personal property, with the assent of the owner, express or implied, shall have a lien thereon for the agreed or reasonable compensation for the service and material while such property is lawfully in the person's possession, which possession the person may retain until such compensation is paid, but such lien shall be subject to all prior liens of record, unless notice is given to all lienholders of record and written consent is obtained from all lienholders of record to the making, repairing, improving, or enhancing the value of any inanimate personal property and in this event the lien created under this section shall be prior to liens of record.

Secured party vs. Article 2 or 2A claimant

Recall Article 2, wherein a seller who was defrauded by an impostor or a person misrepresenting his or her solvency could reclaim sold goods from such a buyer but not from a good-faith *purchaser* for value from the buyer. §§ 2–403(1), 2–702(2) and (3). See Part One, G, 1 supra. A "purchaser" is a person who takes by "purchase," which in turn is any voluntary transaction creating an interest in property—not only a sale, but also a mortgage, pledge, *or security interest*. § 1–201(b)(29), (30) (defining "purchase" and "purchaser"). Thus, an Article 9 claimant falls within the meaning of "purchaser," thus affording an Article 9 claimant BFP status. See § 9–109(a)(1). (As to secured party vs. claimant under Article 2A, Leases, see § 2A–307 esp. (3) and Part Two, F, 2, D supra.)

(b) Goods Held for Sale or Lease—Inventory

Secured party vs. other secured parties, lien creditors, buyers, lessees

A resolution of these priority questions may be analyzed on the basis of whether a purchase-money security interest is involved.

a. Non-purchase-money security interests. As between two secured parties (SP–1 vs. SP–2), security interests in the same inventory rank according to priority in time of filing or perfection. As between SP–1 and a lien creditor (LC), a perfected security interest has priority over later lien creditors. The same result applies to buyers (B) other than buyers in ordinary course of business. A buyer in ordinary course of business "takes free of a security interest created by the buyer's seller, even if the security interest is perfected and the buyer knows of its existence." See §§ 9–322(a)(1), 9–317(a)(2)(A) and (b), 9–320(a) (source of quote). As to lessees and lessees in ordinary course of business, see §§ 9–317(c), 9–321(c). For detailed discussion, see Part Five, C, 5, B, (1), (b) supra. As to after-acquired property and future advances, see Part Five, C, 5, C supra.

Simply: first in time, first in right except as to a buyer (or lessee) in ordinary course of business.

b. Purchase-money security interests. As between two secured parties (SP–1 vs. SP–2) asserting security interests in the same inventory, a perfected purchase-money security interest (SP–1) has priority over a conflicting security interest (SP–2) if (i) the purchase-money security interest is perfected (e.g., by filing) when the debtor receives possession of the inventory, and (ii) the purchase-money secured party (SP–1, e.g., manufacturer of goods) sends an authenticated notification to the holder of the conflicting security interest (SP–2) stating that the person sending the notification has or expects to acquire a purchase-money security interest (PMSI) in the debtor's inventory and describing the inventory. Note: These notification requirements apply only if the holder of the conflicting security interest [SP–2] filed a financing statement covering the same types of inventory (if SP–1's PMSI is perfected by filing) *before* the date of SP–1's filing. § 9–324(b) and (c)(1). (If SP–1 is temporarily perfected, see § 9–324(c)(2) and Comments 4–6.) Also, note that the holder of the conflicting security interest [SP–2] must receive the notification within 5 years before the debtor receives possession of the inventory. § 9–324(b)(3). For detailed discussion, see Part Five, C, 5, A and B, (2), (a) and (d) supra. As to after-acquired property and future advances, see Part Five, C, 5, C supra.

Simply: Second in time, first in right.

Instead of the secured party manufacturer (SP–1) selling goods to the debtor on a purchase-money-security-interest basis, suppose the manufacturer delivered the goods on *consignment.* Will the consignor–manufacturer be required to give notice to an inventory secured party of the consignee who has a security interest in the same goods? Yes. Former § 9–114 required "that where goods are furnished to a merchant under the arrangement known as consignment rather than in a security transaction, the consignor must, in order to protect his position as against an inventory secured party of the consignee, give to that party the same notice and at the same time that he would give to that party if that party had filed first with respect to inventory and if the consignor were furnishing the goods under an inventory security agreement instead of under a consignment." Former §§ 9–114 Comment 1, 9–102(2) (Article 9 applied to consignments intended as security). Revised Article 9, § 9–109(a)(4), applies to consignments as defined in § 9–102(a)(20). Consequently, § 9–324(b) and (c) also determines the priority of a consignor's interest in consigned goods as against a security interest in the goods created by the consignee. Note that § 9–103(d) states, "The security interest of a consignor in goods that are the subject of a consignment is a purchase-money security interest in inventory." §§ 9–324 Comment 7, 9–505 (re: use of "consignor" and "consignee"). See § 9–319 and Comments, Example 1; see Part Five, C, 2, A supra.

As to lien creditors, buyers, and lessees, "[I]f a person files a financing statement with respect to a purchase-money security interest before or within 20 days after the debtor receives delivery of the collateral, the security interest takes priority over the rights of a buyer, lessee, or lien creditor which arise between the time the security interest attaches and the time of filing." § 9–317(e), cf. former § 9–301(2) (ten days as against lien creditors and transferees in bulk).

A buyer in ordinary course of business takes free of a security interest *created by the buyer's seller* even if the security interest is perfected and the buyer knows of its existence. § 9–320(a), see § 9–317(b) and (e). Example of security interest other than that *created by the buyer's seller*: D grants SP–1 a security interest in goods D uses in D's business (i.e., equipment collateral) to secure repayment of a loan. SP–1 promptly files. D sells the goods to Dealer but does not repay the loan to SP–1. Dealer sells the goods to Buyer, a buyer in ordinary course of business. Buyer takes subject to SP–1's security interest; such interest was not created by Buyer's seller (Dealer) but by D. See § 9–315(a)(1). As to lessees in ordinary course of business, see §§ 9–321, 9–317(c) and (e).

Secured party vs. Article 2 or 2A claimant

The discussion above regarding equipment and consumer goods showed that a secured party can come into conflict with certain Article 2 claimants. The same can occur with regard to a secured party with an interest in inventory and an Article 2 claimant—that is, a defrauded seller's rights to reclaim goods are subject to the rights of a good-faith *purchaser* (including an Article 9 secured party) for value. §§ 2–702(3) (seller's remedies upon buyer's insolvency), 2–403(1) (good-faith purchase), 1–201(b)(29) and (30) (defining "purchase" and "purchaser"). (As to secured party vs. claimant under Article 2A, Leases, see § 2A–307, esp. (3) and Part Two, F, 2, D supra.)

Priority of security interests (SP–1 vs. SP–2) created by new debtor

"[Section 9–326] addresses the priority contests that may arise when a new debtor becomes bound by the security agreement of an original debtor and each debtor has a secured creditor." § 9–326 Comment 2. See inventory examples in Comments 2 and 3. Illustration:

1.   SP–X holds a perfected-by-filing security interest in X Corp's existing and after-acquired inventory.

2.   SP–Z holds a perfected-by-possession security interest in an item of Z Corp's inventory.

3.   Z Corp becomes bound by X Corp's security agreement as Debtor (e.g., Z Corp buys X Corp's assets and assumes its security agreement).

See § 9–326 Comment 2, Example 1.

(c) Farm-Related Goods

Priority rules with respect to farm-related collateral (e.g., farm products) may be stated as follows:

1.   Priority among conflicting interests and agricultural liens. "Conflicting perfected security interests and *agricultural liens* rank according to priority in time of filing or perfection." § 9–322(a)(1) (emphasis added). See § 9–322(a)(1) (second sentence), (2), and (3). However, this rule is *subject to* a special rule under an agricultural lien statute, that is, "[a] perfected agricultural lien on collateral has priority over a conflicting security interest in or agricultural lien on the same collateral *if* the *statute* creating the agricultural lien *so provides*." § 9–322(a), (f)(1), (g) (source of quote) (emphasis added). See §§ 9–102(a)(5) and (34) ("agricultural lien" and "farm products" defined), 9–109(a)(2) (agricultural liens within scope of Article 9), 9–308(b) (re: perfection of such liens), 9–310(a) and (c) (re: perfection by filing).

2. Security interest or agricultural lien vs. (i) lien creditors, (ii) buyers, and (iii) lessees. See § 9–317(a)(2), (b) and (c); § 9–201(a).

3. Purchase-money security interests in livestock. Subsections (d) and (e) of § 9–324 "provide a purchase-money priority for farm-products livestock. [§ 9–102(a)(34)]. They are patterned on the purchase-money priority rule for inventory found in subsections (b) and (c) and include a requirement that the purchase-money secured party notify earlier-filed parties. . . ." § 9–324 Comment 10, see Comment 11 (purchase-money security interests in aquatic farm products). Simply, second in time, first in right. For purchase-money security interests in inventory, see Part Five, C, 5, B, (2), (d) supra.

4. Secured party vs. BOCB. "[A] buyer in ordinary course of business [§ 1–201(b)(9)], *other than a person buying farm products from a person engaged in farming operations*, takes free of a security interest created by the buyer's seller. . . ." [Emphasis added.] § 9–320(a) and Comments 3 and 4. But see §§ 9–320 Comment 6, 9–315(a) and Comment 2. Example: Farmer sells certain cattle produced in Farmer's farming operations to BOCB. Farmer had previously granted SP–1 a security interest in the cattle; SP–1 duly filed a financing statement. BOCB takes subject to SP–1's security interest. Note: But for being farm products, the cattle would have constituted inventory, and a buyer in ordinary course of business would have taken free of SP–1's security interest.

Under the Federal Food Security Act, 7 U.S.C. § 1631, notwithstanding any other law (e.g., UCC), a buyer in ordinary course of business who buys a farm product from a seller engaged in farming operations takes *free from* a security interest created by the seller, even if the security interest is perfected and the buyer knows of the existence of such interest. "[T]he Act gave creditors three exceptions to the override; if the creditor fits into any of the three exceptions, its security interest will carry over against the buyer. Two of the exceptions depend upon a state's enactment of a central filing system of a kind specified in the federal act. . . . In the absence of such a federally blessed central filing system enacted by the state, the secured creditor can get protection against an ordinary course buyer only by giving that buyer notice of the creditor's interest in a form specified in the federal law. The notice is much more detailed than a UCC–1 [financing statement]. . . ." UCC Hornbook § 24–9, p. 872.

5. Priority of security interest in crops growing on real property as against an owner or encumbrancer of the real property. See § 9–334(i), (j) and Comment 12.

6. Priority of production-money security interests and agricultural liens.

Former § 9–312(2) gave priority to a new-value security interest in crops based on a current crop-production loan over an earlier security interest in the crop securing obligations due more than six months before the crops became growing crops. This rule "enabled a poor farmer to borrow money to plant current crops by giving a new value secured party a security interest in them which would have priority over a long overdue earlier security interest." Secured Transactions Hornbook § 5–5. Simply: Second in time, first in right.

Appendix II to Revised Article 9 at Model § 9–324A replaced § 9–312(2). It "contains ... priority rules relating to 'production-money security interests' held by secured parties who give new value used in the production of crops. Because no consensus emerged on the wisdom of these provisions during the drafting process, the sponsors make no recommendation on whether these model provisions should be enacted." § 9–101 Comment 4.e.

(d) Goods Affixed to Land or Other Goods—Fixtures, Accessions

In some instances, goods that were sold to debtor (D) by secured party (SP–1) on a secured basis are affixed to real estate or are installed in or affixed to other goods. Upon D's default, SP–1 may seek to remove the affixed goods to satisfy the indebtedness. At the same time, a person claiming an interest in the land (e.g., a land mortgagee) may assert an interest in the goods as *fixtures*; or a person claiming an interest in the "other goods" (e.g., a secured party) may claim an interest in the goods as *accessions.* Who has priority?

(i) Fixtures

Fixtures are defined as "goods that have become so related to particular real property that an interest in them arises under real property law." § 9–102(a)(41). "[Section 9–334] recognizes three categories of goods: (1) those that retain their chattel character entirely and are not part of the real property; (2) ordinary building materials that have become an integral part of the real property and cannot retain their chattel character for purposes of finance; and (3) an intermediate class that has become real property for certain purposes, but as to which chattel financing may be preserved." § 9–334 Comment 3. "To achieve priority under certain provisions of ... [§ 9–334], a security interest must be perfected by making a 'fixture filing' ... [§ 9–102(a)(40)] in the real-property records." Id. See §§ 9–501(a)(1)(B), 9–502(a)–(c). (Of course, "[i]n considering priority problems under ... [§ 9–334], one must first determine whether real-property claimants per se have an interest in ... fixtures as part of real property.... If ... real-property law gives real-property parties an interest in the goods, a conflict arises and ... [§ 9–334] states the priorities." § 9–334 Comment 4.)

Priority of security interests in fixtures

Section 9–334(c) states the *residual* priority rule: A security interest in fixtures is subordinate to a conflicting interest of an encumbrancer or owner of the related real property (other than the debtor). This rule applies *only if* one of the following rules does not. § 9–334(c) and Comment 5. See § 9–334(d)–(h). These other rules are enumerated below:

a. *Usual priority rule: first to file or record.*

Example 1 (secured party of the affixed goods vs. *subsequent* land mortgagee): SP–1 sells a new central air-conditioning unit to D for use in D's business premises and retains a purchase-money security interest to secure the unpaid balance of the purchase price. § 9–103(a) and (b). The unit is installed in a building on land D owns. The unit is a fixture. Later, E, a mortgagee, loans money to D and takes a mortgage on the land, buildings, and fixtures. Does SP–1's security interest in the fixture have priority over a conflicting interest of the mortgagee–encumbrancer (E) of the land and fixture? Answer: SP–1 has priority over E if SP–1 is perfected by a "fixture filing" before E's interest is of record. §§ 9–334(e)(1), 9–102(a)(40) and (41) ("fixture filing" and "fixtures" defined). See §§ 9–501(a)(1)(B) (re: appropriate filing office), 9–502(b) and (c) (contents of financing statement). Simply: First to file or record. § 9–334 Comment 6.

b. *Principal exception to first-to-file-or-record rule: purchase-money security interests.*

Example 2 (secured party of the affixed goods vs. *prior* land mortgagee): E, a mortgagee, loans money to D and takes a mortgage on land D owns. The mortgage, which includes buildings and fixtures on the land, is duly recorded. Later, SP–1 sells D a new central air-conditioning unit for use in D's business and retains a purchase-money security interest to secure the unpaid balance of the purchase price. § 9–103(a) and (b). The unit is installed in a building on D's land. The unit is a fixture. Does SP–1's security interest in the fixture have priority over a conflicting interest of the mortgagee–encumbrancer (E) of the land and fixture? Answer: Section 9–334(d) "contains the principal exception to the first-to-file-or-record rule of subsection (e)(1). It affords priority to purchase-money security interests in fixtures as against *prior* recorded real-property interests, provided that the purchase-money security interest is filed as a fixture filing in the real-property records before the goods become fixtures or within 20 days thereafter. This priority corresponds to the purchase-money priority under Section 9–324(a)." § 9–334 Comment 7.

Note: "It should be emphasized that this purchase-money priority with the 20-day grace period for filing is limited to rights against real-property interests that arise *before* the goods become fixtures. There is no such priority with the 20-day grace period as against real-property interests that arise subsequently. The fixture security interest can defeat subsequent real-property interests only if it is filed first and prevails under the usual conveyancing rule in subsection (e)(1) [first to file or record] or one of the other rules of this section." Id.

(c) *Another exception to the first-to-file-or-record rule: readily removable goods.* See § 9–334(e)(2) and Comment 8.

(d) *Judicial liens.* See § 9–334(e)(3) and Comment 9.

(e) *Special rule: manufactured homes.* § 9–334(e)(4) and Comment 10.

(f) *Construction mortgages.* § 9–334(h) and Comment 11. Note that the purchase-money priority rule of subsection (d) states that it is subject to subsection (h) (Priority of construction mortgage).

(g) *Priority based on consent, etc.* See § 9–334(f) and (g).

Removal of fixtures

See § 9–604, captioned "Procedure if Security Agreement Covers Real Property or Fixtures." Subsection(c) refers to removal of fixtures. Comment 3 states in part,

> Subsection (c) generally follows former Section 9–313(8). It gives the secured party the right to remove fixtures under certain circumstances. A secured party whose security interest in fixtures has priority over owners and encumbrancers of the real property may remove the collateral from the real property. However, subsection (d) requires the secured party to reimburse any owner (other than debtor) or encumbrancer for the cost of repairing any physical injury caused by the removal. This right to reimbursement is implemented by the last sentence of subsection (d), which gives the owner or encumbrancer a right to security or indemnity as a condition for giving permission to remove.

(ii) Accessions

Accessions are "goods that are physically united with other goods in such a manner that the identity of the original goods is not lost." § 9–102(a)(1); cf. "commingled goods." § 9–336(a) and Comment 2. "A security interest may be created in an accession and continues in collateral that becomes an accession. If a security interest is perfected when the collateral becomes an accession, the security interest remains perfected in the collateral." § 9–335(a), (b).

"With one exception, concerning goods covered by a certificate of title ... , the other provisions of ... [Part 3 of Article 9], including the rules governing purchase-money security interests, determine the priority of most security interests in an accession, including the relative priority of a security interest in an accession and a security interest in the whole." § 9–335(c) and Comment 6 (source of quote), which gives this example:

Example 3: Debtor owns an office computer subject to a security interest in favor of SP–1. Debtor acquires memory and grants a perfected security interest in the memory to SP–2. Debtor installs the memory in the computer, at which time (one assumes) SP–1's security interest attaches to the memory. The first-to-file-or-perfect rule of Section 9–322 governs priority in the memory. If, however, SP–2's security interest is a purchase-money security interest, Section 9–324(a) would afford priority in the memory to SP–2, regardless of which security interest was perfected first.

However, § 9–335(d) provides that a security interest in the whole, perfected by compliance with a certificate-of-title statute, takes priority over a security interest in the accession. This rule enables a secured party to rely on a certificate of title without having to check the UCC files to determine whether any components of the collateral may be encumbered. See § 9–335 Comment 7 and Example 4.

As to removal of accessions after default, see § 9–335(e), (f); cf. removal of fixtures, § 9–604 and Comment 3.

(e) Commingled Goods

" '[C]ommingled goods' means goods that are physically united with other goods in such a manner that their identity is lost in a product or mass." § 9–336(a). Examples: (i) flour that has become part of baked goods, (ii) ball bearings installed in an automobile engine. § 9–336 Comment 2; cf. accessions, § 9–102(a)(1).

A security interest does not exist in commingled goods as such. However, a security interest may attach to a product or mass that results when goods become commingled. If collateral becomes commingled, a security interest attaches to the product or mass. If the security interest in collateral is perfected *before* the collateral becomes commingled, the security interest that attaches to the product or mass is perfected. § 9–336(b)–(d). If more than one security interest is perfected, the interests rank equally in proportion to the value of the collateral at the time it became commingled. § 9–336(f)(2); Comment 4 gives this example:

> **Example 1:** SP–1 has a perfected security interest in Debtor's eggs, which have a value of $300 and secure a debt of $400, and SP–2 has a perfected security interest in Debtor's flour, which has a value of $500 and secures a debt of $600. Debtor uses the flour and eggs to make cakes, which have a value of $1000. The two security interests rank equally and share in the ratio of 3:5. Applying this ratio to the entire value of the product, SP–1 would be entitled to $375 (i.e., 3/8 x $1000), and SP–2 would be entitled to $625 (i.e., 5/8 x $1000).

(2) Indispensable Paper Collateral

"Indispensable paper collateral" includes various categories of paper that are either negotiable or to a greater or lesser extent dealt with as if negotiable, i.e., collateral evidenced by an "indispensable writing." Former § 9–106 Comment. This means that the claim is so *merged* into the paper evidencing the claim that the paper is treated as if it were the claim itself. Thus, transfer of the claim can be made only by delivery of the paper (often accompanied by an indorsement); discharge of the claim is made by payment of money, delivery of goods, etc., only to the holder of the paper who surrenders it. See, e.g., §§ 3–602(a) (payment), 3–301 (person entitled to enforce instrument), 7–403(a) and (c) (obligation of bailee to deliver), 7–102(a)(9) ("person entitled under the document"). Accordingly, collateral represented by a writing whose delivery operates to transfer the claim is said to be pledgeable. This type of collateral includes instruments, certificated securities, tangible chattel paper, and negotiable tangible documents.

Instrument

"Instrument" is defined as a negotiable instrument or any other writing that evidences a right to the payment of a monetary obligation, is not itself a security agreement or lease, and is of a type that in the ordinary course of business is transferred by delivery with any necessary indorsement or assignment. § 9–102(a)(47); see § 3–104(a) (drafts, checks, notes, certificates of deposit). The term does not include, e.g., investment property. Id. (Former § 9–105(1)(i) included in the definition of "instrument," a certificated security, e.g., a stock certificate under former § 8–102.)

A security interest in instruments may be perfected (i) by filing (this is new under Revised Article 9), (ii) by taking possession, or (iii) by temporary 20–day perfection. Note: *Sales* of promissory notes are automatically perfected. §§ 9–309(4), 9–312(a) and (e) and (g), 9–313(a); see § 9–102(a)(65) ("promissory note" defined).

Example: Maker issues a note to Payee due in 6 months. Payee pledges the note to SP–1 to secure SP–1's loan to Payee. SP–1 thus perfects its security interest by possession. The note becomes due, and SP–1 delivers it to Payee for the purpose of presentation to Maker for payment. See §§ 3–602(a) (payment), 3–301(i) (person entitled to enforce instrument), 1–201(b)(21) ("holder" defined). The security interest in the note remains perfected for 20 days without filing. § 9–312(g), (h) and Comment 9; see § 9–308(c) (continuous perfection).

SP–1 vs. lien creditor. If, within the 20-day period, LC, a creditor of Payee, acquires a lien in the note by attachment, levy, or the like, SP–1 has priority over LC (and LC's federal counterpart, the trustee in bankruptcy). §§ 9–201(a), 9–317(a)(2)(A), 9–102(a)(52)("lien creditor" defined as including bankruptcy trustee); see Bankruptcy Code § 544(a).

SP–1 vs. purchaser. If, within the 20-day period, P purchases the note, P has priority over any security interest of SP–1 in the note perfected by a method other than possession (e.g., temporary perfection) if P gives value and takes *possession* of the note in good faith and without knowledge that the purchase violates SP–1's rights. §§ 9–330(d) and Comment 7, 1–201(b)(29) and (30) ("purchase" and "purchaser" defined). Further, Article 9 does not limit the rights of a holder in due course (e.g., P) to take free of SP–1's claim to the note. §§ 9–331(a), 3–302 (holders in due course), 3–306 (claims to an instrument). This holder takes priority over an earlier security interest, even if perfected. § 9–331(a) (last sentence). (Note: filing under Article 9 does not constitute notice of a claim or defense to the holder in due course. § 9–331(c).)

As to buyers receiving delivery of instruments vs. secured parties, see § 9–317(b).

Certificated security

A certificated security is a security that is represented by a certificate, e.g., stock certificate. § 9–102(b); § 8–102(a)(4), (16), (18) ("certificated security," "security certificate," and "uncertificated security" defined); see § 9–102(a)(49) ("investment property" defined).

A security interest in certificated securities may be perfected (i) by filing (new under Revised Article 9); (ii) by taking delivery, i.e., acquiring possession (§ 8–301 (a)(1)); and (iii) by 20-day temporary perfection. §§ 9–312(a) and (e) and (g), 9–313(a). Note: a security interest in investment property may be perfected by control. §§ 9–314(a), 9–106, 9–102(a)(49) ("investment property" defined). As to automatic perfection, see § 9–309 (10), (11).

Example: Stockholder D, holder of a stock certificate issued by X Corp., delivers the certificate to SP–1 to secure SP–1's loan to D. SP–1 thus perfects its security by taking delivery. SP–1 then delivers the security certificate to D for ultimate sale or exchange. The security interest in the certificate remains perfected for 20 days without filing. § 9–312(g), (h) and Comment 9; see § 9–308(c).

SP–1 vs. lien creditor. If, within the 20-day period, LC, a creditor of D, acquires a lien on the certificate by attachment, levy, or the like, SP–1 has priority over LC (and LC's federal counterpart, the trustee in bankruptcy). §§ 9–201(a), 9–317(a)(2)(A), 9–102(a)(52) ("lien creditor" defined as including bankruptcy trustee); see Bankruptcy Code § 544(a).

SP–1 vs. purchaser. Article 9 does not limit the rights of a "protected purchaser" of a security (e.g., P) to take free of SP–1's claim to the security certificate. §§ 9–331(a), 8–303. A protected purchaser (a kind of bona fide purchaser) takes priority over an earlier security interest even if perfected. § 9–331(a) (last sentence). (Note: filing under Article 9 does not give notice of a claim or defense to protected purchasers. § 9–331(c).)

As to buyers who receive delivery of a security certificate vs. secured parties, see § 9–317(b).

Tangible chattel paper

Chattel paper consists of (i) a monetary obligation, together with (ii) a security interest in, or lease of, specific goods, if the obligation and security interest or lease are evidenced by a *record* or *records*. Traditional written chattel paper is included in the definition of *tangible* chattel paper. (Electronic chattel paper is chattel paper that is stored in an electronic medium instead of in tangible form.) § 9–102(a)(11), (31), (78) and Comment 5.b ("chattel paper," "electronic chattel paper," and "tangible chattel paper" defined). See definition of "record," §§ 9–102(a)(69), 1–201(b)(31).

A security interest in tangible chattel paper may be perfected (i) by filing, or (ii) by taking possession. §§ 9–312(a) and Comment 3, 9–313(a). (Note: A security interest in electronic chattel paper may be perfected by taking control of the collateral. § 9–314(a).)

Example: Dealer sells goods to User (account debtor). User and Dealer sign a security agreement whereby Dealer reserves a security interest in the goods to secure the unpaid balance of the purchase price. Dealer assigns this security agreement—now called *chattel paper*—to Bank either by outright sale or to secure a loan. Bank is SP–1; Dealer is Debtor re: the chattel paper. §§ 9–102 Comment 5.b., 9–109(a)(1) and (3) and (d)(4) and (5).

SP–1's perfecting by possession of the tangible chattel paper or by filing, will give it priority over later arising competing interests (SP–2, LC, B). § 9–322(a); §§ 9–201(a), 9–317(a)(2) and (b). (As to electronic chattel paper, see § 9–317(d).) However, a purchaser of the chattel paper has priority over SP–1's security interest in the chattel paper if the purchaser gives new value and takes possession of the chattel paper in good faith, in the ordinary course of the purchaser's business, and without knowledge that the purchase violates the right of SP–1. § 9–330(b) and Comment 6, which states in part, "[A] purchaser of chattel paper ... is not required as a matter of good faith to make a search in order to determine the existence of prior security interests.... [I]f a purchaser sees a statement in a financing statement to the effect that a purchase of chattel paper from the debtor would violate the rights of the filed secured party, the purchaser would have such knowledge. Likewise, under new [§ 9–330(f)], if the chattel paper itself indicates that it had been assigned to an identified secured party other than the purchaser, the purchaser would have wrongful knowledge ... , thereby preventing the purchaser from qualifying for priority under ... [§ 9–330(b)].... In the case of tangible chattel paper, the indication normally would consist of a written legend on the chattel paper...."

As to chattel paper as proceeds, see Part Five, C, 5, D, (4) infra; as to assignment of a perfected security interest, see § 9–310(c) and Comment 4 (see Example 2 regarding chattel paper) and Part Five, C, 4, B, (11) supra.

Document

Document means a document of title, e.g., bill of lading or warehouse receipt. § 9–102(a)(30); see § 1–201(b)(6), (16), (42) ("bill of lading," "document of title," and "warehouse receipt" defined) and § 7–201(b) (storage under bond). [Note: The definition of *document* incorporates both tangible and electronic documents of title, § 9–102 Comment 16.] See Part Four, A supra. Documents are issued by third party bailees: i.e., warehouses and carriers. Thus the problem: How does a secured party perfect its interest when goods are in the possession of a person other than the debtor or secured party, who may or not have issued a negotiable document of title?

1. *When a negotiable document is issued*. A security interest in negotiable documents may be perfected (i) by filing, (ii) by the secured party taking possession of a tangible document, (iii) by the secured party taking con-

trol of an electronic document, or (iv) by 20-day temporary perfection. § 9–312(a), (c)(1), (e), (f), (h) and Comments 8 and 9; §§ 9–313(a), § 9–314(a). See §§ 7–104 (negotiable and nonnegotiable documents of title), 7–403 (bailee's obligation to deliver), 7–102(a)(9) ("person entitled under the document" defined). For an example of 20-day temporary perfection, see § 9–308 Comment 4.

While goods are in the possession of a bailee who has issued a negotiable document covering the goods, a security interest in the *goods* may be perfected by perfecting a security interest in the *document*, and a security interested in the document has *priority* over any security interest that becomes perfected in the goods by another method *during* that time. § 9–312(c) and Comment 7 (Examples 1 and 2).

Perfection by possession or control of the document, or by filing or 20-day temporary perfection, will afford priority over a lien creditor (LC) and certain buyers (B). But perfection by filing or by temporary perfection will not limit the rights of a holder to whom a negotiable document of title has been "duly negotiated." The holder takes priority over an earlier security interest, even if perfected, to the extent provided in Article 7. Further, filing does not constitute notice of a claim or defense to the holder. §§ 9–331(a) and (c), 9–317(a)(2) and (b); see § 9–322(a). See discussion of "due negotiation" at Part Four, D, 1 and 2 supra. Even having a security interest in a document perfected by possession has some risks. See, e.g., §§ 7–205, 7–503(a) and Part Four, D, 2, C supra.

As to purchase-money security interests in inventory collateral, see §§ 9–324(c)(2), 9–312(f).

2. *When no negotiable document is issued*. While goods are in the possession of a bailee who has issued a nonnegotiable document covering the goods, a security interest in the goods may be perfected by:

(1) issuance of a document in the name of the secured party (e.g., nonnegotiable warehouse receipt engaging to deliver the goods "to Secured Party").

(2) the bailee's receipt of notification of the secured party's interest (e.g., nonnegotiable warehouse receipt engaging to deliver the goods "to Debtor" and Secured Party notifies warehouse of secured party's interest); or

(3) filing as to the goods. § 9–312(d) and Comment 7. See §§ 7–104 (negotiable and nonnegotiable documents of title), 7–403 (bailee's obligation to deliver), 7–102(a)(9) ("person entitled under the document" defined); cf. § 9–313(c) and Comment 4.

Thus, such perfection will generally give priority over later competing interests. §§ 9–317(a)(2) and (c), 9–322(a); but see §§ 9–320(a) (buyer in ordinary course of business), 9–321(c) (lessee in ordinary course of business).

Example (field warehousing): D (manufacturer or dealer) wishes to finance its inventory. D leases part of its premises to W, a field warehouse, which conspicuously sets off the leased area by wire, signs, etc. This area is the field warehouse and is under the control of W (not D). D delivers its inventory into the warehouse. W issues a nonnegotiable warehouse receipt wherein W engages to deliver the goods "to Bank" (not to the order of Bank). Bank is the "person entitled under the document" to whom W must deliver the goods. §§ 7–403(a), 7–102(a)(9). Thus, Bank has a perfected security interest in the inventory to secure its loans to D. § 9–312(d). Bank's perfected security interest has priority over a creditor of D who seeks to levy on the goods in the warehouse. § 9–317(a)(2). When D seeks to remove certain of the inventory for purposes of sale, Bank will issue a delivery order to W ordering it to deliver the goods to D. § 9–205(b) and Comment 3. See § 9–312(f) and Comment 9. For discussion of "person entitled under the document" and the delivery order, see Part Four, B supra.

As to the priority of a secured party vs. a warehouse or a carrier's lien, see §§ 7–209, 7–307 and Comments.

(3) Purely Intangible Collateral

Purely intangible collateral includes intangibles not evidenced by an indispensable writing, which may be the subject of commercial financing transactions, e.g., accounts and general intangibles.

Account

Account under former Article 9 meant any right to payment for goods sold or leased, or for services rendered, that was not evidenced by an indispensable writing. Under Revised Article 9, it is no longer limited to rights to payment relating to goods or services. § 9–102(a)(2)(i)–(viii) (first sentence). Health-care-insurance receivables are included. § 9–102(a)(2) (second sentence), (46). The term does *not* include rights to payment evidenced by chattel paper or an instrument, commercial tort claims, deposit accounts, investment property, letter-of-credit rights, or rights to payment for money or funds advanced or sold (other than arising out of the use of a credit card). § 9–102(a)(2) (third sentence). Example: Dealer sells goods to users (account debtors) on an open account wherein each have 60 days in which to pay. Dealer (debtor) assigns the accounts to Bank (secured party) either by outright sale or to secure a loan. See § 9–102(a)(2), (3), (28), (72) ("account," "account debtor," "debtor," and "secured party" defined); § 9–109(a)(1) and (3), (d)(4) (re: scope of Article 9). Note: certain accounts are also "as-extracted collateral." § 9–102(a)(6)(B) and Comment 5.a.

Perfection. A security interest in an account is perfected by filing. § 9–310(a). However, "an assignment of accounts ... which does not ... transfer a significant part of the assignor's outstanding accounts" is automatically perfected. §§ 9–310(b)(2), 9–309(2) (source of quote), 1–201(b)(35) ("security interest" defined). Also, health-care-insurance receivables under § 9–309(5) are automatically perfected. See § 9–309 Comment 5.

Priority. As between two secured parties, security interests rank according to priority in time of filing or perfection. § 9–322(a)(1). As to the priority of a secured party vs. lien creditors and buyers of accounts, see §§ 9–201(a), 9–317(a)(2) and (d). As to accounts as *proceeds*, see Part Five, C, 5, D, (4) infra. As to after-acquired accounts and disposition of accounts without accounting, see §§ 9–204, 9–205.

General Intangible

General Intangible is the residual category of personal property collateral (including things in action) that is not included in the other defined types of collateral (e.g., accounts, chattel paper, instruments, investment property, and money). Examples: intellectual property, rights to payment of a loan not evidenced by chattel paper or an instrument, and rights arising under an intellectual-property license. § 9–102(a)(42) and Comment 5.d. The term *includes* "payment intangibles" (a loan not evidenced by an instrument or chattel paper) and "software" (a computer program and any supporting information—but not a computer program embedded in goods). § 9–102(a) (42), (61), (75) and Comments 4.a., 5.d. and 25 ("general intangible," "payment intangible," and "software" defined). See § 9–109(a)(3), (d) (4) and (5) and (7) (scope of Article 9). The definition has been revised to *exclude* (i) commercial tort claims, (ii) deposit accounts, and (iii) letter-of-credit rights. § 9–102 Comment 5.d.

Perfection. A security interest in a general intangible is perfected by filing. § 9–310(a). However, "an assignment of ... payment intangibles ... which does not ... transfer a significant part of the assignor's outstanding ... payment intangibles" is automatically perfected. §§ 9–310(b)(2), 9–309(2) (source of quote). Also, a *sale* of a payment intangible is automatically perfected. § 9–309(3).

Priority. Between two secured parties, see § 9–322(a)(1); between a secured party and a (i) lien creditor or (ii) licensees and buyers of general intangibles, see §§ 9–317(a)(2) and (d), 9–201(a). As to a licensee of a general intangible, see § 9–321(a) and (b). As to *proceeds*, see Part Five, C, 5, D, (4) infra. See also §§ 9–204 (after-acquired property and future advances), 9–205 and Comment 4 (permissible use or disposition of collateral).

Other Intangible Collateral

Investment property includes securities (stocks and bonds), whether certificated or uncertificated, and security entitlements. § 9–102(a)(49). A certificated security is referred to above as "indispensable paper collateral" and is discussed at Part Five, C, 5, D, (2) supra (perfection by filing or taking delivery of the certificated security). A security interest in investment property may also be perfected by "control." See Part Five, C, 4, D supra and §§ 9–310(b)(8), 9–314(a), 9–106 (control of investment property), 8–106 and Comment 1 ("control" defined). As to automatic perfection, see § 9–309(9)–(11) and Comment 6 (§§ 9–309(9), 9–206(c) and Comment 2 codify "broker's lien").

The priority of security interests in investment property can be summed up as follows: a secured party who obtains control has priority over a secured party who does not obtain control. § 9–328 and Comments. As to lien creditors and buyers of investment property, see §§ 9–201(a), 9–317 (a)(2), (b), and (d); Bankruptcy Code § 544(a).

A *deposit account* is a demand, time, saving, passbook, or similar account maintained with a bank. § 9–102(a)(29). Except for proceeds, a security interest in a deposit account may be perfected only by *control*. §§ 9–310(a) and (b)(8), 9–314(a), 9–312(b)(1). A secured party has control of a deposit account if, for example, the debtor, secured party, and bank have agreed in an authenticated record that the bank will comply with the secured party's instructions regarding disposition of the funds *without further consent* of the debtor. § 9–104(a)(2), see § 9–104(a)(1) and (3). See also § 9–109(d)(13) (re: scope of Article 9).

As to priority among conflicting security interests in the same deposit account, see § 9–327 (e.g., security interests perfected by control take priority over those perfected otherwise, § 9–327 Comment 3). As to lien creditors, see § 9–317(a)(2), Bankruptcy Code § 544(a). As to the rights of transferees taking funds from a deposit account, see § 9–332 and Comments. As to the effectiveness of a right of recoupment or set-off against a deposit account, a bank's rights and duties with respect to a deposit account, and a bank's right to refuse to enter into or disclose the existence of a control agreement, see §§ 9–340, 9–341, 9–342.

Security interests in *letter-of-credit rights* may be perfected by control. §§ 9–102(a)(51) ("letter-of-credit right" defined), 9–314(a), 9–107 (control of letter-of-credit right), 9–312(b)(2), see § 9–310(a) and (b)(8). As to priority, see § 9–329.

Security interests in *electronic chattel paper* may be perfected by control. §§ 9–102(a)(31) ("electronic chattel paper" defined), 9–314(a), 9–105 and Comments (control of electronic chattel paper); see § 9–310(b)(8). Also, a security interest in chattel paper may be perfected by filing. § 9–312(a) and Comment 3. [*2010 Amendment.* The amended definition of "control" of electronic chattel paper conforms the Article 9 definition to the Uniform Electronic Transactions Act and the 1999 revisions to Article 7. The amendment provides a safe harbor test, but permits other forms of control as well. §§ 7–106, 9–105, UETA § 16.]

Commercial tort claim. See §§ 9–102(a)(13) ("commercial tort claim" defined), 9–109(d)(12) (scope of Article 9), 9–310(a), 9–504(1) (See § 9–108(e)(1)) (special rules for indication as collateral).

(4) Proceeds of Collateral

Proceeds defined

Proceeds means whatever is acquired upon the sale, lease, license, exchange, or other disposition of collateral. § 9–102(a)(64)(A), see (64)(B)–(E) and Comment 13 (the revised definition expands the definition and resolves ambiguities in former § 9–306(1)). Cash proceeds can consist of money, checks, deposit accounts, or the like. § 9–102(a)(9). See § 9–109(d)(12) (scope of Article 9).

Example: Dealer's inventory of cars is subject to Secured Party's perfected security interest. Dealer sells a car to a buyer in ordinary course of business whose down payment may be his or her old trade-in car and a check or cash. The balance of the purchase price may be payable according to the terms of a security agreement (chattel paper), promissory note (instrument), or promise to pay not evidenced by an instrument or chattel paper (account). The trade-in car, check, cash, chattel paper, instrument, and account are *proceeds* of the inventory collateral.

Secured party's rights on disposition of collateral

1. *Original collateral.* Generally, the security interest (or agricultural lien) continues in collateral notwithstanding sale or other disposition. Exceptions: Purchasers or

other Transferees take free of the security interest (i) if Secured Party authorized the disposition *free of* the security interest; (ii) if the interest is unperfected, § 9–317; (iii) if Transferees are buyers or lessees in ordinary course of business, §§ 9–320, 9–321, 2–403(2); and (iv) in certain other situations: §§ 9–321 (general intangibles), 9–330 (chattel paper and instruments), 9–331 (negotiable instruments and documents and securities), 9–332 (deposit account or money). § 9–315(a)(1) and Comment 2.

2. *Proceeds.* The security interest attaches to any *identifiable proceeds* of collateral. § 9–315(a)(2). As to when commingled proceeds are identifiable, see §§ 9–315 (b) and Comment 3, 9–203(f). Note: Generally, the secured party may proceed against both any proceeds and the original collateral but, of course, may have only one satisfaction. § 9–315 Comment 2.

Perfection of security interest in proceeds

"A security interest in proceeds is a perfected security interest if the security interest in the original collateral was perfected." § 9–315(c) and Comment 4. Thus, the security interest in the proceeds is automatically perfected if the security interest "in the original collateral was perfected." Id. Under § 9–315(d), such perfection is effective for 20 days, after which perfection continues only if (A) a filed financing statement that covers the original collateral, (B) the proceeds are collateral in which a security interest may be perfected by filing in the office in which the financing statement has been filed, and (C) the proceeds were not acquired with cash proceeds. § 9–315(d)(1)(A)–(C).

Example: D is a Florida corporation, and SP has filed a financing statement in Tallahassee, FL that covers "D's inventory of used automobiles." The proceeds are chattel paper from the sale of some of the automobiles. "Since one originally perfecting as to the debtor's chattel paper would file a financing statement in the 'same office' [Tallahassee] and since the proceeds have not been acquired with 'cash proceeds,' the secured creditor is perfected as to the chattel paper without any action by the creditor and despite the fact its financing statement does not list chattel paper. Since almost all filings ... are at the place of a corporate debtor's incorporation, the most common result is that perfection will continue as to proceeds without any action by the secured creditor. [§§ 9–501(a)(2) (re: appropriate filing office), 9–301(1) (re: governing law), 9–307(e) (location of debtor).] Presumably the drafters assumed that any search in the name of the debtor will find the filing as to inventory and will understand that the prior secured creditor likely claimed proceeds as well.'' UCC Hornbook § 23–16b, p. 1245.

As to the other situations involving automatic perfection in proceeds, see § 9–315 Comments 5–7; as to insolvency proceedings and returned and repossessed goods, see 9–315 Comment 8 (see also § 9–330 Comments 9–11); as to proceeds of collateral subject to an agricultural lien, see § 9–315 Comment 9.

Priorities among conflicting interests in proceeds

We have discussed a secured party's right to proceeds and when the interest is perfected. Whether the interest is perfected will often determine priorities between a secured party and various competitors. The competitors may be claiming the proceeds as proceeds of their original collateral (e.g., two inventory secured parties claim the same accounts or chattel paper as proceeds of their inventory collateral), or one competitor may be claiming the proceeds as its original collateral (e.g., SP–1 claims accounts or chattel paper as proceeds of its inventory collateral, SP–2 or purchaser claims the accounts or chattel paper as its original collateral).

The principal rules are as follows:

(i) Conflicting perfected non-purchase-money security interests rank according to priority in time of filing or perfection. The time of filing or perfection as to a security interest in collateral is also the time of filing or perfection as to a security interest in proceeds. § 9–322(a)(1), (b)(1).

(ii) A perfected purchase-money security interest in inventory has priority over an earlier-filed security interest in the same collateral if it fulfills the requirements of § 9–324(b) and (c). See Part Five C, 5, B, (2), (d) supra. "[However,] the special priority of the purchase-money secured interest carries over into only certain types of proceeds.... [T]he purchase-money priority in inventory ... carries over into identifiable cash proceeds ... received on or before the delivery of the inventory to a buyer. As a general matter, ... the purchase-money priority in inventory does *not* carry over into proceeds consisting of accounts or chattel paper." § 9–324 Comment 8. Policy: See § 9–324 Comment 8 (paragraph 3 and 4).

Example 1: On April 1, D grants to SP–1 a security interest in D's existing and after-acquired inventory; the same day, SP–1 files a financing statement covering inventory. On May 1, D grants to SP–2 a security interest in all D's existing and future accounts. On June 1, D sells inventory to a customer on 30-day unsecured credit. When D acquires the account, SP–2's security interest attaches to it (§ 9–203 (a) and (b)) and is perfected by SP–2's financing statement. At the very same time, SP–1's security interest attaches to the account as proceeds of the inventory and is automatically perfected. (See: "Perfection of security interest in proceeds" discussion above.) Under § 9–322(b), for purposes of determining SP–1's priority in the account, the time of filing as to the original collateral (April 1, as to inventory) is also the time of filing as to the proceeds (account). Accordingly, SP–1's security interest in the account has priority over SP–2's. Of course, had SP–2 filed its financing statement before SP–1 filed (e.g., on

March 1), then SP–2 would have priority in the accounts. See § 9–322 Comment 6, Example 5. (Note: § 9–324 governs the extent to which a special purchase-money priority in goods carries over into the proceeds of the original collateral. See Example 2 immediately below.)

Example 2: D creates a security interest in its existing and after-acquired inventory in favor of SP–1, who files a financing statement covering inventory. SP–2 subsequently takes a purchase-money security interest (§ 9–103(a) and (b)) in certain inventory and, under § 9–324(b), achieves priority in this inventory over SP–1. This inventory is then sold, producing proceeds.

SP–1 vs. SP–2. Assume the sale of the inventory produced accounts. "Accounts are not cash proceeds, and so the special purchase-money priority in the inventory does not control the priority in the accounts. Rather, the first-to-file-or-perfect rule of Section 9–322 (a)(1) applies. The time of SP–1's filing as to the inventory is also the time of filing as to the accounts under Section 9–322(b). Assuming that each security interest in the accounts proceeds remains perfected under Section 9–315 [see Perfection of security interest in proceeds discussion above], SP–1 has priority as to the accounts." § 9–324 Comment 9, Example 1. Note: If SP–2 had filed directly against accounts, the date of that filing would be compared with the date of SP–1's filing as to the inventory. The first filed would prevail under § 9–322(a)(1). § 9–324 Comment 9, Example 2; see Example 3.

SP–1 and SP–2 vs. purchaser of chattel paper or instrument. If the sale of the inventory produced chattel paper or instruments, the rights of SP–1, SP–2, and a purchaser of the chattel paper or instruments would be governed by §§ 9–330 and 9–331. Thus, a purchaser of chattel paper has priority over a security interest in it (e.g., of SP–1 and SP–2) which is claimed merely as proceeds of inventory subject to a security interest if the purchaser, in good faith and in the ordinary course of business, gives new value and takes possession of the collateral (if tangible chattel paper) or obtains control of it (if electronic chattel paper), and the chattel paper does not indicate it has been assigned to an identified assignee other than the purchaser. § 9–330(a) and (e) and Comments 2–5. (Note: § 9–330(a) and Comment 5 recognize the common practice of placing a "legend" on chattel paper to indicate it has been assigned.) As to instruments, see § 9–330(d) and Comment 7; § 9–331(a) (Article 9 does not limit the rights of a holder in due course of a negotiable instrument, who takes priority over an earlier security interest even if perfected).

As to other proceeds priorities, see § 9–322(c)–(e) and Comments 7–9 and 12; § 9–324(a), (d)–(f) and Comments 8–12.

E. PRIORITY RULES INVOLVING THE TRUSTEE IN BANKRUPTCY OR A FEDERAL TAX LIEN

(1) Trustee in Bankruptcy

The purpose of the Federal Bankruptcy Code (under what is sometimes called "straight bankruptcy") is (1) to effect an equitable distribution of the assets of a debtor-bankrupt's estate among his or her creditors, then (2) to rehabilitate the debtor–bankrupt by granting him or her a discharge from his or her remaining debts. Thus, a principal function of a trustee in bankruptcy is to collect and reduce to money the property of the debtor's estate for the purpose of distribution to the debtor's general (unsecured) creditors. Bankruptcy Code, 11 U.S.C. § 704 (B.C. § 704). Not only does the trustee succeed to the debtor's interest in assets (except certain exempt assets) (B.C. §§ 541, 522), but the trustee is also the holder of certain displacement powers in the interest of the general creditors. Most important for a UCC Article 9 secured party, the trustee (a) is vested with the rights of a hypothetical lien creditor to reach assets (B.C. § 544(a)), and (b) can set aside certain preferences (B.C. § 547).

Thus, the acid test of a secured transaction is whether the security interest will be valid as against the trustee in bankruptcy. See UCC Hornbook § 23–1.

(a) Trustee as a Federal Counterpart of the Lien Creditor

Hypothetical lien creditor

B.C. § 544(a) states in relevant part as follows:

(a) The trustee shall have, as of the commencement of the case, and without regard to any knowledge of the trustee or of any creditor, the rights and powers of, or may avoid any transfer of property of the debtor or any obligation incurred by the debtor that is voidable by—

(1) a creditor that extends credit to the debtor at the time of the commencement of the case, and that obtains, at such time and with respect to such credit, a judicial lien on all property on which a creditor on a simple contract could have obtained such a judicial lien, whether or not such a creditor exists;

(2) a creditor that extends credit to the debtor at the time of the commencement of the case, and obtains, at such time and with respect to such credit, an execution against the debtor that is returned unsatisfied at such time, whether or not such a creditor exists. . . .

Further, MacLachlan, Handbook of the Law of Bankruptcy § 183 (1956) states that § 70c [now B.C. § 544(a)] "may be regarded as rounding out the concept that bankruptcy is a general levy upon the debtor's assets, so as to cover assets that levying creditors might reach upon the date of bankruptcy if bankruptcy did not take place."

Thus, the trustee, as of the date of filing of the bankruptcy petition, obtains the rights under state law of a hypothetical lien creditor with a lien on the property of the debtor. Thus, an Article 9 secured party (SP–1) who is unperfected as of the date of bankruptcy will lose to a lien creditor under § 9–317(a)(2), and accordingly, will lose to the lien creditor's federal counterpart, the trustee in bankruptcy. Note that, under § 9–102(a)(52), a "lien creditor" includes a trustee in bankruptcy. See § 9–317 Comment 4. Simply: If SP–1 is perfected as of the date of filing the petition, SP–1 wins as against the trustee; if SP–1 is not perfected, SP–1 loses. Winning means SP–1 may "foreclose" upon the security; losing means SP–1 shares in the bankrupt's estate as a general creditor. (See B.C. § 544(a)(3) and fixture security interests at UCC Hornbook § 25–5b.4.)

But what if SP–1 sells equipment to D on May 1 and retains a purchase-money security interest? § 9–103(a) and (b). Assume D files a bankruptcy petition on May 5 and SP–1 files its financing statement on May 8. Will SP–1's grace period under § 9–317(e), which gives it priority over a lien creditor (LC), give it priority over the trustee in bankruptcy under B.C. § 544(a)? Answer: See B.C. § 546(b); B.C. § 362(a)(4) and (b)(3) re: automatic stay.

Actual creditor

B.C. § 544(b) states in part,

> [T]he trustee may avoid any transfer of an interest of the debtor in property or any obligation incurred by the debtor that is voidable under applicable law by a creditor holding an *unsecured claim*.... [Emphasis added.]

Under applicable law (that is, the UCC), an unperfected security interest is not subordinate to [or voidable by] *unsecured* creditors. § 9–201 only. (Such unperfected security interest is subordinate to *lien* creditors. § 9–317(a)(2), (e)). Thus, subject to a limited exception, B.C. § 544(b) may not be used to invalidate Article 9 security interests. See UCC Hornbook § 24–6.

(b) Trustee's Power to Avoid Preferential Transfers

State law generally allows a debtor to pay, and thus prefer, one or more of the debtor's unsecured creditors while leaving other unsecured creditors unpaid. Likewise, under state law, the first unsecured creditor to acquire a lien on property (by attachment, levy, or the like) has priority as to the property even though there may be nothing left for other creditors.

Federal bankruptcy law, on the other hand, is based on the theory that in some instances one creditor should *not* be preferred over others. See B.C. § 726(b). Thus, B.C. § 547 spells out circumstances in which the trustee may avoid certain preferences. Accordingly, even though SP–1 may defeat the trustee under B.C. § 544(a) (since SP–1 was perfected at the date of filing the bankruptcy petition), SP–1 may be vulnerable to the trustee under B.C. § 547.

Five elements of a preference action

B.C. § 547(b) authorizes the trustee to avoid any transfer of an interest in the debtor's property if five conditions are met:

1. The transfer must be to, or for the benefit of, a creditor. B.C. § 547(b)(1).

2. The *transfer* must be for, or on account of, an *antecedent* debt. B.C. § 547(b)(2). (Presumably, if the creditor gives "new value" concurrent with the transfer in the form of money or the release of property, the transfer is not on account of antecedent debt [see B.C. § 547(a)(2), UCC Hornbook § 24–4d].

" '[T]ransfer' means the retention of title as a security interest; . . . or each mode, direct or indirect, absolute or conditional, voluntary or involuntary, of disposing of or parting with property or with an interest in property." B.C. § 101(54). More on *transfer* later. See B.C. § 547(e).

3.   The transfer must have been made when the debtor was insolvent (debts greater than assets, i.e., "balance sheet" test). B.C. §§ 547(b)(3), 101(32). The debtor is presumed to have been insolvent on, and during the 90 days immediately preceding, the filing date of the petition. B.C. § 547(f).

4.   The transfer must have been made on, or within 90 days before, the filing date of the petition. B.C. § 547(b)(4)(A). Note: If the transfer was to an "insider" (e.g., debtor's brother), the trustee may avoid the transfer if it was made between 90 days and one year before the filing date of the petition. B.C. § 547(b)(4)(B).

5.   The transfer must enable the creditor to whom or for whose benefit it was made to receive a greater percentage of its claim that the creditor would receive under the distributive provisions of the bankruptcy code. B.C. § 547(b)(5).

Example 1: D owes ten unsecured creditors $1,000 each. (These debts were incurred several months ago.) D's debts are thus $10,000. D's assets, however, are valued at $1,000. (Thus, D is insolvent under B.C. § 101(32).) To share equally, each creditor should receive $100.

a.   Assume D pays one unsecured creditor, C–1, $1,000 and one month later goes into bankruptcy. Applying the above elements, this transfer, which is on account of an antecedent debt, is voidable by the trustee. (See five elements of a voidable preference above.)

b.   Now assume that, instead of paying C–1, D gives C–1 a security interest in goods valued at $1,000. C–1 promptly perfects by duly filing a financing statement. One month later, D goes into bankruptcy. Trustee can avoid this transfer (giving a security interest), which was for or on account of the antecedent debt. "Transfer" means, inter alia, every mode of parting with an interest in property, including a security interest. B.C. § 101(54). (If

C–1, as a secured party, were allowed to "foreclose" on the collateral, C–1 would receive $1,000, leaving nothing for the other creditors.) Cf. B.C. § 544(a).

Example 2 (delayed perfection): On May 1, SP–1 loans D $10,000 and takes a security interest in D's equipment. See § 9–203 [attachment]. SP–1 perfects [§ 9–308(a)] by filing a financing statement either on May 5 or on June 5. On July 15, D goes into bankruptcy. Applying each filing date, is there a transfer on an antecedent debt? Issue: Did the *transfer* occur when the security interest was created (May 1) or *perfected* (May 5 or June 5)?

a. Re: June 5 filing: Generally, the time of *perfection* (the June 5 filing) is when the *transfer* occurs. B.C. § 547(e)(2)(B) (addressing filings made after 30 days of the creation of a security interest). Thus, the June 5 transfer is for or on account of an antecedent debt (May 1). (See five elements of a voidable preference above.) Note: Under B.C. § 547(e)(1)(B), a transfer of personal property "is perfected when a creditor on a simple contract cannot acquire a judicial lien that is superior to the interest of the transferee." The rights of such a creditor against such transferee are determined by state law, the UCC. Thus, when the transferee (SP–1) becomes perfected (by filing) under §§ 9–317(a)(2) and 9–201, SP–1 prevails over a person who becomes a judicial lien creditor (LC) after the security interest is perfected. See § 9–308(a).

b. Re: May 5 filing: B.C. § 547(e)(2)(A) contains an exception to the rule enumerated in the June 5 example above. It states, "A transfer is made at the time such transfer takes effect between the transferor and the transferee (May 1), if such transfer is perfected at, or within 30 days after, such time." (The May 5 filing is "within 30 days after" such time (May 1).) Accordingly, since SP–1 gave new value concurrently with the creation of the security interest, the transfer is for or on account of a new and contemporaneous consideration, not a transfer on account of antecedent debt. B.C. § 547(e)(1)(B) and (e)(2)(A), see former UCC § 9–301(2).

Nine exceptions to the trustee's avoiding power

B.C. § 547(c) contains nine exceptions to the trustee's avoiding power under B.C. § 547(b). Thus, if a transfer is within one of the following nine exceptions, the trustee cannot avoid the transfer, even if the five conditions of B.C. § 547(b) are met.

1. *Contemporaneous exchange.* This exception is for a transfer that was intended by all parties to be a contemporaneous exchange for new value and was in fact substantially contemporaneous. B.C. § 547(c)(1). Example: S sells goods to B in exchange for B's currently dated check. S presents the check for payment in the normal course of affairs. Cf. Part One, F, 2, C supra.

2. *Debt payment in ordinary course.* This exception is for transfers in payment of ordinary debts made in the ordinary course of business (or "of financial affairs," if a business is not involved). B.C. § 547(c)(2). Example: Payment of monthly utility bills. Policy: To leave normal financial relations undisturbed.

3. *Enabling loan.* This exception is for purchase-money loans given by Lender (SP–1) to enable Debtor to purchase goods. Debtor gives a security interest in these goods to SP–1, who must perfect on or before 30 days after Debtor receives possession of the goods. B.C. § 547(c)(3); see UCC §§ 9–103(a) and (b), 9–317(e).

4. *Net result rule.* This exception codifies the net result rule: If the creditor and debtor have more than one exchange during the 90-day period, the exchanges are netted out according to the formula in B.C. § 547(c)(4).

Any new value the creditor advances must be unsecured to qualify under this exception.

5. *Improvement-in-position test: after-acquired inventory, accounts, proceeds—"floating liens."* Factual setting: To secure a loan on April 1, D grants SP–1 a security interest in "all inventory now or hereafter acquired by D"; "all accounts due or to become due to D" (i.e., after-acquired property, §§ 9–204, 9–205). A financing statement is duly filed on April 2. On November 1, a bankruptcy petition is filed. Issue: Does a *transfer* occur on April 2 when the *perfection* occurs or later, when the property is *acquired*? Importance: If the transfer occurs when property is acquired, all such property acquired within 90 days of filing a bankruptcy petition would constitute transfers on an *antecedent* debt (the April 1 loan) and be subject to avoidance by the trustee. Case law (and former § 9–108) held that after-acquired collateral generally is not security for an antecedent debt.

B.C. § 547(e)(3), however, states, "[A] transfer is not made until the debtor has acquired rights in the property transferred." Thus, items of property acquired by D within 90 days of filing the bankruptcy petition are transfers on antecedent debts and may be subject to avoidance under B.C. § 547(b) (subject to the exceptions of B.C. § 547(c)).

B.C. § 547(c)(5) is a limited exception to the avoidable-transfer provisions of B.C. § 547(b). It states that a trustee may *not* avoid a transfer of a perfected security interest in inventory or a receivable or the proceeds of either, *except* to the extent that the secured party improves its position during the 90-day period before bankruptcy. The test is a two-point test, and requires determination of the secured party's position 90 days before the bankruptcy petition is filed and on the date of the petition. Example:

		Debt	Value of Changing Inventory	Debt in Excess of Inventory
1.	90 days before filing petition	$150,000	$100,000	$50,000
2.	Date of filing petition	$120,000	$110,000	$10,000

Secured Party improved its position by $40,000 ($50,000 minus $10,000) (preferential transfer). Thus, Secured Party can claim only $70,000 ($110,000 minus $40,000) of the $110,000 value of the inventory on the filing date.

[This example assumes that all of Debtor's inventory was acquired within the 90 day period.]

Note: If the "insider" rule applies, the relevant measuring point is one year before the date of filing the petition (not 90 days). B.C. § 547(c)(5)(A)(ii). If new value was first given after 90 days before the filing, see B.C. § 547(c)(5)(B).

6. *Statutory liens.* B.C. § 547(c)(6) excepts statutory liens validated under § 545 from preference attack. Note: " 'statutory lien' means lien arising solely by force of a statute ... but does not include security interest." B.C. § 101(53).

7. *Alimony, maintenance, support payments.* B.C. § 547(c)(7) excepts certain such payments from preference attack.

8. *Small consumer transfers.* B.C. § 547(c)(8) excepts such transfers from preference attack.

9. *Small nonconsumer transfers.* B.C. § 547(c)(9) excepts such transfers from preference attack.

Continuity of perfection

We already know that a security interest is perfected when (1) it has attached and (2) all the applicable steps for perfection have been taken (filing, possession, control, or automatic perfection). If such steps were taken before the security interest attaches, it becomes perfected when it attaches. § 9–308(a).

Now we come to § 9–308(c):

> **Continuous perfection; perfection by different methods**. A security interest or agricultural lien is perfected continuously if it is originally perfected by one method under this article and is later perfected by another method under this article, without an intermediate period when it was unperfected.

Comment 4 to § 9–308 gives the following example illustrating subsection (c):

> Debtor, an importer, creates a security interest in goods that it imports and the documents of title that cover the goods. The secured party, Bank, takes possession of a tangible negotiable bill of lading covering certain imported goods and thereby perfects its security interest in the bill of lading and the goods. See Sections 9–313(a), 9–312(c)(1). Bank releases the bill of lading to the debtor for the purpose of procuring the goods from the carrier and selling them. Under Section 9–312(f), Bank continues to have a perfected security interest in the document and goods for 20 days. Bank files a financing statement covering the collateral before the expiration of the 20-day period. Its security interest now continues perfected for as long as the filing is good.

> If the successive stages of Bank's security interest succeed each other without an intervening gap, the security interest is "perfected continuously," and the date of perfection is when the security interest first became perfected (i.e., when Bank received possession of the tangible bill of lading). If, however, there is a gap between the stages—for example, if Bank does not file until after the expiration of the 20-day period specified

in Section 9–312(f) and leaves the collateral in the debtor's possession—then, the chain being broken, the perfection is no longer continuous. The date of perfection would now be the date of filing (after expiration of the 20-day period). Bank's security interest would be vulnerable to any interests arising during the gap period which under Section 9–317 take priority over an unperfected security interest.

Thus, Bank's interest might become subject to voidable-preference attack under § 547(b), (c) and (d) of the Federal Bankruptcy Code. (Bank would be subject to any interest arising during the gap period which, under § 9–317, takes priority over an unperfected security interest, e.g., lien creditor and trustee in bankruptcy. § 9–102(a)(52)(C).) Thus, if Bank is unperfected at the beginning of the 90-day period before bankruptcy, or allows itself to become unperfected within the 90-day period, a perfection (e.g., filing) within this period would constitute a *transfer* made by the debtor for or on account of an antecedent debt. Accordingly, if the other elements of a voidable preference are established (B.C. § 547(b)), the trustee may avoid Bank's security interest.

Summary

Perfection does not necessarily afford protection as against all third party claimants. Perfection by possession affords the greatest protection; then perfection by filing. Even so, buyers in ordinary course of business and holders of "duly negotiated" documents take free of a security interest perfected by filing. § 9–320(a), § 9–331(a) and (c). Automatic perfection affords less protection than filing, e.g., § 9–320(b). Note: Despite the fact that it has a lower priority than any perfected secured party, even an unperfected secured party prevails in some instances; see § 9–317(b)–(d).

But remember: Although certain methods of perfection give more protection than others, *any* type of perfection will protect a security interest against a lien creditor and, accordingly, the trustee in bankruptcy. §§ 9–317(a)(2), 9–102(a)(52). If SP–1 is continuously perfected (e.g., by possession, then 20 day temporary perfection, then filing within 20 days, then perfecting as to proceeds) the trustee cannot defeat SP–1. B.C. §§ 544, 547 or 551 (avoided transfer is preserved for the benefit of the estate). This is crucial because losing to the bankruptcy trustee is often regarded as SP–1's greatest risk.

(2) Federal Tax Lien

If any person owing tax to the United States neglects or refuses to pay after it is demanded, the United States shall have a lien in that amount (including interest, etc.) upon all such person's property. Such lien arises at the time the assessment is made, but is not valid as against any holder of a security interest until appropriate notice of the lien has been filed. 26 U.S.C. (I.R.C.) §§ 6321, 6322, 6323(a).

As to the validity of an Article 9 security interest securing future advances made *after* a tax lien is filed, see 26 U.S.C. (I.R.C.) § 6323(c), (d). Cf. § 9–323 and Comment 4.

6. PERFECTION AND PRIORITY FOR MULTIPLE STATE TRANSACTIONS

Suppose Debtor, which is incorporated in State A with a chief executive office in State B, gives SP–1, located in State D, a security interest in *goods* located in State C. Alternatively, what if Debtor gives a security interest in *accounts*, an intangible that has no location in any realistic sense? The issue in either case becomes which jurisdiction supplies the applicable law governing perfection and priority of security interests.

A. WHICH JURISDICTION'S LAW NORMALLY GOVERNS

The basic rule of former 9–103(1)(b) was that the law of the jurisdiction where the collateral was located governed the perfection of security interests and the effect of perfection or nonperfection. This rule applied, e.g., to ordinary goods (that is, goods other than those covered by a certificate of title, mobile goods, or minerals). Exceptions to this rule were found at § 9–103(1)(c), (2)(a) and (b), (3)(a) and (b), and (4)–(6). For most accounts and general intangibles, by contrast, the law of the jurisdiction where the *debtor* was *located* governed perfection and the effect of perfection or nonperfection of the security interest.

Law governing perfection: general rule

Revised § 9–301(1) contains a single, general rule covering governing perfection of security interests in both tangible and intangible collateral, whether perfected by filing or automatically: normally, the applicable law is the law of the *debtor's location*. §§ 9–301 Comment 4, 9–307. "[Section 9–307(b)] states the general rules: An individual debtor is deemed to be located at the individual's principal residence with respect to both personal and business assets. Any other debtor is deemed to be located at its place of business if it has only one, or at its chief executive office if it has more than one place of business." § 9–307 Comment 2. This general rule is subject to several exceptions, most notably the following: "Under … [§ 9–307(e)], a registered organization (e.g., a corporation or limited partnership) organized under the law of a 'State' … is located in its State of organization." §§ 9–307 Comment 4, 9–102(a)(70), (76) ("registered organization" and "state" defined).

Law governing perfection: exceptions

The general rule stated above is subject to several exceptions. It does not apply to (i) goods covered by a certificate of title (§ 9–303); (ii) deposit accounts (§ 9–304); (iii) investment property (§ 9–305); (iv) letter-of-credit rights (§ 9–306); (v) possessory security interests (§ 9–301(2)); (vi) security interests perfected by a fixture filing (§ 9–301(3)(A)); (vii) security interests in timber to be cut (§ 9–301(3)(B)); or (viii) security interests in "as-extracted" collateral (§§ 9–301 (4), 9–102(a)(6)). See § 9–301 Comment 5. For example, § 9–301(2) states that perfection of *possessory* security interests is governed by the local law of the jurisdiction where the *collateral* is *located*. § 9–301 Comment 5.a.

Law governing *effect* of perfection and *priority*

Under former § 9–103, the law of a single jurisdiction governed both perfection and priority. Section 9–301(1) generally adopts that approach. Section 9–301 (3)(C), however, divorces questions of perfection from questions of the *effect* of perfection or nonperfection and the *priority* of a security interest. Under paragraph (3)(C), the rights of competing claimants to tangible collateral (tangible negotiable documents, goods, instruments, money, or tangible chattel paper) are resolved by reference to the law of the jurisdiction where the collateral is located. Example: A security interest in equipment located in PA is perfected by filing in IL, where Debtor is located (§ 9–307). If the law of the jurisdiction where Debtor is located (IL) were to govern priority, then the priority of an execution lien on goods located in PA would be governed by rules enacted by the IL legislature. § 9–301 Comment 7; see §§ 9–102(a)(52), 9–317(a)(2). Hence, perfection is governed by IL law; the effect of perfection and priority is governed by PA law. (PA and IL perfection and priority rules should be the same, as both have enacted revised Article 9.) Thus, in the majority of cases, the question will be where one files the financing statement, in IL or PA. Answer: IL.

As to the law governing perfection and priority of agricultural liens, see §§ 9–302, 9–102 (a)(5), 9–109(a)(2).

Note: Sections 9–301 through 9–307 do not address choice of law for other purposes. For example, the law governing attachment, validity, characterization (e.g., true lease or security interest), and enforcement is determined by the rules in § 1–105 [Rev. § 1–301]. § 9–301 Comment 2.

B. WHICH JURISDICTION'S LAW GOVERNS (I) WHEN DEBTOR MOVES FROM THE JURISDICTION WHOSE LAW FIRST GOVERNED, OR (II) WHEN COLLATERAL IS MOVED FROM THE JURISDICTION WHOSE LAW FIRST GOVERNED

"When the *debtor changes* its *location* to another jurisdiction, the jurisdiction whose law governs perfection under ... [§ 9–301(1)] changes as well. Similarly, the law governing perfection of a *possessory* security interest in collateral under ... [§ 9–301(2)] *changes* when the *collateral* is *removed* to another jurisdiction. Nevertheless, these changes will not result in an immediate loss of perfection." §§ 9–301 Comment 6, 9–316(a) and (b). [Emphasis added.]

"[Section 9–316] generally provides that a security interest perfected under the law of one jurisdiction remains perfected for a fixed period of time (four months or one year, depending on the circumstances), even though the jurisdiction whose law governs perfection changes. However, cessation of perfection under the law of the original jurisdiction cuts short the fixed period. The four-month and one-year periods are long enough for a secured party to discover in most cases that the law of a different jurisdiction governs perfection and to reperfect (typically by filing) under the law of that jurisdiction. If a secured party properly reperfects a security interest before it becomes unperfected under ... [§ 9–316(a)], then the secu-

rity interest remains perfected continuously thereafter. See
... [§ 9–316(b)]." § 9–316 Comment 2.

Example: D is a general partnership with a chief executive office in PA. SP–1 perfects a security interest in D's
equipment by filing in PA on May 15, 2002. §§ 9–301(1),
9–307(b)(3). On April 1, 2005, without SP–1's knowledge,
D moves its chief executive office to NJ. SP–1's security
interest remains perfected for four months after the move.
§ 9–316(a)(2) and Comment 2, Example 1. For application of the one-year rule, see § 9–316(a)(3) and Comment
2, Examples 2–5.

Retroactive unperfection

As a consequence of failing to reperfect before perfection ceases under § 9–316(a) (e.g., 4 months), the security
interest becomes unperfected (i) *prospectively* and (ii), as
against purchasers for value, including *buyers* and *secured
parties* (but not donees or *lien creditors*), *retroactively*.
Policy: Although this approach creates the potential for
circular priorities, the alternative—retroactive unperfection against lien creditors—would create substantial and
unjustifiable preference risks. § 9–316(b) and Comment 3
and Examples 6 and 7. See B.C. § 547; §§ 9–317(a)(2), 9–
102(a)(52) ("lien creditor" defined). Cf. § 9–515(c) and
Comment 3.

Possessory security interests

Possessory security interests in collateral (e.g., goods)
moved to a new jurisdiction generally remain continually
perfected; upon entry into the new jurisdiction, the security interest is perfected under the law of the new jurisdiction. § 9–316(c) and Comment 4.

Goods covered by certificate of title

Subsections (d) and (e) of § 9–316 address continued
perfection of a security interest in goods covered by a

certificate of title. See Comment 5 and Examples 8 and 9. Example 8 states,

> Debtor's automobile is covered by a certificate of title issued by Illinois. Lender perfects a security interest in the automobile by complying with Illinois' certificate-of-title statute. Thereafter, Debtor applies for a certificate of title in Indiana. Six months thereafter, Creditor acquires a judicial lien on the automobile. Under Section 9–303(b), Illinois law ceases to govern perfection; rather, once Debtor delivers the application and applicable fee to the appropriate Indiana authority, Indiana law governs. Nevertheless, under Indiana's Section 9–316(d), Lender's security interest remains perfected until it would become unperfected under Illinois law had no certificate of title been issued by Indiana. (For example, Illinois' certificate-of-title statute may provide that the surrender of an Illinois certificate of title in connection with the issuance of a certificate of title by another jurisdiction causes a security interest noted thereon to become unperfected.) If Lender's security interest remains perfected, it is senior to Creditor's judicial lien.

Note: "Section 9–337 affords protection to a limited class of persons buying or acquiring a security interest in the goods [e.g., a buyer of the goods, other than a person in the business of selling goods of that kind] while a security interest is perfected under the law of another jurisdiction but after this State has issued a clean certificate of title." § 9–316 Comment 5.

As to deposit accounts, letter-of-credit rights, investment property, and agricultural liens, see § 9–316(f), (g) and Comments 6 and 7.

[*2010 Amendment. Section 9–316 is redesignated: Effect of Change in Governing Law.*

Security Interests that Attach after Debtor Changes Location. Subsections (a) and (b) address security interests that are perfected (i.e., that have attached and as to which any required perfection step has been taken) before the debtor changes its location. In contrast, new subsection (h) applies to security interests that have not attached before the location changes. § 9–316 Comment 2 (last paragraph), § 9–316(h) and Comment 7, Example 9. (As to change in location of a "registered organization", see E. Smith, A Summary of the 2010 Amendments, UCC L.J. 345 at 360 note 55.)

Collateral Acquired by New Debtor. Subsection (i) to § 9–316 is similar to subsection (h). "Whereas subsection (h) addresses security interests that attach within four months after a debtor changes its location, subsection (i) address-es security interests that attach within four months after a new debtor becomes bound as debtor by a security agree-ment entered into by another person. . . ." § 9–316(i) and Comment 8, Example 10. (See special rules set forth at §§ 9–325, 9–326.

Note: Original Example 5 has been deleted; Examples 6–9 are redesignated 5–8; Example 10 is redesignated 11.]

7. RIGHTS AND DUTIES OF DEBTOR, SECURED PARTY, AND INTERESTED THIRD PARTIES—BEFORE DEFAULT

A. RIGHTS AND DUTIES OF DEBTOR AND SE-CURED PARTY

Security agreement

Except as otherwise provided by the Code, a security agreement is effective according to its terms between the parties (Debtor and Secured Party). § 9–201(a); see § 9–201(b)–(d) and Comments. The terms of a security agree-ment typically include Debtor's obligation to pay the indebtedness, the terms of payment, who bears the risk of loss or damage to the collateral, Debtor's obligation to insure the collateral, Debtor's obligation to maintain and repair the collateral, Debtor's warranty of ownership of the collateral, Debtor's right (if any) to move the collateral to another location, etc. See Part Five, C, 3, A, (2) and (3) supra, especially as to terms that will be given only limited effect or are ineffective.

Article 9 provisions

In addition, Article 9 includes provisions regarding rights, duties, and obligations that apply regardless of whether title to collateral is in the secured party or in the debtor. § 9–202. Some provisions apply only when the security agreement is silent on the question; others apply regardless of the terms of the security agreement. Some examples of both kinds of terms follow:

1. *Rights and duties of secured party in possession or control of collateral.* A secured party with possession of collateral before default is a kind of bailee (pledgee).

a. Duty of care. Generally, Secured Party must use reasonable care in the custody and preservation of collateral in its possession. § 9–207(a) and Comment 2.

b. Specific rules (§ 9–207 Comment 3):

(i) Reasonable expenses incurred in the custody, *preservation,* etc., of *collateral* are chargeable to Debtor and secured by the collateral. § 9–207(b)(1).

(ii) Risk of accidental *loss* or damage is on Debtor to the extent of a deficiency in any insurance coverage. § 9–207(b)(2); cf. § 2–510.

(iii) Secured Party must *keep collateral identifiable*, except that fungible collateral may be commingled. § 9–207(b)(3); cf. § 7–207(a).

(iv) Secured Party may *use* or *operate* the *collateral* to preserve it or its value. § 9–207(b)(4)(A); but see § 9–207(b)(4)(B) and (C) and Comment 4.

(v) Secured Party may hold any proceeds (except money or funds) received from the collateral, as *additional security*. § 9–207(c)(1).

(vi) Secured Party must *apply money* or funds received from the collateral to *reduce* the secured *obligation* (unless the money or funds is remitted to Debtor). § 9–207(c)(2).

(vii) Secured Party may create a security interest in the collateral (*repledge* the collateral). § 9–207(c)(3) and Comments 5 and 6.

[Note: As to *buyers* of certain rights to payment, see § 9–207(d) and Comment 7.]

2. *Additional duties of secured party with control of collateral.* Section 9–208 imposes upon a secured party having control of a deposit account, electronic chattel paper, investment property, letter-of-credit right, or electronic documents of title the duty to *release control* when there is no secured obligation and no commitment to give value. Note: The duty to terminate control is analogous to the duty to file a termination statement imposed by § 9–513. § 9–208 Comments 2 and 3.

Section 9–209 contains analogous provisions when an account debtor has been notified to pay a secured party. See § 9–209 Comment 2.

As to the duty of a secured party with possession (pledgee) to *relinquish possession,* see § 9–208 Comment 4.

3. *Secured party's duty to respond to requests by debtor for information about the secured obligation.* Debtor (D) may request three types of information: (i) D may request SP to prepare and send an "accounting," (ii) D may submit a list of collateral for SP's approval or correction, and (iii) D may submit for SP's approval or correction a statement of the aggregate amount of unpaid secured obligations. See § 9–210(a)(2)–(4). SP is required

to respond to a request within 14 days following receipt. § 9–210(a)(1), (b), (c) and Comments 2 and 4. During a six-month period, D is entitled to receive one free response from SP to a request. § 9–210(f).

As to why requests can be made by debtors only (not, e.g., by other potential secured parties), see § 9–210 Comment 3; if the person claims no interest in collateral or obligations, see § 9–210(d) and (e) and Comment 5; as to waiver of rights and remedies for noncompliance with § 9–210, see §§ 9–602(2), 9–625(f) and (g).

Note: The duty to respond to requests under § 9–210(b) does not apply to a *buyer* of accounts, chattel paper, payment intangibles, or promissory notes, or a consignor.

B. RIGHTS OF THIRD PARTIES

Security agreement

"[Section 9–201(a)] provides that a security agreement is generally effective. With certain exceptions, a security agreement is effective between the debtor and secured party and is likewise effective against third parties.... It follows that subsection (a) does not provide that every term or provision contained in a record that contains a security agreement or that is so labeled is effective.... Exceptions to the general rule of subsection (a) arise where there is an overriding provision in this Article or any other Article of the UCC. For example, Section 9–317 subordinates unperfected security interests to lien creditors and certain buyers, and several provisions in Part 3 [e.g., § 9–322] subordinate some security interests to other security interests and interests of purchasers." § 9–201 Comment 2; see § 1–302 Comment 1 (First paragraph, last sentence). But see § 9–339 (subordination agreement).

Article 9 provisions

"[Part 4 of Article 9 (§§ 9–401 through 9–409)] deals with several issues affecting third parties (i.e., parties other than the debtor and the secured party). . . . This Part primarily addresses the rights and duties of account debtors and other persons obligated on collateral who are not, themselves, parties to a secured transaction." § 9–401 Comment 2. These matters are addressed below.

1. *Alienability of debtor's rights in collateral to third parties.* Generally, whether a debtor's rights in collateral may be voluntarily or involuntarily transferred is governed by law other than Article 9. However, Article 9 does address the issue in §§ 9–401(b), 9–406 through 9–409. § 9–401(a) and Comment 4.

Under § 9–401(b), an agreement between Debtor and Secured Party that prohibits transfer of Debtor's rights in collateral (or makes the transfer a default) does *not prevent* the *transfer* from *taking effect.* § 9–401(b) and Comment 5 and Example 2 (negative pledge covenant).

Example: To secure a $100,000 debt, D gives SP a security interest in D's inventory worth $200,000. The security agreement prohibits any transfer of D's interest in the collateral. A financing statement is duly filed. Later, LC, a judgment creditor of D, levies on certain units of the inventory. Per the above rule, the levy is effective to reach D's equity in the inventory. (Collateral worth $200,000 minus $100,000 debt to SP equals $100,000, which is D's equity.) LC can reach only D's equity because LC's interest is subordinate to SP's prior perfected security interest. §§ 9–201(a), 9–317(a)(2), see § 9–315(a)(1). Determining D's equity in the particular units seized by LC's levy is not a simple matter. The solution to this problem is left to the courts. The doctrine of marshalling may be appropriate. § 9–401 Comment 6. For discussion of marshalling (particularly the "two funds" doctrine), see Nelson & Whitman, Real Estate Finance Law § 10.9 et seq. (5th Practitioner's Ed. 2007).

As to *sales* of receivables, see § 9–401 Comment 7.

2. *Secured party's obligation on debtor's contract.* The mere existence of a security interest, agricultural lien, or authority given to the debtor to dispose of or use collateral does not subject a secured party to liability in *contract* or *tort* for the *debtor's* acts or omissions. § 9–402 and Comment 2.

3. *Account debtor's right to assert defenses against assignee.*

Assume S sells defective equipment to B, who discovers the defect and refuses to pay the purchase price. See, e.g., §§ 2–313 (express warranty), 2–314 (implied warranty of merchantability), 2–601 (buyer's rights on improper delivery), 2–608 (revocation), 2–711 (buyer's remedies), 2–714 (damages for breach; accepted goods). Meanwhile, S assigns the right to the purchase price to Bank as security for a loan. Will B be able to assert its defense (defective goods) against Bank? Rule: The rights of an assignee (Bank) are *subject to* all terms of the agreement between the account debtor (B) and assignor (S) and any defense or claim in recoupment (partial defense) *arising from* the transaction that gave rise to the contract. §§ 9–404(a) and (b), 9–102(a)(3) ("account debtor" defined). Simply: Assignees stand in the shoes of their assignors. (As to any *other* defense or claim, see § 9–404(a)(2).) For exceptions, see § 9–404(b)–(e) and Comments 3–5.

"Of course an account debtor may waive its right to assert defenses or claims against an assignee under Section 9–403 or other applicable law." § 9–404 Comment 2. Section 9–403(b) provides that, with certain exceptions, "an agreement between an account debtor and an assignor not to assert against an assignee any claim or defense that the account debtor may have against the assignor is enforceable by an assignee that takes an assignment: (1) for value; (2) in good faith; [and] (3) without notice. . . ." See § 9–403(a). Example of waiver-of-defense clause: "Buyer/debtor [account debtor] waives the right to assert against any assignee of the seller/secured party [assignor], or any subsequent assignee, any defense, claim in recoupment, counterclaim, or setoff that it could assert against the seller/secured party in an action brought by it upon the debt of the buyer/debtor or upon the security agreement." (These agreements are typical in installment-sale agreements and leases.)

Note that § 9–403(c) does not validate an agreement with respect to defenses that could be asserted against a holder in due course of a negotiable instrument under § 3–305(a)(1) and (b) (the so-called "real defenses"); but only those referred to as "personal defenses" under § 3–305(a)(2) and (3) and (b). § 9–403(b)(4) and (c). Thus, § 9–403 "is designed to put the assignee in a position that is no better and no worse than that of a holder in due course of a negotiable instrument under Article 3." § 9–403 Comment 3. Indeed, if a buyer in an installment-sales agreement signs a negotiable promissory note, it is not an "account debtor" and § 9–403 does not apply to the transaction. Accordingly, if the payee–seller of the note negotiates it to a holder in due course, the latter will take free of buyer's personal defenses (defective goods) as against seller per §§ 3–302, 3–305, 3–306. § 9–102(a)(3) ("account debtor" defined); § 9–403 Comment 2, see Comment 4 and former § 9–206(2).

Section 9–403 takes no position on the enforceability of waivers by *consumers*. § 9–403(e), see § 9–403(d) (FTC notice). See Part Three, B, 2, C supra. Other law not displaced includes "hell-or-high-water" agreements. § 9–403(f) and Comments 4 and 6; see Part Two, D, 10 and E, 4 supra.

4. *Ability of account debtor (e.g., buyer of goods) and assignor (e.g., seller of goods) to modify assigned contract.* Good-faith modification of assigned contracts binds an assignee (e.g., secured party) to the extent that (i) the right to payment has not been fully earned or (ii) notification of the assignment has not been given to the account debtor (e.g., buyer). Section 9–405(a) protects the interest of assignees by (i) limiting the effectiveness of modifications to those made in good faith, (ii) affording the assignee corresponding rights under the contract as modified, and (iii) recognizing that the modification may breach the assignor's agreement with the assignee. Policy: Having the ability to modify assigned contracts can be important, especially in the case of government contracts and complex contractual arrangements (e.g., construction contracts) in which modifications are customary. § 9–405(a) and (b) and Comment 2. For consumer account debtors and account debtors on health-care-insurance receivables, see § 9–405(c) and (d) and Comments 3 and 4.

5. *Account debtor's right to pay assignor until notification.* Generally, an account debtor (e.g., a buyer of goods) may discharge its obligation to pay the assignor (e.g., a seller of goods) by paying the assignor, but only until the account debtor receives appropriate notification that the amount due or to become due has been assigned and that payment is to be made to the assignee (e.g., secured party). After receiving notification, the account debtor may discharge its obligation only by paying the assignee. § 9–406(a) and Comment 2. This rule applies to an account, chattel paper, or a payment intangible. §§ 9–102(a)(3), 9–406(a). With regard to the obligation of the issuer of a negotiable instrument (e.g., note) to pay the "person entitled to enforce," see §§ 1–201(b)(21) ("holder" defined), 3–301, 3–602(a) (re: payment). To be effective, the notification must be authenticated by the assignor or assignee and state that the amount due or to become due has been assigned and that payment is to be made to

the assignee. The notification is ineffective if it does not reasonably identify the rights assigned. §§ 9–406(a), (b)(1). *See* § 9–406(b)(2) and (3) and Comments 2 and 3; as to proof of assignment, see § 9–406(c) and Comment 4.

6. *Contractual restrictions on assignment.* Generally, a term restricting assignment (i) in an agreement between an account debtor and an assignor, or (ii) in a promissory note, is "ineffective." § 9–406(d). The fact that anti-assignment clauses are ineffective "means that the clause is of no effect whatsoever; the clause does not prevent the assignment from taking effect between the parties and the prohibited assignment does not constitute a default under the agreement between the account debtor [e.g., a buyer of goods] and assignor [e.g., seller of goods]." § 9–406 Comment 5 (but see "Example"). "The *policies* underlying the ineffectiveness of contractual restrictions . . . build on common-law developments that essentially have eliminated legal restrictions on assignments of *rights* to *payment* as *security* and other assignments of rights to payment such as accounts and chattel paper." Id. [Emphasis added.] See § 9–406(e)–(j) and Comments 6–9. [*2010 Amendment.* Section 9–406, not § 9–408, governs effectiveness of an anti-assignment term of a promissory note or payment intangible in a sale or other disposition of collateral under § 9–610 or an acceptance of collateral under § 9–620. §§ 9–406(e), 9–408(b).]

See these analogous provisions: 9–407 (restrictions on creation or enforcement of security interest in leasehold interest or lessor's residual interest ineffective); 9–408 (restrictions on assignment of promissory notes, health-care-insurance receivables, and certain general intangibles ineffective); 9–409 (restrictions on assignment of letter-of-credit rights ineffective). § 9–101 Comment 4.g.

8. RIGHTS AND DUTIES OF DEBTOR, SECURED PARTY, AND INTERESTED THIRD PARTIES—AFTER DEFAULT

A. PROCEDURES AVAILABLE TO SECURED PARTY AFTER DEBTOR'S DEFAULT

What constitutes default

The Code does not define *default*. Instead, this is determined by the terms of the security agreement. § 9–601(a) and Comment 3. This agreement will invariably state that Debtor's nonpayment constitutes default. Other common events of default include Debtor's non-insurance of collateral, Debtor's removal of collateral, loss or destruction of collateral, decline in value of collateral unless Debtor furnishes additional collateral, Debtor's bankruptcy or assignment for benefit of creditors, etc. See §§ 1–309, 3–108(b) re: acceleration clauses. As to the time of default for agricultural liens, see § 9–606.

Secured party's alternatives upon debtor's default

Upon Debtor's default, Secured Party may proceed under non-Code law or under Part 6 of Article 9:

1. *Execution, etc. (non-Code law).* Secured Party may reduce its claim to judgment, causing a writ of execution to be issued whereby a sheriff levies on Debtor's property. The property is then sold at an execution sale and the proceeds of the sale applied to satisfy creditors' claims. § 9–601(a)(1), (f) and Comments 2, 5, 6 and 8. See § 9–627(c)(1). *Re: priority:* When Secured Party has reduced its claim to judgment, any subsequent judgment lien *relates back* to the earliest of (i) the date of perfection for the security interest in the collateral, or (ii) the date of filing for a financing statement covering the collateral. § 9–601(e)(1) and (2). As to an agricultural lien, see § 9–601(e)(1) and (3). Execution is a subject of courses called Creditors' Rights, Debtor–Creditor Relations, etc.

2. *"Foreclosure" per Part 6 of Article 9.* Secured Party may take possession of the collateral and "foreclose" (terminate) Debtor's interest in the collateral by either (1) retaining the collateral in satisfaction of Secured Party's claim (strict foreclosure), or (2) selling the collateral (foreclosure by sale) and applying the proceeds of the sale to satisfy the claim. § 9–601 et seq. If the collateral is documents, Secured Party may proceed either as to the documents or as to the goods they cover. § 9–601(a)(2).

3. *Foreclosure when the security agreement covers both real and personal property.* Section 9–604(a) permits the secured party to proceed against both real and personal property in accordance with its rights and remedies with respect to the real property. § 9–604 Comment 2.

Default under Article 2 Sales or Article 2A Leases

Secured Party rights upon the debtor's default under a security interest arising solely under Article 2 (Sales) or Article 2A (Leases) are governed by Article 2 or 2A, not Article 9. § 9–110(3) and Comment 3. See, e.g., §§ 2–401, 2–505, 2–711(3), 2A–508(5) (2A–508(4) in amended Article 2A).

B. FORECLOSURE

(1) Introduction

The big moment for our secured party (SP–1) has arrived. Assume SP–1 has priority over competing claimants and now wishes to apply the collateral toward the debt. Remember: "The rights of a secured party to enforce its security interest in collateral after the debtor's default are an important feature of a secured transaction." § 9–601 Comment 2. These are the rights that distinguish the secured creditor from the unsecured creditor.

After default, a *secured party* has the rights provided in Part 6 of Article 9 and, with certain limitations, those provided by the parties' agreement. § 9–601(a). With some limitations, a *debtor* and an *obligor* also have the rights provided in Part 6 of Article 9 and by the parties' agreement. §§ 9–601(d), 9–102(a)(28) and (59); see §§ 9–601(g), 9–605.

Certain rules found in Part 6 of Article 9, to the extent that they give rights to a debtor or obligor and impose duties on a secured party, may not be waived or varied. See listing in § 9–602(1)–(13) and Comment 3; see § 9–624. Rationale: "With exceptions relating to good faith, diligence, reasonableness, and care, immediate parties, as between themselves, may vary ... [UCC] provisions by agreement. However, in the context of rights and duties after default, our legal system traditionally has looked with suspicion on agreements that limit the debtor's rights and free the secured party of its duties. As stated in former Section 9–501, Comment 4, 'no mortgage clause has ever been allowed to clog the equity of redemption.' The context of default offers great opportunity for over-reaching. The suspicious attitudes of the courts have been grounded in common sense. This section ... codifies this long-standing and deeply rooted attitude." § 9–602 Comment 2.

Simply: "Except for procedure on default, freedom of contract prevails between the immediate parties to the security transaction." Former § 9–101 Comment. See § 1–302. Regarding agreements as to the standards governing the parties' rights and duties, see § 9–603.

When Debtor defaults, Secured Party will follow this sequence: Secured Party takes possession of or control over collateral; Secured Party may either accept the collateral in satisfaction of the debt or dispose of (sell) the collateral and apply the proceeds toward the debt. Any time before disposition, etc., Debtor may redeem the collateral by paying off the debt.

(2) Secured Party's Right to Take Possession or Control of Collateral

Collection rights of secured party

A secured party (if so agreed and in any event after default) may notify an account debtor (the person obligated on an account, chattel paper, or general intangible) or other person obligated on collateral (e.g., maker of promissory note) to make payment to the secured party. § 9–607(a)(1); § 9–102(a)(2), (3), (11), (42), (47), (65) ("account," "account debtor," "chattel paper," "general intangible," "instrument," and "promissory note" defined). Example: Seller–assignor sells goods to various buyer–account debtors, then assigns the several accounts to assignee–secured party. These assignments are on a "non-notification" basis, that is, buyer–account debtor agrees to make the payment(s) to seller–assignor, who in turn agrees to remit the payment(s) to assignee–secured party. See § 9–205. (In fact, buyer–account debtor may not know the account has been assigned.) Assume Seller–assignor defaults in its obligations to assignee–secured party, who notifies buyer–account debtor to make payment to it. Buyer–account debtor thereafter pays assignee–secured party, not seller–assignor. See §§ 9–406(a) and Comments 2 and 3. Note that, if the method of collection contemplated by the security arrangement *before* default was direct (i.e., payment by the account debtor to the assignee, "notification" financing), the assignee–secured party would already be exercising collection rights. § 9–607 Comment 4. Also, a secured party may take any proceeds to which it is entitled under § 9–315. §§ 9–607(a)(2), 9–102(a)(64) ("proceeds" defined); see § 9–607(a)(3)–(5), (b)–(e). See Part Five, C, 5, D, (4) supra.

The secured party may *enforce* the obligations of an account debtor (or other person obligated on collateral) and exercise the debtor's rights with respect to the obligation of the account debtor (or other person obligated on collateral), to make payment to the debtor. § 9–607(a)(3) and Comment 3.

Section 9–608(a) and (b) explicitly provides for the *application* of *proceeds* recovered by the secured party in substantially the same manner as provided in § 9–615(a) and (e) for dispositions of collateral. § 9–608 Comment 2. Note: If the underlying transaction is a *sale* of accounts, chattel paper, payment intangibles, or promissory notes, the *debtor* is not entitled to any surplus, and the *obligor* is not liable for any deficiency. §§ 9–608(b), 9–102(a)(28) and (59). Disposition of collateral is discussed at Part Five, C, 8, B, (3), (b), infra.

Secured party's right to take possession

The secured party is entitled to take possession of collateral after default (if it is not already in possession as pledgee). It may proceed *without judicial process* if it does so "without breach of the peace," *or* it may proceed pursuant to judicial process (e.g., replevin). § 9–609(a)(1), (b) and Comments 2 and 3; see § 1–305(b) (liberal administration remedies). Countless decisions have construed "breach of the peace." See UCC Hornbook § 25–7. Common issues: Was there entry upon Debtor's premises (driveway or house); did Debtor consent to entry and repossession?

After default, a secured party may, without removing the collateral, *render equipment unusable* and dispose of collateral on Debtor's premises. §§ 9–609(a)(2) and Comment 6. Reason: In some cases, such as heavy equipment, removal and storage of the collateral pending disposition may be impractical or unduly expensive. Id.

If so agreed, and in any event after default, a secured party may require the debtor to *assemble collateral* and make it available at a place the secured party designates. § 9–609(c) and Comment 7.

As to a fixture–secured party's right to remove the fixture from the real property after default, see § 9–604(b)–(d) and Comment 3; as to an accession–secured party's right to remove the accession from other goods after default, see § 9–335(e), (f). See Part Five, C, 5, D, (1), (d) supra.

Rights and duties when collateral is in the control or possession of the secured party

The secured party must use reasonable care in the custody and preservation of collateral in its possession. § 9–207(a) and Comment 2; see §§ 9–207(b)–(d), 9–602(1), 1–302(b) (re: variation by agreement). Also, § 9–601(b) provides that a secured party in possession or control of collateral under §§ 9–104 through 9–107 has the same rights and duties provided in § 9–207. See § 9–601 Comment 4. See Part Five, C, 7, A supra.

(3) Strict Foreclosure or Foreclosure by Sale

In the event of a foreclosure sale, the secured party must account to the debtor–obligor for any surplus and, unless otherwise agreed, the debtor–obligor is liable for any deficiency. § 9–615(d) and Comment 4. Example: Foreclosure sale brings $1,000. The debt is $800. Debtor is entitled to the $200 surplus. If the debt were $1,200, Debtor would be liable for the $200 deficiency.

Experience has shown that the parties may be better off without resale of the collateral. Thus, § 9–620 allows an alternative arrangement. In lieu of resale (or other disposition), the secured party may propose to keep the collateral as its own, discharging the obligation and abandoning any claim for a deficiency (strict foreclosure).

Of course, in a strict foreclosure, there will not be a surplus to account for, either. Consequently, if Debtor–Obligor has equity in the collateral (debt of $1,000, collateral worth $2,000) Debtor will prefer a foreclosure sale, so as to realize the surplus. See UCC Hornbook § 26–9.

Discussion follows regarding when the secured party *may accept* the collateral in satisfaction of the debt or when the secured party *may* or *must dispose of* the collateral and apply the proceeds of the disposition toward the debt.

(a) Acceptance of Collateral in Satisfaction of the Debt (Strict Foreclosure)

"[Section 9–620] reflects the belief that strict foreclosures should be encouraged and often will produce better results than a disposition for all concerned." § 9–620 Comment 2.

Consequently, § 9–620(a) provides that, except for certain consumer-goods situations, a secured party may accept collateral in full or partial satisfaction of the obligation it secures. The two conditions necessary to an effective acceptance are as follows:

1. *The debtor's consent.* A debtor consents if (i) the debtor agrees to the terms of the acceptance in a record authenticated *after* default, or (ii) the secured party sends a *proposal* to the debtor and does not receive an objection within 20 days. (Note: Silence is not deemed to be consent with respect to acceptances of collateral in *partial* satisfaction of the secured debt. Thus, a secured party who wishes to conduct a "partial strict foreclosure" must obtain the debtor's agreement in a record authenticated after default.) §§ 9–620(a)(1), (c) and Comments 2 and 3, 9–102(a) (66) ("proposal" defined); see § 9–620(b) and Comment 5.

2. *The absence of a timely objection from a person holding a junior interest in the collateral or from a secondary obligor.* Section 9–620(a)(2) requires that *notice* of a proposal to accept collateral in satisfaction of the obligation it secures be sent to certain other persons who have or claim to have an interest in the collateral: (i) those who notify the secured party that they claim an interest in the collateral, (ii) holders of certain security interests and liens who have *filed* against the debtor, and (iii) holders of certain security interests who have perfected by compliance with a statute (e.g., certificate-of-title statute), etc. under § 9–311(a); if partial satisfaction, see § 9–621(b). §§ 9–620(a)(2)(A), 9–621(a) and Comment 2. See § 9–622(b) and Comment 2 (second paragraph). The secured party may accept the collateral in satisfaction of the obligation if it does not receive, within the 20-day period set in § 9–620(d), a notification of objection to the proposal. § 9–620(a)(2).

For special rules in *consumer cases,* see §§ 9–620(a)(3) and (4) and (e)–(g), 9–624(b), 9–602(12). For example, § 9–620(e)(1) provides for mandatory disposition of consumer goods in which a purchase-money security interest is held, if 60 percent of the cash price has been paid. Also, no partial satisfaction is permitted in a consumer transaction. § 9–620(g).

Effects of *acceptance* of collateral:

1. It discharges the obligation to the extent consented to by the debtor.

2. It transfers to the secured party all of the debtor's rights in the collateral.

3. It discharges subordinate security interests, etc.

4. It terminates any other subordinate interests. § 9–622(a), cf. § 9–617(a).

(b) Disposition of Collateral and Application of Proceeds to the Debt (Foreclosure by Sale)

(i) Secured Party's Right or Duty to Dispose of Collateral

After default, a secured party *may* dispose of the collateral (e.g., by sale or lease) under § 9–610(a). Disposition is *required* (i) in certain consumer-goods situations; (ii) when there is no consent, or an objection, to the secured party's proposal to accept the goods in satisfaction of the obligation (strict foreclosure) under §§ 9–620(a),(e)–(g), 9–624(b) (waiver of mandatory disposition), 9–602(10) and (12) (nonwaivable rights and duties). See discussion immediately above.

(ii) Method, Manner, Time, Place, and Terms of Sale

"After default, a secured party may sell, lease, license, or otherwise dispose of any or all of the collateral in its present condition or following any commercially reasonable preparation or processing." § 9–610(a) and Comment 4 (pre-disposition preparation and processing). In some instances, a secured party may dispose of collateral on a debtor's premises under § 9–610. § 9–609(a)(2). Note: Article 9 default rules do not apply to a surety's exercise of a secured party's rights, under subrogation, with respect to the collateral, as this is not considered a disposition. § 9–618(b)(1) and Comment 2. See § 9–102(a)(71) ("secondary obligor" (e.g., surety) defined).

Commercially reasonable disposition

"Every aspect of a disposition of collateral, including the method, manner, time, place, and other terms, must be commercially reasonable. If commercially reasonable, a secured party may dispose of collateral by public or private proceedings, by one or more contracts, as a unit or in parcels, and at any time and place and on any terms."

§§ 9–610(b) and Comment 8, 9–602(7) (nonwaivable rights and duties); see § 1–302 (re: variation by agreement). [*2010 Amendment*. Section 9–610(b) permits public and private dispositions conducted over the Internet. § 9–610 Comment 2.]

"[A] 'public disposition' is one at which the price is determined after the public has had a meaningful opportunity for competitive bidding. 'Meaningful opportunity' is meant to imply that some form of advertisement or public notice must precede the sale (or other disposition) and that the public must have access to the sale (disposition)." § 9–610 Comment 7. A "private disposition" is one conducted through regular commercial channels. § 9–610 Comment 3. Example: Selling the goods at auction on the courthouse steps vs. selling through a dealer who is engaged in selling goods of the kind. "[Section 9–610] encourages private dispositions on the assumption that they frequently will result in higher realization on collateral for the benefit of all concerned." § 9–610 Comment 2. Remember: The higher the price, the greater likelihood of a surplus and the lesser likelihood of a deficiency. Cf. §§ 2–706 and Comment 4 (Comment 5 in amended Article 2), 7–210 (re: warehouse lien), 7–308 (re: carrier's lien). The secured party may purchase collateral (1) at a *public* disposition, or (2) at a *private* disposition *only if* the collateral is of a kind that is sold on a recognized market or the subject of widely distributed standard price quotations. § 9–610(c) and Comments 7 and 9. [*2010 Amendment*. "A secured party's purchase of collateral at its own private disposition is equivalent to a 'strict foreclosure' and is governed by Sections 9–620, 9–621, and 9–622. The provisions of these sections can be waived only as provided in Section 9–624(b)." § 9–610 Comment 7.]

As to the *time of disposition*, § 9–610 Comment 3 states in part, "This Article does not specify a period within which a secured party must dispose of collateral.... It may, for example, be prudent not to dispose of goods when the market has collapsed. Or, it might be more appropriate to sell a large inventory in parcels over a period of time instead of in bulk.... [I]f a secured party ... holds collateral for a long period of time without disposing of it, and if there is no good reason for not making a prompt disposition, the secured party may be determined not to have acted in a 'commercially reasonable' manner." See § 9–620(f). As to the *relevance of price*, § 9–610 Comment 10, observes, "While not itself sufficient to establish a violation of this Part [6 of Article 9], a low price suggests that a court should scrutinize carefully all aspects of a disposition to ensure that each aspect was commercially reasonable."

Guidance for determining the circumstances under which a disposition is commercially reasonable

Section 9–627 (and see Comment 3) sets forth the guidelines:

1. "The fact that a greater amount could have been obtained by a ... disposition ... at a different time or in a different method from that selected by the secured party is not of itself sufficient to preclude the secured party from establishing that the ... disposition ... was made in a commercially reasonable manner." § 9–627(a) and Comment 2.

2. "A disposition of collateral is made in a commercially reasonable manner if the disposition is made: (1) in the usual manner on any recognized market; (2) at the price current in any recognized market at the time of the disposition; or (3) otherwise in conformity with reasonable commercial practices among dealers in the type of property that was the subject of the disposition. § 9–627(b) and Comment 4.

3. "A ... disposition ... is commercially reasonable if it has been approved: (1) in a judicial proceeding; (2) by a

bona fide creditors' committee; (3) by a representative of creditors; or (4) by an assignee for the benefit of creditors." § 9–627(c), see § 9–627(d).

Warranties on disposition

Section 9–610(d) affords the transferee in a disposition (e.g., sale or lease) under § 9–610 the benefit of any warranties of title, possession, quiet enjoyment, and similar warranties that would have accompanied the disposition by operation of non-Article 9 law. Thus, Article 2's warranty of title would apply to a sale of goods, § 2–312. The analogous Article 2A warranties would apply to a lease of goods, §§ 2A–211. § 9–610(d). These warranties may be *disclaimed* either under, e.g., § 2–312(2) [2–312(3) (2003)] or § 2A–214(4) [2A–211(4) (2003)]; or by a record containing an express disclaimer. §§ 9–610(e), 9–102(a)(69) ("record" defined). Section 9–610(f) provides sample wording that will effectively exclude the warranties in a disposition under § 9–610, regardless of whether the exclusion would be effective under, e.g., § 2–312(2) [2–312(3) (2003)] or § 2A–214(4) [2A–211(4) (2003)]. The wording reads, "There is no warranty relating to title, possession, quiet enjoyment, or the like in this disposition." § 9–610(f) and Comment 11.

A disposition under § 9–610 also may give rise to other statutory or implied warranties of quality or fitness for a particular purpose, as a matter of law other than Article 9. Other law also governs disclaimer of these warranties. Example: A foreclosure sale of a car by a car dealer could give rise to an implied warranty of merchantability (§ 2–314) unless effectively disclaimed or modified (§ 2–316). § 9–610 Comment 11. See also §§ 2–315 (fitness for a particular purpose), 2A–212 (merchantability—lease), 2A–213 (fitness for a particular purpose—lease), and 2A–214 (disclaimer or modification—lease).

(iii) Pre–Disposition Notification

Reasonable notification required

"[Section 9–611] requires a secured party who wishes to dispose of collateral under Section 9–610 to send 'a reasonable authenticated notification of disposition' to specified interested persons, subject to certain exceptions." §§ 9–611(b) and Comment 2 (source of quote), 9–102(a)(7) ("authenticate" defined). "The notification must be reasonable as to the manner in which it is sent, its timeliness (i.e., a reasonable time before the disposition is to take place), and its content." § 9–611 Comment 2, §§ 9–612 through 9–614.

Notification not required

Notification of disposition is not required for perishable collateral or collateral that threatens to decline speedily in value or is a type customarily sold on a recognized market. (e.g., marketable securities.) § 9–611(b), (d) and Comment 7.

Persons to be notified

Section 9–611 requires that notification of a disposition be made to the *debtor* and any *secondary obligor.* § 9–611(b), (c)(1) and (2) and Comment 3; see § 9–102(a)(28) ("debtor" defined), (59) ("obligor"), (71) ("secondary obligor"), (74) ("send"). A secondary obligor includes a guarantor or other surety. See § 9–102 Comment 2.a.

If the collateral is not consumer goods, the secured party also has a duty to send notification to other interested persons (e.g., *secured parties*) as follows:

(i) to any other person from whom the secured party has received (before the "notification date") authenticated notification of a claimed interest in the collateral. § 9–611(a) and (c)(3)(A).

(ii) to any other *secured party* (or lienholder) that, 10 days before the "notification date," held a security interest in (or other lien on) the collateral *perfected* by filing a *financing statement* (pursuant to § 9–611(c)(3)(B)(i)–(iii)) or by, e.g., noting the security interest on a certificate of title (pursuant to a certificate-of-title statute). § 9–611(a) and (c)(3)(B) and (C) and Comments 4 and 8. See § 9–611(e) and Comment 4 (5th paragraph) ("safe harbor" rule). *Policy* of requiring the foreclosing secured party to notify (and thus also to search the files to discover) certain competing secured parties: "Many of the problems arising from the dispositions of collateral encumbered by multiple security interests can be ameliorated or solved by informing all secured parties of an intended disposition and affording them an opportunity to work with one another." § 9–611 Comment 4 (second paragraph).

Timeliness of notification

"The notification must be reasonable as to … its timeliness (i.e., a reasonable time before the disposition is to take place)." § 9–611 Comment 2. Reasonable time is a question of fact. § 9–612(a) and Comment 2. For non-consumer transactions, there is a "safe harbor" rule: "[A] notification of disposition sent after default and 10 days or more before the earliest time … set forth in the notification" is timely. § 9–612(b) and Comment 3.

Contents and form of notification

In a non-consumer-goods transaction, notification of disposition is sufficient if it

(A) describes the debtor and the secured party;

(B) describes the collateral that is the subject of the intended disposition;

(C) states the method of intended disposition;

(D) states that the debtor is entitled to an accounting of the unpaid indebtedness and indicates any charge that is to be made for an accounting; and

(E) states the time and place of a public disposition or the time after which any other disposition will occur.

Section 9–613(1). See § 9–613(2)–(4) and Comment 2.

In consumer-goods transactions, notification of disposition must include the following information:

(A) the information specified in Section 9–613(1);

(B) a description of the recipient's potential liability, if any, for a deficiency;

(C) a telephone number from which the amount that must be paid to the secured party to redeem the collateral under Section 9–623 is available; and

(D) a telephone number or mailing address from which additional information concerning the disposition and the secured obligation is available.

Section 9–614(1); see § 9–614(2), (4)–(6) and Comments 2 and 3.

If properly completed, the sample forms found in § 9–613(5) (general) and § 9–614(3) (consumer-goods transactions) are sufficient. See §§ 9–613 Comment 2, 9–614 Comment 3. [*2010 Amendment*. Section 9–613 applies to a notification of public disposition conducted electronically; thus, for example, an electronic location can be provided. § 9–613 Comment 2.]

Waiver of disposition notification

A *debtor* or *secondary obligor* may waive the right to notification of disposition of collateral under § 9–611, but only by authenticating an agreement to that effect *after* default. §§ 9–624(a), 9–611 Comment 9, 9–602(7) and (12); see § 9–102(a) (7) ("authenticate" defined), (28) ("debtor"), (59) ("obligor"), (71) ("secondary obligor").

(iv) Application of Proceeds of Disposition, Debtor's Right
     to Surplus, and Obligor's Liability for Deficiency

Application of proceeds

The secured party must apply the cash proceeds of a
disposition under § 9–610 in the following order:

First, to the expenses of disposition, that is, the reasonable expenses of retaking and disposing of the collateral.
Also—if provided for by agreement and not prohibited by
law—reasonable attorney's fees, etc. § 9–615(a)(1) and
Comment 2.

Second, to the secured obligation. § 9–615(a)(2).

Third, in specified circumstances, to interests that are
subordinate to the secured party's interest—that is, to
satisfy any subordinate security interest (or other subordinate lien on the collateral) *if* the secured party receives
from the holder of the subordinate security interest (or
other lien) an authenticated demand for proceeds before
distribution of the proceeds is completed. §§ 9–
615(a)(3)(A), 9–102(a)(7) ("authenticate" defined). See
§ 9–615(b) (proof of subordinate interest).

With respect to consignors of the collateral, see § 9–
615(a)(3)(B) and (4); as to application of noncash proceeds, see § 9–615(c) and Comment 3 and § 9–602(4); as
to cash proceeds received by a junior secured party, see
§ 9–615(g). Note re: collection rights of a secured party:
§ 9–608(a) and (b) provides for application of proceeds
recovered by the secured party in substantially the same
manner as provided in § 9–615(a) and (e). § 9–608 Comment 2. See Part Five, C, 8, B, (2) supra.

Surplus or deficiency

If the security interest under which a disposition is
made secures payment or performance, after making the
payments and applications required by § 9–615(a) as dis-

cussed immediately above, (1) the secured party is required to account to and pay the *debtor* for any surplus; and (2) the *obligor* is liable for any deficiency. §§ 9–615(d) and Comments 4 and 5, 9–602(5).

The "debtor" is the person whose property secures the debt. The "obligor" is the person owing payment or other performance of the obligation. § 9–102(a)(28), (59). In all but a few cases, the person who owes the debt (obligor) and the person whose property secures the debt (debtor) will be the same. Occasionally, one person (debtor) furnishes security for another's (obligor's) debt. In this case, the "debtor" is entitled to the surplus, but the "obligor" is liable for any deficiency.

Example: X borrows $10,000 from SP–1 and grants SP–1 a security interest in certain equipment as collateral. X is both "obligor" and "debtor." X defaults. SP–1 takes possession of the collateral under § 9–609, and conducts a commercially reasonable foreclosure sale under § 9–610. The sale brings $15,000. Before SP–1 applies the cash proceeds of the sale, it receives SP–2's authenticated demand for payment of $2,000 X owes to it on a subordinate debt. The expenses of the sale are $200, and attorney's fees are $500. The proceeds of the sale are applied as follows: (1) $700 for reasonable expenses and attorney's fees (assuming they were agreed to); (2) $10,000 to pay SP–1's claim; and (3) $2,000 to pay SP–2. The surplus of $2,300 ($15,000 minus $12,700) is paid to X. If the sale brought $8,000, the proceeds would be applied as follows: (1) $700 for expenses, and (2) $7,300 toward the interest of SP–1. X is liable to SP–1 for the $2,700 deficiency ($10,000 minus $7,300) and is liable to SP–2 for $2,000.

As to consumer protection legislation restricting deficiency judgments in consumer credit sales, see Uniform Consumer Credit Code (1974) (UCCC) § 5.103. See also

UCCC §§ 2.507, 3.310, 3.302, 3.303, 3.306, 3.308, 3.401, 3.402, and 5.108.

No surplus or deficiency in *sales* of certain rights to payment

"If the underlying transaction is a sale of accounts, chattel paper, payment intangibles or promissory notes: (1) the debtor is not entitled to any surplus; and (2) the obligor is not liable for any deficiency." § 9–615(e), see § 9–109(a)(3); cf. § 9–608(b).

Calculation of surplus or deficiency in disposition to "person related to" secured party

Section 9–615(f) deals with calculation of a deficiency or surplus when a disposition is made to a secured party, a "person related to" the secured party, or a secondary obligor (e.g., guarantor). In such a case, the secured party may lack the incentive to maximize the proceeds of disposition. Thus, if the proceeds of disposition are " 'significantly below the range of proceeds that a complying disposition to a person other than the secured party, a person related to the secured party or a secondary obligor would have brought,' then instead of calculating a deficiency (or surplus) based on the actual net proceeds, the calculation is based upon the amount that would have been received in a commercially reasonable disposition to a person other than the secured party, a person related to the secured party, or a secondary obligor." § 9–615(f) and Comment 6 (source of quote) and 7; see §§ 9–102(a)(63) ("person related to" defined), 9–602(8) (nonwaivable rights and duties).

Explanation of calculation of surplus or deficiency

"[Section 9–616] reflects the view that in every consumer-goods transaction, the debtor or obligor is entitled to know the amount of a surplus or deficiency and the basis

upon which the surplus or deficiency was calculated."
§ 9–616 Comment 2 (duty to send information), Comment 3 (explanation of calculation), Comment 4 (liability for noncompliance). See § 9–602(9) (nonwaivable rights and duties).

(v) Rights of Transferees of Collateral Upon Disposition

"A secured party's disposition after default: (1) transfers to a transferee [T] for value all of the debtor's rights in the collateral; (2) discharges the security interest [SP–1] under which the disposition was made; and (3) discharges any subordinate security interest [SP–2] or other subordinate lien [LC]. . . ." §§ 9–617(a) and Comments 2 and 3, 1–204 ("value" defined). As to warranties on disposition, see § 9–610(d) and (e).

Example: D owns goods free from all liens, security interests, etc. D gives SP–1 a security interest in the goods to secure a loan. SP–1 duly files. Then, D gives SP–2 a security interest to secure another loan. SP–2 duly files but is subordinate to SP–1. § 9–322(a)(1). Later, LC, a creditor of D, gets a judgment and levies on the goods. See §§ 9–201(a), 9–317(a)(2). D then defaults as to SP–1. SP–1 forecloses on the goods, and T purchases the goods at the foreclosure sale. T gets title to the goods free from any claims of D, SP–1, SP–2, and LC. (Note: If T purchased at SP–2's foreclosure sale instead of SP–1's, T would take free from any claims of D, SP–2, and LC, but subject to SP–1's senior security interest.)

A transferee acting in good faith *takes free* from the rights and interests described in § 9–617(a)—and discussed above—*even if* the secured party fails to comply with Article 9 or the requirements of any judicial proceeding. §§ 9–617(b) and Comments 2 and 3, 9–102(a)(43) ("good faith" defined). (See also 1–201(b)(20) and Comment 20). Otherwise, the transferee takes *subject to* the rights of debtor (D), the enforcing secured party (SP–1), other security interests (SP–2), and other liens (LC). § 9–617(c) and Comment 4.

(c) Right to Redeem the Collateral

Redemption, which is not defined in the Code, means to free property from a lien or encumbrance and regain absolute title by paying the amount the property secures. A debtor, any secondary obligor, or any other secured party or lienholder may redeem collateral. § 9–623(a).

Requirements for redemption

To redeem collateral, a person must tender fulfillment of all obligations the collateral secures, plus reasonable expenses and attorney's fees as described in § 9–615(a)(1). If the entire balance has been accelerated, the entire balance must be tendered. § 9–623(b) and Comment 2; see §§ 1–309 (option to accelerate at will), 3–104(a)(2) ("date certain" requirement for negotiable instruments), 3–108(b) (acceleration clauses). Remember: Secured Party's interest in the collateral is only to secure a debt. Once the debt is paid off, the collateral should be freed from the security interest.

When redemption may occur

Redemption may occur any time *before* a secured party

1. has collected collateral, e.g., accounts from account debtors, under § 9–607 (see Part Five, C, 8, B, (2) supra);

2. has disposed of collateral or entered into a contract for its disposition, under § 9–610 (foreclosure by sale) (see Part Five, C, 8, B, (3), (B) supra); or

3. has accepted collateral in full or partial satisfaction of the secured obligation under § 9–622 (strict foreclosure) (see Part Five, C, 8, B, (3)(a) supra). § 9–623 (c) and Comments 2–4.

Waiver of redemption right

In a non-consumer-goods transaction, a debtor or secondary obligor (e.g., surety) may waive the right to redeem collateral, but only by an agreement to that effect entered into and authenticated *after* default. §§ 9–602 (11), 9–624(c). "[N]o mortgage clause has ever been allowed to clog the equity of redemption." § 9–602 Comment 2 (quoting former 9–501 Comment 4).

(d) Remedies for Secured Party's Failure to Comply With Article 9

A secured party may fail to comply with Article 9 provisions in several ways, e.g., if it made a non-commercially reasonable disposition, failed to give notice of disposition, breached the peace in repossession, did not exercise reasonable care as a pledgee, did not allow redemption, did not furnish or file a termination statement, did not respond to a request for accounting, etc. These matters were addressed above. See § 9–625 Comment 2.

Judicial orders concerning noncompliance

If it is established that a secured party is not complying with Article 9, a court may order or restrain collection, enforcement, or disposition of collateral. § 9–625(a).

Damages for noncompliance

Basic Remedy: A person is liable for any loss caused by a failure to comply with Article 9. Such damages may include loss resulting from the debtor's inability to obtain, or increased costs of, alternative financing. § 9–625(b) and Comment 3.

Person entitled to recover damages

Damages may be recovered by any person who (at the time of the failure) was a *debtor* or *obligor*, or held a *security interest* in or other *lien* on the collateral. § 9–

625(c)(1). Note the *statutory damages* in a consumer-goods transaction: "A person that was a debtor or a secondary obligor ... may recover ... in any event an amount not less than the credit service charge plus 10 percent of the principal amount of the obligation or the time-price differential plus 10 percent of the cash price." § 9–625(c)(2) and Comment 4.

Statutory damages

In addition to any damages recoverable under the basic remedy provision at § 9–625(b), discussed above, § 9–625(e)–(g) imposes an additional $500 liability upon a person who fails to comply with the provisions specified in § 9–625(e)(1)–(6),(f) and (g) (e.g., "a person who ... fails to comply with a request for an accounting or a request regarding a list of collateral or statement of account under Section 9–210"). § 9–625 Comment 5.

Action in which deficiency or surplus is in issue

Section 9–626 addresses situations in which the amount of a deficiency or surplus is in issue. Courts construing former Section 9–507 disagreed about the consequences of a secured party's failure to comply with the requirements of former Part 5. Three approaches emerged:

1.   Some courts did not allow the noncomplying secured party to recover a deficiency (the "absolute bar" rule).

2.   A few courts allowed the debtor to offset its former Section 9–507 damages resulting from the secured party's noncompliance against any deficiency claim (the "offset" rule).

3.   A plurality of courts considering the issue barred the noncomplying secured party from recovering a deficiency unless it overcame a rebuttable presumption that compliance with former Part 5 would have yielded an amount sufficient to satisfy the secured debt.

Section 9–626 Comment 4.

Section 9–626(a) establishes the "rebuttable presumption" rule for nonconsumer transactions. Comment 3 explains:

> Under paragraph (1), the secured party need not prove compliance with the relevant provisions of this Part as part of its prima facie case. If, however, the debtor or a secondary obligor raises the issue (in accordance with the forum's rules of pleading and practice), then the secured party bears the burden of proving that the collection, enforcement, disposition, or acceptance complied. In the event the secured party is unable to meet this burden, then paragraph (3) explains how to calculate the deficiency. Under the rebuttable presumption rule, the debtor or obligor is to be credited with the greater of the actual proceeds of the disposition or the proceeds that would have been realized had the secured party complied with the relevant provisions. If a deficiency remains, then the secured party is entitled to recover it. . . .

> Unless the secured party proves that compliance with the relevant provisions would have yielded a smaller amount, under paragraph (4) the amount that a complying collection, enforcement, or disposition would have yielded is deemed to be equal to the amount of the secured obligation, together with expenses and attorney's fees. Thus, the secured party may not recover any deficiency unless it meets this burden.

"[T]he limitation . . . to transactions other than consumer transactions is intended to leave to the court the determination of the proper rules in consumer transactions." § 9–626 Comment 4.

"A debtor whose deficiency is eliminated under Section 9–626 may recover damages for the loss of any surplus. However, a debtor or secondary obligor whose deficiency is eliminated or reduced under Section 9–626 may not otherwise recover ... [under the basic remedy under § 9–625(b) discussed above.]" § 9–625(d) and Comment 3 (the last sentence of subsection (d) eliminates the possibility of double recovery). Note: "Like neutrinos, surpluses are believed to exist but are never observed." UCC Hornbook § 25–13e.

See § 9–605 and Comment 2, and § 9–628 and Comment 2 regarding duties, nonliability, and limitation of liability to unknown persons. Also note that, under § 9–602(13), a debtor or obligor may not vary or waive the rules stated in §§ 9–625 and 9–626, which address a secured party's liability for failure to comply with Article 9.

Note on Transition, §§ 9–701 through 9–709

Problems have arisen involving transactions and relationships entered into under former Article 9 that remained outstanding on the effective date of revised Article 9 (July 1, 2001, in almost all jurisdictions). The difficulties have arisen primarily because revised Article 9 expands the scope of former Article 9 to cover additional types of collateral and transactions and because it provides new methods of perfection for some types of collateral, different priority rules, and different choice-of-law rules governing perfection and priority. Sections 9–701 through 9–709 address these problems. § 9–701 Comment. *[2010 Amendment*. The transition rules for the 2010 Amendments to Article 9 are contained in §§ 9-801 through 9-809. They establish a uniform effective date of July 1, 2013. For a summary of the transition rules, see E. Smith, A Summary of the 2010 Amendments, 42 UCC L.J. 345 at 368-73 (2010).]

PART SIX

THE ENTIRE TRANSACTION MADE PURSUANT TO A LETTER OF CREDIT

Introduction to letters of credit

The concept of the Uniform Commercial Code is that "commercial transactions" is a single subject of the law notwithstanding its many facets. This is best illustrated by the commercial transaction made pursuant to a letter of credit, the subject of UCC Article 5. §§ 5–101 and Comment, 5–102(a)(10) ("letter of credit" defined). In this letter-of-credit transaction, the goods are sold per Article 2. A draft is issued per Article 3 and collected per Article 4. A bill of lading is issued per Article 7. The goods are financed per Article 9. Thus, "every phase of commerce involved is but a part of one transaction, namely, the sale of and payment for goods." General Comment to UCC.

The Comment to § 5–101 observes in part,

The Official Comment to the original Section 5–101 was a remarkably brief inaugural address. Noting that letters of credit had not been the subject of statutory enactment and that the law concerning them had been developed in the cases, the Comment stated that Article 5 was intended "within its limited scope" to set an independent theoretical frame for the further development of letters of credit. That statement addressed accurately conditions as they existed when the statement was made, nearly half a century ago. Since Article 5 was originally drafted, the use of letters of credit has expanded and developed, and the case law concerning these developments is, in some respects, discordant.

Revision of Article 5 therefore has required reappraisal both of the statutory goals and of the extent to which particular statutory provisions further or adversely affect achievement of those goals.

The statutory goal of Article 5 was originally stated to be: (1) to set a substantive theoretical frame that describes the function and legal nature of letters of credit; and (2) to preserve procedural flexibility in order to accommodate further development of the efficient use of letters of credit. A letter of credit is an idiosyncratic form of undertaking that supports performance of an obligation incurred in a separate financial, mercantile, or other transaction or arrangement. The objectives of the original and revised Article 5 are best achieved (1) by defining the peculiar characteristics of a letter of credit that distinguish it and the legal consequences of its use from other forms of assurance such as secondary guarantees, performance bonds, and insurance policies, and from ordinary contracts, fiduciary engagements, and escrow arrangements; and (2) by preserving flexibility through variation by agreement in order to respond to and accommodate developments in custom and usage that are not inconsistent with the essential definitions and substantive mandates of the statute. No statute can, however, prescribe the manner in which such substantive rights and duties are to be enforced or imposed without risking stultification of wholesome developments in the letter of credit mechanism. Letter of credit law should remain responsive to commercial reality and in particular to the customs and expectations of the international banking and mercantile community. Courts should read the terms of this article in a manner consistent with these customs and expectations.

It should be noted that letters of credit often state,

This credit is subject to the Uniform Customs and Practice for Documentary Credits, 2007 revision, International Chamber of Commerce Publication No. 600. [See §§ 1–303 (trade usage, etc.), 1–103(b) (applicability of supplemental principles).]

Further, the Comment to Revised UCC § 5–101 states,

The subject matter in Article 5, letters of credit, may also be governed by an international convention that is now being drafted by UNCITRAL, the draft Convention on Independent Guarantees and Standby Letters of Credit. The Uniform Customs and Practice is an international body of trade practice that is commonly adopted by international and domestic letters of credit and as such is the "law of the transaction" by agreement of the parties. Article 5 is consistent with and was influenced by the rules in the existing version of the UCP. In addition to the UCP and the international convention, other bodies of law apply to letters of credit. For example, the federal bankruptcy law applies to letters of credit with respect to applicants and beneficiaries that are in bankruptcy; regulations of the Federal Reserve Board and the Comptroller of the Currency lay out requirements for banks that issue letters of credit and describe how letters of credit are to be treated for calculating asset risk and for the purpose of loan limitations. In addition there is an array of anti-boycott and other similar laws that may affect the issuance and performance of letters of credit. All of these laws are beyond the scope of Article 5, but in certain circumstances they will override Article 5.

For additional information on the UNCITRAL Convention on Independent Guarantees and Standby Letters of Credit, as well as the International Chamber of Commerce's Uniform Rules for Demand Guarantees (URDG) and International Standby Practices ISP98, see Kristen

David Adams, Commercial Transactions 18–10—18–12 (2007).

The following discussion will provide an overview of a commercial transaction made pursuant to a letter of credit.

Recall the prior discussion in Part Four, B involving the documentary sale. Because Seller was unwilling to deliver goods to Buyer without receiving payment, Buyer and Seller agreed to exchange a document of title for the purchase price. This was accomplished per a term in the sales agreement providing for a "sight draft against order bill of lading." The transaction was outlined thus: (1) Seller delivered the goods to Carrier in return for a seller's order bill; (2) Seller drew a sight draft on Buyer and indorsed and delivered the draft and bill to Seller City Bank for collection; (3) Seller City Bank forwarded the draft and bill to Buyer City Bank; (4) Buyer City Bank notified Buyer of their arrival, and Buyer paid the draft and received the bill (exchanged the document for the price); (5) Buyer—as the *holder* and consequently the "person entitled under the document" to whom Carrier must deliver the goods—surrendered the bill to Carrier and received the goods; (6) Buyer City Bank transmitted the proceeds to Seller City Bank; and (7) Seller City Bank remitted the proceeds to Seller.

The significance of the documentary sale is that Buyer cannot obtain the goods from Carrier without surrendering the bill, and Buyer cannot obtain the bill from Buyer City Bank without paying for the goods. However, what if Seller ships the goods, but Buyer cannot or will not pay the draft in exchange for the document? Even though Seller is not in the position of having Buyer obtain the goods without paying for them, the goods are in Buyer City, and Seller may incur considerable expense disposing of them there. If the goods are perishable, the problems become aggravated. Accordingly, Seller may desire assurances, *before* shipping the goods, that some responsible person will pay for them. This is where the letter of credit enters the picture.

In the context of the above transaction, a *letter of credit* is a definite undertaking by a bank (Buyer City Bank) made at the request of an *applicant* (Buyer) that the *issuer* (Buyer City Bank) will *honor* the documentary presentation by payment upon compliance with the conditions specified in the credit. See § 5–102(a)(6) and (10) ("document" and "letter of credit" defined); UCP 600, Arts. 7, 2. Thus, when the *beneficiary* of the letter of credit (Seller) draws a draft on Buyer or Buyer City Bank, the issuer (Buyer City Bank) will honor the draft upon compliance with the conditions specified in the credit. See § 5–102(a)(8) ("honor" defined). These conditions include presentation to Buyer City Bank of the draft, bill of lading, and certain other documents, e.g., invoice, inspection certificate, insurance certificate, etc. See § 5–102(a)(6), (10), (12) ("document," "letter of credit," and "presentation" defined). §§ 3–104(e) ("draft" defined), 4–104(a)(6) ("documentary draft" defined). [Note: "Article 5 contemplates that electronic documents may be presented under a letter of credit and the provisions of this Article should be read to apply to electronic documents as well as tangible documents." § 5–102 Comment 2 (Conforming amendment to Revised Article 7 (2003)).] Note that a bank-issued credit card (e.g., MasterCard, Visa) is similar to a letter of credit.

Accordingly, a letter of credit accomplishes the following:

(1) Seller's "credit" risk is minimized. Seller knows that, if Seller ships the goods and forwards the appropriate papers to Buyer City Bank, Bank will pay for the goods.

(2) Buyer's "goods" risk is minimized. When Buyer gets the bill from Buyer City Bank after paying the price to the

bank, Buyer knows it will be able to obtain the goods from Carrier. Further, the inspection certificate (issued by a disinterested third person certifying that the goods conform to the contract) will minimize the risk of receiving nonconforming goods. Finally, the insurance certificate will minimize Buyer's loss if the goods are lost or damaged in transit after risk of loss has passed to Buyer. See § 2–509; also see INCOTERMS (2010).

The letter-of-credit transaction outlined

A letter-of-credit transaction involves relationships between (1) the applicant (Buyer) and beneficiary (Seller); (2) the issuer (Buyer City Bank) and applicant (Buyer); and (3) the issuer (Buyer City Bank) and beneficiary (Seller). § 5–102 Comment 3 (paragraphs 3 and 4):

1. *The underlying sales transaction.* Seller and Buyer enter a sales contract with a term like this:

It is agreed that Buyer shall, within _____ days after the date of this agreement, establish with Buyer City Bank an irrevocable letter of credit in the amount of the purchase price, naming Seller as beneficiary. The terms and conditions of the letter shall provide that Seller will present to Buyer City Bank the following documents on or before _____ 20 __:

    a.   Commercial invoice.

    b.   Ocean bill of lading adequately describing the goods sold under this agreement.

    c.   Consular invoice.

    d.   Inspection certificate issued by _____.

    e.   Certificate or policy of insurance governing the goods described in this agreement.

Any confirmation of the letter of credit shall be by Seller City Bank.

UCC Section 2–325 states that a letter of credit must be irrevocable; Seller's delivery of a proper letter of credit suspends Buyer's obligation to pay; and Buyer's failure to furnish a letter of credit seasonably is a breach of the sales contract. § 5–106 (a) (second sentence). See Amended § 2–325 (2003) (conforms to revised Article 5); see also § 2–703(2)(e) (2003) (re: seller's remedy).

Note that the above transaction involved an Article 2 sale of goods. However, the underlying transaction could just as well involve the sale of investment securities (per UCC Article 8), the transfer of negotiable instruments (per UCC Article 3), the transfer of documents of title (per UCC Article 7), or a security interest (per UCC Article 9). Former § 5–103 Comment 3.

2. *The Buyer (applicant) and Buyer City Bank (issuer) transaction.* Buyer applies to Buyer City Bank for a letter of credit, and the parties enter into an agreement whereby Buyer City Bank agrees to issue an irrevocable letter of credit to Seller, and Buyer agrees to pay the bank a sum for this service and to reimburse the bank immediately for payment made under the credit. § 5–108(i). If the bank is to lend money to Buyer on what is now called an Article 9 security agreement (formerly called security-basis-trust-receipt financing), § 9–109(a)(1), Buyer will obtain the bill of lading without paying for the goods, but Buyer City Bank will obtain a purchase-money security interest in both the bill and the goods. §§ 1–201(b)(35), 9–103.

Note well: Buyer City Bank (issuer) must honor a draft that complies with the terms of the credit, *regardless* of whether the goods or documents conform to the underlying contract for sale. §§ 5–103(d), 5–108 (a) and (f). See Uniform Customs and Practice for Documentation Credits, 2007 Revision, ICC Publication No. 600 (UCP 600), Articles 4 and 5. Buyer City Bank's obligation to Buyer (applicant) includes good faith and the observance of any general banking usage, but *not* liability or responsibility for the underlying contract between Buyer (applicant) and Seller (beneficiary). § 5–108(f)(1). Instead, the basic obligation of Buyer City Bank is to examine the documents with care, so as to ascertain whether, on their face, they appear to comply with the terms of the credit. § 5–108 (a). See UCP 600, Arts. 14, 2 (5th Sen.); 18c and 14e.

Thus, a letter of credit is essentially a contract between the issuer (Buyer City Bank) and beneficiary (Seller), and is recognized by Article 5 as being independent of the underlying contract between the applicant (Buyer) and beneficiary (Seller). In view of the independent nature of the engagement, the issuer is under a duty to honor drafts that comply with the terms of the credit without concern for their compliance with the terms of the underlying contract. § 5–108. See UCP 600, Arts. 4 and 5. This is called the "independence principle."

The above rules rest on the following assumptions: Issuer (Buyer City Bank) had no control over the making of the underlying contract or the selection of the beneficiary (Seller); the issuer is paid to provide a payment service, not a guaranty of performance; the small charge for the issuance of a letter of credit suggests that the issuer assumes minimum risks as against its applicant; and normally, an issuer performs a banking service, not a trade function. Former § 5–109 Comment 1.

3. *The Buyer City Bank (issuer) and Seller (beneficiary) transaction.* Pursuant to the agreement with Buyer, Buyer City Bank issues an irrevocable letter of credit naming Seller as beneficiary. As we have observed, this is essentially a contract between Buyer City Bank and Seller and is independent of the underlying contract between Buyer and Seller. See §§ 5–104 through 5–106. The key language of the credit states,

We hereby agree with the drawers, indorsers, and bona fide holders of drafts drawn under and in compliance with the terms of this credit that such drafts will be duly honored on presentation to the drawee.

The credit is forwarded to Seller City Bank (the *adviser* bank) which advises Seller that Buyer City Bank has issued a letter of credit in favor of Seller. An adviser does not assume any obligation to honor drafts drawn under the credit. §§ 5–107(c), 5–102(a)(1); see UCP 600, Arts. 9, 2. If, by contrast, Seller City Bank is a *confirmer* bank, the bank becomes directly obligated on the credit as though it were the issuer. §§ 5–107(a), 5–102(a)(4); see UCP 600, Arts. 8, 2. (Seller may not wish to rely on an engagement of a bank in distant Buyer City without an engagement from its local bank.)

Seller now has assurance that Buyer City Bank will honor Seller's draft, so long as the conditions specified in the credit are met, namely, by presenting the following documents to the bank: the draft(s), commercial invoice, bill(s) of lading, consular invoice, inspection certificate, and certificate of insurance. See §§ 2–320 (C.I.F. and C. & F. terms), 2–503 (manner of seller's tender), 2–504 (shipment by seller), 2–509 (risk of loss where there is no breach), 3–106 (unconditional promise or order), 7–304 (tangible bills of lading in a set).

4. *Performance.* Seller now performs its obligations: It procures the appropriate inspection and insurance certificates; it delivers the goods to Carrier and receives appropriate bills of lading; it draws a draft on Buyer City Bank (or Buyer); and it prepares and procures appropriate invoices. These documents are forwarded to Seller City Bank, which sends the documents to Buyer City Bank.

Upon presentation of the documents, Buyer City Bank is called on to honor the draft drawn under the credit. If the presentation appears on its face strictly to comply with the terms and conditions of the letter of credit, Buyer City Bank will honor the draft; if not, Buyer City Bank will dishonor it. § 5–108(a). Strict compliance does not mean slavish conformity to the terms of the letter of credit, and is determined by the standard practice of financial institutions that regularly issue letters of credit. "For example, standard practice (what issuers do) may recognize certain presentations as complying that an unschooled layman would regard as discrepant. By adopting standard practice as a way of measuring strict compliance, ... [Article 5] indorses the conclusion of the court in New Braunfels Nat. Bank v. Odiorne ... (beneficiary could collect when draft requested payment on 'Letter of Credit No. 86–122–5' and letter of credit specified 'Letter of Credit No. 86–122 S' holding strict compliance does not demand oppressive perfectionism)." § 5–108(a) and (e) and Comment 1 (source of quote).

Note that, if the documents do comply, yet Buyer City Bank (issuer) dishonors the draft, the bank may be liable to Seller (beneficiary.) §§ 5–108(a), 5–111(a) (remedies). If, by contrast, the documents do not comply, yet Buyer City Bank (issuer) honors the draft, the bank may be liable to Buyer (applicant). § 5–108(i) and Comment 1 (paragraphs 1–3) see § 5–109. (If a presentation is made that appears on its face strictly to comply with the terms and conditions of the letter of credit, but fraud or forgery is involved, see §§ 5–109, 5–110.)

See also UCP 600, Arts. 14–16, 2 (5th Sen.); 18c and 14e, and illustrative case:

S and B contracted for the sale of Alicante Bouchez grapes. Bank issued a letter of credit agreeing to honor S's draft when tendered with accompanying documents. The credit referred to Alicante Bouchez grapes; the invoice specified Alicante Bouchez grapes; but the bill of lading said "grapes." Bank honored the draft; the court upheld Bank's decision, stating that, taken together, the documents were adequate. Laudisi v. American Exch. Nat. Bank, 239 N.Y. 234, 146 N.E. 347 (1924).

Buyer City Bank has a reasonable time after presentation (but not beyond the end of seven business days) to either honor the draft or notify the presenter of discrepancies in the presentation. § 5–108(b) and (h), UCP 600, Art. 14b. Buyer City Bank may be precluded from asserting any discrepancy as a basis for dishonor if (i) timely notice is not given, or (ii) the discrepancy is not stated in the notice. § 5–108(c) and (d), UCP 600, Art. 16.

Assuming the documents comply with the terms of the credit and Buyer City Bank honors the draft, Buyer City Bank is entitled to reimbursement from Buyer. § 5–108(i). See § 2–707 and Comment (re: "person in the position of a seller"); see also UCP 600, Art. 13. After Buyer reimburses the bank, Buyer obtains the bill of lading, presents it to Carrier, and gets the goods.

King, Kuenzel, Stone & Knight, Commercial Transactions under the Uniform Commercial Code 382 outlines the above letter-of-credit transaction thus: Reprinted from King, Barnhizer, Knight, Payne, Starnes & Stone, Commercial Transactions Under the Uniform Commercial Code and Other Laws, with permission. Copyright 2011 Matthew Bender & Company, Inc., a member of the LexisNexis® Group. All rights reserved.

1. Contract for sale of goods from S to B, containing letter of credit term.

2. B applies to Issuing Bank for letter of credit, and B and Issuing Bank enter into letter of credit agreement.

3. Issuing Bank issues letter of credit and forwards it to Adviser [or Confirmer] Bank.

4. Adviser [or Confirmer] Bank issues Advice [or Confirmation] of Credit to S.

5. S secures insurance policy covering the goods while in transit.

6.   S has goods inspected (by Inspection Agency designated in letter of credit) and secures inspection certificate.

7.   S delivers goods to Carrier and receives negotiable bill of lading covering the goods.

8.   Carrier transports goods to destination.

9.   S draws draft upon Issuing Bank [or B] for purchase price, insurance and freight, and forwards draft and documents (bill of lading, insurance policy, and inspection certificate) to Adviser [Confirmer] Bank. (If Bank is Confirmer Bank, S will receive payment at this point; if Adviser Bank, S may receive immediate credit as the draft is forwarded to Issuing Bank for collection.)

10.   Adviser [Confirmer] Bank sends draft and documents to Issuing Bank.

11.   Issuing Bank examines draft and documents, and if in compliance with the letter of credit, remits payment to Adviser [Confirmer] Bank.

12.   Adviser Bank remits payment to S, deducting any credit already advanced to S upon the draft. (If Confirmer Bank, S has already received payment under 9 above.)

13.   B pays the amount of the draft to Issuing Bank and receives the documents (and the draft, if B is drawee).

14.   B turns bill of lading over to Carrier and receives the goods.

"Trust receipt" secured financing of buyer

What if Buyer City Bank has agreed to finance Buyer's purchase of the goods on a secured basis? In this situation, Buyer will sign "trust receipts" (now deemed a security transaction under Article 9). An example of this transaction is given in § 9–308 Comment 4:

Debtor, an importer, creates a security interest in goods that it imports and the documents of title that cover the goods. The secured party, Bank, takes possession of a tangible negotiable bill of lading covering certain imported goods and thereby perfects its security interest in the bill of lading and the goods. See Sections 9–313(a), 9–312(c)(1). Bank releases the bill of lading to the debtor for the purpose of procuring the goods from the carrier and selling them. Under Section 9–312(f), Bank continues to have a perfected security interest in the documents and goods for 20 days. Bank files a financing statement covering the collateral before the expiration of the 20-day period. Its security interest now continues perfected for as long as the filing is good.

If the successive stages of Bank's security interest succeed each other without an intervening gap, the security interest is "perfected continuously," and the date of perfection is when the security interest first became perfected (i.e., when Bank received possession of the tangible bill of lading). If, however, there is a gap between stages—for example, if Bank does not file until after the expiration of the 20-day period specified in Section 9–312(f) and leaves the collateral in the debtor's possession—then, the chain being broken, the perfection is no longer continuous. The date of perfection would now be the date of filing (after expiration of the 20-day period). Bank's security interest would be vulnerable to any interests arising during the gap period which under Section 9–317 take priority over an unperfected security interest.

See Part Five, C, 5, E, (1), (b) supra.

Financing of seller: transfer of letter of credit; assignment of proceeds

A typical transaction might involve an exporter who has contracted to sell goods to a foreign buyer and is the beneficiary of a letter of credit initiated by the buyer, especially if the goods in question are still to be manufactured. The exporter is frequently in need of the wherewithal not only to finance payment to its supplier, but also to protect against cancellation of the order during manufacture. For this purpose, either (i) transfer of a letter of credit, or (ii) assignment of the proceeds of a letter of credit, may be desirable. See former § 5–116 Comment 1.

As to assignment of proceeds, § 5–114(b) provides,

A beneficiary may assign its right to part or all of the proceeds of a letter of credit. The beneficiary may do so before presentation as a present assignment of its right to receive proceeds contingent upon its compliance with the terms and conditions of the letter of credit.

With respect to transfers, § 5–112(a) states,

Except as otherwise provided in Section 5–113 [transfer by operation of law], unless a letter of credit provides that it is transferable, the right of a beneficiary to draw or otherwise demand performance under a letter of credit may not be transferred.

Caution: "By agreeing to the issuance of a transferable letter of credit, which is not qualified or limited, the applicant may lose control over the identity of the person whose performance will earn payment under the letter of credit." § 5–112 Comment 2 (last paragraph).

See UCP 600, Art. 38. (Transferable Credits) and Art. 39 (Assignment of Proceeds).

Standby letter of credit

"[S]tandby letters of credit include every letter of credit . . . that represents an obligation to the beneficiary on the part of the issuer . . . [t]o make payment on account of any default by the party procuring the issuance of the letter of credit [applicant] in the performance of an obligation." 12 CFR § 208.24. Example: Issuer engages to pay

Buyer (Beneficiary) who is purchasing telephone poles from Seller (Customer/Applicant) upon Issuer's receipt of Buyer's authenticated cable certifying that Seller has not performed its obligation to deliver the poles per purchase order #4229. KMW International v. Chase Manhattan Bank, 606 F.2d 10 (1979). See International Standby Practices (ISP98).

Conclusion

This nutshell confirms the statement in the General Comment to the Code that "[t]his Act purports to deal with all the phases which may ordinarily arise in the handling of a commercial transaction, from start to finish." These phases involved (1) selling or leasing goods; (2) paying for goods with negotiable instruments or wire transfers; (3) shipping and storing goods covered by documents of title; (4) financing the sale of goods: the secured transaction; and (5) constructing the entire commercial transaction pursuant to a letter of credit.

This nutshell should provide a base from which both law students and practitioners can embark on an enlightened study of the Uniform Commercial Code.

INDEX

References are to Pages

---

†